Th

TE ⊲ IRISH FAMINE

1845–52

This Great **Calamity**

THE IRISH FAMINE
1845–52

Christine Kinealy

ROBERTS RINEHART PUBLISHERS

Published by
ROBERTS RINEHART PUBLISHERS
5455 Spine Road, Boulder, Colorado 80301

First published in Ireland in 1994 by Gill & Macmillan Ltd.

Distributed in the U.S. and Canada to the trade
by Publishers Group West

Cover illustration courtesy of Radharc Films

Manufactured in the United States of America

For Kieran and Siobhán

Contents

List of Illustrations

List of Maps

List of Tables

Acknowledgments

A number of debts have been incurred in the research and writing of this book.

Firstly, I am grateful to the Public Record Office of Northern Ireland, the Public Record Office in London (at Kew), the Newspaper Depository at Colindale, and, in Dublin, to the National Archives, the National Library, the Custom House, the Library of the Society of Friends, and St Mary's Hospital, for access to, and permission to quote from, the records in their possession. Throughout Ireland, a number of county and local libraries have provided much appreciated assistance. They include Trinity College Library, Dublin; the Linenhall Library, Belfast; the County Library, Lifford, Co. Donegal; the Dunfanaghy Workhouse Library, Co. Donegal; the County Library, Galway; the County Library, Kerry; the Dingle Library, Co. Kerry; the County Library, Meath; Tramore Library, Co. Waterford; the County Library, Wexford. A special mention should also be made of the staff of the former State Paper Office, Dublin Castle (now absorbed into the National Archives) where, in an office formerly used as a jail, I passed many fruitful hours.

Financial support was provided initially by the Department of Education and subsequently by the Twenty-Seven Foundation. I am obliged to both of them. Thanks are owed to Louis Cullen for initially guiding my research in the direction of the Famine. Raymond Gillespie provided any additional persuasion that was necessary. Peter Roebuck, Patrick Buckland and Patrick Hickey have also provided support. Special mention must be made, however, of Cormac Ó Gráda for his encouragement, advice and insightful comments. I am also grateful to Paul Ferguson for allowing me to make use of his maps of Poor Law unions in Ireland. This, of course, does not mean that these people necessarily agree with my conclusions. I fully accept responsibility for both them and any mistakes that may be present.

Eileen Black and Seán Egan have provided helpful and incisive comments throughout the writing of this book. Friends have also provided welcome encouragement, especially, Angela Farrell, Bernadette

Barrington, Rita Egan, John McHugh, Sarah Ward-Perkins, Linda Christiansen, Maureen Curran and Valerie Smith. An even larger debt is owed to my parents, Andrew and May.

Finally, I am especially grateful to Arthur Luke. He not only provided expert guidance in the field of statistical analysis but also, as a hard-headed Ulsterman, encouraged a more in-depth examination of the impact of the Famine on that province than might otherwise have been the case.

Note on Currency

Money values are expressed throughout in contemporary pre-decimal terms. A pound (£) comprised twenty shillings (20s). A shilling comprised 12 pence (12d). Sometimes, commodity prices were expressed in shillings only, even though the sum in question exceeded £1 (for example, a commodity might be quoted at 25s 6d per cwt). This customary usage has been retained in the text.

Introduction

The major tragedy of the Irish Famine of 1845–52 marked a watershed in modern Irish history. Its occurrence, however, was neither inevitable nor unavoidable.

This book explores several important dimensions of the Famine, an event which dramatically changed the economic and social structure of Ireland, and which imprinted a lasting perception on the minds of the Irish people. The complexities of the Famine have been well illustrated in recent studies of its local effects, which have increased our understanding of its practical consequences. Yet for a significant period the debate on the Famine has produced controversy on the extent of its inevitability, uniqueness, and its importance as a pivotal event in Irish history. In this context, there is clear need and scope for a fresh examination of the critical issues. What were the forces which shaped the actual impact of the Famine and how did they interact?

In seeking to contribute to an understanding of the Famine, the main focus of this book provides an overview of the years in which external relief was provided to Ireland, that is 1845–51. Certain specific objectives and approaches can be identified. First, there is an exploration of the actual incidence of the Famine throughout the country, revealing the diversity of its impact. Secondly there is an examination, in some detail, of how the Famine evolved chronologically, exploring the contemporary perceptions of Ireland, and the intentions of the key players—individuals, groups and organisations—involved in shaping the events of that time. Thirdly, there exists an enhanced understanding of the official response to the Famine, revealing the interplay of the Dublin and London spheres of influence and reflecting variations in the philosophy and objectives of those involved in decision-making. That analysis considers the constraints and opportunities confronting those with the will and capacity to act.

It is not possible to understand adequately the official response to the Famine in the absence of a detailed appreciation of the British context for the provision and management of relief. This organisational and inter-personal complexity was informed and influenced by populist opinions and political/economic theory. The backdrop of complex economic, social, political and cultural factors that surrounded the Famine added to an intricate mixture of influences on the government of the United Kingdom. An important question to be considered is whether, through this multi-dimensional situation, it is possible to discern a coherent policy in the government's response to the Famine. Consequently, there is extensive reference to the British sources of evidence, both about perceptions of the situation in Ireland and of the context for decision and action in Westminster and Whitehall.

To a large extent, writings on the Famine have been polarised. There exists a strong 'revisionist' tradition of Irish writing on the Famine, which plays down the negative role of the British government, so beloved of vernacular folklore. It holds the view that the Famine was not a pivotal event and argues that many of the changes in its wake were occurring anyway as a consequence of market forces. This strand of thinking is generally thought to have commenced in the 1960s with Raymond Crotty, and in the 1990s finds its main proponent in Roy Foster. Some of these conclusions have recently been challenged by Joel Mokyr, James Donnelly Jnr and Cormac Ó Gráda, amongst others.

This book seeks to go beyond the parameters of that debate. Through a detailed examination of local and national sources, it re-assesses the short-term impact of the Famine in the context of the long-term aspirations of many key members of the British establishment. It is contended that the way in which relief policies were conceived and implemented was crucial. These policies transformed the Famine into a mechanism which, in many parts of Ireland, explained the rapidity and scale of change that took place in the years immediately following the onset of the blight. Relief policies were much more important than market forces in this respect. A synthesis of the evidence presented in this book argues that the potato blight and the official response to it made the Famine one of the most significant events in the economic and social history of modern Ireland.

The popular imagery of the Famine remains vivid even today. Mass graves, wholesale evictions, emaciated people helplessly and hopelessly searching a barren land for potatoes, desperate and diseased masses flocking to the ports in an effort to be anywhere but Ireland, and the so-called 'coffin ships' leaving the country alongside corn-laden vessels— these are powerful and enduring images of the Famine.

The origins of other Famine traditions are more elusive. One misleading belief has been that following 'Black 47' the Famine was over. This was first stated to be the case by some members of the British government as early as 1848, and was accepted as a cut-off point for studies of the Famine for many years. However, it was far from reality—in some parts of the country the demand for relief and the levels of emigration, disease and mortality were far higher in 1848 than they were in the more recognised Famine years. The widespread deterioration of conditions after 1847 began increasingly to mirror regional differences in economic structure and development within Ireland. The plight of those localities most dependant upon a peasant, subsistence agriculture, which had evolved around the cultivation of the potato, defined a geographically distinct and desperate community.

Most myths possess their own heroes and villains. Sir Robert Peel is generally considered to fall into the former category. Peel was Prime Minister in 1845 when the potato blight appeared throughout the United Kingdom. His government fell in the summer of 1846 in the wake of his decision to repeal the Corn Laws, despite the opposition of a formidable group of protectionists within his own party. Peel's decision to repeal the Corn Laws is widely believed to have been prompted by the Famine in Ireland and his desire to provide cheap food for the Irish people.

The timing of this action, however, makes such an altruistic motive unlikely. The Corn Laws were repealed too late to have any impact on the shortages resulting from the blight of 1845, and as their dismantling took a further three years to achieve, their repeal cannot be viewed as an immediate solution to food shortages and expensive corn in any part of the United Kingdom. Furthermore, in the spring of 1846, when the decision to repeal the Laws was made, there was no conception of the impact and longevity of the potato blight. The distress and shortages resulting from the blight of 1845 had not been transformed into a Famine. This was only apparent following the more widespread blight of autumn 1846 and the way in which the government (now led by Russell) chose to respond to it. Peel's decision to repeal the Corn Laws, therefore, was not prompted by a 'famine'. Was it rather the response of an opportunist and pragmatic politician who, for a number of years, had been moving closer to a policy of free trade in corn and not, as had frequently been implied, an act of political suicide largely motivated by a desire to alleviate the situation in Ireland?

Queen Victoria is often depicted as one of the villains of Famine mythology. A popular belief is that she gave a mere five pounds to help the starving people in Ireland but simultaneously donated a far larger amount to a dogs' home. In fact, the Queen donated over two thousand pounds to Famine relief and, in the face of hostile British public opinion, issued a Queen's Letter asking for more public donations. Furthermore, when Victoria visited in Ireland in 1849, she was given a rapturous welcome.

The reaction of the British authorities to the shortages within Ireland was a crucial factor in the context of Famine relief. It was patently inadequate. To nationalists, the response of the government has provided a profound example of calculated landlord and British oppression, culminating in an inadequate response to a starving people. This view has been largely discredited in recent years. None the less, popular perceptions and easily memorable shibboleths have continued to reinforce this monolithic image. However, throughout the Famine, there was considerable diversity amongst relief officials regarding the provision of relief. During the latter years of the Famine, a major division within the government machinery was apparent, which reflected divergent views on the type and quantity of relief to be given to Ireland. The advice of those who argued that more financial assistance was necessary to reduce mortality was repeatedly ignored. Edward Twistleton, the Chief Poor Law Commissioner, eventually resigned in frustration at the frugal policies being pursued by the government; however, Charles Trevelyan, Permanent Secretary at the Treasury and advocate of ever increasing parsimony (and villain 'in extremis' of Famine mythology), received a knighthood at the beginning of 1848, when the Famine had officially been designated as over, even though the demand for relief, the rate of emigration and mortality levels were still rising.

Against this background of popular perceptions, academic study of the Famine is surprisingly sparse. It has also tended to use only the most readily accessible sources, which are not necessarily the most revealing. As a consequence, the extensive documentation detailing the events of the Famine years has been greatly underemployed. In recent years also, academic research on the Famine has tended to be dominated by historians who have been anxious to dispel the old myths—pathos and emotion have been removed with surgical precision. Controversial issues have been replaced with cautious reasoning. Even the significance of the ubiquitous potato—which on the eve of the Famine was almost single-hand-edly feeding over one-third of the population—has been undermined.

Most significantly, the suffering and human degradation which accompanied the food shortages have been moved from centre stage. Consequently, an attempt has been made to play down essential components of the Famine—the levels of suffering, disease and mortality have been reduced and the long-term adverse impact of the Famine years on the Irish economy and society has been minimalised. Significantly also, the crucial role played by the British government and its key agents has also been softened by appeals to view their actions within the context of the period. Overall, this interpretation has reduced the amount of accusation and blame directed at government for its response to the food shortages. Simultaneously, revised interpretations have failed to acknowledge the real extent of the trauma that accompanied the great calamity that was the Famine, thus anaesthetising accounts of these pivotal events. In presenting this sanitised image, proponents of the 'school of suffering' have been mocked and unceremoniously tossed aside. Although this revised view of the Famine has raised some interesting and 'politically correct' questions, its main contentions are ultimately unconvincing. Too frequently, the starving baby has been thrown out with the purified bath water. A move away from this interpretation is now emerging.

This book acknowledges the contribution of recent studies on the Famine, but challenges many of the conclusions of these researches. Through an examination both of traditional and previously unused evidence, it reassesses the causes and impact of the Famine, and the reaction to the disaster. At the same time, it re-evaluates the management of the official response to what was, indisputably, a human catastrophe of major proportions. Although Ireland was a poor country, a disaster such as the potato blight was neither expected nor inevitable. The potato blight, in fact, was an unforeseen ecological disaster, the longevity of which could not have been predicted. In some areas seven successive years of potato blight ensued. This persistent problem provided a major challenge even to the government of what probably was the wealthiest empire in the world at the time. But was a famine the inevitable outcome of this failure?

The way in which the government responded to the challenge of such large-scale, prolonged distress is a major theme of this book. This raises the issue of whether a failure to meet the needs of the problem was ignorance of its nature, lack of resources, incompetence or some other less obvious reason.

One of the conclusions of this book is that the challenge posed by the Famine could have been met successfully and many of its worst excesses

Map 1: Ireland, showing counties and principal towns

avoided, had the political will to do so existed. The question is then raised of why this political will did not exist. This question leads to the consideration of a further issue, expressed as an underlying theme of this book, of whether the capability to provide relief was distorted by an even greater desire to seize the opportunity presented by the Famine to bring about economic and social changes in Ireland that were considered to be desirable by a ruling class who, for the most part, did not even reside there. If the Famine was to be utilised as an instrument of change, these purposes could be brought about only if it was regarded as a local responsibility, rather than the shared burden of the larger and more prosperous economic unit of which Ireland had been part since 1801, namely, the United Kingdom.

Background:
The Rags and Wretched
Cabins of Ireland

1845

In the three decades from the end of the Napoleonic Wars to the onset of the Famine, there was a debate amongst the influential classes in Britain about economic conditions in Ireland, the latest addition to the recently-constituted United Kingdom. The debate included a consideration of the most appropriate policies to adopt in Ireland, especially in view of its relative under-development.

To a significant extent, the received and common wisdom in Westminster and Whitehall about the Irish situation was determined by the fashionable philosophy of political economy, rather than by the facts of the situation. This populist model of political economy produced an interpretation of Ireland as an over-populated country where sub-division of land and dependence on the potato left an excessive amount of idle time to peasant and landlord alike. The lack of economic progress was interpreted as a failure by landlords to undertake their responsibilities properly. Consequently, the solution to the perceived Irish problem was to break-up the system of 'easy existence' through a diversification of economic activity, an end to sub-division, a reduction in the role of the potato, and the introduction of men of energy and capital to the country.

To members of the British establishment, political economy provided a number of accessible theoretical propositions and behavioural assumptions that could be readily applied to the Irish situation. Moreover, the theory was both diagnostic and prescriptive, although at a necessarily broad level of generality. The most commonly discussed features of

Ireland (consisting primarily of problems) could easily be made to fit into a predetermined stereotype. This analysis of the Irish situation was able easily to accommodate the onset of the Famine. Yet, the widely accepted notion of a rapidly growing population that could no longer be maintained by a potato monoculture was both inaccurate and misleading. Malthus's reference to 'the rags and wretched cabins of Ireland' took no account of the heterogeneity of the Irish economy where a commercial and a subsistence economy existed side-by-side, often intertwined. On the eve of the Famine, approximately 5,000 country fairs were held each year dealing in livestock, and Ireland was exporting a large surplus of food—mostly corn—to Britain annually. Since 1800 also, Ireland had been joined in union with the wealthiest country in the world.[1]

The roots of prejudice about Ireland are evident. The realities of the Irish economy in the decades before the Famine contrast sharply with a simplistic view of Ireland, based more upon theoretical abstractions and pragmatic considerations than the reality of the situation. A distortion of the nature of Irish social and economic conditions became accepted as truth by a number of leading economists. Hypotheses about human reproductive behaviour, for example, in the context of the provision of poor relief, were popular among the intellectual elite, linking high birth rates to indolence and the inactivity associated with poverty on the one hand, and too generous a system of poor relief, on the other. These assumptions on human behaviour were used to justify a particular system of Poor Law provision both in England and Ireland, in the face of compelling evidence that such ideas often were in conflict with reality, for example, declining Irish birth rates. The pervasive influence of populist but unsubstantiated views derived from political economy contributed to attitudes and views of Ireland whose prejudicial character resulted in a widening gulf between simple and dogmatic perceptions of the country and the truth of its actual diversity. During a period of crisis as represented by the Famine, prejudice and fear were easily translated into policy prescription. Influential contemporary theories, produced a caricature of the Irish economy. Yet these misleading theories were invoked (when convenient) to define the nature of the problem of the Famine, not as a human disaster, but as an unfortunate situation where non-interference was seen as the best hope of bringing about long-desired changes in Ireland. Paradoxically, this invocation of *laissez faire* principles in the observation of the process of Famine-induced change increasingly was characterised by a type of pernicious 'intervention' which simultaneously paid lip-service to the benefits of non-intervention. Thus, the government used popular theories, which were sufficiently flexible to adapt to the needs of an evolving situation, to justify its chosen course of action. Simultaneously, these theories were offered as providing a solution to the alleged problems identified in the same theories. Significantly, however, these metaphysical considerations helped to determine an economic policy ordained by the government but comprehensively implemented by its agent, the Treasury.

To understand the Famine, it is necessary to appreciate this web of theory, its development and distortion. Although such theories may have passed their zenith in Britain by the 1840s, in the context of Ireland they were still influential. They provided a 'received wisdom' of the nature of the alleged problems of the Irish economy and at the same time were sufficiently flexible to be tailored to the exigencies of the situation. Moreover, political opportunism, cynicism, and an abstract view of societies founded on theoretical 'models' of behaviour, created a dehumanised view of how governments might deal with social forces. This was especially the case in Ireland, which was simultaneously caricatured for its poverty and characterised as a potential threat to the economic development of Great Britain. The timing of these theories was significant. Britain, on the verge of industrial and imperial ascendancy, was perhaps susceptible to the belief that its potential could be hampered by the closeness—both geographical and political—of a poor, over-populated, potato- and priest-ridden Ireland. This political closeness, however, fostered by the Act of Union and the amalgamation of the parliaments of Ireland and Britain, provided the instrument with which to control the dangers inherent in the situation.

This is the general context for an examination of Ireland, concentrating on the development of those theories which shaped the actions of the key policy-makers. Within this context, the introduction of a Poor Law to Ireland is significant. Its development highlighted attitudes within Westminster to the problem of poverty in Ireland. The debate which led to the passing of this legislation in 1838 provided many of the theoretical antecedents which were subsequently translated into practice during the course of the Famine. The 1838 Poor Law itself, however, proved to be hopelessly inadequate in meeting the challenge of the Famine years.

Economic Conditions and the Role of the Potato

On the eve of the Famine, Ireland was a country of considerable social and economic diversity, between both social groups and regions. An image of Ireland as a poor, backward, potato-based country only partially represents its pre-Famine economy. Irish agriculture was more commercialised than sometimes has been depicted. By the 1840s, approximately three-fifths of all agricultural output ended up in the market place. The most industrially advanced parts of the country were situated in the east, facilitated by proximity to Britain, the undisputed 'workshop of the world', and helped by developments in shipping and other transport in the early part of the nineteenth century.

Following the ending of the Napoleonic Wars in 1815, there was dislocation both in the Irish and British economies as prices began to fall. Yet sections of the Irish economy did expand and there was a noticeable growth in exports. During the period 1815–45, for example, there was a marked growth in the export of grain from Ireland to Britain, facilitated by the existence of the protectionist Corn Laws which guaranteed minimum prices for home-produced corn. Britain, at this stage, was a net importer of corn and Ireland was her largest single supplier. The widespread growth and consumption of potatoes within Ireland allowed the export of a high portion of the grain that was grown. On the eve of the Famine, an estimated two million people within Britain were, in fact, fed with food imported from Ireland, and the demand for this food was increasing. In this way, agricultural Ireland was described with some accuracy as a granary for the remainder of the United Kingdom.[2]

The economy of the eastern part of Ulster was generally held to be the most commercially advanced and prosperous region in the country. This was due partly to the existence of the domestic linen industry since the eighteenth century which, although present elsewhere in the country, was most concentrated and developed in this region. Ulster was also the most advanced region (with the exception of Dublin) in terms of industrial development based upon the British model. As a consequence of such commercial development in some sections of the local economy, the north-eastern corner of Ireland had more in common with the industrialising regions of Britain than with areas in the remainder of the country. A similar diversification was also present within the agricultural sector of the economy of the north-east. Although potatoes were grown by a substantial portion of the population, the people in this region tended to eat more oats than elsewhere in the country. Flax growing also existed side by side with more traditional agricultural pursuits and many small farmers were able to supplement their income as part-time weavers. This alternative source of income was particularly beneficial during periods of crop failure. As the nineteenth century progressed, however, this occupation declined in importance, even in the flax-rich north of the country.[3]

Regardless of the diversity of the Irish economy, within Ireland the position of the potato was unassailable. The humble potato was grown throughout the country and was eaten—and apparently enjoyed—by rich and poor palates alike. Even famine and emigration did not sever the Irish people's loyalty to the potato. It was also fed to animals—pigs, horses, cattle and hens consuming from one-third to a half of the annual crop. In years of low yield, therefore, the animals were the first to feel the impact of the shortages.

The potato is believed to have reached Ireland in the late sixteenth century. Initially it was used as a supplementary vegetable by nearly all social groups. For the poorest sections of society, however, it gradually replaced other foodstuffs and, together with skimmed milk or buttermilk, became the main component of their daily diet. This was occasionally supplemented with fish, oatmeal, cabbage and carrots. By the 1840s, approximately two-fifths of the Irish population, that is over three million people, were relying on the potato as their staple food.

There were many advantages to the growing of potatoes in the place of other crops. They were easy to cultivate and to cook. They were impervious to the inclement climate of Ireland and were able to proliferate even in bogs and rocky hillsides. Because potatoes could be grown in poor quality, marginal land, the expansion in the consumption of this vegetable also helped to increase the volume of land under cultivation. Potatoes were also very nutritious and taken in sufficient quantities with buttermilk, could supply all of the proteins, nutrients and calories necessary for a healthy diet.[4] The size, fertility and longevity of the Irish population provided evidence of this. There were, however, a number of disadvantages. High dependence on a single crop meant that during the intermittent periods of crop failure, the local population was particularly vulnerable to food shortages. Because potatoes were predominantly a subsistence crop, those who grew them were likely to have accumulated little in the way of capital. Potatoes could not be stored over long periods of time, and their bulk made them difficult and expensive to transport. The very ease with which they were grown and consumed, however, had incurred the wrath of a number of influential people. Potatoes were held responsible for the twin evils which permeated the west of Ireland: subdivision and ever-increasing population growth. Moreover, the little effort required to grow them supposedly encouraged the Irish people in their alleged favourite pastimes—indolence and the production of children.[5]

These so-called 'potato people' had a number of factors in common: they were generally the poorest sections of a community, were amongst the least literate members of society, predominantly resided along the western seaboard, and lived in what were officially designated 'fourth-class hovels'. Traditionally also, these were the people who were most vulnerable not only during the intermittent failures of the potato crop, but also in the 'hungry months' or 'meal months' which occurred every year between the old and new crop of potatoes becoming available. Although those who were most dependent on potatoes chiefly lived in the western portion of the country, this did not mean that potatoes were grown in this area to the exclusion of other crops. In fact, there was considerable diversity within the economy of this region, and only approximately one-third of all tilled land was devoted to potatoes. Consequently, subsistence and commercial agriculture existed side-by-side. Corn was also widely grown, although largely for commercial reasons, including export. Small-holders sometimes used it for the payment of rent, with the exception of a small portion discreetly held back for use in distillation.[6]

By the 1840s, the dependence on the potato showed no sign of abating and was even increasing in some parts of Ireland, including Ulster, the wealthiest part of the country.[7] The extent of land under the potato crop reached a peak in 1845, when 2,516,000 acres of land, approximately one-third of the total acreage tilled, was for the use of this crop. In this year, which marked the first of a series of harvests ruined by a mysterious potato blight, an estimated 50 per cent of the potato crop was lost. By 1846, the extent under cultivation had fallen only to 1,999,000 acres, and blight had extended to all parts of Ireland. Twelve months later, the size of the crop had fallen drastically and disastrously to an estimated 284,000 acres, ironically a year of relatively limited blight.[8]

The 'Condition of Ireland' Question

Since 1801, Ireland had been part of the United Kingdom. Economically, it was an unequal union. For Ireland, being associated with such a rich country could have brought many advantages. However, the fruits of being part of the most powerful and industrially advanced empire in the world were illusory, and the benefits proved to be elusive. During the period from the Union to the Famine, the total income of Ireland did rise, but the benefits of this were uneven and the bottom third of the population probably grew more impoverished. As a result, the demarcation between both social groups and regions grew during these years.

Politically, the relationship between Ireland and Britain in the wake of the Union was also uneven. Following the dissolution of the Irish parliament, the island became subject to the parliament at Westminster. Of the 658 MPs who sat in the House of Commons, only 105 represented Irish constituencies, regardless of the fact that Ireland represented over 40 per cent of the population of the United Kingdom. The parliamentary reforms of the 1830s did not redress this imbalance. The 1832 Parliamentary Reform Act and subsequent legislation almost doubled the size of the franchise throughout the United Kingdom. Again, the impact of the changes was uneven. Following the reforms, Scotland, which possessed approximately three times the population of Wales, was given less than twice as many seats. Ireland, however, fared even worse. Although the population of Ireland was approximately three times that of Scotland, Ireland received less than double the representation. As a result of this, the electorate in England comprised of one person in five, compared with one in eight in Scotland, and only one in twenty in Ireland.[9]

Regardless of the high level of commercial activity within some sections of the Irish economy, the overwhelming contemporary perception of Ireland was that of a poor, backward country. The Act of Union meant that the British government had a vested interest in ensuring that the condition of Ireland did not deteriorate further. The early decades of the nineteenth century marked the emergence of an official obsession with investigations into the condition of society. The first national census of Ireland was taken in 1821, and subsequent censuses were taken every ten years. For the British government, the censuses and the numerous other official enquiries provided an opportunity to find out more about its new partner in the Union. Most of the information obtained confirmed the pessimistic view of the Irish economy. To official observers in Westminster and Whitehall, the Union with Ireland presented both a challenge and an opportunity to bring about change.

Inquiries into the condition of Ireland in the nineteenth century were concerned predominantly with its poverty, the system of landholding, the size of its population and the backwardness of its agricultural sector, especially the continuing dependence on potatoes. Poverty and how it should be relieved, not merely in Ireland but throughout the United Kingdom, was a major concern of the British government. To a large extent, the terms of reference of this debate were both shaped and constrained by the writings of a number of leading economists. One of the most influential doctrines was that of political economy. Adam Smith was generally acknowledged as the father of this philosophy. He believed that the wealth of a nation could be increased if the market was free from constraints and government intervention was kept to a minimum. He also applied this principle to the relationship between the government and the individuals within society, employing it to justify individualism and self-help. Smith outlined this in his influential book, *An Inquiry into the Nature and Causes of the Wealth of Nations*, stating:

The natural effort of every individual to better his own condition, when suffered to extend itself with freedom and security, is so powerful a principle, that it alone, and without any assistance, is not only capable of carrying on the society to wealth and prosperity, but of surmounting a hundred impertinent obstructions with which the folly of human laws too often incumbers its operation.[10]

Smith believed that if this philosophy was adopted, it would bring increased wealth to the whole country. The ideas of Adam Smith were complex, but they were frequently reduced to the simple slogan of *laissez faire* or non-interference.

Smith's ideological heirs included such luminaries as Thomas Malthus, Edmund Burke, David Ricardo, Nassau Senior, Harriet Martineau and Jeremy Bentham. Each of these writers developed their own individual interpretation of political economy, which were all too frequently contradictory, despite being delivered with 'ex cathedra' assurance. Jeremy Bentham, the utilitarian philosopher, summed up simultaneously the principles which underpinned this doctrine and the justification for not always using it when he stated: '*Laissez faire*, in short, should be the general practice: every departure, unless required by some great good, is a certain evil.'[11] Government ministries from William Pitt to Lord John Russell were inspired by this philosophy although their understanding of it was sometimes simplistic and dogmatic. Edmund Burke, a fervent disciple of Smith, in a memorandum to Pitt concerning the duty of a government not to intervene during a period of scarcity, assured the Prime Minister that even God was on their side when he informed him:

It is not by breaking the laws of commerce, which are the laws of nature, and consequently the laws of God, that we are to place our hope of softening the divine displeasure to remove any calamity under which we suffer.[12]

Paradoxically, political economy existed in a period of increasing government intervention. This intervention, however, was frequently piecemeal, pragmatic, measured, and parsimonious, and as in the case of the 1834 English Poor Law, carried out with a view to reducing costs. If it suited the purposes of the government, *laissez faire* could be raised to the status of dogma; on the other hand, as in the case of the Corn Laws and the Navigation Acts, it could be discarded when convenient. One of its main attractions, therefore, was that 'ministers could take whatever suited them from political economy and reject whatever did not'.[13]

Overall, the doctrine provided a useful and flexible shield with which to deflect any untoward demands being made on the resources of the government. During the Famine, the ideas of political economy were invoked to justify non-interference in the grain trade, following the disastrous blight of 1846. This philosophy appeared to give a scientific basis to what were, essentially, culturally derived ideas of economic behaviour and social needs. It had the strong support of political economists in the Whig cabinet including Charles Wood and the Colonial Secretary, Earl Grey. At the height of distress, the works of Smith and Burke were sent to relief officials in Ireland, and they were encouraged to read them in their spare time.

The Census of 1841 created a certain amount of concern about Ireland amongst members of the government. They were especially concerned about the on-going dependence on potatoes—'the lazy crop'—and the size of the Irish population. The Census showed that the population of Ireland now stood in excess of eight million persons—a figure which equalled the population of England in 1801. This meant that the Irish population had grown by approximately 50 per cent in the four decades since the Act of Union. As a consequence, it represented a substantial portion of the population of the United Kingdom. Although there were some signs that the rate of growth in Ireland was decelerating by the 1840s, this was having least impact in the poorest, most densely populated western portions of the country, in particular, counties Galway, Clare, Cavan, Kerry and Mayo.[14]

The 1841 Census Report confirmed the pre-eminence of agriculture within the Irish economy. It also showed that Ireland, unlike Britain, was not undergoing a transition to industrialisation. In fact, in strong contrast to the British example, industrialisation in Ireland was actually decreasing in relative importance, the percentage of the labour force engaged in industry declining from an estimated 43 per cent in 1821 to 28 per cent in 1841 although again there were marked regional contrasts.[15] Between 1821 and 1841, for example, the rural workforce within Ireland increased by an estimated 50 per cent. This was in strong contrast to the situation in Britain where, since 1820, the number of persons employed in industrial production had overtaken the number employed in agriculture, while industrial output had started to exceed agricultural output. Although agriculture had declined in relative importance, output continued to increase, mainly as a result of improvements, including the enclosure movement and technological innovations, which had been transforming the rural landscape since the seventeenth century. None the less, demand for agricultural produce had been sustained by the needs of the fast growing industrial sector. As a consequence, demand continued to exceed supply and, after 1770, Britain became a net importer of grain—Ireland being a major exporter to this apparently insatiable market. On the eve of the Famine, Ireland was supplying Britain with sufficient grain to feed approximately two million people per annum. This meant that in addition to feeding her own large population, Ireland was also producing a large surplus of food for export.[16]

At the beginning of the nineteenth century, Britain was the leading agricultural, industrial and commercial power in the world. The transformation of the British economy was unique and not easy to replicate elsewhere. The changes which had been taking place in British agriculture and had transformed much of the rural sector in the eighteenth century, for example, had made little headway in many parts of Ireland. Outside the commercially successful corn-growing areas, reliance on the potato proved resistant to change. Dependence on this form of mono-agriculture—so well suited to much of the marginal land in the west of the country—was even increasing in parts of Ireland on the eve of the Famine. The impact of this was to increase pressure on the land, and to make the division between those who had access to the land and those who did not even more marked. Although some efforts had been made to 'modernise' agricultural production in the west of the country, partly in the manner of the British 'improving landlords', this frequently met with resistance—both passive and violent. Attempts to put an end both to the wasteful rundale system of production, based on farming in strips similar to the system used in England prior to the enclosure movement, and to end sub-division were also opposed.[17] The improvements which had transformed British agriculture had made little headway in Ireland.

Despite the diversity of pre-Famine Ireland, much attention was focused on its poverty and its fast-growing population. This contributed to a view that Ireland was growing ever more impoverished and was potentially an economic liability to the Union. The problems of the country were being reduced to the fashionable Malthusian equation of fast-increasing population and heavy dependence on a single resource— the potato—which made vice and misery inevitable. Despite this simplistic and depressing view, not even the most pessimistic observers—not even Malthus himself—regarded a major famine as imminent. A number of commentators were even optimistic regarding the prospects of the country. The Halls, who toured Ireland on the eve of the Famine, were generally sanguine about the prospects for the country. They provided a favourable, if at times idiosyncratic, impression of the country and concluded that:

A material change for the better has therefore taken place through-out Ireland, which is perceptible even in the remotest districts, but very apparent in the seaport towns. The peasantry are better clad than they formerly were, their cottages much more decent and their habits far less uncivilised . . .[18]

Official observers within Britain, many of whom were coloured with a Malthusian tint, tended to take a more pessimistic view of the situation in Ireland. The Census returns and other government enquiries appeared to confirm that the country was suffering from the multiple evils of heavy dependence on one crop, extensive poverty, and a fast growing popula-tion. These circumstances, which were confined to the poorest sections of society, tended to overshadow any improvements among other social groups. The recently introduced Poor Law, which had been intended to facilitate a major transformation of Irish society, from early evidence was having little impact. The workhouses were greatly underused. Consequently, it was perhaps both convenient and pragmatic to see Ireland as representing a Malthusian model of a society in crisis. Within this gloomy context, the pessimistic view of many British officials appeared to be justified. To depict Ireland as a monolithic economy, trapped in a spiral of poverty and hurtling towards disaster, perhaps owes more to post-hoc rationalisation, seen through Famine-tinted lenses, rather than to the reality of the situation. At the same time, by regarding the Famine as inevitable and the outcome of years of improvidence, it lifted much of the blame for the impact of such a disaster from official shoulders, either individual or collective.

Population, Poor Relief and Political Ideology

Thomas Malthus was one of the most influential disciples of Adam Smith. He predicted that if the population was allowed to grow unchecked, it would increase more rapidly than food supplies. If moral restraint was not exercised, particularly by the poorer classes, it could eventually lead to famine. Malthus's dismal prognosis was helped consid-erably by the results of the first English Census in 1801 which proved how rapidly the English population was increasing. In keeping with other political economists, Malthus believed that state intervention was unde-sirable. He believed that this intervention was particularly dangerous in the realm of social welfare, notably that of poor relief. He alleged that poor relief, in fact, exacerbated the problem of population growth by encouraging the poor to breed recklessly. He believed, therefore, that no poor person should expect to receive poor relief from the state on the

11

grounds that 'if he cannot get subsistence from his parents, on whom he has a just demand, and if society does not want labour, has no claim of right to the smallest portion of food, and in fact, has no business to be where he is'.[19] Poor relief, by providing a safety net for poor (and implicitly, profilgate) people, only helped to facilitate further unnecessary population growth. State intervention in the relief of poverty was, therefore, both futile and counter-productive.

In England, which had possessed a Poor Law since the reign of Elizabeth I, Malthus's denial of the need for state involvement in this area was controversial. Malthus's arguments, however, not only appeared to dovetail with the thoughts of other leading economists, but also managed to encapsulate the mood of the period. In the second half of the eighteenth century, poor rates had been increasing in England and the need for a change in the system of relief was generally accepted. Malthus, encouraged by the reception his ideas had received, in the second edition of his successful book argued even more forcefully that the poor, rather than being encouraged to expect poor relief, should be persuaded to exercise moral restraint as a way of reducing population expansion. Hunger, and even famine, should be used as a deterrent to those who refused to curb their tendency to irresponsible procreation.

A number of leading political economists, including David Ricardo, John Ramsay McCulloch, Harriet Martineau and Robert Torrens, championed and extended Malthus's ideas on poor relief, agreeing that expenditure incurred for this purpose was money squandered. Not only did the expectation of relief perpetuate poverty, it also contributed to an unregulated and dangerous growth in population. Even more seriously, unless relief expenditure was tightly controlled, it would eventually swallow up the whole income of a country. Instead, the political economists argued, an unfettered economy in which state intervention was kept to a minimum would provide jobs and so make poor relief unnecessary. Social policy, therefore, neatly complemented economic theory to the satisfaction of the authors of political economy. By the 1830s, as state intervention in a number of areas became necessary, differences regarding some of the details of Malthus's arguments were apparent, but many of his general principles were still accepted. The subtleties of the debate were also generally lost on many of the self-confessed supporters of this philosophy, although it could conveniently be reduced to a few facile slogans. More importantly, however, the ideas of political economy continued to have a hypnotic effect on many members of the government.[20]

Many political economists, while approving of a total abolition of the

Poor Laws, realised that this was not practicable. After 1815, as poor rates began to rise sharply, a number of official enquiries were held on poor relief as the government searched for a compromise between non-intervention and making poor relief unattractive. General unrest throughout Britain after 1815, culminating in the agrarian riots of 1830—which coincided with a year of revolution in Europe—forced the British government to reassess the question of poverty. The domestic agitation took place predominantly in the areas where poor relief—particularly the much maligned Speenhamland System—was most extensive. A connection between a liberal system of poor relief and social unrest, therefore, appeared immutable. It was generally accepted that the whole system of poor relief needed to be reformed, but the problem for the government was how to do so in accordance with the principles of political economy and with the acquiescence of the local ratepayers. A solution appeared to be provided by reference to the way in which the 'old' Poor Law was managed by two local administrators—Rev. Thomas Whately, Rector of Cookham and Maidenhead, and George Nicholls, overseer of Southwell parish. These two men were to be influential in shaping the outcome of the poor relief debates not only in England, but also, ultimately, in Ireland.

Both Whately and Nicholls were sympathetic to the ideas of political economy. They also shared a draconian approach to poor relief which had resulted in a substantial reduction in the poor expenditure in their local areas. The secret of their success was attributed to the fact that they had both attempted to end outdoor relief. In its place, they had offered paupers indoor relief, that is, relief within the confines of the local workhouse. At the same time, Whately and Nicholls had been determined to make life within the workhouses as unattractive as possible, as a further deterrent to seeking relief. To the government, the advantage of extending workhouse relief was that it would help to end the demoralising effects of outdoor relief, whilst ensuring that only the truly destitute would seek the alternative relief being offered.[21]

The Royal Commission on Poor Laws in England sat between 1832 and 1834. It was the most extensive enquiry into poor relief ever undertaken in the country. The Commission was dominated by members sympathetic to the ideas of political economy. The evidence which it accumulated, not surprisingly, demonstrated that all poor relief, but especially outdoor relief, was extremely demoralising. It recommended that a system of relief be introduced that would provide a subsistence to those genuinely requiring assistance, whilst eliminating the abuses which were prevalent under the former system. In 1833, the Commission produced an interim report which formed the basis of the subsequent Bill. Although these generally found favour with both sides in parliament, the government wanted to ensure that any new legislation on Poor Laws, especially as it was potentially controversial, had a broad base of support. With an impressive determination to create a popular awareness for its product, whilst convincing the public of the need for greater stringency in Poor Law administration, the government secretary engaged the services of Harriet Martineau, popular writer, political economist and government propagandist.

Martineau was offered an advance fee of £600 by Henry Brougham, the Lord Chancellor, to write a number of stories that would demonstrate the corruptness of the old system of poor relief. To make the stories authentic, Martineau was allowed access to the evidence collected by the Commission. Martineau, who had already undertaken a similar task in 'popularising' the writings of the political economists, agreed. Within a few months, she had produced a number of tales with a strong moral—the moral being that unless poor relief was stringently controlled, the deserving poor would rapidly increase and become the undeserving poor. It was a cynical, but effective, public relations exercise by a government determined to create a system of poor relief in accordance with the ideas of political economy. They conveniently glossed over information which did not conform to this image, including the fact that since 1822, the cost of poor relief both in absolute and relative terms had actually dropped.[22]

The Report of the Commission formed the basis of the 'new' Poor Law of 1834. In many ways it was a classic Malthusian document with glimmers of Benthamite influence. This is not surprising as the Report was written predominantly by Nassau Senior, a leading political economist, and Edwin Chadwick, an admirer of Bentham. The Report reflected an obsession with population growth and the pernicious effects of state intervention in areas of social welfare. It paid scant attention, however, to some of the areas which did require reform, notably, the type of assistance to be provided during periods of temporary unemployment and periodic depressions, and how to deal with long-term shortages or famine.[23] The 1834 Act, therefore, had more in common with the preconceived ideas of political economy, based on influential abstractions, than the realities of life in England in the 1830s.

Following the introduction of the English Poor Law in 1834, the attention of the government turned more fully to the problems of poverty in Ireland. In some respects, Ireland appeared to fulfil the requirements of a perfect Malthusian economy—a fast-growing population, high levels of poverty, over-dependence on one crop. However, there were significant areas in which it differed from the Malthusian model. In the first part of the nineteenth century, the Irish population was regarded as one of the fastest growing in Europe, a fact that was continually referred to by contemporary commentators. What was ignored, however, was the fact that the rate of growth had been decelerating since the ending of the Napoleonic Wars and possibly earlier. In the decade from 1831 to 1841, the rate of population growth in Ireland has been estimated to be as low as 5.5 per cent, compared with 14.3 per cent in the decade from 1821 to 1831. In Britain during the same period, the rate of population growth was 15.2 per cent in the decade from 1821 to 1831, and 13.3 per cent in the decade ending in 1841.[24] The fact that no national system of poor relief existed in Ireland until 1838 meant that the procreative habits of the poor could not be attributed to too generous a system of relief. Furthermore, despite the high level of dependence on the potato, the Irish economy demonstrated considerable regional diversity and even managed to produce a surplus of food which was exported to feed the grain-hungry English population. Moreover, despite a large portion of the population being poor in a material sense, usually measured in terms of income and housing, by other standards they were better off than agrarian workers elsewhere. For example, Irish people tended to live longer, were healthier, better fed, grew taller and were more literate than many of their European counterparts. The potato was also held responsible for both the strength and handsomeness of the Irish people. The dispassionate economist, Adam Smith, observed that:

> The chairmen, porters and coalheavers in London, and those unfortunate women who live by prostitution, the strongest men and the most beautiful women perhaps in the British dominions, are said to be, the greater part of them, from the lowest rank of people in Ireland, who are generally fed with this root. No food can afford a more decisive proof of its nourishing quality, or its being particularly suitable to the health of the human constitution.[25]

Irish people also had more leisure time than other workers, partly due to the relatively few man-hours required to grow potatoes which were frequently referred to as 'the lazy crop'. The growth of population was sometimes attributed to the poor Irish not having sufficient labour to occupy their time. In addition to a plentiful supply of food, even poor people had access to a ready and plentiful supply of fuel in the form of turf or peat. Finally, the potato, derided and undeniably victim to intermittent disease and periodic failures (as indeed were all crops), had an impressive record of production and probity which far outweighed periods of shortages. The shortages apparent in the years 1845 to 1851 were remarkable because so many consecutive years of blight were unprecedented.

To official observers in London, a number of aspects of the Irish economy were worrying and they were repeatedly referred to the numerous government enquiries into the condition of Ireland. The main preoccupations of the British bureaucracy appeared to be the system of land tenure, the size of the population, the tendency of unskilled Irish paupers to emigrate permanently to Britain (although seasonal migrants were generally welcomed), the apparent apathy of the Irish landlords, and the continuing dependence of a large (and, seemingly, ever growing) part of the population on the potato. Regardless of this interest in the affairs of Ireland within Britain, the political economists generally paid relatively little attention to Ireland, except when it impinged on Britain.

Malthus himself showed little interest in the problems of Britain's new partner in the Union. He appeared not to recognise Ireland as a model for his gloomy predictions and, in his writings on population, tended to use the evidence provided by the Swedish and Norwegian economies more readily than the Irish example. His two main articles concerning Irish population, written in 1808 and 1809, were published anonymously and only in response to the demands of the *Edinburgh Review*, who promised to pay him 'substantial fees' in return.[26] One of Malthus's main concerns was that the excess population in Ireland would eventually have serious implications for Britain, due to the proximity of the two islands. The surplus Irish population would be tempted to emigrate to Britain, especially as wages were far higher on the mainland. Malthus warned that the outcome of this would be to depress both wages and moral standards within Britain. The need to protect Britain was obvious. Malthus, however, offered a solution. The population of Ireland, particularly in the poorest part of the agricultural sector, had to be reduced. In a widely quoted comment to Ricardo he explained that:

> . . . the land in Ireland is infinitely more peopled than in England; and to give full effect to the natural resources of the country, a great part of the population should be swept from the soil.[27]

Unlike England, where Malthus attributed the fast-growing population to the existence of poor relief, the lack of a Poor Law in Ireland until 1838 meant that Malthus had to look elsewhere for the cause of population growth and extensive poverty in the country. Instead, he blamed the reproductive tendencies of the poor, the land tenure system, and the existence of a corrupt landlord class who perpetuated all of this. In regard to the breeding habits of the Irish poor, he explained that they were so degraded that they were apt to 'propagate their species like brutes' and therefore should not be considered as human. Ironically, for an advocate of political economy, Malthus accepted that state intervention was necessary to force the landlords to change, but admitted, 'I do not know how the government can interfere to force them'.[28] Following the ending of the Napoleonic Wars, even some political economists were arguing that state intervention in the affairs of Ireland was necessary in a number of areas. This U-turn was justified on the grounds that Irish landlords, especially absentee ones, had persistently shown that they were unlikely to perform their rightful duties voluntarily. A leading political economist, John Ramsay McCulloch, explained that in Ireland it was necessary for the government to ensure that those:

> . . . who have property in the country have a strong direct pecuniary interest in repressing the spread of pauperism, and in taking care that the poor are not improperly multiplied.[29]

The increasing realisation amongst members of the government that a system of poor relief needed to be introduced in Ireland was due largely to a belief that Britain needed to be protected rather than to any concern for the problems of the native poor. British officials feared that if the disparity between the condition of the Irish and British poor grew too great, the former might be attempted to abandon their potato patches and seek refuge (either in work or poor relief) within Britain. If this was not controlled, a number of prominent economists predicted that the population of Britain would be reduced to the same level of poverty as their Irish counterparts.[30] Thomas Malthus, the oracle on all issues concerning the relationship between poverty and population growth, confirmed the danger that Ireland presented to Britain. In 1826, he warned a Parliamentary Committee on Emigration from Britain that:

> It is vain to hope for any permanent and extensive advantage from any system of emigration which does not primarily apply to Ireland, whose population, unless some other outlet be opened to them, must shortly fill up every vacuum created in England or Scotland, and to reduce the labouring classes to a uniform state of degradation and misery.[31]

Poor Relief

Prior to 1838, the poor in Ireland were assisted almost totally by private charity. Periods of sustained, extraordinary shortages were alleviated with a combination of both local and central involvement. The distress of 1782–4, for example, was mitigated by a mixture of local and central intervention including a successful embargo on exports of food.[32] The Executive in Dublin Castle frequently played a key role in providing this relief. After the Act of Union, however, Westminster increasingly became involved in the issue of poor relief in Ireland. Following the ending of the Napoleonic Wars in 1815, there were intermittent crop failures and slumps in both Britain and Ireland. Select Committees were appointed in 1819, 1823 and 1829 to examine the question of how poverty should be relieved in Ireland. Between 1825 and 1837, seven Poor Law Bills for Ireland were introduced unsuccessfully into the House of Commons by private members.[33] By the 1830s, even the political economists agreed that state intervention in the arena of poor relief was necessary in Ireland. This was motivated largely by the widely held view that Irish landlords had failed in their duty to the Irish poor. However, they disagreed as to what form a system of poor relief should take. The example of the 'old' Poor Law in England had discredited the idea of giving outdoor relief in any form to paupers.[34]

In 1833, a Royal Commission, chaired by Archbishop Whately, was appointed to enquire into the condition of the poorer classes in Ireland. Many of the members of the Commission were handpicked by the Whig government. Richard Whately was a well-known political economist. He had succeeded Nassau Senior as Professor of Political Economy in Oxford University in 1829, but had resigned the chair two years later upon being appointed Archbishop of Dublin. As a result of his move to Dublin, he also had to be replaced from the Commission of Inquiry on the English Poor Laws. Whately's appointment as chairman of the Commission of Inquiry on the Irish poor appeared, therefore, to be a safe choice on the part of the Whig administration. The Commissioners carried out the most extensive survey of poverty ever undertaken in either Britain or Ireland. In the course of three years, 1,590 persons were interviewed. The picture which the Commissioners presented of Irish poverty was even more bleak than the British government had anticipated. The Commissioners also showed themselves to be more sympathetic to the problems of the Irish poor than had been expected. They estimated that the number of persons out of work and in need of assistance for thirty weeks of each year was not less than 2,385,000—approximately 30 per cent of the population. The Commissioners agreed that state intervention was essential but they rejected a Poor Law modelled on the newly amended Law in England, based on relief inside a workhouse. Instead, the Commissioners recommended that the government should introduce a number of schemes to promote the economic development of the country, including land reclamation and development of fisheries. They also suggested that large-scale emigration (to the colonies, not Britain) be used to reduce the population.[35]

The recommendations of the Commissioners were greeted unenthusiastically in Westminster. The assertion by Whately's Commission that under no circumstances should the government grant a 'right' to relief to the Irish poor, as existed under the English Poor Law, met with the approval of leading political economists. Yet the proposals for extensive financial support from the state for both public works and assisted emigration overshadowed and discredited the general findings of the Commissioners. The Commission's estimate of the extent of poverty in Ireland was also regarded with scepticism. At the request of the government, a number of leading political economists commented on the Report. Overall, they were critical of it. Nassau Senior, a former student of Whately and his personal friend, condemned the scale of government involvement envisaged by the Commissioners. Senior, who had held the first Chair in Political Economy at Oxford University, regarded poverty as the fault of the individual and believed that it was not the duty of the government to alleviate it. Senior also pointed out that as the inactivity of Irish landlords had contributed to the poverty of Ireland they, rather than the British government, were primarily responsible for relieving it.[36] George Cornewall Lewis, an English Poor Law Commissioner, criticised the high level of government intervention proposed by the Report. He warned that if the suggestions were implemented, they would remove individual responsibility from the Irish population for improving the condition of their country and this, ultimately, would serve to exacerbate the problems which already existed. Furthermore, ignoring the recommendations of the Commissioners, Cornewall Lewis also proposed that the English Poor Laws should be extended to Ireland.[37]

One of the most vociferous critics of the Poor Inquiry was the Home Secretary, Lord John Russell. Russell was an influential member of the government who was regarded as a key reformer in the 1830s, having played an important role in the passage of the Reform Act of 1832. Russell would replace Peel in 1846 and remain Prime Minister for the rest of the Famine. He regarded the recommendations of the Poor Inquiry Commissioners as not only inappropriate, but extremely expensive to implement. He criticised the Commissioners for having gone beyond their remit by looking at the whole question of poverty rather than merely the problem of destitution. As a consequence, Russell accused the Commissioners of having:

> . . . bestowed too great a consideration on the question by what means, by what state resources, they could improve the general welfare of the country, and have not confined themselves entirely to the question as to the destitute classes, which was more particularly put into their hands.[38]

Russell believed that the solution to the problems of Ireland lay in closer assimilation with Britain. This, he believed, would only be possible if Irish landlords were forced to assume more responsibility for providing employment and supporting the poor, as was the case in England and Scotland.[39]

Overall, the recommendations made by the Commission were not popular: they did not accord with contemporary economic thought, they would be expensive to implement, and, as a consequence of the high level of government intervention, they would allow the Irish landlords to continue to neglect their duties towards their estates and the poor who resided on them. The antagonism exhibited towards Whately's Report by both influential political economists and leading members of parliament resulted in it being by-passed. Its timing was also significant: the new English Poor Law, based on a stringent 'workhouse test', had been introduced recently into England and, despite some resistance, provided a readily-available model of how poor relief should be administered. The relief of the poor, however, was not to be the only purpose of a Poor Law for Ireland. The British government also desired to introduce a law that would bring about the various changes which were considered to be both desirable and necessary in Ireland. Legislation for the relief of the poor, therefore, was needed to facilitate change, but in such a way as to keep the role of the government to a minimum, whilst forcing those who held property in the country to play an active role in the process. In general, the government regarded a well-designed Poor Law as a vehicle for bringing about much desired social changes in Ireland:

> Instead of tending to increase the population and attach it more firmly to the soil, a properly designed Poor Law could be made to facilitate the transition from a cottier economy to capitalist farming by giving the cottier another alternative besides land or starvation.[40]

The government, dissatisfied with the results of three years of painstaking and thorough inquiry, commissioned a fresh investigation. They were increasingly coming to the opinion that the English Poor Law was, in fact, suitable for Ireland. George Nicholls, a Commissioner of the English Poor Law, was despatched to Ireland. Nicholls had come to the notice of the government as a result of his frugal policies and the reduction which he had brought about in Poor Law expenditure as overseer of the Southwell union. This had provided a prototype for the English Poor Law and in recognition of this, he had been asked to be a Commissioner in the 1834 Poor Law. He was regarded as a dependable representative to evaluate the situation in Ireland. Nicholls, who had no prior knowledge of Ireland, viewed his familiarity with the English Poor Law as sufficient to allow him to assess its suitability for Ireland. He was told to take copies of the Poor Inquiry Report with him and judge its accuracy. He was also told to pay particular attention to whether he believed the workhouse system could be extended to Ireland. Even before he set foot in the country, Nicholls announced that he was convinced that the English Law would be as effective with the Irish as it would be with the English poor.[41]

Within three months of being sent to Ireland, Nicholls submitted his findings. He had spent only nine weeks in the country, during which time he had visited parts of the south and west. He considered it unnecessary to visit the north of Ireland on the grounds that the people living there were, he assumed, similar to English people.[42] Not surprisingly, he concluded as a result of his brief and partial investigations that the English Poor Law system would be suited to Ireland. However, he regarded the function of a Poor Law as being only to relieve persons who were utterly destitute. He estimated that approximately 1 per cent of the population fell into this category. The Poor Inquiry Commissioners, on the other hand, had set themselves the much larger task of suggesting how to alleviate poverty in Ireland. Nicholls regarded the role of the Irish Poor Law as extending beyond the provision of mere relief. He suggested that if the workhouse system of relief was introduced, it would bring about the changes desired by the government, claiming that the introduction of the workhouse system would not only solve the immediate problem of destitution, but would also help Ireland through its 'transition' period. During this period, Ireland would change from being a country of small-holdings, low productivity and absentee landlords, to one in which the holdings would be consolidated, the labourers would become wage-earners, and men of energy and capital would take an interest in their estates.[43] Furthermore, Nicholls alleged, the introduction of stringent, well-managed and disciplinarian workhouses would also improve 'the character, habits and social condition of the people'.[44] All of these changes, he believed, were necessary prerequisites for the introduction of capital to Ireland. In the face of such optimism both for the short- and long-term prospects of Ireland, the inquiry undertaken by Whately appeared even more inadequate. The workhouse system, on the authority of Nicholls, not an impartial observer, was decreed not only to be suited to Ireland but also, by implication, to be the saviour of the whole economy.

Nicholls' Report, although criticised, found favour with the most influential members of government. Nicholls was asked by Lord John Russell to prepare it for presentation to parliament as a Bill. The death of the King, William IV, in 1837 meant that parliament was prorogued. During this time, Nicholls took the opportunity to revisit Ireland. Following his second visit, Nicholls admitted that Irish poverty was more extensive than he had originally estimated and he concluded that it could prove to be more difficult to introduce the workhouse system than he had initially anticipated. Regardless of this reservation, he remained convinced that a Poor Law system similar to the English one could succeed in Ireland if it was strictly and stringently administered. In order to ensure that this was the case, he recommended that each district should be made responsible for the maintenance of its own poor. The effect of this would be to force landlords to take an interest in their estates and this, in turn, would lead to the consolidation of property and the investment of capital in the country. As a result of these revisions, a slightly amended Bill was introduced into the House of Commons in December 1837.[45]

A number of amendments were suggested during the Bill's passage through the Commons. These were predominantly from Irish members. Daniel O'Connell oscillated between support for and total opposition to the idea of a Poor Law. For the most part, however, Irish amendments were unsuccessful and the Bill passed through the House with no substantial changes being made.[46] In the House of Lords, opposition to the Bill was more successful. This was partly due to the existence of a substantial Irish interest—one in four peers owned property in Ireland. Most of the opposition was concerned with financing the new Law. It was ultimately decided to make the payment of poor rates as local a responsibility as possible.[47] In general, the Irish Poor Law Bill had a relatively easy passage through both Houses: in the House of Commons it passed by a majority of 175 and in the Lords by a majority of 62 votes.[48] As a result of this, in July 1838, a Poor Law closely based on the recommendations of Nicholls was introduced to Ireland. In recognition of the work that he had done, Nicholls was appointed the first resident Poor Law Commissioner in Ireland. He was assisted by four English Poor Law Commissioners, thus establishing a pattern which was to exist through most of the nineteenth century, that is, that the administration of Poor Law was dominated by men who were English and trained in the English system.[49]

The Irish Poor Law was modelled to a large extent on the 'new' English Poor Law of 1834, but there were a number of significant differences which indicated that pauperism in Ireland was to be treated more harshly than in England. Ireland provided a blank page in terms of poor relief, upon which the government could impose policies that would have proved unacceptable in England. Furthermore, as poverty and pauperism in Ireland were so extensive, it was felt that only a stringent application of a draconian law would keep the problem under control. In Ireland, therefore, unlike in England, relief could only be provided within the confines of a workhouse, no provision being made for outdoor relief; also, there was no 'right' to relief—it was to be discretionary and dependent on the availability of workhouse places. If a workhouse was full, there was no obligation on the Poor Law to provide alternative relief.[50] Overall, both in principle and in underlying ethos, the Irish Poor Law was intended to be more stringent than its English counterpart. Its provisions illustrated an approach to policy that underpinned the government's response to the onset of famine in Ireland only seven years later.

In addition to alleviating pauperism, the Irish Poor Law was regarded as a medium through which a number of changes could be introduced which would, the government hoped, transform Ireland into a more productive society and protect Britain from an influx of Irish paupers. This was to be achieved in a number of ways, but the imposition of a new, local tax known as poor rates was regarded as particularly important. The 1838 Act deliberately made poor rates a local responsibility in an attempt to force landlords to take a greater interest in the affairs of their estates. After 1843, an Act was passed making landlords liable to pay poor rates on land valued at under £4 per annum. This burden fell most heavily on landlords, predominantly situated in the west, whose property was highly subdivided. It was hoped that the Act would provide them with an incentive to consolidate their property. It was not until after 1847, facilitated by the punitive Quarter-Acre Clause and the soaring burden of poor rates, that some landlords commenced the desired large-scale clearance of their estates.

The Poor Law Commission governed both the English and the Irish

Poor Law. It was an autonomous, non-party body which worked through intermediaries in the Home Office and the Executive at Dublin Castle. During the Famine, however, the roles played by the officials in Dublin Castle, the Home Office, the Poor Law Commission and all other relief agencies were minimised, as the Treasury became the primary agent of the government.

Before the Poor Law could be implemented, Ireland was divided into 130 new administrative units known as 'unions'. Each union consisted of a group of electoral divisions made up of a number of townlands. In accordance with an attempt to make the poor rate as local a charge as possible, electoral divisions were made the unit area of taxation. The size of the unions was far from uniform: those situated along the western seaboard were far larger than those in the east, with the smallest unions lying in north-east Ulster (see Map 2, p. 176). Each union was to have its own workhouse, centrally situated near to a market town. This was to be administered by a board of guardians who were a mixture of elected and *ex officio* local men. Inevitably, the wealthy and propertied classes dominated each board room. The weekly meetings providing a convenient forum for the enactment of local politics. Involvement by the local landlords in the day-to-day administration of the Poor Law, both as tax-payers and guardians, was felt to be essential in Ireland. By making the tax burden a local charge, it was hoped to encourage the landlords to either take a greater interest in the management of their estates or sell them to people who would.[51] Local involvement was also an important aspect of political economy. John Stuart Mill, a disciple of Jeremy Bentham, and a third-generation political economist, advised that:

> We have observed that, as a general rule, the business of life is better performed when those who have an immediate interest in it are left to take their own course . . . the individual agents have so much stronger and more direct an interest in the result, that the means are far more likely to be improved and perfected if left to their uncontrolled choice.[52]

After 1847, the British government again employed this argument to justify making Famine relief as local a burden as possible.

Nicholls recommended that the workhouses should be able to hold approximately 1 per cent of the total Irish population, or an estimated 100,000 paupers. The 130 workhouses which were finally built varied from being able to accommodate 200 to 2,000 inmates. In the years before the Famine, few workhouses were full and some were even empty for long periods. During periods of extraordinary distress, however, the workhouses lacked the capacity to provide sufficient relief. At the height of the Famine, for example, almost 50 per cent of the population required poor relief. Partly due to the inflexible way in which it had been conceived, the workhouse system proved totally inadequate.

The government desired that the new system of relief should be implemented as quickly as possible, to forestall the sort of opposition that the 1834 Poor Law had received in England. Also, as outdoor relief was expressly forbidden, the Law was inoperative until the workhouses were ready. The speed with which the country was divided, guardians elected, and the workhouses built and opened was impressive. By the beginning of 1842, eighty-one workhouses had been declared ready to receive paupers; by the beginning of 1845, 118 workhouses were providing relief.[53]

The workhouses, in a number of ways, embodied the whole ethos of the 1838 Irish Poor Law. Not only were they the sole medium for the provision of relief, they were also expected to provide a 'test' of relief, through being administered in such a way as to deter all but the truly destitute from applying. The architect who designed the workhouses was directed to make them uniform and cheap, durable and unattractive. Life within the workhouse was to reflect the deterrent aspect of the actual buildings. The regime was to be based on the principles of order, classification, regimentation and discipline. Individuals could not enter the workhouse, but paupers had to enter as whole family units. Once inside, families and sexes were to be strictly segregated. As their name suggested, nobody was to be idle within the workhouse. Work of an 'irksome' nature was to be used as a further deterrent to any pauper remaining for too long. Diet was to be inferior to that of independent labourers or, if that was not possible in the poorest areas, it was to be deliberately monotonous.[54] Destitution (as opposed to poverty) was the only criterion for receiving relief. A successful workhouse was one which deterred all but the genuine destitute from applying for relief and ensured that those who did chose not to remain for long. The punitive nature of poor relief permeated all aspects of workhouse life and applied to all categories of paupers, including the infirm, aged and young. Again, this reflected contemporary economic thought.

An important area in which the Irish Law differed from the English Poor Law lay in the sensitive areas of 'removal' and 'settlement'. The Irish Poor Law did not include a Law of Settlement. This meant that an Irish pauper could obtain relief in any union within Ireland, provided the criterion of destitution was met. In England, on the other hand, the existence of a Law of Settlement meant that unless a pauper applying for relief had obtained a 'residency' in a union—either by virtue of being born in the union or having worked there for a number of years—he or she could be forcibly removed to his parish of birth. The Law of Settlement could be invoked against Irish paupers who settled in England and Wales and, after 1846, also in Scotland.

For the most part, paupers removed from Britain to Ireland were not returned to their own union, but were unceremoniously dumped at the nearest port of entry in Ireland. The Guardians of the Belfast and Dublin unions complained about this repeatedly but unsuccessfully. During the latter years of the Famine, thousands of Irish emigrants were returned to their native land as a result of this legislation.[55] Although the government was requested to change the Law in regard to removal, they refused to do so. Privately, they admitted that the existence of this legislation would be useful to apply during economic slumps in Britain, to protect the native workforce.[56] During the Famine, this law was invoked frequently and sometimes illegally, the protection of the native British workforce and ratepayers again being considered more important than the needs of the Irish emigrants.

Distress and Food Shortages

The Poor Law, and the various enquiries which preceded it, showed relatively little concern with periods of extraordinary scarcity or famine. June, July and August were recognised as the 'hungry' months between the old crop of potato being exhausted and the new crop becoming available. George Nicholls recognised that during these months, demand for workhouse relief would be highest. He stated categorically, however, that it was beyond the power of the 1838 Poor Law to deal with a period of protracted distress or famine. This is perhaps surprising as crop failures and localised distress were not unusual within pre-industrial societies. In the eighteenth and early part of the nineteenth centuries, intermittent crop failures and food shortages were an integral part of the agrarian life-cycle, not only in Ireland, but throughout Europe.

The Famine of 1740–41 in Ireland was particularly severe and, unusually, it resulted in a massive loss of life. In relative terms, it has been suggested that more lives were lost during this period than even during the Great Famine.[57] Again, these were years of food shortages throughout Europe, although Ireland was one of the worst affected. During the following hundred years localised crop failures, often accompanied by potentially fatal 'famine diseases', were familiar occurrences within the Irish economy. In the years following the Act of Union with Britain, there were a number of food crises within Ireland, notably in 1800–1801,

1816–19, 1821–2 and 1830–31. Ireland, however, was not alone. These were years of shortages in many other parts of Europe, those of 1830 contributing to agrarian unrest in Britain and attempted revolution in some parts of Europe.[58]

Precise figures are not available for these periods of shortages. It would appear, however, that resultant mortality was relatively light. Distress in the years 1800–1801 and 1817–19 was possibly the most severe, with mortality averaging approximately 50,000–60,000 lives. Yet even during these periods, Irish mortality was less than that suffered in a number of European countries.[59] In the years 1821–2 and 1830–31, mortality appeared to have been even lower. This success reflected a high level of intervention from the Executive in Dublin, and a prompt and generous response to the suffering by private individuals and charitable organisations in both Ireland and England. The response to the shortages during these years—both private and public—was, in fact, not unlike that shown in 1845, which met with a similar degree of success.[60] In each of the years that followed the introduction of the Poor Law to Ireland localised extraordinary distress was reported from the west of Ireland. This was not unusual, and the resultant low mortality suggested that Ireland was able to deal with periodic, short-term and localised crop failures. The less frequent, yet more serious, long-term and widespread crises required external assistance, usually in the form of government intervention.

Before the Poor Law became fully operative, it was confronted by a series of poor harvests which raised the issue of whether to permit outdoor relief to be employed as a temporary expedient. In both 1839 and 1842, there was exceptional distress in some parts of the country. This was particularly severe among the potato dependent population of the south and west and, to a lesser extent, with the handloom weavers in the north of the country.[61] As only a few workhouses were open, the distressed population resorted to the traditional practice of requesting the Lord Lieutenant to intervene and provide aid to the affected areas. As the 1838 Act had expressly forbidden outdoor relief, the government had to decide whether the Poor Law should be extended to meet the temporary, localised distress, or whether it should be by-passed altogether. If it were, responsibility for providing relief would fall upon external resources, as had traditionally been the case.[62]

Although admitting that it was beyond the resources of the Poor Law to deal with long-term shortages or famine, Nicholls had not specified the form that relief should take during such periods. When it became apparent that the distress of 1839 was going to be unusually severe, the government faced the problem of how to employ the services of a Poor Law that was not operative. The government decided to leave to the discretion of the Poor Law Commissioners the extent to which the new Law should be used to meet the shortages. The Commissioners insisted on a dogmatic adherence to the 1838 Act, ruling that they could not 'deviate in the slightest degree from the course the Act prescribed'.[63] This decision was made on the grounds that if any deviation from the Law was permitted, a dangerous precedent would be created. Government intervention would also stifle all voluntary effort and allow the local landlords to continue to be apathetic. Instead, the distress was met with a traditional mixture of local voluntary effort and subscriptions, and centrally provided government funds. With what was to become a familiar dictum during the Famine, the relief officials were told to stress to the local population that government intervention was intended to supplement, but not replace, local responsibility.[64]

In 1842, there was again severe distress in parts of the west of Ireland. Eighty-one workhouses were operative, but those that were not yet open were situated predominantly in the west, where the distress was most severe. In counties Clare, Kerry and Mayo, where the shortages were having most impact, only one workhouse, Kilrush, was open. Again, following the precedent established in 1839, the Commissioners refused to allow any deviation from or extension of the Poor Law Act.[65] They insisted that only a workhouse, with its emphasis on order, discipline and employment, could act as a true test of destitution. At the same time, the Commissioners demonstrated an obsessive yet not uncommon fear of the consequences of outdoor relief. They warned that any slackening in the provision of relief would be interpreted as sanctioning outdoor relief, 'a recognition of which in any shape would be full of peril and ought by all means be avoided'.[66] The Commissioners, with the approbation of the government, again defended a narrow interpretation of the role of the Poor Law. In doing so, they refused to acknowledge that the Poor Law had failed to make any provision for the large number of small-holders who during periods of crop failure required temporary relief, yet who did not meet the criterion of being destitute.

The determination of the Poor Law Commissioners and the government to adhere rigidly to their chosen method of poor relief occasionally bordered on obsession. To a large extent, this was because outdoor relief, even if used as a temporary expedient, was regarded as an evil that had to be avoided. Not only, as the English example had shown, was it expensive, but it was regarded as demoralising and a destroyer of the spirit of self-reliance. Nicholls had stated unequivocally that outdoor relief, even for a short period, would destroy the whole system of poor relief in Ireland.[67] Also, no less an authority than Malthus had warned of the link between outdoor relief and procreation. In the short term, therefore, outdoor relief would be financially ruinous for Ireland and in the long term would add to the existing population problems of the country.

By the beginning of 1845, only twelve of the 130 workhouses remained unopened. This was not regarded with undue alarm. The Annual Report of the Poor Law Commissioners for 1845 was self-satisfied and optimistic, almost to the point of being smug. Within a relatively short space of time, a national system of relief had been introduced into Ireland which was working more smoothly than even its supporters had predicted.[68] The success of the workhouse 'test' in deterring false claimants for relief was evident from the fact that no workhouse was full, and most were almost empty. In fact, the majority of inmates were not able-bodied paupers, but the sick and infirm seeking medical care within the workhouse infirmaries. On the eve of the Famine, a number of boards of guardians were even complaining that their workhouses were too large and requesting that they be amalgamated.[69]

Regardless of this spirit of optimism—perhaps surprising in a country that was, retrospectively, judged by some to have been hurtling towards a Malthusian catastrophe—there were obvious limitations to the system of poor relief chosen for Ireland. To a large extent, these could have been overcome if a more liberal and flexible approach to the Poor Law had been permitted. This was particularly necessary during the crop failures that were a feature of the economy. The shortages of 1839 and 1842, however, demonstrated that this was unlikely to be the case, these years establishing a pattern that was adopted in 1845. In 1838, 1842 and again in the years following 1845, the government regarded its role, and that played by the various relief agencies, as secondary to the role of the localities in meeting the distress. They adhered, at times dogmatically, to the idea of the social responsibility of the propertied classes.

To a large extent, the constraints imposed on the Poor Law in its early years of existence meant that it was ill-equipped to deal with large-scale distress or famine. The refusal to permit outdoor assistance meant that Poor Law relief was limited by the amount of inmates a workhouse could accommodate; furthermore, persons who were not destitute but only temporarily dislocated were excluded from receiving relief, no provision being made for short-term hardship. Significantly also, the principle of local chargeability, even during periods of crop failure, meant that the amount of relief available was restricted financially by what could be raised locally from poor rates. Finally, as George Nicholls had correctly realised, the Irish Poor Law was not capable of dealing with a crisis such as a famine. All of these factors were to have serious repercussions in the years following the appearance of potato blight, especially after August 1847, when responsibility for providing relief was vested almost exclusively in the Poor Law. Despite its recent introduction to Ireland, the operation of the Poor Law on the eve of the Famine exposed many underlying attitudes not only to Irish poverty but to the whole country.

A Blight of Unusual Character

1845–6

Initially, reports describing the appearance of a mysterious disease on the potato crops in various parts of Europe in 1845 were regarded with curiosity rather than alarm within Ireland. In the previous year, a number of Irish newspapers had carried reports from American journals and newspapers concerning a disease which had attacked the potato crop there for the second consecutive year. Within Ireland, however, there was little response to the news that the same disease had apparently spread to Europe in 1845.[1]

In August 1845, there were reports of the appearance of the mysterious disease in parts of England, notably on the Isle of Wight and in the vicinity of Kent. Many Irish newspapers reprinted articles from an English journal, *The Gardener's Chronicle and Horticultural Gazette*, edited by the eminent botanist, Dr John Lindley, which described the disease or blight. The observations of one subscriber to the journal from the Isle of Wight were widely published:

> A blight of unusual character, which almost universally affects the potatoes in this island, have been the last few days, repeatedly, brought to the notice by several gardeners.[2]

Although the *Gardener's Chronicle* quickly became the recognised authority on the potato disease, they were unable to identify either the cause of or a remedy for it. The disease still had no name but was variously referred to as the disease, the blight, distemper, the rot, the murrain or the blackness.

Throughout August, the *Gardener's Chronicle* carried reports of sightings of the potato disease in other parts of England. The blight had also appeared in Scotland, Belgium and Holland. These reports were extensively reprinted in the Irish newspapers. At the beginning of September, sightings of the disease were also being reported in Ireland.[3] On 16 September, Dr Lindley made an official announcement that 'the potato murrain has unequivocally declared itself in Ireland.' At the same time, he posed the question, 'Where will Ireland be in the event of a universal potato rot?'[4]

For the most part, within Ireland, general digging up of the potato crop did not take place until October—later than in many other countries. Because of this, the extent to which the Irish crop had been affected by the blight was not immediately obvious. Apart from some concern arising over the appearance of the mysterious blight, agricultural reports in general were very promising, predicting that the potato crop of 1845 would be exceptionally abundant. Two disquieting features of this type of blight were, however, beginning to emerge: in some cases, although the potato stem appeared luxuriant, upon digging it became apparent that the root was rotten, and potatoes which had appeared to be sound upon digging had, when stored, decomposed into a putrid, black mass.[5] Because of this, early estimates of the loss of the potato crop tended to understate the problem.

Initially, it was estimated that approximately one half of the Irish potato crop was unfit for human consumption. Within Ireland, potatoes were the main, if not the only food of about three million people who were, in general, the poorest sections of society. The remainder of the population also ate potatoes in varying quantities. No other country in Europe depended on the potato as extensively as the people of Ireland. On average an adult male in Ireland would, during the nine months following the harvest, consume from 10 to 12 lbs of potatoes daily. During the so-called 'hungry months' of June, July and August, the quantity consumed would have been less until the new harvest was ready. The diet of potatoes and buttermilk, consumed in such large quantities, and occasionally supplemented with a bowl of oatmeal, contained all the nutrients and vitamins necessary for a healthy diet.[6] Apart from being consumed by humans, potatoes were also extensively fed to pigs and farmyard fowl. Approximately 50 per cent of the yearly crop was used in this way. During periods of scarcity, therefore, it was the animals who bore the initial brunt of the shortages.[7]

Potato disease was not unknown in Ireland. Prior to 1845, the potato crop was periodically attacked by two main diseases commonly referred to as 'curl' and 'dry rot'. Neither of these diseases had ever been as destructive as the blight. The unknown blight which was attacking the potato crop throughout Europe in the summer of 1845 was, in fact, caused by a fungus 'phytophthora infestans'. The disease was thought to have originated in South America from where, facilitated by improvements in sea transport, it eventually made its way to Europe. The fungus initially attacked the potato leaves and then spread through the foliage to the actual potato. Some contemporary accounts described the blight on the potatoes as having the appearance of soot. Thereafter, the plant decomposed rapidly, the potatoes withering, turning black and finally rotting, during which process a putrid smell emitted from them.[8]

Although numerous hypotheses were propounded as to the cause of the disease and a remedy to it, none of the suggestions were successful in stopping the advance of the blight. Explanations for its dispersion ranged from there being surplus water in the diseased potatoes to the unusual coldness and wetness of the weather. One school of opinion believed that God was displaying his wrath for the granting of Catholic Emancipation whilst another held that God was extracting a penance for the Irish people accepting money from the British government to finance Maynooth College. The real cause—a fungus which fed on even healthy potatoes—had few supporters and their ideas were subsumed beneath more popular orthodoxies. Remedies for the disease were equally diverse and included soaking the diseased potatoes in bog water or putting the newly dug potatoes in well ventilated pits which were covered with a thatched roof. The latter was favoured by Dr Lindley and had the official support of the government. In spite of such eminent backing, it proved to be unsuccessful in keeping the potatoes free from disease. This led one newspaper to observe that the government's advisors 'know nothing whatever about the causes or remedy for disease'.[9] It was not, in fact, until the 1880s that an effective antidote to the blight—a solution consisting of copper sulphate—was applied.

As the national dimensions of the blight became increasingly apparent, there were signs of public panic as to its consequences. Although the effects of the disease were unlikely to be felt until the following spring and summer, there was a general feeling that the government should act quickly to meet the anticipated crisis. At the end of October, the Mansion House Committee was established, with Lord Cloncurry as its chairman. Meetings were also held in Dublin and other major towns in Ireland and demands were made for immediate (and very traditional) measures to be taken by the government. They were, that employment on public works be commenced, the export of corn be stopped, and distilleries be closed.[10]

By the middle of October, the Prime Minister, Sir Robert Peel, had privately acknowledged that Ireland appeared to be on the brink of a major disaster.[11] Peel was familiar with the problems caused by crop failure in Ireland, having served as Irish Chief Secretary during the 1817, and as Home Secretary during the 1822, food shortages. Although he realised that some additional legislative measures were necessary to alleviate the inevitable distress, he was reluctant to act until he had full and accurate information as to the extent of the loss. Both Peel and the Home Secretary, Sir James Graham, established daily contact with the Irish Executive at Dublin Castle and they in turn requested detailed reports describing the local situation from members of the coastguard, the constabulary and the Poor Law Board.[12]

The Prime Minister decided to appoint a Scientific Commission which was to enquire into the cause of the blight and suggest a palliative for it. The Commission consisted of an eminent Scottish chemist, Dr Lyon Playfair, and the English botanist, Dr (later Professor) Lindley. They were subsequently joined by the Irish scientist Sir Robert Kane. Peel also asked them to suggest ways in which potatoes which were partly diseased could be used.[13] Furthermore, Peel desired their opinion, as independent observers, as to the true extent of the loss caused by the potato blight, believing:

> there is such a tendency to exaggeration and inaccuracy in Irish reports that delay in acting upon them is always desirable.[14]

Within two weeks of arriving in Ireland, Playfair and Lindley had submitted their first report. In private correspondence to Peel, Lindley described the situation as 'melancholy' and advised that the problem had been understated rather than exaggerated.[15] For the purpose of the official report, Lindley and Playfair had examined the potato crop in the relatively prosperous counties of Dublin, Louth, Meath, Westmeath and Kildare. In these areas, approximately half the crop was considered unfit for human consumption. Although in some places the situation was considerably worse than this, elsewhere it was much better. They could not, however, give any guarantees for the continuing safety of the unaffected part of the crop.

The Scientific Commissioners found no evidence that the size of the potato crop was, as had been widely reported, any larger than usual, but they considered it to be an average size crop. From the portion of the crop that was unaffected by the blight, on average a quarter (rather than the usual one-eighth) needed to be left aside for seed for the following year.[16] This left only three-eighths of the usual crop available for general consumption. The report of Playfair and Lindley estimated the blight as being far more extensive than local reports from the constabulary suggested. In a private letter, Peel admitted that he found the report of the 'men of science', 'very alarming'.[17] It is probable that the Commissioners, in fact, overstated the amount of potatoes lost and understated the overall size of the crop, particularly by their emphatic declaration that the size of the crop was not larger than usual, as had been widely anticipated. By doing this, they may, inadvertently, have influenced the government into providing more relief than they otherwise would have.

Playfair and Lindley made various suggestions for protecting the unaffected part of the crop, with particular emphasis on the storing of it in dry, well ventilated pits. They also recommended that if only part of a potato was diseased, the remainder could still be consumed by humans. Potatoes in which the blight was too extensive to allow this were to be used for the production of starch, which although inedible by itself, could be mixed with flour to make wholesome bread. The recommendations of this report were widely publicised. Seventy thousand copies were distributed by the government, including thirty to each Roman Catholic priest. Smaller abstracts were also made which the constabulary were to distribute to 'the cottiers on the land'.[18] Overall, Lindley and Playfair were doubtful that their suggestions would be followed for a variety of reasons: the want of means on the part of the Irish peasant, the wetness of the climate, the dispute between landlord and tenants, and perhaps the despair or other feelings of the poor cultivators.[19]

Within Britain also, there had been concerns about the size of the harvest. The summer of 1845 had been unusually wet and cold and, even before the blight appeared, there was some apprehension that the harvest would be poor. As a consequence, food prices, particularly of wheat, were expected to rise. Some members of the government believed that unless the weather improved, there would be severe distress within Britain and the task of feeding so many people would be formidable. In a pessimistic letter to the Prime Minister, the Home Secretary Sir James Graham confided that:

> I know not that the state of affairs is really sound when Ministers are driven to study the Barometer with so much anxiety, but under no Law will it be found easy to feed twenty-five millions crowded together in a narrow space, when heaven denies the blessings of abundance.[20]

Weather conditions did improve within Britain, although the potato crop was almost totally lost. However, fears about the size of the British crop gave way to news of the widespread destruction of the potato crop in Ireland. At the same time, there were reports of crop shortages in many parts of Europe; the potato blight had appeared in Belgium and Holland and the wheat harvest in many countries was poor. The governments of Belgium, Turkey, Alexandria, Russia and Sweden responded quickly to this news by prohibiting exports of food, particularly corn.[21] This meant that within Europe there was less food than usual available for import into Britain. At the same time, several overseas traders continued to buy in the British market; in a single day, agents of the Belgian government cleared the Liverpool market of its supplies of rice which resulted in a 75 per cent price rise.[22]

Within Britain, the problem of food supply, particularly during a period of scarcity, was inextricably linked with the Corn Law question. The Corn Laws restricted the importation of corn into the United Kingdom until the price of grain in the home market had reached a fixed price. These Laws had many opponents within Britain who regarded them as an impediment to free trade, and the Anti-Corn Law movement was a powerful lobby within the country. The Tory party, which was in power in 1845, was traditionally regarded as the defender of the Corn Laws but by this stage Peel and some of his supporters, including Graham, were of the opinion that they should be repealed.[23] Peel, in fact, had been moving closer to a policy of free trade since 1841. The impending distress within Ireland (and to a lesser degree, in Britain) provided the perfect opportunity for Peel to attempt to repeal the Corn Laws:

> Can we vote money for the sustenance of any considerable portion of the people, on account of actual or apprehended scarcity, and maintain in full operation the existing restrictions on the free import of grain? I am bound to say my impression is that we cannot.[24]

The Home Secretary, Graham, agreed that free importation was necessary in order to keep provisions within Ireland as cheap as possible, and warned that 'the peasantry without potatoes cannot go to market and must starve at home'.[25] This view, however, did not have the support of the majority of the Tory party and only three members of the Cabinet supported Peel.[26] Without majority support Peel was aware that repeal of the Corn Laws would be political suicide for him and would probably lead to the downfall of the government. Despite the approach of widespread distress within Ireland, during the winter of 1845–6 the question of whether or not to repeal the Corn Laws dominated British political life, both in and out of Westminster. Within Ireland also, the Corn Law issue was widely discussed. Again, the debate frequently cut across party lines. It was vehemently opposed by a determined Protectionist lobby— mostly consisting of successful Irish merchants—who stated that the reports of scarcity had been exaggerated. The supporters of the repeal denied this and described the issue as 'not as a political question, but one of charity'.[27]

In December 1845, Peel tendered his resignation over this issue, but remained in office as his opponent, Lord John Russell, was unable to form a government. The Corn Law debate, therefore, continued to dominate the British political scene throughout the early months of 1846. It was not finally resolved until June 1846 when the Corn Laws were repealed. As expected, this resulted in the fall of Peel's government, his Party refusing to support him on the question of Irish coercion. The Tory party was replaced by a Whig government led by Lord John Russell. The timing of repeal, however, meant that this action came when almost a year had passed since the first appearance of the blight and when the 1846 crop would soon be available.

The relief measures introduced by Peel's government in 1845–6 were generally held to be effective. The following, frequently quoted, opinion printed in the *Freeman's Journal* (a frequent critic of the government) provides perhaps the most important measure of the effectiveness of his policies: 'no man died of famine during his administration'.[28] As early as October 1845, Peel had become convinced of the need to repeal the Corn Laws as soon as possible, but this action alone was unlikely to supply the deficit resulting from the potato blight, nor could it guarantee that those who had lost their usual source of food would have access to other supplies. In October 1845, the Lord Lieutenant of Ireland, Lord Heytesbury, had warned the government that prices were already beginning to rise in Ireland and that meetings were being held in Dublin and other large towns calling for the prohibition of distillation from grain and for the opening of the ports to foreign corn.[29] Peel was sceptical about the real benefit of such actions:

> I have no confidence in such remedies as the prohibition of exports or the stoppage of the distilleries. The removal of impediments to import is the only effectual remedy.[30]

Despite this conviction, there was such a long delay before the Corn

Laws were finally removed that the contribution of the repeal to relieving the distress was severely limited. It also took a further three years before the change in policy was implemented fully.

Because the main pressure for relief was unlikely to be felt until the following spring and summer, Peel and Graham were determined to proceed cautiously, acting on as much information as possible. To this end, they both engaged in private correspondence with contacts in Ireland, not trusting the information which they received through official channels. As Graham explained to one of his correspondents:

> . . . in the haze of exaggeration which surrounds you in Dublin, every object is either magnified or distorted.[31]

A few measures, however, were taken promptly to prepare Ireland for the impending distress. In addition to the Scientific Commission already constituted, in November 1845 a temporary Relief Commission was established which was to organise food depots and co-ordinate the efforts of local relief committees. At about the same time, Peel and the Chancellor of the Exchequer, Henry Goulburn, arranged for the purchase of £100,000 of Indian corn which was to be secretly imported into Ireland, and in December it was decided to give an additional grant of money to the Board of Public Works. Neither the food nor the additional public works were to be made available until the following spring, and during the interim, the government hoped to obtain an accurate assessment of the need for relief. The Poor Law, which was the permanent system of poor relief in Ireland, was not to be extended, although a new Commissioner, Edward Twistleton, was appointed.

The measures introduced by Peel's government in response to the first appearance of blight has generally been praised, both then and subsequently, for its effectiveness. To a large extent, however, the relief measures employed in 1845–6 were similar, although on a larger scale, to those adopted in 1817, 1822, 1831, 1839 and 1842, which had also been regarded as successful. In 1817, 1822 and 1831, the government had imported supplies of food into the country (corn and potatoes) to compensate for the temporary deficit. It is perhaps significant that Peel was directly involved in the temporary relief programmes of 1817 and 1822. In 1839 and 1842 local relief committees had been encouraged to provide the distressed areas with food and employment. On each occasion public works had also been provided. In 1845, the government considered the potato failure as being little different from earlier crop failures, although they acknowledged that the scale of the problem was larger.

Essentially, however, it was regarded as a temporary failure; temporary measures, which in the past had proved to be successful, were felt to be sufficient. As late as May 1846, the government was convinced that it was 'applying merely a temporary remedy to a temporary, though widespread, calamity'.[32]

The British government viewed its role in the relief operations of 1845–6 as it had done on earlier occasions, that is, as 'stimulating, directing and supporting but not superseding' the duties of the local landlords. They were anxious that the whole burden of relief should not be thrown upon them, when it rightfully should be performed by the landowners of Ireland.[33] Everyone involved in the provision of relief agreed on this point. Charles Trevelyan, who was Permanent Secretary at the Treasury during the whole of the Famine period, repeatedly warned the officers involved in providing relief of the dangers of allowing Irish landlords and large farmers to abdicate from their duty and instead throw the burden on the 'public purse'. Trevelyan cautioned the Relief Commissioners:

> the landlords and other ratepayers are the parties who are both legally and morally answerable for affording due relief to the destitute poor . . . the measures to be adopted by you, and the officers employed under you are, therefore, to be considered as merely auxiliary to those which it is the duty of persons possessed of property in each neighbourhood to adopt.[34]

Sir Randolph Routh, the Chairman of the Relief Commission, agreed that if given the least encouragement to depend on government funding, 'the people would rest on their oars and throw the whole labour on the government'. He was, nevertheless, unsure if this could be totally avoided.[35] Trevelyan had no such doubts, and viewed the relief measures as a struggle between landlords and government, the outcome of which depended upon:

> whether the officers of government firmly oppose themselves to such selfish dereliction of duty, and make the persons who are possessed of property in each locality feel the full extent of their responsibility, or whether they yield to it and take the entire responsibility of providing the relief upon the government.[36]

To ensure that the first course was followed as far as possible, Trevelyan insisted that no money should be spent in Ireland without it initially receiving the sanction of the Treasury. Also, rather than work through the intermediary of the Relief Commission in Dublin, Trevelyan chose to correspond directly (and sometimes secretly), with the officers in the field. From the very beginning, therefore, Trevelyan approached the provision of relief with a rigour and conviction that seldom wavered. For the most part, he enjoyed the support and full concurrence of both Chancellors of the Exchequer (Goulburn was replaced by Charles Wood in June 1846) and by the ministers of both the Tory and Whig governments under which he served. If, occasionally, his views were at variance with the Tory Chancellor of the Exchequer, Henry Goulburn, Trevelyan's ideas found a more sympathetic audience in Goulburn's successor, Charles Wood. Charles Wood and Charles Trevelyan presented a formidable duo at the Treasury. They shared a common strength of conviction and commitment to economic orthodoxy that set them apart from a number of leading members of the Whig administration, including Russell himself.

From the very outset, it was obvious that the policies of the British government had been created and were to be implemented with a view to bringing home to the landed interest within Ireland the fact that, ultimately, it was their responsibility to finance and distribute the relief necessary. At the same time, the responsibility for administering these policies lay with the British government. It was generally believed that a rigorous pursuit of the chosen policy would have long-term advantages for Ireland. Trevelyan was in no doubt as to the correctness of this policy:

> That indirect permanent advantages will accrue to Ireland from the scarcity, and the measures taken for its relief, I entertain no doubt. . . . Besides, the greatest improvement of all which could take place in Ireland would be to teach the people to depend upon themselves for developing the resources of the country, instead of having recourse to the assistance of the government on every occasion . . . if a firm stand is not made against the prevailing disposition to take advantage of this crisis to break down all barriers, the true permanent interests of the country will, I am convinced, suffer in a manner which will be irreparable in our time.[37]

From the very beginning, therefore, members of the British government saw themselves as being involved in a crusade to bring about social changes within Ireland, the enemies to such changes being the recalcitrant landlords on one side, and the perfidious potato on the other.

The Relief Commission and Local Relief Committees

The temporary Relief Commission, established by Sir Robert Peel, first met on the 20 November 1845. It consisted of some of the most influential and able members of the Irish administration. Edward Lucas, the Under-Secretary at Dublin Castle, was appointed Chairman and was assisted by Sir James Dombrain, the Inspector General of the Coast Guard. Also appointed were Colonel Harry Jones of the Board of Works; Edward Twistleton, the newly appointed Poor Law Commissioner; Sir Randolph Routh, officer in charge of the Commissariat Department of the Army; John Pitt Kennedy, former Secretary of the Devon Commission which investigated all aspects of land tenure in Ireland; and Sir Robert Kane, the distinguished scientist, who also had the distinction of being the only Catholic member of the board. In January 1846, the temporary Relief Commission was re-organised, with Randolph Routh as Chairman. Colonel Harry Jones was removed from the board.

The duties of the Relief Commission were to advise the government, through the medium of the Treasury, as to the amount of distress within Ireland and to supervise and co-ordinate the activities of local relief committees. The local relief committees were voluntary bodies comprised of notables within a district, including landlords, clergy, merchants and large farmers. The main functions of the local committees were to act as a medium for the purchase and re-selling of the Indian corn imported by the government from America and to oversee the provision of employment on small works of local utility. These activities were to be financed by voluntary subscriptions from the local community. This money could be matched by a grant provided by the government of up to 100 per cent of the amount donated. Requests for this grant were to be made to the Lord Lieutenant who was in charge of its distribution. It was the Treasury, however, acting on the information provided by the Relief Commission, which made the ultimate decision as to the amount of money to be provided. In order to qualify for a government grant, the local committees had to comply with the printed instructions provided by the government.[38]

The instructions, which were intended to advise on the formation of the temporary relief committees and their duties, were not issued until the 28 February 1846. By this time there was considerable distress in some parts of the country. This was particularly severe in many of the areas along the western seaboard, notably, counties Clare, Kerry, Galway, Mayo and west Cork, and the adjoining counties of Tipperary and Roscommon—the areas which traditionally suffered most during crop failures. In addition to this, however, the impact of the blight was also being felt in counties Louth, Meath, Kilkenny and Waterford, and local reports referred to the expectation of heavy demand for relief.[39] The exceptional wetness caused by heavy rain since the end of January also appeared to exacerbate the spread of the blight which, prior to this, had seemed to have reached a plateau.[40] Reports about the extent of the blight were contradictory, owing to the amorphous nature of the blight itself. Routh described the country as being like a chequer-board, as it was black and white in close juxtaposition.[41]

The capricious nature of the blight and the erratic way in which it appeared, even during the early months of 1846, made it difficult to gauge accurately the extent of loss. From the constabulary reports of March 1846, it appears that it was most virulent in counties Antrim, Clare, Kilkenny, Louth, Monaghan, and Waterford, where it affected over 40 per cent of the crop. Counties Armagh, Fermanagh and Wicklow were amongst the least affected counties. Unfortunately, incomplete data was provided to the constabulary for some counties, including Co. Mayo.[42] (See Appendix 1.) Although these reports provide an insight into the potato losses sustained, they do not necessarily relate to levels of incipient distress in each area. The official reports do not take into account the size of the crop, nor do they measure the dependency on the potato within the area, or the relative social position of the growers of the blighted crops. Overall, this meant it was difficult to judge the amount of relief required in each area. Also, as local reports stated and Routh explained, the 'chequered' nature of the blight meant that even adjoining fields were differently affected. Inevitably, this meant that there was considerable local variations in the demand for relief in the spring and summer of 1846.

The delay in the issuing of the government's instructions filled the Chairman of the Relief Commission, Edward Lucas, with alarm, particularly as he doubted whether the amount of relief envisaged would be sufficient to meet the approaching distress. In a report to the government on 20 January he was critical of various aspects of the government's relief policy:

> numerous cases of distress are likely to occur, and some are near at hand, for which the Act [Extension of Public Works Act] nor any other, as far as we know, in existence or in the contemplation of the government, can provide an effectual remedy'.[43]

Lucas confirmed that potato blight was present in every county and every Poor Law union in Ireland. Out of the 2,049 electoral divisions in the country, over 1,400 had reported the appearance of blight and there was no way of being sure that the other 600 electoral divisions had escaped. Because the loss caused by the blight was patchy rather than continuous, Lucas believed that the system of public works envisaged was not suitable. He also doubted:

> . . . whether any adjustment of public works can be made to meet the need wherever it may occur; and it must be met, or death from famine may be the result.[44]

It is perhaps no coincidence that shortly afterwards, Lucas, who had been so critical of the policies of the government, was replaced as Chairman of the Relief Commission.

The delay in issuing the instructions to the local relief committee was, in fact, a deliberate policy intended to 'postpone the assistance of government to the latest possible period'.[45] The Relief Commission, the Treasury and the Home Office—the government departments which were primarily involved in the relief of the distress—were afraid that if they did not strictly control government spending, funds would appear to be limitless, which would result in further demands being made on the public purse. At the same time, a generous provision of relief would be a disincentive to attempts at self-exertion.[46]

The decision on the choice of the date for issuing the guidelines for the committees was in the hands of the Treasury. The involvement of the Treasury in the various temporary relief measures increasingly took on a more central position. The Treasury was responsible for the issuing of all sums of money required by the various relief departments, but its influence also spread rapidly into all matters associated with everyday administration. To a large extent, such a pervasive presence reflected the personality of the Permanent Secretary at the Treasury, Charles Trevelyan. His enthusiasm, thoroughness and high level of personal involvement ensured that the Treasury played an important role in all decisions in relation to the provision of relief. He quickly became an authority on the Irish situation by insisting that he personally receive a full and detailed application on each request for relief. As a result, Trevelyan's role went far beyond that of a neutral administrator of public finances. His advice was initially sought by several of the people involved in the provision of relief. Sir Randolph Routh, the Chairman of the Relief Commission, at one stage informed Trevelyan, 'I am most anxious to be guided by your instructions.' Routh, nevertheless, like many of the other relief officials based in Dublin, fell foul of Trevelyan over a difference of view on the relief policies. Routh, like Lucas before him, was eventually replaced. Trevelyan, however, remained in position throughout the whole course of the Famine.

On 20 February, Trevelyan informed Routh that he considered that the time had arrived for the 'authoritative promulgation of the plans of government'.[47] A week later, copies of the instructions were sent to all local areas through the usual channels (constabulary, boards of guardians, clergy, magistrates) and to other interested parties. The instructions required that the Lieutenant of each county should oversee the formation of local relief committees. It was recommended that they should consist of the county Lieutenant or his deputy, local magistrates, an officer of the Board of Works, clergymen of all persuasions, the chairman of the Poor Law union, other Poor Law Guardians and, where possible, a coastguard officer. The Lieutenant could also select other 'active and intelligent gentlemen' to join a committee.[48]

The committees were to be responsible for districts where there had been a 'very considerable' loss of the potato crop.[49] During the spring and summer of 1846, almost 700 relief committees were established according to the instructions of the government. The majority of these committees were in the south and west of the country. There were fewer in the midlands, only a handful in the province of Ulster and none whatsoever in counties Armagh, Down, Fermanagh, Londonderry or Tyrone. The formation of relief committees was therefore most frequent in areas where there was a high level of dependence on potatoes, even if the effects of the blight had been below the national average, or where the effects of the blight had been very severe. The relief committees did not conform to any uniform geographic or administrative boundaries; in some places, the unit of the barony was used; elsewhere, smaller electoral divisions or parishes were preferred. In general, the committees formed in 1846 tended to be larger than those formed in the second year of distress.

The main function of the relief committees was to raise funds with which to purchase and distribute the food imported by the government. The amount of money provided by local subscription could be matched by an equal amount from funds especially put at the disposal of the Lord Lieutenant by the Treasury. In practice, the amounts provided by the Lord Lieutenant were often smaller than those raised locally. The committees could purchase this food at cost price from various depots situated around the country. The government believed that by adhering as far as possible to these procedures, an important principle was being followed, namely, that the government was not seen to be directly involved in the sale or distribution of food. In cases where a person did not have the means to purchase food, a task of work of 'public improvement' was to be demanded in return for it. If the relief committee so desired, they could instigate and oversee their own public works, although these were expected to be on a smaller scale than the public works introduced by the government.

Another principle which the government regarded as important was that the relief committees should not give relief in the form of money unless absolutely necessary (absolutely necessary, in this case, meant when the alternative was starvation). Even in cases where a task was performed, the government stipulated that payment had to be in the form of food. In each case, the food provided was to be sufficient only to feed the workman and his dependants and was to be given on a daily basis (Sunday excepted). Only in 'extreme' cases could the food be given gratuitously. By 'extreme', the government meant when the person had no money, was unable to work, and was unable to obtain a place in the local workhouse, due to it being full. Starvation, therefore, was the alternative.[50]

The government believed that it was essential to involve the local community, via the relief committees, in the provision of relief, as their local knowledge made them ideally suited to detect imposters. This was something which agents of the government would have found it far harder to do. To this end, the committees were to obtain lists of the residents of each townland together with 'minute reports of the circumstances of each family from whom application for relief may be made'.[51] A register was to be kept of all persons given a ticket or certificate entitling them to relief. Records were also to be kept at the depots, by a member of the constabulary if possible, in which details of all transactions were to be recorded. Overall, the various instructions issued to the relief committees are indicative of the extreme caution with which the government implemented its relief policy, and the fact that in their attempt to prevent a misuse of their funds, procedure often took precedence over provision.

From 26 March to the beginning of August 1846, the relief committees raised a total of £98,003 1s 2½d, the largest amount ever raised by voluntary subscriptions for the relief of distress in Ireland. To this, the Lord Lieutenant added a further £65,914 10s 0d. Most of this money was raised by committees in the south and west of the country, particularly in counties Cork, Limerick, Tipperary and Waterford. Not surprisingly, the largest individual amounts from local committees came from those situated in large towns. Within counties Clare, Galway and Mayo, smaller relief committees were established, which although they did not individually raise as much as the committees of the larger towns, still appear to have been very active. There were far fewer relief committees in the midlands and east of the country, and hardly any in Ulster. This suggests that the formation of the local committees was a response to a local and varied call for help. An article on the national scarcity in a Dublin newspaper in June 1846 praised the response of the majority of landlords in Ireland to the prevailing situation, particularly those in Co. Clare where it judged the distress to be most severe. Within Britain, however, the positive response of many landlords to Irish distress was generally overshadowed by a persistent belief that Irish landlords were continuing to evade their responsibilities.[52]

The largest amount raised by any individual relief committee was £2,300 collected by Cork city. To this, the Lord Lieutenant donated £1,500. The largest amounts of money provided by the committees were raised in April, May and June, following which the amounts contributed began to taper off even before the official closing date of 10 August. If the largest donations were made by the towns, the smallest donations appear to have been raised in the small islands situated off the west coast of Ireland. Aran Island (Inishmore), near Galway, raised £7 18s 0d, to which the Lord Lieutenant added £7 10s 0d. Lettermore Island made two donations of £8 1s 0d and £4 8s 0d, to which were added £8 0s 0d and £4 8s 0d respectively by the Lord Lieutenant.[53] The relative smallness of these amounts partly reflects both the scale of the blight in these areas, and the fact that these islands appear to have escaped from the worst effects of the distress in 1845–6. This was because blight was not widespread in the islands in 1845, whilst the diversity of the local economies meant that the local population was not totally dependent on potatoes anyway.[54]

The Food Depots

One of the first actions of Peel, acting with the Chancellor of the Exchequer, Goulburn, had been to arrange for £100,000 worth of Indian corn and corn meal to be secretly purchased in America and shipped to Ireland at the beginning of 1846. The trading house of Baring Bros and Co. acted as agents of the government in this transaction. This decision had been taken by Peel even before the official sanction of the Treasury had been given. The public were to be kept in the dark about the corn for an even longer period as the government wanted to keep its actions secret until the last possible moment. In this way, the government hoped they would not stifle private enterprise nor would their actions be a disincentive to local relief efforts.[55]

Due to unfavourable weather conditions, the first shipment of Indian corn did not arrive in Ireland until the early part of February 1846. In the first instance, all the imported corn was to be unloaded and stored in Cork. This was because the corn had not been ground and was inedible. The government recognised that this task was unlikely to be carried out locally, as it involved a long and complicated process if it was to be done correctly. It was therefore to be carried out in Cork where it could be supervised by Commissary-General Hewetson, an officer of the Relief Commission. The following description of the process, written by Routh, shows what a complicated and delicate process the grinding of Indian corn was:

> First to keep the corn eight hours on the kilns, and turn it twice, so as to be thoroughly dried without parching. It was then allowed to cool for forty-eight hours. In grinding it, the stones were kept wider apart than for wheat, and not driven too rapidly lest it should heat the meal. . . . The meal was then ordered to remain seventy hours to cool before it was dressed, it was again left to cool for a day or two before it was sacked.[56]

Before the Indian meal was actually consumed, it had to be 'very much' cooked again, otherwise its consumption could result in severe bowel complaints.[57] Sir Randolph Routh who, during sixteen years service in America, had become acquainted with these processes, regarded himself as an authority on Indian corn. He produced a pamphlet containing simple recipes for its use, which was sold throughout the country. Not surprisingly, the demand for this small book was great in a country where Indian corn was hardly known. The decision to import Indian corn, however, was based partly on its very strangeness. The government, wishing to keep its own involvement in food importation distinct from that undertaken by private traders, deliberately chose a food that was not generally imported into the country. Some Indian corn had been imported during earlier crop failures, also by the government, but on a far smaller scale than in 1845–6.[58]

Routh, who became a public advocate of the use and benefits of Indian corn, advised that one meal in the morning was sufficient to support a labourer throughout the whole day. He also claimed that it had the added benefit of reducing the likelihood of fever, no mean feat as fever inevitably followed during periods of distress. By the end of August, Routh pronounced that the Irish people now preferred Indian corn to oatmeal, particularly in the form of 'mush, or stirabout', which was cooked in large quantities and then eaten cold in slices. Indian corn had also the significant advantage of being bulky and filling, therefore 'its cheapness and nutritious qualities were calculated to replace advantageously the loss of the potato crop'.[59] By this stage, however, many people had found that a judicious mixture of Indian corn with oatmeal made the former considerably more palatable.

Initially, however, there was resistance to this alien, bright yellow, hard grain, which was derisively referred to as 'Peel's brimstone'. The contrast with the traditional potato diet was stark. Even Routh admitted privately to Trevelyan that the Irish people 'are accustomed to potatoes, which satisfy by repletion, and a more nourishing substance, which does not fill the stomach, leaves a craving sensation, a want of support and strength, as if they had not eaten enough'.[60] Routh, without intending to, had touched unintentionally on the comparative nutritional value of certain foodstuffs. The traditional diet of potatoes, particularly when consumed in large quantities, was nutritionally far superior to an exclusively grain-based diet. Indian corn, especially when mixed and diluted with water, may have appeared to fill stomachs, but nutritionally did little else. By engineering this change of eating habits upon some of the Irish people, the government inadvertently was increasing the vulnerability of those people to nutritional deficiencies and diseases.[61]

In order to prepare the poor people of Ireland for a diet of Indian corn, even before the depots were open, an experiment was made of introducing corn into the diet of a number of workhouses. Initially, the inmates refused to eat it.[62] Such resistance was short-lived and seems to have almost disappeared as people became more familiar with the correct way to cook the corn. However, although the government wanted to dispel the early prejudices, they did not want their bounty to appear too attractive. Trevelyan decreed that it was necessary to grind the Indian corn twice in order to make it more palatable and employed his oft-repeated argument that 'it would do permanent harm to make dependence on public charity an agreeable mode of life'.[63]

Although the main Indian corn depot was in Cork, the government also established other depots in various parts of the country. The 'out-depots' were at Limerick, Kilrush, Galway, Westport, Sligo, to serve the west; Athy, Banagher, Tullamore, and Longford in the midlands; and Waterford, Dublin and Dundalk to serve the east coast. The Limerick and Dublin depots were the largest, reflecting the regional breakdown of areas where the government anticipated most demand for relief. No out-depot was situated in Ulster. The grain was transported to these depots from Cork by sea. There were also a number of smaller sub-depots.

Seventy-six of these were based at coastguard stations which were situated along the western seaboard, as far north as Dunfanaghy in Co. Donegal. A further twenty-nine were managed by the constabulary, mainly in the interior of the country. The coastguard performed the new duties assigned to them for no additional remuneration. About 11,000 members of the constabulary were put in charge of the sale of the corn, the government regarding them as more trustworthy than local members of the community. For this service they received 2s 6d per day, in addition to their usual pay.[64]

The government decided to postpone making the corn available until the last possible moment in order to conserve the limited supplies which they had. They also wanted the Irish people to depend on their own resources for as long as possible. In this they were helped by the size of the potato crop. Despite the early and pessimistic predictions of Lindley and Playfair, the crop, in general, was a third larger than usual. Also, in spite of the private and public concerns expressed about them, many landlords involved themselves in the relief operations with both 'activity and outlay'.[65] Some proprietors maintained their tenants from their own resources or provided additional employment for them. The government was also pleasantly surprised by the amounts raised voluntarily by the relief committees, which made the issue of free corn virtually unnecessary. In fact, from March to August 1846, the local committees raised over £98,000, which was the largest amount ever contributed voluntarily by Irish landlords for the relief of distress.[66] The attitude of the recipients of relief was also a contributory factor. Routh realised and admitted that the success of the government's policies was because 'the people submitted patiently to great sacrifices'.[67]

The date chosen for the opening of the food depots and the sale of corn was 15 May. Due to local pressure, some did have to open at the end of March although most, in keeping with the policy of the government, did not open until May. The demands on the depots exceeded expectations. The Limerick depot was particularly busy, issuing approximately 500 tons of corn per week compared to 300 tons per week in Cork. The relief committees were only allowed to purchase corn in quantities ranging from five to twenty tons. They then could only resell it in small quantities from one to seven pounds. Most of the demand was, however, for small quantities.

Due to the clamour to buy Indian corn, particularly in small amounts, many local depots had to remain open from six o'clock in the morning to nine o'clock in the evening. The corn was generally paid for in small coppers and coins. Initially, the price of the corn was fixed at cost price but the eagerness with which the corn was purchased and the apparent ease with which the population could afford it, resulted in a change of policy; after 3 June, the Treasury decreed that the price of the corn was no longer to be cost price but was to be fixed at the local market price which was inevitably higher. Local relief committees were slow to respond to this instruction, or ignored it altogether. This resulted in an admonishment of Routh by Trevelyan. In a strongly-worded letter, Trevelyan pointed out that while Routh might be the chairman of the Relief Commission in Dublin, the control of local sales prices was the preserve of the Treasury and changes could not be made without prior sanction.[68] In this letter, Trevelyan demonstrated that he clearly believed in the primacy of central government decisions over local knowledge.

By the end of June—only six weeks after the official opening dates of the depots—the supplies of Indian corn were beginning to run low. As July was expected to be the month of most distress, the government was forced to purchase a further supply of corn. Trevelyan warned Routh that the government would not be willing to purchase a third quantity.[69] An additional 3,000 tons of Indian corn, believed to be inferior to that from America, was purchased from the Mediterranean countries. At the same time, the army was requested to keep a supply of biscuits available in the Ordnance stores in the event of the corn running out.[70]

In total, the government expended £185,432 7s 7d for the purchase, freight and grinding of Indian corn. Of this amount, only £50,481 5s 5d was not to be repaid. The government also absorbed other costs such as shipping and labour. The amount of Indian corn which was provided was 44,121,574 ½lbs which could feed 490,240 persons daily for a period of three months, at the government recommended level of one pound of grain per adult, per day.[71] This amount compared poorly with the average quantity of 10 lbs of potatoes consumed in normal years. In total quantity, it also compared badly with the overall deficit in food supply caused by the potato blight. The government insisted that only the officers employed by the government should be informed of the amounts which were available. They also wanted the amount of corn which they considered sufficient to feed each person to be kept a secret, in case it became necessary to reduce the size of the recommended rations.[72]

The intention of the government in framing this policy had not been to provide sufficient food for the affected section of the population. Rather, their actions were meant to act as a disincentive to private traders from hoarding their supplies until the last possible moment and then charging exorbitant prices.[73] In this regard the government was successful as grain prices did not rise substantially until the end of 1846. Also, from early in that year, private merchants began to import Indian corn in substantial quantities, as the government had hoped they would. At the same time, the Irish merchants began to import grain in far larger quantities than they had done prior to 1845. As a result, during the Famine period, Ireland switched from being an exporter of grain to being a large scale importer.[74] By the government's own criteria, therefore, the policy was successful and appeared to have provided the necessary 'kick-start' to the importation of foodstuffs.

Although Routh had recommended that the depots should stay open until 1 September, the government decided to close them on 15 August.[75] Again they used the argument that if they did not restrict the amount of relief available, they would encourage a false dependency on the resources of the government.[76] During their busiest period the officers of the Relief Commission were working a twelve-hour day. When Routh mentioned an indisposition caused by this amount of work, he was told by Trevelyan, in his usual brusque manner, that, given the prevailing circumstances, there was no time to be ill.[77] At the beginning of July 1846, the Treasury decided that the supplies in the various food depots should be allowed to run out and not be replenished. If necessary, however, supplies could be transferred from the depots with unused supplies to depots in the most distressed areas.[78] As the relief operations began to wind down, there was a general mood of optimism and self-congratulation amongst the officers involved in providing relief.[79] In typical and strangely prophetic manner, Trevelyan warned that it was too early to celebrate.[80]

The relief provided by the government through the temporary Relief Commission in the summer and spring of 1846, was held to be successful, both by contemporaries and subsequently by many historians. Not only had there been no fatalities, but the government had the satisfaction of knowing that its policies, based on caution and secrecy, had been successful. At the same time, the government believed that the need to show Irish people—from peasant to landlord—that self-dependence was always preferable to provision by the government, had worked. The role performed by the local relief committees was particularly satisfactory. Up to 1 August 1846, they had raised over £98,000, to which the government contributed a further £66,000.[81] The amount of money raised by the committees had exceeded all expectations and they had proved effective agents in the local distribution of relief. In addition, many landed proprietors had also provided additional employment on their estates, thus reducing the demand for employment on the government-sponsored relief works. Furthermore, since 1838, the largest proprietors in Ireland had been responsible for paying the poor rates with which to finance the workhouses.[82] This positive demonstration of landlord activity implies the existence of a moral economy, and it contrasts sharply with the image traditionally assigned to Irish landlords, most notably by non-Irish members of the government. A distinction should perhaps be made, however, between landlords who, by being present on their estates, were willing and able to become involved in the various measures for providing relief, and those who, due to their absenteeism, were able to avoid any direct calls on their resources.

Apart from the immediate success of their policies, some of the officials engaged in providing relief believed that the policies of the government would be of longer-term benefit to the people of Ireland. The introduction of Indian corn into the Irish diet was seen as a positive step in moving sections of the population away from their dependence on the potato, which was blamed for many evils within Irish society. Routh put this very clearly when he stated:

> The little industry called for to rear the potato, and its prolific growth, leave the people to indolence and all kinds of vice, which habitual labour and a higher order of food would prevent. I think it very probable that we may derive much advantage from this present calamity.[83]

There was also a general feeling among the British relief officials that what Britain had effected during the emergency would help to foster more positive relations between the two countries. One senior officer of the Relief Commission confided to Trevelyan:

> I know it to be an opinion among reflecting Irishmen that more will have been done in these few months to counteract the efforts of agitators, than years could have accomplished under ordinary circumstances.[84]

Routh was similarly optimistic, believing that the efforts of the British government would earn them a place in history:

> A practical relief of this description, distributed to a nation in small issues, to reach the poorest families, is an event of rare occurrence, even in history . . . a deep feeling of gratitude has risen up in return for the paternal care of her Majesty's government.[85]

Overall, therefore, the agents of the Treasury and of the Relief Commission were well pleased with their efforts on a number of fronts, not least of which was the 'small comparative expense at which this large quantity of food has been made to supply a whole population'.[86]

One of the less satisfactory elements of the government's relief policies was the fact that some Irish merchants were dissatisfied with them. As early as April 1846, even before many government depots were open, some of the smaller merchants complained that they could not get a sufficiently high price for their goods.[87] Their reservations had much support within the government, as the prevailing belief was that private traders, and not the government, should be the main providers of subsistence for the people.[88] Only exceptional circumstances warranted a deviation from this philosophy.

Charles Trevelyan was sympathetic to the situation of the Irish traders. In the spring of 1846, he sent copies of a book by Edmund Burke, *Thoughts on Scarcity*, to various relief officers, urging them to read it and comment on it. In his book, Burke had warned of the great evils which could arise from allowing people to depend on the government for subsistence. Burke's ideas received a sympathetic hearing from the members of the Relief Commission, all of whom felt that government interference should be limited to cases of extreme urgency and should be of as short a duration as possible.[89] The general consensus of feeling was that if there was again a crop failure in Ireland, the actual purchase of food should be left to private competition, and the role of the government should, as far as possible, be confined to giving people the means with which to purchase the food.[90]

By the summer of 1846, there were scattered reports about the reappearance of blight and the possibility of further food shortages became a reality. Routh and Trevelyan discussed the future role of the government in depth. Although at this stage the extent of crop loss was not known, they agreed on the general principles which should determine future policy. Both men abhorred the idea of the government again interfering in the market place and purchasing food. They agreed that 'if it should unfortunately be indispensable to revert to those measures', the role of the government should be more limited than it had been in 1845–6. Food should not be imported into the east of Ireland which, apart from its proximity to the ports of Liverpool and Bristol, possessed its own 'mercantile facilities'. Furthermore, if it did prove necessary to import food to parts of Ireland in the following year, purchases should be made in the United Kingdom rather than from overseas markets. This would help to stimulate British trade rather than depress it, as had been the case during the early part of 1846.[91] Even before the first year of distress had drawn to a close, therefore, some relief officials were aware that a second year of government intervention might prove necessary.

The Public Works

If the contribution made by the Relief Commission was generally praised, the role played by the public works was deemed to be less than satisfactory. Public works, like relief committees, were a traditional way of relieving periods of exceptional distress within Ireland. In 1822, for example, extensive relief had been provided throughout the south and west of Ireland through the construction of roads and, to a smaller extent, piers and harbours.[92] In 1831, the British Treasury had provided £11,000 for relief work, to be used in the distressed counties of Mayo and Galway.[93] The responsibility for public works was shared by various departments which, in 1831, were consolidated into the Board of Works.[94] The use of public works to help mitigate the effect of the potato blight had been discussed by Sir Robert Peel and the Irish Executive in Dublin Castle in early November 1845. They agreed that by introducing public works to provide immediate relief, they would simultaneously be promoting the longer-term welfare of Ireland. The measures which they particularly favoured were drainage and navigation, including the linking of the lakes of Ulster to those of Connacht, and giving a stimulus to the fishing industry by the building of larger boats and the making of better nets.[95]

The Irish Board of Works did not become involved in the actual provision of relief until December 1845, when the Lord Lieutenant requested that the government place £5,000 at the disposal of the Board for the provision of employment in the distressed areas. This was agreed to, although, at the same time, the longer-term role of the public works was under consideration. It was not until the beginning of March 1846 that legislation was introduced which confirmed the role of the Board in the relief measures. Four separate Acts were passed which were intended to promote the development of fisheries and harbours, to encourage drainage and other improvements on estates, and to facilitate the construction and repair of roads.[96] These various works of utility were to be financed in one of two ways, depending on the nature of the work undertaken. The repair and construction of roads could receive a 50 per cent grant from the government, whereas the other works were to be financed by the local Grand Juries. In the first instance, a Memorial was to be sent from the local district to the Lord Lieutenant asking for work on the roads to be undertaken. Following an inspection, the Treasury could then provide the requisite grant, half of which was to be repaid by the local barony, the other half being a free grant. If any of the other works of improvement were to be undertaken, an application was made through the local Grand Jury to the Lord Lieutenant. If approved, an advance would be issued by the Treasury, but this time the whole amount was to be repaid by the local area.[97] In view of the financial incentives offered by the first method, it is not surprising that road construction and repair were overwhelmingly preferred to the other types of improvements as a method of providing public employment. During the year, a total of £476,000 was spent in the improvement of roads, compared with the expenditure of £126,000 in other works of utility.[98]

Even before the public works commenced, Trevelyan expressed reservations about the wisdom of making the public works so attractive through the introduction of the 'half-grant' system. Within a few days of the Acts being passed, it became obvious that most of the requests were from people whose main interest was to avail of this grant. Trevelyan accused the landlords of promoting their own interests rather than trying to provide relief and he urged that a distinction should be made between 'what is indispensably required for the relief of the people, and what is demanded under the pretext of that scarcity'.[99] Trevelyan's reservations were shared by Lieutenant-Colonel Harry Jones, Chairman of the Board of Works, who believed that the funds 'so generously allocated by the government' were being used for individual benefit rather than for the public good. He urged that either some further checks should be imposed or that a different system be introduced.[100]

The Irish Executive, through whom this money was to be channelled, were less critical of the availability of the fund. They were shocked by Trevelyan's suggestion that, in order to reduce any possibility of abuse of the funds, he would withhold the money for as long as possible. The Irish Executive informed Trevelyan that this was contrary to both the intentions of parliament and the terms of the Acts. Furthermore, they warned, if Trevelyan attempted to push this policy too far, it would act as a total check on the activities of the proprietors and thus throw an even larger burden on the government.[101] The pessimistic reports of the Commissioners of Public Works in the weeks after the Acts were introduced appeared to confirm Trevelyan's suspicions. In a report published concerning the grants made for the relief of distress, Trevelyan publicly condemned the financing of the public works, stating that:

Instead of a test of real distress, we have a bounty on interested exaggeration . . . not for the sake of the remedy, but the sugar in which it is coated . . . and the appeal thus made to the selfishness of the proprietors was irresistible.[102]

There was also considerable dissatisfaction with the way in which the Acts were being implemented in the various localities. Again, there was a conflict of opinion amongst the key relief personnel, with the Irish Executive on one side and the Treasury, together with the Boards of Works, on the other side. Lord Lincoln, the Lord Lieutenant, praised the Irish landlords for having behaved even better than had been expected. By doing so, he believed that they had successfully averted the threat of famine.[103] The perspective of the Board of Works and of the Treasury was clearly stated by Lieutenant-Colonel Jones in his declaration that, 'farmer, priest, landlord and tenant all make strong attempts to squeeze something out of the government purse'.[104]

Administratively, there were many problems in trying to implement public works on such a large scale. From the outset, the Board of Works had difficulty in finding a sufficient number of trained personnel, notably engineers and superintendents. Jones subsequently admitted to Trevelyan that the small amount of work actually done was primarily due to the 'inattention and ignorance' of those who superintended them. He did, however, praise the work of the engineers and county surveyors.[105] The procedure for commencing the public works was also cumbersome. The distressed area had to send a memorial to the Lord Lieutenant in Dublin Castle requesting assistance. This was forwarded to the Relief Commissioners who were then asked to comment on it. Next, it was passed on to the Board of Public Works where the application was again examined and officially registered. Following this, it was given to either a local surveyor or engineer for local inspection. He proceeded to the area, inspected the proposed work, obtained more local information and made a report on it. Upon receiving this report, the Board of Works finally decided whether or not to accept the application. If it was accepted, they would make a recommendation to the Lord Lieutenant about the amount of money to be provided. The Lord Lieutenant, acting on this recommendation, would then ask for the sanction of the Treasury. Upon receiving this, official approval could be given and an officer of the Board of Works despatched to the area.[106]

Even the Commissioners of the Board of Public Works realised that this long-drawn out process was not suitable when immediate relief was required. For the most part, in the spring and summer of 1846, the demand for relief was not as immediate as it was to become in subsequent years. In a few instances, however, the Irish Executive and the Relief Commission felt compelled to intervene and request the Board of Works to provide immediate relief as they considered the situation to be urgent. The Board of Works did not approve of this interference and complained to Trevelyan that they were being 'forced to do what they feel ought not to be done'.[107]

The role of the local relief committees was also included in the general criticism of the public works. The committees were responsible for issuing tickets of employment to destitute persons, but the Board of Works considered that they did this in an 'irregular manner'.[108] They were accused of not having paid sufficient attention to the circumstances of each applicant and thereby greatly adding to the difficulties of the officers of public works. Jones recommended that if this form of relief ever needed to be provided again, 'arrangements of a very different nature must be made'.[109] The people employed on the public works were paid a daily rate usually of 9d or 10d per day. In a Treasury Report of 3 April, this was condemned as being too high especially as a system of task work—payment by results—had not been introduced. The Report warned that by making the public works so attractive, labourers would not seek private employment or even undertake work on their own farms. As evidence, the Treasury pointed to the fact that seasonal migration to England had almost stopped. The Treasury Report recommended that, as far as possible, food should be given instead of money wages. Furthermore, if wages were paid, they were to be below the usual rates of pay in the neighbourhood and were only to be sufficient to keep a workman and his family from starvation.[110]

This Treasury Minute caused some controversy within the government. It appears to have been the personal work of Charles Trevelyan and to have been issued without prior consultation. The recommendations contained in the Report relating to the rate of wages was condemned by Lord Lincoln, the Lord Lieutenant, James Graham, the Home Secretary, and Henry Goulburn, the Chancellor of the Exchequer. Although Trevelyan was criticised for interfering in matters of government policy, his actions were dismissed (not for the first time) as being part of his zealous nature.[111] Subsequent government policy may have vindicated the recommendations of Trevelyan. In a Treasury Minute of 26 June, it was declared that 'numerous' persons who did not really require relief had been employed on the public works. It also stated that the wages which had been paid, by being above what was absolutely necessary, had tempted the people to abandon their normal means of employment.[112] Although the Irish Executive again protested about the insinuations contained in the Minute, it appeared that Trevelyan's suggestions now had the support of the newly installed Whig government.[113]

The amount of money expended on an individual public work ranged from £500 to £6,000, although the average expenditure tended to be in the region of £2,000. The popularity of the half-grant scheme was such that by the end of May, applications had been received from eighteen different counties, namely Clare, Cork, Galway, Kerry, Kildare, Kilkenny, King's, Leitrim, Limerick, Louth, Mayo, Meath, Queen's, Roscommon, Sligo, Tipperary, Waterford and Westmeath, for 203 separate works, the anticipated cost of which was over £1m. Of this, only £250,000 worth of works was finally actually sanctioned.[114] As had been expected, after June 1846, the number of persons employed on the works began to rise sharply. In June, the number of people daily employed on the works was approximately 21,000. In July it increased to 71,000 daily, and in the second week of August it peaked when almost 98,000 people were employed on the public works. At this stage, only five counties, all situated in Ulster, were not involved in the scheme. They were counties Armagh, Down, Derry, Fermanagh and Tyrone.[115]

The number of persons employed on the public works showed a marked diversity in its geographic distribution. Demand was highest in counties Clare, Galway, Kerry, Limerick, Mayo, Roscommon and Tipperary, areas which had suffered periodic distress even before 1845. In counties Monaghan and Waterford, both of which experienced a heavy loss of the potato crop, demand was relatively low. This would suggest that the level of demand for relief was due to a combination of partial loss of the potato crop, together with a more general economic vulnerability. The largest number of people employed within Ireland on the public works was in Co. Clare. In the course of one week in July 1846, 109,052 people were locally employed on the public works out of a total of 385,633 employed in the whole country. Clare therefore accounted for almost 30 per cent of the total number employed within Ireland. At this time, of the counties involved in the scheme, the lowest number were employed in Co. Dublin—approximately 13 people per day.[116]

The number of people employed on the public works peaked in the first week of August when, in a six-day period, 560,000 people were engaged on them. Again, the regional contrasts are startling. Co. Clare was, once more, in the lead, employing 119,943 persons during the course of the week. Limerick and Galway were the next highest users of public works, employing 78,495 and 69,777 respectively during the week. The lowest number of people employed was in counties Donegal and Dublin which employed a mere 103 and 157 respectively. In Co. Monaghan, during the same week, 1,811 people were employed, and in Co. Waterford, 4,495.[117] The demand for relief, therefore, was concentrated in those areas which had consistently displayed a high level of vulnerability. In areas which had suffered an extensive loss of the potato crop, yet made relatively little use of the public works, other factors may have been at work. In general, the economies of the east and midlands of the country tended to be less dependent on the potato. In addition, their local economies were more diversified than those in the west of the country and more integrated into the markets of both Dublin and Britain. A further factor which was significant was that the local landlords in the east and midlands of the country were providing more private employment than their counterparts in the west were reputed to be doing. Overall, therefore, the level of demand for the public works in some degree reflected employment opportunities within the local economy.

In Co. Clare, during the first week of August, 18,175 persons were employed daily on the public works. This represented 6.3 per cent of the total population of the county as calculated in the 1841 Census. This Census classified the number of people who were employed in the production of food, primarily on the land, within Clare as 73,600.[118] Even discounting any increase in population between 1841 and 1846, this figure meant that a maximum of 24.6 per cent of people employed in agriculture availed of the public works. This left three-quarters of the agricultural workforce free to pursue their usual occupation during any one day. This would suggest that the impact of the public works was distinctly limited, even in Co. Clare where the demand for employment was highest. Even at its peak in August, public works only employed 1.2 per cent of the whole population of Ireland each day. The fact that employment was heavily concentrated within a few areas gave credibility to the government's allegations that the scheme was over-subscribed and was keeping people away from their usual agricultural pursuits.

In a Treasury Minute of 21 July 1846, it was announced that all the public measures which had been introduced to meet the emergency were to be brought to a close as soon as possible. The Minute repeated many of the criticisms which had already been made by Trevelyan and Jones. If it was absolutely necessary for the works to continue within an area, to prevent any further abuses, they were to be inspected by an officer of the Board. The lists of labourers were to be revised and labourers only allowed to remain on the works if no other form of subsistence was available. In addition, a date for closure was to be fixed and each officer of the public works was to keep a daily journal, a copy of which was to be sent weekly to both the Lord Lieutenant and the Treasury. The Minute repeated Trevelyan's earlier dictum that the wages given were to be below the local average. The Treasury once more employed the argument that if this were not done the people would not be able to carry out their usual harvest work.[119]

In private correspondence with the officers of the Board of Works, the Treasury ordered them to reduce all wages as a means of forcing the people off the public works. This resulted, in some instances, in rioting and protest meetings in various parts of the country. In Westport, there was a crowd of a few hundred people but in Castlebar, an estimated 10,000 people assembled in a 'show of physical force' which was encouraged by 'several mob orators'. They were protesting about the reduction in their wages, particularly as the local potato crop was again showing signs of blight. This show of strength came to an end with the sending of a Memorial to the new Prime Minister, Lord John Russell. They believed that if they made him aware of their situation, the government would again come to their aid.[120] The fact that the reduction of wages on the public works now had official sanction suggests that Trevelyan's ideas found more favour with the new Chancellor of the Exchequer, Charles Wood, than they had done with his predecessor, Goulburn. In fact, even before the relief operations of 1846 had come to a close, a new rigour and stringency was evident within the government.

In spite of continuous criticisms from the Treasury and the Board of Works alike regarding the temporary system of public works, the works do appear to have been introduced in areas where the distress was most widespread. In this way, like the relief committees, they appear to have been an effective response to a genuine local need. The fact that they never employed more than 2 per cent of the population of the country indicates that they were a limited response to a widespread, although uneven, period of distress. For government officials, with the exception of the Irish Executive at Dublin Castle, the alleged abuses of the public works provided a convenient means through which the greed of the local landlords could again be highlighted. Close public scrutiny before a work commenced, together with a 50 per cent contribution from the local landlords, meant that the 'sugar coating' talked of by Trevelyan could be bitter-sweet.

The Poor Law

The policy adopted in relation to Irish distress in 1845–6 was based on the decision that the temporary and the permanent systems of relief were to be kept separate. A Poor Law had been introduced into Ireland in 1838 which for the first time had provided the country with a permanent and national system of poor relief. Immediately following its introduction, there was distress in Ireland in 1839 and again in 1842. During these two years and again in 1845, the government made a clear distinction between the temporary measures that were necessary to meet the additional distress, and the permanent relief measures already in existence to meet the customary distress. Routh, the Chairman of the Relief Commission established in 1845, was particularly anxious that this distinction should be observed:

> I have no doubt, and indeed it is already visible, that claims will be made on the government on account of the distress of the people rather than their want of food proceeding from the losses of the potato crop, and it is very necessary to maintain this distinction, for the former may be said in a greater or lesser degree constantly to exist, whereas our duty is immediately directed to the scarcity arising from the diminished crop.[121]

In 1845 therefore, the Poor Law was to remain separate from other relief agencies within Ireland, following the precedent established in 1839 and 1842.[122]

In both 1839 and 1842, few of the workhouses in the south and west of Ireland, where the crop failure had been most severe, were providing relief. As outdoor relief had been expressly forbidden by the 1838 Poor Law Act, the question was whether the Poor Law should be extended to meet the extraordinary demand for relief. George Nicholls, the Irish Poor Law Commissioner who had been responsible for introducing the Law to Ireland, saw its role as being very clearly defined. He believed that it was beyond its scope to deal with a famine or extended periods of additional distress. When questioned on this point by the government, he stated categorically that in his view the Poor Law 'could not deviate in the slightest degree from the course the Act prescribed'.[123]

To ensure this separation was observed, the government had encouraged the formation, in 1839, of local relief committees under the aegis of Captain Chad of the Royal Navy. These committees raised subscriptions to meet the distress which could be matched by equal grants from the government. The government viewed its role as supplementary to local efforts, fearing that if they did not make this clear, local self-reliance would be undermined.[124]

In 1842, there was again distress in parts of Ireland, predominantly along the west coast, particularly counties Clare, Kerry and Mayo. Although eighty-one workhouses were providing relief within this area, only the Kilrush workhouse was open.[125] The Under-Secretary, Edward Lucas, suggested to Nicholls that temporary workhouse accommodation be made available in the distressed areas. Again, the Poor Law Commissioner refused to allow this, informing Lucas that not only was his proposal impracticable, it was also 'dangerous', as it could have long-term implications for the administration of the workhouses.[126] In 1842, therefore, local relief committees became the main medium for providing relief and again the government provided grants equal to sums raised by voluntary contributions. Although the local Assistant Poor Law Commissioners were allowed to give their professional advice to the relief committees, they were warned not to look like 'the official dispensers of government bounty' or in any way to appear to sanction the giving of outdoor relief:

> . . . a recognition of which in any shape would be full of peril and ought by all means be avoided.[127]

In both 1839 and 1842, the Poor Law Commissioners refused to allow any deviation from the provisions of the recently introduced law, believing that if they did so, a precedent for outdoor relief would be established.[128] Instead, they insisted on a dogmatic adherence to the terms of the 1838 Act, not wishing the Poor Law to become involved in any temporary, extraordinary, and extensive provision of relief.

Following the precedent of 1839 and 1842, the official response to the partial failure of the potato crop in 1845 was to introduce extraordinary relief measures rather than extend the existing administrative machinery of the Poor Law. By the beginning of 1846, all but two of the 130 workhouses were open, which meant that virtually the whole country had been brought into the Poor Law network. However, the 1838 Act had stipulated that Poor Law relief was limited to the number of people who could be accommodated within the confines of the workhouses. As no statutory 'right to relief' existed in Ireland, when a workhouse became full the guardians were not obliged to provide additional relief. The consequence was to restrict relief to the 100,000 inmates that the workhouses could contain. Although this was usually adequate—many of the workhouses were less than half full and some had no inmates at all—it was unlikely to be sufficient during periods of exceptional distress. George Nicholls had made it clear when he introduced the Act that one of the Poor Law's limitations was its inability to provide sufficient relief during a period of acute distress or famine.[129]

In 1845, the government decided to supplement the permanent system of relief with additional temporary measures. Although it had considered the possibility of extending the Poor Law and permitting outdoor relief, it judged that the outcome of such an action would be of 'uncertain expediency'. If outdoor relief was permitted even temporarily, there was a danger that it could become a permanent feature of the Law. The principle of outdoor relief had been emphatically rejected in 1838 and the government did not want it to be introduced in 1845, even as a temporary measure. The government regarded the means of financing the Poor Law, from local rates or taxes, as finite and not sufficient to subsidise a period of prolonged distress. Sir James Graham, the Home Secretary, also believed that it was not feasible to expect the ratepayers to provide sufficient funds to finance the emergency:

> It could not be expected, that by a compulsory rate, on the basis of poor rates, introduced suddenly, any large fund could be obtained for the relief of the poor in Ireland during the present scarcity.[130]

Each workhouse was financed by special 'poor rates' which were levied within the confines of a poor law union. The rates were paid by all occupiers of land except those valued under £4, who were exempt. In these cases, the responsibility for the payment of the rate fell on the landlord. The poor rates, therefore, were a relatively new tax and the government was determined that there should be no resistance to their payment. Widespread resistance to the rates had already occurred in 1843—a period known as 'the rate war'—and had, forced the government to change its policies and introduce a £4 exemption clause. In 1845, the government did not wish to increase further the burden on the taxpayers, as they were worried that this might again result in extensive resistance.[131]

The role to be played by the Poor Law and by the local ratepayers in 1845–6, therefore, was deliberately to be restricted. Occasionally, this made the role of the local Poor Law administrators ambiguous, especially as there was considerable overlap between the people who were active on the relief committees and those who had been elected Poor Law guardians—they both being dominated by the resident landlords. Sir Randolph Routh, the Commissioner in charge of the temporary relief measures, requested that the local guardians be used as agents to receive and distribute the Indian meal imported by the government in 1845–6. The guardians were initially to purchase grain with the money raised from the poor rates, and then re-sell it at cost price. Edward Twistleton, the new Poor Law Commissioner, however, refused to allow such a scheme. He regarded Routh's suggestion as being tantamount to the involvement of the guardians in the provision of outdoor relief which, he believed, was contrary to the role envisaged for the Poor Law by the government. He also considered that it contravened the provisions of the 1838 Act.[132] Twistleton informed Trevelyan that he considered it 'illegal' to involve 'the Poor Law Guardians in the administration of outdoor relief in any shape'.[133]

The function of the Poor Law, nevertheless, was extended in one specific way, namely, in the provision of relief for fever victims. Fever appeared sporadically in Ireland and always in the wake of a period of extraordinary distress. In 1845, there were 101 fever hospitals throughout Ireland, but their distribution throughout the country was uneven. There were none in counties Longford, Louth and Roscommon, and only one in counties Antrim, Leitrim, Queen's, Mayo, Meath, Sligo and Westmeath. In contrast, counties Tipperary and Cork had twelve and thirteen respectively.[134] To some extent, this gap was filled by the workhouses. Each workhouse was built complete with an infirmary; in areas where there was no existing fever hospital, the board of guardians could provide one. In 1843, an amendment had been made to the original 1838 Act which permitted workhouse facilities to be used to treat fever patients who were poor, but not necessarily destitute.[135] The guardians could also make separate provisions for people suffering from fever. They were able to do so in three ways: the poor rates could be used to pay for an inmate suffering from fever to be conveyed to the nearest fever hospital; the guardians could rent a house within the union for the treatment of fever patients; or they could erect a separate building on workhouse grounds for the same purpose. As the first two options were only of temporary benefit, the Poor Law Commissioners preferred that, as far as possible, the third one should be adopted.[136]

By 1845, only one-third of the boards of guardians had established either separate buildings or separate wards for the treatment of fever patients, but in eighty-eight of the unions, nothing had been done. In cases where the workhouse had no facilities for the treatment of fever, the guardians could remove the patient to the nearest fever hospital, the cost of which was to be borne by the local poor rates.[137] The criterion for receiving relief within the workhouses was destitution rather than the broader category of poverty, but a more liberal approach was allowed in the case of people suffering from fever. This apparent broadening of the terms of the original Act probably had more to do with the widespread fear of contagion rather than a liberalisation of attitude towards poor relief.

Initially, no changes were made to the existing provisions for the treatment of fever victims although, in December 1845, the Commissioners reminded all local boards of guardians in a circular of their responsibility to provide fever care. The Commissioners recommended that a separate building for this purpose should be built on the grounds of the workhouses. In emergencies, temporary sheds made from timber could be built, but the longer-term solution was preferred. To finance these buildings, the guardians were allowed to borrow the amount required, but the government was not willing to provide finance, even as a loan. This circular, and a second one on the same subject sent in January 1846, appears to have been largely ignored by the guardians.[138] On 24 March 1846, a Fever Act was introduced which established a temporary Board of Health in Dublin. Its remit was 'to make temporary provision for the treatment of destitute poor persons afflicted with fever in Ireland'.[139] The Board of Health consisted of five commissioners who were to be responsible for all fever hospitals, whether established by the Poor Law guardians or provided by medical charities. This Act was to expire on 1 September 1847. The temporary Board of Health could require the local Poor Law administrators to establish fever hospitals as they deemed necessary. Within two months of the Act being passed, a further fifty boards of guardians had initiated the building of a fever hospital.[140]

Overall, the central Poor Law Commissioners and the local guardians felt no particular apprehension about the impact of the potato blight on the workhouses. In the short term, they believed that it could be advantageous, as the unusually high price of agricultural produce would make poor rates easier to collect. They therefore urged the local guardians to make the poor rates as high as the circumstances of the union would allow. By May 1846, the guardians were collecting rates to the value of £260,000, which the Commissioners described as 'satisfactory'.[141] Although the numbers in the workhouses began to increase, it was not very substantial: in December 1845, there were 38,232 inmates in the Irish workhouses, compared with 37,736 a year earlier. By the end of March 1846, the number had risen to 47,403, compared with 40,931 for the same period in December 1845.[142] The workhouses, therefore, were still less than half full.

The main impact that the potato blight had initially on the administration of the Poor Law was in influencing a change in the workhouse diet. In 1838, it had been decided that the diet to be given to the inmates should be monotonous and, as far as possible, inferior to that of the poor outside the workhouse. In most workhouses, the inmates were fed potatoes every day, mixed with buttermilk. This had the advantage of being cheap, nutritious and easily available. At the beginning of November

1845, the guardians were given permission to depart from the potato diet, and provide other food such as rice, soup or bread instead. Through the use of a greater variety of foods, the Poor Law Commissioners hoped to reduce the general demand for potatoes in the market place. By May 1846, sixty-nine of the 130 unions had modified their diet in this way.[143]

The Lord Lieutenant also requested that the guardians be used to oversee the manufacture of farina, starch, flour etc., from diseased potatoes, in order to implement one of the recommendations made to the government by Playfair and Lindley. It was thought that such manufacture would provide suitable employment for the workhouse inmates while, at the same time, offer a useful service to the local community. Only diseased potatoes were to be converted. Although some guardians attempted to introduce this facility into their workhouses, like many of the other ideas of the Scientific Commission, it proved to be expensive and impractical and was quickly abandoned.[144]

The eating of diseased potatoes was not only confined to the workhouses, but appeared to be general throughout the west of Ireland in the winter of 1845–6. At the beginning of 1846, the medical officers of the various public institutions throughout the country, including the workhouses, recorded an increase in disease. The incidences of influenza, jaundice and smallpox had all increased markedly, but the most common complaints were bowel and stomach ailments, notably diarrhoea and dysentery. The medical officers attributed the increase in disease to the scarcity of provisions, a shortage of fuel supplies, and the eating of diseased potatoes. One person who was known to have eaten diseased potatoes was described as having 'bowel complaints, painful and violent griping, with other violent symptoms continuing eight to twelve hours'.[145] In Newmarket-on-Fergus in Co. Clare, the whole village had eaten diseased potatoes, as a result of which they were 'attacked with colic, purging and vomiting'.[146]

The eating of diseased potatoes was confined to the poorest sections of society, who had been deprived of their subsistence diet. To a large extent, the increase in disease correlated with areas in which the population had suffered the greatest loss of their staple food. Counties Cavan, Clare, Cork, Galway, Kerry and Waterford recorded the greatest increase in diseases, with counties Armagh and Donegal showing a less marked increase. In each of these areas, the local medical officers warned the government that if demand for medical assistance continued to increase, they doubted their ability to deal with it. Although the rate of mortality showed no significant increase following the first appearance of blight, it left a large portion of the population physically more vulnerable when the potato crop failed again in 1846. The localised distress of 1845–6 also indicated that in the poorest areas the medical resources were stretched to the limit and would be unable to cope with a more extensive demand for medical relief if the need should arise.[147]

Although the role officially assigned to be played by the Poor Law was deliberately limited, within the local workhouses, the potato blight inevitably had an impact. The situation in the local unions varied considerably. In the Longford Poor Law union, the guardians were unable to purchase potatoes as early as 3 August 1845, despite having 'done everything in their power to procure them'. In October, a contractor was found who promised to supply 'good cup potatoes' although their price had risen from 1s 6d to 2s 2d per cwt. The price of oatmeal had also risen and was 14s per cwt. By the beginning of December, even the potatoes which had appeared sound had started to rot. The Longford union was one of the few unions to purchase a 'potato machine' for the conversion of the diseased potatoes. When this process quickly proved to be ineffective, the guardians decided to replace the potatoes with oatmeal, despite its cost. It had now risen to 17s per cwt. At the same time, the paupers were allowed to eat the existing potato stocks before they rotted. Despite the difficulties being experienced by the Longford guardians, the paupers were still given their usual beef dinner on Christmas Day.[148]

In the Ballymoney union in Co. Antrim, a third of the local crop was estimated to be lost in October 1845. By the December following, potatoes had risen to 3s a cwt. Despite their expense, the guardians continued to use potatoes within the workhouse until June 1846.[149] In the Enniskillen union in Co. Fermanagh, where there had been few instances of blight, potatoes continued to be used in the workhouse until July 1846, when the children were given oatmeal instead. It was not until a month later that potatoes were also withdrawn from the adult inmates. They were instead to be given 7½oz of oatmeal instead of their usual daily allowance of 3½ lbs of potatoes.[150] In the neighbouring Lowtherstown union, potatoes were also available, although they had risen sharply in price. In November 1845, the Lowtherstown workhouse contained only four inmates, a situation which the guardians blamed on the 'harsh regulations' of the central Commissioners, particularly the prohibition of tobacco, which many poor people enjoyed. The guardians warned that some of the local people would 'perish from famine' unless the regulations were changed. In January 1846, the guardians were still able to obtain potatoes and were admonished by the central Commissioners for giving the inmates three meals a day.[151]

It was not, in fact, until March 1846 that many local unions began to feel the effects of the potato shortages. By this stage, the cost of potatoes had begun to rise sharply, although prices varied in different parts of the country. The average price had risen to 4½d per stone, compared with 3d per stone only twelve months earlier. The increase in potato prices was not uniform, and reflected the largely localised nature of the market for potatoes. Natural economic forces were evident as the highest prices were recorded in areas which had been little affected by the blight or where the local population was least dependent on potatoes for subsistence, most notably in the north east of the country, but where cash incomes were greatest. Some of the smallest price increases were recorded in the poorest unions in the West of Ireland, although in these areas, the ability of the population to afford even these comparatively low prices was probably more restricted.

For the Poor Law guardians, the increase in the price of potatoes provided an incentive to substitute them with other foodstuffs in the workhouses. This was most apparent following the opening of the government food depots. Although the government had hoped that the guardians would not make use of these depots, the cheapness of the corn meant that many of them did. Indian corn was cheaper than either potatoes or oatmeal and unions which were situated near a government depot increasingly began to give the workhouse inmates Indian corn. The unions in counties Clare, Cork, Kerry, Louth and Tipperary made the most extensive use of the facility of the grain depots. In a number of workhouses, Indian corn was sometimes mixed with oatmeal, to make gruel or stirabout.[152] Some unions which were not situated close to a grain depot, particularly those in the north east, made their own arrangements for the purchase of Indian corn from England, mostly the port of Liverpool.[153]

During the spring of 1846, before the temporary relief measures became fully effective, many boards of guardians were put under considerable pressure to provide additional relief; not, however, inside the workhouse, but the more attractive temporary relief which had been promised. Although the guardians invariably responded to such requests with an offer of workhouse relief, this was always refused; the incipient relief measures which were about to become effective appeared far more attractive than the stringencies of the 'workhouse test'.[154] Occasionally, the demands for immediate (although not workhouse) relief, were organised on a large scale. In Clanwilliam in Co. Tipperary, for example, 100 heads of families attended the local workhouse asking for employment to be provided. In the town of Tipperary, a similar deputation was made to the guardians, during the course of which, 'the spokesman respectfully hinted . . . that it was only to avoid more serious consequences that the application had been made'. In the town of Sligo, about 100 persons were reported to have marched through the streets to the local workhouse, with loaves of bread fixed on poles. When the local guardians promised to give them both work and increased wages, the crowd dispersed. In the town of Kilkenny, the local guardians offered nothing except relief inside the workhouse to the 100 'labouring men' who assembled outside it. The men refused but informed the guardians that 'unless relieved they must resort to violence'.[155]

Although, for the most part, these actions were peaceful, the poor were exerting a form of moral force on the authorities. In some instances, more direct action was resorted to. In the towns of Cork and Waterford, for example, supplies of potatoes were 'seized by the mob'; in Co. Monaghan, a meal store was robbed; and in Co. Roscommon, a party of ten men travelled around demanding money for the relief of distress. In the city of Derry, a shot was fired into the local police station. Some of the threats were directed at the landlords or their agents. For the most part, the landlords were asked to provide additional money or employment, although some were asked to give up their land. More often, the anger of the people was directed at the absentee landlords who were safely removed from any threats that could be made. One group in Tipperary actually wrote to the absentee landlords, appealing to them to do something.[156] In general, this type of activity was short-lived and reflected an impatience with the slowness in establishing the temporary relief measures. As both the government meal and the public works became available, however, they tended to dissipate and were not revived until August 1846, when the government attempted to reduce wages on the public works. Although there were some instances of the officers of the public works being attacked in the summer of 1846, these were isolated. The government may have had many reservations about its various temporary relief measures, but, to a large extent, the people of Ireland were satisfied.

In July 1846, there were increasing sightings of potato blight in various parts of the country. These were worrying as not only was the blight appearing at an earlier date than in the previous year, but it had manifested itself in counties such as Wicklow which had been virtually blight-free in 1845. Increasingly, the necessity for government intervention for a second year appeared inevitable, although the extent of required assistance could not be gauged. The repeal of the Corn Laws in July 1846 had resulted in the fall of Peel's government and its replacement by a Whig administration led by Lord John Russell. Russell's administration came to power when the demand for relief was at its maximum. He therefore allowed the relief operations already in progress to continue, as they were due to expire at the harvest period anyway. The reappearance of blight, however, even before the relief operations had been completed, inevitably raised the question as to whether the relief measures should be allowed to continue. In this matter, the advice which the government received from the men in the field was very clear. The relief operations must be brought to an end:

> or you run the risk of paralysing all private enterprise and having this country depend on you for an indefinite number of years.[157]

3

We Cannot
Feed the People

1846–7

During the winter of 1846–7, the localised food shortages that had been a characteristic of the previous year gave way to widespread distress on a major scale. A general lack of anticipation and readiness to tackle a greatly increased scale of need was evident. Yet, as awareness grew, there was no commensurate response from the government. Excessive mortality was probably inevitable given the extent of the shortfall in food following the 1846 blight. However, the tardy, frugal, short-sighted and ideologically-bound policies adopted by the Whig administration made inevitable the slide from distress to the national calamity of famine.

The temporary relief measures which had been introduced by Peel's government following the first appearance of potato blight in 1845–6 were to be phased out from mid-August 1846, when the new crop of potatoes would start to be available. The Whig administration, under the leadership of Lord John Russell, which had come to power in June 1846, allowed these arrangements to stand in the expectation that they would close at the end of August. However, even before the relief measures had started to wind down, there were reports of an even more widespread appearance of blight. In 1845, the blight had been localised and variegated, but in 1846, from early reports it was obvious that blight had affected the potato crop throughout Ireland. In 1845 also, it had been difficult to obtain an accurate estimate of the damage caused by the blight as its appearance was spread over a number of months, but in 1846, the destruction of the potato crop was as rapid as it was comprehensive.[1]

The recently appointed Lord Lieutenant of Ireland, Lord Bessborough, informed the new Prime Minister early in October, 'I verily believe that by Christmas there will not be a sound potato in the country'.[2]

In spite of the impending food shortages within Ireland, the British parliament was prorogued on 28 August 1846 and Russell decided not to re-assemble it earlier than the appointed date in January 1847. He justi-fied this on the grounds that it would enable the Irish landlords who sat in parliament to remain in Ireland and become more fully involved in the affairs of their country.[3] In a similar manner to their Tory predecessors, many members of the new Whig government believed that the Irish landlords needed to be forced into taking more responsibility for alleviat-ing the impending distress. Arising from this view, a new philosophy was evident in the measures introduced by the government in 1846. More of the financial responsibility for providing relief was to be placed on the landlords. As one member of the government declared: 'the exertions and sacrifices necessary for this purpose must fall upon the Landed Property of Ireland'.[4]

The relief measures introduced in 1845 had been regarded as tempo-rary expedients to meet a widespread although essentially localised period of scarcity. In this regard, the official response to the potato blight of 1845–6 was not unlike the response of the government to earlier peri-ods of distress. The more virulent blight of 1846 transformed the situation from being merely temporary and localised distress into an extended national calamity. The relief officials in Ireland were aware that unless they responded swiftly to this crisis, there was likely to be wide-spread famine. In early September, the Irish Executive warned the government that intervention in the affairs of Ireland was imperative 'to save the people from starvation'.[5] In London, there was less consensus about the impact of a second year of blight. To some extent, this reflected differences both within the cabinet and in the government as a whole regarding Ireland. Although there was some support for more extensive state investment in public works, railways and for subsidised emigration schemes, these were overshadowed by the more popular policies suggest-ed by the political economists, including Lord Brougham, the economist Nassau Senior, and Charles Wood and Charles Trevelyan at the Treasury. The philosophy of non-intervention, which underpinned political econo-my, stressed that during a period of shortage or famine, it was the responsibility of a local area, aided by private charity, to alleviate the situ-ation. In the short term, the government's commitment to non-intervention might appear cruel but, as *The Times* pointed out, 'There are times when something like harshness is the greatest humanity'.

Furthermore, the political economists had the satisfaction of believing that, in the long term, adherence to this policy would facilitate the economic development of Ireland.

The Treasury was sceptical about the real extent of the losses sustained and the impact which they would have. This drew a slight rebuke from the Prime Minister to Charles Wood, the new Chancellor of the Exchequer, when he informed him that 'the only fault I ever find with your reasonings about Ireland is that you treat the destruction of £10m. worth of food as if it were an ordinary calamity'.[6]

The type of relief measures to be introduced in 1846 were to a large extent shaped by the relief policies of the previous year. Although these were generally held to have been successful, it was felt that this had been achieved at a high cost—not only in financial terms, but also because it had raised the expectations of the people about the role of the government in such a situation. The government's policies were formed by a conviction that the Irish people, if allowed to, would again expect 'good wages, little labour, and a low price of food; they must be resisted and all such expectations should be crushed'.[7] Whilst the government accepted that continuing relief would be necessary, at the same time they believed that the Irish people needed to be taught a lesson in self-reliance on the grounds that:

> The common delusion that government can convert a period of scarcity into a period of abundance is one of the most mischievous that can be entertained. But alas! the Irish have been taught many bad lessons and few good ones.[8]

The government also believed that it was essential that any new relief policies introduced should not interfere with the role of the traders and merchants. In the previous year, this powerful lobby had been angered by the interference of the government in the importation of foodstuffs into the country and sought a commitment that this would not occur again. Overall, the government hoped that the measures introduced in Ireland during the second year of distress would bring long-term benefits to Ireland. They viewed it as their moral responsibility to use the failure of the potato crop in 1846 to force economic change within Ireland, including the capitalisation of the Irish agricultural sector. As Russell informed Wood:

> The future is no doubt perilous. But if there is capital in Ireland, as I believe there is, the country will be made to produce food for eight millions of Irish and four millions of English in a few years.[9]

The Government Food Depots

An important element in the government's relief measures in the spring and summer of 1846 had been the provision of food through a number of especially established grain depots. Although this measure had been popular with those in receipt of relief, the intrusion of the government into the market place had annoyed many merchants, who believed that their profits and ultimately their livelihoods had been threatened.[10] This point of view had many sympathisers within the government. Trevelyan thought that even limited interference by the government disturbed the natural balance of supply and demand. He was confident that 'The natural adjustments which take place under a system of perfectly free trade are always more than sufficient to counteract any inconveniences arising from such a system'.[11] Russell confirmed the allegiance of the Whig government to a policy of non-interference as far as possible in the provision of food, on the grounds that 'the interference of the state deadens private energy, prevents forethought, and, after superseding all other exertion, finds itself at least unequal to the gigantic task which it has undertaken'.[12] The intervention of the government in 1845–6 was blamed for, allegedly, having led to a reduction in the activities of private merchants. If this occurred again, it was feared that it would damage the mercantile interests of the whole country. Repeated government intervention would not only paralyse all private enterprise, but would increase the dependence of the Irish people on the government. In the second year of distress, therefore, the government compromised. They assured the Irish merchants that there would be no government interference in the import of food into the eastern part of the country. They would, however, intervene in the west of the country where there were fewer traders anyhow, if it proved to be absolutely necessary.[13] Responsibility for overseeing the import and distribution of food was placed in the hands of the Treasury, thus confirming the increased importance of Wood and Trevelyan in the relief operations.

Following the first appearance of potato blight, the government had attempted to keep the purchase of Indian corn a secret for as long as possible. In the second year of distress, this secrecy was no longer possible, and many people regarded the provision of food by the government as inevitable. The new Whig government believed that a dangerous precedent had been established in the previous year. It had not been the intention of Peel's government to feed the distressed people, but rather to keep the price of food down and to provide a stimulus to private trade, but the success of the scheme created an expectation that the government would again supply food but on an even larger scale. Russell had no intention of allowing his government to repeat the experiment and stated unequivocally: 'It must be thoroughly understood that we cannot feed the people. It was a cruel delusion to pretend to do so.'[14]

The government ordered that no new depots were to be established and that the existing ones—now confined to the west coast, from Donegal to Skibbereen in west Cork—were only to be used as a last resort.[15] The various sub-depots which in the previous year had been superintended by the constabulary and coastguard were not to be re-opened as they had 'embarrassed the accounts considerably'. Instead, only central depots were to be operative, controlled by the Commissariat Office under Sir Randolph Routh. Routh, using Biblical imagery, elaborated on the minimalist policy of the government:

> I take a leaf out of Joseph's plan, who established central depots, and enjoined the people to come with their money in their sacks for their supplies. He did not send it to them.[16]

In the autumn of 1846, the government engaged as their agent a Mr Erichsen to import Indian corn into Ireland. As far as possible, the purchase of corn was to be carried out within the home market, that is, within the United Kingdom. Although the government had initially asked the firm of Barings again to act on its behalf, Barings had declined to do so as they felt that the conditions which were to govern the purchase of food in the coming year were too restrictive. In their place, they recommended the London-based company of Erichsen. Due to a general shortage of corn within the United Kingdom, it subsequently proved necessary to make additional purchases in Europe and, eventually, in America. By the time this was decided, the corn buying season was almost over and the unusually high competition provided by other European countries had not only pushed the price of corn up but had also made supplies unobtainable in some markets. To help compensate for this, Erichsen was also permitted to import other foodstuffs including wheat, barley and barley-meal.[17] A portion of the food imported by Erichsen was for distribution in Scotland, which had also been affected by the potato blight. The far greater portion, however, was intended for use in Ireland. The Lord Lieutenant justified this on the grounds that:

> In Scotland, there will be great distress for the want of potatoes, but its population have always been accustomed to other articles of food. In Ireland, potatoes have been the sole food, and I am confident that a very large portion of the people have never had any other food in their mouth.[18]

In spite of the comparatively greater need of the Irish people, the government decided that Scotland should first be supplied with imported food. This caused some anxiety in Ireland and at the end of October Sir Randolph Routh admitted, 'I shall be very glad to hear that Scotland is supplied, and that your resources are turned towards us.'[19]

Between 26 August 1846 and 15 January 1847, seventy-two separate purchases of food, mostly Indian corn, were made by Erichsen on behalf of the British government. The first shipments were due to arrive in November 1846 and the final ones in May 1847. Initially, most of the food was purchased in London, Liverpool, Antwerp and Venice. However, by the end of September, as supplies of Indian corn within Europe were providing difficult to obtain, Erichsen was allowed to make purchases in America, even though these supplies would take a longer time to arrive in Ireland. The prices paid for the Indian corn varied greatly, it becoming more expensive as the season progressed. The lowest price was paid on 26 August 1846 when the corn cost 33s 6d per quarter in London. By 28 December, it had risen to 63s per quarter in London. The highest price paid by Erichsen was on 3 January 1847, when he purchased corn at 70s per quarter in Liverpool.[20]

Between late August and the end of October 1846, Erichsen purchased 16,420 tons of food on behalf of the government. This quantity was estimated to be sufficient for the whole year. These purchases are detailed in Table 1.

Table 1: Government Food Purchases, August–October 1846[21]

	Tons
Indian Corn	13,200
Indian Corn meal	180
Egyptian Wheat	1,340
Barley	900
Barley meal	800
	Total 16,420

This, however, was only a small portion of the 1,438,324 tons of Indian corn which the Relief Commissioners estimated would be required in Ireland in the coming year.[22] Most of the corn and other food purchased by Erichsen was initially stored in Portsmouth or Plymouth in England, although some was sent directly to the Irish ports of Sligo,

Westport, Galway, Limerick and Ballina, with only one shipment being sent directly to Kilrush. The port of Cork was not used as it had been in the previous year, because it was decided that it did not lie within the west of the country. The east of the country was to be left to commercial enterprise. The corn was stored in ships which lay off the west coast until the government was ready to sell it.[23]

A problem which confronted the government in the second year of distress was the milling of corn. In the previous year, this had been carried out in Cork by officers of the Relief Commission, but in the second year of distress, the government left this essential process in the preparation of Indian corn to private enterprise. In the West of Ireland, this was virtually impossible as there were so few mills. One local government inspector warned Trevelyan that the consequence of this could be to give a monopoly to mill-owners who were only interested in 'profitable speculation'.[24] The corn which was stored in Portsmouth and Plymouth could be ground on the spot, but the problem remained with corn that was imported directly into Ireland. The solution proposed by the government was that handmills should be made available in the west of Ireland. Trevelyan was unenthusiastic about this idea, but with his usual thoroughness immediately began to experiment personally with different types of handmills, including the Irish quern.

Although the end result was corn that was 'granulated' rather than ground Trevelyan declared that such food, made on the 'machine of our ancestors', was suitable for making into a porridge.[25] A circular sent to the local relief committees suggested that corn could be sold unground, and as long as it was subsequently cooked, it would still prove to be nutritious and wholesome.[26] Eventually, a variety of mills were recommended to be used in Ireland and, if they possessed sufficient funds, the relief committees were encouraged to purchase their own model. The price charged for a stone quern ranged from 10s to 12s, and for a small steam-mill (which the government hoped the merchants would purchase) from £3 to £5 each.[27]

Due to the widespread appearance of blight, the demand for relief manifested itself in the weeks immediately following the harvest. Despite this, the government was determined not to be forced into opening the food depots earlier than it considered absolutely necessary. Although many local relief committees had recommenced their activities as soon as the blight re-appeared, they had to rely on private traders for their supplies of food. Initially, the leading dispensers of government relief were satisfied with the transfer to private enterprise. Routh admitted that he was pleased with the effect of forcing the committees to depend on 'home supplies'.[28] Trevelyan agreed that the revised policies, committed to allowing the primacy of private enterprise, were already having the desired effect. He cited as proof 'the great diminution of the export of provisions, and especially of corn from Ireland to England, and of the great increase in the exportation from England to Ireland'.[29] Nevertheless, by the end of October, Routh had become less sanguine about the effect of deliberately continuing to delay making government supplies available. In a fraught, yet typically apologetic letter to Trevelyan, he explained:

> I sometimes tremble when I think of the number of empty depots which we have to fill . . . Could you speak with Mr Erichsen on this subject; some immediate purchases on the spot of any description of food . . . If we do not look to this and consider it, I am afraid we shall be in difficulties . . . It is really a subject worthy of reflection, and you will excuse me if I press it upon you in the midst of ten thousand affairs that are pushing upon you.[30]

Despite this plea, Trevelyan would not allow the plans of government to be changed. As had already been agreed, grain would not be sent to Ireland or any depots opened until the government believed it to be absolutely necessary. Moreover, Scotland was to be supplied with imported food before any could be sent to Ireland.[31]

As predicted by the government, the Irish merchants did import additional supplies of food, including Indian corn, into the country. In the months following the harvest, food prices rose drastically. To some extent this was due to speculation and hoarding by a number of merchants, resulting in exorbitant 'Famine' prices. This was most prevalent in the midlands and west of the country. Within one week at the end of October 1846, prices of wheat, flour, and oatmeal in the city of Cork— not considered by the government to be a distressed area—rose by approximately 50 per cent.[32] The price of imported Indian corn was also higher than it had been a few months earlier. In August, it had been as little as £10 per ton, but by the beginning of October it had risen to £14 a ton and a few weeks later to £18 a ton. Even when the price had risen to £14 a ton, the local relief committees complained that the price was 1½d per pound, thus displaying an increase of 50 per cent on the average prices earlier in the year. The government predicted that prices were likely to rise even higher and that it might be January 1847 before the market mechanisms would correct themselves and prices begin to fall.[33] In many distressed areas, however, prices did not begin to fall until April

1847, by which time wages from the public works were being replaced by direct relief in the form of soup.

The final two months of 1846 were remarkable for a spiralling demand for relief in any guise, that is, in food, on the public works or even in the workhouses. There was also an inability of the supply to keep pace with the demand. A mood of panic, despair and desperation was apparent within the country, amidst growing reports of death from starvation. The high price of food was generally regarded as a major factor in contributing to the widespread distress and the verdict given at some inquests was 'Wilful murder against Lord John Russell'.[34] Despite being urged by the relief committees and various officers employed in the west of Ireland to open the government food depots earlier than the fixed date of the end of 1846 or later if possible, the government refused to deviate from this policy. Even in Skibbereen, Co. Cork, which in the last few months of 1846 achieved an unenviable international reputation due to almost daily reports of deaths from starvation, no exception was to be made. In the closing weeks of 1846, Routh persistently appealed to the Treasury to allow the food depots to be opened. The Treasury, however, refused to bring forward the appointed date of 28 December. Trevelyan explained to Routh:

> You must . . . draw out the resources of the country before we make our own issues. In the execution of this important duty you must be prepared to act with great firmness and to incur much obloquy . . . these principles must be kept in view in reference to what is now going on in Skibbereen, for if we were to commence a lavish issue there, we might find it difficult to adopt a safe course elsewhere.[35]

Within a few weeks of the depots being opened, Routh and Trevelyan were again in conflict. Routh believed that the Treasury's decision to sell the grain at the market price was a mistake. Again, the Treasury proved impervious to the advice of the Relief Commissioner. Trevelyan, not even attempting to disguise his impatience with Routh, informed him: 'If we make prices lower, I repeat for the HUNDREDTH TIME, that the whole country will come upon us.'[36]

Although Skibbereen achieved international notoriety at the end of 1846, other areas along the west coast were also suffering because relief, either in the form of food or public works, was not yet available. The policy of withholding grain supplies was judged by many of the local relief officials to be a mistake and a number of them informed the government that it was having a detrimental effect on the local economies.

In Kilrush, Co. Clare, the local officer wrote to Trevelyan concerning 'the welfare of the poor creatures about here, whose sufferings can scarcely be described in a letter'. There were few local merchants and those who were present, were exporters only. Because of this, the area had to depend on Limerick for supplies. This meant 'the hucksters take advantage, and prices range higher in consequence'.[37] In Burtonport, Co. Donegal, there was great distress, again resulting from the non-availability of food, which caused the local relief officer to write:

> The distress of the wretched people here is heart-rending. Something ought to be done for them; they can get nothing to purchase. The carters have stopped bringing supplies . . . The people in Arranmore Island are living on seaweed . . . It strikes the people as being very unfeeling on our part to keep the corn in store without issuing it . . . I hope I may soon get the authority to issue. I would think little of my trouble if, by issuing from morning until night, I could relieve their distress.[38]

Some Irish landlords were concerned about the policy of leaving the provision of food in the final months of 1846 in private hands. A concerned proprietor in Co. Down, one of the most commercially developed parts of Ireland, believed that:

> The government have shown a great want of foresight in not laying up stores and depots of grain through the country, owing to which I fear, many thousands in the south and west will perish from starvation.[39]

Sir James Graham, who had been Home Secretary in the Peel administration twelve months previously, was critical of the policies adopted by the Whig administration. He did not think that the Whigs were willing to admit the full extent of the distress and the remedies which they were applying were therefore inappropriate. Graham confided to Peel that 'The real extent and magnitude of the Irish difficulty are underestimated by the Government, and cannot be met by measures within the strict rule of economical science'.[40]

Such accounts and misgivings did not deter the faith of a number of members of the government in their policy of non-interference, and the high prices and scarcity which had resulted. Nor was this faith shaken by numerous accusations that the Irish merchants contributed to this hardship by charging high prices for foodstuffs. The commitment to private enterprise appeared unassailable. Trevelyan was a vociferous defender of both the private traders and policies of the government. He defended the actions of the merchants on the grounds that:

> They cannot help either the excessive demand or the very insufficient supply, and these and not the cost price, are the circumstances which regulate the selling price of articles . . . It can, however, hardly be necessary to remind you that high prices are the natural check upon the over rapid consumption of an insufficient stock of food, and that, greatly as we suffer now, we might suffer before long still more intensely if this check were to be removed by any artificial interference.[41]

At the beginning of January, however, on the eve of the reconvening of parliament, Russell, less dogmatic than his colleagues at the Treasury, admitted that he was reluctant to face parliament with prices continuing to be so high and he suggested that any final remaining duties on corn be removed in an attempt to bring prices down.[42] Wood, the Chancellor of the Exchequer, disapproved of Russell's proposal and urged that if such a measure were to be introduced, it should be temporary only.[43]

Although the Whig government undoubtedly desired to restrict its forays into the market place to a minimum, the situation which they faced at the end of 1846 was different from that which had existed twelve months previously. Apart from a general failure of the potato crop in both Ireland and Scotland, the grain harvest throughout Europe was poor: this inevitably pushed prices up. Although the government considered importing other foodstuffs from further afield, such as yams, they were regarded as too expensive or, as Trevelyan stated, the price was be 'beyond our limits'. By December, Routh could no longer disguise his disillusionment with the policies of the government and accused the Treasury of not having made sufficient effort to obtain food for the distressed of Ireland. Trevelyan insisted that it was no longer a question of money but rather one of supply. The food shortages were not merely confined to Ireland, but were apparent in the whole of the United Kingdom. This meant that the supplies which they had obtained had to be strictly controlled, for 'it was only by carefully husbanding it, that it could be made to last to harvest'.[44] Trevelyan maintained that it was not within their power to procure additional supplies of grain and corn as, in the previous few months 'the whole world was ransacked for supplies'.[45] Charles Wood confirmed this when he stated at the beginning of 1847, 'I am inclined to think that there is no corn now in the world unbought.'[46]

By the end of 1846, therefore, despite obvious disquiet within Ireland regarding the relief policies being pursued by the British government, the belief amongst relief officials in England was that they had done all that it was possible to do for Ireland.

The Local Relief Committees

There were three main components to the relief policies of the government following the second year of crop failure: public works, relief committees and the local workhouses. Again, the first two were intended to be purely temporary measures which were to supplement the permanent system of poor relief. In a shift of emphasis, however, the public works were to be regarded as the main agency of relief. This reflected a greater commitment to the idea of relief in return for labour. Relief committees were to play a less significant role, the government hoping that private merchants would provide most of the additional food to meet the expected shortfalls. The role of the workhouses was not to be increased, but they were expected to deploy their resources more fully than they had done in the previous year.

Although the role undertaken by the local relief committees was to be subordinate to the public works in the second year of distress, these voluntary bodies were still expected to perform a wide range of duties. Their main functions were to raise subscriptions for a local relief fund, to provide small works of local utility and, where possible, to promote works of more general improvement such as drainage or land reclamation. These duties were similar to those undertaken by the local committees in the previous year. Significantly the contribution of the government was to be reduced from a maximum 100 per cent to 50 per cent. This act of financial retrenchment by the Whig government was an early indication of their determination to throw more of the responsibility for providing relief on the local districts. As the extent of the distress became known, however, this contribution was again raised to 100 per cent. One further aspect of the work of the committees had been modified. They no longer had the authority to issue tickets of employment to distressed persons; instead they were to compile lists of people whom they considered eligible for employment. These lists would then be scrutinised by officers of the Board of Works, who were to control the issue of tickets.

Table 2: Sums Exceeding £500 raised by Relief Committees 25 March–1 August 1846

Relief Committee 1846		Donations from Lord Lieutenant £	Amount Raised by Relief Committee £
Limerick	25 March	400-0-0	500-0-0
Loughrea Union	11 April	350-0-0	820-0-0
Killarney	14 April	300-0-0	650-0-0
City of Cork	14 April	500-0-0	1005-0-0
Clonmel	14 April	500-0-0	500-0-0
Clanmurriss (Kerry)	18 April	500-0-0	803-0-0
Waterford	28 April	750-0-0	1016-0-0
Cork	28 April	1550-0-0	2300-0-0
Fermoy	2 May	600-0-0	787-0-0
Thurles	2 May	400-0-0	571-1-0
Kilkenny	2 May	400-0-0	609-0-0
Town of Galway	6 May	350-0-0	508-0-0
Ennis District	11 May	200-0-0	611-0-0
Wexford Ed	13 May	410-0-0	626-0-0
Corkaguieney Kerry	15 May	350-0-0	521-0-0
Waterford	16 May	750-0-0	1000-0-0
Youghal	25 May	400-0-0	565-0-6
Tralee	28 May	800-0-0	1203-10-0
City of Limerick	1 June	800-0-0	1211-18-0
City of Cork	3 June	900-0-0	1323-12-5
Killarney	3 June	400-0-0	591-13-4
Decies within Drum, Waterf'd	12 June	375-0-0	558-13-0
Clonmel	17 June	670-0-0	1006-8-6
Shillelagh	22 June	670-0-0	1003-7-2
Drogheda	22 June	500-0-0	743-17-10
Killarney	20 June	150-0-0	1277-0-0
Total		**£13,975-0-0**	**£22,342-1-9**

Total £36,317-1-9

As in the previous year, relief committees which wanted to avail of donations from the Lord Lieutenant had to comply with the printed instructions of the government. The original instructions had been published in February 1846 but these were superseded by a revised set published on 8 October 1846.[47] Again, government grants would only be given to committees which were recognised by the lieutenant of a county. The more widespread appearance of blight in 1846 resulted in the formation of nearly twice the number of committees as in the previous year, although not all of them were successful in obtaining grants from the government. In general, the local committees covered a wider geographic spread than in the previous year, reflecting the more general need for relief. At the same time, the newly established committees tended to be responsible for smaller geographical areas, perhaps reflecting a greater intensity of distress. Although there was no uniformity regarding the size or location of the committees, the instructions did stipulate that they should comprise at least two parishes.

The first duty of a relief committee was to raise funds by voluntary subscriptions. In general, this money was raised through public appeal such as the distribution of handbills or the insertion of a notice in a local newspaper. From September 1846 to January 1847, the local relief committees raised £30,062 10s 8d, to which the Lord Lieutenant added a further £20,629 16s 0d. Overall, the sums raised by individual committees tended to be smaller than in the previous year, but again, the largest contributions came from the towns. In the south of Ireland, Cork raised the largest individual amount. In the north of Ireland, Derry and Belfast raised the largest sums. The Belfast local relief committee did not raise this money with a view to receiving a government grant—Belfast never, in fact, received money from the government. Rather, it was used to establish the Belfast General Relief Fund which proved to have sufficient funds at its disposal to offer aid to other parts of Ireland.[48]

The amounts raised in the rural areas were frequently smaller than those collected in the towns. Usually, an appeal was made directly to all landed properties in a district, both resident and absentee. Absentee landlords were generally less responsive to such appeals. Not surprisingly, the most active committees were in areas where there was an interested and resident landlord class. In such cases, the largest landlords were invariably chosen as chairmen of the committees and it was they who acted as intermediaries between the local committees and the government, either in Dublin or London. In the rural areas, it was also the resident landlords who made the largest donations to the relief funds, although members of the local clergy were also regular contributors.

An in-depth examination of the relief committees in the Dunfanaghy union in Co. Donegal, provides an interesting insight into how the local committees responded to the situation. Table 3 shows the major contributors to the Crossroads relief committee in the Dunfanaghy area of Co. Donegal. Although a poor locality (Dunfanaghy had one of the lowest Poor Law valuations in the country) for the most part, the local landlords and clergy worked successfully together to raise funds for the provision of relief. The majority of the local landlords were resident and already active as either Poor Law guardians or private benefactors to local charities. This high level of interest and involvement by resident gentry, supported by local clergy, appears to have been a decisive factor in ensuring the success of the relief policies. However, even these men became frustrated with the bureaucratic stranglehold imposed by the government.

The Crossroads committee made monthly subscriptions to relief, which appears to have been the general practice in the area. Many of the following subscribers also contributed to other committees in the vicinity.

Table 3: Crossroads Relief Committee (at Falcarragh) 16 January 1847[49]

William Forster (Society of Friends)	£25
Wybrants Olphert (chairman, P.L. Guardian, large landowner)	£ 4
Rev. C. F. Stewart (Stewart of Hornhead, large landowner, C. of I. minister, philanthropist)	£ 5
Rev. A. Nixon (large landowner, C. of I. minister)	£
Thomas Olphert (landowner, P.L. Guardian)	£ 1
Rev. R. Gibbings	£ 2
Rev. Mr. Friel (R.C. priest)	£ 1
Miss A. Humphrey	£ 7
Guernsey Fund	£ 5
J.O. Woodhouse, Esq. (landowner)	£ 3
Total	£54 [sic]

Although the fund-raising activities of this committee appear to have been successful, problems in obtaining sufficient food for distribution to the poor proved to be more difficult. A Memorial from the area in October begged for a government food depot to be opened in the district, as the people had been reduced to 'the lowest extremity of destitution'. It accused the government's promises of being 'illusory . . . no better than, "live cow and you'll get grass"'.[50] Although a depot was opened at the end of the year in the nearby village of Bunbeg, its supplies were soon exhausted. In mid January, the Chairman of the Crossroads relief committee warned Routh:

> the poor of this area are now living on sea-weed, and many don't even taste that for 24 hours . . . it is impossible for one relief committee to keep one half of this population alive.[51]

The money raised by the local relief committees, in the first instance, was to be used for the purchase of food either from private merchants or from the government's relief depots. The committees were able to purchase supplies from the government's depots at cost price. This food was then to be re-sold in the distressed areas, usually by the issue of ration tickets by the committees. But the food imported by the government was only to be used as a last resort. The revised instructions of October 1846 stated that the food provided by the committees sold and in small quantities only. They also stipulated that food could only be sold to people who had 'no other means' of procuring it. Giving food gratuitously was to be avoided as far as possible. It could only be given to those who were incapable of employment on the public works and only if the local workhouses were full.

One aspect of the instructions which was particularly disliked by the local relief committees was the order which stated that the committees should charge for the food a price as near as possible to the local market rate. Prices were high throughout Ireland in the months following the harvest. The charging of market prices was regarded as being of no real benefit to the poor, nor was it felt to be using the financial resources of the committees for the purpose for which they had been raised. In fact, if this policy were strictly adhered to, some committees could actually have made a substantial profit on their sales.[52]

Some of the most outspoken critics of this policy were in Ulster, even though the local retail trade was well developed and demand for relief was less severe than in parts of the south and west. Indeed, it may have been due to their relative financial buoyancy that they felt able to disagree with or flout some of the rules of the government. Following the first appearance of potato blight, relatively few relief committees had been established in Ulster. Although a larger number were established in the second year of distress, most of these were confined to the west of the province. With the exception of parts of Co. Donegal, the population of Ulster was less dependent on potatoes than other parts of Ireland. A large number of the inhabitants of Ulster were both weavers and small farmers, often growing a combination of flax, potatoes and oats. A number of Ulster men were also seasonal migrants, crossing the sea every summer to Scotland, where they earned their rent for the coming year. The bad harvests in Scotland after 1845 reduced the demand for this type of labour. The market for linen in 1847, was depressed and many weavers were earning less than 10d per day. As the price of grain in January 1847 had risen to 2d per lb, it was beyond the reach of many poor people.[53] The combination of the failure of the potato crop, combined with a downturn in the demand for linen, meant that small farmers in the north-east of Ireland were in a far more vulnerable position that they had been in the previous year.

Along the north-west coast of Co. Donegal, potatoes had been the staple food of the local population. Although oats were also grown, they were traditionally used for the payment of rent and rarely consumed. Little corn had been imported to the area and what was available was beyond the means of the local population. By the end of 1846, there were increasing reports that the population was living on seaweed.[54] Lord George Hill, who was the chairman of the Gweedore relief committee, felt that the policy of selling at market price was detrimental to the well-being of these people. Hill, who had earned a reputation as an energetic and improving landlord, spoke from a privileged position as one of the few well-regarded Irish landlords.[55] Perhaps because he knew that he was well respected within the government, Hill felt able to point out the shortcomings of its policies. He informed Routh that because there was so little commercial activity in his area, food prices were very high. The price of meal was 2d per pound although wages were rarely higher than 9d per day. Because of this, he felt that there was no justification for charging market prices, and informed Routh that neither his committee nor any of the local committees had been doing so anyway. Nor was this response limited to relief committees in the north of the country. When a number of relief committees in counties Kerry and Cork made a unilateral decision to reduce the price of food below the market price, the local merchants and millers reacted angrily, complaining to the government that their prices were being undercut unfairly.[56]

In January 1847, Hill, together with the local Church of Ireland minister, published an appeal on behalf of the Gweedore relief committee in which he stated categorically that the committee was selling food 'at a reduced price'.[57] In addition to putting food beyond the reach of the poorest members of society, Hill believed that the government's policies were shortsighted in that they forced even small farmers to dispose of all their assets, including seed, for the following year. He warned that 'if the

Committee are not allowed to sell to any but the absolutely destitute, the whole of the population will be without seed'.[58]

Of all the difficulties which confronted the relief committees, the most serious constraint was caused by the limited amount of food available, even following the opening of the depots. In an attempt to conserve limited supplies, no depot was to open before 28 December 1846, the date chosen by the Treasury. As this date approached, Routh confided in Trevelyan that he was increasingly uneasy regarding the quantity of food purchased by the government. There were only 4,800 tons of grain in store in the depots, although a further 2,770 tons were expected to arrive before the end of the year, bringing the total to 7,570 tons. From the beginning of 1847, approximately 1,000 tons of food was scheduled to arrive monthly. However some of this supply was to be sent to Scotland. In the previous year, although many depots had not opened until May, the supply of 8,000 tons of Indian corn had only lasted for two months. In the second year of distress, the depots would have to provide for a period of eight months, during the course of which the demand was likely to get increasingly heavier. Routh did not believe that the quantity of food imported by the government would be sufficient to meet this demand.

Trevelyan's impatience with Routh's misgivings was scarcely disguised. He explained to him, 'Our own purchases have, as I have more than once informed you, been carried to the utmost limit, short of seriously raising the price in the London market'.[59] He insisted that the government had done everything that could reasonably be expected of them. That this might not prove to be enough, Trevelyan felt was not the fault of Britain, 'the greatest trading nation in the world'. Not for the first time, Trevelyan laid much of the blame for the situation on the Irish themselves. In a long, didactic letter to Routh, he elaborated on this point:

. . . for a numerous people like the Irish to be fed from foreign countries is a thing unheard of. I hope that it may turn out to be easier than I expect, but my fears are stronger than my hopes . . . . The ordinary mercantile interests of even the greatest trading nation in the world is unequal to such a novel emergency . . . and even supposing it to have arrived on the shores of Ireland in sufficient quantity, can it be brought into consumption in all the different parts of the interior in sufficient time to meet the wants of the people? . . . The ordinary social machinery by which the necessary supplies of food are distributed in other countries is, as you well know, lamentably deficient in Ireland.[60]

In the early months of 1847, there were increasing reports of deaths caused by disease and starvation in all parts of Ireland. There was also an upsurge in instances of pilfering and plundering of grain supplies. In a number of areas also, crowds of hungry people attempted to exert their moral authority on the local officials by marching to the town centre or local workhouse, carrying poles adorned with loaves of bread. Although police and troops were frequently employed to disperse the crowds, for the most part the demonstrations were peaceful, their purpose being, as one newspaper stated, 'to show themselves as a memento of their destitution'. Occasionally, this form of moral force did have a short-term impact, the marchers being given bread by the local bakers. To official observers in London, however, these demonstrations were yet a further indication of the ingratitude of the Irish people.[61]

Regardless of the fact that the policies being pursued by the government were inadequate, the government refused to deviate from its chosen course. At this stage, a short-term solution such as placing a temporary embargo on exports from Ireland or purchasing additional supplies in the markets used by the private merchants could have been introduced to provide immediate assistance to Ireland. But the government refused to do so. It was unwilling to attempt a temporary and immediate, although undoubtedly radical, and expensive solution. The fall of Sir Robert Peel's government over the repeal of the Corn Laws was perhaps too recent a memory for the Whigs to risk upsetting the merchant lobby. Instead, the government chose to adhere to a policy of either limited (in the west of Ireland) or total (in the east of Ireland) non-interference. The continuation of this policy could be justified on the grounds that not only was it ideologically acceptable, but it had also become a matter of honour. As Trevelyan explained, 'We attach the highest public importance to the strict observance of our pledge, not to send orders abroad which would come into competition with our merchants and upset all their calculations'.[62] The promises made to a small but powerful group of merchants and traders were put above the need of many Irish people to obtain food. Although the government did not consider it possible to deviate from this policy, they did make a few minor concessions to the local relief committees. They were permitted to provide relief to the poor in the form of soup, in an attempt to eke out their dwindling resources. At the same time, the donations made by the Lord Lieutenant to the relief committees was increased to a maximum of 100 per cent, as it had been in the previous year. That such measures were inadequate can be judged from the fact that even after the food depots were opened, in the first months of 1847, mortality within Ireland continued to increase.

The Public Works

By the end of 1846, the relief committees were not alone in experiencing problems, as the public works became increasingly unable to meet the demands being placed on them. In March 1846, four new Public Works Acts had been introduced, which had been extended by additional legislation passed in August 1846. Within a few months of this, however, even the Commissioners of Public Works described the relief works as having become 'a system strained beyond its proper limit'.[63] The most important of the Public Works Acts passed in March 1846 had provided for the construction and alteration of roads. This was to be equally financed from both local and central taxation: half the cost was to be paid by the local barony and the other half was to be provided as a grant by the Treasury.[64] Although there had been much dissatisfaction with the way in which these Acts had been implemented in the spring and summer of 1846, following the second appearance of potato blight, the government chose to make the public works the main agency for providing relief.

The new public works legislation which was passed in August 1846 was popularly known as the 'Labour Rate Act'.[65] It was based on the proposals of Trevelyan and was designed with the intention of eliminating all of the alleged waste, abuses and mismanagement which the government believed to have been prevalent in the previous year.[66] The Act was in many ways an extension of its predecessor. Again, the onus was on the local Grand Juries to apply to the Lord Lieutenant, through a special presentment session, for a work of public utility to be introduced to the area. As had been the case under the previous Act, the construction and maintenance of roads was regarded as the most useful way of providing simple yet extensive employment. Yet again, the Treasury had the final say regarding the issue of monies and they exercised their right to withhold their sanction until the work had been visited and approved by an officer of the Board of Public Works.

Although it was still the responsibility of the local Grand Juries to initiate the introduction of public works to an area, the Board of Works then assumed responsibility for the management of the project. The local relief committees were no longer permitted to issue tickets for employment on the relief works. Instead, their role was limited to compiling lists of people whom they considered to be suitable candidates for employment. Final approval then had to be obtained from an officer of the Board of Works. To facilitate the larger role which they were to play and the subsequent increase in bureaucratic procedure, more staff were necessary. The size of the Board of Works was increased substantially as an additional 10,000 overseers, 5,000 check clerks, extra engineers, inspecting officers, valuators, office clerks, draftsmen, and pay clerks were all employed.[67] The cost of financing the additional staff was shared between the local barony and the government, with the former paying the larger portion. The cost of so closely superintending the local works could occasionally be as high as 25 per cent of the total cost of labour on the roads and as high as 50 per cent of the cost of the drainage works.[68] Already, by 31 December 1846, the cost of employing the additional staff at the Board of Works was £48,000. This, combined with the expense of tools costing a further £10,000, made a total of £58,000 expenditure compared with the £8,000 provided.[69]

The most significant change made regarding the extension of the public works was in regard to funding. While there was a move towards more centralisation in the administration of the relief works, there was simultaneously a decentralisation in the method of financing them. The Act of March 1846 had provided for the cost of the relief works to be shared equally between local taxation (through Grand Juries) and imperial taxation (through the British Treasury). Following August 1846, local taxation in the form of county cess was to bear the whole cost of all such relief although, in the first instance, it could be provided by the Treasury in the form of a loan. The Treasury charged interest on these loans at 5 per cent per annum payable in half-yearly instalments of not less than four and not more than twenty payments. This change of policy marked a significant, additional step in making Irish distress the financial responsibility of Irish local taxation. Inevitably, this burden fell most heavily on the landlords. The government could sanctimoniously justify this on the ground that, at last, Irish property was being forced to support Irish poverty. In fact the policy meant that Irish property was being forced to bear the cost not merely of ordinary Irish poverty, but also to finance the relief of the extraordinary distress brought about by an unforeseen act of nature. Nor was this burden a light one. The relief works carried out on the roads in the spring and summer of 1846 had cost £476,000, half of which was a grant from the government. The relief works carried out in the wake of the Act of August 1846 cost a staggering £4,848,000, all of which was ultimately to be borne by the localities in which they were carried out.[70] For the Board of Works, this represented a growth of gargantuan proportions in their duties, as the usual expenditure on public works was £500,000 per annum with which they employed 20,000 men each year.[71] For the property of Ireland, it represented a large portion of the total Poor Law valuation of the country, which had been estimated at just over £13,000,000.[72]

In spite of the enormous expenditure and the large increase in staff of the Board of Works, in the second year of distress the public works proved inadequate to the task which confronted them. In the months following August 1846, demand for employment on the works continually outstripped supply, whilst for those who did obtain employment, the wages were frequently insufficient to pay for food prices, which continued to rise until February 1847. Initially, however, the main concern of the government was to restrict the numbers employed on the public works and was particularly anxious to introduce more control over the rate of wages. Earlier in the year, a fixed wage had been paid which had averaged from 10d to 1s per day. Both the Board of Works and the Treasury had regarded this as being too generous and an encouragement to people to abandon their own farms in favour of a guaranteed wage on the works. At the same time, fixed wages were believed to encourage and reward idleness. Therefore, after August 1846, a system of task work—that is, payment by results—was introduced. The local Board officials were urged to devise a system which permitted average labourers to earn between 10d and 1s per day, and exceptional labourers up to 1s 6d per day. Indolent or troublesome workers, on the other hand, were to be paid as little as 8d per day.[73] This general advice was given without regard to prevailing prices within a locality. As food prices spiralled towards the end of 1846, the inflexible wages set by the Board of Works meant that persons employed on the works experienced a substantial drop in their real incomes.

The most frequent complaints made against the public works by the distressed people who sought employment on them concerned the tardiness in the payment of wages, the delays involved in introducing them, and the imposition of task work. The former was partly attributable to the introduction of task work which meant that all work completed had to be measured and valued. A general shortage of silver also impeded the work of the pay clerks. Although the wages were occasionally stolen and pay clerks attacked, this was a relatively rare occurrence. These delays were usually of a few day's duration. The delay in commencing a public work could sometimes be as long as five weeks. In many cases, this delay was caused by the bureaucratic procedures involved in the establishment of any relief work, particularly the inability of a local relief committee to issue tickets for employment. This new regulation frustrated the efforts of even the most dedicated of local relief committees. In Dunfanaghy in Co. Donegal, for example, the chairman of a local relief committee regarded the delays as rendering the public works totally inadequate. He did, however, personally absolve the officers of the works and admitted that:

. . . notwithstanding every exertion on their part, the calls of the engineers and officers of the Board of Works to lay roads are such that only 150 have as yet been set to work . . . I fear it will be some time yet before tickets can be issued for the remaining 332, for I know that the inspecting officer who issues them, has engagements for a fortnight at least, and the calls upon the engineers in every direction are as pressing as possible.[74]

On many occasions, these delays served only to exacerbate the already debilitated state of the people. One Board officer from Castlebellingham in Co. Louth, which was not one of the most distressed parts of the country, noted that 'the works in aid of relief were not commenced until the people were almost starving'.[75] In this case, the shortcomings of the public works system forced some of the local people to seek relief in the local workhouse.

The introduction of task work was resisted in many parts of the country. Although the system of payment by results potentially meant that the labourers could earn more than in the previous year, this was rarely the case. Task work could only benefit those who were healthy and strong or people who did not depend on public works as the only means of income for their family. However, in the counties which lay along the western seaboard, an increasingly debilitated population had no other source of income but relief works. Task work was disliked on the grounds that it increased the delays in the payment of wages and also penalised people who were unable to work quickly. This dislike increased as food prices soared and the wages paid were no longer sufficient to maintain a labourer and his family. By the end of 1846, the price of Indian corn had risen to 3s per stone (14 lbs) in some areas. Even allowing an average wage of 1s per day for a six day week, this meant that a family, which could consist of a man, his wife and four or five children, had to survive on 2 lbs of corn each day. Nor did this allow for other necessities such as turf or milk. What was intended to be a subsistence wage had, in fact, deteriorated into a starvation wage. This contributed to a downward spiral of depression. As the labourers became weaker and more debilitated, so they were less capable of performing enough task work to earn an adequate day's wage. At the beginning of December 1846, Jones had declared that task work had failed in its purpose as 'the men are receiving much larger sums than they ought to do'.[76] A month later, in January 1847, even Jones was aware that the situation had changed dramatically and admitted, 'In some districts, the men who come to the works are so reduced in their physical powers as to be unable to earn above 4d or 5d per diem'.[77]

Protests against task work had commenced immediately following its introduction in the harvest of 1846. The first incident was reported at the end of August in Westport, Co. Mayo, when a 'mob' of between 3,000 to 4,000 persons 'forced' the labourers employed of the works to leave them and listen to 'inciting addresses'. The situation was diffused following the intervention of the local Roman Catholic priest.[78] From the end of August 1846 to the beginning of February 1847, 140 separate incidents of outrage or violence were reported to the Board of Works. The majority took place in the most distressed parts of the country, notably counties Clare and west Cork and, to a lesser extent, counties Galway, Kerry, Mayo and Limerick. They were mainly concerned with the lowness of wages due to task work. Despite this, surprisingly few instances of stealing or robbery were reported. Instead, the majority of outrages were threats made to the officers of the public works, with fewer acts of violence being committed.[79] One threatening letter given to a relief officer in Co. Clare was signed 'Captain Starlight' in a manner reminiscent of earlier Rockite threats.[80]

ENCLOSURE.

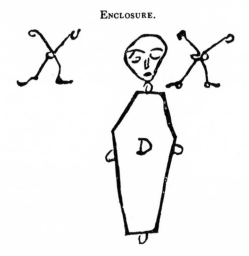

CAPTAIN WYNNE,

CAPTAIN STARLIGHT sends you notice to lave thes parts, or if you dont i give you the end of Mesters carrige blood and c'o. they say your a undanted man, but i have forty rifel men as kind as ever puled a thriker, so go an with the works a truan and quit the country, af you dont wish to go home to the mistres a corpes, which by the mortel i'l send you if you come to thes parts agin, take this warnin or youl be a ded man in no time, i'l wach you.

Your obed' Ser'
CAPTAIN STARLIGHT.

For the most part, threats were rarely carried out. One of the most unusual outrages occurred on the Pullough Road in Co. Limerick when an officer of the public works was 'brutally attacked by two armed men in women's clothes'.[81] The government recommended to their local officials that if a group of labourers gathered in a potentially threatening situation, they should ask the local parish priest to intervene and calm the situation down. This policy met with a high degree of success, but in cases where an act of violence was actually perpetrated, the works were sometimes suspended as occurred in Ruan, Co. Clare, and additional troops or police were sent to the area.[82] As the situation progressively deteriorated, it is perhaps surprising that more acts of violence were not committed.

In some areas the scheme of task work was not rigidly enforced but even where the average wage of 1s per day was paid, this was increasingly insufficient to meet the requirements of a family. Many workers earned far less than this, however, as from October 1846 to the close of the scheme in June 1847, the average daily wage paid on the public works was a mere 7¼d—even lower than the punitive rates originally envisaged by the Board of Works and Treasury.[83] As the winter progressed, both heavy rain and snow interfered with the ability of labourers to earn a full wage in the course of a week. As early as September, the three main government bodies involved in the provision of relief—the Irish Executive, the Board of Works and the Treasury—had decided that on the days when inclement weather prevented any work, the labourers were to be sent home and receive only a half day's pay.[84] The exceptionally cold conditions of December 1846 and January to April 1847—severe frost followed by heavy snowfalls—meant that many work days were inevitably lost. A member of the Society of Friends who was in Co. Donegal in February 1847, where snow had been falling for almost two months, observed 'the ground is now deeply covered with snow, and I fear all the public works will be stopped, and how those poor creatures can exist I know not'.[85] Although some people attempted to continue to work despite the weather, road construction was not possible during heavy rain or snow, and they were forced to undertake stone-breaking for a lower wage. What in September had been provided as a minimum wage was, three months later, insufficient to keep a family alive.

Regardless of the inadequacy of the wages paid on the public works, the demand for employment continued to exceed the number of places available. Reports from the officers in the field in areas where there was a high level of dependence on the public works indicated a system which could no longer provide for the demands being made on it. The officer in Swinford, Co. Mayo, described the prospects of the county as 'frightful' and complained that:

My life is a constant worry; from morning until night my house is beset with men, women and children, all crying together and saying I can save them by giving them an order to work; they have an idea that my power is unlimited.[86]

In Co. Clare, where public works were heavily relied upon, a Board officer reported, not for the first time:

The people are starving, notwithstanding the enormous extent of employment . . . I have stated this frequently but I consider it my duty to repeat it again and again; the supplies of food available from day to day, do not give the people a meal a day.[87]

Impervious to such reports, the official philosophy of the Board of Works continued to be 'to keep the numbers as low as the existing calamity will permit'.[88] It is not surprising, therefore, that during this period, many women and children began to crowd on to the public works in an attempt to supplement the meagre incomes available for a family. In one district in Co. Louth, the number of women and girls employed increased from 81 during the week ending 26 December, to 7,042 a month later. Although, as the table below shows, their earning power was less than an adult male, their wages must have provided an important supplement to a diminished family income. Inevitably, a price was to be paid for this. Whole families being employed in manual labour during a particularly severe winter, took its toll on the health of the people.

Table 4: People Employed in Castlebellingham, Co. Louth from the Period at which the Works commenced on 5 December 1846 to 30 January 1847, and Average Rate of Daily Wages[89]

Date	Men	Wages s.d	Women/Girls	Wages s.d	Boys	Wages s.d
5 Dec.	133	1- 1	2	0-4	2	0-4
12 Dec	824	0- 8	13	0-7¾	6	0-7¾
19 Dec.	2080	0-10½	7	0-7	23	0-6
26 Dec	2129	0-11	81	0-7¼	113	0-6¼
2 Jan.	3803	0-11¾	184	0-7	273	0-7
9 Jan.	4849	0-11½	397	0-6	744	0-7½
16 Jan	4930	1- 1¾	2011	0-5¾	1137	0-6¼
23 Jan.	5644	1- 1¾	2455	0-6¼	1765	0-7¾
30 Jan.	9608	0-10¾	7042	0-6	3606	0-4¾

Although many aspects of the public works were disliked, the number of people engaged on them continued to grow, not peaking until March 1847. In one week at the end of September 1846, 26,000 men had been employed on relief works and, within a month, this had increased to approximately 114,000. By November, it had reached 286,000. By the end of December, it had swollen to 441,000 persons. In January 1847, the weekly average number of people employed was 615,000 people, but this fell slightly in February due to appalling weather. The amount of money expended on the public works also increased sharply during those months.

Table 5: Expenditure on the Public Works from September 1846 to February 1847

September/October	£ 54,878
November	£298,799
December	£545,054
January	£736,125
February	£944,144

The number employed reached a maximum at the beginning of March 1847 when 714,000 persons were employed on the works during the course of a week. Jones, the Chairman of the Board of Works, predicted that if this trend continued, as many as 900,000 people could be seeking employment within a few months.[90]

Jones believed that as a result of the overwhelming demand for employment on the relief works, he and his colleagues were 'no longer Commissioners of Public Works, but administrators of outdoor relief to nearly a million families'.[91] Jones doubted that the Board possessed the means to provide this level of relief. He informed Trevelyan that road building had already 'reached the utmost point to which we can find work' and that if increased demands were made on the Board of Works, they would find 'we have neither the staff nor the work upon which we can employ them'.[92] Even more seriously, Jones realised that the public works were no longer providing a bulwark against the impact of the Famine. In the west of Ireland, an increasing number of verdicts of death from starvation were blamed upon the inadequacy of the relief works. Jones admitted that the condition of these people meant that relief in return for labour was starving the people who 'their bodily strength gone and spirits depressed, they have not the power to exert themselves suffi-ciently to earn the ordinary day's wages'.[93] Many deaths from starvation and famine-related diseases had already occurred in some parts of Ireland and Jones warned that if this system continued, even heavier mortality was likely in counties Clare, Cork, Galway, Kerry, Leitrim, Mayo, Roscommon, Tipperary and Wicklow.[94]

As in the first year of shortages, the regional distribution of relief was varied. Again, there was a marked correlation between areas which had a low valuation and high degree of dependence on potatoes, with areas which required a large amount of assistance in the form of public works. Even in Ulster, more areas were dependent on the relief works than had been the case during the distress of 1845–6. This was due to a temporary dislocation in the linen industry, which resulted in a short period of hardship for the small farmers who also supplemented their income with flax-growing or weaving. The actual numbers employed, however, still remained small. For example, the daily average number of labourers employed in Co. Antrim from October 1846 to June 1847, when the works came to an end, was 270 labourers. This compares starkly with the daily average of 42,134 labourers employed in Co. Cork during the same period.[95]

Although the public works were used less in eastern Ulster than in other parts of the country, more use was made of the Drainage Acts than in any other area. Nevertheless, as Table 6 demonstrates, there was considerable diversity throughout the country in levels of dependence on relief. The geographic distribution of relief followed a similar pattern to the previous year, continuing to be highest in counties along or near the western seaboard, that is, counties Cork, Clare, Galway, Mayo, Tipperary and Limerick. As the table below shows, there was a marked diversity between demand for relief in the four counties which employed the maximum numbers of persons on relief works and the counties which employed the lowest numbers.

Table 6: Average Number of People Employed Daily on the Public Works from October 1846 to June 1847[96]

County	Daily Average No. Employed
Highest Users	
Cork	42,134
Galway	33,325
Clare	31,310
Mayo	29,221
Lowest Users	
Carlow	1,414
Dublin	725
Down	335
Antrim	270

Table 7: Average Number of Labourers Employed Daily as a Percentage of the 1841 Workforce

Cork	13.9%
Galway	17.8%
Clare	26.0%
Mayo	17.2%
Tipperary	15.2%
Limerick	20.9%
Roscommon	20.1%

During the period from October 1846 to June 1847, the average daily number of labourers on the public works was 363,400, which was equivalent to 10.3 per cent of the total Irish labour force as enumerated in the 1841 Census. Again, however, as Table 6 demonstrates, there existed a significant geographic concentration of the use of this scheme to provide relief through employment. In particular, the top seven counties, that is those with an average number of daily labourers in excess of 20,000, accounted for over half (56.7 per cent) of the total employment generated by the public works, although their share of the total labour force in 1841 was 33.8 per cent. Within these counties, dependence on the public works was relatively most important in Co. Clare, where an average of 26 per cent of the workforce were so employed.

The Public Work Act of August 1846 was supplemented by a further provision which was intended to provide employment of a more specialised nature which, at the same time, would help to modernise the system of agriculture within the country. This was embodied in 'Mr Labouchere's Letter' of 5 October 1846. The letter, from the Chief Secretary of Ireland, provided for drainage and sub-soiling to be added to the public works already being undertaken. These particular relief works were popularly known as the Labouchere works or the drainage works. Unlike the works carried out on the roads, their cost was to be a charge on electoral division rather than the larger barony unit, thus placing their funding on the same basis as Poor Law rating. The consequent reduction in the size of the unit of taxation was regarded as a way of encouraging landlords to provide relief employment whilst simultaneously undertaking lasting improvements on their estates. The intention was to bring taxation more within the control of individual landlords by giving them a direct and permanent benefit.[97] This was of most relevance in the north-east of Ireland, where the electoral divisions were smaller than in other parts of the country and sometimes were coterminous with estate boundaries. It is, therefore, not surprising that, unlike the ordinary relief works, the greatest concentration of drainage work was carried out within the province of Ulster and the smallest portion within Connacht.

Table 8: Number of People Employed on Drainage Works in Ireland in March 1847[98]

Leinster	5,622
Munster	5,794
Ulster	7,366
Connacht	2,194

To enable this legislation to be implemented, an initial period of training was considered essential. The Board of Works regarded it as necessary to 'instruct not only the ordinary farm labourers, but fishermen, unaccustomed to spade labour, and the inhabitants of towns who are proverbial for idleness and hated exertion'.[99] Within a month of the Labouchere Letter being introduced, sixty-eight applications for this form of relief were received. In December, this rose to 122 applications and peaked in February 1847 when 134 presentments were made. But even at its maximum, no more than 5 per cent of all people on relief were engaged on the drainage works. However, as public works on the roads started to be phased out after March 1847, the numbers engaged on the drainage works actually increased slightly. This was because the government considered that important reproductive work was being undertaken and, at the same time, that the skills which had been learned in the laying of drains would be of permanent advantage to Ireland. As a result of this, the drainage works did not start to be phased out until July 1847 and were fully closed in August. Unlike the relief provided by employment on the roads which was widely condemned by labourers, cess payers and government alike, there was a 'universal expression of satisfaction, with the way in which the drainage works were executed' and even the Board of Works praised them for having been implemented with 'system and success'.[100]

By the end of 1846 even the most ardent supporters of the public works realised that the system of providing relief in return for labour had failed. Trevelyan regarded the main problem as being one of over-centralisation. He described the public works as having developed into a 'monstrous system of centralisation' the burden of which was 'fearful in the extreme'. The government had not anticipated that the demand for employment would be so great, although they believed that some of this demand came from people who were not genuinely destitute. A further result of this policy had been to use up the limited resources provided by the government in encouraging people to neglect their ordinary agricultural pursuits.[101] Jones realised that the failure of the public works system was even more serious than his superiors in London realised when he stated that 'the question had become one of food not labour'.[102] He realised that the public works, although successful on previous occasions, were unable to meet the demands made on them in the winter of 1846–7. Essentially, the temporary relief measures introduced only a few months earlier had failed in the most basic requirement of all, that is, in providing a distressed people with food.

At the beginning of 1847, the government announced a major change of policy. It had two basic components. In the short term, people in the western counties of Ireland needed food. This was to be provided through soup kitchens which were to be introduced in the spring and summer of 1847. They were to provide relief directly in the form of food, usually soup. In the longer term, labour and relief were to be separated. Public works and other temporary measures were no longer to be the main means of providing relief. Instead, the permanent system of poor relief in Ireland, the Poor Law, was to be extended to meet any future demands. By doing this, a greater responsibility for the provision of relief was to be placed on the localities through the administrative unit of the Poor Law unions. Jones welcomed this transfer in the responsibility for the provision of relief. He hoped that public works would never again be resorted to as a means of relieving extraordinary distress. In the Final Report of his Board he recommended that 'labour will not in future be lowered to serve the purpose of relief, nor relief deprived of its character of benevolence'.[103]

Although the Public Works Acts were not due to expire until 15 August 1846, the government decided to start to wind them down in March in order to facilitate a gradual transfer to the new relief measures. On 22 February 1847, the Board of Works issued a circular stating that relief by labour was shortly to cease and was to be replaced by relief in the form of food. To facilitate a smooth transfer, landlords were asked to provide as much private employment as possible. On 11 March, the Treasury directed that employment on the works was to be reduced by 20 per cent. The only exception to this was the drainage works. A month later, a further 10 per cent reduction was to take place, with a view to a total cessation on 1 May.[104] A corresponding reduction was also made in the number of staff employed on the public works. In April, 9,817 people had been employed as overseers, but by June this had been reduced to

518. In areas of intense distress, there were to be no sudden stoppages of relief. Delays in the opening of the soup kitchens meant that in some areas, the public works had to remain in operation. At the end of May, 111,696 people were still employed on the road works and a further 22,089 on drainage. The Board of Works considered that any further reductions would be imprudent and admitted that the reductions already implemented had not been 'wholly effected without suffering'.[105] The areas which were experiencing most problems in the establishment of the new relief measures were those situated in the remotest and most inaccessible parts of the country, that is, counties Galway, Cork, Mayo and Donegal. In many other parts of the country, notably counties Roscommon, Leitrim and Fermanagh, the sudden closure of the public works and the tardiness in opening the soup kitchens resulted in a hiatus in relief provision. In these areas, an additional burden was placed upon the already overfull workhouses and forced some relief committees to reconvene hastily to provide relief—usually soup. These ad hoc relief measures were generally inadequate to meet the demands placed on them and, in the spring of 1847, emigration and mortality rose dramatically. The increase in deaths from starvation became so commonplace that many newspapers stopped reporting them in detail. It led the local newspaper in Roscommon to pose the question, 'What will become of our peasantry?' The Roman Catholic clergy of Derry, led by their Bishop, Dr Maginn, blamed the increase in mortality very firmly on the British government. For the period November 1846 to April 1847, they compiled a separate list from the parish registers of all deaths that were attributable to starvation. On 1 May 1847, they placed this list in the diocesan archive, rolled in black crepe, and inscribed:

> The Records of the Murders of the Irish Peasantry, perpetuated in A.D. 1846–47, in the 9 and 10 Vic., under the name of economy during the administration of a professedly Liberal, Whig government, of which Lord John Russell was Premier.[106]

In the middle of July, the Board of Works announced that the only people remaining on the works were those employed on essential tasks. This meant that all 'relief employment' on the public works was officially at an end. The policy of dismissing large numbers from the relief works regardless of whether or not an alternative form of relief was available was widely criticised within Ireland. The Kerry Grand Jury described the decision to strike 20 per cent of labourers off the relief lists as a 'death warrant'. William Smith O'Brien, the MP for Co. Limerick and a member of the Repeal Association, viewed this policy as a further proof of England's indifference to Irish distress. He estimated that 240,000 persons had died of starvation unnecessarily, as the government possessed the means of preventing this. This theme was taken up by Archbishop MacHale of Tuam, who also supported a Repeal of the Act of Union. MacHale viewed the change in policy as 'a melancholy proof of the hatred of Ireland'.[107]

As the Board of Works began to close down its relief operations, numerous complaints were made that many roads were being left in an unfinished state and that some were in a worse condition than before the work had commenced. Jones excused this on the grounds that they had received so many demands for employment that close supervision had been impossible. Also, if the public works had not been closed earlier than originally anticipated, many of these 'deformities and inconveniences' could have been eliminated.[108] Jones believed that neither his Board nor the government should be held responsible for any work which had not been completed. The main purpose of the public works had been to provide relief, and to this end 'work, at any cost, was paid for, as the only means of saving the people from famine, and the property of the country from the alternative of pillage'.[109]

By the beginning of 1847, not only was the inadequacy of relief provided by the public works generally recognised, but the system was also increasingly criticised by central government for being mismanaged. Much of the blame for this alleged ineffectiveness was attributed to the local relief committees, who were accused of not having been sufficiently ruthless in the compilation of relief lists. Jones personally regarded the local committees as being 'very troublesome' and interested only in 'getting as many persons employed as possible, instead of anxiously endeavouring to keep the number as low as the existing calamity will permit'. Captain Norris, the local Inspector in Thurles, Co. Tipperary, complained that in his area, Catholic priests dominated the relief committees and, because they had no personal interest in keeping taxes down, they allowed people onto the relief lists indiscriminately.[110] Apart from the relief committees, there was a general belief that, where possible, people were still attempting to take advantage of the government or, as Jones warned Trevelyan, 'everybody considers the government fair game to pluck from as much as they can'. This theme was taken up in England by *The Times* which repeatedly drew a comparison between the ungrateful and feckless poor of Ireland and the 'respectable' poor of England, cautioning that:

What is given to the Irish is so much filched from English distress . . . The English labourer pays taxes from which the Irish one is free —nay, he pays taxes by which the Irishman is enriched.[111]

The Irish landlords were selected for particular criticism. Again, they were accused of not having made sufficient effort to help the distressed people. The government had hoped that 'the pressure of a great public calamity would have led to increased exertions on the part of the upper and middle classes of society'. Public opinion in Britain deemed that this had not been the case, and, consequently a larger number of people were forced to seek relief on the public works than had been anticipated.[112] This contributed to widespread reports of the public works being used by people who were not genuinely in need of relief. At the beginning of December, the Relief Commissioners had tried to combat this by ordering the local committees not to place people on the relief lists if they occupied land valued at over £6. The relief lists were to state the rating of each person included on the list.[113] The committees were also directed to make 'searching local investigation' in order to discover the true means of every applicant for relief, as not to do so would be 'productive of ruinous consequences'.[114]

The introduction of more stringent tests of destitution did not end the rumours of abuses on the public works. The following report was reprinted in a number of Irish newspapers:

It is but proper the English people should be told that the sons of a broken down gentry—a gentry full of beggarly pride but utterly destitute of the spirit of manly independence—are deriving the chief advantage from the present enormous expenditure of public money.[115]

The *Northern Whig*, a Belfast newspaper, in a series of editorial comments and articles, criticised the way in which relief was being provided in the west of the country, and highlighted in particular the alleged apathy of the landlords. In an article on the relief measures in Skibbereen, the paper accused the local landlords of encouraging public works in full expectation that:

. . . the sum voted will be advanced by government and never repaid, and so jobbing and knavery and laziness meet and scheme and luxuriate, making a benefit of the starved dead.[116]

Within Ireland, such stories were supported by sympathisers of the Whig government, perhaps in an attempt to draw attention away from the more serious problem of starvation due to the inadequacy of the public works. Similar stories also appeared in some of the English newspapers, notably *The Times* and the *Morning Chronicle*, which not only discredited the relief measures operating in Ireland but also at times cast aspersions on the character of the Irish people. In a report published in *The Times* in March 1847, Irish people were described as 'a people born and bred from time immemorial, in inveterate indolence, improvidence, disorder and consequent destitution'. The newspaper also accused them of showing indifference to the burial of their dead:

> The astounding apathy of the Irish themselves to the most horrible scenes under their eyes and capable of relief by the smallest exertion is something absolutely without a parallel in the history of civilised nations . . . the brutality of piratical tribes sinks to nothing compared with the absolute inertia of the Irish in the midst of the most horrifying scenes.

The inhabitants of the west of Ireland were accused of being too indolent to give their dead a 'decent Christian burial'. They added that even in places such as Skibbereen, plenty of money was still available, citing the fact that deposits in the local Savings Bank had doubled, and concluded:

> Could anything make it clearer that it is not money but men that Ireland wants—real men possessed of average hearts, heads and hands.[117]

The reports in *The Times*, the most influential newspaper of the day, had an impact on parliamentary and public opinion. In helping to shape the public perception of events in Ireland, this paper was ably supported by the satiric articles and caricatures that appeared in *Punch* magazine. However, much of the information upon which these stories were based was supplied by Wood and Trevelyan who used the powerful medium of the press to their own political advantage.

Edward Twistleton, the Chief Poor Law Commissioner in Ireland, however, was worried that such reports were having a negative impact on the policies of the British government in Ireland. Twistleton felt sufficiently alarmed to warn Sir George Grey, the Home Secretary, that the articles which had appeared over a number of weeks in *The Times* and the *Morning Chronicle* had created 'a considerable impression on the public mind'. He felt that the article on the increase in bank deposits was being used inappropriately as 'a proof of successful swindling on the part of the Irish people during the past year'. Twistleton was aware of the effect that such adverse publicity could have on both the policies of the government and the work of private charities. He felt such an accusation should not be left unanswered especially as, in his opinion, bank deposits were not an accurate indication of distress. He cautioned the government:

> I know well, however, the thorough fallacy of the assumption on which the article was based, and could not but deplore the mischief which such views were likely to occasion. Now it would be a serious misfortune if Her Majesty's government, admitting the multiplicity of subjects which are likely to occupy their attention, were led to suppose that these views rested on a foundation of truth.[118]

The Poor Law

The government responded to the re-appearance of potato blight in 1846 by extending the temporary relief measures which had been used so successfully in the previous year. Again, they hoped to keep the temporary and the permanent systems of relief separate. The public works and the local relief committees continued to be employed by the government as, 'the principal means of contending with the calamity'.[119] The Poor Law, which was the permanent relief system in Ireland, was to be subsidiary to this, although more use was to be made of it than in the previous year. No right to relief existed in Ireland and relief provided by the Poor Law was to be limited to the number of people who could be accommodated within the local workhouses. No extension of this was contemplated. To prepare for an increased demand on their resources, in September 1846, the Poor Law Commissioners advised each board of guardians to review their stocks, contracts and finances with a view to the full capacity of their workhouse being used in the coming year. They were also told to base all financial estimates, especially the amount of poor rate to be levied, on the same assumption. If the demands for workhouse relief exceeded its capacity, the guardians were to send the excess numbers to the local relief committees. The guardians were to give priority in providing workhouse accommodation to those whom the 1838 Act had declared to be 'the primary objects of the Irish Poor Law', that is, the aged, infirm and otherwise disabled persons. This was regarded as being particularly necessary because:

The recent measures of parliament enacted for the employment of labour, apply only in an indirect manner, and who may, therefore, be expected to form the class most liable to destitution on consequence of the present calamity.[120]

The impact of the potato blight in 1845 on the local workhouses had been unremarkable. The second, more widespread, appearance of blight in 1846 had an immediate effect on Poor Law relief. As early as October 1846, the number of inmates in many of the workhouses began to rise sharply. By the end of November, the workhouses of the Ballina, Cork, Granard and Waterford unions were full. This pressure for Poor Law relief so soon after the harvest was unusual, indicating the severity of the distress. It also partly resulted from the tardiness with which the temporary relief measures were being implemented. This forced the destitute to turn to the permanent system of poor relief, which was sometimes the only relief agency within an area. By Christmas 1846, over half of the 130 workhouses were full. The number of workhouse inmates continued to rise until February 1847, at which time almost all of the workhouses were full, and some even contained more inmates than their official limit. After February, the numbers in the workhouses started to decline slowly, partly as the government soup kitchens began to open.[121]

As the shortcomings of the public works and other temporary relief measures became obvious, the boards of guardians were increasingly used as a medium through which the poor people could air their grievances. In addition to being Poor Law guardians, these men were frequently also members of the local relief committees and were, especially in the west of the country, generally the largest resident landowners in the union. As a consequence, they had a vested interest in seeing that their taxes were properly spent. On occasions, threats of violence were made against the guardians, but as in the previous year, instances of actual violence against them were rare. In some areas, troops were deployed to disperse crowds of hungry people who were surrounding the workhouse. It was to these guardians and the local machinery of the Poor Law that the distressed people turned when the other relief proved to be either inadequate or bureaucratically impenetrable. Many boards of guardians responded to the distressed condition of the people swiftly and compassionately. Even if their workhouse was full and their legal obligation to provide relief therefore at an end, they continued to provide additional relief. This took a variety of forms. Free meals were sometimes provided on the workhouse premises to people who were not inmates of the house, poor people were given food to take to their homes, parts of families were given temporary accommodation and, even after a workhouse became full, the guardians admitted people whom they considered required relief. All of these actions were totally contrary to the provisions of the 1838 Act and drew the immediate wrath of the Poor Law Commissioners upon the boards of guardians involved. Edward Twistleton, the Chief Poor Law Commissioner, believed that a literal application of the law was necessary, not only because the provision of a more liberal form of relief would establish a dangerous precedent, but also because, in his opinion, the local poor rates could not bear this increased financial burden. When a workhouse became full, Twistleton believed that it was the responsibility of either the relief committees or 'individuals possessed of property' to relieve it. He informed the government that:

> I confess that it does not appear to me that . . . the responsibility of deaths from starvation outside the workhouse rests either with the board of guardians or the Commissioners.[122]

Notwithstanding the official policy of the Poor Law Commissioners in regard to outdoor relief, this form of illegal relief continued to be provided during the winter of 1846–7. The giving of outdoor relief was generally held to be an undesirable aspect of any relief policy. The 'new' English Poor Law of 1834 had attempted to eliminate outdoor relief as far as possible and the Irish Poor Law Act of 1838 had deliberately excluded it. Outdoor relief was believed to be demoralising and beyond the resources of a country as poor as Ireland. Despite this, in the months following the harvest of 1846, many guardians throughout the country provided a system of relief which had neither precedent nor statuary backing in Ireland. Many local guardians, when confronted with a deepening crisis to which they were ill-equipped to respond adequately, embarked upon pragmatic action that breached the formal limits of their responsibilities. The Commissioners, unable to eradicate this, were determined to draw as little public attention to it as possible. In their Annual Report for 1847, the Poor Law Commissioners stated that towards the end of 1846, some Poor Law guardians in counties Cork, Kilkenny and Tipperary had attempted to introduce a system of outdoor relief. If allowed to continue, they believed that this would have led to a system of 'abuse and confusion'. The Commissioners added that the guardians involved, when asked to discontinue, had done so.[123] In reality, however, the giving of outdoor relief and other forms of illegal relief was a lot more extensive than the Commissioners admitted publicly.

The Cork guardians were one of the first boards to introduce a system of outdoor relief. This had commenced at the end of September in response to delays in the introduction of public works, when the guardians provided breakfast to approximately 1,440 persons daily who were not inmates of the workhouse. They stopped on 6 October because the relief works were about to open, but promised to continue to give relief to the wives and children of men employed on the works for a few more days. By the end of the month, despite numerous promises, the public works still had not opened. Although the workhouse was full, the guardians continued to admit all destitute applicants for relief. They also introduced a system of outdoor relief in the area. The Poor Law Commissioners repeatedly asked the guardians to stop, but they refused to until public works were commenced. The guardians added that, although they were opposed to outdoor relief in principle, they regarded their activities as a temporary, though necessary, expedient. Notwithstanding the commencement of public works in Cork at the end of 1846, demand for relief inside the local workhouse continued to increase and the guardians again started to provide a daily meal to people who were not inmates of the workhouse. At this stage, the workhouse contained 4,400 inmates, even though it had only been built to accommodate 2,000 persons. Although the Poor Law Commissioners advised the guardians that they should find additional accommodation, the guardians responded that they had insufficient funds to do so. The Cork guardians, like many other boards of guardians throughout the country, had lost faith in the various relief measures. They passed a resolution stating that the Poor Law did not have sufficient resources to meet the prevailing distress, and condemning the government for imposing such a heavy burden of taxation on an impoverished country.[124]

In other unions, the local guardians responded in a similar manner. In the nearby Fermoy union, between 400 to 500 people who were not inmates of the workhouse were given a daily breakfast of stirabout.[125] The Kilkenny guardians provided almost 2,000 people each day with a meal after their workhouse became full. They pointed out that, as food was consumed on the premises, they were acting within the spirit of the 1838 Act. Furthermore, if this relief was discontinued, they predicted that the 'wretched people' would starve.[126] The Skibbereen guardians described the distress in their union as 'heartbreaking' and supported the Reverend Caulfield when he opened a soup kitchen in an attempt to alleviate it. On average, over one thousand people were fed one pint of soup each day, gratuitously in this way.[127] Similar actions were repeated in unions throughout the west of Ireland. They were also adopted in unions which were situated outside those areas officially considered to be distressed. In the New Ross union in Co. Wexford, the Dunshaughlin and Trim unions in Co. Meath, the Edenderry union in King's County, the Abbeyleix union in Queen's County, the South Dublin union in Co. Dublin, the Bailieborough union in Co. Cavan, the Ballymoney union in Co. Antrim, and the Banbridge and Kilkeel unions in Co. Down, and possibly more, the guardians were providing outdoor relief and thus contravening the most fundamental aspiration of the 1838 Act.[128] The Commissioners responded to this flouting of the regulations alternately with persuasion and threats. They also sought legal opinion on the provision of outdoor relief, which confirmed that such actions were illegal under the provisions of the existing Poor Law legislation.[129] When urged to discontinue, however, the guardians either ignored the Commissioners or promised they would stop when other forms of relief became available. Outdoor relief provided by the Poor Law guardians, therefore, was widely resorted to in the winter of 1846–7 as a way of compensating for the inadequacies of government's temporary relief measures.

The Poor Law Commissioners were hopeful that where threats and conciliation had failed in bringing outdoor relief to an end, financial considerations would be more successful. At the end of 1847, they observed that a lack of finance was forcing some guardians to reconsider the amount of relief which they were able to provide. This was confirmed by a report from Edward Senior, the Assistant Poor Law Commissioner in eastern Ulster, who was highly regarded for the thoroughness with which he administered the unions in his charge. Senior used the example of the Kilkeel union in Co. Down. The Kilkeel guardians were finding themselves in financial difficulties as a result of providing such extensive relief. Senior provided a detailed description of the pecuniary difficulties which would ensue from providing outdoor relief: in his unions, the poor rate was levied annually, generally took up to six months to be collected and was generally done during the winter months. This meant that income derived from a poor rate could not be increased swiftly. In many unions, estimates for the current year were already proving to be too low, and Senior estimated that in his district about one-third of the rate had been lost due to the blight and a more general economic depression. As a result, Senior was convinced that only two or three unions in the east of Ulster could sustain the additional burden of paying for outdoor relief.[130] As Senior's district contained some of the wealthiest unions in Ireland, the Commissioners believed that his argument applied even more forcefully throughout the rest of the country. In Munster and Connacht, therefore, which included some of the poorest unions and where outdoor relief was most extensive, the financial difficulties confronting the guardians would be on an even larger scale. In these areas, the Poor Law Commissioners hoped that the guardians would discontinue the system of outdoor relief and transfer the responsibility to the relief committees on whose shoulders, they believed, it correctly belonged.[131]

In addition to providing outdoor relief, an even larger number of boards of guardians were admitting more paupers than the legal limit. With the exception of a handful of unions in the north-east of the country, in January 1847 workhouses throughout Ireland contained more inmates than they were intended to accommodate.[132] Again, the Commissioners regarded this as not lying within the legal responsibility of the guardians. They warned them that by acting in such a way, they were converting their limited resources to evil rather than beneficial ends and increasing the risk of infection in the workhouses. The Commissioners urged the guardians to contact the local relief committees with whom lay the legal responsibility for providing the necessary relief.[133] Although this advice may have been legally correct, the practical consequences of it soon became obvious. The Ballina guardians refused admission to some persons to the workhouse because it was full—the correct procedure and the one recommended by the Commissioners—but these people were found dead shortly afterwards. The government, whilst acknowledging that the Poor Law Commissioners were in a difficult position, severely criticised them for allowing this to happen. The Commissioners were warned that 'a very heavy responsibility' rested on officials who refused relief in such circumstances.[134]

By the end of 1846, it was obvious that the temporary relief policies introduced by the government in the autumn of 1846 were not succeeding. Although the government had intended to keep the temporary and permanent relief systems separate, this clear division was no longer possible in the general clamour for relief. Regardless of the increased demands being made on its resources, the government refused to provide any financial support to the Poor Law. They regarded it as being vital to the success of their policies that the Poor Law should remain totally self-financing. Both Routh and Trevelyan agreed that if any deviation from this was permitted, it would bring upon the government 'the expense, and as a necessary consequence, the charge and care for all the poor in the workhouses in addition to those outside'.[135] Trevelyan admired the fact that the Poor Law made the people who owned property financially responsible for the relief of their local destitute, and he was determined that this additional burden should not be placed on the government. His assessment of the situation was consistent with the writings of Edmund Burke, whom he greatly admired.[136] However, in the months following the 1846 harvest, the demarcation between the various systems of relief was less well defined as demand for relief continued to grow, whether it was in the form of labour, food or workhouse shelter. This choice, in fact, was usually limited by the availability of a particular form of relief within an area. It was also limited by the financial resources available to the relief administrators which resulted in an unofficial, yet generally harmonious alliance. Many local relief committees increasingly provided food in the form of soup—chosen for its cheapness—as their funds became exhausted. Several used the facilities of their local workhouse for making the soup. The relief committee in Carrick-on-Suir requested the local guardians to provide people who were not inmates of the workhouse with breakfast and dinner, as they no longer had the means to provide food. A similar request was made by the Cavan relief committee.[137] In the Ennistymon union in Co. Clare, when the local contractor stopped supplying food to the workhouse due to unpaid debts, the guardians personally paid for five tons of Indian meal to be delivered to the union.[138] In spite of the disapproval of the Commissioners and the government, the guardians and relief committees—who frequently included the same people—often responded with flexibility and imagination in a desperate attempt to stem the flood of distress.

A number of guardians were increasingly sceptical about the ability of any of the existing relief measures to meet the demands being placed on them. Nor was this belief confined to the guardians in the poorest western unions. The guardians of the New Ross, Wexford, Kilkenny and Carlow unions jointly petitioned the government to the effect that the relief being provided was insufficient. They also felt the central administration of the relief policies was ineffective, and criticised the fact that no provisions had been made for the infirm or people with large families.[139] The Galway board of guardians was also dissatisfied with the way in which the government had responded to the second year of shortages. Within the union, the potato crop had almost totally failed, thus depriving the people of 'this densely populated union of their only sustenance'.[140] Co. Galway was one of the largest employers of people on the public works, but the employment provided was insufficient to meet the demand. This threw more of the responsibility for providing relief on the local workhouses, but the guardians doubted their own ability to provide this additional relief. Their finances were already low despite all local taxes having been paid with 'cheerful alacrity'. Scenes of distress in the union were 'daily and hourly becoming still more numerous and more painful'. In spite of this, the poor people remained peaceful and law-abiding. The Galway guardians appealed to the Whig government to show some generosity to the union on the grounds that:

> In so general a calamity, the state should contribute its fair propor-
> tion of the General Burden, a principle recognised by Sir Robert
> Peel last year.[141]

By December 1846, the Galway guardians were facing a deepening
crisis. The workhouse was full and mortality within it was very high. The
funds of the union were almost exhausted and food prices were exorbitant. The guardians considered that it would be impossible to collect
another rate under prevailing circumstances as the ratepayers were
already 'over-burdened'. They asked the government to give them assistance and provide them with a supply of Indian corn and a loan. This
request was refused.[142] The guardians repeatedly appealed for external
assistance, and informed the Commissioners that they were unable to
purchase basic provisions. The standard reply of the Commissioners to
this and similar requests was to direct the guardians to make a greater
effort to collect the poor rates. At the beginning of March 1847, the liabilities of the union amounted to £1,000. The Galway guardians
threatened to discharge the inmates of the workhouse and resign as a
board. Again, the guardians expressed the view that:

> they conceive it to be the duty of government, in a crisis like the
> present when distress is so universal, to come forward and aid the
> Board in supporting the overwhelming mass of paupers.[143]

By June, the debts of the union had risen to £3,711 0s 8d, and some of
the contractors were refusing to allow any further credit. The guardians
considered the collection of any further poor rates impossible 'in the
deplorable state of the country'. The guardians threatened that they
would definitely resign within the week unless they received assistance.
This time, the government provided the union with a small advance of
money. The Galway guardians were simultaneously informed that, in
future, they should make a more determined effort to collect rates.[144]

The unprecedented and, largely unexpected, demands being made on
workhouses throughout the country at the end of 1846 resulted in a
modification in the role to be played by the Poor Law. Although the
Commissioners and the government recognised that an extension of
Poor Law relief was necessary, they were still reluctant to permit outdoor
relief to be granted. Indoor relief was still held to be the most effective
safeguard against abuse. From December 1846, the Poor Law

Commissioners recommended that each board of guardians should take steps to obtain additional accommodation. This could be achieved in a number of ways: either by erecting additional sleeping galleries within the workhouses, building sheds in the grounds, or by hiring additional accommodation within the union. The Commissioners did not recommend the extension of existing workhouse accommodation as this would take too long to implement. It was impressed upon the guardians that they were not to expect any financial assistance from the government but must raise the necessary money within the union.[145] This change of policy did not have the approval of Twistleton, who was convinced that an extension of workhouse accommodation should not be viewed 'as a material resource in the general relief arrangements of the country'.[146] In a private communication to the Home Secretary, Sir George Grey, he expressed alarm at the possibility of the local unions being expected to provide additional relief. In his opinion, the unions could not afford to finance any additional demands on their finances as the resources of the small ratepayers were already exhausted. This action, he believed, would ultimately result in even more demands being made on the Treasury. The government disagreed. Twistleton was informed by Grey that the government had the:

> . . . strongest objection to any grant from the Public Treasury, in aid of or as a substitute for the rate for the relief of the poor.[147]

The government believed that the Irish ratepayers had more resources available to them than they were admitting. Grey unequivocally lent support to this when he stated:

> Many persons liable to be rated are, if my information is correct, at the present time, placing their money in the Savings Banks, and by their refusal to employ any labourers in the cultivation of their land, are increasing the existing distress. To acquiesce in their exemption from the burden legally and morally attaching to them, would, I think, be most objectionable in principle and more injurious in effect.[148]

By the beginning of 1847, several Poor Law unions were without funds. This was most notably the case in those in the south and west of Ireland which had a low Poor Law valuation. In some unions, the Poor Law had not been long enough in operation to be on a secure economic footing: the workhouses in counties Mayo and Clare had only just opened when the blight struck. Also, the loans for the workhouse build-ings were still outstanding and had to be repaid in regular instalments. Although, as the table below shows, the amount of poor rate collected during the year October 1846 to September 1847 increased by approxi-mately 100 per cent, and increased even further in the following year, this was not sufficient to meet the demands being made on it.

Table 9: Amount of Poor Rate Collected During Each Month in the Three Years ending September 1848[149]

	1846	1847	1848
October	£27,605	£26,805	£121,255
November	30,792	36,639	151,684
December	33,262	46,440	168,850
January	36,229	52,439	194,054
February	41,885	47,264	187,064
March	38,909	52,561	138,449
April	38,436	63,110	111,981
May	31,230	64,865	114,518
June	30,630	59,436	121,571
July	24,185	62,197	95,452
August	17,173	53,389	102,107
September	21,510	73,358	120,715
Total	**£371,846**	**£638,503**	**£1,627,700**

The amount of poor rates collected rose sharply in 1847 and 1848, but it remained insufficient to meet increased union expenditure. Prior to 1845, many workhouses had been less than half full but at the end of 1846, for the first time, boards of guardians were having to purchase suf-ficient food for a capacity number of inmates. In March 1846, the cumulative credit balances of all of the unions had been £52,115 but, in March 1847, their total liabilities were £4,619 and continuing to rise. In Co. Mayo, the unions were experiencing particularly severe problems in the period immediately following the harvest. The Ballina workhouse had contained 344 inmates in January 1846 but twelve months later, this had increased to 1,101. Since September 1846, their funds had been exhausted and they had appealed to local landlords, agents and large farmers for assistance.[150] In the adjoining Castlebar union, the guardians were deeply in debt to their contractors who were refusing to supply any more provisions as early as October 1846. The chairman of the board, Lord Lucan, had been personally paying the current expenses of the workhouse for a month. The guardians threatened that they would not admit any more paupers unless they received financial assistance from the government. Lucan's subsequent policy of evicting his small tenants overshadowed his earlier generosity and earned him national notoriety and enduring opprobrium.[151]

As early as October 1846, even though a new harvest rate had only recently been made, the funds of the Westport union were exhausted, and the guardians were pessimistic that this situation was unlikely to improve until the following harvest. The workhouse was only kept open as a result of the financial contributions of individual guardians. Various economies were introduced. For example, all new inmates had to wear their own clothes as the union could no longer afford to purchase the special workhouse uniform. The guardians warned, however, that they would have to close the house altogether unless they received financial assistance.[152] The problems experienced in Co. Mayo appear to have been due to a combination of factors: the local workhouses were amongst the last ones in the country to open; the almost total failure of the potato had left the area without its local subsistence crop; a low Poor Law valuation reflecting the general poverty of the area; large Poor Law unions which meant that the guardians were responsible for a large number of paupers who might have to travel up to thirty miles to a workhouse; a landed class which was notorious for its high level of absenteeism. In spite of the criticisms frequently directed at the landlords in the west of Ireland, for a few weeks during the winter of 1846–7, the workhouses of Ballina, Castlebar, Gort, Swinford and Westport were only able to remain open due to the financial support and personal generosity of individual guardians.[153]

In these and similar cases, the guardians were told that they should raise a second rate in order to meet the increased financial demands being made on them. This appears to have been a government initiative as Twistleton continued to be opposed to any extension of the Poor Law. Even in unions where a second rate was levied, it would take some time to be collected. In the unions of counties Mayo, Galway, Clare, Kerry and west Cork, the guardians believed that it was hopeless to impose a second rate when so much of the first one was outstanding. In certain instances also, the local rate collector had been threatened or physically assaulted.[154] In some areas, the collection of a second rate so shortly after the first appeared unreasonable and some guardians asked to be relieved of the burden of poor rates until the following harvest.[155] Unions throughout the west of Ireland were experiencing similar difficulties and the Assistant Commissioner in the south-west of the country informed the government that in his area, the ratepayers of the Cahirciveen, Bantry, Dunmanway, Kenmare, Kanturk and Skibbereen unions did not have the means to pay any further rates.[156] A few weeks later, he warned the Commissioners that these unions would soon be unable to bear the burden of providing for the destitute within their workhouses.[157]

In unions without either money, credit or provisions, the boards of guardians sometimes threatened to resign unless they received some external aid. In such cases, the Commissioners responded dogmatically, even though they personally sympathised with the guardians. They reiterated that there was no hope of external assistance as the guardians possessed ample means to raise money.[158] The guardians were told that they had adequate powers to enforce the collection of rates and should use these to the utmost. Several guardians appealed to the Lord Lieutenant to intervene on their behalf, but he responded that, although he could not give them a loan, he would provide them with military or police support where necessary. A number of boards of guardians were concerned that a show of force would not be addressing the root of the problem. In the Athlone union, the chairman and vice-chairman of the local board refused to continue to hold office under such circumstances. The chairman of the Boyle union, Viscount Lorton, who had been much praised for his generosity towards his tenants, resigned in protest at the continual refusal of the Poor Law Commissioners to provide the union with a loan. Shortly afterwards, he moved his household to London. The guardians were also encouraged to borrow more money in order to provide for the increased demand for relief. The 1838 Act had, however, made it illegal for the guardians to pay interest out of the poor rates for any money that was borrowed to pay for current expenses. The Commissioners suggested to the boards of guardians that they should pay the interest out of their own pockets. This idea was resisted by many guardians who refused to do so. To overcome this, the Lord Lieutenant agreed that the Irish government would act as guarantor for any interest to be paid.[159]

Privately, both the Commissioners and the Irish Executive were apprehensive about the ability of some unions to raise sufficient funds by whatever means.[160] They realised that the demands for financial support from the government would increase as the season progressed and they predicted that before long a number of Poor Law unions would not be able to survive without external financial assistance. The problem, however, was to convince their superiors in London of the seriousness of this situation. Labouchere, the Chief Secretary, contacted the Prime Minister directly as he was deeply concerned about the condition of some of the Poor Law unions. He informed Russell:

> The workhouses are full and the people are turned away to perish. It is impossible to allow this state of things to continue without making some effectual effort to relieve it. The mortality in the workhouse is rapidly increasing, both from the crowded state of the unions and the exhausted state in which the applicants are received.[161]

The Irish paupers and ratepayers, however, did not receive a sympathetic audience in London. Grey, the Home Secretary, informed the Dublin-based relief officials that it was the opinion of the government that most people could still afford to pay the rates. He added that the guardians should be encouraged to use every means at their disposal to collect them. The government were afraid that if they provided financial assistance to even the most distressed unions, a dangerous precedent would be established. Grey also expressed the government's disappointment at the lack of exertion shown by the landed proprietors in Ireland.[162] Increasingly, a gulf between how the Famine was viewed by the relief officials in Dublin and how it was viewed in England was opening. Again, there was some exasperation about the way in which the Irish people managed their affairs. Charles Wood, the Chancellor of the Exchequer, despaired of the state of Ireland. He saw the solution in there being less, rather than more, government interference:

> What has brought them, in great measure at least, to their present state of helplessness? Their habit of depending on government. What are we trying to do now? To force them upon their own resources. Of course they mismanage matters very much . . . If we are to select the destitute, pay them, feed them and find money from hence, we shall have the whole population of Ireland upon us soon enough. It is tending very fast to that already and we must beware of taking further responsibility . . . Let us do all we can to improve the local machinery, but for God's sake do nothing so fatal as cast it aside.[163]

As the situation deteriorated the Treasury was given additional responsibility for the control of the various relief policies. It was Trevelyan, the Permanent Secretary, rather than Wood who increasingly began to exert his influence over Irish affairs. One visitor to the Treasury acerbically confided in Sir Robert Peel:

> If you were to come over to the Treasury, you would not know yourself. Trevelyan is First Lord, and Chancellor of the Exchequer; has a new room, with four private secretaries and three Commissariat clerks, and the whole has been left to him.[164]

The policies of Russell's government were increasingly being compared unfavourably with the policies of his predecessor. Contrary to the outward appearance of confidence, both Wood and Trevelyan were privately concerned about the relief being provided. They even unofficially sought the advice of leading members of the Tory party, including Peel himself. The general consensus within Britain was that the Irish people must be made to learn to depend on their own resources, despite the problems that had become apparent. Wood, however, was increasingly disillusioned with the fact that although so much assistance had already been provided to Ireland the situation had deteriorated rather than improved. He confided to one member of the opposition that 'everything seems to go wrong in Ireland' and that he did not see 'what could be done to carry the country through'.[165]

In January 1847, the leading members of the Irish Executive, the Under-Secretary and the Lord Lieutenant, informed Sir George Grey that the situation within the Irish workhouses had reached a crisis point. Almost a hundred workhouses already contained an excess number of inmates and this was likely to increase. The overcrowded conditions within the workhouses was already proving to be detrimental to the health of all of the inmates. Fever was rampant and many medical officers had warned of the likelihood of the spread of other pestilent diseases. Mortality within the workhouses was already high and still rising. They urged the government to intervene.[166] At this stage, the government was receiving over 100 reports each day of deaths from starvation, and they believed this to be an under-estimation. Within Ireland, the policies of the government were increasingly held to blame. Russell, who was less doctrinaire than his colleagues in the Treasury and Home Office, was privately less sanguine than he publicly appeared to be. He referred to the situation as 'the horrible famine which presses so cruelly on some parts of Ireland'. He realised that some new relief measures were necessary which 'if they are not immediate remedies, must at least go in the right direction'. Again, however, despite the evidence of overwhelming distress, Russell's government was unwilling to introduce any measures that went against current economic orthodoxies or that would upset the powerful lobby opposed to giving any additional relief to Ireland.[167]

Even before the new relief proposals had been debated in parliament, unofficially and unobtrusively the government introduced some minor modifications in the provision of relief. The Whig administration tried not to draw attention to these changes as they believed that if they did so, it would further increase the demands being made on them. One change which was to have long term implications for the government's relief policy was the official sanction given to the establishment of soup kitchens. Towards the end of 1846, some relief committees and unions, in an attempt to make maximum use of their limited resources, were providing food in the form of soup. The Society of Friends had already used soup kitchens as a means of providing relief in Cork and it was generally regarded as being effective. In the Edenderry union, in King's County, to solve the problem of overcrowding in the workhouses, the guardians had opened a soup kitchen in each electoral division. The initial cost for the food was paid out of the poor rates, and the guardians then sold the soup at cost price. The Poor Law Commissioners regarded this system as tantamount to providing outdoor relief. They forbade the guardians to continue and refused to sanction any expenditure for this purpose. They also informed the guardians that if they wanted to continue to provide this form of relief, they should encourage the establishment of a local relief committee. The Edenderry guardians responded by pointing out one of the major flaws in the relief policies of the government: 'there is most poverty where there is least means of getting funds.'[168] The actions of the Edenderry guardians, however, came to the notice of the Home Secretary. George Grey regarded soup kitchens as an effective way of providing a large amount of relief very cheaply. He therefore recommended that soup kitchens, organised by local relief committees, should be established in areas of intense distress. By placing the soup kitchens under the control of the relief committees, the government was ensuring that at least part of the cost should be paid from local funds. Special consideration would, however, be given to areas where only a small amount of money was raised.[169]

The use of soup kitchens formed a major part of the government's relief policies in 1847. In February, legislation was passed for soup kitchens to be used as the principal means of relief in the summer of 1847. This legislation was known as the Temporary Relief Act. It was intended to facilitate the transition from relief based on the public works and other temporary measures to a system provided almost exclusively by the Poor Law. Even before this Act was implemented, soup was increasingly provided by officials involved in the administration of relief. Within many workhouses also, soup was used as a substitute for other forms of food. Recipes for numerous varieties of soup appeared frequently in the national newspapers, all claiming to be nutritious and generally aiming at the production of a maximum quantity for a minimum outlay. The most famous recipes were devised by Alexis Soyer, a famous French society chef, who claimed to have tested them out on noblemen and members of parliament. One of his recipes, which was widely published, made up to 100 gallons of soup for under £1. Much of the flavour was provided by the recommended addition of mint, bay leaves, thyme and marjoram. In the spring of 1847, when soup kitchens as a means of providing relief had received the official approval of the government, Soyer visited Ireland in order to promote his recipes. Initially he was funded by private subscriptions, but the Relief Commissioners retained his services following the success of this experiment. In the midst of much publicity, Soyer opened a number of 'model' kitchens in Dublin. When he left Ireland in April, with a show of ostentation, Soyer was presented with a snuff box as a gift for making cheap soup 'palatable'.[170] A diet composed almost exclusively of soup was regarded as an easy and acceptable way of providing food to a large number of people. This meant that even before the introduction of the Temporary Relief Act, a large number of people were eating little else. During the summer months, the transition from stirabout to soup was a reality for approximately half of the population.[171] In the short term, this provided a solution to one of the government's most pressing problems: how to provide food to a large number of people using a small amount of money. In the long term, a diet based almost exclusively on liquids may have actually damaged the health of the people dependent on it. In nutritional terms, it is probable that 'filling famine bloated bodies with watery soup did more harm than good'.[172]

In addition to permitting the opening of the soup kitchens, the government also agreed to provide limited financial assistance to some of the most distressed unions. This was based on certain conditions. It was only to be provided where the alternative was starvation. It was to be given in such a way that it would not supersede the ordinary means of relief but would merely be a temporary expedient to supply a local deficiency. The collection of rates would still be rigorously enforced and, as far as possible, their actions would be kept secret.[173] In February 1847, the Lord Lieutenant, acting on behalf of the government, began to issue small sums of money to the most distressed unions. This was carried out as discreetly as possible and was provided for the purchase of bedding, clothing etc. Relief was also given to the guardians in the form of Indian meal.[174] The Treasury, under the direction of Trevelyan, regarded it as of the utmost importance that charges which rightly belonged on the local rates should not be thrown on the national funds. He commanded the Lord Lieutenant to confine 'within the narrowest possible limits the advances authorised by him for the support of the poor in workhouses whether in food or money'.[175] Notwithstanding the smallness of the grants made, Trevelyan informed Routh that much improvement had resulted from 'the liberal, practical extension lately given to all relief measures', and that he was satisfied that the government was doing everything possible to help the poor Irish.[176] These changes, however, were grossly inadequate and as 1847 progressed, distress, disease and mortality continued to rise.

Descriptions of the condition of the inmates of the Irish workhouses in the early months of 1847 depict an appalling scene of destitution. Many guardians continued to admit paupers to workhouses that were already overflowing and often full of disease. Again, this was because paupers in many unions in the south and west of the country were unable to obtain any other form of relief. The Galway guardians described the applicants for relief to their workhouse as being 'living skeletons'. In the Gort workhouse, also in Co. Galway, one quarter of inmates were all sick, mostly suffering from fever or dysentery. The guardians suggested that it was safer to close the house before all of the inmates and officers perished.[177] In many workhouses, the rate of mortality was high, which the Medical Officers usually attributed to the debilitated state in which the people entered them. The conditions in the workhouses sometimes exacerbated rather than improved their condition. Fever was prevalent in many, but cases of dysentery, influenza, whooping cough and smallpox were also present. The insanitary conditions of the workhouses contributed to the spread of diseases. At the beginning of 1847, deaths in the Irish workhouses reached approximately 2,700 per week, following which it continued to decline slowly, falling to about 500 deaths per week during the summer. In the early months of 1849, however, mortality again reached in the region of 2,700 per week although by this time, the workhouses had become the principal means of relief and workhouse accommodation had been substantially increased. For the poor people who had no alternative but to seek Poor Law relief, especially those who were already sick or belonged to the most vulnerable groups—the old, the young, pregnant or lactating women—a stay in a workhouse could prove fatal.[178]

The British government may have been geographically removed from the scenes of distress in Ireland, but throughout the winter of 1846–7 they received numerous reports from a wide variety of sources which testified to the appalling situation in parts of the country. Although the impact of a second year of blight was felt in all parts of Ireland, in the west coast of the country, the distress had clearly become a famine. The unprecedented increase in mortality, disease and emigration in 1847 became remembered in folk memory as 'the Famine year' or 'Black '47'. Many reports at this time depicted a people in whom physiological manifestations of distress were becoming apparent. Physically, they appeared wizened, old and shrunken, regardless of their actual age. They also were listless, depressed and apathetic. Although it was not officially recognised at the time, these were the classic symptoms of malnutrition. This was due to not only an insufficiency of food, but also a dietary deficiency caused by a sudden change of diet. The effect of this was to deplete the poor Irish people of several essential nutrients, many of which had been plentiful in the traditional potato and buttermilk diet.[179]

Each of the counties along the western seaboard was affected in varying degrees by the Famine, although the descriptions from west Cork were particularly harrowing. In the village of Skibbereen, the suffering of the local population appeared to be particularly severe. In Skibbereen, as elsewhere in the west, reports referred to the apparent indifference of the poor people to death:

> A terrible apathy hangs over the poor of Skibbereen . . . and they sullenly await their doom with indifference and without fear . . . Death is in every hovel; disease and famine, its dread precursors, have fastened on the young and old, the strong and feeble, the mother and the infant.[180]

In the nearby village of Schull, the reports of a government inspector were similarly melancholy:

> In the village of Skull [sic] three-fourths of the inhabitants you meet carry the tale of woe in their features and persons, as they are reduced to mere skeletons, all their physical powers being wasted away.[181]

Conditions in west Cork, particularly in Skibbereen, were brought to the attention of people in Britain primarily through the publication in both islands of the journals of a Church of Ireland minister, the Rev. Richard Townsend. His reports attracted a number of visitors to the area, including British newspaper reporters. They also attracted the attention of some of the students of Oxford University who collected £50 for the village. This money was taken in person by two of the students, Lord Dufferin and the Honourable Mr Boyle, who wanted to view the distress themselves. During their visit, the Rev. Townsend acted as their guide. He took them to what had become a typical burial scene, in which the dead bodies were emptied into a pit in the ground from a shell coffin which was to be used again. The graves were so shallow that, 'a few scrapes of a shovel soon laid bare the abdomen of the one that was uppermost'.[182] Only people who died whilst in the local workhouse were able to be buried in a coffin. The visitors admitted that they were 'completely sickened' by what they had witnessed and decided to leave the following day, although they left an additional donation of £10. The Rev. Townsend admitted that he only remained in Skibbereen out of 'a stern sense of duty'. He blamed the policies of the British government for much of the suffering of the people, and described the local population as victims of 'a most mistaken national policy on whom the principles of political economy have been carried out in practice to a murderous extent.'[183]

An independent account of the situation was provided by a young midshipman whose ship had landed at various ports in west Cork. In Baltimore, he witnessed 'hundreds of beings begging for bread who, we know, will not live another week'. In Schull, he found the situation was just as awful and was appalled when he encountered a group of 500 persons 'half naked and starving' who were waiting for a meal of soup:

> Fever, dysentery and starvation stare you in the face everywhere—children of 10 and 9 years old, I had mistaken for decrepit old women, their faces wrinkled, their bodies bent and distorted with pain, their eyes looking like those of a corpse.

He was informed by a local doctor that death from disease and starvation were averaging forty to fifty persons daily, and that from the 500 people queuing for soup, 'not a single one of those you now see will be alive in three weeks: it is impossible.'[184]

Similar reports were received from many other parts of the west of Ireland. An exception was parts of Co. Donegal which provides an interesting insight into the diversity of relief provision in Ireland. The potato blight of 1845 did not appear in all parts of this county, and where it did appear, the resultant distress and mortality was not as acute as in other counties in the west of the country. A noticeable exception to this was the

Glenties union in Co. Donegal which experienced much of the suffering prevalent along other areas of the southern and western seaboard. This appears to have been due to an interaction of various factors, both economic and social. The presence of an active and interested landlord or gentry class in many unions helped to ameliorate some of the worst effects of the potato blight. At the beginning of 1847, however, it was evident that within Co. Donegal, a portion of the people were without sufficient food. Members of the Society of Friends who had travelled through Ireland at the end of 1846 and the beginning of 1847 were dismayed by what they saw and carefully reported it back to the central committee in Dublin. Mr. James H. Tuke visited north Donegal in December 1846. In the vicinity of Dunfanaghy, nine-tenths of the population had subsisted entirely on potatoes prior to 1845, but now, Tuke observed, many of them were living upon 'a single meal of cabbage, and even, a little seaweed'. Tuke, a Yorkshireman who had considerable experience in the provision of poor relief within his own country, declared that 'nothing can, indeed, describe too strongly the dreadful conditions of the people.'[185]

Tuke visited some of the homes of the poor and was shocked by the scenes that he witnessed. Not only were the people without food, but they could not afford turf for a small fire which, due to heavy falls of snow, was especially necessary. He described the appearance of the poor people as being 'almost beyond belief'. Tuke visited one small cabin not more than twelve feet square, in which seventeen persons lived including 'two or three half-naked children'. In another house, he observed:

> In addition to the poor family who owned the house, I saw in one corner, crouched upon her knees over a little turf fire, a very old and superannuated woman, constantly rocking to and fro, and muttering to herself. Her matted grey hair hung raggedly over her dirty, shrivelled face, adding to her wild and wretched appearance. She was hardly clothed at all . . . It appeared that this sad object was no relative of the poor widow of the house but, with noble kindness, she allowed her to remain here, and shared with her, her last morsel.

Tuke repeatedly referred to the inadequacy of relief provided by the government, particularly the inadequacy of the food depots and the public works. However, in spite of their lack of food, fuel, clothes and even shelter, Tuke praised the people for maintaining their 'good feeling, patience and cheerfulness under privation'.[186]

Tuke noted the apparent contradiction in the fact that even though many people in the west were starving, the local populations did not eat more fish. He described the bay of Dunfanaghy in north Donegal as 'teeming with fish of the finest description, waiting, we might say, to be caught'. But in Dunfanaghy and many other villages along the coast, the people were unable to take advantage of this asset because:

> so rude is their tackle and so fragile and liable to be upset are their primitive boats or coracles, made of wickerwork over which sail cloth is stretched, that they can only venture to sea in fine weather and thus, with food almost in sight, the people starve.[187]

In spite of the desperate poverty which he found in Dunfanaghy, Tuke was favourably impressed with the activities of the local landlords, merchants and clergy in providing relief. Within the Dunfanaghy Poor Law union, three separate relief committees had been established, each of which was energetically chaired by a local landlord, namely, Alexander Stewart (Stewart of Ards), Wybrants Olphert Esq. and Lord George Hill. Apart from their participation in the government relief schemes, many of the members of the committees were also providing additional relief, often from their own pockets. The task of keeping the population from starvation was, Tuke admitted, a formidable one. Out of a population of 15,270 persons, only 639 people held land valued over four pounds. At the beginning of 1847, Tuke estimated that nearly twelve thousand people were, 'in the greatest possible distress, without resource of any kind'.

When visiting other parts of the west of Ireland, Tuke was very critical of failure of the landlords to become involved in the provision of relief. He was particularly uncomplimentary about absentee landlords, many of whom had not subscribed even 'one farthing' to help the distressed people. This, he believed, was because some landlords regarded the poor cottiers who resided on their estates as 'a great injury to their properties and are therefore discountenanced in every way'. In a total contrast to the series of articles that had been printed in *The Times*, Tuke was full of praise for the behaviour of the Irish people under such circumstances:

> I regret that I feel so incompetent to express or describe the state of total helplessness that those gentle, suffering people are reduced to. Tenants of an absentee landlord are neglected by those who are living in luxury from the rents collected from these wretched people. Their patience is beyond belief.[188]

Within individual unions, the sanitary condition of the workhouse could vary greatly. The Members of the Society of Friends who visited Ireland at the beginning of 1847 noted the great variations within workhouses. The Quakers believed the effectiveness of workhouse relief to a large extent was dependent on the involvement of, and interest shown, by the local landlords. In the unions of Co. Donegal, demand for workhouse relief was not as great as in some other unions along the western seaboard. Within the Dunfanaghy union in north Donegal, the Quakers were impressed with the energy of the local landlords, clergy and merchants who were active not merely as guardians and members of the local relief committees, but also in providing additional private relief. One of the most active of these was Lord George Hill who, since his purchase of a large estate in Gweedore in the 1830s, had shown a keen interest in improving the condition of his property. The interest of the local landowners etc. was reflected in the efficiency of the local workhouse:

> We found the poor house in excellent order and the inmates appeared to be in good health. The diet was 17 oz of oat and Indian meal mixed half and half with three-quarters a quart of buttermilk daily for the able bodied, varied with rice twice a week. This is only a small poor house and the number of inmates was 116; the same period in the last year there was only five. Few of the inmates could read or write and hardly any could speak English, indeed the Erse is the prevailing language in this district. Near the poor house, a fever hospital has been erected by private charity; it contained 16 patients. During the year, 100 patients had been admitted, and only three deaths had occurred.[189]

In the neighbouring union of Glenties, the Quakers noted the absence of any landlords or merchants in the provision of relief. On the estate of one absentee proprietor they found people 'crying from hunger and starvation' and stated, 'no statement can be too strong with respect to the wretched condition, the positive misery and starvation in which the cottiers and small farmers in this immense domain are found'. The Quakers believed that 'the extreme wretchedness of this district must, in part at least, be attributed to the want of a resident proprietor.' Again, conditions within the union generally were reflected by conditions within the local workhouse:

> We visited the poor house at Glenties, which is in a dreadful state; the people were, in fact, half-starved and half-clothed. The day

before, they had had one meal of oatmeal and water, and at the time of our visit had not sufficient food in the house for the day's supply. . . . Their bedding consisted of dirty straw, in which they were laid in the rows on the floor; even as many as six persons being crowded under one rug; and we did not see a blanket at all. The rooms are hardly bearable for filth. The living and dying were stretched side by side beneath the same miserable covering.[190]

The number of people receiving workhouse relief peaked in February 1847, although some workhouses remained full until the harvest. Demand for this form of relief continued to be highest in the unions within counties Clare, Cork, Galway, Kerry, Limerick and Mayo, and these workhouses were the last ones to empty. In these unions also, demand for employment on the public works was high although, by the beginning of 1847, the local bureaucracy involved in providing relief works was collapsing.

Although the demand for relief was highest in the west, severe distress was also apparent in other parts of the country, including even some of the wealthy unions in the north-east of Ulster. The Belfast union, for example, which had the fourth highest Poor Law valuation in Ireland, was regarded by the Poor Law Commissioners as having one of the most efficient—by which they meant, frugal and disciplinarian—boards in the country. At the end of 1846, nevertheless, it was experiencing many of the problems common to all workhouses at this time: rapidly increasing pauper numbers, and a high rate of disease and mortality within the workhouse. Like many other institutions, the Belfast workhouse suffered from periodic outbreaks of fever and other diseases, but this was exacerbated following the harvest failure of 1846 as many persons flocked to the town, seeking work or relief or simply en route to another country. By the beginning of 1847, fever and dysentery were present in all parts of the workhouse. Pauper mortality continued to increase, especially amongst children under the age of two. In one week alone, sixteen instances of infant mortality were reported. Mortality amongst the older inmates was also far higher than usual, averaging between fifty to sixty people per week. This was made worse by an outbreak of measles and smallpox amongst the paupers. Nor were the diseases confined to the inmates of the workhouse. The medical officer, the schoolmaster, the schoolmistress and the cook all died from fever. The rapid spread of these diseases within the workhouse was attributed by various medical officers to the poor quality of the diet, the damp and crowded state of the place, and its insanitary condition. For example, dead bodies remained in the same room as sick inmates until they could be buried, and many burials still took place on the workhouse grounds.[191]

In an attempt to redress the situation, in the early months of 1847 the Belfast guardians increased the amount of workhouse accommodation available and enlarged the fever hospital. This had originally been designed for 150 people but was regularly being used for up to double that number. The guardians estimated that approximately one-third of these people came from other unions but, as no Law of Settlement had been introduced into Ireland, the Belfast guardians were legally bound to relieve them.[192] The guardians asked the Poor Law Commissioners for a loan to finance this venture. The Commissioners, however, whilst congratulating the guardians for their 'efficiency and zeal', refused to give one. They justified their decision on the grounds that:

> The town of Belfast is so wealthy and its inhabitants so enterprising, and the funds and the credit of the union are in such excellent condition, that if assistance were given to the Belfast Board from the Public Purse by way of a loan, it would be impossible to refuse a similar application from any union in Ireland.[193]

Within Belfast, a number of relief committees had been established in response to the re-appearance of blight. These committees, with the exception of the Ballymacarrett Committee, were self-financing, choosing not to avail of the government's half grant scheme. As a result of their independent stance, they were held up by the government as examples to be followed in other parts of the country. A Belfast General Relief Fund was also established in the town which gave grants to various relief committees, primarily in the south of Ireland.[194] In addition to this, in early 1847, a day asylum was established in Belfast which provided relief during the day although not at night time. By April 1847, the asylum was admitting on average 900 persons per day, an estimated two-thirds of whom were described as 'strangers' who came from outside Belfast.[195] This sharp increase in demand for relief following the second potato blight reflected the fact that the effects of the distress were being felt even in the wealthiest parts of the country. The impact of the potato blight of 1845–6 on Belfast had been limited, although there had been a slight increase in disease and an influx of paupers from outlying areas for work, relief, or a passage to a different country. The impact of the second blight, however, was both immediate and unrelenting. This was not due to the impact of the potato blight alone. In 1846 and 1847, there was a general economic slump throughout western Europe which had a short-term impact on the industries within the eastern parts of Ireland, especially the linen industry in Belfast. As linen had its base in the cottage industries of small farmers, this slump had repercussions in many parts of Ulster. In March, an editorial in the *Northern Whig* stated:

> We are sorry to have to announce too that some of our mills will be put on half time after next week and we fear that many of them will, at a not too distant date, work still shorter hours, and some of them perhaps, cease work.[196]

Regardless of the apparent wealth of Belfast, and the general praise which it received for its efficiency, there is no doubt that some people slipped through the relief net in 1847, particularly those who were suddenly thrown out of work due to the trade depression or illness. One visitor to the Old Lodge Road came across a young teacher who was unable to work due to illness. He was 'lying upon a handful of straw, on the earthen floor of a damp kitchen' and had not eaten for forty-eight hours. He had been unable to obtain any government relief due to 'some obstacle existing to his admission to the poor house or hospital'.[197] During the trade depression, many weavers were forced to take a drop in wages. The fact that they had some income, however, made them ineligible for workhouse and other forms of relief. An example of this was a weaver named McAnnaly whose income, by March, had dropped to 3s 6d per week, although he had a large family of five to support. His dwelling was described as being:

> . . . utterly devoid of light, fire and food, and the house was without furniture, bed or bedding except a heap of carpenter's shavings in a corner. On a handful of these shavings we found outstretched (when we lighted a candle) the emaciated corpse of an infant, towards the remains of which the hapless parents were too poor to provide a shroud and there lay the little wasted body with no other covering than a fragment of rug thrown over the limbs.[198]

Belfast was not the only union in the north-east of the country that was experiencing problems in the provision of relief. In the Lurgan workhouse, in October 1846, even before the full demands for relief were felt, the guardians were in debt. In January 1847, the numbers of deaths within the workhouse rose from 18 at the beginning of the month to 68 at the end. The main causes of this were fever and bowel complaints. The medical officer attributed this increase in mortality to overcrowding, a poor diet, and the fact that many people were seriously debilitated before they entered the workhouse—factors which appeared to be common to all workhouses throughout the country. On the advice of the Poor Law Commissioners, the Lurgan guardians refused to admit any more paupers, directing them instead to the local relief committees.[199] Even the Armagh union, frequently referred to as having the best managed workhouse in Ireland, was finding it difficult to meet the increased and sudden demands made on it. In the summer of 1846, the Visiting Committee described their visit as 'a pleasure' due to the 'cleanliness, order, and good conduct observed throughout, as well as the cheerful appearance of the inmates generally'. By March 1847, the workhouse was described as 'crowded and unhealthy'. Not only were many of the inmates ill, but some of the workhouses officers had also caught the fever, including the medical officer himself. To protect themselves, the guardians started to hold their weekly meetings at the court house rather than the workhouse. The Armagh guardians, acting on the advice of the Commissioners, decided that when the workhouse was full, they would make the excess paupers the responsibility of the local relief committes.[200]

In parts of the north-east of Ireland, therefore, in the second year of distress, many unions were experiencing problems similar to those experienced by the unions in the south and west of the country. The north-east was remarkable, however, for the fact that many voluntary bodies were also providing relief and the relief measures introduced by the government for the most part were still able to offer an alternative form of relief. In contrast to this, in many unions in the west of the country, the local workhouse was frequently the final sanctuary of desperate people. In these districts, the public works, the relief committees and the workhouses increasingly had to prop each other up and attempt to compensate for both their individual shortcomings and the overall inadequacy of the local relief provisions. In several unions in the north, however, the local relief committees were financially buoyant even though many of them were self-financing and did not avail of the government's grant. This, and the fact that it had been unnecessary to establish any government food depots in this part of the country, seemed to be proof that self-reliance was the key to success in the provision of relief.

Not all unions in the north of Ireland conformed to the image of healthy self-reliance and efficiency so beloved by the Poor Law Commissioners and many members of the government. This was particularly the case in unions in which the potato blight had been especially severe. In the Enniskillen union in Co. Fermanagh, mortality was high and the union was financially embarrassed. The guardians, who had frequently been in dispute with the Commissioners, blamed the latter for this situation. The workhouse could accommodate 1,000 paupers and, in January 1846, contained only 119 inmates. By January 1847, this had changed dramatically. There were 991 inmates and deaths from fever averaged fifty each week. The majority of the officers of the workhouse had also contracted this disease. The guardians, anxious to avoid catching fever themselves, decided to meet in the town hall in Enniskillen. The medical officer believed part of the problem was the recent change of diet within the workhouse. The traditional potato diet had been replaced by stirabout (made from Indian corn) and buttermilk. He recommended that this should be changed again to one based on rice and new milk. At the same time, he warned that the conditions in the workhouse were totally unsanitary. Water from the local lake, which was not always clean, was used in the preparation of all food. The guardians could not afford to purchase any supplies of clothing or shoes which meant that the inmates were forced to 'wear their own filthy rags'. The local contractors were refusing to give them more supplies. The guardians believed that the ratepayers did not have the resources to pay an even larger rate. They warned that unless they were given financial assistance, they would be forced 'however painful to their feelings, to close the workhouse and put out the unfortunate paupers'.[201]

By May 1847, the Enniskillen workhouse was full, and the guardians were forced to turn paupers away. Fever was also increasing throughout the union. The guardians were over £5,000 in debt and they asked the government for a loan of £3,000 or £4,000. The government responded by sending them a loan of £100. Inevitably, they were also told to make every effort to collect the present rate and immediately levy a further one. The guardians, although they complied in striking an additional rate, simultaneously declared that such an action would be disastrous. They put their grievances on record, believing 'it is right that the Public should know how the government is acting towards the guardians of the Enniskillen union'. The annual valuation of the union was just over £95,000. In January 1847, they had made a rate of £4,500. In August 1847, although £800 of this rate remained uncollected, the guardians struck a further rate of £9,500—or 10 per cent of the total Poor Law valuation. At the same time, they stated that this would be almost impossible to collect because the potato blight of 1846 had left many local farmers without financial resources. The guardians believed that the collection of such heavy rates would be accompanied by:

... ruinous severity from the most industrious farmers in the country and would thus cripple the means of employment and of production of our most useful men . . . The guardians believe that no system could be more dishonest in principle or more mischievous in its commercial consequences than to lay such frequent and large rates on the country.[202]

The conflicts between the Poor Law Commissioners and the Enniskillen board of guardians continued until the latter were finally dissolved at the end of 1847.

The changes in policy announced by the government at the beginning of 1847 meant that, following the harvest, the responsibility of relieving the destitute would devolve almost totally on the Poor Law. To prepare for these increased demands, the guardians were warned that they should immediately bring their finances into order. In the early months of 1847, however, boards of guardians throughout the country were finding it difficult even to meet the current Poor Law expenses, and several boards expressed a conviction that they did not possess the resources to meet any increased demands which would be made on them. Many Poor Law unions were without funds and had exhausted their local credit, and some contractors were refusing to supply any further goods unless they were paid. The bank which represented thirty unions announced that they were no longer willing to advance any further loans to them.[203]

In some unions the inability of the guardians to obtain credit had an immediate impact. The contractors of the Kenmare guardians took a law suit against the union and the local sheriff threatened to distrain their personal goods and chattels. Although the Kenmare guardians agreed to levy an additional rate, they were convinced of 'the utter hopelessness of collecting it'.[204] The amount of rates levied was already considerably higher than in the previous year and some guardians believed that if they tried to raise them further, some ratepayers would stop paying altogether. The Lisburn guardians, whose union had been badly affected by the slump in the demand for linen, warned that if, as the Commissioners suggested, they attempted to make 'an increased and vigorous' collection of the rates, they would be reducing some of the current ratepayers to paupers.[205] The Ballina guardians reported that many people were already fleeing from the land due to the burden of high poor rates. In the Banbridge union, the guardians stated that they considered it impossible to collect further rates until the following harvest.[206] The Westport union was again being kept open through the personal subventions of the chairman of the board. The guardians threatened to resign unless the

Commissioners provided them with a loan. The Tralee board of guardians did actually resign in protest at their financial situation. Again, the workhouse was without funds and was only being kept open through the generosity of one of the guardians.[207] In general, the correspondence of the various boards of guardians to the central Commissioners at this period refers to the inability rather than unwillingness of many ratepayers to pay their rates.

Notwithstanding the financial difficulties of the unions in all parts of the country in the early months of 1847, the government was determined that the Poor Law should become almost exclusively responsible for providing relief after August 1847. This decision, made at the beginning of the year, came in response to the fact that the relief measures introduced only a few months earlier had failed. Even more seriously, in the eyes of the government, the effect of these policies had been to demoralise the Irish people and further encourage their tendency to 'helpless dependence'.[208] A change was necessary, and government was determined any new relief policies would facilitate change within Ireland, rather than perpetuate the existing faults evident in Irish society. Leading members of the Whig administration favoured a relief policy that would increase self-reliance of the people and force the landlords to realise that property had its duties as well as its rights. The Poor Law, with its emphasis on local chargeability and union responsibility, was regarded as an ideal mechanism for facilitating these changes. The extended Poor Law, therefore, was regarded not merely as an agent for the provision of relief, but also as a catalyst for facilitating important economic and social improvements in Ireland. This was felt to be particularly necessary in the south and west of Ireland because:

> The owners and holders of land in these districts had permitted or encouraged the growth of the excessive population which depended upon the precarious potato and they alone had it in their power to restore society to a safe and healthy state'.[209]

The fact that the Poor Law was proving unequal to the demands made on it in the early part of 1847—when officially it was still playing a subsidiary role in the provision of relief—did not deter the government from a determination to make it the primary agency for providing relief following the harvest of that year.

In February 1847, the government announced its new relief measures in which the Poor Law was to play such a vital role. It simultaneously announced that half of the advances made to the public works, due to be repaid out of local taxation, were to be remitted. The fact that it had proved necessary for new relief measures to be introduced midway through the agricultural year was indicative of the failure of the relief policies introduced in 1846, and the fact that the government had misjudged the extent of the problem.

The new relief policies introduced consisted of a temporary and immediate measure, and a more long-term policy. The Temporary Relief Act was to operate during the summer of 1847 and was to provide direct relief in the form of food through soup kitchens which could either sell or provide soup gratuitously. After 15 August 1847 an extended Poor Law, which for the first time ever permitted outdoor relief, was to be responsible for providing relief. Both of these measures were to be financed by the poor rates. In the case of the Temporary Relief Act, in the first instance, the money would be loaned by the Treasury to the local area on the security of the poor rates. Following this, the guardians were to levy sufficient rates, not only for the current rates of the union, but also to repay any advances which had been received from the government.

Even before August 1847, therefore, the local poor rates were to be used for the financing of relief. In pursuing this policy, the government chose to ignore the fact that some Poor Law unions were already facing bankruptcy. A small clique within the Whig administration had decided that local resources were to bear the responsibility for financing local poverty, regardless of the ability of these resources to meet the new demands.

The Deplorable Consequences of This Great Calamity

1846–7

By the beginning of 1847, it was obvious that the temporary relief measures introduced only a few months previously had failed. The public works introduced in the first year of distress had cost £476,000 and were regarded as having been effective. In the second year of distress, the cost of maintaining them rose to £4,848,000, which was originally intended to be repaid from the areas that had benefited. Donations to the local relief committees and Poor Law expenditure also increased, and charitable donations were at their highest. However, in spite of the enormous public and private expenditure, distress, disease and mortality continued to increase in Ireland.[1] The government admitted that, by this stage, 'serious evils' were apparent in the system of relief. To a large extent, the government claimed that these resulted from the 'unexpected magnitude of the calamity'. As a consequence of this, they acknowledged that:

> Although upwards of two million persons, either directly or indirectly, obtain assistance from the Relief Works, there are other multitudes who stand equally in need of relief . . . and instances of starvation daily occur.[2]

A new system of relief was considered to be 'indispensably necessary' with the result that at the end of January and beginning of February 1847, a new temporary relief measure was rushed through parliament. This Act was known as the Temporary Relief Act or, more popularly, as the Soup Kitchen Act and, occasionally, as Burgoyne's Act. It provided that, for the first time, direct relief was to be supplied by the government in specially established soup kitchens in the form of cooked food or soup.[3] At the same time as this new temporary measure was introduced, the government also announced a further change in the system of relief: after August 1847, the permanent Poor Law was to be extended and was to become responsible for providing both ordinary and extraordinary relief. As a result of this change, after the autumn of 1847 all relief would be financed by the local Poor Law rates. The Temporary Relief Act was also ultimately to be financed from the poor rates, although in the first instance, the government was willing to make advances on the security of the local rates, in addition to a number of grants to the poorest unions. The Temporary Relief Act was therefore intended as an interim measure to facilitate the transition from temporary relief to relief based on the Poor Law. At the same time, it was hoped it would end both the expense and the mortality which had accompanied the Labour Rate Act.

Both the Soup Kitchen Act and the extended Poor Law were significant steps in the government's aim to make all relief a local charge as far as possible. Since the first appearance of blight in 1845, the various members of the government had attempted to force the landed proprietors of Ireland into playing a more active role in the affairs of their country, not merely in the immediate provision of relief, but also in trying to effect more long term improvements in Ireland. The Labour Rate Act, apart from being expensive, had failed, in the opinion of the government, to encourage landlords to exert themselves and provide additional employment. As a result of this, the demand for employment on the public works was much higher than had been anticipated. By making the soup kitchens and the extended Poor Law almost exclusively dependent on local poor rates, the government was ensuring that there would be a high level of local involvement and accountability. The new Relief Commissioners were told that the only way to avoid severe and protracted suffering and place Irish society in a 'self-supporting and, therefore, in a safe and permanent condition', was through the 'personal exertions, on the spot, of the upper and middle classes, to check abuse and increase the productive powers of the country'.[4] Some members of the government believed that the salvation of Ireland depended on a transfer to local interest and accountability. In his book on the Irish Famine, written in 1848, Trevelyan, repeating many of the arguments made by Edmund Burke half a century earlier, explained this as follows:

There can be no doubt that the deplorable consequences of this great calamity extended to the Empire at large, but the disease was strictly local, and the cure was to be obtained only by the application of local remedies.[5]

To some extent, the Temporary Relief Act marked a radical departure from the relief policies which had preceded it. Relief and labour were now to be separated. The system of public works, considered to be 'so injurious and demoralising', was to be discontinued. In a complete turn of face, the government now desired that labour should revert to 'the wholesome condition of being applied solely to objects that shall be indisputably worthy of it, and of being only paid for in proportion to the full value of work done'.[6] Instead, gratuitous relief in a liquid form was to be made available to the destitute of Ireland. Since the end of 1846, cooked food in the form of soup had increasingly been used by relief committees, boards of guardians, charitable bodies and private individuals as a means of feeding a large number of starving people economically. Initially the government had disapproved of the relief committees supplying the destitute with cooked food, but in January 1847 they gave it official approval. The change-over to relief in the form of soup helped to augment the limited supplies of Indian meal, while making food accessible to many starving people.[7] The decision by the government to introduce soup kitchens in response to a mounting crisis has generally been praised by historians for being both innovative and successful.[8] In the short term there is no doubt that soup kitchens did provide an effective form of relief to a massive number of persons. In the longer term, however, it may have served to exacerbate some of the shortcomings of the various relief systems: it probably further weakened the health of an already debilitated people and increased the financial burden on the already heavily burdened Irish taxpayers on the eve of the transfer to Poor Law relief.

In recognition of the urgency of the situation, the Temporary Relief Act was implemented immediately, although it was estimated that it would take approximately six weeks for the new administrative machinery to become operative. At the beginning of February, even before the Act was on the Statute Books, a new Board of Temporary Relief Commissioners was established. The composition of the new Commission was very similar to that established in 1845. It consisted of Thomas Redington, the Under-Secretary of the Irish Executive, Sir Randolph Routh of the Commissariat, Colonel Harry Jones of the Board of Works, Edward Twistleton, the Poor Law Commissioner, and Colonel McGregor, the Inspector-General of the Constabulary. One significant change was that Routh was no longer chairman but was effectively

Sir Robert Peel.

Poor crop yields were a perennial hazard, even before the Famine. This engraving from the *Illustrated London News* of 18 June 1842 shows an attack on a potato store by starving people.

Interior of a cabin.

This image taken from the *Illustrated London News* of 16 December 1848, is entitled 'The Day After the Ejectment'.

Alexis Soyer's model soup kitchen in Dublin.

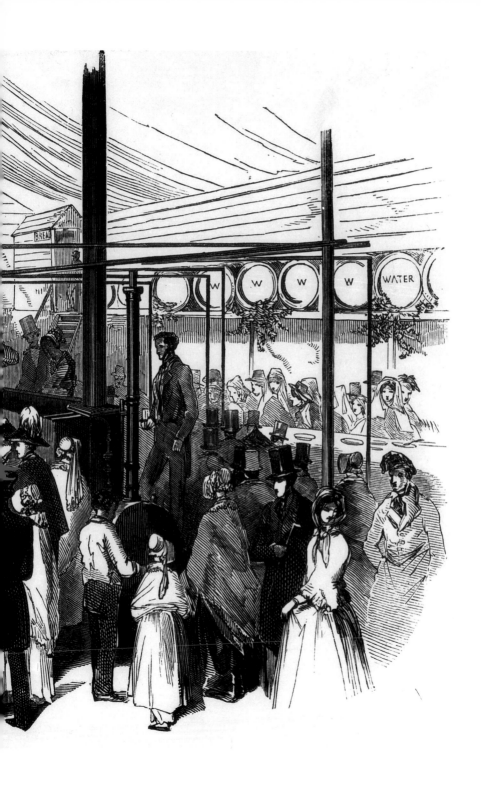

A woman begging at Clonakilty, Co. Cork.

Clifden workhouse, Co. Galway.

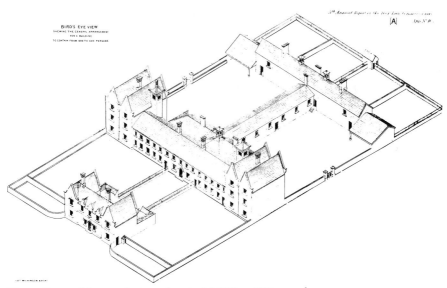

Plan of a workhouse designed to hold 400 to 800 people.

Bridget O'Donnell and her children, Famine beggars.

demoted and replaced by Major-General Sir John Burgoyne, a former chairman of the Irish Board of Works. A further aspect of continuity was that the new relief Commission, like its predecessor, was to be directly answerable to the Treasury not merely in regard to expenditure, but also more generally on all matters of policy.[9]

The inspecting officers employed under the Temporary Relief Act were men who had already gained experience of the relief measures, either with the Board of Works or the Commissariat. The officers selected were to possess 'in the highest degree, the qualifications necessary to ensure success'. They were to commence work immediately even if this was inconvenient to the Board of Works.[10] They were to liaise closely with the local committees and visit them frequently. They were also to submit weekly reports to the government. Again, their role was regarded not merely as facilitating the short-term provision of relief, but also to help to bring about long-term improvements in the country. The two objectives that the inspecting officers were to bear continually in mind were:

> to afford relief to the greatest number of the present really destitute population under the most economical arrangements, and with the smallest amount of abuse . . . and to encourage such principles of feeling and action as shall prospectively tend rather to improvement of the social system and, consequently, of Ireland itself.[11]

The rates of pay for the various employees of the new Commission were established by the Treasury and were relatively generous. The inspecting officers were handsomely reimbursed, receiving 21s each day. They were also to receive an additional overnight allowance of 10s for each night spent away from their base, plus an extra 3s lodging money. Travelling expenses were also to be paid in addition to this. Each local finance committee was to employ a clerk whom the Treasury decreed could receive up to 30s per week. The people employed in the soup kitchens were not to be paid more than 1s 6d per day.[12]

In an attempt to eliminate the alleged abuses of the previous relief systems a rigid and cumbersome bureaucratic infrastructure was created to ensure strict financial accountability at all levels. This undoubtedly contributed to delays in the introduction of the new system of relief and consequently ensured the continuance of high levels of mortality throughout April and May 1847. Within six weeks of the Act being passed, over 10,000 account books, 80,000 sheets and 3,000,000 card tickets had been distributed throughout the country. The total weight of these papers (as calculated by the Relief Commissioners) was in excess of fourteen tons.

Regardless of the urgent need for soup kitchens to be opened in a number of districts, the relief committees were informed that they would not receive money until all the requisite forms were filled in correctly. The Relief Commissioners realised that this regulation could leave them open to the accusation of 'withholding food from the starving population'.[13] They believed, however, that it was necessary from the outset to enforce a strict adherence to correct procedures.

The method of constituting the new temporary relief committees was also subject to more central control than had previously been the case. This reflected the desire of the government for a closer supervision of local administration. Two tiers of administration were to be established: a finance committee which was coterminous with each Poor Law union and whose duty it was to regulate all expenditure: and a smaller relief committee, which operated at the level of electoral divisions, and which was to oversee the distribution of food. At the beginning of March, the Lord Lieutenant issued instructions regulating the membership and duties of both of these committees. He also appointed personally the members of the finance committes.[14] Although the issuing of cooked food could commence as early as 15 March, this was rarely the case. To some extent, the complicated new procedures contributed to this delay. In some of the distressed areas the delay was so protracted that the Society of Friends offered to continue to provide relief in the interim although they stipulated that they would do so for no longer than two weeks.[15]

The administrative machinery of the Temporary Relief Act closely conformed with the geographic divisions of the Poor Law. The area of responsibility of each newly appointed finance committee was the Poor Law union. There were 130 of these in Ireland, but the unions of Antrim, Belfast and Newtownards, all within the north-east of Ulster, chose not to avail of the provisions of the Act. The local relief committees were more numerous and when the system was at its maximum, there were almost 2,000 of these operating under the Act. The area of responsibility of the relief committees conformed to the electoral divisions within a Poor Law union. There were, in total, 2,049 electoral divisions within Ireland which meant that approximately fifty of these divisions did not open government soup kitchens, although, for the most part, they operated privately funded soup kitchens.[16] Electoral divisions were far from being either a uniform economic or geographic unit. The size of these divisions varied greatly. The smallest one was the Blackrock division of the Rathdown union in Co. Dublin, which was only 257 acres in extent, whilst the largest was 145,598 acres in size and was situated in the Belmullet division of the Ballina union in Co. Mayo. The population of individual electoral divisions varied from the Seacor division of the

Letterkenny union in Co. Donegal, which had 514 residents, to the South City division of the South Dublin union, containing 135,661 residents. The Poor Law valuation of the electoral divisions also showed similar diversity. The lowest valued division was Mullaghderg in the Glenties union in Co. Donegal valued at only £331 10s; the electoral division with the highest Poor Law valuation, of £402,516 3s 4d, was situated in the south Dublin City union.[17] In general, the unions which covered the largest geographic areas tended to have the lowest valuation and were situated in the west of the country. In contrast to this, the smallest and wealthiest unions were situated in the east, predominantly in the eastern part of Ulster.[18]

The role of the finance committees was to be an important one and they were constantly warned that 'it is to them that the country must look for carrying out this measure'. The responsibility for appointing the 127 finance committees lay with the Lord Lieutenant. The committees were to comprise between two to four 'resident gentlemen having a great interest in the welfare of the districts'.[19] Although the Lord Lieutenant initially hoped to achieve a mixture of creeds and political parties on the finance committees, this proved to be impracticable. The Relief Commissioners hoped that in the prevailing state of the country, this was probably less necessary than usual. They claimed that people were putting their differences to one side, with the result that there was a 'happy amalgamation of feeling for the public good' and 'a spirit of social feeling generally prevalent now amongst the people of this country'.[20] The finance committees were to communicate with the central Relief Commissioners each week, in an attempt to prevent them from allowing 'lavish expenditure' within the union.[21] In addition to looking after the financial affairs of the various local relief committees within the union, the finance committees were also to keep an eye on the general administration of the local committees and prevent them from providing relief with 'too great an extent of liberality'. Communication between the local committees and the central Relief Commissioners was only to be carried out through the channel of the finance committees.[22]

The composition of the new local relief committees was also to be more tightly controlled than previously had been the case. Although it was impossible for the Lord Lieutenant to select personally the members of these committees, on 4 March he issued a promulgation which regulated their composition. Their membership was confined to resident Justices in the electoral division (or a representative nominated by them, subject to the approval of the Lord Lieutenant), the local Poor Law Guardians, resident archbishops of either the Catholic or Established church, the chairman of the local union, the three principal clergymen, the three highest ratepayers and the local relief inspector.[23] The fact that the majority of the members of the committees were to be resident property holders within the electoral division reinforced the move towards local responsibility. The Relief Commissioners received many requests from interested parties to be allowed membership of these committees. However, their policy was to refuse these applications unless, due to insufficient numbers, it was 'absolutely necessary' to appoint additional members.[24] The heavy responsibility which lay on these committees was continually impressed on them. They were warned that only through 'the most strenuous, uncompromising, and disinterested operation of every individual', could even 'partial alleviation' be afforded. If funds were misapplied or, as was thought to be more likely, relief provided too generously, the consequences would be dire as 'every farthing of food or atom of food applied unduly, would be so much abstracted from a starving population'.[25] Regardless of these and other warnings, the Relief Commissioners frequently expressed their disappointment with the operation of the relief committees. They complained that, due to either local influence, apathy, or misplaced humanity, the local committees were often too liberal in the provision of relief. Although the Relief Commissioners implied that there had been instances of 'actual connivance at the grossest frauds', the only actual cause of deceit occurred in the Bantry union in Co. Cork.[26] The relief committees, however, provided a convenient scapegoat for any deficiencies in the provision of relief.

The increase in mortality in the early months of 1847 and the public attention which it received made the government anxious to implement the Temporary Relief Act as quickly as possible. At the end of March, the inspecting officers were ordered to introduce the Act 'with the least possible delay'. Nevertheless, it was not until the middle of June that it was operative in all the unions participating in the scheme. Various factors, including an initial reluctance to transfer to a system of gratuitous outdoor relief, failure to conform with the correct bureaucratic procedures and the practical problems associated with attempting to provide cooked food for so many people, contributed to the delays.[27] In some instances, even following the opening of a soup kitchen, the local take-up of relief was slow. This was due to the widespread belief amongst many of the poor that, in the manner of Poor Law relief, they would have to give up all of their possessions, including their cabins, in order to be eligible for gratuitous relief. Instances of prosletyism or souperism—that is, providing food in return for a conversion to Protestantism—were rare and tended to be perpetrated by individuals rather than organisations or relief officials. Where souperism did occur, however, it tarnished the reputations of those providing relief and left a legacy of enduring bitterness.[28]

By the middle of May, the Relief Commissioners admitted that they were 'disappointed' in the delays in implementing the Act, as only 1,248 electoral divisions (out of 2,000 participants), had opened government soup kitchens.[29] For the most part, the unions where distress was most intense were the last ones to open soup kitchens. The government responded to these delays by stipulating still further reductions in the number employed on the public works. This policy, however, served to leave some people without any relief whatsoever as, rather than expediting the introduction of the new relief measures, in several districts it left the local population without any relief at all.

The sluggish opening of the soup kitchens and the response of the government to the delays undoubtedly contributed to the continuation of distress and mortality in some unions. This was particularly true in areas where there was a high level of dependence on external relief which was temporarily no longer available. In the Galway union, the government inspector reported that the closing of the public works together with a delay in opening the soup kitchens was the direct cause of a further increase in local mortality.[30] The Relief Commissioners contributed to the delays in opening the soup kitchens by insisting on a more rapid closure of the public works, regardless of the impact of this policy in several areas. In the Roscommon union, the local population relied heavily on the support of external aid, particularly the public works and charitable donations from the British Relief Association. This assistance ended at the commencement of summer, in the expectation of soup kitchens being operative. The delay in introducing the Temporary Relief Act, however, left the population without any relief. By mid-June, the local inspector stated that he was maintaining the distressed people out of his own pocket.[31]

The number of people employed on the relief works reached its maximum at the beginning of March. By then, the government departments involved realised that they no longer were able to control the way in which it was managed. They admitted that all their attempts to limit the numbers employed on the works had proved to be 'utterly inefficacious' and that attempts to monitor the work carried out 'has for the moment, been lost'.[32] The transfer of responsibility to a different system appeared to be the only way to salvage and control the provision of relief. This provided a further incentive for the transfer to be implemented as quickly as possible. A further concern of the government was that the public works diverted the poor from their normal agricultural pursuits. It was therefore essential that the relief works should be closed as early as possible to allow an immediate return to the usual harvest preparations. The Treasury anticipated that if this return to normal agricultural pursuits was not facilitated 'evils must ensue which . . . would produce calamities even greater than those which have hitherto been experienced'.[33]

On 20 March 1847, the Treasury ordered a 20 per cent reduction in the numbers employed on the relief works. The first people to be discharged were those who occupied over ten acres or more of land, even if this exceeded the 20 per cent quota. A second reduction of 10 per cent was to take place on 24 April. A week after this, with what appears to be undue haste, all public works were brought to a close unless the Treasury deemed the circumstances to be exceptional. If prior to these dates a soup kitchen was opened in the vicinity, then the public works were to be closed immediately.[34] The timing of these reductions aimed to allow the resumption of normal harvest work as soon as possible. The contraction of the public works, however, was sometimes enforced without any due regard to the availability of other forms of relief. The poorest electoral divisions were frequently the last ones to open soup kitchens. For example, in the notorious Skibbereen union, the final soup kitchen was not opened until 15 June, while in the impoverished electoral division of Ballycastle in the Ballina union, the local soup kitchen was not operative until 24 June, almost two months after the public works were closed.[35] Inevitably, such delays left some people even more vulnerable than they had been during the previous winter.

The compulsory reductions in the number of people employed on the public works in March and April 1847 resulted in a period of spasmodic disturbances and outrages in some parts of Ireland. These were most numerous in counties Clare, Cork, Limerick and Galway—areas which had a high level of dependency on external relief agencies—although isolated instances did occur elsewhere. Most of the disturbances took place between the closing of the public works and the opening of the soup kitchens, although some were a response to the provision of relief in the form of cooked rather than uncooked food. The continuation of these disturbances even after the new system of relief was operative suggests that they became absorbed into a more general set of grievances. In early April, the *Cork Reporter* described an outbreak of violence in Youghal:

We are sorry to learn that the consequences of dismissing bodies of men from the public works before measures for their temporary relief were in operation, have already manifested themselves in Youghal, where it will be recollected outrages of a most violent character occurred some months ago, arising from want of employment.[36]

In Co. Galway there was a marked increase in the number of attacks on meal depots as public works were closed down. A number of vessels off the coast were also boarded and plundered. The local Coast Guards suspected that most of the attacks were carried out by the inhabitants of Kildownet and Currane and were able, therefore, to retrieve a portion of the stolen meal. In the union of Ballinasloe in Co. Galway, the last soup kitchen was not opened until 16 June 1847. In some parts of the union, between 500 and 800 labourers protested against this by holding daily marches through the local towns. They were described as being a 'rueful and famine-worn band' who daily visited the local relief committee to ask if they could have either bread or employment. When it became obvious that the relief committees were unable to provide them with either, the marches occasionally developed into attacks on the local food stores. Following this, the police and dragoons were employed to protect all food stores in the local vicinity. The protracted delay in opening the soup kitchens resulted in half of the people who had been dismissed from the public works being reinstated again.[37] In the Gort union in Co. Galway, the first soup kitchen was opened on 3 April, although the final one was not operative until 15 May.[38] Some of the disturbances which followed the closure of the public works became violent and were described by one local newspaper as having descended to 'wholesale butchery'. In Ballinskelligs a group of dismissed labourers resorted to eating a horse which they flavoured with salt in order to disguise the nature of the meat.[39]

A number of outrages were directed against the actual soup kitchens themselves or, occasionally, the officials who administered them. In Castlemartyr in Co. Cork, a local mob threatened to 'smash all the soup boilers in the country', because they wanted no more 'greasy kitchen stuff but should have either money or bread'. A local landlord, Lord Shannon, agreed to meet a small delegation but refused to have any communication with a mob.[40] Throughout Co. Limerick, dismissals from the public works had resulted in many 'tumultuous meetings' being held. Again, these sometimes led to public disturbances, particularly to the plundering of food stores. The police were usually called to put down these disturbances although occasionally they required reinforcements from the military.[41] Even after soup kitchens had been opened, the disturbances continued throughout Co. Limerick. The Relief Commissioners attributed this to the fact that cooked food was 'extremely unpopular with all classes'.[42] In the city of Limerick, soup kitchens were opened as early as 3 April. Despite this, disturbances continued throughout April and May. In one incident, the soup boilers in one kitchen were 'smashed to atoms' and a meeting room of the relief committee was broken into and all documents and papers therein were destroyed. When the ringleader was arrested, the crowd attacked the local barracks with stones. This resulted in shots being fired into the crowd.[43]

The provision of cooked rather than uncooked food, as had previously been the case, was initially unpopular with many of the distressed populace. In Corofin in Co. Clare, for example, the local soup kitchen was destroyed by a number of people who demanded uncooked meal in the place of cooked 'porridge'. In the town of Kells in Co. Meath, a mob refused to allow anybody to receive their soup ration, again on the grounds that they did not like the indignity of receiving cooked food. The reporter on the local newspaper, the *Meath Herald*, described this incident as 'a stirabout rebellion'. He personally tested the soup and stated that it was 'excellent stirabout, made of Indian meal, rice and oatmeal'. He predicted that as the local population became more used to receiving cooked rations, they would grow to like them. Cooked food, however, was regarded by the government as being a more accurate test of genuine destitution than relief in either uncooked meal or money and was also considered to be less open to abuse. The relief commissioners claimed that during the previous eighteen months, there had been a number of instances of uncooked food being exchanged or sold for 'tea, tobacco and EVEN spirits'. It was alleged that some men had sold their rations of uncooked meal which they had received for their family and then got 'drunk upon the proceedings, leaving their children to starve'.[44] Some of the local relief committees responded to the attacks on their soup kitchens by returning to the provision of uncooked food. The Relief Commissioners realised that many ratepayers were 'intimidated' by the threats of violence and acknowledged that 'the peasantry are turbulent, and having had their own way for so long, the gentlemen of the country anticipate great violence if they attempt any reform in the issue of food.[45]

Instances of intimidation were believed to be particularly numerous in areas where there were no resident landlords. The Relief Commissioners ruled that in areas where people on the relief lists were found to be involved in cases of bad behaviour or intimidation, they were to be struck off the lists. This was felt to be a more effective solution than the use of the police or the military. The Relief Commissioners believed that they were morally justified in striking people off on the grounds that if they were truly starving, they would be grateful for this food, and therefore it was 'unreasonable to require force to be employed for compelling people who are reputed to be famished to receive wholesome food provided for their subsistence'.[46]

The attacks on the soup kitchens occasionally became interwoven with more general outrages. One local newspaper believed a general state of lawlessness was apparent in counties Limerick and Clare and warned that 'the whole country is swarming with armed parties, and in the shebeen houses, juries meet to decide on attacks on life and property. Impunity makes the assassin confident.'[47] Additional troops were despatched to the troubled areas and in May the Lord Lieutenant issued a proclamation of 'caution and admonition'. In England, the increase in outrages and corresponding increase in the sale of firearms was viewed as further evidence of the lawlessness and ingratitude of Ireland.[48]

The delays in opening the soup kitchens were invariably blamed on the local relief committees. Some were accused by the Relief Commissioners of being apathetic. Others, however, were regarded as being unwilling to introduce a system of outdoor relief which had the effect of 'feeding vast numbers of able-bodied men, who will be kept in idleness'. At a public meeting held in Roscommon, the landowners asked the government to make the able-bodied undertake employment in order to receive soup. They complained that the soup kitchens were contributing to the increase in crime, by allowing the people so much free time.[49] A suggested alternative was the provision of relief as a supplement in aid of wages. This, however, was strictly forbidden as it was felt to have been the cause of 'very great evils in England' prior to the new Poor Law being introduced in 1834.[50] In the tradition of Malthus, they argued that relief in aid of wages had encouraged 'early marriages and their natural result, large families' whilst wages had been determined by 'the caprice of the employer'.[51]

The provision of gratuitous outdoor relief to able-bodied men was at variance with contemporary attitudes to the provision of poor relief. It had been expressly forbidden by the poor relief system of 1838 and had been excluded from the temporary measures introduced since 1845. The Temporary Relief Act, therefore, marked a radical departure from previous forms of relief. The government was opposed in principle to any system of outdoor relief. They regarded the Temporary Relief Act as a short term expedient which was 'necessarily of a nature contrary to all sound principles'.[52] In order to help counteract the inevitable 'degradation', the quantity of relief provided was to be 'miserable and scanty'. At the same time, it was to be made clear to each able-bodied man 'how unmanly it is to abandon his independence, and all hopes of bettering the condition of his family'.[53]

The Temporary Relief Act was undoubtedly the most liberal and extensive form of relief used at any time during the Famine. Unlike the public works, labour was not demanded in return for relief and, contrary to the basic ethos of the Poor Law, recipients did not have to be absolutely destitute. In fact the Act, albeit temporarily, broadened the definition of what constituted 'destitution'. When asked if, under the Temporary Relief Act, a person who possessed a horse or a cow could be considered eligible for relief, the Commissioners replied that he could, 'if, by retaining it, there may be a prospect of his hereafter being able to provide for his own support'. They believed that it was possible to justify the provision of temporary relief if the outcome was 'to avoid driving [the recipient] into permanent destitution'.[54] Most of the relief provided under the Temporary Relief Acts was to be gratuitous. The Relief Commissioners described three categories of people who were eligible for this form of relief: firstly, 'destitute, helpless or impotent persons'; secondly, 'destitute, able-bodied persons, not holding land'; and thirdly, 'able-bodied persons who held small portions of land'. A further category of people was allowed to purchase food at the soup kitchens, namely, employed able-bodied persons whose wages were insufficient to maintain their families.[55]

Relief under the Temporary Relief Act was provided in the form of soup, by which was meant 'any food cooked in a boiler, and distributed in a liquid state, thick or thin, and whether composed of meat, fish, vegetables, grain or meal'.[56] Soup was to be made according to one of the various prescribed recipes and was to be accompanied by either one and a half pounds of bread, or one pound of biscuit, flour, grain or meal. If the soup had been thickened by grain, only a quarter ration of these was provided. It was recommended that the rations should be varied as often as possible to promote good health. This advice, however, did not appear to be widely adopted. Persons over the age of nine were to receive one full ration, and those aged under nine a half ration.[57] Although there was some dissatisfaction with the size of the rations, the Relief Commissioners stated that it had received the approval of the Board of Health. Furthermore, they pointed out that 'under the present dearth, it would be impossible to afford relief to the degree that every charitable person would desire'.[58]

The Relief Commissioners had consulted the Board of Health regarding the nutritional implications of providing cooked food in the form of soup. The Health Commissioners were concerned that the replacement of potato by other forms of food could have a detrimental impact on the health of the Irish people, particularly those who, prior to 1845, had had a high level of dependence on potatoes. The Board of Health recognised that the potato 'although not containing a large proportion of nutrient, is remarkable in containing within itself all the varied elements necessary for forming healthy blood'.[59] The dramatic change in diet for those who were forced to depend on external relief had resulted in an increase in dysentery and diarrhoea. The Board, however, felt that this had been exacerbated by unfamiliarity with the proper cooking processes of the replacement foods. They had received many reports of rice and meal being undercooked and some instances of it being eaten raw.[60]

As a result of the experience of the previous eighteen months, the Board of Health fully approved of relief being provided in the form of cooked food. Its main concern was that the cooked food should be varied and nutritious. It cautioned the Relief Commissioners against mistaking 'bulk for nutrient', and recommended that the soup should be in a 'solid' rather than a 'very fluid form'.[61] The Relief Commissioners were optimistic about the effects of the new Act and in mid-June, declared that as a consequence of the introduction of cooked food, cases of starvation had become rare. Even in Skibbereen, which had suffered greatly during the previous few months, the Relief Commissioners stated that 'the population is gradually amending from their former emaciated state'. This assertion appears to have been correct. A detailed examination of six parishes in Skibbereen has demonstrated that following a period of high mortality from September 1846 to May 1847, mortality fell to almost zero during the summer months when the local soup kitchens were fully operative.[62]

Although the incidence of diseases such as dysentery diminished over the summer months, there was an increase in others. The Board of Health noted an increase in a disease which resembled 'sea scurvy'. They attributed this to 'defective nutrition' which, they believed, was caused 'not from deficiency of quantity, but from deficiency of quality and variety in the food'.[63] Rice or meal alone could not provide the nutrients necessary for health. Again, they warned that the relief provided from the soup kitchens should be varied. They recommended that onions, leeks, scallions and shallots should be added to the soup and that fresh vegetables, peas and beans should be used more often. The *Roscommon and Leitrim Gazette*, in response to reports that the instructions of the Board of Health were not being followed, undertook an experiment with rations of soup obtained from soup kitchens in their vicinity. In general, they found that the quality of the soup was not good and they suggested that it should be replaced with 'nutritious meat soup'. There were a few exceptions, however, and they commended the Mullingar relief committee for providing each adult with 3 lbs. of 'well cooked and wholesome stirabout'.[64]

The procedures for obtaining relief from the soup kitchens were precisely outlined by the Relief Commissioners. The local relief committees were again to compile lists of people who were eligible to receive relief.

The Relief Commissioners estimated that each adult male on the list had an average of three dependants, including his wife. The person named on the relief list was to attend the soup kitchen daily, bringing with him a suitable can or vessel for transporting the rations. The only exception to this was the sick or impotent poor, who were allowed to receive up to two weeks' rations at a time.

Small holders of land were allowed a fixed period of time for tilling their land, during which their wives or other nearest relatives could attend the depot on their behalf. Double rations were provided on a Saturday as the kitchens were closed on Sundays.[65] Soup kitchens were to be centrally located within an electoral division and more than one could be opened if necessary. The Relief Commissioners were anxious that the soup kitchens should not become a focal point for discontent and that large numbers of people should not be allowed to congregate at any given time.[66] To avoid 'the serious evil of crowds', each person on the relief list was given a number and the relief rations were provided according to these numbers. Also, to expedite the distribution of food, and to 'help preserve order and decorum at the depot', each kitchen was to have two doors, an entrance and an exit. Any person who caused a disturbance whilst waiting at the soup kitchen was to be forced to wait until the end of the day for their rations. Rations which were left over at the end of the day, could be sold by the relief committees.[67]

The number of people in receipt of soup continued to rise throughout May and June 1847, as more electoral divisions came under the provisions of the Act and more people were provided with rations.[68] As the table below shows, the number of people receiving rations was at its maximum at the beginning of July.

Table 10: Statistics for Soup Rations, Summer 1847[69]

	Electoral Divisions	Gratuitous Rations	Rations Sold	No. of Persons Relieved Gratuitously
8 May	1063	777,884	48,441	
5 June	1677	1,923,361	92,326	2,729,684
3 July	1823	2,342,900	79,636	3,020,712
31 July	1707	1,845,868	45,839	2,520,376
28 Aug.	1098	772,725	9,795	782,520
11 Sept.	563	442,739	–	505,984

The Temporary Relief Act was at its peak at the beginning of July when over three million people were in receipt of free rations of soup. The overall number of people receiving this relief, however, disguises the fact that there were large regional diversities in its distribution (see Appendix 3). Again, it was the unions along the western seaboard— notably counties Mayo and Galway—where the highest proportion of the population depended on the assistance of the government for subsistence. However, in some individual electoral divisions in these areas, the number of people daily in receipt of the government rations exceeded the local population. The Relief Commissioners attempted to impose a ceiling on the numbers receiving relief by restricting it to 75 per cent of the local inhabitants. In some of the most distressed unions, however, this upper limit proved to be impossible to maintain.[70] In the east of the country, particularly in the north east, dependence on this form of relief was lightest. Three unions—Antrim, Belfast and Newtownards—did not avail of the provisions of the Temporary Relief Act at all. The table below demonstrates the disparity between the ten unions with the highest dependence on the Temporary Relief Act and the ten unions with the lowest.

Table 11: Temporary Relief Act: regional variations[71]

Union	Maximum No. of People in union dependent on rations as a % of the population
Ballinrobe	94.41
Clifden	86.62
Gort	85.84
Westport	85.72
Swinford	84
Tuam	83.74
Ballina	78.70
Newcastle	76.44
Castlebar	75.90
Galway	74.67
Newtownlimavady	9.12
Downpatrick	9.05
Lurgan	8.16
Coleraine	5.84
Londonderry	5.53
Ballymena	5.23
Dunfanaghy	4.63
Lisburn	3.3
Kilkeel	2.12
Larne	1.15

The average take-up of soup rations throughout the Poor Law unions was 36 per cent which tended to fall into an east/west spatial divide. However, even within the electoral divisions of individual unions, there could be considerable diversity in both the demand for and dependence on soup kitchens. In both the Dunfanaghy and Larne unions, for example, only one electoral division out of a possible ten and thirteen respectively, opened a government soup kitchen. The fact that an electoral division did not operate under the Temporary Relief Act did not necessarily mean that relief was not being provided in an area but, as in the case of the Belfast, Newtownards and Antrim unions, indicated that relief was being funded privately without the intervention of the government. The Malone relief committee in Belfast, for example, refused to operate under the provisions of the Temporary Relief Act on the grounds that they wanted to maintain their own autonomy whilst avoiding the cost of employing government inspectors.[72] In the west, south and many parts of the midlands of Ireland, the provisions of the Temporary Relief Act were fully availed of, making this relief measure the most widely used form of assistance during the Famine.

Although the advances from the Treasury were not due to cease until 30 September, it was decided to begin reducing them from early August. Relief provided in the soup kitchens was to be discontinued on 15 August in fifty-five unions, most of which were situated in the east and the midlands of the country. In the remainder, mostly in the west, it was to end on 29 August. The 'impotent' sick or poor in the forty-six most distressed unions could continue to receive relief until 30 September.[73] Although there were some objections to the early closure, the Relief Commissioners believed that it was necessary not to delay as, after the harvest, the people would either have to depend on their own resources or obtain relief from the Poor Law.[74]

The cost of providing a full ration in the soup kitchen was initially 2½d. The great increase in food imports to Ireland during the late spring and summer of 1847 contributed to a sharp decrease in food prices. As a result, the average price of rations dropped to 1d each, although prices in the unions near to a port tended to be lowest and those in the midlands were generally the highest overall. In 1847, Ireland changed from being a net exporter of grain to a net importer of grain: an estimated 145,000 tons being exported compared with 836,000 tons being imported.[75] The large amount of grain available helped to reduce its price—perhaps six months too late for many poor people. The sharp fall in prices meant that costs under the Temporary Relief Act were less than had been anticipated by the government: out of the £2,255,000 voted by parliament, only £1,724,631 17s 3d had been expended.[76]

152

The final report of the Temporary Relief Commissioners stated that they were content with the operation of the system which they had administered over the preceding six months. The inspecting officers were praised for their dedication and even the local relief committees were congratulated for their 'zealous and honourable exertions'.[77] With barely concealed satisfaction, the Relief Commissioners were able to assert confidently 'that the measure has fully succeeded in its object, there can be not the slightest doubt'.[78] The relief had not been extravagant: it had conformed to the government maxim that it should be limited 'to the bare support of the thoroughly destitute', yet it had succeeded in bringing to an end deaths from starvation while simultaneously it had improved the 'hitherto haggard appearance of the population'.[79] This had contributed to a general feeling of well-being within the community and over the summer the crime rates had decreased. Many people appeared grateful for what had been done for them and the Relief Commissioners stated that 'the poor pray God's blessings upon the Queen and the government for sending them food in the time of their latter need'.[80] As a result of all of these favourable factors, the Relief Commissioners believed that the transfer to Poor Law relief could not have occurred at a better time. Regardless of the success of the temporary measures, the Whig administration and the Relief Commissioners viewed the soup kitchens as a temporary expedient which had been necessary to meet a unique situation. They did not believe that such circumstances would ever reappear and thus justify the continuation of the Temporary Relief Act:

> On the contrary, we are fully aware of its many dangers and evils, and that it could only be justified by such an extreme occasion, including a combination of circumstances that can hardly be expected to occur again.[81]

The committees themselves were generally satisfied with the impact of the Temporary Relief Act; not only had it saved more lives than the public works, it had also operated at approximately one-third of their cost. The committees of ninety-two unions forwarded to the Relief Commissioners 'resolutions or expressions of approbation', some adding that they wished that the Temporary Relief Act had been introduced earlier.[82] Regardless of the popularity of this measure, however, it did not establish a precedent for the provision of extensive outdoor relief. The Commissioners were worried that the success of the measure might encourage the committees to ask for its extension, which they believed would reduce the country to 'universal pauperisation'. They were pleased to observe that the provision of such 'large and discriminate' relief had, however, provoked a 'salutary re-action' by showing people at first hand the evils associated with providing indiscriminate relief.[83]

Apart from the immediate benefits of the Temporary Relief Act, a number of long term benefits were also evident. The British government was delighted with this aspect of their policies, and believed that the changes which they had desired for so long were gradually taking place within Ireland. One manifestation of this was that for the first time farmers and labourers were emerging as two distinct groups, a division which was apparent in 'all other well regulated countries'. A distinction between ratepayers and paupers was also apparent, that is, those who depended on relief and those who financed it. It was hoped that the creation of distinct groups or classes within Ireland would increase productivity and wealth and, at the same time, would help to 'break through that terrible band of secrecy, hitherto the bane of Ireland'.[84]

The general optimism and mood of self-congratulation evident amongst the relief officials did not disguise some disquieting factors which were evident as the temporary system was drawing to a close. The money for financing the Temporary Relief Act was in the first instance to be provided by the Treasury, on the security of money to be raised from the local poor rates. A number of the poorest electoral divisions also received a grant from the Treasury. A total of £953,355 17s 4d in loans was advanced on the credit of the rates, to be repaid by the respective unions. If an electoral division raised a subscription for poor relief, the Treasury could make a donation of an equal amount. The sum of £45,740 1s 11d was raised by voluntary donations in the local electoral divisions.[85] Initially, the money lent by the Treasury was to be repaid in one payment. The Relief Commissioners believed that this would not be possible even though expenditure had been less than anticipated and advised that repayments should be allowed to be made in instalments. They also warned that although the average repayment for the Temporary Relief Act would be 2s 6d in the pound, some areas would only have to make repayments of a few pence, whereas in other unions the repayments would be far higher. Inevitably, the heaviest burden on the local taxpayers would be in the unions in the west of Ireland, those which the Commissioners described as being 'the most suffering', where dependency on the soup kitchens had been highest.[86] The Commissioners acknowledged that in some of the poorest unions, even before the repayments were demanded, 'the mass of the tenantry, hitherto ratepayers, are in a state of pauperism, while the proprietors themselves, from the impossibility of obtaining rents, will be very unequal to meet such extra demands'.[87] They informed the government that some unions, through no fault of their own, would be unable to afford any additional expenditure in the foreseeable future.[88]

Again, a disagreement was apparent between the attitudes of the relief officials in Dublin and those in London; the latter being far less sympathetic to the financial embarrassments of some districts. The Treasury disapproved of the suggestion that repayments should be made in instalments. Their objections were based on the fact that since January 1847, the poorest unions had received regular advances from the Treasury and therefore should not be encouraged to believe that this would continue indefinitely. Trevelyan was convinced that tenacity was required by the British government to force the Irish ratepayers to meet their responsibilities on the grounds that, 'whatever local suffering may be occasioned, the welfare of the whole community requires that all further assistance either by way of a loan or grant, should be withheld until the rates are properly put in course of levy'. [89] Reluctantly, the Treasury conceded that the repayments could be made in instalments and the first one did not have to exceed 3s in the pound. By September 1847, it was obvious that the harvest was far smaller than had been predicted. Reluctantly, the Treasury conceded that the first repayment did not have to be made until 1 January 1848.[90]

The Temporary Fever Act of 1846 had made the local boards of guardians responsible for establishing additional fever hospitals, but the guardians had been hamstrung by the general lack of funds.[91] Aware of the shortcomings of the health system in Ireland, the government established a Central Board of Health at the beginning of 1847. The Board was empowered to establish temporary fever hospitals and pay for the purchase of coffins, whitewashing buildings, fumigating the houses of sick people etc. from government advances similar to those made for the establishment of soup kitchens. The local relief committees were made responsible for implementing the fever regulations in their areas. Ultimately, loans for this purpose were to be repaid from the poor rates.[92] These powers were due to expire at the end of September, after which the Poor Law guardians would again be responsible for fever hospitals. The Board of Health was concerned that the advances which they had been receiving from the government were also to cease on 30 September 1847. At the beginning of the month, they warned the Irish government that a number of diseases, including dysentery and scurvy, were likely to increase over the winter, and that fever had already reappeared in an even more malignant form than previously. They therefore considered it essential that financial assistance should continue to be provided for the provision of medical relief, as poor rates alone could not carry this burden.[93]

The Irish Executive were also worried about the transfer of so many heavy responsibilities to the poor rates. The new Chief Secretary, Sir William Somerville, was especially pessimistic regarding the implications of making poor rates responsible for medical relief. He believed that the means at the disposal of the guardians was more limited than had previously been the case and warned that as the original Medical Relief Act:

> was found to be ineffectual for its object in 1846, owing to the want of funds under which the unions then laboured, its failure might be expected to be still more complete now, when the pressure upon the rates is much more severe under the provisions of the Poor Law Extension Act of last season, and when fever has increased to the alarming extent stated.[94]

The Irish Executive suggested to the British Treasury that the money which had been saved during the operation of the Temporary Relief Act could be used for the support of medical relief. The Treasury rejected this suggestion. They were of the opinion that the taxpayers of Britain had already subsidised Irish poverty to a large extent, especially with the recent influx of fever-infected Irish migrants to Britain. Therefore they considered it vital to the whole success of their new relief policy that, after 1 October 1847, financial dependence on the British Treasury should be ended and instead responsibility should be placed upon the ratepayers of Ireland.[95]

Although the Treasury assured the Irish Executive that they would not leave the fever hospitals without funds, they stressed that this was rightfully the responsibility of the boards of guardians and the local ratepayers.[96] This answer did not reassure the officials in Dublin. Somerville privately admitted 'I tremble at the thought of what may happen'.[97] The Treasury, however, felt that the new relief measures, which the government had specifically intended to be financed from the local poor rates, should not be compromised at such an early stage. Trevelyan was convinced that the transfer to local responsibility would be persistently resisted unless the Treasury acted resolutely. He viewed the ensuing struggle as 'a trial of strength . . . to decide whether the necessary measures for relief are to be taken by the Poor Law guardians, or all thrown back on the government'.[98] By October 1847, however, as optimism about the situation in Ireland was giving way to pessimism, the Treasury did relent and in a measure which they described as 'considerate liberality' agreed to subsidise expenses arising from the Fever Acts.[99]

Although the prospects for the 1847 harvest had appeared promising during the summer, the actual yield was disappointing, even though potato blight was on a far smaller scale than in the previous year. The Relief Commissioners, who had previously expressed their optimism at the prospects of the country in the coming year, now warned that during the winter of 1847–8, they believed that neither potatoes nor wages would be available to the poor. Based on their experiences, they predicted that distress would be highest where the land was sub-divided and conacre was used extensively. They also recognised that as people entered their third year of distress, their resources and capital would probably be exhausted. Many people had already pawned their few possessions. In the town of Kilkeel, by no means one of the poorest areas, £8,500 worth of clothing had been pawned since 1845. In the east of Ireland, the resources of the poorest people had disappeared even earlier and wealthier people were also affected: pigs had become almost extinct; the number of horses had fallen to half its prevous level; and black cattle had been reduced by approximately a third.[100] The Relief Commissioners, aware of the inverse relationship between dependence on poor rates and ability to pay them, were worried that in the unions where relief was most necessary, the local resources for providing it were no longer available. As the size of the 1847 harvest became apparent, the former optimism of the Relief Commissioners also changed to pessimism. They believed that the government would have to continue to provide financial aid to several unions, regardless of its stated intentions. Demand for relief was highest in the unions with the least resources to finance it. In these unions, they warned 'the property and the society were less in a condition to support the masses; and the means . . . of alleviating the charge will be smaller'.[101]

Public Subscriptions and Private Charity

During the intermittent periods of distress before 1845, in addition to the relief provided by the government, a considerable amount of assistance was also provided both by philanthropic individuals and charitable organisations. The activities of these bodies were regarded as being of particular importance in the years prior to the introduction of a Poor Law in Ireland. During the Famine of 1845–51, but especially in the aftermath of the total potato failure of 1846, Irish distress attracted donations from all parts of the world. Some of the larger charitable organisations even employed representatives to oversee and facilitate the distribution of their largesse. The provision of charitable relief, as with government relief, was frequently governed by an underlying philosophy: the giving of alms was to be done in such a way as not to demoralise the recipient or dampen self-exertion. If possible, the relief given was to have a longer-term benefit, not only to the individual, but also to the country. There also existed an underlying belief that unless strict controls were enforced, the relief provided would be abused and taken for granted. Each system of relief, therefore, was to incorporate various tests of genuine destitu-tion. In general, relief was believed to be less open to abuse if it was pro-vided in the form of cooked food, bedding or clothing, rather than in money.

One of the most important and highly regarded charitable organisa-tions was the Society of Friends, or Quakers. They first became involved in Irish Famine relief in November 1846, when some Dublin-based members of the Society decided to establish a Central Relief Committee. The Quakers had a long tradition of philanthropic activity and were well regarded for their avoidance of proselytism. Although the Quakers were numerically small in Ireland, their numbers did include a relatively high proportion of successful businessmen. They also had the support of co-religionists throughout the world. Initially, the role of the Central Relief Committee was to be mainly advisory, as they believed that it was impor-tant for accurate information to be provided by disinterested experts. They intended that any assistance which they gave was to be merely sup-plementary to other relief. However, in the early months of 1847, the relief provided by the Society of Friends often proved crucial in keeping people alive, as other systems of relief failed in this basic purpose. This was particularly so during the vacuum in relief provision following the closure of public works in some areas.

At the end of November 1846, two Englishmen, James H. Tuke and William Forster, with the assistance of local Quakers, commenced a tour of the most distressed parts of Ireland. During the course of this journey, they visited counties Roscommon, Leitrim, Fermanagh, Donegal, Sligo, Mayo, Galway, Longford and Cavan. The Quakers admitted that their extensive experience in working with distressed people in England had not prepared them for what they saw in Ireland. They reported to the Central Relief Committee that they were appalled by the scenes which they witnessed and had never encountered such suffering before. Tuke was driven to record: 'the scenes of poverty and wretchedness are almost beyond belief . . . notwithstanding all my experience derived from my years service in the Poor Law Commission, three of which were spent in Yorkshire and Lancashire during the extremity of distress there'.[102]

A number of Quakers criticised the relief policies of the government, holding them to be inadequate and misjudged. As the Quakers who were touring the west of Ireland quickly realised, the distress was often most severe in the areas where the administrative machinery for the distribution of relief was most limited. They believed that absentee or irresponsible landlords were to a large extent responsible for this. Consequently, although the Quakers identified the most severe distress as existing in the province of Connacht, the amount of relief which they provided was restricted because of the absence of an interested middle and landlord class in some places through which to channel this assistance. Joseph Bewley, the Secretary of the Society of Friends, realised that government policies meant that the relief taxes were heaviest in the districts which were least able to afford them. He judged these policies to be short-sighted and incapable of bringing any long-term benefit to the people of Ireland.[103] During his visit to Co. Donegal, Tuke was delayed for weeks by heavy snowstorms. He realised the implications that this had for people who were employed on the public works: bad weather reduced the amount of money which could be earned. Also, the effort to remain warm and dry—through the wearing of warm clothes or the lighting of a small fire—proved an additional drain on the limited resources of the people. Those who attempted to continue working during the bad weather invariably increased their propensity to fall ill. Apart from the relief provisions, Tuke was also critical of the social structures within Ireland. He regarded the abject poverty and wretchedness of the small farmers and cottiers as not being surpassed even in the 'most barbarous nations'.[104] Tuke saved his most severe criticisms for the role played by absentee landlords, particularly those who, although they owned large estates, had not 'subscribed one farthing' to help alleviate the suffering of their tenants.[105]

The Society of Friends had undertaken to import supplies of food mostly from America into Ireland in 1847. Even before it arrived, it was obvious to Tuke and Forster that in many areas more extensive and immediate assistance was required than that envisaged by their colleagues in Dublin. In each of the areas which they visited, Tuke and Forster distributed both food and cash. Although the Quakers had intended that their provisions should be sold at cost price, they realised that if they adhered to this, it would still be beyond the means of the most distressed people. Increasingly, the relief provided by the Quakers in the field was given gratuitously even though in doing so they offended both the central committee in Dublin and the Treasury. As far as possible, the Quakers worked through the local relief committees or local gentry or clergy. Money was not to be provided directly to the destitute people. The money which they provided was frequently used for the establishment of a soup kitchen, the purchase of seed, or the provision of local employment. In Dunfanaghy, for example, money was given to the local minister for the purchase of boilers for a soup kitchen and the purchase of materials for the local women to knit Guernsey shirts.[106]

Apart from food and cash, the Quakers donated clothes and bedding. They also imported boilers for soup kitchens, being one of the first organisations to favour the use of soup kitchens as a means of providing large-scale relief. This was approved by the government, which disliked giving either money or uncooked food. The government, who regarded the involvement of the Quakers as very valuable, paid the freight and warehouse charges of all goods imported by the Quakers and waived all port duties. Most of the food was imported directly into the area where it was to be distributed. It included Indian meal, flour, rice, biscuits, peas, Scotch barley, American beef and tapioca.[107] During 1846 and 1847, the Quakers provided approximately £200,000 for the relief of distress in Ireland, which was spent almost exclusively in the west of the country. The following statistics which refer to Co. Donegal provide an insight into the assistance afforded by the Quakers:

Table 12: Quaker Relief in Co. Donegal[108]

Estimated number of grants:	266
Number of boilers:	19
Quantity of food, in tons:	400
Value of food and boilers:	£6,659 0s 0d
Amount of money grants:	£1,429 5s 9d
Total Value	£8,088 5s 9d

During the summer of 1847, as the Temporary Relief Act was implemented, the Quakers began to wind down their operations with a view to ending them totally when the extended Poor Law became operative in the autumn. Instead, they decided only to provide relief which would contribute to developing the industries and resources of the country. However, in the winter of 1847–8, the government asked them if they would consider again becoming involved in the provision of relief, particularly in the re-establishment of soup kitchens. The Quakers were reluctant to do so. As one official explained, providing this form of relief would be similar to 'giving the criminal a long day'. They believed that it was better if they used their energies to contribute to the long-term improvement of Ireland and leave the provision of immediate relief to the government. In 1849, Trevelyan, at the request of the government, offered the Quakers £100 if they would provide direct relief as they had previously done, but again they refused.[109]

The main form of relief provided by the Quakers in 1848 was the distribution of seed, primarily on behalf of the government. The Relief Commissioners had a supply of seed but the government would not permit them to become involved in the direct sale of it. Instead they requested the Quakers to distribute it in the most impoverished districts in Ireland. The Quakers agreed, as they felt that this would be of permanent benefit to the country. In total, they distributed nearly 200,000 lbs of seed which was estimated to result in the cultivation of approximately 800 acres of green crops. The vast majority of the seeds were turnip, although carrot, parsnip and cabbage seeds were also distributed.[110]

Another philanthropic organisation involved in providing relief in Ireland was the British Relief Association. Its founders were primarily wealthy English businessmen and merchants, including the Baron Lionel de Rothschild. The British Relief Association was established in London in January 1847 for 'the relief of extreme distress in remote parishes of Ireland and Scotland'. One of its main purposes was to help people who were beyond the reach of the government. The Association, like the Society of Friends, intended to provide relief only in the form of food, clothing and fuel, but not in cash. Unlike the Quakers, however, the Association did not establish its own independent local relief organisations but operated through the machinery already created by the government. They appointed Count Strzelecki, a Polish nobleman, as their agent in Ireland. At the end of January, he travelled to Westport in Co. Mayo and confirmed that the distress was even more severe than they had anticipated.[111]

The British Relief Association raised money primarily in England and America, although it did raise some from as far away as Australia. In England, its fund-raising activities were helped by the publishing of a 'Queen's Letter' in early 1847, in which Victoria appealed for money to relieve distress in Ireland. This raised contributions from, amongst others, the Secretary of State, the Chancellor of the Exchequer (£200), Charles Trevelyan, William Thackeray (£5) and £2,000 from the Queen herself. The total raised was £171,533. A second Queen's Letter, launched in October 1847, reflecting a hardening in British public opinion, raised hardly any additional funds for the Association. In the summer of 1849, in response to continuing distress in a number of western unions, the government initiated a private subscription from within its ranks, to which the Queen contributed £500. The £10,000 raised was given to the British Relief Association which, although it never achieved as high a profile as the Quakers, raised approximately £470,000—over double the amount provided by the Society of Friends. Count Strzelecki initially worked closely with the Treasury and agreed to distribute all funds in the manner considered to be most appropriate by them.[112] In the early months of 1847, most of this money was used by the Treasury to provide loans to the most distressed unions. In August 1847, the Association had a balance of approximately £200,000. Strzelecki suggested that as the Poor Law was officially responsible for providing relief, this balance should be used to help schoolchildren in the west of Ireland. Trevelyan, however, had already drawn up a programme for the distribution of the remaining funds of the Association. He warned Strzelecki that it would be dangerous to set up any new administrative machinery as it might 'produce the impression that the lavish charitable system of last season was intended to be renewed'.[113] When Strzelecki proved to be adamant on the question of feeding the schoolchildren, Trevelyan conceded that a small portion of the funds could be used for this purpose. Most of the money raised by the British Relief Association, however, was spent in the way directed by the Treasury.[114]

Within Ireland itself, a number of relief organisations were also established. At the end of 1845, the Mansion House Committe was reconstituted, having been active in the provision of relief during the food shortages in 1831. It had the support of various Dublin dignitaries including the Mayor and the Lord Lieutenant. In September 1846, the Irish Relief Association, which had also been active in 1831, was reformed. It raised approximately £42,000 for the relief of distress.[115] In December 1846, the General Central Relief Committee was established in Dublin, the President of which was the Marquess of Kildare. It raised approximately £63,000. The two Archbishops of Dublin, the Catholic Archbishop Murray and the Church of Ireland Archbishop Whately, also worked together to raise funds from their co-religionists throughout the world. Most of the money collected by these bodies was raised in 1846 and in 1847, after which time, the level of subscriptions raised fell considerably. Disillusionment and distrust of Irish distress was apparent. A notable exception to this, however, was the Irish Catholic Church which continued to make donations from its limited resources to priests in the distressed western unions throughout the latter stages of the Famine.[116]

In addition to the main philanthropic organisations which were active in Ireland in 1846 and 1847, a number of societies, groups, civic authorities, religious bodies and individuals also contributed to the relief of Irish distress. Donations for the Irish Famine came from distant and unexpected sources. The first contribution received is thought to have come from Calcutta in 1846 and amounted to £14,000. In July 1847, Calcutta sent a further £2,500 for Irish relief via the Society of Friends. A sum of £3,000 was also sent from Bombay.[117] Subscriptions for the distressed Irish were also raised in Florence in Italy, where an Irish Relief Fund was established and a society ball was held for this purpose. The Society of St Vincent de Paul in France sent 110,000 francs, and 'the negroes of Antigua . . . from their own scanty resources' raised £144. The House of Assembly in Jamaica voted £2,000 towards the mitigation of Irish distress in remembrance of the fact that, 65 years earlier, Ireland had sent £2,000 to Barbados when that island had been destroyed by hurricanes.[118] A Famine Relief Committee was established in Hobart in Van Diemen's Land which throughout 1847 sent both regular cash donations and also wheat for the relief of Irish distress. Their final donation was sent in November 1847.[119] In 1847, when most of the charitable donations had ceased, an unusual one was sent by a tribe of Red Indians from Oklahoma in America. The Choctaw tribe, which had been forced from their own lands in 1831, had heard of the suffering of the population in the Doolough district in the Westport union. They sent a donation of $170 for distribution among the local population.[120]

A large proportion of private donations came from North America, which had been a favourite destination for migrants in the century prior to the Famine. In 1846, an estimated million dollars was sent from the United States. Large donations of food were also sent. Russell, the Prime Minister, publicly praised America for giving so much to Irish relief. To encourage further contributions, meetings were held in major cities within North America and 'Relief Committes for Ireland' were established. In February 1847, a letter from Philadelphia appeared in many Irish newspapers which stated that 'our whole country is aroused and all feel that out of the abundance with which God has blessed us, we should contribute largely to those who want'.[121] The town had committed itself to raising $50,000, approximately £10,000, in addition to possible private contributions. The generosity of the donations was partly due to the fact that America had experienced a rich harvest in 1846. The letter went on to say that for those Irish domestic servants employed in every city in America 'their only desire at present appears to be to give every farthing they possess'. It concluded on a philosophical note: 'of course, the misery of Ireland is our prosperity, and the prices obtained by producers are far beyond anything every dreamed of.'[122] In addition to money sent privately or channelled through relief associations such as the Quakers in the winter of 1846–7, the following amounts were raised by towns in America:

Table 13: Relief Funds Raised in American Cities[123]

New York	$170,150
Newark and State of New Jersey	$ 35,000
Boston	$ 45,000
Baltimore	$ 40,000
Philadelphia	$ 50,000
New Orleans	$ 25,000
Albany	$ 25,000
Washington	$ 5,000
Total	$395,150

In Britain also, private subscriptions were raised for Ireland and Scotland. By May 1847, private donations from Britain were estimated to have reached £200,000.[124] The 'Queen's Letter' appealing for donations had encouraged this philanthropic spirit. Fund raising bazaars were held, Ladies Relief Committees were established and pullovers were knitted to help the distressed people of both countries. Some money was also raised through various church groups, the most significant one being the Church of England. The funds collected were entrusted to the bishops of the Church of Ireland, who undertook to distribute to people of all religions. In a letter of thanks published by the Irish bishops in May 1847, they thanked the people of England for these donations but added:

> In several districts of the country, the distress of the poor is still of the most urgent kind and, in some parts, is even increased by reason of the removal of a number of persons from employment on the public works.[125]

The response of the Irish landlords living in England—the universally detested absentees—was varied. Sir Robert Palmer, an absentee landlord from Co. Sligo, was attacked for his 'luxurious living' while people died of starvation in the hovels on his estate.[126] In contrast to this, the Adair family who held an estate in Ballymena, Co. Antrim, regularly made 'munificent donations' to the local relief committee. As a result of these latter contributions, the relief committee was able to avoid seeking assistance from the government. The fact, however, that a number of absentee landlords chose not to return to their estates during such a crisis was generally indicative of their indifference to the condition of their tenants, and that this was reflected in the absolute wretchedness of their tenants was remarked upon even by such neutral commentators as the Quakers. A large number of resident landlords not only gave of their time generously in sitting on relief committees, grand juries, boards of guardians etc. but, especially in the years 1845–7, provided private assistance in the form of food, money, seed or rent abatements.[127]

As 1847 progressed, the relief effort for Ireland was tempered by the hordes of Irish people who were daily arriving at British ports. Initially, they were regarded as creatures to be pitied, but increasingly were viewed as carriers of disease and heavy burdens on the local poor rates. In the space of two years, the British Treasury had advanced almost £6,000,000 in aid of Irish distress. Although most of this money was a loan to be eventually repaid, many British taxpayers felt that they had contributed enough money towards Irish distress. The fact that the government was planning to advance even more for the operation of the Temporary Relief Act may have added fuel to this particular flame. The failure of a second Queen's Letter in October 1847 to elicit many subscriptions for Ireland indicated the end of the honeymoon period for providing financial assistance. Furthermore, the fact that a second appeal was even made aroused a vitriolic debate in the columns of *The Times*, one protagonist asking 'Why should the United Kingdom pay for the extravagance of Ireland?' One Anglican minister from London stated that giving any more money to Ireland would be 'about as ineffectual as to throw a sackful of gold into one of their plentiful bogs'. *The Times'* editorial columns added weight to these arguments by declaring itself to be against 'begging for Ireland' and suggesting that any money raised by the Queen's Letter should be given to the English poor. [128]

In Ireland itself, groups were formed and functions were held to raise money for the distressed people. In 1847, for instance, the Royal Irish Art Union held a loan exhibition of Old Masters in Dublin, the admission charge being donated to Famine relief.[129] In a number of towns, the formation of Ladies Relief Societies proved to be particularly popular. The Dublin Ladies Relief Association raised funds from England, including £3,000 from the soldiers in Regents Park Barracks in London. The Belfast society was very active, and even attracted a donation from Lady Byron, widow of the illustrious poet. The money raised was distributed not only in Belfast but in parts of the south and west of the country, mostly for the establishment of industrial workshops, for knitting, weaving and similar activities. The Belfast Ladies Committee provided clothing for poor emigrants who were passing through the town. They also gave food each day to approximately eighty schoolchildren, although the demand for this was much higher. Some of the children had been without food for several days before receiving this provision and the effect of providing them with a meal resulted in 'sickness and loathing during several successive days'.[130]

The Belfast Ladies Committee regarded the encouragement of self-reliance and industry amongst the poorer classes as a crucial aspect of their endeavours. To this end, a large portion of their funds was used for the establishment of work rooms and knitting shops. This was believed to be of especial value to females in Belfast, some of whom had been affected by the trade depression, which meant that:

> Many respectable women and girls are rapidly sinking into destitution from low wages, want of employment and high price of food; their decent raiment is passing to the pawn shops and, they themselves, daily adding to the squalid wretchedness of our streets.[131]

Although some of these women were already in receipt of rations at the soup kitchens, the Ladies Committee believed that the provision of gratuitous relief would ultimately do more harm than good because it would not 'improve them in habits of self-helpfulness and industry', but reduce them to 'hopeless idleness'.[132] By the autumn of 1847, the funds at the disposal of the Belfast Ladies Relief Committee were exhausted. Convinced of the value of the work which they had undertaken, they applied to the British Treasury for financial assistance. By return they were informed that such intervention lay beyond the scope of the government. Following this, many of the activities of this committee were wound up.[133]

Apart from the larger relief organisations, a number of smaller contributions were made. Among these, the workmen employed at Messrs Coates and Young in Lurgan, decided to contribute about £1 each week from their wages for the support of the poor in the Ballymacarret district of Belfast.[134] The principal proprietors of Ballynure in Co. Antrim voluntarily imposed a relief tax upon themselves, based on the Poor Law valuation. In parts of eastern Ulster, the local relief committees prided themselves on their self-reliance and ability to manage without contributions from the government. The Malone relief committee in Belfast passed 'strong resolutions' in which they determined to do without financial help from the government (and therefore, they reasoned, costly government officials) for the opening of soup kitchens in the summer of 1847.[135] A local newspaper praised both the local people and the local landlords for the contributions which they had voluntarily made to the provision of relief and recommended that:

> If such examples of wise and generous assistance on the part of the landlords, and local effort and self-reliance on the part of the people were more generally followed, such scenes of fearful misery as the present season has disclosed would be prevented and greatly lessened.[136]

A spirit of self-help had manifested itself most evidently in the north-eastern part of the country. To a large extent, it successfully embodied the perceived ideal of the government. Comparisons with the south and west of the country inevitably were made. To Trevelyan, the distressed parts of the country were 'peccant' and characterised by their 'habitual dependence' on the government. He believed that the solution to this lay in the introduction of an extended Poor Law in August 1847, with its emphasis on local responsibility for financing of relief.[137]

Mortality

The exact number of people who died during the Famine years (1845–51) is not known. In the first year of distress, no one was believed to have died from want; however, by the end of 1846, this had changed dramatically. In April 1847, an editorial in an Irish newspaper asked:

> What has become of all the vast quantity of food which has been thrown into Ireland? Where are the effects which it might have been expected to produce? How are the millions of pounds of money voted and subscribed been used that the march of famine, instead of being saved, has apparently been quickened.[138]

By this stage, it was obvious that the various relief measures employed since the appearance of the second blight had failed. The most telling manifestation was the great increase in mortality in the winter of 1846–7.

In 1851, the Census Commissioners attempted to produce a table of mortality for each year since 1841, the date of the previous census. Their calculations were based on a combination of deaths recorded in institutions and recollections of individuals (civil registration of deaths was not introduced into Ireland until 1864). The statistics provided were flawed and probably under-estimated the level of mortality, particularly for the earlier years of the Famine: personal recollections are notoriously unreliable and such methods did not take into account whole families who disappeared either as a consequence of emigration or death. In the most distressed areas, therefore, the data is the most incomplete and the information was sometimes based on indirect evidence. The table below, which was compiled by the Census Commissioners, does offer some insights into the fluctuations in mortality in these years. Because the rates of mortality were computed at the county level, with the exception of the larger towns, the disparities within each county cannot be measured and thus it is difficult to identify pockets of particularly severe distress. Local reports and increased numbers of local studies revealed a complex picture of local diversity, exposing pools of distress and excess mortality in parts of the midlands, whereas areas in the west of Ireland were little affected. Furthermore, excess mortality was evident even in some of the wealthiest parts of the country.

Table 14: Irish Mortality, 1842–50 [139]

Year	% of the Total Number of Deaths Occurring in Each Year
1842	5.1
1843	5.2
1844	5.6
1845	6.4
1846	9.1
1847	18.5
1848	15.4
1849	17.9
1850	12.2

The number of deaths during the Famine has variously been calculated as lying between half a million and one and a half million fatalities. The correct number probably lies in between. It is more generally accepted that in the region of one million people died during these years. Excess mortality as a result of the Famine, however, did not end in 1851. In addition to deaths, the Famine also contributed to a decrease in the birthrate, by contributing to a decline in the rate of marriage and in the the level of fertility and fecundity. The number of deaths in Ireland in 1847 was double the number in the previous year. This increase in mortality affected all parts of Ireland. The high rates of mortality were not prolonged and some areas in Ulster and the east coast showed signs of recovery in 1848, which was maintained despite the reappearance of blight in the same year. By this time, the local economies were recovering from the temporary industrial dislocation apparent in 1847. In parts of the west, however, mortality remained high and reached a second peak in 1849, a cholera epidemic providing the final, fatal blow to an already vulnerable people.[140]

Mortality was particularly severe in the first three months of 1847, peaking in March and then starting a slow decline after April. This peak coincided with public works being used as the main vehicle for relief and is a clear testament to the failure of this system. The continuing high mortality of April and May 1847 coincides with the period during which public works were being wound down, even though their replacement was not always available. After May, the level of mortality began to decrease significantly, although it remained higher than its pre-Famine levels. This reduction is generally associated with the opening of soup kitchens in the summer of 1847 and the relatively generous provision of relief. The impact of mortality was most severe among the lowest economic and social groups within Ireland—those who, lacking their own capital resources, depended on external assistance for relief. The most vulnerable individuals within this group were children under five, old people and pregnant and lactating women. Overall, however, women tended to be more resilient than men to the effects of the Famine.[141]

At the end of March 1847, Lord George Bentinck, leader of the Tory opposition, questioned the government regarding the number of deaths in Ireland and accused the Whigs of attempting to conceal the truth. No official figures had been released to parliament, although he suspected that there were:

> . . . tens of thousands and hundreds of thousands of deaths—they could not learn from the government how many, for there was one point about which the government were totally ignorant or which they concealed, which was the mortality which had occurred during their administration of Irish affairs.

Bentinck continued by attacking an underlying economic philosophy of the government:

> They know the people have been dying by their thousands and I dare them to enquire what has been the number of those who have died through their mismanagement, by their principles of free trade. Yes, free trade in the lives of the Irish people.

In a private communication to the chairman of the Limerick Assizes, Bentinck laid blame for the high levels of mortality on the Whig administration's dogmatic pursuit of *laissez faire*, concluding that, 'the British government, reined, curbed, and ridden by political economists, stands alone in its unnatural, unwise, impolitic and disastrous resolves'.[142]

Various analyses have sought to explore a general correlation between areas in which during the Famine years there was a high level of distress and areas which suffered from high rates of mortality. The areas which were most vulnerable to Famine mortality appear to be those that had experienced the most consistent poverty prior to 1845. This poverty was indicated for example by a low Poor Law valuation, small farms, few capital resources, and a high level of dependency on the potato. These areas, which were concentrated in the west of Ireland but included also pockets of distress in other counties, tended to be most vulnerable to the inadequacy of the government's relief systems following a second year of potato blight. In 1847, the median rate of mortality for each county was 2.6 per cent. The median is the middle value of a range of numbers. For a simple comparison of the ranking of county mortality rates, the median allows avoidance of some of the difficulties associated with other measures, for example the weighted mean. The counties (not including the towns) which exceeded this national average are shown in Table 15.

Table 15: Mortality in 1847 as a Percentage of 1841 Population: counties[143]

County	%
Armagh	3.3
Clare	3.6
Cork, East Riding	5.0
Cork, West Riding	3.3
Fermanagh	3.2
Galway	3.0
Kerry	3.1
Leitrim	3.9
Longford	3.0
Louth	3.1
Queen's County	3.0
Roscommon	3.1
Tipperary, North Riding	4.2
Tipperary, South Riding	4.1
Waterford	3.3

This expression of vulnerability was, however, mitigated in areas where the relief mechanisms—either public, private or individual—were effective. Thus, in counties Donegal (2.4 per cent mortality), Tyrone (2.3 per cent mortality) and Londonderry (2.3 per cent mortality), areas in which landlord activity had been remarked upon, the rates of mortality were lower than the median rate for the country as a whole. In these counties, it is possible that actions of landlords helped to keep rates below the national average, by providing relief and avoiding eviction. An example is the Dunfanaghy union in Co. Donegal which had one of the lowest Poor Law valuations in the country. During the winter of 1846–7, high levels of distress were recorded in the union.[144] Despite this, some of the electoral divisions in the west of the union actually recorded an increase in population between 1841 and 1851.[145] The presence of a resident landlord class which was actively involved in the provision of relief would appear to have been significant. In addition, seasonal migration to Scotland continued, especially after 1847 when the Scottish economy began to improve in the wake of a number of poor harvests.[146]

Table 16: Mortality in 1847 as a Percentage of 1841 Population: towns

Town	%
Belfast	6.9
Cork	5.5
Galway	11.1
Limerick	7.0

Mortality in towns was exceptionally high in 1847. For example, on the same basis of calculation as for counties, Belfast recorded 6.9% mortality, Cork 5.5% and Galway 11.1%. In periods of distress, there was traditionally an exodus to the towns. Some went in search of work or relief, others emigrated. The fact that the 1838 Poor Law Act had not included a Law of Settlement meant that relief provided by the Poor Law did not depend on length of residency within a district. The day asylum in Belfast admitted 569 people in one day alone, three-quarters of whom were reported to be from the south and west of Ireland. The crowding of people into districts which were already congested and impoverished placed further demands on the relief available, particularly in the workhouses and hospitals, and this facilitated the spread of disease. Mortality in the Irish workhouses rose to 2,706 inmates during the week ending 3 April 1847, compared with 159 deaths for the same period in the previous year.[147] Disease, in fact, accounted for many more fatalities during the Famine than deaths from starvation, although the two are inextricably linked. Nor was the risk of infection from diseases such as fever confined only to the poorest classes. Many boards of guardians began to hold their weekly meetings at a distance from the workhouse. Other people who were more directly involved in providing relief were less fortunate and numerous medical officers, relief administrators and members of the clergy died whilst tending to the poor and sick.[148] In February 1847, the Board of Health was reappointed, but although they appointed overseers for the largest towns to check for cleanliness and the existence of disease, they made little impact and reports of cases of dysentery and fever continued to increase until June 1847.[149] In Belfast the local fever hospital, which had been built to house 150 patients, contained 400 people and its administrators informed would-be applicants that its 'doors are shut'. A local newspaper warned:

> Fever is spreading with a rapidity which leaves scarcely a chance of its being overtaken without a strenuous and unanimous effort, and it is certain that in so spreading it will not confine its ravages to the poor alone.[150]

In the town of Galway, there were reports of a virulent malignant typhus fever and spotted typhus. In Cork city, the spread of infectious diseases, thought to be brought in by migrants from the countryside, was rampant, much to the consternation of the residents. The mayor requested that a proclamation be implemented for the exclusion of infected persons from the city. Following this, men were employed to stand at the city gates to prevent the further influx of paupers from the countryside. Even this did not prove to be a totally effective deterrent:

> Poor wretches come from the country in multitudes and it is said that they linger about the suburbs until the evening and then carry in their famine and disease under the cover of dark . . . many cases lay themselves down and die . . . but though they thus pass away, they leave behind them the pestilential influences under which they at last sank.[151]

The volume of migrants to Cork did not reduce significantly and in May 1847, there were an estimated 20,000 'strangers' in the city.[152] The volume of mortalities also provided the authorities with a further problem regarding the burial of the dead. In Cork city, the presence of dead bodies in the street had become a frequent sight. One of the local newspapers described a common burial scene:

A hearse piled with coffins—or rather undressed boards slightly nailed together—passed this office today unaccompanied by a single human being, save the driver of the vehicle.[153]

Some of the smaller towns in the west of Ireland were experiencing similar problems. In Tralee, Co. Kerry, for example, a visitor was informed that the local distress was 'quite beyond their means of relief' even though the town was situated on the estate of 'a rich, unencumbered landlord who draws about £12,000 a year out of it but whose subscription for the relief of his starving tenants was paltry in the extreme'. He further observed:

While I write this note, there is a child about five years old lying dead in the main street of Tralee opposite the windows of the principal hotel, and the remains have lain there several hours on a few stones by the side of a footway like a dead dog.

During the early months of 1847 also, reports of dogs eating the flesh of dead bodies became commonplace.[154] The sudden withdrawal of the customary diet of many Irish people and its replacement by far less nutritious fare undoubtedly contributed to the spread of epidemic diseases such as fever, typhus, diarrhoea and cholera. The number of vitamin deficiency diseases such as scurvy, pellagra, and xerophthalmia (commonly referred to as ophthalmia) also increased.[155] During the Famine, epidemic diseases were a far greater cause of the loss of life than diseases caused by starvation.

The link between famine and infectious diseases is a complex one: people suffering from malnutrition are more susceptible to the development of such diseases and once caught, tend to develop a more severe form of the disease than would otherwise be the case. As a result, people suffering from malnutrition have a higher propensity to die from such diseases. Their spread was also facilitated by the social dislocation which accompanies any period of distress, such as overcrowding, queuing and lack of sanitation; all facilitate the transmission of such diseases.[156] In the winter of 1846–7, many factors were present simultaneously, exacerbating the transmisson of disease and increasing the people's vulnerability to infection. A medical superintendent in Crossmaglen in Co. Armagh warned the local landed proprietors of the reasons for the increase in mortality caused by fever and dysentery in his district in terms applicable to many parts of Ireland:

Dysentery prevails to an alarming extent . . . The causes of dysentery are well known: exposure to the cold and wet, improper food, want of clothing . . . But a great source of dysentery in this locality during the winter months was where persons on the public works were exposed to the inclemency of the weather from want of clothing . . . Fever of a low type is increasing also. Unfortunately, in many cases, the poor have not sufficient nutriment to assist their recovery. Want of cleanliness and the effluvia arising from the decomposition of putrid animal and vegetable substance assisted by cold are the most common causes of fever.[157]

The potato blight of 1845 and 1846 deprived many Irish people of their staple food and forced them to depend on external assistance. Sometimes, this proved elusive. But even for those who did obtain relief in the winter of 1846–7, there was no guarantee of survival. As food prices soared at the end of 1846, relief was often inadequate and mostly only given in return for hard, physical labour. Labour on the public works was increasingly undertaken by women, children, the old and the infirm during periods of severe weather, including prolonged snow falls, often while wearing inadequate clothing. The replacement of potatoes by stirabout or increasingly by watery soup deprived the Irish people of many of the essential proteins, vitamins, fats and minerals, in the correct proportions, necessary to maintain health and which they had been accustomed to in the years prior to the appearance of blight.[158] Adults who had, prior to 1845, an average daily intake of ten to twelve pounds of potatoes and buttermilk during the winter months were expected in 1846–7 to survive on one pound of Indian meal daily or one bowl of soup and a piece of bread. The high mortality at the beginning of 1847 was due to the fact that the relief system had failed to deliver even this minimum to an already famished and debilitated people.

Expedients Well Nigh Exhausted

1847–8

The third consecutive year of Famine distress in Ireland coincided with an extension of Treasury control over the mechanisms as well as the finances of social policy. The philosophy of referring to the Famine as being 'over' and stating that any on-going distress was a local problem that should be resolved locally, indicated a further distancing of the central government from the provision of relief. At the same time, a renewed emphasis upon the restructuring of agricultural holdings became more central to the official response to the Famine. All of these strands of thinking had been evident in the previous two years. However, a strengthened position of Wood and Trevelyan in the Treasury, and a general lack of sympathy in Britain for Irish distress, facilitated the enactment of a significantly more rigorous approach to relief policy.

Central to this opportunity for economic orthodoxy in Ireland was an increasing focus on the Poor Law and its institutions as the most important mechanism for forcing the local rates to pay for the local impact of the Famine. The implications of this policy included the collection of escalating levels of poor rates to pay both for current relief and to meet the cost of past government loans for relief. Pressure on the Poor Law, landlords, tenants, and the destitute themselves was a feature of this year of intensifying retrenchment.

The failure of the government's relief policies in the winter of 1846–7 resulted in a change of emphasis in the provision of relief. Public works were no longer to be the primary means of alleviating distress as the idea of providing relief in return for labour had been discredited. The local

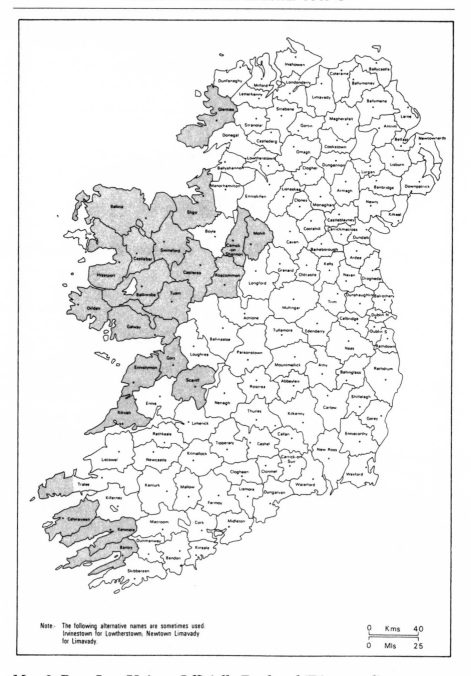

Note:- The following alternative names are sometimes used:
Irvinestown for Lowtherstown; Newtown Limavady
for Limavady.

Map 2: Poor Law Unions Officially Declared 'Distressed'
Ballina, Ballinrobe, Bantry, Cahirsiveen, Castlebar, Castlerea, Clifden, Dingle (part of Tralee Union), Ennistymon, Galway, Glenties, Gort, Kenmare, Kilrush, Mohill, Roscommon, Scariff, Sligo, Swinford, Tuam, Westport, Carrick-on-Shannon

relief committees, frequently the object of derision by members of the government, were also to be disbanded. Instead, the administration of relief was to be channelled through the medium of the local Poor Law. Each board of guardians was to be responsible for the provision of all relief within their union. Local responsibility was further reinforced by the manner in which relief was to be financed. Each Poor Law union, through the mechanism of levying poor rates, was to be responsible for the relief of all distress within the union. The only exception to this was twenty-two unions situated along the western seaboard that were officially designated 'distressed', in recognition of the fact that they would probably require external financial assistance in the approaching year. The 'distressed' unions were Ballina, Ballinrobe, Bantry, Cahirciveen, Carrick-on-Shannon, Castlebar, Castlerea, Clifden, Dingle, Ennistymon, Galway, Glenties, Gort, Kenmare, Kilrush, Mohill, Roscommon, Scariff, Sligo, Swinford, Tuam, Westport, all of which were situated in the west of the country (see map).

The transfer to Poor Law relief in August 1847 marked an end to the various temporary measures which had been employed by the government with varying degrees of success in the previous two years. Instead, both ordinary and extraordinary distress were amalgamated and made the responsibility of the Poor Law. The original Poor Law Act of 1838 had to be considerably extended to make this possible. This was a significant step towards the government's aim of making relief as local a responsibility as possible, rather than a charge on the national or even imperial revenue. At the same time, by making relief a local charge, the government was able to realise the long-held aspiration that Irish property should support Irish poverty.

The type of relief envisaged to combat distress after the autumn of 1847 had been decided even before the extent of the crop yield was known. In general, the harvest of 1847 was a healthy one and in many parts of the country the potatoes were completely free from blight. Large quantities of food, including Indian meal, had been imported into the country during the spring and summer which had resulted in a drop in food prices. Unfortunately, however, as the government had anticipated, the extent of potatoes sown in some districts was considerably less than usual. This meant that only a small quantity of potatoes were available for consumption, whilst those that were sold in the markets were expensive and beyond the reach of the peasantry and even those in low paid employment.

In 1847–8 the demand for relief was less uniform than it had been in 1846–7. In 1847–8, in the districts where employment was available and food prices low, labourers were in a stronger economic position than in any year since the first appearance of the blight. In contrast, in areas where there was little employment and potatoes were scarce, the population was unlikely to have the resources to avail of the cheap, imported food. In these areas, a third year of distress was inevitable. However, in spite of the government's recognition that famine was going to continue in at least twenty-two unions, the official picture presented by some people involved in the relief operations was that the Famine was over.[1] It is perhaps no coincidence that much of the fund-raising which was previously evident was greatly reduced after this period, thus reinforcing dependence on local resources.

British public opinion was largely in favour of the transfer of fiscal responsibility from the Treasury to the local unions. There was a general belief—which was reinforced by the columns of *The Times* and *Punch*—that the Irish were insufficiently grateful for the assistance which they had received from Britain during the previous two years. Moreover, by permitting this dependence to continue, the Irish would never develop the habits of self-reliance which were venerated by the framers of the government's relief policies. In the general election which had taken place during the summer of 1847, an increased number of Repeal candidates had been returned in Ireland. One supporter of the Whig party described the election result as an act of disloyalty, coming as it did:

> just after two or three millions of Irish have been saved from famine and pestilence by money which, if the Union had not existed, their own parliament would never have been able to raise. This is not natural.[2]

The results of the 1847 General Election were to have important implications for subsequent relief policies in Ireland. Much of Russell's support was eroded as the balance of power moved away from the traditional Whig aristocrats to middle-class radicals led by Cobden and Bright, the former leaders of the Anti-Corn Law League. As a consequence, those members of the Whig administration, including Russell himself, who were sympathetic to a continuation of limited intervention in Ireland were outnumbered by supporters of non-intervention. This latter philosophy had the support of a number of key members of the government, including Charles Wood and Lord Clarendon (the Lord Lieutenant of Ireland). It also had the support of the influential Irish landlord, Lord Lansdowne, who was regarded as particularly valuable on the grounds that 'he knows Adam Smith and Ireland'. Russell, on the other hand, was increasingly isolated within his own party. His main ally, Lord Bessborough, the former Lord Lieutenant of Ireland, had died in May 1847 and Russell had reluctantly appointed Clarendon in his place. The resultant policy conflicts between Russell and Clarendon in the latter part of 1847 further weakened Russell's position.

A further significant factor which helped to determine the provision of relief after 1847 was the state of the money market in Britain. The 1847 harvest in many parts of Europe, including Britain, was poor. This coincided with a short-lived depression in a number of British industries and a run on the Bank of England which resulted in a temporary embargo on the issue of money. These events contributed to a short-term, yet severe, financial and monetary crisis in Britain in the autumn of 1847, just as the new Poor Law was becoming operative. This crisis, brief though it was, contributed to a determination that Ireland should not be allowed to make further demands on an already hard-pressed Treasury. There is some evidence, however, that Wood and Trevelyan used the financial crisis as an opportunity to exercise more personal control over various aspects of social policy—both English and Irish. George Cornewall Lewis asserted, 'Economy is the order of the day in all public departments. The Treasury thinks a grant of £100 is now a great concession to anybody . . . The demand for retrenchment is now the public cry.' The demand for financial retrenchment and 'cheap government' was popular in Britain and, ironically, it was most closely associated with Peel's policies of fiscal rectitude. During its one year in power, Russell's administration had gained a reputation for high expenditure on a wide range of social issues. In Ireland, over £4,000,000 had been spent on public works alone (although much of this was initially provided as a loan), and this was generally considered to have been largely squandered, providing neither long-term benefit to Ireland, nor short-term relief to the poor.

Within Ireland, Clarendon used the financial crisis to justify a new spirit of retrenchment in the relief policies of the government, emphasising at the same time the concurrent suffering of the English working classes. He explained to a meeting of landlords and large farmers in Galway that:

> The government, as guardians of the public purse, and bound to watch alike over the interest of the whole community, must necessarily find itself incapacitated from doing all that under more prosperous circumstances it would desire, and would think it a duty to do for Ireland.[3]

Trevelyan was a vociferous advocate of transferring the financial burden for relief to the Poor Law. He felt that by placing the responsibility upon the local ratepayers, fewer instances of abuse and over-spending were likely to occur. Trevelyan, a disciple of both Adam Smith and Edmund Burke, sent copies of their writings to relief officers in Ireland, recommending them to read them when sick or on holiday. Like Smith and Burke, he regarded gratuitous relief during a period of sustained distress as having a demoralising effect on the recipients. He believed that the only way to bring this dependence to an end was by making local landlords financially responsible for providing relief and, at the same time, to make relief so unpalatable that only the genuinely destitute would avail of it. The Poor Law, with a similar underlying ethos, was considered to provide an ideal mechanism for relieving the continuing distress within Ireland. In his book, *The Irish Crisis*, published in 1848 when he officially proclaimed the Famine to be over, Trevelyan accused the Irish landlords of selfishness, neglect and apathy. The transfer of Poor Law relief would end this dereliction of duty and force them to realise that property had its duty as well as its rights. Furthermore, Trevelyan believed that poor rates, if rigorously collected, would act as a tax on absenteeism by providing landlords with a direct incentive to reside, or at least take an interest in, the affairs of their estates. If they were not willing to do so, he recommended that they should sell their property to men of capital and energy who would take an interest.[4] The idea of using the Poor Law as a means for bringing about social reform within Ireland was not new, but had been suggested by George Nicholls in 1837 and 1838.[5] Following the introduction of the Amendment Act in August 1847, it was to play a significant part in shaping the way in which relief was provided.

To facilitate the transfer to Poor Law relief, it was necessary to extend the provisions of the original 1838 Act which had stipulated that relief could only be provided to inmates of a workhouse.[6] Outdoor relief, that is, relief provided outside the workhouse, was expressly forbidden. The criteria for receiving workhouse relief was that the recipients were destitute and entered the establishment in entire family units. Within the workhouse, life was to be 'less eligible' than life outside, through the adoption of an inferior and monotonous diet and the enforcement of discipline, regimentation and labour. This constituted what was known as the 'workhouse test', the purpose of which was to deter all but the genuinely destitute from applying. The workhouses had been originally built to accommodate 100,000 inmates, or just over 1 per cent of the population. Although accommodation had been extended throughout 1846,

Irish workhouses could still only accommodate 157,977 inmates, which fell far short of the three million people who had received relief during the summer from the government soup kitchens.

The transfer to Poor Law relief was achieved through the introduction of three new pieces of legislation in June and July 1847.[7] The Poor Law Amendment Act of 1847 allowed outdoor relief, subject to various conditions, to be provided for the first time by the Poor Law. It recognised the right of certain groups to relief either inside or outside the workhouses. This category included persons disabled by old age or infirmity, destitute persons who, due to ill health, were unable to work, orphans and destitute widows who had two or more legitimate children dependent upon them. Able-bodied persons who were destitute could only receive outdoor relief as a last resort, and only if the workhouse was full or unable to accommodate them. Outdoor relief could only be provided upon the issue of a Sealed Order by the Poor Law Commissioners, and for no longer than two months. As far as possible also, it was to be provided in the form of cooked food. The Commissioners hoped that it would not be necessary to issue many Sealed Orders but recommended that, as far as possible, the guardians should acquire additional accommodation and empty their workhouses of the infirm, the sick and the old (the so-called 'impotent poor') to make room for the able-bodied destitute.[8] The most notorious section of the 1847 Amendment Act was the 'Gregory' or 'Quarter Acre Clause', which stated that any occupier of more than a quarter of an acre of land could not be deemed destitute and therefore was ineligible to receive relief paid for by the poor rates.[9] Simultaneously, an Act was passed for the punishment of vagrants which also provided for the conviction of persons who had neglected to maintain their wives and children.[10]

The Poor Law Extension Act altered the structure of the Poor Law Commission and provided for the establishment of a separate authority in Ireland, with autonomy from the Poor Law Board in England. This separation gave official recognition to what was, in fact, already a reality as the English Commissioners had never taken an interest in the affairs of Dublin and the two Boards had rarely communicated with each other.[11] Edward Twistleton, the resident Commissioner in Ireland, was to continue in office as Chief Commissioner. Twistleton approved of the separation from the English board. He believed that as the provisions of the Irish Poor Law were more stringent than those of its English counterpart, it was embarassing for the English board even nominally to continue in control of the Irish Poor Law.[12] Twistleton was joined in the new Commission by the Chief Secretary, Sir William Somerville, the

Under-Secretary, Thomas Redington, and Alfred Power, an English Poor Law official who was appointed Assistant Commissioner. This Board was to meet daily in the Dublin Castle headquarters of the Irish Executive. Continuity was maintained through the continued involvement and increased prominence of the Treasury, notably Charles Trevelyan, in the provision of poor relief.[13]

This role was adopted with relish and enthusiasm by Trevelyan. If his outspokeness and lack of tact occasionally offended more senior members of the government, no one could doubt his efficiency and dedication to the cause of Irish distress. The Whig administration, in particular the Chancellor of the Exchequer, Wood, realised that with Trevelyan at the helm, the relief policies would be implemented dispassionately and with an absence of lavishness or sentimentality. This confidence was shared by members of the Irish Executive in Dublin. As the third year of distress commenced, the Lord Lieutenant urged Trevelyan to take care of his health, 'as I don't exactly see how the public can get on without you'.[14] To the officers in charge of implementing the various relief policies, notably Routh and Twistleton, Trevelyan's interest increasingly bordered on over-interference. He insisted on communicating with the officers in the field directly, urging them to be frank with him, rather than going through the channel of the central Commissioners. This resulted in Routh's wry response, when asked for some details regarding the implementation of the government's policies, that Trevelyan was better informed than he was on all such matters regarding relief. Trevelyan's self-importance was clearly demonstrated in October 1847 when he wrote to *The Times*—without any prior consultation with his colleagues or superiors—and urged them to publish a letter from Burgoyne, the Relief Commissioner, explaining the need for further assistance to Ireland. Trevelyan used this opportunity to promote his own views on Ireland—'my principal study for a long time past'. He explained that limited financial assistance was necessary if the economy of Ireland was ever to be reformed, because:

> The change from an idle, barbarous isolated potato cultivation, to corn cultivation, which frees industry, and binds together employer and employee in mutually beneficial relations . . . requires capital and a new class of men.[15]

The transfer to Poor Law relief coincided with an apparent hardening in the attitude of some British officials towards Irish distress. To a large extent, however, the Amendment Act consolidated certain strands which were already evident early in 1847. This legislation marked the final stage in the shift from central to local responsibility. The local Poor Law administration was given a more central role to play, reflecting the belief that as the potato blight was essentially a local disaster, its cure should be financed from local resources. The 1847 Amendment Act, therefore, gave official recognition to the idea that relief of distress was a local rather than a British or even an imperial responsibility. Also, although outdoor relief was to be allowed to continue after the harvest of 1847, it was hoped that by bringing it under the umbrella of the Poor Law administration, it would be more closely regulated and tests of destitution more rigorously enforced. It was anticipated that the change of policy would bring about an immediate reduction in the applicants for outdoor relief. Twistleton described the intentions of the legislature when framing the Amendment Act as being 'to extinguish such relief as soon as possible; merely to tolerate it for a time when deaths from starvation could not be prevented without it, and ultimately to extinguish it'.[16]

The Whig administration realised that the transition to Poor Law relief, particularly when the financial implications of it became evident, would not be achieved without a struggle. Many Irish members of parliament were opposed to an extension of the permanent Poor Law, arguing that the increased tax burden as a result of outdoor relief would ruin them financially. Henry Grattan MP blamed the change of policy on the fact that 'the Lord Lieutenant had no power and Downing Street had no heart'. Within the British government, however, there was a general consensus that after two years of distress and financial dependence on the state, a firm resolve was required to force the Irish people to depend on their own resources. Russell, the Prime Minister, did have some reservations. He was apprehensive that unless a determined effort was made to support the Poor Law, 'we shall utterly fail from not getting a wind to take it out of harbour'.[17] He predicted that when the ratepayers realised that they would be financing all relief, 'The relief lists will be cut considerably. In fact, it will be a fight between Landlord, Tenant and Co. versus Priest, Labourer, Burgoyne and Co'.[18]

It was also anticipated that Poor Law relief would be unpopular with the recipients. Under both the Labour Rate and Temporary Relief Acts, many poor people were believed to have hidden some of their resources, but a well regulated Poor Law made this difficult.[19] Again, the character of the people was cited both as a justification for a stringent application of relief and for the need for social change. One government officer blamed the failure of the various relief policies on the fact that, 'Outside Dublin, the country is uncivilised'.[20] The Inspector of the Granard union took a cynical view of the condition of the small occupiers in his district, informing the Commisioners that:

> The whole of them, with a few exceptions are, as usual, idle, reckless, lazy and improvident; many of them I could see as I passed along sitting idly smoking on the back of a ditch, without making the slightest attempt even at digging their gardens. They appear to depend on some future contingency like the public works or a temporary relief measure, to feed themselves and their families.[21]

Lord Clarendon, who had been appointed Lord Lieutenant in May 1847, agreed that many people were 'utterly demoralised' by two years of living from charity, and anticipated a number of outbreaks of violence. He attributed this to the fact that in areas of high distress, the population was idle and showed a complete lack of any industrial habits. Clarendon hoped that the government's policies would result in a change in the entire social system which would bring to an end the dependent condition of the Irish people.[22]

During the summer of 1847, the boards of guardians were repeatedly advised to prepare for their new responsibilities by finding additional accommodation and reviewing their stocks of bedding and clothing. As each local union was to be financially responsible for maintaining the destitute within their union, they were urged to make adequate rates, not only to finance an increase in relief expenditure, but also for the repayment of the various government loans.[23] In recognition of the increased duties devolving on the Poor Law, the number of Assistant Commissioners—now to be called Poor Law Inspectors—was increased from five to nine. For the most part, the new Inspectors were men who had been employed as officers under the Labour Rate Act. Within the local unions, the Act also provided for the appointment of new officials known as Relieving Officers. The guardians were directed to appoint these officers as soon as possible. Even in the unions where it seemed unlikely that outdoor relief would be required, the Commissioners recommended that at least one of these officers should be employed, in order that relief could be provided immediately in cases of emergency.

The main duty of the Relieving Officers was to compile lists of applicants for relief for the perusal of the guardians. In cases of urgent necessity, the Relieving Officers could provide immediate, provisional relief.[24] A number of the more prosperous unions in the north and east of the country regarded the cost of appointing a Relieving Officer as an unnecessary charge on the ratepayers. The boards of guardians of the

Antrim, Downpatrick, Inishowen, Larne, Lisburn, Lurgan and Newtownards unions refused to appoint a Relieving Officer as they did not anticipate that it would be necessary for outdoor relief to be provided. In these and other cases where the guardians refused to appoint a Relieving Officer, the Commissioners threatened to instruct Law Agents to proceed against the boards for neglect of duty. As a result of this threat, the majority of guardians acquiesced although, as late as May 1848, the Commissioners were taking legal action against some recalcitrant boards.[25]

Financing the Poor Law

The effectiveness of the Poor Law and the ultimate success of the government's new policy largely depended upon the levying and collection of adequate poor rates. If Irish property was truly to be made to support Irish distress—both ordinary and extraordinary—the income from the poor rates needed to be higher than had previously been the case. As a consequence of this, any problems in the collection of rates was taken seriously by both the government and the Poor Law Commissioners. Many local relief administrators, however, were apprehensive about the financial implications of transferring to Poor Law relief in the autumn of 1847. They pointed to the fact that some unions had no funds in hand and that the means at the disposal of the local ratepayers was exhausted. A number of guardians suggested that the soup kitchens should be allowed to remain open. The government was adamant that this should not be the case; they believed that they had already contributed substantially to Irish relief and it was now the turn of the Irish ratepayers. The Relief Commissioners responded to the requests of the guardians by publishing a letter in the national newspapers which stated that:

> The Temporary Relief Act was passed, not as a remedy for any embarrassments in the unions, nor for any general poverty in the country, but solely to replace, for one season, the food of which the people were deprived by the failure of the potato crop.[26]

The government was willing to provide a reduced form of relief during an interim period to the most distressed unions but, overall, the local ratepayers were to make greater exertions than had previously been the case. Also, the money distributed by the government following the harvest of 1847 was, as far as possible, to be drawn from the funds of the British Relief Association rather than from the imperial Treasury.[27]

As early as May 1847, a new stridency was apparent in the attitude of the various officials regarding the collection of the poor rates. The Poor Law Commissioners, acting on the advice of the Lord Lieutenant, issued a series of directives to each board of guardians concerning the future handling of this matter. The guardians were ordered to commence preparations immediately for the levying of the harvest rates. When the rate collection started, they were to show an active interest in the amounts which had been paid and who had paid them. The collectors' ratebooks were to be examined more frequently than had previously been the case. The Commissioners also recommended that rates should, in the first instance, be obtained from the gentry and largest ratepayers. The guardians were advised to publish the names of the ten highest defaulters in an attempt to embarrass them into paying. The police and the military were also to be made available if necessary to enforce the collection.[28]

As the paucity of the 1847 harvest became more obvious, the government officials in Ireland responsible for the implementation of the new relief policies were increasingly apprehensive about the ability of some of the unions to finance the requisite amount of relief. Even Clarendon suggested that the guardians should be allowed a 'liberal extension' of the time required to repay all government advances. The Chief Secretary, in a frank admission to Trevelyan, confessed that he found the prospect of providing relief through the machinery of the Poor Law as the season progressed 'terrifying'.[29] Twistleton was also increasingly pessimistic. Although he was willing to enforce the collection of rates to the utmost of his ability, he increasingly believed that this money alone would not be sufficient. He anticipated a continuation of deaths from starvation for which, he believed, he would be held responsible.

Because Irish distress had attracted so much negative publicity Burgoyne, the Relief Commissioner, felt compelled to write to *The Times* and point out that 'Absolute famine still stares whole communities in the face'. In the long term, he believed that the new Poor Law would help to make Ireland self-supporting, but in the short term, he asked for further financial assistance. Significantly, the letter was timed to be printed a few days before the second Queen's Letter was published, appealing for subscriptions for Ireland. Although these sentiments were endorsed in a separate letter by Trevelyan, their impact on British public opinion appears to have been negligible. Within the columns of *The Times*, Burgoyne's letter initiated a backlash against Irish relief, in which the distress was blamed repeatedly on the population's lack of 'industry and enterprise'. Nor was this attitude confined to the British press. A German newspaper, the *Frankfurter Allegemeine Zeitung*, described the Irish people as 'lawless and ungrateful', and predicted that no matter how much was done to help them, they would 'criticise the begging box tomorrow'.[30]

Regardless of the personal disquiet of the Irish Poor Law Commissioners concerning the finances of the local unions, they mounted a relentless campaign to enforce as high a collection as possible in the months following the introduction of the Amendment Act. Guardians who did not comply with the high expectations of the Commissioners were frequently replaced with vice-guardians, who were paid officials employed by the Commissioners.

The Commissioners employed a variety of tactics to ensure a vigorous collection of rates in each union. Even the unions which had been officially declared 'distressed' were not to be allowed any advances until the Treasury was satisfied that they had exhausted their rate collection. The demands for external financial assistance came from these unions even sooner than the government had anticipated. At the beginning of September 1847, the Ballinrobe union in Co. Mayo was so deeply in debt that the local sheriff seized the property of the workhouse and threatened to sell it.[31] The neighbouring unions of Castlebar and Westport had also financially collapsed and were seeking assistance from the government.

The Poor Law Commissioners were anxious to nip such demands in the bud by making an example of these unions. The three boards of guardians were dissolved and the newly-installed vice-guardians of the Ballinrobe, Castlebar and Westport unions were told that it was essential 'to the interests of the Empire' that even in these impoverished unions sufficient rates should be collected to relieve the local destitution.[32] When, in October, it proved essential to give an advance of £100 to the Glenties union in Co. Donegal, it was stipulated that this money was only to be used to prevent actual starvation, and even then only with 'the utmost secrecy'.[33]

The unions which had been officially designated 'distressed' were not the only ones to require external assistance during the harvest period. In the Granard union, in Co. Longford, the local Poor Law Inspector warned the Commissioners that if advances stopped even for a short period, all relief would cease and deaths from starvation would follow.[34] Twistleton, although anxious to prevent any further deaths from starvation, was afraid that if it became generally known that the government was providing advances to a number of unions which had not been declared distressed, other boards of guardians might be encouraged to relax their exertions in the collection of rates.[35] Advances were made, therefore, only if there was evidence that the guardians had made an 'increased and vigorous' effort to collect the rates. At the same time, the

Commissioners stipulated that applications for a loan were to be accompanied by a statement of the people whose rates were outstanding and the methods which had been employed to enforce their collection. Also, all loans were to be repaid at the first possible opportunity.[36]

Many boards of guardians viewed their role in the new relief measures with alarm. This was particularly true in the impoverished western unions where the poor rates were already the highest in the country. Although in the first two years of distress, the Poor Law had only been designated a subsidiary role in the provision of relief, the shortcomings of the other relief measures had placed an unexpected strain on its resources. Consequently, the workhouses had played a vital, if undervalued, role during these years. In addition to the ordinary Poor Law expenses, after August 1847, the guardians were also expected to levy taxes for the repayment of earlier loans from the Treasury. The regressive fiscal nature of the various policies introduced by the government meant, in fact, that the unions which experienced the highest level of destitution were liable to pay the largest amount of taxes. In the unions of Ballina, Ballinrobe, Clifden, Kenmare and Westport, the rates for ordinary relief were in excess of 10s in the pound, and in the Scariff union as high as 12s 6d in the pound. The guardians of the Kenmare union claimed that local rates alone would be insufficient even to pay for the current expenses of the union. They appealed to the government to re-introduce public works into the area.[37] The Ballina guardians warned that although they had exhorted the local ratepayers to pay as much as was 'humanly possible', they believed their income would still be insufficient and feared that they might be forced to close the workhouse. Again, these difficulties were not confined to only the distressed unions. The Dunshaughlin, Enniscorthy, Inishowen, Lowtherstown, Rathdown, Trim and Wexford guardians were amongst the boards that passed resolutions stating that they would be unable to meet the repayments for the Temporary Relief Acts. Increasingly, the Commissioners threatened the dissolution of boards of guardians which refused to strike adequate rates.[38]

In Co. Tipperary, the guardians of five local unions—none of which had been designated 'distressed'—met to discuss the weight of taxation on their unions. They agreed that if taxes were imposed for the repayment of all outstanding loans—for advances made under the Temporary Relief Act, for workhouse construction and for public works loans—and if this were followed by an increase in the poor rates, then the whole produce of the land would be swallowed up. They suggested that the government should instead introduce a system of relief which provided employment and assisted emigration. The Fermoy guardians were also critical of the latest government policy as it placed a punitive burden on the local ratepayers. They recommended that the Imperial Treasury should bear the cost of all previous relief measures which would leave the poor rates free to finance current pauperism. The Enniskillen guardians were also critical of the government's handling of the relief operations. They suggested that the Treasury should wait until the country had recovered from the impact of the blight before any repayments were demanded.[39]

Initially, the Treasury insisted that the repayment for the advances for the Temporary Relief Act were to be included in the 1847 harvest rate. The smallness of the 1847 harvest, however, together with the insolvency of some local unions, resulted in a re-scheduling of the repayments. None were demanded before 1 January 1848. As a further concession, if the rate for ordinary expenditure exceeded 3s in the pound, the repayments for the Temporary Relief Act would not be demanded immediately and an upper limit of 3s in the pound was also placed on these repayments. Furthermore, repayments for the presentments, or public works, were not to be demanded until Spring 1848. These concessions were allowed as the Treasury was anxious that the amended Poor Law should be seen to be working well during the first few months of its operation.[40] Not all boards of guardians, however, approved of these changes. The Omagh and Donegal guardians objected to the new ruling on the grounds that it was most beneficial to unions which had obtained large amounts of money from the government rather than those which had made an effort to rely on their own resources.[41] The Poor Law Commissioners agreed that it was often the case that the better managed unions were penalised rather than unions with lax administrations.[42]

The burden of repayments on the various unions varied considerably. The average rate of repayment per pound of Poor Law valuation for the Temporary Relief Act alone was 2s 6½d in the pound. Again, the unions in the west of the country made the highest repayments. In the Westport union, the repayments for the Temporary Relief Act alone were 22s 5d in the pound which exceeded the rate of valuation of the union. Within the province of Ulster, with the exception of a few unions, the repayments did not exceed 1s in the pound. Table 17 below shows the diversity in the level of repayments of the Temporary Relief Act within the country, using the example of the unions with the highest and lowest repayments. The Treasury had agreed, however, that a portion of the advances made for the opening of soup kitchens could be a grant, and no repayments for this purpose were to exceed 3s in the pound.

Table 17: Poundage Rating of Repayments for Loans Advanced Under Temporary Relief Act[43]

Union	Poundage Rate
Ballina	11s 11½ d
Castlebar	10s 8¼ d
Clifden	10s 9½ d
Kenmare	11s 5½ d
Swinford	16s 8¼ d
Westport	22s 5 d
⋮	
Ballymena	2 d
Celbridge	1½ d
Dunshaughlin	2½ d
Edenderry	2½ d
Kilkeel	1 d
Larne	0½ d

Some guardians were pessimistic about their ability to collect sufficient rates even for ordinary Poor Law purposes. Where land was valued under £4—as was the case in many western unions—the landlord was liable for the payment of the whole rate. This was a heavy burden on landlords whose property was much subdivided and had not yielded any rents since 1845. In the Swinford union, some landlords refused to pay the rates until payment of their rents had been secured.[44]

Increasingly after September 1847, a solution to the financial difficulties of some landlords was to evict tenants who occupied small holdings of land. In a number of unions, the increase in abandoned and empty farms and cabins made rate collection and the distraint of goods more difficult.[45] The Poor Law stipulated that in cases where farms or tenements were left vacant, the subsequent occupier was liable to pay all poor rates due as long as it was carried forward in the ratebooks as an arrear. The Assistant Commissioner, Alfred Power, believed that the carrying forward of this arrear was a disincentive to new tenants to occupy the property and suggested that such rates should be declared irrecoverable.[46] In some of the unions in the north-east of the country, where many of the small farmers supplemented their income with weaving, the guardians warned that if the rates became too high, the people would sell their looms, and thus become paupers themselves.[47] Even several of the newly-appointed vice-guardians admitted that they were experiencing problems in collecting the poor rates. The vice-guardians of the Ballinrobe, Castlebar and Westport unions echoed what had been pointed out already by the elected board of guardians, that the poverty of the local ratepayers made it impossible to collect a high rate. In a similar manner to their predecessors, they asked for the burden on the local taxpayers to be reduced.[48]

The reluctance of the ratepayers to pay such heavy rates was apparent in many unions. A number of guardians warned the Poor Law Commissioners that if they attempted to collect the requisite high rate, there would be a breakdown in law and order within their unions.[49] This was reflected in many unions where the rates were high and, in the months following the 1847 harvest, the Commissioners were informed of numerous instances of attempts to resist payment of rates, which occasionally involved physical attacks on the rate collectors.[50] Again, this was not confined to the poorest unions in the west of the country. In the Carrick-on-Shannon union, the guardians admitted that they were unable to find collectors who were willing to face the opprobrium of the local ratepayers. The vice-guardians of the Mohill union in Co. Leitrim also experienced difficulties in employing rate collectors. They attributed this to a number of factors:

> The extreme poverty of the area which, we regret to say, is retro-grading still further each day, every description of chattel property fast disappearing, its lawless state, the unusually high rates, and the previous irregular habits formed in meeting this species of demand, seem to deter proper persons from seeking the office, unallured by the extravagant rates of fees (two shillings in the pound) we offer. If we fail in this second effort, our expedients are well nigh exhausted.[51]

The majority of Poor Law Inspectors shared the pessimism of the guardians and vice-guardians. Joseph Burke, the Inspector in the south-east, agreed that the high rates made by the guardians would be impossible to collect. He warned the Commissioners that if they tried to force an additional collection for the repayment of the government loans, some boards of guardians would relinquish their duties and thus throw the whole burden for providing relief on the government.[52] The Inspector in Connacht attributed the difficulties in collecting the rates in his district to the diminished resources of the local landed proprietors. This was due to a fall in the income which they had derived from rents, combined with a large increase in local taxation.[53] Charles Crawford, the

Inspector in west Cork, believed that the high level of local taxation was self-perpetuating, as it was pauperising small occupiers who had previously paid rates and making them, in turn, dependent on the poor rates. Like many other Inspectors, he did not regard the Poor Law as a suitable method of providing relief on such a large scale.[54]

Notwithstanding the vicissitudes in the levying and collection of rates, the financial position of the Irish Poor Law unions did improve in the months following the 1847 harvest. In the twelve months ending December 1847 over £1m was collected in poor rates alone.[55] This was out of a total Poor Law valuation of just over £13m. Poor Law expenditure in 1847 amounted to approximately £1,700,000, leaving a relatively small short fall of £500,000. At the end of 1847, the financial position of the unions appeared stronger than ever before, with 119 out of 130 having balances in their favour. The unrelenting attitude of the government in making local rates responsible for local relief ostensibly was working. These figures, however, disguised the fact that many unions were still deeply in debt, owing money for the building of the workhouses, for the public work advances, for the Temporary Relief Acts and miscellaneous loans which had been made to the poorest unions. Arrears of poor rate were also far higher than they had been in the previous year. In December 1847, £890,639 of rates remained uncollected, compared with £243,384 in December 1846.[56] This figure did not include repayments for the Temporary Relief Act which were to commence in January 1848. By February 1848, all but six of the 127 unions which had participated in the scheme had made a rate for this purpose.[57] To a large extent, the willingness of the guardians to impose these repayments in spite of their previous protests was due to the fact that in many of the poorest unions, where repayments were heaviest, the elected guardians had been replaced by paid officers.

Regardless of the fact that the Irish poor rates were being better collected than they had ever been, *The Times* began to publish a series of deprecating articles on the finances of the Irish unions, their lack of financial independence, and the consequent drain on the resources of the imperial Treasury. These articles caused some disquiet within the government and prompted Twistleton to reassure Trevelyan that the newspaper was misrepresenting the facts and that, in spite of some problems in the collection of the rates, overall the Irish poor rates were better collected than they had ever been in England. Ironically, much of the information upon which these articles were based was supplied secretly to *The Times* by Wood and Trevelyan. In May 1848, the collection of poor rates continued to display a remarkably high level of return despite the heavy and unexpected burdens which had been placed on it: throughout the country, the national amount of rates collected since the commencement of the Poor Law was 92 per cent, the amount carried forward was 6 per cent, and the amount declared irrecoverable was a negligible 2 per cent. As expected, wealthier unions such as Antrim and Newtownards had paid all their poor rates, and the lowest payments were in the west of Ireland; the Castlebar union had paid 67 per cent and the Galway union 68 per cent of their poor rates. However, even in some of the distressed unions, the payments—despite the image frequently portrayed—was surprisingly high. The Kilrush union in Co. Clare had paid 100 per cent of all poor rates due, and neighbouring Ennistymon had paid almost 98 per cent.[58]

Regardless of the high return from the poor rates, the Treasury continued to criticise both the guardians and vice-guardians for not striking sufficiently high rates. The Poor Law Commissioners were more sympathetic to the local unions, realising what hardships had to be endured for such a large amount of rates to be collected. They pointed out that many unions would be unable to continue to pay such high rates for much longer and suggested that some of the repayments be waived to ease the general burden of taxation. The Prime Minister, Russell, was willing to consider this but the Treasury emphatically resisted such an idea. Sir Charles Wood, the Chancellor of the Exchequer, believed that to do so, at a point when their uncompromising policies appeared to be successful, would be regarded as a sign of weakness. He advised Russell:

> Firstly, it would encourage the belief that nothing was to be repaid in Ireland. Secondly, the Irish received the value of the money, not in mending their roads, but in saving the lives of their people. 3,000,000 of people at one time lived on wages thus obtained.[59]

The government had already remitted half of the money loaned for Famine relief and Wood was convinced that any further concessions would mean that the Irish taxpayers would never again take any mention of repayments seriously. Not for the first or last time, Russell allowed his own instincts to be over-ruled by the uncompromising vision and determination of the officials at the Treasury.[60]

During the summer of 1848, as the demand for relief increased, several unions again found themselves unable to meet even their current financial demands. Reluctantly, the Treasury was forced to modify its policy regarding repayments. In the poorest unions, they agreed that the produce of the rates could be used exclusively for the maintenance of the destitute, and no further repayments were to be made until the harvest of 1848.[61]

As the 1848 harvest approached, it was obvious that the financial position of several Poor Law unions was precarious. In September 1848, out of the 130 Poor Law unions in the country, only 45 had balances in hands. There was, however, considerable regional diversity in the financial condition of the unions, only one union in Connacht possessing a balance-in-hand (a mere £168), compared with twenty unions in Ulster. In Munster, the balances in the hands of the guardians amounted to £20,996, although this was concentrated in twenty of the thirty unions in the province. The reappearance of the potato blight in many parts of the country in 1848 meant that the finances of the local unions and their ability to maintain their poor and also to make repayments for the various government loans continued to be a problem in the fourth year of shortages.

Table 18: Financial Condition of Poor Law Unions
29 September 1848[62]

Province	Debits(£)	Balances-in-hand(£)
Ulster	£ 25,666	£21,036
Leinster	£ 38,206	£12,120
Munster	£109,568	£20,996
Connacht	£ 94,833	£ 168

The Provision of Poor Relief

Following the harvest of 1847, the responsibility for providing relief devolved almost exclusively on the Irish Poor Law. In some of the distressed western and southern unions, the demand for admittance to the local workhouses commenced in September, far earlier than was usually the case. This was an ominous warning that the demand for relief was likely to grow even higher even as the season progressed. This was confirmed by reports from the local Poor Law officers which overwhelmingly painted a negative picture of the condition of the unions. The state of the people in these areas was invariably described as 'wretched' and 'debilitated'.[63] Overall, the reports of the local relief officials indicated that the condition of the applicants for relief had deteriorated markedly since the previous year. In the Castlebar union, the vice-guardians described the applicants for relief as 'a wretched mass of human misery' and felt that they had no alternative but to admit them to the workhouse, even though it was already full. The vice-guardians believed that it would be fatal to refuse them this form of relief. The

Inspector of the Cahirciveen, Kenmare and Skibbereen unions regarded the prevailing 'mass of destitution' as being beyond the power of the Poor Law alone to relieve, and he suggested that government food depots should again be established in the area.[64]

Regardless of the increase in demand for relief immediately following the harvest of 1847, both the Poor Law Commissioners and the government refused to permit outdoor relief to be granted until it was absolutely necessary. Outdoor relief to the able-bodied destitute was regarded as being particularly undesirable. The 'workhouse test'—using admittance to the workhouse as a test of destitution—was to be employed as far as possible. A circular from the Commissioners informed all boards of guardians that 'the evil which is to be most guarded against is the necessity of granting outdoor relief to able-bodied men'. During the previous year, both the Labour Rate Act and the Temporary Relief Act had allowed people who were not genuinely destitute to obtain relief and consequently 'numerous persons have had a share of the public alms who ought to have subsisted on their own resources'. The Commissioners added that they 'confidently predicted' that if the workhouse test was strictly adhered to, all cases of imposition would be brought to light and only the genuinely destitute would obtain relief.[65] Guardians who asked for an order permitting them to provide outdoor relief were told that they should 'spare no exertion' to find additional accommodation. If this was not possible, the guardians were to discharge the old and infirm paupers who were already in the workhouse to make way for able-bodied applicants for relief. This policy was not achieved without difficulties, however. A condition of entry to the workhouses was that the applicants had to be destitute, that is, without either possessions or property. As a consequence, some paupers were reluctant to leave the shelter of the workhouse, on the grounds that they no longer had either a home or land to which they could return.[66]

As the winter progressed and the demand for relief increased, the policy of forcibly emptying the workhouses of certain categories of inmates to create room for able-bodied applicants continued to cause problems. Throughout the country, there were reports that many of the old, young and infirm paupers were reluctant to vacate the workhouses, some pointedly refusing to do so. The most common reason given was that they and their families and friends no longer possessed either homes, lodgings, farms, bedding or clothing. A further problem was that the Poor Law only provided for relief to be given in food. No recognition was given of the need for other basic necessities such as soap, clothes, fuel or lodgings. A few boards of guardians defied the Commissioners and refused to empty their workhouses. The Rathkeale guardians, for example, unanimously decided to resign in protest against the policy of making the most vulnerable categories of paupers leave the shelter of the workhouses. Other guardians, including the Galway board, were threatened with dismissal unless they implemented the ruling without delay.[67]

Privately, Edward Twistleton, the Chief Poor Law Commissioner, regarded this aspect of the Poor Law as particularly severe, although he agreed that the workhouses should be preserved for the use of the able-bodied. A modification in this policy was made when large numbers of people refused to leave the workhouse or, if they left, they applied for readmittance within a few days. The Commissioners recommended that in such cases, the guardians should first try to ascertain in advance whether lodgings with friends or relatives might be obtained for them.[68] The effect of emptying the workhouses of the old and infirm did occasionally have the desired effect. In the Castlebar union many vacancies were created in the workhouse by transferring its inmates onto the outdoor relief lists. Many of the able-bodied destitute who had applied for relief refused the indoor relief offered to them. The Poor Law Commissioners regarded cases such as this as proof of the efficacy of the workhouse test.[69]

In a number of unions, even when destitute, some persons were reluctant to enter their local workhouses. In some instances, this was due to the prevalence of fever and other diseases in the workhouses and the consequent fear of infection. At the beginning of 1848, out of 120,172 inmates of the workhouses, 7,007 persons were being treated for fever. During the course of one week, 1,460 inmates died. Again, mortality was highest in the distressed western unions where a hungry population was more vulnerable to disease. More frequently, the unwillingness to enter workhouses was due to people's reluctance to give up their few remaining possessions in order to become eligible for Poor Law relief. Since 1845, the pledging of articles with pawnbrokers had steadily increased, although the redeeming of articles had decreased considerably. The Poor Law Inspector of the Kilrush union attributed the high level of mortality in his locality to the fact that many people delayed their entry to the workhouse for as long as possible. One consequence of this was that many people did not apply for poor relief, 'till their health and constitution are broken down beyond repair'.[70] Some of the destitute discharged themselves within a few hours of being admitted to a workhouse, in order to return to their cabins 'where they have that combination of dirt, smoke and warmth which they love. They will cling to them in many cases to the death'.[71]

To facilitate the transfer to Poor Law relief, the 1847 Act had extended the powers of the guardians to obtain auxiliary accommodation. Some boards of guardians, however, taken unaware by the unexpectedly early demand for relief, were unable to obtain additional accommodation in sufficient time to meet the demand. Occasionally, this resulted in relief being provided in a way not permitted by the legislature. In the distressed western unions, the local guardians repeatedly contravened the provisions of the new Poor Law Act in an effort to make their limited resources stretch as far as possible. In Cahirciveen, for example, the guardians permitted the paupers to sleep up to four in each bed. When the Listowel and Ballina workhouses became full, each applicant for relief was provided with a supply of food to take away with them, even though no order for outdoor relief had been issued. In the Ballina union, the numbers receiving this form of ad hoc relief rose from an initial 260 to over 2,000 paupers within a few weeks. Guardians who persisted in providing this illicit relief, regardless of the admonitions of the Commissioners, were summarily replaced by vice-guardians, many of whom, to the dismay of the Poor Law Commissioners, acted in a manner similar to their predecessors.[72]

It was not only in the distressed western unions that this form of illicit relief was provided. In a number of other unions, including those of Waterford, Thurles, Clogheen and Dungarvan, the guardians provided outdoor relief without first obtaining the requisite order, explaining that to do so would waste valuable time. They regarded their actions as a necessary, although temporary, response to a desperate situation. The Kilkenny guardians felt that the provision of immediate assistance was absolutely necessary because conditions in their union had deteriorated so badly that the able-bodied destitute could more accurately be described as infirm.[73] In a few instances also, illegal outdoor relief was provided in the northern unions, which were generally regarded as the most compliant in all matters of administration. To a large extent, distress in the north of the country was primarily caused by a temporary depression in trade, rather than the shortcomings of the 1847 harvest. In Dungannon, for example, the guardians could not afford to provide additional accommodation. They responded to the sudden increase in pressure, which they attributed to a temporary slump in the local linen industry, by providing the destitute with food and shelter in the workhouse during the day and allowing them to return to their own homes in the evening.[74] The Ballymoney union in Co. Antrim was also affected by the short-term slump in the linen industry. The guardians provided applicants to the workhouse with relief in money, despite the exhortions of their Inspector who warned that their actions would 'prove fatally injurious to the well-working of the law'.[75] In general, however, the northern unions were reluctant to provide outdoor relief of any description. An extreme example of this occurred when the Lurgan workhouse became full. The guardians purchased canvas tents in order to avoid giving outdoor relief. In September 1848, when outdoor relief had been available for a year, out of the twenty-five unions which had avoided outdoor relief altogether, seventeen were situated in Ulster.[76]

Despite the introduction of a Vagrancy Act at the same time that the amended Poor Law became operative, reports from the local Inspectors in the west of the country in 1848 suggested that begging was still widespread. The new Act had stipulated that the punishment for begging was up to thirty days hard labour, but this was rarely enforced. The Poor Law Commissioners, however, continually urged that vagrancy should be suppressed as they feared that it would undermine the Poor Law.

Landlords who continued to provide private charity rapidly obtained a reputation for their benevolence and as a result of this even more demands were made on them. The local Inspector of the Carrick-on-Shannon union witnessed the scenes outside the home of one such benevolent landlord:

> . . . the unenviable position that they are living in—having their house surrounded from morning to night by hundreds of homeless, half-naked, famishing creatures, who, from my own conversation with them, I ascertained to have much stronger claims on others.[77]

Some persons were believed to have resorted to begging in the hope that they would be sentenced to gaol. The Inspector of the Galway union reported that ninety-two paupers, most of whom were from Connemara, had been committed to gaol for a month, having deliberately been caught begging in order to be sent to prison. Elsewhere, there were reports of people caught stealing for the same reason.[78]

The Poor Law Commissioners and the Treasury agreed that outdoor relief was not to be allowed until it became absolutely necessary in order to prevent deaths from starvation. By November 1847, as reports of such deaths were again increasing, the Commissioners reluctantly began to issue outdoor relief orders. The first unions to receive the order were the Oldcastle and Newcastle unions, neither of which had been designated 'distressed'. By the beginning of 1848, over half of the unions in Ireland had been permitted to provide outdoor relief to able-bodied persons.[79] In the first week of February 1848, 445,456 persons were in receipt of outdoor relief, 107,811 of whom were classed as able-bodied persons. By the beginning of April, this had risen to 638,141, 211,580 of whom were able-bodied. By September 1848, when the new relief system had been operative for a year, an estimated 1,433,042 persons, from all categories of pauper, had been in receipt of outdoor relief. A further 525,263 had received relief within the confines of the workhouse.[80]

In the unions in which it proved necessary to allow outdoor relief to the able-bodied, it was provided in such a way as to minimise all opportunities for abuse. The 1847 Extension Act had confined the order permitting outdoor relief to a maximum period of two months. As far as possible, it was only to be given in food and rations were to be cooked, as a precaution against their being re-sold. Due to the large amount of relief being provided daily, this was not always possible; some guardians provided a combination of cooked and uncooked food. The Commissioners also ordered the guardians to publish the names of all recipients of outdoor relief in an attempt to reduce any possibility of fraud.[81]

The Poor Law Commissioners believed that the most effective way to detect any unnecessary demands on the Poor Law was to insist that work be demanded from all recipients of relief. Since the introduction of the Poor Law, the Commissioners had been determined that the paupers in the workhouses should be kept employed in some way. This was regarded as an integral part of the 'workhouse test', which endeavoured to make all aspects of life in the workhouses less attractive than life outside. Any items manufactured by the paupers, however, could only be used within the workhouses and not be sold for profit. The reasoning behind this was that the Commissioners did not want to undermine the workings of the free market economy and thus undermine—or even pauperise—the livelihood of independent labourers. Furthermore, paupers could not be employed on works of improvement such as land reclamation, as had been proposed by a number of landlords, as it was feared that unscrupulous landlords would use this type of labour for their own profit.[82]

Although the system of demanding labour in return for relief under the amended Poor Law appeared to be similar to public works used in the previous year, different philosophies underlay the two systems. The public works had provided the destitute with a daily wage and the work carried out by them was to be of benefit to the public. The Poor Law Commissioners were critical of the way in which the public works had operated in 1846–7, and described the outcome of a lax administration thus: 'immense numbers of labourers were attracted; discrimination became impractical; work could not be exacted; an enormous expenditure took place, and the works which were begun remained to a great extent unfinished'.[83] The Commissioners omitted to mention that the public works had also failed in their objective of saving lives. The Poor Law differed from the public works in that it separated relief from labour and thereby ensured that a man would either wholly be supported by his employer or by the Poor Law union. Relief in aid of wages had been totally discredited under the old English Poor Law, in particular, under the notorious Speenhamland System. The separation of labour and relief had, therefore, been regarded as an important element of the 'new' English Poor Law of 1834, the Irish Poor Law of 1838 and the Amendment Act of 1847.[84] Initially, able-bodied paupers in receipt of outdoor relief from the Poor Law were expected to work for at least eight hours a day, but in April 1848, this was increased to ten hours per day. The guidelines laid down by the Poor Law Commissioners for this type of labour were that:

> It should be as repulsive as possible consistent with humanity, that is, that paupers would rather do the work than 'starve', but that they should rather employ themselves in doing any other kind of work elsewhere, and that it would not interfere with private enterprise or be a kind of work which otherwise would necessarily be performed by independent labourers.[85]

Choosing a task of work that did not put the paupers in competition with independent labourers was difficult, and stone-breaking was the one frequently chosen. Although stone-breaking did not fully meet the criteria of the Commissioners, they stated that it did so more completely than anything else. Stone-breaking also had the further advantage that the amount of work which had been carried out could be easily measured; it could be more easily superintended than the public works; and it required fewer tools than other forms of labour.[86] For a people who were already debilitated by three consecutive years of shortages, however, the physical exertion of stone-breaking undoubtedly proved exhausting and possibly the last straw for those already weakened by hunger and a diet lacking in nutrition. During the winter of 1847–8, there were again heavy snowfalls in many parts of Ireland, a further calamity for the many people whose clothes were increasingly ragged or had long since been pawned. Since 1845, no provision had been made for the purchase of soap, fuel, or clothes, relief frequently being equated merely with the provision of food. For these persons, stone-breaking represented a particularly harsh test of destitution.

Stone-breaking was unpopular with many of the recipients of outdoor relief, especially those who had to travel a long distance to their workplace and then remain there for up to ten hours without food. Many paupers were also aware that the amount of relief which they received compared unfavourably with that enjoyed by workhouse inmates who, in addition to food, were provided with fuel, soap, clothing and shelter.[87] Paupers in receipt of outdoor relief were further disadvantaged in not being provided with a coffin if they died which, again, was provided to paupers receiving relief in the workhouses, although there were instances of paupers being buried three to a coffin or in re-usable coffins. This anomaly regarding the burial of paupers was brought to the attention of the Commissioners by the guardians of the Lismore and Rathkeale unions, who requested that it be changed. The Killmallock board even offered to pay an additional rate for this purpose.[88] The requests to change this regulation were supported by the Poor Law Commissioners and many members of the government. In June 1848, it was made legal for paupers who died whilst in receipt of outdoor relief to be provided with a coffin paid for out of the poor rates.[89]

The cost of providing Poor Law relief, particularly outdoor relief, was cheap, especially as the price of meal and corn was low in the months following the harvest of 1847. Adults in receipt of outdoor relief were provided with a pound of Indian corn, or some other type of grain, a day, which cost approximately one penny. This compared very favourably with 1s 5d per day, the average cost of nine pounds of potatoes, which the adult inmates of the workhouses had received prior to 1845. It also compared favourably with the cost of indoor relief, each adult inmate costing on average between 1s 6d and 2s per week. The cost of indoor maintenance for the year ending September 1848 was £603,035, and the cost of outdoor relief for the same period was £725,449, regardless of the far higher number of recipients.[90]

The Poor Law Commissioners were worried about making public the cost of providing outdoor relief. They were afraid that the cheapness of this form of relief might give an unfavourable impression of the Poor Law regarding the adequacy of the relief provided by it. They justified the low cost of relief on the grounds that as Ireland was such a poor country and the extent of the deficit so large, it would be irresponsible to provide anything more lavish. At the same time, the cost of Indian corn was very cheap. The Commissioners also pointed out that the Poor Law diet had also received the prior approval of the Board of Health.[91]

For the poor who were the recipients of this form of relief, whether they resided in one of the distressed western unions or elsewhere, the prospect of a third consecutive year of distress was devastating. Nor was the consequential suffering confined exclusively to the western unions.

The Inspector of the Carrick-on-Shannon union in Co. Leitrim, who had been employed in a western union in the previous year, felt that it was necessary to emphasise this point:

> I fear the extent of destitution in this union has never been fairly represented, it is perfectly frightful; accustomed as I am to scenes of misery in the western counties, I have never met with so extensive and hopeless destitution.[92]

Although there were some intermittent protests against the new system of relief, these were neither concerted nor sustained. The Cahirciveen, Galway, Kilrush, Nenagh, Scariff and Sligo unions all reported instances of crowds gathering regularly at the meetings of the guardians and vice-guardians and troops were regularly used to disperse these people.[93] The most frequent demand of the paupers was for outdoor relief to be introduced, or if it already had been introduced, for it to be extended. Occasionally, their attitude was belligerent. In the New Ross union, for example, a crowd of approximately 300 people threatened to attack the workhouse unless they received either food or employment. In the Newcastle union, a group of paupers forced their way into a board meeting demanding relief, but refused to accept admittance to the workhouse when it was offered. In the Kilrush union, about 3,000 people gathered outside the workhouse to demand outdoor relief. When this was refused, the crowd became disorderly and attacked the building. Police and troops had to be called to restore order. Although there were threats of violence against some workhouse buildings or individual guardians, few acts of violence were actually perpetrated against Poor Law officials, and those that did take place were usually directed against rate collectors.[94]

The state of the country was of concern to the authorities in Dublin. The Lord Lieutenant, Lord Clarendon, regarded his position as a struggle between satisfying hunger and quelling outrage. Describing the situation at the end of 1847, he stated 'I felt as if I was at the head of a Provisional government of a half-conquered country'.[95] By 1848, Clarendon believed that there was a determination to rebel in Ireland. This had been exacerbated by the situation throughout Europe and the Chartist agitation in Britain. Clarendon realised that the British government no longer could depend on the support of the Irish gentry or landlords who had been alienated by the government's most recent relief policies. Despite the introduction of the Treason Felony Act in April 1848, an uprising, which was quickly quelled, took place during the summer. Many of the ringleaders were transported and the Habeas Corpus Act was suspended. Clarendon, however, did not fully support the repressive response of the government. Clarendon's attitude to Irish distress had softened since his appointment as Lord Lieutenant. He believed that the distress was at the root of much of the dissatisfaction and suggested that the government should address the problem of Irish poverty. He advised the Prime Minister, Russell, to attempt to remove the cause of discontent 'and that will be best done by relieving distress which causes much of the bad feeling now, and if we can pay off a revolution in that way, it will be an economy'.[96]

The pessimism of the Dublin administration was echoed in the localities. Some of the local relief officials believed that the insistence on utter destitution as a qualification for relief prevented the Poor Law from functioning successfully as the primary means for relieving distress. Furthermore, the policy of trying to extend the system of indoor relief left the poor people vulnerable in the long term: if they entered the workhouse, their own houses would probably be pulled down and it was unlikely that they would ever again be able to regain a foothold in the land. One of the Inspectors in the south-west of the country warned that the consequence of pursuing such a policy:

> If such persons are once admitted into the workhouse, it becomes afterwards a matter of the greatest difficulty to support them by outdoor relief as, on coming into the workhouse, they leave their houses which they would be unable to gain possession of should the guardians be disposed to alter the kind of relief afforded to them.[97]

For a number of members of the Whig administration, however, the clearance of smallholders from the land coincided with their long term aspiration to bring about improvements in the system of land-holding in Ireland. A necessary pre-condition for the economic transformation of Ireland was that smallholders should voluntarily relinquish their claims to the land.[98]

A further aspect of the government's policy which worried some people was the fact that the lives of the destitute were dependent on the ability or willingness of ratepayers to pay their taxes. The underlying principle of the amended Poor Law was that persons who possessed property should not be allowed to evade their duties. A Church of Ireland minister in Carrick-on-Shannon, one of the distressed unions, claimed that as a consequence of this policy the poor people, through no fault of their own, were being held to ransom in pursuit of the government's ends. Following many desperate and unsuccessful attempts on behalf of his poor parishioners to receive additional aid, he questioned, 'Is the government satisfied to have the lives of one class at the disposal of the other? If so, further interference is utterly useless.'[99]

Increasingly, boards of guardians in the south and west of Ireland were sceptical about the ability of the Poor Law to bear the whole burden of providing relief, despite the recent extension of its powers. The Killarney guardians felt that the latest government policy would have a divisive effect in the country by putting the interests of property and poverty in conflict with each other. Again, there were calls for the soup kitchens, the public works or the food depots to be re-opened. The Skibbereen guardians, who had witnessed such severe distress in the previous winter, were particularly vociferous in their condemnation of the relief policies in general and the Poor Law in particular. They disliked the fact that the amended Poor Law did not distinguish between people who were long term destitute and those who were temporarily distressed due to the condition of the country. Furthermore, they believed that the policy of emptying the workhouses of the old and infirm in order to create more room for the able-bodied destitute was unnecessarily harsh. The Skibbereen guardians warned that there would again be widespread suffering in their union and they asked to be replaced by paid officials who would have more time to dedicate to the granting of relief.[100]

The Kilrush guardians were also outspoken in their criticism of the new policies which they were expected to administer. They considered that Poor Law relief alone would be inadequate to meet the anticipated distress and suggested that the government should procure food for the poor, rather than leave them to the whim of 'mercantile caprices'. In a memorial to Russell, which was also printed in *The Times*, the Kilrush board stated:

> That we record as our unequivocal opinion that all money in the imperial Treasury is valueless compared to that of thousands of lives lost in Ireland last year by starvation that could have been easily prevented by a liberal policy on the part of Her Majesty's government'

Furthermore, the Kilrush guardians questioned the whole basis of the Act of Union, on the ground that Irish distress was not regarded in the same way as either English or Scottish distress. Unlike the other boards, however, they viewed the question of relief of the poor in political terms and discussed the issue of 'tenant right' at their meetings. Increasingly, they denounced Ireland's connection with Britain.[101]

Although the Poor Law Commissioners were criticised for the paucity of relief which they provided, they defended themselves on the grounds that the lives of many people had been saved by the Poor Law in such a way that the industrial energies of the country had not been damaged and that the recipients of relief had not been any further demoralised.[102] In May 1848, over one million people daily were being relieved by the Poor Law, four-fifths of whom were in receipt of outdoor relief. The numbers dependent on Poor Law relief continued to increase; numbers in the workhouses peaked in June, while those on outdoor relief reaching its maximum in July 1848. Following this, the numbers on poor relief continued to decrease until the end of September 1848, when it again began to rise. During the summer of 1848, the guardians were informed that outdoor relief would not be permitted after 15 August. As soon as a pauper left the workhouse, his or her place was to be made available to someone on outdoor relief. Persons whom the guardians believed would be able to find employment during the harvest were to be discharged from the workhouse. The advances which had been made by the government to some of the poorest unions were also to cease at the harvest. Following that, every Poor Law union would be expected to depend on its own financial resources.[103]

The Distressed Unions

Following the introduction of the extended Poor Law in the summer of 1847, the government had hoped that the responsibility for financing relief would devolve totally on the Poor Law. The smallness of the 1847 harvest, however, again forced the British government to assist in the provision of relief in Ireland for the third consecutive year. The government were reluctant to do this as they believed that a continuation in their involvement, on a similar scale to the previous two years, would perpetuate the dependence of the Irish on external aid. This would not be beneficial to Ireland in the long term and, in the short term, it would be injurious to the finances of the whole Empire. In the previous year alone, over £4½m had been unprofitably spent on the public works in Ireland—half of which had been paid for by the British Treasury.

The government was determined that such a waste of resources should not occur again. They therefore decided that, after 1847, they would only give assistance to areas in which destitution exceeded the ability of the local ratepayers to finance it. Using this criterion, the government estimated that it would be essential to provide external financial assistance to twenty-two unions which they designated 'distressed'. At the same time, they privately admitted that approximately twenty-five other unions might require similar assistance. In the first instance, the money provided for these unions was to come from the funds raised by the British Relief Association, although they agreed to leave its distribution in the hands of the Treasury. The money advanced on behalf of the British Relief Association was to be provided as a mixture of grants and loans. If it proved necessary to provide assistance beyond this, the government determined that it should be in the form of a loan rather than a grant from the Treasury. Local taxes, however, were expected to contribute the major share of financial assistance. The government emphasised that they would only give assistance if all possible local exertions had been made to collect rates and the amount raised was still insufficient to prevent starvation.[104]

The distressed unions were all situated along the western seaboard. These unions had a number of other features in common: they were geographically extensive; they had low Poor Law valuations; they supported large populations, many of whom had depended on the potato for subsistence prior to 1845; and they contained a substantial proportion of small-holdings. Each had also experienced a high level of distress in both 1845 and 1846, not all of which had been met effectively. Significantly, by 1847 each of these unions had a large number of people who no longer possessed the resources to support themselves and their families. Inauspiciously, they had all accumulated heavy debts as a consequence of two years of high taxation. At the same time, their rates for current expenditure continued to be heavier than those in the unions to the east of the country, even though the means of financing them had already decreased considerably. Regardless of this high level of vulnerability, funds for the purpose of relieving the destitute poor were not to be issued until they were proved to be absolutely essential for the purpose of saving life. This time-consuming process involved at least one letter, often more, from the local Poor Law Inspector to the central Commissioners. If satisfied that the application was justified, the Commissioners would ask the Treasury to allow the requisite amount of money required. The policy of the Treasury in these applications was to provide the minimum sum which they considered to be necessary to prevent the loss of life in the union, sometimes independently of the advice of the Commissioners.[105] This drawn-out process was regarded as essential to reduce unnecessary expenditure. It undoubtedly also contributed to further suffering, and probably to additional mortality, while the bureaucratic niceties insisted upon by Whitehall were observed.

The Poor Law Commissioners were anxious to keep as close an eye as possible on the unions which were in receipt of external funds or which were giving outdoor relief to the able-bodied. In each of the twenty-two distressed unions, a separate Poor Law Inspector was appointed to oversee the provision of relief, and additional ones were appointed as outdoor relief increased. The Commissioners believed this to be necessary on the grounds that:

> They cannot reckon on out-door relief being properly administered to able-bodied men in any union in a distressed district, unless an Inspector constantly resides there, to stimulate the guardians, to prevent abuses, and to see that the Commissioners' regulations are duly observed.[106]

The approval of the Treasury was required before the appointment of any new Inspector and Trevelyan, with typical thoroughness, recommended various men to this position. There was also a direct correlation between unions which received external funds and those in which the elected boards of guardians were replaced by paid officials. In each of the poorest unions, therefore, paid government officials were in charge of the distribution of relief. In recognition of the heavy demands which were to be made for relief in the distressed unions, depots were to be established in which the food for outdoor relief could be cooked and distributed. People in receipt of outdoor relief were to receive their rations at these buildings. The Commissioners recommended that the able-bodied should receive relief in the form of bread, as this commodity had little resale value.[107]

Within the distressed unions, special provision was made for school children. They could obtain relief, paid for by the British Relief Association, from their local schools. This scheme was introduced by Count Strzelecki, the agent of the Association in Ireland. He had already introduced a pilot scheme in the Westport union which had proved to be both popular and successful. Trevelyan did not support an extension of this, as he felt that it would be difficult to administer effectively. Strzelecki, however, remained adamant that a portion of the funds of the British Relief Association should be used for this purpose. Twelve thousand pounds was allocated from the funds of the Association for the extension of the scheme to feed schoolchildren throughout the distressed unions. A grant from this fund was given to each union according to the number and size of the local schools. It was then distributed to the children with the assistance of the local clergy, the school inspectors or the school masters. It was recommended that each child should receive a daily ration of rye bread and warm broth, which was considered to be more nourishing than Indian meal. Count Strzelecki estimated that the cost of feeding each child was a third of a penny per day.[108] The extension of the scheme met with considerable success. In a few unions, however, there were so few schools that it appeared impractical, although this initial difficulty was soon overcome. In the Swinford union, for example, the local Inspector reported that schools were springing up like 'mushrooms'. Whereas previously there had only been three schools in the union with a total of 176 pupils, since the introduction of the scheme the number of pupils had increased to 2,138.[109] The Inspector of the Skibbereen union reported:

> You can have no idea of the great good the British Association bounty is doing to this union: hundreds of lives have been saved by it, and were it not for this, the scenes of last year would have been witnessed in Skibbereen again.[110]

The government wanted to avoid giving regular advances to any union, as they did not want the assistance to appear automatic. Although it had originally been anticipated that financial assistance would be limited to the twenty-two distressed unions, this never was the case. Apart from these unions, which received the largest number of advances, throughout the year it proved necessary to provide another twenty-five unions with financial aid. Most of these were situated in the west or midlands, usually adjoining the distressed unions. In the forty-seven unions which received intermittent financial assistance from the Treasury, advances were usually provided as a provisional loan to be repaid when a new rate was collected.[111] As the year advanced, it became increasingly obvious to the Poor Law Commissioners that the situation in many unions was far worse than had been anticipated or was being acknowledged publicly. Twistleton privately confided to Trevelyan that no repayments were likely to be made to the government before the 1848 harvest at the very earliest.[112]

Regardless of the fact that distress in the poorest unions continued to increase in the early part of 1848, and was unlikely to abate during the summer months, the Treasury urged the Commissioners to start reducing the amount of relief being provided. This was partly motivated by a desire to encourage people to cultivate the land and avoid a small harvest as in the previous year. In March 1848, the Commissioners suspended outdoor relief to the able-bodied in twenty-four unions to encourage a return of labourers to the soil. The Commissioners believed that this could be achieved without too much hardship as approximately 200,000 children were receiving relief from their local schools. The British Relief Association agreed to help the Commissioners by making relief to the children contingent on their parents working on the land. By summer, however, the funds of the Association were almost exhausted and, as the most intense months of distress approached, they were forced to begin to contract their school rations. This resulted in an immediate increase in the number of people seeking relief from the Poor Law. Twistleton found this development disturbing as July and August were traditionally the most intense months of distress and he feared that the Poor Law alone would not be able to provide sufficient relief.[113]

By July 1848, the funds of the British Relief Association were almost completely spent and they started to wind down their activities in Ireland. Since October 1847, they had advanced £143,518 in aid of local rates to the distressed unions and had spent £92,968 in providing relief to schoolchildren. When the Association closed its operations in Ireland, they had a balance in hand of £12,900 which they decided to donate to the Poor Law Commissioners. The Commissioners agreed to use these funds to help the poorest unions. This meant that during the year from the harvest of 1847 to that of 1848, the British Relief Association had provided £249,386 for the relief of Irish distress and had assisted an estimated 300,000 paupers. This compared with a mere £156,060 spent by the British government in the same period.[114]

The reduced involvement of the British Relief Association in 1848 meant that it again became necessary for the government to provide financial assistance. Over the summer months, not merely the twenty-two distressed unions but other, previously independent, unions in the midlands and south of Ireland made desperate appeals to the Treasury for assistance. Although advances were made, it was on the clear understanding that all issues of money were to cease in August 1848. The Treasury also decreed that outdoor relief was to end on 15 August. As this date approached, the relief officials in each of the distressed unions informed the Poor Law Commissioners that they believed that this was not possible. Reluctantly, the Treasury permitted the date to be extended to 31 August 1848, but Twistleton doubted if even this was realistic. In private correspondence with Trevelyan, he expressed his concern as to the financial prospects of all of the distressed unions. Regardless of the intentions of the Treasury, he did not believe that these unions would be able to manage without financial assistance even following the harvest.[115]

Trevelyan was appalled at Twistleton's pessimistic predictions. He accused the Poor Law Commissioners of encouraging the unions to make claims on the public purse. Trevelyan warned that while the Treasury was willing to issue advances to each of the poorest unions, they would not do so indiscriminately. Twistleton, not for the first time, was admonished by Trevelyan, the latter assuming the role of the final arbiter of the way in which relief should be administered. From London, Trevelyan informed Twistleton:

> A broad line can be drawn between those unions which, if the guardians choose to exert themselves, could maintain their own poor, and those which, even if they were to make every practicable effort, could not so maintain them.[116]

The guardians and vice-guardians who were administering the policies of the government found themselves caught between the fiscal rectitude of the government on the one hand, and the demands of the destitute poor on the other. The financial position of some unions continued to be precarious in the spring and summer of 1848, as they became increasingly dependent on the intervention of the Treasury for survival. Even when such assistance was forthcoming, the various bureaucratic controls meant that there was often a time lapse before relief became available. In some of the western unions, food for the inmates of the workhouses was being purchased daily, sometimes only as a result of the benevolence of a vice-guardian or other relief official. Occasionally, the Commissioners, anticipating that such a delay could prove fatal, intervened to provide immediate assistance. In these instances, the Treasury refused to make any further advances if the Commissioners continued to behave in this manner.[117] Relief to the most distressed unions, therefore, lay very firmly in the hands of the Treasury. The role of the Poor Law Commissioners became increasingly marginalised.

The Dissolution of Boards of Guardians

As the summer of 1848 advanced and the burden on the Poor Law became heavier, many guardians were forced to devote an increasing amount of time to the duties of the office. Before 1845, boards of guardians had generally met weekly, but this was no longer sufficient as the demands on the Poor Law increased. Following the transfer to Poor Law relief, some boards met daily, whilst others, although recognising the necessity to do so, were unable to, as they had also to tend to their own affairs.[118] The transfer of the Poor Law relief was disliked by many impoverished people who had been reduced to the level of paupers. Some of the recipients of relief protested against the scantiness of that provided. Some guardians and vice-guardians received threatening letters which demanded an increase in relief. Actual instances of violence, however, continued to be rare. An exception to this occurred in the Nenagh union, where an assassination attempt was made on the chairman of the board of guardians because he had refused to extend outdoor relief. This incident caused alarm amongst various other boards of guardians, and in the Rathkeale union, where outdoor relief had not been introduced, the guardians decided to resign as a precautionary measure.[119] The desire of the Rathkeale board to resign was not unique: the Athlone, Ballina, Carrick-on-Shannon, Kanturk, Newcastle, and Skibbereen guardians all offered to do so at various stages. In each case the guardians were informed that a board could only be dissolved if they failed to discharge their duties.[120]

Following the harvest of 1847, however, the Poor Law Commissioners increasingly used the threat of dissolution when dealing with boards of guardians whom they believed had not performed their duties adequately. The 1847 Extension Act had facilitated this process by providing for the immediate replacement of elected guardians by paid officials. As a result, each of the twenty-two distressed unions was dissolved together with the boards of twenty others. The most common reasons for the dissolution of a board were its failure to collect a sufficient rate, refusal to repay advances from the government, the provision of illegal relief (such as outdoor relief without first having received an order permitting it), or instances of death from starvation within the union. The latter reason was of particular concern to the Commissioners because, if recorded in a Coroner's Court, it would sometimes attract a lot of publicity. In such cases, the government required the Irish Executive to initiate an enquiry into the circumstances of death.

Most of the dissolved boards were from unions situated in the west of Ireland where the impact of the potato blight since 1845 had been most severe, whilst no board was dissolved in the north-east or east of the country. Unions in the south-east, including Kilkenny, New Ross, Thurles and Waterford; those in the midlands, including Granard, Mullingar, Trim and Tullamore; and four unions in Ulster, Cavan, Cootehill, Enniskillen and Lowtherstown (also known as Irvinestown), were also dissolved.[121] Although the most common reason for dissolving a board was the fact that the guardians were deemed not to have made sufficient rates or were financially insolvent, guardians who had not implemented the Poor Law in strict accordance with the rules prescribed by the Commissioners also found themselves rewarded with dissolution. In the case of the Kenmare union, for example, the local Inspector recommended that the board be dissolved as some of the guardians had not paid their poor rates, whereas the board of the Trim union were dissolved for providing outdoor relief illicitly.[122] Inevitably, perhaps, the boards of guardians who had been outspoken critics of either the Commissioners of the Poor Law in general were amongst the first to be dissolved.

In their Annual Report for 1848, the Poor Law Commissioners professed themselves reluctant 'in the highest degree' to interfere, even temporarily, with the system of local self-government. Notwithstanding this, they believed it was their duty to do so if poor relief was not being administered effectively.[123] Unofficially, however, the Commissioners regarded the appointment of paid officials, particularly in the distressed unions, as crucial to the well working of the law. They also believed that it was vital as a way of protecting the Treasury from continued unwarranted demands which were rightfully the responsibility of local taxation. The government considered this to be of paramount importance, even if it required interference with the system of local government. Twistleton was aware of the government's priorities and privately explained to Trevelyan: 'The principle of local government is excellent, but it seems to be of less importance for the present year than to protect the national finances'.[124]

The Commissioners believed that there were considerable advantages in the appointment of paid guardians: they would not be swayed by local considerations when levying and collecting the poor rates; they would be able to devote all of their time to the affairs of the union; and most importantly, they would be directly answerable to the Commissioners.[125] The Commissioners also realised that the request for a loan on behalf of the paid vice-guardians would be regarded more sympathetically than one on behalf of elected guardians.[126] At the beginning of 1848, Twistleton unofficially admitted that he wished that twice the number of elected boards had been dissolved, as he believed that it was the only way of ' . . . preventing Irish unions from making demands upon the national funds at a time when such demands, if carried to a very great extent, might be seriously injurious to the Empire'.[127]

The Treasury and the Whig administration, however, believed that it was essential that they should not be seen to be over-interfering in the delicate relationship between local taxation and representation. They warned Twistleton that he should adopt a more cautious approach to this problem. Twistleton felt that, not for the first time, he was being placed in an impossible position by the British government. He did not believe that it was possible to pursue the new relief policies unless they were able to employ the threat of dissolution. Twistleton regarded the fears of the government as groundless but realised that they had been prompted by criticisms of the relief policies within parliament. As a consequence of the Whig administration's sensitivity to such criticism and the many personal attacks that had been made on Russell, Twistleton believed that the discretion of the Poor Law Commissioners was constantly being interfered with. He warned that the Irish local government system should not be judged by that which pertained in England.[128] As Twistleton pointed out to Trevelyan, he regarded his personal position as invidious:

> It is wished that the Irish should not come upon the national finances for the relief of their destitute. It is also wished that deaths from starvation should not take place. But these wishes are as unreasonable as if you ask us to make beer without malt, or to fly without wings.[129]

The first example of dissolution was the much publicised case of the Lowtherstown board of guardians who were dissolved on 14 September 1847. The Lowtherstown guardians were remarkable in that they fiercely resisted their dissolution until they were reinstated on 25 March 1848. The reason given for dissolving them was the financial condition of the union. The financial problems of the board had started in the previous year, following the disastrous potato harvest of 1846. Like many other unions in the country, at this stage, the income from the local poor rates proved insufficient to meet the demands being made on them. A year later, the transfer to Poor Law relief ensured that in unions where the local harvest was poor, demands on local rates continued to increase. Additionally, repayments for various government loans, notably the Labour Rate and Temporary Relief Acts, were to be raised from local taxation. The burden of poor rates was not particularly high in the Lowtherstown union, especially when compared with the unions in the west of the country. During the operation of the Temporary Relief Act, only 16 per cent of the population of the Lowtherstown union had depended on the soup kitchens for relief, whereas in many of the western unions it exceeded 80 per cent, rising to over 93 per cent in the Ballinrobe union. In the Lowtherstown union, the rate for the repayment of the Temporary Relief Act was 1s 5½d in the pound, far below the repayments due from many of the distressed unions. The rate for the current expenditure of the union ranged in the various electoral divisions from 11d to 1s 10d in the pound.[130]

Despite the relatively low composite rate required in this union, the Lowtherstown guardians considered the burden on the local taxpayers to be too high. Instead, they offered to make the repayments in five yearly instalments. When the board of guardians refused to compromise on this proposal they were dissolved. The new vice-guardians immediately levied a rate sufficient both for the current rates and the government's repayments. The new rate was resisted by some of the ratepayers and threats of violence were made against the vice-guardians. The Commissioners urged the new officials to adopt a stricter approach with the rate collectors as they were anxious that the vice-guardians should be seen to be effective. Throughout the course of these events, the guardians of the Lowtherstown union continued to protest vociferously against their dissolution. Their adroit use of publicity resulted in a parliamentary enquiry, as a result of which they were re-instated.[131]

Most other boards of guardians accepted their dissolution without demur and some actually welcomed it. Although the alleged incompetence of the elected guardians continued to be the main cause of dissolution, this was not always the case. The Clogheen guardians were dissolved, not through any dereliction of duty, but because they could not devote sufficient time to the needs of the destitute. The local Inspector described them as an efficient and dedicated board but doubted if they, as a voluntary body, could carry the union through the difficult times ahead.[132] The Kinsale and Ennistymon boards were dismissed respectively for not making sufficient poor rates and providing poor relief too liberally. In each case, the local Inspectors believed that they had been dismissed unfairly, describing the boards as hard working and diligent and suggesting that the Poor Law Commissioners had not taken sufficient account of the extreme difficulties they faced.[133]

The men who were chosen to act as vice-guardians invariably came from outside the union. Frequently they were persons who had been employed previously under the Poor Law or on one of the earlier relief systems. The usual practice was to appoint two or three men simultaneously who were in charge of up to three adjoining unions; for example, the Ballinrobe, Castlebar and Westport unions were all administered by the same vice-guardians.[134] Upon receiving an order of dissolution, the board of guardians was requested to remain in office until the paid officials arrived. Following their arrival in a union, the vice-guardians were provided with a loan—usually from the funds of the British Relief Association—to enable them to provide relief until a new rate could be put in course of collection. Before this was granted, the Commissioners recommended that a new valuation of the union should be undertaken. The Commissioners believed that the collection of poor rates was the most important aspect of the vice-guardians' duties on the basis that:

They regard it of essential importance to the interests of the whole Empire that it may be distinctly shown to be possible, even in the most distressed unions in Ireland, to collect a sufficient amount of rates to relieve their destitution at the present season.[135]

The Commissioners, aware that the failure of the policies of the government was increasingly being blamed on the local administrators, declared that the appointment of vice-guardians in the distressed unions was highly satisfactory. The number of deaths from starvation decreased during the summer of 1848 compared with the earlier months of the year, and the Commissioners attributed this to the removal of elected boards of guardians and their replacement with paid officials. As a result of the appointments, the collection of rates also improved. Overall, the Commissioners believed that the whole administration of relief had become more efficient as a result of the change.[136] The use of paid guardians, however, was not the unqualified success portrayed by the Commissioners. Frequently, the vice-guardians encountered problems similar to those encountered by their predecessors. The most pressing and recurrent problem was the on-going shortage of funds, especially in the distressed unions. Sometimes this became a matter of life and death. In these cases, when the funds of the vice-guardians were exhausted, many of the officers did as the elected guardians before them had done: they made themselves personally liable for the debts of the union or even provided financial relief from their own pockets. The Commissioners totally disapproved of these actions and, as they had done with the elected guardians, urged them to deploy their full powers to collect the poor rates.[137]

Another problem frequently encountered by the vice-guardians was the sheer volume of work with which they had to contend. In some unions, they were employed on union business until 11 p.m. every day. One Inspector informed the Commissioners that the vice-guardians who were jointly responsible for the Ballinrobe, Castlebar and Westport unions—probably the most impoverished unions in the country—were not very efficient. He did not blame them personally but attributed this to the fact that they had to divide their time between the three unions and therefore could only devote two days a week to each. The Inspector suggested that a larger number of vice-guardians be employed and paid lower wages.[138] Some vice-guardians, such as those appointed to the Clonmel, New Ross and Scariff unions, proved to be incompetent and had to be replaced. The vice-guardians of the Kenmare union fought among themselves and the Inspector described them as being no better than the late board. Complaints against the vice-guardians could also be politically inspired as in the case of the Mohill and Loughrea unions which were brought to the attention of the government. Twistleton, when asked to explain these particular claims of incompetence, stated that the allegations were unfounded. Privately, he suspected that they had originated from two landlords associated with the unions, Lords Clements and Clanricarde, who were personally opposed to the administration of the Poor Law. Despite these and other complaints against the vice-guardians, however, Twistleton repeatedly assured the government that the administration of Poor Law relief was working well.[139]

The restoration of the dissolved boards was to take place in March 1848 or, if not then, twelve months later. The re-establishment of elected boards could not take place at any other time. At the beginning of 1848, the Commissioners announced that, with the exception of the Lowtherstown guardians, they were not going to restore any other board. The re-appearance of the potato blight in 1848, and the necessity for continued external financial assistance, confirmed the Commissioners in this decision. In March 1849, a further sixteen boards of guardians were restored. At the same time, the Vice-Guardians Act was passed which reinforced the existing powers of the Poor Law Commissioners regarding dissolution.[140] This Act allowed the Commissioners to prolong the dissolutions to either November 1849 or, if this did not appear appropriate, in March 1850.[141] As a result, it was not until 1850 that the administration of the Poor Law was returned to its elected representatives, in recognition of the fact that demand for poor relief had stabilised. The only exception to this was in Co. Clare, where severe distress continued to cause problems for the administration of the Poor Law.

Eviction and the Quarter-Acre Clause

Prior to 1845, there had been several attempts to restructure and modernise a number of estates in Ireland. It was generally agreed that the most effective way of achieving such a purpose was through the consolidaton of the small holdings which proliferated in many parts of the country, most notably the west. Politicians, economists and social commentators believed that such changes were essential if the economy was to improve. One of the most famous 'improving' landlords was Lord George Hill of Gweedore in Co. Donegal.[142] His attempts to improve his estate were generally unpopular, and met with passive resistance. Elsewhere in the country, agrarian violence and the activities of secret societies slowed down the process of change and modernisation.

The Famine, however, provided the necessary preconditions and impetus for economic and social change. The repeal of the Corn Laws in 1846 contributed to a shift from tillage to cattle farming. Increasingly after 1847, the process of change was facilitated by the relief policies of the government. As the relief entered its third year and financial demands continued to be made on the Treasury, a restructuring of the Irish economy and society were regarded as essential. Subsequent relief policies, therefore, were used as a means to facilitate change and improvement in Ireland. After 1847, also, the social dislocation caused by emigration, eviction, spiralling taxation, disease and mortality made further changes inevitable. To that extent, the Famine was the point of no return.

The financial burden on the taxpayers, especially after the transfer to Poor Law relief, provided a clear economic rationale for a restructuring of Irish society. The Poor Law made landlords rather than tenants liable to pay the poor rate on all holdings valued at under £4 on their property. The burden on landlords whose estates were highly sub-divided and who had not received rents since 1845 was therefore extremely heavy. This burden increased after August 1847 when the poor rates became responsible for financing all current poor relief and for the repayment of various government loans. In several of the distressed unions, the repayments for the Temporary Relief Act alone was 3s in the pound, and to this had to be added repayments for the Labour Rate Act, in addition to ordinary Poor Law expenditure. The burden of these combined taxes fell most heavily in the west and was lowest in the north and east. The unions situated in the midlands tended to fall, in varying degrees, between the two extremes although there were a number of pockets of distress, notably in counties Leitrim and Roscommon. For some landlords, years of financial mismanagement finally caught up with them. In 1847, out of a total rental of just over £13,000,000 approximately £1,3000,000 was in the hands of the receivers. By 1849, that amount had risen to £2,000,000.[143]

In 1848, the Encumbered Estates Act was introduced to facilitate the transfer of property from, the government hoped, impoverished landlords to men of capital. Sir Charles Wood, the Chancellor of the Exchequer, explained the government's underlying premise:

> There is no real prospect of regeneration and substantial amendment for Ireland until substantial proprietors possessed of capital and the will to improve their estates are introduced into the country.[144]

For a number of landlords, the combination of falling rentals and increased taxation proved a powerful incentive to clear their estates of all smallholders. Yet, at the same time, a number of Irish landlords were advertising in Scotland for new tenants for their estates. In several areas, once the movement to evict small tenants had commenced, it proved irresistible and evictions continued to increase until 1850 and continued at a high level for some years after this. Even at its peak, however, the number of people evicted did not amount to more than 2½ per cent of all agricultural holders.

Table 19: Number of Families Evicted, 1847-51[145]

1847	6,026
1848	9,657
1849	16,686
1850	19,949
1851	13,197

The evictions showed marked regional contrasts. Until 1848, most of the evictions were concentrated in the relatively prosperous counties of Armagh, Antrim, Leitrim and Monaghan. After 1848, there was a change and evictions primarily took place in the poorer counties of Clare, Galway, Limerick, Mayo and Tipperary, reflecting the continuation of high distress and consequently high taxation in these districts. It was in these counties that the decline in agricultural holdings was also highest: the national average was 20 per cent, whereas in counties Tipperary and Limerick it was 30 per cent, and in Co. Clare almost 40 per cent.[146]

The transfer to Poor Law relief undoubtedly contributed to the increase of evictions within Ireland. Before this change, earlier relief legislation had permitted the distressed people to retain their smallholdings whilst in receipt of relief. The government believed that to refuse to do so would increase long-term destitution within Ireland. The Poor Law, however, insisted that all recipients of workhouse relief had to be totally destitute. This did not allow for the same return to 'normality' after the crisis was over. The Poor Law Extension Act of 1847 increased this process by making the workhouse the primary method of providing relief. It also contributed to an increase in the number of evictions, most notably through the introduction of the controversial Quarter-Acre Clause. This was popularly known as the Gregory Clause, after the eponymous Irish landlord who introduced it, William Gregory, a landlord from Galway, who held a parliamentary seat for Co. Dublin. The Clause received support from other Irish members of parliament (only two, in fact, voted against it) who believed that it would safeguard their property and their pockets against people claiming poor relief unnecessarily.

The Gregory Clause stipulated that any person who occupied more than a quarter of an acre of land could not be deemed destitute and was not entitled to receive relief. A number of Irish landlords viewed this Clause as a protection against holders of land valued at under £4, as on these properties, it was the landlord who was liable to pay the poor rates. Since 1845, although the burden of poor rates had increased substantially, the income from rents had generally decreased. The sharp increase in evictions following the introduction of the Gregory Clause and the ruthlessness with which they were occasionally carried out resulted in a further Act being passed for the protection of evicted persons.[147] The main purpose of this Act, however, was not to bring evictions to an end, but merely to regularise the process. Some members of the Whig administration including the Prime Minister, Russell, recognised that aspects of the Poor Law, particularly eviction, were harsh. Notwithstanding this, they believed that the changes resulting from the legislation would ultimately be beneficial to the country. As a leading member of the government stated:

> It is useless to disguise the truth that any great improvement in the social system of Ireland must be founded upon an extensive change in the present state of agrarian occupation, and that this change necessarily implies a long, continued and systematic ejectment of small holders and of squatting cottiers.[148]

The Gregory Clause was regarded as a necessary safeguard against the abuses which had existed under both the Labour Rate Act and the Temporary Relief Act. It was anticipated that the Gregory Clause would put an end to these abuses by forcing the destitute people to choose clearly between property or relief. This was because the Clause stipulated:

> No person who shall be in occupation of any land of greater extent than a quarter of a statute acre shall be deemed and taken to be a destitute poor person . . . and if any person so occupying more than the statute quarter acre shall apply for relief, it shall not be lawful for any board of guardians to grant such relief within or out of the workhouse, to any such person.[149]

Within the Poor Law Commission, a clear division emerged concerning the impact which this Clause would have on the people seeking relief. Edward Twistleton was outspoken in his criticism of the Clause, believing that it imposed too rigid a test of destitution given the prevailing condition of the country. Alfred Power, the Assistant Poor Law Commissioner, on the other hand, saw its introduction as a necessary precaution against further abuses in the provision of relief. Following this, a clear division emerged within the Poor Law Commission and there were increasingly divergent opinions regarding the way in which relief was to be administered.[150] The legislation also received a mixed reception generally within Ireland. Some people viewed it as the salvation of the property of the country; others as draconian, fearing that it would merely contribute further to the general destitution. The *Dublin Evening Post*, a Catholic newspaper which regarded itself as a champion of the poor, condemned the Gregory Clause for being 'very cruel' and alleged that some landlords were interpreting its provisions in a way not intended by the legislature. The *Evening Mail*, a Protestant, establishment newspaper, described the Clause as providing a necessary test against deceit, which it believed had been extensive. At the same time, it criticised the Poor Law Commissioners for allowing too lax an interpretation to be put on the Clause. In a similar manner, the *Kerry Evening Post* declared that, without the protection of the Gregory Clause, the whole country would be swamped by taxation and eventually ruined.[151]

A similar polarisation of opinion was evident amongst local relief officals also, several believing that the Clause would ensure that relief was only given to deserving cases, others claiming that it allowed landlords to take unfair advantage of their tenants' vulnerability. Two of the most outspoken critics of the legislation were the Killarney and the Kells guardians, both of whom had been in dispute with the Poor Law Commisioners on many previous occasions. The Killarney board of guardians were outspoken supporters of tenant right. They regarded the Gregory Clause as both unjust and injurious to the poor in their union. They further observed that the Clause had introduced a 'spirit of ejectment' into the country, which was contrary to the principles of a benevolent Poor Law. As a consequence, they described the Poor Law as no longer protecting the poor. Instead, it was making permanent paupers of those whom, when the Famine was over, would otherwise have been able to support themselves unaided by the rates. Although the Killarney guardians agreed to administer the law, they did so reluctantly. The guardians of the Kells union had also been critics of various aspects of the Poor Law since its introduction. They believed that the Gregory

Clause would exacerbate the faults already present in the law and would be exploited by unscrupulous landlords. In an attempt to reduce the possibility of abuse by greedy landlords, they warned that if they found evidence of forcible entry into the home of any person in their union, they would lay information before the local magistrates. At the same time, they petitioned parliament for a complete change in the Irish Poor Law.[152]

The way in which the Gregory Clause was interpreted varied greatly, not only within individual Poor Law unions, but also amongst members of the Commission and within the government. Inevitably, this resulted in much confusion. One of the most frequent areas of dispute arose over the ability of a Relieving Officer, in cases of emergency, to give immediate relief to a person who occupied more than a quarter of an acre of land. Although Edward Twistleton did not like the Clause, he felt bound to adopt a literal interpretation of the law which meant that, even in cases of starvation, relief could not be provided to persons holding more than a quarter of an acre of land. His interpretation was based on the original 1838 Act which stipulated that only persons who were deemed to be destitute could be given relief: no person who occupied this much land, he argued, could be deemed to be destitute. Some leading members of the government, however, were concerned that if, as a consequence of a literal interpretation of the Clause, there was an increase in deaths from starvation, they might be held to blame. George Grey, the Home Secretary, informed Twistleton that in his opinion, it should be possible to obtain some relief in the case of a sudden and urgent necessity. Although Twistleton, a solicitor, believed this interpretation to be incorrect, he did promise to take a legal opinion on the Clause if any problems arose regarding its implementation in the local unions.[153]

A further problem arose in trying to decide what constituted a 'surrender' of land. Several persons who occupied more than a quarter an acre of land offered to relinquish the excess quantity if they could retain their cabins. In some cases, however, they had been forced to give up everything by their landlord. The majority of these cases occurred in the impoverished western unions where numerous instances were brought to the notice of the Poor Law officials. An example of this, concerning a widow with six children, occurred in the Westport union. Catherine Murray, who resided on the estate of Sir Robert Palmer, a notorious absentee landlord, was repeatedly refused relief from the local vice-guardians. Following her death, there was an investigation into her case which reported that she:

. . . went to obtain a hearing at the Board-room on the 27 December, going a distance of 27 miles in sleet, storm and rain; failed to get a hearing; went with a like result on the 5 January, when her case was brought before the chairman by an ex-officio guardian, who mentioned the fact of her having buried her child Bridget without a coffin on Christmas Eve at night, unassisted, in a snow-storm . . . The chairman refused all evidence being tendered . . . this poor widow could only reach home when she found her son Michael dead from hunger.[154]

This inquiry found that this woman had been refused relief on the grounds that her landlord's bailiff had informed the Relieving Officer that she possessed two and a half acres of land and was ineligible. This was proved subsequently to be untrue, but had been said to force the woman to give up all claim to her home. The inquiry found that this sort of deception, used against poor people with small holdings, had been repeated throughout the Westport union, the only exception being the estates of Lord Sligo. The person who brought this case to the notice of the Poor Law Commissioners regarded the impact of the Gregory Clause as disastrous for small-holders of land because:

The paid chairman, Relieving Officer, and bailiff, form one of the most arbitrary, life-destroying courts of ejectment (from which there is no appeal) ever yet established in Ireland'.[155]

Although less common, there were some instances of collusive arrangements occurring between landlords and tenants. Some guardians had received certificates of surrender from the applicants for relief but suspected that the landlords were still allowing the tenants to remain in their property illicitly. In some cases people sublet the excess quantity of land to friends or relatives. As a result of this, many guardians asked the Commissioners to clarify what proof of surrender was required in order for a person to become eligible for relief.[156] To resolve the numerous irregularities arising over the implementation of the Quarter Acre Clause, the Poor Law Commissioners decided to take legal advice on a number of issues. The resultant legal opinion surprised the Poor Law Commissioners. It ruled that the refusal of a landlord to accept a surrender did not disqualify a person from receiving relief and, further to this, the method of surrender was irrelevant as the occupation or the non-occupation of land was the only criterion necessary for obtaining relief. Following this ruling, the guardians were no longer bound to investigate the question of title in cases where a surrender had been declared. They were also informed that:

> No additional unbending condition should be insisted on such as a certificate of surrender from a landlord, or the cessation to occupy even a quarter acre of any land of still less extent.[157]

Regardless of the apparent liberalisation in the implementation of the Gregory Clause, many cases of suffering and privation continued to be reported in the early months of 1848. These included people who had held onto their land, even though this made them ineligible for relief. Death was sometimes the result. The Quarter Acre Clause and high poor rates were frequently blamed for the increase in the number of evictions after 1847, although the process was also facilitated by the fact that the protective activities of the agrarian societies were almost non-existent during these years. The consequences were often devastating. The Inspector of the Ballina union visited the remains of what had been a village on the estate of Mr Walsh of Castle Hill. Walsh had not paid poor rates for two years. Despite this, the Inspector discovered that eighty families had been ejected within two months from Walsh's estate, and their houses destroyed on Walsh's order. The impact of the evictions on the residents was that 'some were in their graves, others under ditches; others begging shelter from house to house, and plundering whatever they could lay hands on'.[158] Not all landlords, however, behaved in this way. In the same union, the neighbouring landlords—the Earl of Arran and Colonel Vaughan Jackson—were commended by the Inspector for showing the 'greatest forbearance and liberality' to their impoverished tenants.[159]

The main incentive for landlords to evict tenants was to avoid liability for the full amount of poor rate which was on all holdings valued at under £4. Consequently, evictions were most numerous in counties that possessed a high proportion of holdings valued at under £4, such as Leitrim, Clare, Mayo and Galway. Again, the attitude of individual landlords played a significant part in determining the level of evictions in any particular area. Some unions such as Kilrush in Co. Clare achieved national notoriety for the number of evictions taking place there daily.[160] Numerous evictions merely added to the problems facing local guardians. In the Carrick-on-Shannon union, for example, the workhouse was swamped by applicants who had been forcibly evicted from their homes which were then destroyed. The local workhouse was full and the guardians could not offer them outdoor relief because these persons no longer possessed homes to which they could return. Due to lack of finance, the guardians were unable to afford additional accommodation. Their only solution was to squeeze the poor people into an already over-crowded workhouse. Apart from the immediate difficulties caused by this eviction, the guardians doubted that these people, once admitted to the workhouse, would ever again be able to acquire a holding on the land.[161]

The eviction of large numbers of people threw a heavy burden on the poor rates within a union. For unions which were already in financial difficulties and dependent on piecemeal contributions from the Treasury, this burden was particularly severe. Some cases of eviction attracted widespread publicity, especially if they were known to be illegal. In the Swinford Poor Law union, twenty-three families were simultaneously evicted from the estate of Lord Lucan, even though the majority of tenants had paid their rents and cropped their lands. This eviction was widely publicised. As a result, the case was brought to the notice of the government who, in turn, requested the Lord Lieutenant to enquire further into the incident. It was not that the government disapproved of the eviction of small tenants, but they feared that there would be a public outcry if they were callously or illegally carried out. The investigation concluded that although the evictions carried out by Lord Lucan appeared to be harsh, in the long term such evictions would help to reduce the poverty by encouraging more capital investment in the land.[162]

One of the most common causes of suffering arising from the Gregory Clause was the fact that the families of a person occupying more than a quarter acre of land were denied relief. This punitive regulation was thought to contribute to an increase in the number of deserted wives and abandoned children. The Commissioners believed that such cases constituted neglect by the head of the family and wanted the guardians to be provided with additional powers to prosecute the father. Again, the Commissioners felt compelled to take legal advice. The legal opinion returned by the Attorney General, Jonathan Henn QC, was both unexpected and controversial. Henn interpreted the Quarter Acre Clause in a way which had not been envisaged by the Poor Law Commissioners and was contrary to the underpinning philosophy of the government. Henn ruled that in cases where a man held on to more than a quarter of an acre of land, the wife and children could be relieved, either inside or out of the workhouse, if they became destitute. Furthermore, if the occupier of land was genuinely without the resources to maintain his family, then Henn did not believe that he could be prosecuted for failing to do so. The Poor Law Commissioners, worried about the implications of such an unexpected ruling, sought a second legal opinion. This, however, reiterated that a father could not be convicted of failing to maintain his wife and children who were entitled to receive relief, regardless of the quantity of land held by the occupier. The two legal opinions also concurred that a Relieving Officer could provide provisional relief in the case of sudden and urgent necessity to the families, but not the actual occupier, of a quarter acre or more of land.[163]

As a result of these opinions, the guardians were told that neither they nor the Relieving Officers should permit the wife or child of a person occupying more than a quarter an acre of land to suffer any hardship because the occupier had refused to surrender his land and thus qualify for relief. At the same time, the guardians were warned not to allow too liberal an interpretation of the recent judgment because:

> It would be an extreme perversion of the meaning of the law, and of the language and meaning of the circular, to give relief systematically and indiscriminately to the wives and children of persons occupying more than a quarter acre of land, when the Legislature has expressly declared that such persons are not to be deemed destitute.[164]

The guardians were also warned against deception: if they suspected that an occupier of a quarter of an acre or more of land had the means to maintain his family, they were to prosecute him.[165]

The two legal opinions were regarded with suspicion by a number of members of the government. Charles Wood and Charles Trevelyan were particularly outraged by the outcome of this opinion and the subsequent instructions of the Poor Law Commissioners to the local guardians. They believed that any relaxation in the provision of relief would bring increased demands on the Treasury. To avoid this, Trevelyan demanded that the Commissioner's instructions to the local unions should be modified in such a way as to protect the Treasury from any undue demands.[166] The Home Office was also apprehensive about the implications of the recent interpretation of the Gregory Clause. Sir George Grey, the Home Secretary, feared that the legal opinions had gone too far and would give the families of a man occupying more than a quarter of an acre an unduly high expectation of relief. Although he did not doubt the correctness of the legal opinion, Grey informed the Commissioners:

> It appears to the government that it would be obviously contrary to the spirit and intentions of the provisions of the law and tend to

defeat the object with which it was enacted if the families of persons owning more than a quarter of an acre of land were to be considered as indiscriminately entitled to relief.[167]

The Poor Law Commissioners were not surprised at the alarm that the new interpretation of the Quarter Acre Clause caused, especially amongst members of the government. Edward Twistleton personally disliked the outcome of the legal advice, but he acknowledged that many people had already died of starvation and this would have continued without a change in the law. He believed that over the summer many lives would be saved by this legal opinion, especially as occupiers of land would not want to surrender their holdings so near to the harvest. Twistleton, therefore, felt that it was unfair of the government to suggest that he should attempt to deviate from the course prescribed by the legal opinion. Twistleton was becoming increasingly disillusioned with the demands being made on him by the Whig government and their officers at the Treasury. He informed the Treasury that if they did not like the legal interpretation, they should ask the government to amend the Act.[168] However, the Quarter Acre Clause, despite official misgivings, remained in place. Regardless of the controversial legal opinion, the number of evictions and surrenders of land did not decrease. Evictions in 1849 were almost double the number in 1848 and continued to increase until 1851. Even after this date, however, the numbers evicted remained far higher for a number of years than they had been prior to the Famine.

The Quarter Acre Clause sharpened the developing contrast between those whose main motivation was to tackle social distress and those who viewed the distress as an opportunity to bring about a measure of economic restructuring. The latter's concern, unofficially expressed by some leading members of the government and the Treasury, was to increase the size of agricultural holdings and introduce new capital into Ireland. This vision of the economic transformation of rural Ireland encouraged a policy of minimal intervention which, together with the Quarter Acre Clause, clearly facilitated the amalgamation of small holdings. A number of landlords, though by no means all, also used the prevailing social disruption as an opportunity to go beyond the letter of the law and evict at will. The impact of government policies was a clear instance of economic opportunism: of achieving a perceived benefit, the social cost of which was paid by the destitute. At the same time, the primary concern of the government and the Treasury continued to be to minimise their financial exposure to the consequences of the distress. The Quarter Acre Clause represented de facto a dogmatic concern to place the integrity of public finance and socio-economic engineering above the human consequences of famine.

Relief During the Summer of 1848

During the early months of 1848, the relationship between the Poor Law Commissioners in Dublin and the Treasury in London deteriorated considerably. The Poor Law Extension Act of 1847 had provided for the Treasury to play an active role in the affairs of the Poor Law, even to determine the number and salaries of employees of the Poor Law Commission. Moreover, monies provided by both the British government and the British Relief Association were channelled through the Treasury. Trevelyan, who had been involved in the provision of relief since 1845, was determined to control its distribution as far as possible. Since the first appearance of blight, he had increasingly taken upon himself the role of commander-in-chief of Irish distress. By 1847, he was firmly entrenched in this role, especially as no one within the British government expressed any interest in removing the mantle from him.

The introduction of the amended Poor Law in 1847, of which Trevelyan fully approved, presented him with even more opportunities for directing the way in which relief was to be provided. Trevelyan sent each of the newly appointed relief officials a copy of his book, *The Irish Crisis*. He also unofficially asked them to send him privately a full report on local destitution, including their frank opinion on the general administration of the Poor Law. Trevelyan further requested that Twistleton should send him a copy of all Poor Law correspondence and insisted that he should be involved in the appointment of all Poor Law personnel. Twistleton resented the constant intrusion of Trevelyan into the affairs of the Poor Law Commission. He did not want to allow him any additional involvement in the appointment of Poor Law officials other than that prescribed by the government. He also refused to forward copies of Poor Law correspondence to him, on the grounds that it was concerned with individual points of administration and therefore not relevant to Treasury business.[169]

As the year progressed, the personal relationship between Trevelyan and Twistleton grew increasingly more fraught. Twistleton, supported by the members of the Irish Executive, was concerned that the Poor Law alone did not possess the financial resources to provide the relief necessary. He believed that if the government continued to insist that local rates must support local poverty, they were running a risk of increased deaths from starvation. He warned the Whig administration that if they pursued this policy 'some risks must be run, you cannot fight a great battle without some loss'.[170] To officials within the Treasury, however, the success of the Poor Law depended upon the enforcement of the collection of rate after rate. Trevelyan explained that the policy of the government had been purposely designed to make the people choose between:

> . . . a lamentable loss of life of the lower classes, and the temporary distress of those classes whose duty it is to give employment to able-bodied poor and gratuitous relief for the impotent poor.[171]

The gradual withdrawal of the funds by the British Relief Association during the summer of 1848 occurred at a time when demand for relief was increasing. Twistleton was apprehensive that during the critical weeks between the beginning of July and the beginning of September, the Poor Law alone would be insufficient to meet the expected distress. He felt that during these weeks it might even prove necessary to provide relief to previously unassisted unions.[172] Although financial assistance was provided by the government, they again adopted the policy of only providing the minimal amount of relief necessary to prevent deaths from starvation. Twistleton was informed that the Treasury would intervene in 'desperate cases' only, where it was absolutely necessary to save the lives of the destitute. Also, this assistance was to end on 15 August 1848, the date which had been fixed for outdoor relief to be stopped.[173]

The plans of the government for a cessation of all financial assistance following the harvest of 1848 were destroyed by the reappearance of the potato blight. By August 1848, it was obvious that not only had blight appeared in many parts of the country, but that in the areas in which it had appeared it was already as virulent as in 1846. Twistleton no longer believed that it would be possible to end outdoor relief in August, and asked the Treasury to allow an extension to September, as in the previous year. He also believed that the reappearance of blight would mean that even beyond this date, many unions would again require external financial assistance.[174] The response to these suggestions indicated how wide the gulf between the Poor Law Commissioners and the Treasury had become. The Treasury was appalled by the Commissioners' assessment of the situation, and reprimanded them for contemplating such a large role for the government in the coming months. Notwithstanding the reappearance of the blight, the Treasury reiterated that assistance would only be provided if absolutely necessary, on the grounds that 'we do not profess to aim at saving the unions from serious embarrassments'.[175]

They believed that if they allowed any deviation from this 'The demands upon us would become infinite and the habit of depending upon the assistance from the national fund would be extended and confirmed'.[176] In a further long, explicit letter to Twistleton, Trevelyan painstakingly explained the policy of the government regarding aid to Poor Law unions. He stated, with thinly veiled sarcasm, that he considered it necessary to make these instructions very clear to the Commissioners, because the latter's repeated misinterpreting of the government's intentions had resulted in many embarrassments and misunderstandings. Trevelyan concluded with a direct criticism of the way in which the Poor Law Commissioners had administered relief. He cited the examples of the Galway and Tuam unions, which had received advances from the Treasury on the recommendation of the Commissioners, yet they had made very small poor rates.[177]

This unprecedented attack on the Poor Law Commissioners marked a further step in the deteriorating relationship between the Treasury and the relief officials in Ireland. Twistleton was particularly angry that the Commissioners had been accused of mis-spending the funds of the government without first being asked for an explanation. He pointed out that without this money many thousands of people would have died. In the Galway union, even with the support of the military, both the elected guardians and vice-guardians found it difficult to collect the rates. Galway was a very poor union and, if the Commissioners had withheld financial assistance, they considered that it would have achieved the same notoriety as the Skibbereen union had in the previous year. In the Tuam union also, financial assistance had been necessary to prevent deaths from starvation. In both unions the Commissioners believed that relief had been provided with due economy and only where absolutely necessary to save lives. They therefore were adamant that there had been no departure from the rules by which assistance was to be granted.[178] In a separate private communication to Trevelyan, Twistleton asked him not to reproach the Commissioners publicly without first giving them a chance to explain their actions. With undisguised annoyance, he added that Trevelyan should demonstrate more confidence in the administration of the Poor Law Commissioners and should not interfere in the manner in which they chose to distribute grants to the unions.[179]

The increase in the number of deaths from starvation in the early months of 1848 resulted in the Poor Law Commissioners increasingly questioning the effectiveness of the policies which they were administering. The Treasury continued to insist that rates be collected to 'the utmost practicable point', but Twistleton admitted that he no longer knew where this point lay. If this system of relief continued, Twistleton predicted that there was a risk of further deaths from starvation. He suggested that if the government wished to reduce this, they should revive the Temporary Relief Act—the soup kitchens—used in the previous year. Twistleton was pessimistic that this would not occur. The government—and public opinion in Britain—was committed to the idea of local Irish taxes maintaining the Irish local poor, considering it 'inexpedient that the poor of Ireland should again be maintained from the public purse'.[180] The inability of the Poor Law to meet the demands which would be made on it, Twistleton feared, would provide its opponents with a weapon which would create mischief for him personally. He concluded that the government was pursuing its chosen policy so single-mindedly, regardless of the risks involved, because:

> It seemed to be a less evil to the Empire to encounter the risk than to continue the system of advances from the public purse. If the system pursued during the last four months is continued, there will be a continuance of the same risk . . . But the success of the Commission in preventing deaths from starvation must not be judged by a comparison with another system of relief, which is wholly distinct in its fundamental principles.[181]

Over the summer of 1848, the Treasury reluctantly provided additional financial assistance to the distressed unions. The Treasury felt that there were certain advantages in continuing to support Poor Law relief: notably, it was cheap and could be centrally monitored more easily than the earlier systems of relief. More importantly, the Poor Law did not encourage a feeling of dependence on the government but—even more positively—was helping to promote 'the national remedial process which is in rapid progress amongst all orders of society in the distressed unions'.[182] The money advanced to the distressed unions was to be in the form of loans which, the Treasury insisted, were to be repaid from the local poor rates as soon as possible.

Although the Commissioners were pleased that additional money would be forthcoming, they were concerned that in the long term this policy would place the dependent unions in a difficult position. As a consequence of government policy, the ratepayers in many unions, particularly the poorest ones, were deeply in debt—often through no fault of their own—as the produce of the land was absorbed almost totally in the provision of relief.

Twistleton and the Irish Poor Law Commissioners were not the only people to worry about the impact of this policy. George Nicholls, who had framed the 1838 Act, introduced it to Ireland, and been the first Irish Poor Law Commissioner, was adamant that it was beyond the scope of the Poor Law to deal with any period of extended distress. He felt that during a famine it was the duty of one part of the Empire to come to the rescue of another, recognising the existence of a special relationship between a famine and a Poor Law:

> Although in one sense intimate, it is in other respects limited; for where the land has ceased to be reproductive, the necessary means of relief cannot be obtained from it, and a Poor Law will no longer be operative, or at least not operative to the extent adequate to meet such an emergency as then existed in Ireland.[183]

The year 1847–8 was a period of widening gulfs. The divide in opinion on how the official response to relief should be handled meant that there was a distancing between the Treasury in London and relief officials in Ireland, to the increasing frustration and despair of the latter who were unable to match their policy prescriptions with the level of assistance that they believed to be necessary. The Treasury, in command of both policy and resources, pursued its own vision of the improvement of Ireland. Underpinning this was a strong conviction that God's purpose, with the help of the political economists, was to be served by forcing the inadequacies of the poorest parts of Ireland to be met from within their own resources.

The focus of the organisation of relief on the Poor Law produced a gulf between good intention and practical achievement. The Poor Law system had not been devised, designed or financed to cope with widespread starvation such as existed in the most severely afflicted areas. Finally, after a brief interlude of soup kitchen relief in the summer of 1847, the gulf widened between the nutritional requirements of the destitute and the availability of relief. The ultimate recipients of the relief remained victims to a system of parsimony that viewed their very existence as part of the problem.

Making Property Support Poverty

1848–9

In the spring of 1848, the prospects for the approaching harvest appeared good. In April of that year, the Poor Law Commissioners requested information from each of their local Inspectors regarding the prospects of the crops, especially potatoes, in their unions. In general, the replies were favourable and reflected a widely-held optimism regarding the harvest. The Inspectors reported that in many areas large tracts of land, previously left as waste, had for the first time in years been planted with crops. Also, potatoes had been cultivated to an extent unknown for many years. This was mostly due to an almost total lack of blight in the previous year, which had contributed to a renewed confidence in the potato as a crop. These reports were all the more reassuring because the distress of the previous year had been due, not so much to blight, but to the smallness of the crop sown. The encouraging prospects for the harvest persuaded small farmers to endure severe privation during the summer, rather than relinquish their holdings and so become eligible for Poor Law relief.

At the same time, some factors were present which suggested that a degree of caution was necessary. Although small farmers were reported to be showing renewed enthusiasm in cultivating their properties, this had little impact on the cottier or labouring classes, as it provided little additional employment. Some of the smallest holdings remained uncultivated as their occupiers had long since taken refuge in the local workhouse, emigrated or died. The very large extent of potatoes sown in some areas excluded other crops, indicating a willingness amongst many people to rely again solely on the potato for their livelihood. One Inspector, while admitting that the people in his area were in better spirits and more energetic than they had been for over three years, cautioned that if blight appeared again, it would result in a total ruination of small farmers. Furthermore, the claims of the local Inspectors regarding the extent of the potato crop, had little basis in reality. The statistical returns of agricultural produce that were kept annually after 1847, indicate that the acreage of potatoes under cultivation continued to be below its pre-Famine levels for many years. In 1845, the acreage under potatoes had exceeded two million; it dropped to just over one million in 1846, to 0.3 million in 1847, and rose to only 0.7 million in 1848. Tillage also remained far below its pre-Famine levels for a number of years.[1]

The optimism regarding the state of the potato crop was short lived. At the beginning of July 1848, there were sightings of the blight along the west coast of Ireland. By August, it was obvious that in the areas where blight had re-appeared, it was as virulent as in 1846. Local reports from around the country showed that the blight of 1848 was localised, being particularly evident in the west of the country and some parts of the north-east, with only isolated instances elsewhere.[2]

The potato blight of 1848 was in many ways a watershed in the relief operations. This was due not only to its uneven distribution but also to a more general economic recovery in various parts of the country. This resulted in an even greater demarcation between the 'distressed' and 'non-distressed' unions, that is between those that were able to depend on their own resources following the 1848 harvest and those that were unable to provide relief without external aid. In some parts of the country, notably in the north-east and on the east coast, the worst of the Famine was over. But along the western seaboard, the effects of a fourth year of distress and shortages were devastating. As usual, the majority of unions in the midlands of the country fell between these two extremes.

In 1848, there was severe blight in many parts of the north-east. Despite this, the financial prospects of many northern unions were better than they had been for a number of years. This was mostly due to the role of the potato in the local economy. The north-eastern part of Ulster differed from the rest of the country, as most small farmers were also involved in the linen industry, usually as part-time weavers. Oats were also more widely grown than in other parts. This meant that the level of distress in the area not merely depended on the yield of the local crops but also on the state of the linen trade. A downturn in the linen trade in 1847, combined with the smallness of the potato crop, resulted in severe distress in parts of counties Antrim, Derry and Down. The spread of fever in many northern unions had contributed to this distress. These factors had, however, been short lived and, reflecting the general prosperity of the area, the unions had been able to provide relief without requiring assistance from the Treasury.[3]

By the end of 1848, the linen trade in Ulster had recovered almost totally from the temporary dislocation. Despite the appearance of blight in a number of unions, the local Poor Law Inspector, Edward Senior, was optimistic about the prospects of the unions in his district. He attributed his optimism to a number of factors. Although potatoes were not available in many of his unions, both breadstuffs and corn had been imported in large quantities from Europe and America. Also, although the potato crop had been blighted, there had been a large yield of other crops within the area. Furthermore, the local linen trade had almost totally recovered, enabling farmers and other individuals to provide additional employment. Senior believed that improvements in the provision of relief had also taken place. Workhouse accommodation had been increased by up to a third and the sanitary condition of the workhouses had improved.

In general, Senior believed that the changeover to Poor Law relief had been beneficial. Whereas earlier systems of relief had been lax and demoralising, the Poor Law could be closely monitored and strictly administered. Senior admitted that in the approaching year there would be distress, some of it severe, in many of his unions. Regardless of this, he anticipated that it would not prove necessary to give outdoor relief to the able-bodied and local rates would be sufficient to finance the distress.[4] Overall, Senior was pleased with the prospects of the Poor Law in his unions for the approaching year. He felt there was a great difference between the unions in the north of the country and those in the south. Consequently, he believed it was unfair that the whole country should be regarded as diseased and corrupt by many persons living outside Ireland.[5]

As Senior's assessment of the situation indicated, the potato failure was not as decisive a factor in rural welfare in the north-east as in other parts of the country. The revival of the linen industry in mid-1848 meant that the small-holders in Ulster were able to weather the storm of a further potato blight and small crop yields. In the parts of the east and midlands which also possessed a diversified economy, the end of the international trade slump brought an improvement in local economic conditions. In parts of the north-west, seasonal migration, which had been temporarily in abeyance due to unemployment in Britain, again revived. These factors helped to provide a safety net against the appearance of blight in the locality. But in areas where the potato was the mainstay of the subsistence economy, as in many parts of the west, the impact of a fourth year of blight was devastating. The Poor Law Commissioners were inundated with correspondence from the twenty-two distressed unions, all of which pointed to a deepening crisis within them. As the Commissioners were aware, this situation was likely to worsen as the year progressed.

The Treasury had decided that all external financial assistance to the unions was to end in September 1848. By this time, however, the situation in the distressed unions was worrying as demand for relief was even higher than it had been in the previous three years. The vice-guardians were amongst the first to express alarm. Apart from the potato blight, there had been a more general crop failure within their unions which left the local population without food. A variety of other factors meant that the distress was likely to be more severe than in previous years: widespread eviction and the throwing down of houses had increased the number of homeless families; small-holdings had been left uncultivated as people had voluntarily surrendered their property in order to be eligible for relief; large-scale emigration, some by men who had left their wives and families behind; the wetness of the season, which meant that there was a scarcity of fuel; and, most importantly, the cumulative impact which three years of shortages, sickness and suffering had made on the local population.

The Inspector of the Kenmare union described the population in this union as being without any resources as a consequence of three years of distress. He believed this to be evident from the fact a number of inmates of the workhouse had refused to change to outdoor relief because their homes had been knocked down and they had no resources with which to obtain other shelter.[6] The prospects of the Skibbereen union, which had achieved such notoriety in 1846, had also worsened. Apart from the potato blight, the local turnip crop had failed and the fishing industry had collapsed. In the previous year, the British Relief Association had provided food to over 20,000 children in the union, but this relief had now ceased altogether. Many small farmers had, only a few months earlier, sold or pawned what few possessions they had remaining in order to procure seed potatoes, in the hope of a good harvest. The reappearance of blight had made these sacrifices meaningless. Instead, these people were likely to become applicants for Poor Law relief which, the Inspector believed, was the only hope left to the poor and destitute.[7]

In the Kilrush union, in the six-month period from July to December 1848, 6,090 people were evicted from their holdings. This figure did not include families who had voluntarily surrendered their holdings. None of these people even possessed the means with which to emigrate. The local Inspector described these evictions as 'inhuman' acts which had been perpetrated on a 'helpless, hopeless people'. In November 1848, between 1,000 and 3,000 new applicants for relief were applying to the Poor Law daily. The workhouse quickly filled and the Inspector requested that out-door relief be permitted as quickly as possible.[8] The Inspector of the Ballina union was pessimistic about the ability of the Poor Law to pro-vide sufficient relief for the needs of the people. He observed that, although poor rates might appear to an outsider to be light, they had brought the union to virtual ruin. In his opinion, if a further high rate was struck, there would be no solvent tenants left in the union. He believed that this situation was being repeated in every other union in Co. Mayo. In an insightful comment on the whole operation of the Poor Law and its underlying ethos, he concluded:

> The question must now be determined whether the experiment of making property support poverty is to be continued in the west of Ireland, and I have no doubt whatsoever, such an experiment must ultimately fail, and I therefore think it would be most cruel to per-severe in it.[9]

Throughout the west of Ireland, relief officials, members of the clergy and ratepayers doubted the ability of the Poor Law and the local rates to bring the unions through the ordeal ahead. Apart from the reappearance of the potato blight and more general crop failure, a number of other factors contributed to the general feeling of pessimism. Limited employ-ment was available and the fishing industry had almost totally disap-peared. The little capital possessed by the poor had long since gone, so that many of the population possessed neither the means to purchase food, pay their rents, or even to emigrate. The continued evictions only added to the suffering and vulnerability of the poor. The funds of the British Relief Association and various other charitable organisations were exhausted and the goodwill which had accompanied the giving of dona-tions had disappeared. As the fourth year of shortages commenced, the only outlet available to many people was the Poor Law, and many Poor Law officials no longer believed that it possessed the resources to rise to the challenge.

The Provision of Relief

Following the harvest of 1848, the Poor Law was again to play a central role in the provision of relief in Ireland. This role was further increased because the activities of many other bodies, which had been actively involved in providing relief in earlier years, had been brought to an end, either through lack of funds or by order of the government. The food depots which had been controlled by the Commissariat Department under Sir Randolph Routh, had been gradually closed down over the previous year. In 1847, the Board of Ordnance had provided the Poor Law Commission with a large supply of bedding and clothing for distribution in the distressed unions. In 1848, the Commissioners had asked if this could be repeated, but the Treasury refused to sanction the request. They explained that if they did so, they would only perpetuate and prolonging the habit of dependence on the government.[10] The government also decided not to import additional foodstuffs to the country, stating that private trade would be stimulated by the public declaration that they would again not interfere in the market place, even in a limited form.[11]

Of more significance was the fact that, increasingly, the assistance provided by various charitable associations, particularly the British Relief Association, was no longer available. For the most part, donations to Irish distress had been most numerous in the winter of 1846–7, but had quickly dried up thereafter. The Society of Friends, one of the largest charitable organisations involved in the provision of relief, had decided to disengage themselves from this role during the summer of 1847. They claimed that their members were exhausted and they did not want to undermine the work of the Poor Law. Although the government had requested them to revive some of their activities, they had refused to do so on the grounds that this would be similar to 'giving a criminal a long day'. Instead, they chose to limit their resources to bringing about long-term improvement within Ireland through the distribution of seed.[12] The British Relief Association, in the year following the 1847 harvest, had contributed significantly to the relief of Irish distress. Apart from feeding thousands of children in the west of Ireland, they had also given direct aid to the twenty-two distressed unions and had provided intermittent grants to twenty-five other impoverished unions. The Association had agreed to allow this money to be channelled through the Treasury. By the autumn of 1848, however, their funds were totally exhausted.[13] The withdrawal of their support meant that, after 1848, the provision of relief was further centralised in the hands of the Poor Law, pushing the burden on the local poor rates even higher.

In 1848 the country was entering its fourth successive year of distress. Yet the government continued publicly to express faith that the Poor Law, with the help of private resources, could provide sufficient relief in the difficult months ahead. Accordingly, the relief provided after 1848 was, as in the previous year, the responsibility of local taxation. Poor rates were again to be the main means of financing local destitution.

Privately, however, the reappearance of blight in the distressed unions was a matter of grave concern to the government, the Treasury and the Poor Law Commissioners. The government had planned to stop all advances to the Irish unions at harvest and no contingency plans had been made in the event of a return of the blight. At the end of September 1848, the government announced that it had less than £3,000 in hand and that grants to the distressed unions would cease when this was exhausted. Following this, the poor rates would be expected to finance all relief.[14] This money was put in the hands of the Treasury, who increasingly played a game of brinkmanship in an effort to ensure that local taxes bore the primary responsibility for financing local relief. Again, the main sufferers in this game were the poor and destitute whose lives depended on the provision of this relief.

In November 1848, the Poor Law Commissioners warned the Treasury that extraneous financial assistance was required immediately in the majority of the distressed unions, and possibly in a few adjoining ones. In the course of the previous few weeks, mortality had increased throughout these unions, mostly as a result of fever and dysentery, the spread of which the Commissioners believed was exacerbated by the debilitated condition of the population. They considered that there would be an even greater loss of life if the government continued to insist that local poor rates alone were to finance the relief. The Commissioners estimated that 100 of the 131 unions (an additional union had been formed in Dingle from the Tralee union) would not require external financial assistance. Of the remaining thirty-one unions, they calculated that ten or eleven of them 'by dint of exertion' might be able to survive from their own resources. This meant that twenty unions would definitely require assistance from the government or some other source.[15]

Although the Treasury acknowledged that it would be necessary to continue with external aid to the distressed unions, they repeated that such money was to be limited to cases of 'absolute emergency'. They insinuated that this had not always been the case, citing the example of money which had recently been forwarded to the Gort union by the Poor Law Commissioners. They also accused some of the vice-guardians of having been 'lavish' in their expenditure of government money. Twistleton was furious with such accusations, which he considered ill-founded and unjustified. He responded that, in his opinion, the vice-guardians deserved full credit for having brought to an end deaths from starvation. The fact that these men had not been lavish in their expenditure could be judged from the emaciated appearance of such a large portion of the population. Justifying the grant to the Gort union, Twistleton explained:

> What I think of Gort union is that they were really hurt when they cried—in many parts of Ireland, especially the east, men have cried without being hurt.[16]

In spite of their personal reservations regarding the policies of the Whig government, the Poor Law Commissioners continued to urge the local administrators to do everything in their power to enforce an immediate collection of poor rates. Privately, however, they expressed considerable sympathy with the predicament of the local guardians and vice-guardians. They described the blight as having reduced the condition of the people in the west of Ireland 'to nearly the lowest point of squalor and want at which human beings can exist'.[17] Contrary to the public declarations of the government, they no longer believed that local poor rates would be sufficient to alleviate the incipient distress. Already, the financial situation in several unions meant that the receipt of external aid had become a matter of life and death. In the Bantry union, the situation deteriorated so rapidly that the Commissioners were forced to send the vice-guardians £300 which had been earmarked for another union. Following this, the Commissioners appealed directly to the government, rather than through the usual medium of the Treasury, for further subventions. They believed that unless these were forthcoming, the prospects for parts of Ireland were dismal. Twistleton warned:

> Unless funds from some extraneous sources are placed at their disposal for the aid of the Distressed Unions it cannot be doubted that deaths from starvation will occur in some of these unions as in the winter of 1846–7.[18]

By this stage, it was apparent that no system of relief on such a large scale had ever before been administered so cheaply. Twistleton, aware of this, was worried as to how far the limited resources at the disposal of the Poor Law could be stretched. He believed that the relief provided was so cheap because the underlying ethos of workhouse life, even before the Famine, depended on the principle of 'less eligibility'. The introduction of outdoor relief continued the principle of providing minimal relief. Although this was partly defensible given the general poverty of Ireland, the Irish Poor Law Commissioners realised that it was totally contrary to the principles on which relief was administered in England. Twistleton was afraid that if the precise details about the quantity of relief provided were made public, 'others might say that we are slowly murdering the peasantry by the scantiness of the relief'.[19] The Poor Law Commissioners became increasingly defensive about the way in which they were administering Famine relief. Their recommendations had been repeatedly ignored, and the Commissioners wanted to dissociate themselves from the relief policies being implemented. They tried to ensure that any material published relating to the Poor Law, particularly in their Annual Reports and in Parliamentary Papers, was as uncontroversial as possible, even to the extent of occasionally omitting certain details about the relief provided.[20]

As the Poor Law Commissioners were aware, the system which they were administering was particularly unpopular in the latter months of 1848 and early months of 1849, in both England and Ireland. The opposition was mostly concerned with the way in which relief was managed although a number of its opponents were critical of the way in which it was financed. In England, the opposition centred around *The Times* newspaper. Since the first appearance of blight in 1845, *The Times* frequently accused the Irish people of doing little to help themselves, and claimed that they preferred to depend on external assistance from the British Treasury. Its sympathy towards the Irish distress did not improve with the passage of time. In the early months of 1847, when distress was most severe, *The Times* argued against continuing financial support from Britain on the grounds that, 'whatever might be done now, would only increase the necessity, and hasten the occasion, for doing more hereafter'. When, at the beginning of 1849, parliament proposed to give Ireland a further grant of £50,000—a relatively small figure when compared with the £4½m which had been expended in 1846–7 on the public works alone—*The Times* described this money as 'breaking the back' of English benevolence.[21]

In Ireland also, some of the Tory newspapers which had been vociferous critics of the Poor Law since its introduction by a Whig government in 1838, repeatedly attacked its operation. Opposition was not confined merely to the Tory press. In Dublin, the *Evening Post* suggested that certain changes were necessary in the administration of the Poor Law. The *Evening Mail* was even more scathing and used the excuse of a fourth year of distress to demand a complete abolition of the Poor Law system.[22] The Poor Law even had its critics in the north of Ireland, where its administration was most successful. The *Northern Whig* described the operation of the law in the west of Ireland as a 'cruel and useless experiment', which it considered had failed in its declared purpose of bringing about an economic and social transformation.[23]

Within the Poor Law unions, there was both individual and collective dissatisfaction with the Poor Law, and a number of boards of guardians petitioned parliament demanding its repeal. This opposition was not restricted to the poorest unions, but also was evident in some of the unions situated in other parts of the country. Towards the end of 1848, the Kells board established a Poor Law Amendment Committee, with headquarters in Northumberland Buildings in Dublin. In December 1848, this committee convened a meeting to which boards of guardians from all parts of Ireland were invited. The meeting was attended by guardians from as far apart as Tralee and Belfast, although it received most support from guardians of unions in the midlands and south-east of Ireland: many of the unions in the west of the country were still being administered by vice-guardians, and the majority of elected guardians in the north-east distanced themselves from such agitation. At the meeting, the Kells guardians, who for many months had advocated a complete change in the Poor Law system, proposed a motion to this effect. The proposal was, however, rejected on the grounds that a Poor Law was nec-essary for the ongoing relief of distress. Despite this, the Poor Law was criticised because it was believed to have acted as a disincentive to land-lords to improve their property, while simultaneously degrading the recipients of relief. At the beginning of March 1849, the Poor Law Amendment Committee met for the last time, as its members considered that they had achieved their objective in the preparation of various peti-tions to parliament. The more militant faction of the anti-Poor Law movement was defeated; a complete repeal of the Poor Law was not demanded, only a modification of some aspects of it.[24]

The opposition to the Poor Law was not limited to the boards of guardians, nor was it confined to the poorest districts where the burden on local rates was highest. The Poor Law was held responsible for a wide variety of ills. In the North Dublin union, the ratepayers held a meeting to discuss the sending back of Irish paupers from England and Scotland, often in an impoverished condition. The large landowners in Co. Westmeath jointly suggested the Poor Law should be amended as they considered that it was a hindrance to the trade of Ireland. The ratepayers of Co. Clare petitioned parliament for a change in its method of taxation, which they regarded as demoralising and expensive. A number of magis-trates in Dublin accused the Poor Law of encouraging the people to revolt.[25] Much of this dissatisfaction was fragmented, and was concen-trated in a few months during the winter of 1848–9, following which it tended to disappear. It was quickly succeeded by a far more concerted and sustained campaign by the usually passive northern boards, arising from the controversial Rate-in-Aid Bill.

To a large degree, the most vehement opposition to the Poor Law existed in parliament itself. Some of this antagonism was directed against Twistleton, who was personally unpopular for his increasingly outspoken criticisms of the government's policies. He was also a convenient scapegoat for the failure of the government's relief policies. Much of the opposition revolved around the Irish members of parliament, many of whom had landed interests in Ireland. These men had frequently been blamed, even before the potato blight, for the economic backwardness of the country. The burden of poor rates during the Famine, especially on estates which were already impoverished and highly sub-divided, was regarded by Irish MPs as punitive and unfair. Several of the Irish members formed a committee to discuss possible amendments to the Poor Law. This discontent was not, however, confined to the Irish members of parliament. The debate concerning the funding of distress for a fourth year showed the extent of the unpopularity of the Poor Law in particular, and Irish distress in general, in parliament. The decision, reached in February 1849, to provide the relatively small amount of £50,000 to Irish distress was vehemently opposed.[26] These parliamentary deliberations resulted in the appointment of twin select committees of the House of Commons and the House of Lords. The purpose of the committees was to examine the administration of the Poor Law and decide how, in future, it should be funded. Russell, who had carefully handpicked the members of the Commons committee, used it as a forum to suggest a further change in the policy for financing Irish distress, proposing a national 'Rate-in-Aid' to be levied on every union in Ireland, for the relief of the poorest unions.[27] This suggestion confirmed the fact that Irish poor rates were still to be responsible for financing Irish distress, although this shifted the emphasis from local to national taxation.

Regardless of the unpopularity of the Poor Law and its inability to finance local relief in the poorest unions, the Whig government continued to express its faith in the ability of the Poor Law to bring Ireland through a fourth year of distress. The reduced parliamentary majority of the Whigs and the public outcry against continuing aid to Ireland, meant that Russell's government had to find a solution to Ireland's ills that would not be regarded as a burden on the British taxpayers. The Poor Law, assisted by the proposed Rate-in-Aid, continued to be regarded as the safest way of doing this.[28] As a method of providing relief, the Poor Law also had the support of the Treasury which, despite being frequently in dispute with the Commissioners, regarded it as the most effective and economic way of relieving distress in Ireland. To the leading members of the Treasury, the cheapness of Poor Law relief, the stringency with which it could be provided, and the emphasis on local accountability, all made it preferable to other systems of relief. The relief committees, public works and food depots had been both costly and demoralising, and had encouraged the people to expect unending assistance from the government. The Treasury was determined that this should not be the case again. The Poor Law, on the other hand, apart from providing Famine relief, was believed to be facilitating the much-needed social and economic reform within Ireland. The burden of poor rates, the workhouse test, and the Quarter-Acre Clause were all believed to have contributed to this. Wood, the Chancellor of the Exchequer, advised the government unequivocally not to be persuaded to return to the earlier systems of relief. These, he believed, would 'only prolong the expense and consequent expenditure by enabling small-holders to hold on'. He explained:

> The plea of helping the Poor Law preserves us from the calamity of that admirable institution breaking down under the pressure of local and temporary distress, prevents extreme destitution, and does not in the least retard the national remedial process which is in rapid progress amongst all orders of society in the distressed districts.[29]

Financing Poor Relief

By the beginning of 1849, it was obvious that some additional finance would have to be allocated to the relief of distress. Charles Wood suggested to the Prime Minister, Russell, that the government should ask parliament for no less than £50,000 for this purpose. This, he admitted, was a small sum in view of the number of unions requiring support. Already only a few months after the 1848 harvest, the finances of twenty unions were totally exhausted and he estimated that a further eleven unions, situated close to the distressed unions, would require external aid at some stage during the year. Wood also admitted to Russell that this money would probably be insufficient to support the unions until the following harvest, but he felt that, given the general opposition within parliament towards Irish distress, it would be unwise to ask for any more. Russell was aware, however, that even this relatively small amount would meet strong opposition both inside and outside parliament, including from some members of the Whig party. In a debate in the House of Commons at the beginning of 1849, this antagonism manifested itself.

Again, it was stated that the Irish people had done nothing to help themselves. Regardless of the fact that over £1m. had been raised in poor rates since the extension of the Poor Law in August 1847, the blame for Irish distress continued to be laid firmly at the feet of the Irish themselves. A powerful grouping of Whig moderates, middle-class radicals and Peelites argued against continuing financial intervention. Even more important, however, was British public opinion, which appeared antagonistic to any further measures to help Ireland. The Prime Minister was less doctrinaire than many of his followers, but Russell was increasingly isolated within his own party. Although he would have liked to provide more relief to Ireland, he realised this was not possible. He informed Clarendon, the Lord Lieutenant:

> The great difficulty this year respecting Ireland is one which does not spring from Trevelyan and Charles Wood but lies deep in the breasts of the British people. It is this—we have granted, lent, subscribed, worked, visited, clothed the Irish; millions of pounds worth of money, years of debate etc. etc.—the only return is calumny and rebellion—let us not grant, clothe etc. etc. any more and see what they will do . . . Now, without borrowing and lending we could have no great plan for Ireland—and much as I wish it, I have got to see that it is impracticable.[30]

On 12 February 1849, £50,000 was made available for the relief of Irish distress. The debate which preceded the granting of this money was indicative of a further hardening of attitude by many Members of Parliament towards the ongoing problem of Irish distress. This small sum of money was passed by a majority of 220 to 143 votes, after a rough passage through parliament.[31] Between 1845–8, the amount of government money provided for the relief of Irish distress had been £7,918,400, although almost half of this was a loan. Although the £50,000 was provided as a grant towards the poorest Irish unions, it indicated a real reduction in government expenditure.[32] At the same time, the government desired to make it clear that there were limits to its largesse. Parliament was eager to find a way of ensuring that this would be the final grant made to relieve Irish distress. A scheme to end this dependence which was suggested by George Graham and supported by Disraeli, both members of the Tory opposition, was therefore eagerly seized upon by many members of the two main parties. Sir Robert Peel, the former Prime Minister, however, was an outspoken critic of this proposal. The scheme proposed that when the £50,000 was exhausted, if further monies were required for the relief of distress, they should be raised by a national tax levied in Ireland, to be known as 'Rate-in-Aid'. To win support for this proposal, Russell circulated a copy of it to members of the two select committees on the Poor Law.[33]

As in earlier years, the money granted by the government was under the control of the Treasury who, in turn, allocated it to the Poor Law Commissioners. The Treasury used the unpopularity of the Poor Law to reassert its authority over the Commissioners. Apart from providing advice on purely financial issues, the Treasury increasingly interfered in matters concerning the day-to-day administration of the Poor Law. Trevelyan made it clear to Twistleton that unless he was satisfied with the local management of the Poor Law he would not authorise the granting of any money. Once more, the distressed people were held as hostages to a dogmatic government policy, as interpreted by its most powerful agent, the Treasury. Balancing the imperial ledgers appeared to be more important than saving lives. The Treasury also hoped to encourage a new spirit of financial separation. Trevelyan deemed that it was the responsibility of the Commissioners and their local officers to enforce the rate collection in order to prevent:

> . . . the great injustice of the burden which belongs to the rate-payers of each [Poor Law] union being unnecessarily transferred to the tax-payers of the United Kingdom.[34]

Again, the Treasury assumed total control of the provision of relief. They insisted that the Commissioners should provide support only to those unions in which poor rates had been collected to 'the utmost extent' but where none the less income was still insufficient for the needs of the union. The money advanced by the Treasury could only be used for the current expenses of the union, and not for the repayment of any debts. The 'social evil' of outdoor relief was to be avoided as far as possible but if it did prove essential, it was to be provided in such a way as to prevent all but the genuinely destitute from applying for it. In a further tightening up of the bureaucratic process, the Treasury also insisted that at the commencement of each month the Commissioners were to submit an estimate of the sum likely to be required. This was to be accompanied by a detailed financial statement of each union in receipt of a grant from the government, including its progress in the collection of rates. On the basis of this information, the Treasury would then decide whether or not to issue a grant.[35]

Twistleton was relieved that further government aid would be forthcoming to the poorest unions. Nevertheless, he admitted that he was disappointed that parliament had shown so little understanding of, or even sympathy with, the condition of the unions. In particular, he felt that some recognition should have been given to the general inability in parts of Ireland to pay poor rates—something which was recognised by the English Poor Law, but not by the Irish one. Twistleton had additional reservations regarding the recent directives of the Treasury which, he believed, trespassed on areas that were the exclusive concern of the Poor Law Commissioners. At this stage, it was apparent that Twistleton regarded the level of interference by the Treasury as unacceptable. When, shortly after this, Trevelyan suggested to the Poor Law Commissioners that all children should be put out of the workhouses to make additional room for able-bodied men, Twistleton replied in a terse note. He declined to do so adding, 'it is a Poor Law point and not a Treasury point'.[36]

Regardless of the £50,000 grant made available to the Irish unions in February 1849, the condition of several western unions continued to deteriorate. Some of the vice-guardians did not possess sufficient capital with which to purchase food for the paupers. In a number of unions, some of the local tradesmen and food suppliers were on relief lists, because so many people—including the vice-guardians—owed them money. Within the poorest unions, the repayment of the Temporary Relief Acts continued to be a heavy burden on the poor rates. It also proved to be an ongoing source of conflict between the Poor Law Commissioners and the Treasury.

Following the harvest of 1848, the policy of the Treasury regarding repayments was that if the combined amount of Poor Law expenditure, together with the amount of repayments, exceeded 5s in the pound in any electoral division or union, the level of repayments could be reduced by a sum equal to the excess. Within Ireland, this concession by the Treasury was regarded as insufficient. Both the Commissioners and the Irish Executive were increasingly pessimistic that the reappearance of the blight would mean that even this amount would be too heavy a burden for many unions, and they suggested that the upper limit should be reduced to 3s. They also felt that this policy would have little impact in the poorest unions, where ordinary Poor Law expenditure was far in excess of the 5s ceiling.[37] The Treasury, however, refused to act on this advice or deviate from the schedule of repayments. Wood expressed the view privately, that the government, by insisting on a high rate, hoped that an increased number of small farmers would be forced to emigrate. This was considered to be highly desirable and had been one of the aims of the government when deciding to channel all relief through the administrative machinery of the Poor Law.[38] Not for the first time, therefore, the Poor Law Commissioners found themselves forced to implement a policy with which they disagreed. The local Poor Law Inspectors were told that no deviation from the amount required could be permitted. Therefore, all possible exertion was to be made to collect a sufficient rate promptly so that 'the money so liberally advanced by the government during the distress of 1847 should be punctually paid'.[39]

Reports of increasing mortality within some unions forced a modification in government policy and the Treasury reluctantly reduced its ceiling to 3s as had been recommended by the Commissioners. Twistleton was pleased with this change of policy as he was convinced that it would have been both morally incorrect and physically impossible to insist on the higher rate. He believed that more money would actually be realised by insisting on a smaller rate. Although he accepted that the government hoped, through its policies, to bring about a number of long-term changes in Ireland, he was afraid that these policies were being carried too far. While he agreed that it would benefit the country if the tenants and small farmers emigrated, if the poor rates were too high, the more substantial farmers would also emigrate and this would be detrimental to the country.[40]

Within the most impoverished unions and those which were only marginally better off, the concession made by the Treasury in practice made little difference to the financial problems which they were facing. For many unions, with the exception of a limited number situated in the east and north of the country, the repayments of the Temporary Relief advances continued to be a heavy burden. Many boards of guardians, especially in the poorest parts of the country, protested that this additional demand on the ratepayers was particularly harsh in view of the reappearance of the blight. In the Donegal union, the guardians and local ratepayers complained that the enforcement of these rates would spell ruin for the union as there were still arrears of rent and cess unpaid.[41] Other boards of guardians asked for a postponement in the repayment of the additional rate until the condition of the country improved. The Wexford guardians made the radical suggestion that the government repayments should be paid by the levying of an income tax on all landlords who were absent from the country for more than four months of each year.[42] The problem was most acute in the distressed unions. Even before the 1848 potato blight, each of these unions was in debt. The vice-guardians feared that the burden of yet another high rate would make many of the ratepayers themselves insolvent. Many of the paid guardians had exhausted all of their local credit and several of the vice-guardians doubted their ability to feed the paupers in the coming year.[43]

During the period from the harvest of 1848 to February 1849, the amount of repayments made by the local unions varied greatly throughout the country. To a large extent, this reflected the financial resources at the disposal of the various unions—those in Ulster repaying the highest amount, whereas many of the unions in Connacht had made no repayments whatsoever. Overall, the Treasury was dissatisfied with the amount which had been collected, especially from the unions situated in Munster and Leinster whom the Treasury considered should have paid far more than they had done. In recognition of the fact that the coming months were likely to be ones of considerable hardship in many unions, the Treasury again permitted a further change in policy. They agreed that no further repayments would be demanded until following the harvest of 1849. The Treasury also acknowledged that the policy of demanding large repayments when ordinary Poor Law expenditure was already high could be counter-productive, as it only resulted in further demands being made on external funds. Following the harvest of 1849, they anticipated that the resources of the Poor Law unions would be in a better position to meet external financial demands.[44]

The Commissioners blamed the precariousness of the situation within the poorest unions on the meagreness and piecemeal nature of the advances made by the Treasury. As a consequence, the vice-guardians were getting more deeply into debt. They considered that this situation was putting the lives of the poor people in these unions at risk through no fault of the local administrators. Again, the differences in the interpretation of the government's policy between the main protagonists, the Treasury and the Commissioners, were obvious. The Commissioners demanded to know upon what principle the Treasury was basing their estimates, and they appealed to the government to intervene on their behalf. The government, however, declared that it was satisfied that the Treasury was acting in accordance with its wishes. In frustration, Twistleton concluded that:

> The extent of the calamity which affects the Distressed Unions and the intensity of the distress in them, do not seem to be fully understood in England.[45]

The main ideological battleground became the Treasury in London and the Poor Law Commission in Dublin, led on one side by the officious and doctrinaire Charles Trevelyan and, on the other, by the increasingly doubtful Edward Twistleton. But if Twistleton was losing his faith in the policies of the British government towards Ireland, Trevelyan remained convinced that the policy of minimal government interference had the support of an even higher authority: God, he believed, had ordained the Famine to teach the Irish people a lesson, and the machinations of man should not seek to reduce the effects of such a lesson. Again, this philosophy had much in common with the earlier writings of Adam Smith and Edmund Burke.[46]

The Treasury remained impervious to the pleas of the Commissioners. Not for the first time, the Poor Law Commissioners were admonished for not acting in total accordance with the regulations of the Treasury and for expecting too much money. They were told that if they only spent money as stipulated by the Treasury—that is, where it was absolutely necessary for the saving of lives—the funds would be sufficient. The Treasury accused the Commissioners of a 'too prevalent disposition to make exorbitant demands on the national funds for the relief of local distress'.[47]

In private, Trevelyan was even less sympathetic to the situation in which some of the unions found themselves. He admitted that the starving condition of some of the people in the western unions had not been exaggerated and that, however disagreeable, it was the duty of the government to relieve the worst aspects of this. If the government did not provide even this minimal form of relief, Trevelyan believed that 'the deaths would shock the world and be an eternal blot on the nation, and the government will be blamed'. At the same time, he used Biblical imagery to justify his actions, likening the paupers in the distressed unions to 'the prodigal sons' who could not be abandoned but who should not be given a 'fatted calf'. Instead, 'the workhouse and one pound of meal per day' was to be offered to them.[48]

In the middle of March 1849, a final grant of £1,000 was given by the British Relief Association to the Poor Law Commissioners. At the same time, it was made clear that these grants were now definitely at an end. A few weeks later, the Commissioners received an additional £6,200 from the Treasury, which was the last instalment of the £50,000 grant. The Commissioners were aware that this money would last no more than a few weeks, yet external aid to the distressed unions would be required until the harvest. At this time, the proposed Rate-in-Aid was being discussed by the government, but they showed no sign of making any further advances to Irish distress. The seriousness of the situation became obvious on 26 April 1849, when the Commissioners found themselves in a situation of having absolutely no money in hand and not knowing when any more would be available.[49]

The months of April and May 1849 were remarkable for a succession of pleas from the Poor Law Commissioners to the Treasury seeking additional assistance for the distressed unions. The Commissioners regarded the situation in the Bantry, Castlebar, and Westport unions as particularly precarious, but warned that in any of the twenty-two distressed unions a sudden discontinuance of external aid would result in an immediate loss of life. These entreaties appeared to have had little impact on the Treasury. In response to their applications, the Commissioners were provided with small, piecemeal grants, the amounts of which were decided upon by the Treasury. Repeatedly, the Commissioners were urged to distribute the advances of the government with 'greater care', with 'rigid economy', and 'as stringently as will serve to prevent disastrous consequences affecting human life'. The Commissioners were further informed that 'loss of life' and not 'severe privation' was to be the only criterion for providing any future aid.[50] The Commissioners regarded these grants as insufficient for the needs of the distressed unions and feared more deaths from starvation would follow. Because of the refusal of the Treasury to heed their advice, the Commissioners informed the Treasury that they considered themselves to be:

> absolved from any responsibility on account of deaths which may take place in consequence of those privations.[51]

Disease and Mortality

Although many official accounts of the Famine tended to view it as being 'over' by 1848, for a large number of people, notably in the west of Ireland and in some pockets of distress in the midlands, the impact of food shortages remained an enduring hardship. After 1848, the regional diversity of the Famine became more striking, but many parts of Ireland continued to be in the grip of a vicious cycle of poverty, poor rates, eviction, emigration and mortality. The Census Commissioners, acting on behalf of the government, stated that in 1849 mortality reached a new peak. They calculated that, as a percentage of the 1841 population, in 1845, mortality was 6.4 per cent; in 1846, it was 9.1 per cent; in 1847, 18.5 per cent; in 1848, 15.4 per cent; in 1849, 17.9 per cent; in 1850, mortality was 12.2 per cent.[52] A feature of the 1849 mortality was that it was concentrated in the three provinces of Connacht, Leinster and Munster, while it actually declined in Ulster. Mortality was highest in the counties which included a number of the distressed unions, that is counties

Clare, Cork, Galway, Kerry and Mayo. In Co. Galway, the increase was most marked, growing from 12,582 deaths in 1848 to 15,939 deaths in 1849. Overall, mortality was higher in 1849 in the three most affected provinces than it had been in 1847, the frequently-called 'Famine Year':

Table 20: Mortality Rates, 1847–9[53]

	1847	1848	1849
Leinster	59,208	50,536	60,360
Munster	82,496	69,715	92,737
Ulster	64,586	46,222	42,742
Connacht	43,045	41,779	44,958
Ireland	**249,335**	**208,252**	**240,797**

The returns of deaths in the 1851 Census are not totally reliable. They were recorded retrospectively and the Commissioners, for the most part, assumed that throughout the 1840s both population growth and decline were constant. The Census calculations were also based on details provided by people living in Ireland at the time it was made. Inevitably, it was distorted by the extreme social and geographical dislocation of the previous few years and therefore tended to be most deficient for the most affected areas. Families who had disappeared without a trace either through emigration or death obviously left no spokesperson to provide information on their behalf. The Census Commissioners realised the difficulties of their estimates and admitted that 'a correct statement of the number of deaths, their causes, etc. can never be procured by means of such an enquiry'.[54] The Census Commissioners realised that their figures were probably an underestimation, although they themselves tended to favour emigration as the primary reason for the drop in population between 1841 and 1851. The estimates of the Census Commissioners, however, do provide a useful contemporary impression of the overall patterns of mortality, particularly its regional dimensions many of which are consistent with subsequent historical research. The extent of additional mortality in Ireland caused by the Famine (excess mortality) remains an issue that attracts analysis and much counter-factual speculation. The lack of reliable contemporary sources means that total accuracy is not possible. However, Cormac Ó Gráda's estimate of approximately one million excess deaths, which lies between both the higher and lower calculations of the impact of mortality, appears to be the most accurate calculation to date.[55]

Within the local workhouses, in the early months of 1849, mortality again was as high as it had been in the winter of 1846–7, rising to 2,500 deaths per week, showing an approximate increase of 1,000 deaths per week over the same period in the previous year.[56] This is partly explained by the increase in workhouse accommodation throughout the country, especially following the harvest of 1847. It is also indicative of the increased vulnerability of certain sections of the population. Furthermore, in accordance with government policy, the workhouses were used to accommodate the able-bodied, rather than the old, young, sick and infirm who had previously occupied them, but who had been removed wholesale to outdoor relief in an effort to preserve the workhouses for the most undeserving group. Able-bodied paupers, therefore, were the main victims of the rise in workhouse mortality in 1849. The incidence of mortality in 1849 followed a similar regional pattern to 1846–7. Areas in which the general economic situation had improved following the harvest of 1848 showed the lightest mortality. The causes of the mortality, however, appeared to have changed. By 1849, so-called 'famine diseases' had declined substantially, and outbreaks of fever and typhus tended to be both intermittent and localised.[57] The appearance of cholera in some parts of Ireland in the early months of 1849, had a short-term but dramatic impact on local mortality rates and the provision of poor relief.

Initially, cholera was brought into Ireland from Britain and was first noticed in the various sea ports. It quickly spread to the distressed unions. The way in which cholera was treated, regardless of the general advice of the Board of Health, varied from union to union, often reflecting the financial buoyancy of each area. In some of the wealthier unions, the guardians appointed local Officers of Health even before any case of cholera had been reported. In general, in the poorer unions, the local administrators took no precautions until after cholera had appeared, and then, due to lack of funds, responded by admitting the cholera victims to the local workhouse.[58] One of the first reports of the disease was made in Belfast towards the end of 1848. By December 1848, it had spread to many parts of the town, including the workhouse. The local guardians responded to the situation promptly; from the income of the poor rates, they paid for cholera victims to be treated at the local hospital and provided a treatment grant to the Belfast Dispensary Committee. The Poor Law Acts contained no provision which permitted the poor rates to be used in such a way. The Commissioners, therefore, intervened on behalf of the Belfast guardians, and requested that the government sanction the expenditure of this money.[59]

At the beginning of 1849, the Central Board of Health warned each board of guardians that a cholera epidemic was imminent. The disease struck its victims very suddenly and the guardians were asked to take preparatory steps in anticipation of its appearance. Two main components were recommended to the guardians; those concerned with promoting general cleanliness and improving sanitary conditions for the purpose of preventing or limiting the dispersion of cholera, and those centred around providing additional medical relief to the victims following its appearance. The former was facilitated by the recent introduction of the Nuisance Removal and Disease Prevention Act, which made the guardians responsible for general cleanliness within their unions. Increasingly, therefore, the boards of guardians were assuming the role of local boards of health. The cost of this service, including the expense of both preventing and treating cholera, was to be paid for out of the poor rates. The appearance of cholera, therefore, placed an additional charge on the already high poor rates.[60]

By March 1849, cholera had appeared in each of the distressed unions and many of the adjoining ones in the west of Ireland. The guardians and vice-guardians, who were already deeply in debt, appealed to the Poor Law Commissioners for additional financial aid with which to treat the disease. In turn, the Commissioners asked the Treasury for permission to apply a portion of the government's grant to defray this expense if no other funds could be obtained. They urged the Treasury to reach a decision quickly, as cholera was spreading rapidly.[61] The Treasury did agree that, in extreme situations, government funds could be used in this way, but emphasised that it was to be allocated 'with caution'. Within a few weeks, however, the Commissioners were accused by the Treasury of having allocated the money too liberally. In the majority of cases, the Commissioners had given grants of £50 to the distressed unions to be for the treatment of cholera, but in the Galway and Westport unions they had issued £288 and £264 respectively. The Treasury admonished the Commissioners for failing to act on their instructions, and threatened that they would not sanction any further advances for the treatment of cholera. They also suggested that the vice-guardians involved should be removed from office. This resulted in a bitter dispute between the officers of the Treasury and the Poor Law Commissioners. The Commissioners stressed that the money had only been provided in cases where not to have done so would have resulted in loss of life. Furthermore, they pointed out, if the Treasury refused to issue any more grants for the relief of cholera, there would be an immediate increase in mortality in the poorest unions. The Commissioners pleaded with the

Treasury to reconsider their decision and authorise further advances of money. Although the Treasury agreed to overturn its decision, at the same time, they caustically informed Twistleton (not for the first time) that the parameters of government aid were more limited than those obviously envisaged by the Poor Law Commissioners.[62]

The cholera epidemic reached its peak by the beginning of April 1849. By June, it had almost totally disappeared from the country, with only a few isolated instances being reported in July. Within the poorest Poor Law unions and the sea ports of Ireland, the epidemic had been particularly virulent. In these areas, many persons who were already debilitated or dependent on the meagre resources provided by the Poor Law died. The unions in which the disease proved to be most deadly were those of Carlow, Clare, Cork, Dublin, Galway, Kilkenny, Limerick and Waterford. In each, the Poor Law Commissioners attributed the high levels of mortality to the insufficiency of funds which were made available for the prevention and treatment of cholera.[63]

The impact of cholera on mortality within Ireland was a short-term but significant one. In some unions, it contributed to an overall rise in mortality in 1849 compared with the previous year. The cholera mortality was heaviest in the western parts of Ireland and lightest in Ulster, thus reflecting the general trend. To a large degree, mortality in 1849 reflected the uneven impact of the 1848 potato blight, together with the fact that within some areas, the local economy was experiencing an upswing which made it less susceptible to the combined effects of disease and distress. In the poorest unions, which depended on a fixed and, as was increasingly obvious, finite supply of funds, the impact of the Famine continued to be as devastating in 1849 as in the disastrous winter of 1846–7.

The Rate-in-Aid

The financial situation in the poorest Poor Law unions was a continuing concern to the Poor Law Commissioners in the spring of 1849. By April of that year, the £50,000 advanced by the government only two months earlier was exhausted. Reluctantly, parliament permitted a further £6,000 to be granted from the Civil Contingencies Fund as an interim measure. This money, however, was well short of the £10,728 estimated by the Commissioners to be necessary. The Commissioners increasingly despaired of the parsimonious and fragmentary way in which sums of money were put at their disposal. They warned the Treasury that an absolute stoppage of relief was imminent in some unions.[64] When the

Treasury did not respond to this statement, the Poor Law Commissioners persisted with a stream of daily correspondence to the Treasury—both the government department and Trevelyan personally—requesting that further advances be made without delay. They also pointed out the fatal consequences of not providing the Commissioners, and thereby the unions, with sufficient resources. Several workhouses already appeared to be on the verge of closing, and the Commissioners had been forced to inform the vice-guardians that, in the foreseeable future, no additional financial assistance would be forthcoming.[65]

In London, the Treasury continued to criticise the Commissioners for advancing money 'too liberally'. Also, as May was generally a favourable month for the collection of rates, they told the Commissioners to avail of this resource for financing the provision of relief. They further advised that, in the first instance, rates should be collected from the largest landlords, especially in unions such as Kilrush, where there had been numerous evictions. The Treasury approved of the long-term effects of evictions but, in the short term, regarded them as placing an additional burden on the local poor rates and making external aid necessary. The Treasury was unwilling to make any more advances of money to the distressed unions, but agreed to allow a supply of biscuits from the Commissariat Stores to be distributed to them.[66]

Other government departments, including the Home Office, appeared to be equally immune to the pleadings of the Commissioners. To a large extent, this was due to the timings of the requests. The Rate-in-Aid Bill was in the process of being introduced into parliament for the purpose of providing funds to the poorest unions. If the Bill was successful, the government agreed to provide a further—and it hoped, final—advance to Irish distress. This money was to be repaid from the produce of a national rate to be known as 'the Rate-in-Aid'. The government did not want to compromise the success of its Bill by continuing to issue further money to Ireland.[67]

The idea of an additional rate had first been broached in parliament in February 1849 during a debate on the provision of further aid to Ireland. The general mood of the House was opposed to providing further assistance. Good will towards the apparently never-ending problem of Irish distress appeared to be exhausted: millions of pounds from the imperial Treasury had already been expended in Ireland and still Ireland expected more. The Prime Minister, Russell, adverted to the fact that some parts of Ireland were no longer enduring 'extreme distress', therefore they were as capable as England and Scotland of bearing part of the burden of taxation for the relief of distress.[68] In trying to find a means of transferring part of the burden to Ireland, Russell tentatively suggested that income tax could be introduced to Ireland, despite the fact that it had been specifically omitted from the Act of Union. This aroused a storm of protest from Irish Members of Parliament. It may have been a tactical ploy by Russell. The alternative suggestion of a temporary system of taxation, known as Rate-in-Aid, to be levied equally on all parts of Ireland, although unpopular, was felt to be preferable to the introduction of a permanent system of taxation.[69]

The main purpose of the Rate-in-Aid was to allow additional relief to be provided to the distressed unions while, at the same time, severing financial dependence on the Treasury. The Rate-in-Aid was intended to be a tax of 6d in the pound to be levied on all rateable property in Ireland. The proceeds from the rate were expected to be £332,552. In the first instance, a portion of this money was provided as a loan from the government, but it was to be repaid by December 1849. An advance of £50,000 was to be made available for this purpose. The Rate-in-Aid Bill was passed on 24 May 1849. Shortly after this, a subscription was started by the government, each Member of Parliament contributing £100 and the Queen £500 to the relief of distress. Almost £10,000 was raised in this way. The subscription was viewed by the government as a way of providing immediate aid to the distressed unions without encouraging further demands on the Treasury. The distribution of the subscription was entrusted to Count Strzelecki of the British Relief Association. All other money raised for the purposes of the Rate-in-Aid was to be distributed through the medium of the Treasury. The Whig administration hoped that this Act would mark the beginning of a disengagement from financing relief in Ireland.[70]

The Rate-in-Aid Act was intended to end, finally, the dependence of the poorest unions on the government. It marked a significant change in the policy of the British government to Irish distress: the financial responsibility for relieving distress within Ireland was now to be a national rather than local charge, but definitely not an imperial charge. Within the Treasury, the Act was welcomed as being an effective way of relieving distress without continuing the burden on the imperial taxes. No new administrative machinery was necessary as the Rate-in-Aid would be levied with the poor rates. Significantly also, the demands of the poorest unions would be made on their fellow countrymen, who would be in the best position to detect fraud and resist undue applications for assistance, which was not possible for officials based in Westminster or Whitehall. Trevelyan believed that the introduction of this Act would ensure that the key principle of the Poor Law was finally realised, which was 'to make the burden as near local as possible in order that it may be locally scrutinised and locally checked'.[71] He also was hopeful that the Act, by making Irish property more responsible for the relief of distress, would simultaneously help bring long-term benefits to the country, notably the transition from small-scale to large-scale farming. This would be achieved because the Rate-in-Aid would make it difficult for small farms which were no longer economically viable to survive.[72]

The most vehement critics of the proposed Rate-in-Aid were the Members of Parliament who had a vested interest in Ireland. In March 1849, a meeting was convened of all members connected with Ireland to consider the implications of the Bill. Although the proposed Act had some supporters, the majority passed a resolution stating that:

> The tax to be levied upon the present rateable property of Ireland is unjust in principle and dangerous in its tendency, and that we will oppose its enactment by every means which the Constitution affords us.[73]

The members from Ulster were the most outspoken opponents of the Bill. They continually and misleadingly chose to see the rate as a straight transfer of taxes from the hard-working people of Ulster to the indolent poor of Connacht. A successful propaganda campaign reinforced this interpretation although, in fact, the provinces of Leinster and Munster were more heavily taxed for the Rate-in-Aid than Ulster. The new rate was based on a uniform levy of 6d in the pound. The valuation of the four provinces in 1849 is shown in Table 21.

Table 21: Net Annual Value of all Rated Property, 1849[74]

Province	Net Annual Value
Ulster	£3,320,334
Munster	£3,777,112
Leinster	£4,624,530
Connacht	£1,465,643

Of the twenty-two distressed unions which were to benefit from the Rate-in-Aid, fourteen were situated in Connacht, seven in Munster, one in Ulster (Glenties), and none in Leinster. Notwithstanding this, the propaganda machine of the Ulster Members of Parliament was very effective.

The prudence, loyalty and industry of the ratepayers of Ulster was continually contrasted with the improvidence, fecklessness and inefficiency of the ratepayers of the west. The member for Co. Antrim, Sir Edward Macnaghten, stated his objections uncompromisingly when he described the rate as having the effect of making the innocent pay for the guilty.[75] Another MP, Joseph Napier, QC, reinforced the Ulster versus Connacht, industry versus sloth argument, when he described the rate as 'keeping up an army of beggers, fed out of the industry of Ulster'.[76]

Some of the opposition to the Rate-in-Aid was based on the unconstitutionality of the Bill, although this tended to be overshadowed by the 'Ulster subsidising Connacht' debate. The debate also raised a further question, however: if the Act of Union was a true union between kingdoms, then all parts of the United Kingdom shared an equal responsibility for helping to relieve the distress in another part. The Rate-in-Aid, however, placed the burden of relieving Irish distress very firmly on Ireland itself. At the same time, the decision to introduce the Act tended to detract from the very significant contributions which had already been made in all parts of Ireland, in the form of voluntary subscriptions, taxation and poor rates. One of the most eloquent proponents of the view that the Irish Famine was constitutionally an imperial responsibility was William Sharman Crawford. He attempted, unsuccessfully, to introduce an amendment to the Bill, on the grounds that:

> It is unconstitutional and unjust to impose on Ireland separate national taxation for the wants of particular localities, so long as the public general revenue of Ireland is paid into an Imperial Treasury and placed at the disposal of an Imperial Legislature for the general purposes of the United Kingdom.[77]

Only a minority of the members of the House of Commons opposed the Rate-in-Aid. The majority supported the Bill, believing that a change of direction was necessary in relation to Irish distress. Again, the argument was employed that the impact of the Famine would not have been as severe if Irish landlords had discharged their duties. As a consequence of their not having done so, the taxpayers of Britain had been forced to subsidise Irish distress, both through the taxes paid to the imperial Treasury, and as a consequence of the increased burden on local taxpayers due to the recent influx to Britain of Irish paupers.[78] The arguments in favour of the Rate-in-Aid received the overwhelming support of the House of Commons and it passed at the beginning of March, with a majority of 206 votes to 34.[79] The Bill had a more difficult passage

through the House of Lords, many of whose members had landed interests in Ireland. The second reading passed with a majority of only one
vote.[80] In addition to the resistance to the Rate-in-Aid bill in parliament,
there was active, extra-parliamentary opposition to it within Ireland.
This opposition was most overt in Ulster. The *Northern Whig*, in a series
of editorials, repeatedly objected to the introduction of the Bill and
warned the government that the people of the north would not comply
with its provisions. The paper described the Bill as an 'anti-Union
scheme' which would have the effect of increasing the separation
between Britain and Ireland. Following the lines of the parliamentary
debates, the *Northern Whig* also viewed the distress in terms of the north-
east versus the west of Ireland, and it warned its readers that 'Antrim,
Armagh and Down are to be made the preserves for the paupers of
Connacht to graze on'. The implication of the newspaper's argument was
that the people of the west of Ireland did not deserve to be helped in this
way and criticised the Bill for being:

> ... simply and avowedly an attempt to make the industrious, peace-
> able, hard-working portion of Ireland pay towards the support of
> the idle and turbulent.[81]

Within the local unions of the north-east of Ulster, both the guardians
and ratepayers were angered by the proposed legislation. Many of these
unions had received little or no aid from the government over the previous few years, and they felt that it was unfair that they should now be
expected to subsidise the affairs of unions which had already received
substantial financial support. Many boards of guardians passed resolutions condemning the Bill and sent petitions to both Houses of
Parliament. They mostly based their objections on the constitutional
argument: if Ireland was truly an integral part of the United Kingdom
and ultimately, of the British Empire, then Ulster had no relationship
with Ireland that was not shared equally by other parts of the Empire.
Thus there was no moral obligation on the people of Ulster to provide
assistance to the paupers in the west of Ireland. A number of guardians
predicted that the bill would lead to the economic ruin of the north-east
of Ireland as it would act as disincentive to ratepayers to pay their rates
promptly.[82]

In addition to the individual protests of the boards of guardians in the
north-east of the country, some of the northern unions also took the
unprecedented step of forming a combination in an attempt to prevent
the Bill from being introduced. Meetings of ratepayers and guardians

were held throughout the district. At the end of February 1849, at a large meeting in Co. Fermanagh, it was suggested that instead of introducing the Rate-in-Aid the government should levy a tax on goods imported from England. An even larger meeting, attended by an estimated 4,000 people, took place in Lurgan on 2 March. This was followed by further meetings at Armagh, Downpatrick, Hillsborough and Lisburn, but attendance at each meeting was lower than had been anticipated. A delegation from the town of Belfast, which included the Lord Mayor, travelled to London to meet Lord John Russell, but to no avail. Although additional meetings were held in Belfast on 11 and 24 May, by this time the Act had been introduced, and the opposition movement appeared to have lost some of its momentum.[83]

Regardless of the strength of feeling against the Rate-in-Aid in parts of Ulster, by July the local Poor Law Inspector reassured the Poor Law Commissioners that the worst of the crisis was over. The Commissioners were relieved. If the ratepayers of Ulster had refused to pay this rate, the resistance could have escalated and the administration of Poor Law could have been paralysed. This fear, however, had proved groundless. The rate was in course of collection in the majority of unions in Ulster, and even the most overtly militant unions of Belfast and Larne had taken steps for the rate to be collected.[84] Overall, resistance to the Rate-in-Aid from unions in the north-east of the country, although it had appeared initially concerted and determined, quickly seemed to dissipate following the introduction of the Act. The opposition to the Bill, however, after it became law, reasserted itself in a more subtle way. The province of Ulster was traditionally the area in which poor rates and government repayments were paid most promptly. By the end of 1851, however, the repayments of the Rate-in-Aid showed the highest amount of arrears in Ulster; the average arrears were 16 per cent, compared with 4 per cent in Leinster, 6 per cent in Munster and 9 per cent in Connacht.[85] The Ulster unions may not have won the war against the Rate-in-Aid, but they ensured that the battle continued.

Outside Ulster, the reaction to the Rate-in-Aid was less uniform. Meetings in counties Wicklow and Wexford, held to discuss the issue, concluded that it was the duty of the Empire at large, rather than one portion of it, to come to the assistance of Irish distress. In other unions, meetings were held in which the ratepayers stated that although they agreed with the Rate-in-Aid principle, due to the current state of the country they were unable to pay it. In the Carlow Poor Law union, at a meeting called by the opponents of the rate, all of the proposals made by the conveners of the meeting were overturned and a motion supporting the Bill was passed by a large majority.[86] This division of opinion was reflected in the national and local newspapers. The *Morning Chronicle* objected to the Rate-in-Aid on the grounds that the imposition of yet another tax would not help to reduce pauperism, but would actually increase it. The newspaper predicted that if the rate was introduced, the number of distressed unions would double within six months and this would continue until all of the wealth of the country had been absorbed into rates.[87] The *Dublin Evening Post*, on the other hand, regarded the introduction of the new rate as unavoidable. Although the newspaper acknowledged that the new rate would be unpopular, it regarded it as 'a national tax to prevent a national loss'.[88] As was the case in Ulster, following the introduction of the Act most of the opposition disappeared.

Some of the fiercest objections to the Rate-in-Aid came from the Poor Law officers themselves, based on a variety of reasons. In fact, the only Poor Law official who gave support to the bill was Alfred Power, the Assistant Commissioner. Power supported the new policy of the government on the grounds that relief, in its present form, could not be allowed to continue. Many of the local officials opposed the new change of policy. Joseph Burke, the Poor Law Inspector in the south-east of the country, which included some of the poorest unions in Ireland, regarded the rate as unnecessary and punitive. In three-quarters of his unions he considered the Poor Law was working well: the distress was financed through the collection of local rates and the government finances were starting to be repaid. If the additional burden of 6d in the pound rate was imposed on these already burdened unions, he predicted that it would be resisted and would result in solvent unions becoming insolvent. He suggested that rather than introduce a Rate-in-Aid, the government should provide financial assistance in the form of a loan, as the ratepayers had proved most willing to pay earlier advances.[89] Both Edward Gulson and Edward Senior also opposed the introduction of the Rate-in-Aid, although for different reasons to Burke. They argued, in a similar manner to the Ulster MPs, that the proposed Rate would, in effect, be forcing the industry of the north to pay for the indolence of the west. They warned that not only would its payment be resisted, it would also act as a disincentive to farmers to employ labourers.[90]

George Nicholls, the first Poor Law Commissioner in Ireland and the main framer of the 1838 Poor Law Act, was also deeply critical of the Act. He thought that the change of direction by the government in introducing a new dimension to the Poor Law had no precedent or, he believed, justification. He described the introduction of the Rate-in-Aid as an 'alarmist response' by the legislature to the on-going problems of distress in Ireland. This had made the government desperate to find a way to make the property of Ireland responsible for the relief of its poverty. Nicholls calculated that the British government had already contributed almost £10m to Irish distress and they were determined to provide no more financial assistance. Despite this, Nicholls regarded the Rate-in-Aid Act as objectionable on the grounds that the distress was both widespread and severe. The potato blight was an 'imperial calamity' which, in Nicholl's opinion, deserved special treatment from the imperial Treasury. He unequivocally believed that it was the duty of the British government to provide extraneous aid to Irish distress which would make the imposition of the Rate-in-Aid unnecessary.[91]

One of the most outspoken opponents of the Rate-in-Aid, however, was the man who was to implement the new policy, Edward Twistleton, the Chief Poor Law Commissioner. Twistleton was a fervent supporter of the Act of Union between Great Britain and Ireland and regarded the proposed Rate as being contrary to this Union. In his view, where the local poor rates proved to be inadequate for the provision of relief, it was the responsibility of the state to provide additional financial assistance. Twistleton believed that the opprobrium directed at the ratepayers of Ireland was also misplaced as, despite the general distress and consequent heavy burden of taxation, the poor rates had been well paid in most instances. Twistleton was concerned that an additional rate would act as a disincentive to farmers to invest capital in their properties. Edward Twistleton, who had so often been in conflict with the government regarding the amount of external assistance to be provided to Irish distress, saw the Rate-in-Aid issue as the final straw, and he resigned in protest at its introduction. He explained:

> Strongly disapproving as I do of the Rate-in-Aid Bill . . . I could not, with honour, have carried it into execution.[92]

Twistleton was replaced by Alfred Power.

Following his resignation, Twistleton made a number of uncompromising statements describing his frustrations with the policies of the British government towards Irish distress. In giving evidence before the select committee of the House of Lords in 1849, Twistleton used the public platform to criticise the policies which the Whig administration had been pursuing. He made it very clear that, in his opinion, the main problem confronting the poorest unions was a financial and not an administrative one, and that this was a problem which, if the political will to do so existed, the government could solve. He estimated that in the twenty-two poorest unions of Ireland, the total amount required for the payment of both debts and current expenses until 1849 was £700,000, which he regarded as 'very trifling indeed'. Twistleton also stated very clearly that, if the additional money was forthcoming, there would be no further deaths from starvation:

> I wish to remark that it is wholly unnecessary that there should be a single death from starvation this year in the Distressed Unions in Ireland. The machinery for the administration of relief is now tolerably complete and all that is requisite is that the necessary funds should be furnished to those that are entrusted with the administration of relief.[93]

Twistleton refused to compromise on the question of how suffering and mortality could have been prevented. He emphasised the fact that the various policies introduced by the British government were not due to a shortage of funds but to an unwillingness to continue providing support to Irish distress. He made an unfavourable comparison with the amount of money that the government was willing to expend on fighting various wars. He believed that by acting in such a way, the government had brought 'deep disgrace' on the country. He emphasised:

> . . . the comparatively trifling sum with which it is possible for this country to spare itself the deep disgrace of permitting any of our miserable fellow subjects in the Distressed Unions to die of starvation. I wish to leave distinctly on record that, from want of sufficient food, many persons in these unions are at present dying or wasting away; and, at the same time, it is quite possible for this country to prevent the occurrence there of any death from starvation, by the advance of a few hundred pounds, say a small part of the expense of the Coffre War.[94]

The number of people in Irish workhouses peaked in June 1849, with 227,329 inmates receiving relief daily. The maximum on outdoor relief occurred in July when the lists reached 784,370 persons. Following this, the numbers continued to decrease until the beginning of October.[95] This meant that in the summer of 1849, over one million people were in receipt of poor relief. Although this figure was far below the three million people dependent on the government soup kitchens two years earlier, it was indicative of the fact that severe distress still continued in parts of Ireland.

In the middle of the crisis, Queen Victoria visited Ireland. The visit had originally been planned for 1846, but had been postponed due to the potato blight. In recognition of the continuation of distress in some parts of Ireland, the Queen's visit in 1849 was not to be a state visit, and the need for economy was stressed. Significantly also, her visit was to be brief, well orchestrated, and confined to the east of Ireland, that is, Cork and Dublin. Although there were criticisms of the expense which the visit would entail, overall the government considered that the benefits would outweigh the disadvantages. One leading Whig predicted:

> I shall be much mistaken in Paddy's character if the Queen is not satisfied with the demonstration of joy and loyalty with which her arrival in Ireland will be greeted.[96]

The Queen's visit was a success, which was attributed to the weather, her manner, and most importantly 'the inexhaustible fund of good humour of the people here when it is not perverted for mischievous purposes'.[97] It did not, however, result in the anticipated investment of British capital in Ireland.

Notwithstanding the imposition of the Rate-in-Aid in 1849 for the use of the distressed unions, the financial position of many unions continued to be precarious. The amount of money which the Treasury released was always a bare minimum, usually less than the amount sought. Again, some vice-guardians resorted to subsidising the provision of relief from their own pockets, regardless of the disapproval of the Commissioners.[98] The money provided to the distressed unions from the Rate-in-Aid could only be used to discharge current debts, which meant that it did not help to improve the indebtedness of these unions. Even though the prospects for the 1849 harvest appeared to be good, the Poor Law Commissioners realised that it would take more than one sound harvest to solve the financial problems of the distressed unions. They privately warned the government that, in their estimation, in at least twenty-three unions it would be necessary to continue to provide external financial assistance even after the harvest.[99] As the 1849 harvest approached, therefore, despite official reports to the contrary, the Famine in Ireland was far from over.

The General Advancement of the Country

A gradual release of rural Ireland from the extremities of distress became more apparent in 1849. Yet a more general availability of food was accompanied by a further polarisation: both in the geographical incidence of severe distress, and in the official response to the Famine. Despite an overall reduction in the demand for relief, large areas of the country faced a further year of distress and shortages. Almost the only system of support available to these people was the local Poor Law. The Poor Law, however, was financed by a system of taxation that was burdened by the need to pay high current expenses and past loans for Famine relief, both from within the resources of a devastated local economy.

Even more starkly than had been apparent in previous years, the management of the Famine relief was concentrated in the hands of the Treasury in London, and was delivered almost exclusively through the Poor Law administration in Ireland. Within this system, the Poor Law Commission and the Irish Executive in Dublin had no independent control or resources and effectively became, at local level, a mechanism for the implementation of Treasury directives.

Compared with earlier years, the organisation of relief after 1849 became concentrated in the hands of the permanent system of poor relief in Ireland. The official management and dispersal of relief, therefore, can be tracked substantially through a study of the operation and evolution of the Poor Law.

The harvest of 1849 was mostly healthy, with only isolated instances of potato blight. Many local relief officials reported that a new spirit of optimism was apparent in many parts of the country and there was a general belief that the prospects for the following year were auspicious. The government and the Poor Law Commissioners used the improved conditions as an opportunity to return to a system of providing a more limited amount of relief. Their basic premise was that abundant employment would be available to the labouring classes. The primary objective of the Poor Law Commissioners following the 1849 harvest, therefore, was to achieve a 'stabilisation' in the provision and administration of poor relief.

An essential component of the stabilisation was believed to be a transition from large-scale outdoor relief to a system of indoor relief only. The original 1838 Poor Law Act had only permitted poor relief to be provided within the confines of a workhouse but the 1847 Extension Act had, in response to an extreme situation, permitted the provision of outdoor relief. Two separate parliamentary enquiries into the administration of the Poor Law appointed at the beginning of 1849 had both recommended that outdoor relief should be brought to an end as soon as possible. They considered that unless the circumstances were exceptional, poor relief should be provided only within the confines of a well-regulated workhouse. Such a shift in policy would, however, require additional accommodation. Consequently, the parliamentary enquiries had recommended that the number Poor Law unions and hence, permanent workhouses, should be increased. The Poor Law Commissioners were optimistic that following the 1849 harvest the transfer from outdoor to indoor relief would be achieved. They felt that this was possible because in the previous year, workhouse accommodation had increased substantially and the building of new, permanent workhouses would increase their capacity. In the period following the 1849 harvest, therefore, the Commissioners refused to issue any further orders permitting outdoor relief to the able-bodied on the grounds that:

> . . . we consider a matter of the utmost consequence to the future as well as the present working of the Poor Law to avoid, if possible, the issue of these orders in a season which has been marked by an abundance rather than a scarcity of food, and thus to prevent any expectation being created that these powers will be exercised, excepting under extraordinary circumstances.[1]

As a consequence of the two parliamentary enquiries, certain legislative changes were made to the Poor Law in the autumn of 1849. Most of these changes were concerned with financing relief, particularly with increasing the power of the guardians in respect to the collection and

Lord John Russell.

A deserted Famine village.

Interior of a workhouse.

Impoverished children.

Potato diggers.

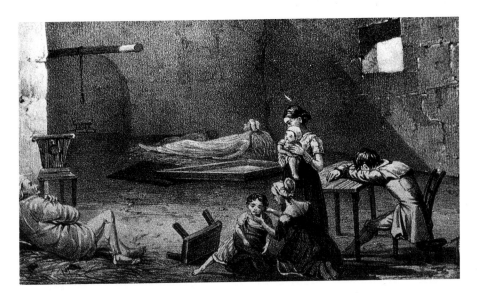

Two cottage interiors from Famine times.

The Irish Relief Squadron distributing stores from HMS *Valorous* in the West of Ireland.

Charles Edward Trevelyan.

recovery of outstanding poor rates. Significantly also, occupiers of land were no longer permitted to deduct from their rent half of the poor rates which they paid. This meant that the burden of poor rates was redistributed in favour of landlords rather than occupiers of property. The 1849 Amendment Act also facilitated the emigration of Irish paupers to the British colonies, paid for out of the poor rates. At the same time, the Act provided for the formation of new Poor Law unions.[2] By providing for an increase in permanent workhouse accommodation, the centrality of indoor relief within the Irish Poor Law was confirmed.

The changes introduced into the Poor Law during the harvest of 1849 were largely based on the assumption that there would be less distress to relieve in the approaching year than in the previous years. The 1849 potato crop was not totally free from blight, however, although blight was more localised than in any year since 1845. The average crop yields, still tended to fall below their pre-Famine level. The Poor Law Commissioners deliberately chose to emphasise the positive aspects of the apparent improvement in the prospects of the country, and in their Annual Report optimistically referred to 'the abundant harvest in 1849, which suffered less from blight than in previous years'.[3] They did not mention the implications for the areas in which blight had appeared for the fifth successive year. In 1849, it was most severe along the western seaboard, most particularly in Co. Clare. Thus there was an increasing division between areas in which the Famine could be said to be 'over' (although its impact was still evident) and those in which it continued to have a devastating effect on the local population.

Following the harvest of 1849, there were marked regional contrasts within Ireland in the extent and impact of distress. In most parts of Ulster, the area which had suffered least during the Famine, the local Poor Law Inspector observed that he had never before seen such an abundant harvest, the potato crop being especially luxuriant. In many other parts of the east and midlands, the news was similarly positive. An improvement in agricultural conditions was also, for the first time since 1845, apparent in some parts of the west. In Co. Mayo, in which each of the unions had been designated 'distressed', the reports made by the local Inspectors were, for the first time in many years, favourable. A new spirit of activity was described as being apparent within the county, and this had resulted in a reinvestment of capital in the land. The optimism of the local relief officials appeared to be well founded because, by the end of 1849, plenty of food and fuel were reported to be available for the first time in five years. Although 1849 marked the first of a series of good harvests in many parts of Ireland, in counties Clare, Kerry, Limerick and

Tipperary the reappearance of blight made on-going distress inevitable. In counties Clare and Kerry, where it was most severe, the demand for relief was even higher than it had been in the previous year.[4] In the spring of 1850, 12,000 people were in receipt of workhouse relief in Co. Clare alone and a further 30,000 were on the outdoor relief lists. This was nearly twice the number receiving relief in the whole of Connacht during the same period.[5] Following the 1849 harvest, therefore, the demarcation between the areas in which the condition of the population was improving and those in which it was getting worse, was considerable.

The Restoration of Boards of Guardians

An important feature of the return to a more normal system of relief was the restoration of elected boards of guardians. Although a number of boards had been restored in March 1849, the Commissioners had decided that in the unions where relief was still extensive, it was preferable if the vice-guardians remained in place. In November 1849, however, eleven of the remaining sixteen dissolved boards of guardians were reinstated.[6] In recognition of the fact that in the poorest unions the difficulties facing the guardians had not disappeared totally, the new office of assistant guardian was created. These new administrators were to be appointed in the poorest unions in order to facilitate a change from paid to elected guardians.[7] Many of the reinstated boards welcomed the presence of an assistant guardian as the duties devolving on them continued to be heavy. The appointment of these officers, however, proved disappointing. No provision had been made for their wages to be raised from local poor rates and the government refused to pay for them. This meant that unless the assistant guardians were willing to provide their services voluntarily—which was the case in the Kenmare union—this new class of administrator did not emerge.[8]

The restoration of the boards of guardians was not without difficulties. The main problem was that many of the restored boards declared that they were dissatisfied with the condition in which they found their unions. A number of boards of guardians continued to resent the fact that they had been dissolved at all. The restored guardians in the Lowtherstown union, the first board to be re-appointed, criticised the vice-guardians for their 'lax' administration of union affairs and described the union as:

> . . . much demoralised, the poorer classes being impressed with a doctrine that instead of finding employment it must be found for them, and that the decree of the Almighty, that man must live by

the sweat of his brow, is changed to the effect that man is to live by Act of Parliament.[9]

The Westport guardians also felt that during their absence, the workhouse had become 'a hotbed of laziness and vice'.[10] The Mohill guardians had viewed their dismissal as a denial of their basic democratic rights. The chairman, Lord Leitrim, described it as 'a most unbounded, arbitrary and despotic' exercise of the power of the Poor Law Commissioners. Lord Leitrim recommended to his fellow guardians that they should not accept the control of their union, as it had been handed back to them in such a disreputable manner.[11]

A frequent complaint made against the vice-guardians was that they had mis-spent or squandered union funds, or levied rates in an unfair manner. This allegation was often based on the fact that the restored boards were generally confronted by large accumulated debts, which they were expected to repay. These persistent complaints resulted in the appointment of a select committee. Following an investigation, the committee ruled that neither the Poor Law Commissioners nor the vice-guardians had displayed either the activity or judgment which the public had the right to expect.[12] The conclusions of the committee regarding the administration of the Poor Law between 1847 and 1849 appeared harsh, particularly in the light of the various difficulties with which the vice-guardians had had to contend, most notably a continual shortage of funds. The Poor Law officials provided a convenient scapegoat for all shortcomings in the administration of relief during the Famine.

Not all boards of guardians, however, were dissatisfied with the administration of the vice-guardians. Many boards, including those of the Enniskillen, Galway, Gort, New Ross, Scariff and Tullamore unions, passed resolutions thanking the vice-guardians for the way in which they had managed their unions. The guardians of the Athlone, Kenmare, Mullingar and Waterford unions took this a step further and declared that they could not have provided relief more efficiently during such a difficult period and asked if the vice-guardians could be retained for a further period of time. This request, however, was refused.[13]

Financing the Poor Law

The cost of providing Poor Law relief was higher in 1849 than in 1848. In 1849, total Poor Law expenditure was £2,177,651 compared with £1,732,597 in the previous year. This was partly explained by the fact that the number of people in receipt of poor relief increased from 2,043,505 people in 1848 to 2,142,766 in 1849. At the same time, there was an increase in the proportion of people receiving indoor relief compared with those on outdoor relief. This shift was regarded by the Commissioners as being desirable even though the cost of providing indoor relief *per capita* was higher.[14] Most of the expenditure in 1849 was concentrated in the spring and summer period. Following the good harvest, a reduction in Poor Law expenditure was apparent. By March 1850, income from poor rates exceeded expenditure by £426,470. Poor Law expenditure for the twelve month period ending September 1850 had fallen also to £1,430,108. The Poor Law Commissioners were confident that this year marked the beginning of a permanent reduction in Poor Law expenditure.[15]

The reduction in relief expenditure in 1850 was due to an overall decrease in the number of people receiving relief in the twelve months following the harvest of 1849, most especially the number of people in receipt of outdoor relief. By September 1850, the number of people who had received indoor relief in the previous twelve months was 805,702, whilst the number of people on outdoor relief was only 363,565. In forty Poor Law unions, it did not prove necessary to provide any outdoor relief. Again the regional contrasts in the number of people receiving relief were marked, with almost 10 per cent of the total number of people in receipt of poor relief being concentrated in merely three unions.

Table 22: Poor Law Unions Providing Most Relief, 1849–50 [16]

Union	Population in 1841	Indoor Relief	Outdoor Relief
Kanturk	61,538	14,214	16,111
Kilrush	64,429	12,860	19,863
Newcastle	44,737	13,040	17,033
Total in Ireland	**8,175,124**	**805,702**	**363,565**

The general amelioration following the harvest of 1849, and the consequent reduction in the demand for poor relief, was regarded by the government as an opportune time to enforce the payments of the various debts which were due to them. The Treasury agreed, advising the government that even the poorest unions could now afford to repay their debts. After the harvest of 1849, therefore, the Treasury decreed that the repayments to be made by each Poor Law union, in order of priority, were the Rate-in-Aid, the Temporary Relief Advances, and the loans made for the building of the workhouses. In the past, the amount of repayments which had been demanded from the local unions had been a source of conflict between the Treasury and the Poor Law Commissioners. However, Twistleton's successor, Alfred Power, was more acquiescent than his predecessor and he agreed to give the latest policy of the Treasury his full support. Although Poor Law expenditure for the country as a whole decreased following the harvest of 1849, a small number of unions in the south-west corner of Ireland continued to require external financial assistance.[17]

The repayments made by the local unions in the final months of 1849 were below the levels expected by the Treasury. This was partly because the financial recovery of the Poor Law unions was less rapid than the Treasury had calculated that it should be, but also because, in addition to ordinary Poor Law expenditure, the burden of repayments was heavy. In December 1849, the combined liabilities for all unions in Ireland were £2,525,315 out of an estimated valuation of £12,565,953. Again, the burden was most onerous on the unions with the least resources with which to meet the demands. In each of the twenty-two distressed unions, for example, the total amount of liabilities was approximately 50 per cent of the valuation, although in some unions it was far higher: in the Bantry union, liabilities were £25,877 out of a valuation of £36,920 and in the Kenmare union, total liabilities were £17,706 out of a valuation of £24,552; in contrast, the Antrim union had total liabilities of £8,656 out of a valuation of £101,280, over £7,000 of which was owed for the building of the union workhouse.[18]

Many of the guardians were alarmed at the pecuniary demands being made on them, especially as the burden of current expenditure was still abnormally high. Even unions such as Londonderry, Omagh and Waterford, which had escaped the worst effects of the potato blight, regarded these repayments as a heavy burden on their resources. The Waterford guardians had £8,000 in hand, £6,000 of which they were directed to repay to the government. The guardians refused to pay on the grounds that if they did so, they would not be able to meet current expenditure. The Commissioners responded to the complaints of the guardians unsympathetically, warning them that if this money was not paid voluntarily, the government would take the money from the Treasurer of the union directly. In the Waterford union, the dispute continued until April 1850 when the Commissioners invoked their statutory powers to force the guardians to make the requisite repayments.[19]

In the unions in which distress had been consistently high for a number of years, not only did the government repayments prove to be a heavy burden but in some unions the guardians were without sufficient funds to provide ordinary poor relief. By the beginning of 1850, there were again reports of deaths from starvation in some of the unions in which blight had reappeared in 1849. In the Scariff union in Co. Clare, the local Poor Law Inspector blamed the recent increase in deaths from starvation on the irregularity in the supply of food to paupers in receipt of outdoor relief. In one case, in which the head of the family had died, the family had received only 3½ lbs of meal during one week compared with their usual supply of 21 lbs. Similar cases were also reported from the nearby Ennistymon union, where the quantity of food provided to the paupers fluctuated greatly. The guardians attributed this to the fact that the rate collection had been so low that they were unable to afford to purchase sufficient provisions.[20]

The financial problems of the poorest unions deteriorated noticeably in the months following the 1849 harvest. When the elected guardians of the Scariff union resumed office in November 1949, the union was £11,996 6s 6d in debt and had no funds in hand. The guardians estimated that even if the full rate was collected, they still would not have sufficient funds to pay the everyday expenses of the union. At the beginning of 1850, due to a shortage of funds, only one-third of the supply of food required by the union had been purchased. As a result of this, many of the people on the outdoor relief lists were not receiving their full supply. Within the workhouse, conditions were little better. The workhouse was overcrowded and fever, malaria, and other infectious diseases were reported to be rampant. This was exacerbated by the fact that there were insufficient clothes to allow any change of clothing for the inmates. The supply of food was also irregular and milk had not been delivered to the workhouse for six weeks. Regardless of such conditions, the demand for admittance was still growing.[21]

The debts of the Scariff union continued to increase in the months following the harvest and the guardians found it increasingly difficult to obtain credit. At the beginning of February 1850, the meal contractor refused to provide any further supplies to the workhouse. The local sheriff also seized all of the provisions in the workhouse in order to repay some of the debts of the guardians to the meal contractor. The sheriff then took possession of the main workhouse and its various auxiliaries and threatened to auction all of the disposable goods within them. The guardians immediately informed the Commissioners that it was now impossible for them to discharge their duties effectively and they warned that unless the Commissioners intervened immediately, deaths from starvation would occur daily. The guardians also pleaded with the Lord Lieutenant to intervene on their behalf as their situation was so desperate. Both the Poor Law Commissioners and the Lord Lieutenant promised to bring the situation in the union to the attention of the Treasury.[22]

As had been the case in earlier years of the Famine, the amount of money at the disposal of the Poor Law Commissioners for distribution to the poorest unions continued under the control of the Treasury with Wood and Trevelyan still at the helm. Despite the general improvement within the Irish unions, the Treasury continued to maintain a close control over all money provided for the purpose of relieving the distress. In the early months of 1850, the Commissioners appealed to the Treasury to provide financial assistance to the Kilrush, Scariff and Tralee unions, stressing that in each instance it was a matter of life or death. Regardless of the urgency of the case, the Treasury refused to provide assistance until they had received further details outlining the exact condition of the unions. In the case of Tralee, the Treasury pointed out that despite the poverty of some parts of the union, they believed that it had sufficient resources to come to its own rescue. The intractability of the Treasury on this issue again brought it into conflict with the new head of the Poor Law Commission, Alfred Power.[23] The Treasury, who were now in charge of the allocation of the Rate-in-Aid funds, proved as parsimonious in their allocation as they had been with the money provided by the government. Power, like his predecessor Edward Twistleton, quickly found that it was the Treasury who not only held the purse strings but acted as final arbiter in the provision of assistance to the poorest unions.

Regardless of the general amelioration in the condition of the country, at the end of 1849 the amount of rates which had been collected was less than had been expected by the Commissioners. They regarded this as being particularly disappointing as the powers of the guardians to collect poor rates had been increased. In the poorest unions, the Poor Law Commissioners were worried that their insistence on the collection of a high harvest rate would make it more difficult for the most impoverished unions to collect the spring rate, and this would result in some areas continuing to require the assistance of the government in the following spring and summer. The fears of the Commissioners proved to be well founded as in the months prior to the harvest of 1850, many of the distressed unions continued to require external financial assistance. Regardless of the stringency with which the Treasury applied the income from the Rate-in-Aid, by the beginning of July 1850, these funds were exhausted. Not for the first time, the government had underestimated the amount of money which would be required to relieve Irish distress. Consequently, in the summer of 1850, for the fifth consecutive year, the British government was forced to intervene and come to the assistance of the poorest Irish unions.[24]

The necessity of continuing to provide many of the distressed unions with further financial aid forced the government to amend its policy towards Irish distress. Although continuing to provide assistance to a number of unions, at the same time the government announced that a more determined effort was to be made to force the unions to repay all of their accumulated debts. This was to be achieved through the Consolidated Annuities Act introduced in May 1850. This Act empowered the Treasury to issue to the poorest unions, by way of a loan, advances not to exceed £300,000. The largest portion of this money was allocated for use in the unions in Munster, most particularly those in Co. Clare, which received £176,487 of the £300,000 loan. Only £334 was allocated to the province of Ulster, for the use of the Glenties union.[25]

The Consolidated Annuities Act provided for the Treasury to ascertain and consolidate the debts of each electoral division within each Poor Law union. These debts were then transformed into annuities which were to be paid directly from the Treasurer of each union to the Treasury. This money was to be repaid over a period of between five to forty years, depending on the circumstances of each individual union. September 1850 was the date agreed on for the first consolidated repayment to be made. The total accumulated debt of the Irish unions was £4,422,953. In the first year, from September 1850 to September 1851, the annuity payable was £245,061, which was a national average of 5d in the pound on the poor rates. Inevitably, this burden was heaviest on the provinces in which many of the distressed unions were situated.

Table 23: Annuity Charges, 1850–51 [26]

Province	Amount of Annual Charge Sept. 1850-51	Total Charge
Ulster	£41,510 8 2¼	£ 541,847
Munster	£95,925 7 1¼	£1,952,885
Leinster	£56,385 3 9	£ 811,810
Connacht	£51,240 7 0½	£1,116,411
Total	**£245,061 6 1**	**£4,422,953**

Alfred Power admitted that he would watch the payment of the first annuity order 'with some anxiety', and he privately warned Trevelyan not to be over-optimistic. Power realised that the annuity repayments would be a heavy burden on the poorest unions. Even in the wealthier unions, however, the guardians would be reluctant to pay a rate directly to the Treasury which would be of no benefit to the union.[27] The government had hoped that their policies would act as an incentive to smallholders and impoverished landlords to relinquish their holdings and sell them to men with capital, but the Poor Law Commissioners warned that if poor rates were too high, this would act as a deterrent to capital investment in the land. In some parts of the country, as a result of five years of distress and the consequent high levels of mortality, eviction and emigration, land prices had fallen and a lot of property lay waste. In 1841, the net annual value of land in Ireland was over £13m but by 1851, this had fallen to less than £12m with no immediate signs of recovery. To facilitate the sale of land, the government had introduced the Encumbered Estates Acts of 1848 and 1849. Within a few years of these Acts being passed, approximately five million acres of land—a quarter of Ireland—had changed hands. The expectation regarding the investment of British capital into Ireland never materialised. The purchasers were overwhelmingly Irish: by 1857, out of the 7,489 transactions that had taken place, 7,180 were from Irish capitalists, the remainder being of English, Scottish or other origin.[28] The Encumbered Estates Acts, however, did not address the problem of who was liable for arrears of poor rates on land which had changed hands. The Poor Law Commissioners were forced to take legal advice on this question. The legal opinion ruled that the first occupier within two years of the property becoming vacant was legally bound to pay the arrears of poor rates. The Commissioners believed that, in the short term, this ruling would act as a disincentive to the purchase of land, particularly in the unions in which the distress had been most severe.[29]

As the date fixed for the first repayment of the annuity approached, some guardians began to doubt their ability to raise a sufficient rate and asked if the payments could be spread over a longer period. Unofficially, the Poor Law Commissioners sympathised with the guardians, but they responded that it did not lie within their power to comply with such requests. The stance adopted by the Treasury was less sympathetic. Trevelyan privately thought that the time had arrived for the government to adopt a hard line on the question of repayments as, in his opinion, all of their previous attempts to obtain them had been successfully resisted by the guardians. If the repayments of the Consolidated Annuities were launched with a suspension of payments in some unions, Trevelyan considered that this would establish a dangerous precedent and unions which could afford to make the payments would be discouraged from making any. He also believed that it was essential for the government to stand firm on this issue and to recognise that 'our last position is a very strong one and we should not allow ourselves to be forced from it.[30]

The Treasury did realise that the poorest unions would not be able to make these payments unless they were given external financial assistance. On the suggestion of Trevelyan, it was decided that all further money provided to the unions should be given on the understanding that it could be used for the purpose of making repayments. Under the provisions of the Consolidated Annuities Act, therefore, for the first time the money which had been simultaneously advanced by the government was allowed to be used to discharge debts and liabilities of the unions, but only if the prior consent of the Treasury was obtained. This marked a radical departure from all earlier government policy which had stipulated that all advances of money could only be used for the provision of relief. Trevelyan believed that in allowing advances to be used in this way it would help to 'preserve the integrity of our Annuity'. The primacy of the Treasury, in particular Trevelyan, in the provision of relief during the latter stages of the Famine, was helped by the internal disarray of the Whig party and Russell's increasingly precarious position within it. This was marked by a further deterioration of relations between Charles Wood and Russell who fought a number of bitter battles over budget estimates for all aspects of public expenditure. Wood's demands for more financial retrenchment had the support of both the influential Peelites (free trade Conservatives) and middle-class Radicals. In an effort to strengthen his own personal position, Russell introduced the anti-Catholic Ecclesiastical Titles Bill in 1851. This ill-conceived legislation lost Russell the support of Catholic MPs and caused a crisis within the government that made his own downfall a few months later virtually inevitable.[31]

In September 1851, the first government annuity was due for repayment. For the most part, the guardians wanted a postponement of the repayments but, in a few cases, total exemption was demanded. In the west of Ireland, many boards of guardians believed that insisting that these repayments be made before the country had recovered from the effects of the Famine would further prolong the impact of the distress. The guardians of the Oughterard union in Co. Galway described the annuities as a further penalty on areas which had already suffered a great deal. This union had recently been formed from some of the poorest parts of Ballinrobe and Galway unions and a large portion of it was either bog or wasteland. The annuity repayment demanded from the electoral divisions in the union averaged 2s in the pound. This, the guardians believed, when added to its current expenses, would ruin the new union financially before it had a chance to establish itself.[32]

The ratepayers of the impoverished Belmullet union in Co. Mayo also objected to these repayments and appealed to the government for exemption. They based their objections on the fact that although the worst of the Famine was now over in their union, as in many other unions in the west its effects were still evident. In the Belmullet union, the population had fallen by 29 per cent since 1845 and many smallholdings were unoccupied and unproductive. The guardians believed that the annuities would only increase the burden on the already hard-pressed ratepayers. This would act as a disincentive to a revival in the local economy and would encourage even more people to emigrate.[33]

In Co. Roscommon, the boards of guardians joined together to protest against the annuities. They believed that these payments would be impossible to meet as current expenditure remained high and the state of the country was still depressed. The value of rateable property in the county had dropped on average by between 25 and 40 per cent.[34] The various Roscommon guardians agreed that if repayments were demanded at this particular moment, the value of land would drop even further and more properties would be abandoned.[35]

The protests of these and other boards of guardians resulted in a relaxation in the terms of repayment. In October 1851, the Treasury acknowledged that in several unions the rates were insufficient to meet both ordinary Poor Law expenditure and the repayments required. In these unions, the Treasury would not require a rate to be levied for the payment of the annuities for a further year. In the greater portion of unions, however, it was convinced that no exemption was necessary. The Treasury added that it had decided on this course of action as it believed that in the aftermath of the years of distress in some parts of Ireland, it was necessary to take measures to help to restore the confidence of both the owners and occupiers of land. Again, the Treasury was determined that the idea of the annuities should not be abandoned altogether. Instead, a new scale of remission was introduced which was based on the individual circumstances of each area.[36] In keeping with the policy of the government, Irish property was still to be forced to pay for Irish distress, even if it proved to be a long-term proposition.

Both the distribution of the money provided by the Annuities Act and the collection of the government annuities were put under the control of the Treasury. The burden of current Poor Law expenditure combined with the annuity repayments continued to bear heavily on many unions, even those which had not been affected by the blight in 1849. In some of the western unions, where localised instances of blight continued into the early 1850s, the local guardians were unable to meet these repayments.

The continuation of distress in some unions, and the aftermath of distress in others, forced a further modification of government policy although, as had so often been the case, it proved to be insufficient. In 1851, the government permitted the annuities to be remitted in any union in which current Poor Law expenditure exceeded 4s in the pound. For many unions, however, the burden of the annuities hindered their recovery from so many consecutive years of Famine and distress. In 1853, the government finally decided to abandon the repayment of annuities by the Poor Law unions. Instead, an income tax was introduced in Ireland. At this stage, Russell's government had been replaced with a Peelite Coalition led by the Earl of Aberdeen, committed to a more rigid economic policy and a reduction in public expenditure.[37]

The harvest of 1850 was largely a healthy one but, as in the previous year, there were localised instances of potato blight, mostly in counties Clare and Limerick. As a result, the government realised that, yet again, some of the poorest unions in Ireland would require their assistance. The £300,000 which had been provided earlier in the year was almost exhausted and parliament, which since 1847 had been attempting to force Ireland to depend on its own resources, was reluctant to provide any additional money. The government sought a solution to its dilemma through the introduction of a second Rate-in-Aid. This was introduced in December 1850 and imposed an additional rate of 2d in the pound on all rateable property.

The introduction of a second Rate-in-Aid was unpopular with many boards of guardians, although the opposition to its introduction was not as uniform or vociferous as it had been to the first Rate-in-Aid. The Strabane guardians were one of the first boards to object to the introduction of this rate. Their main objection was the fact that they were being called upon to pay a second rate when some unions had not even paid the first one. Again, the general dissatisfaction of the northern guardians was based on the fact that they believed that they were being asked to subsidise unions in the west of the country which had paid no portion of the Rate-in-Aid to date. The Poor Law Commissioners had repeatedly to reassure the northern guardians that this was not in fact the case and that only three unions in the whole of Ireland had not made a contribution to the Rate-in-Aid.[38]

Some of the opponents of the second Rate-in-Aid objected to it on the grounds that originally the Rate-in-Aid had been introduced as a temporary measure only and that its date of expiration had passed. The Limerick guardians submitted their objections to Joseph Napier, QC for his opinion. Napier had been opposed to the introduction of the initial

Rate-in-Aid Act and he agreed with the Limerick guardians that 'the rate may be (as I think it is) most objectionable in principle, and there may be much hardship in levying it'. Regardless of this, Napier viewed the rate as being a legal charge and he recommended that the guardians should pay it.[39]

The Cork board of guardians also sought legal opinion, from Isaac Butt. Butt had held the first Chair in Political Economy at Trinity College, Dublin. Although initially a Tory, he eventually became a constitutional nationalist. Throughout the course of the Famine, Butt was an outspoken critic of the policies of the government. He argued that in the midst of such an extensive calamity it was morally wrong to treat Ireland as a separate entity rather than as an integral part of the Union. Butt was also critical of the way in which the Whig government and its key advisers were misinterpreting the rules of political economy, in particular, 'The folly of relying on private enterprise to supply the deficiency . . . Private enterprise has not saved us from the horrors of Famine'. He also questioned the Whigs' financial policies and asked, 'What can be more absurd, what can be more wicked . . . than talking of Ireland being a drain on the English Treasury?' The legal opinion given by Butt, however, was similar to the one provided by Napier. Butt warned the Cork guardians that legal action could be taken against them if they did not impose the second rate. The opinion of Jonathan Henn, QC, who had frequently been employed by the Poor Law Commissioners on earlier occasions, was sought by the Belfast board of guardians. Henn could only confirm what had already been stated. He believed that the provisions of the Act were now legally in force and advised the Belfast guardians to collect the rate. Again, however, as had been the case with the first Rate-in-Aid, very little opposition to the second one actually emerged following its introduction.[40]

Boundary Changes in the Poor Law

The various boundary changes which commenced at the beginning of 1850 added to the existing financial and administrative problems of the Poor Law unions. These changes provided for the establishment of new Poor Law unions and permanent workhouses in Ireland. The building of a new workhouse inevitably placed a further financial burden on the unions in which they were necessary, especially as the loans for the original workhouses had not yet been paid. The formation of the new Poor Law unions was felt to be necessary to bring an end to the system of outdoor relief, which had been permitted by the 1847 Extension Act. The granting of outdoor relief had been introduced in response to exceptional circumstances, and the government, the Treasury and the Poor Law Commissioners were determined that it should be brought to a close as quickly as possible. A Poor Law Boundary Commission was appointed in 1848 to examine the problems caused by excessively large unions and recommend how their size could be reduced. It was also to suggest how outdoor relief could be brought to an end.[41]

The original 1838 Poor Law Act had only permitted poor relief to be provided within the confines of one of the 130 workhouses situated throughout the country. This was known as 'indoor relief'. Prior to 1845, many workhouses were less than half full, some were virtually empty, and several boards of guardians suggested that too many workhouses had been built. Following the devastating potato blight of 1846, the local boards of guardians were encouraged to acquire additional workhouse accommodation in order to prepare for an increased demand on their limited resources. As a consequence, workhouse accommodation was extended, but still proved insufficient to meet the increased demand for Poor Law relief. The resultant overcrowding contributed to an increase in disease and mortality within these institutions. Outdoor relief was made legal by the Extension Act of 1847, but the local guardians were advised to continue to acquire additional accommodation in an attempt to maintain the workhouse test as far as possible. This was due to a deep-seated conviction that outdoor relief, even in the midst of a famine, was demoralising. By the beginning of 1848, this policy had resulted in work-house accommodation increasing from approximately 100,000 places (its pre-Famine level) to over 150,000 places. A year later, workhouse accom-modation had increased to approximately 250,000 places. The Poor Law Commissioners attributed the willingness to extend indoor accommoda-tion to the realisation by the relief officials that:

> The abuses incidental to outdoor relief are not to be contended with by any administrative agency, when such relief is conducted on a large scale; and that a system of workhouse relief is preferable, not alone in ordinary times, but in the seasons of the severest distress . . . [42]

In several unions, the overwhelming demand for Poor Law relief caused some problems in workhouse administration. The overcrowding apparent after 1846, when many workhouses admitted paupers beyond their official capacity, contributed to the spread of disease and an increase in workhouse mortality. Regardless of the prevalence of disease amongst workhouse inmates, however, the Poor Law Commissioners still contin-ued to regard indoor relief as preferable to relief provided outside the workhouse.[43] The benchmark of good Poor Law administration after 1847 was measured by how little outdoor relief was provided by a board of guardians. In this respect, Ulster was generally regarded as having the most efficiently managed unions in the country. In the first year that outdoor relief was permitted, only twenty-five unions did not provide it, seventeen of them situated in Ulster.[44] The avoidance of outdoor relief in many parts of Ulster was due to a number of factors: distress was less severe in the north-east, the local economy was more diversified, private charities were effective, and land cultivation was generally regarded as being more advanced than in other parts of the country. There is also evidence that within Ulster, the leaseholders with substantial holdings were able to offset any losses in the potato crop by the even more profitable sales of grain and dairy produce. Additionally, the local Poor Law unions in Ulster were also more numerous and far smaller than in the rest of the country, the largest unions being situated in Connacht. In Ulster there were forty-three unions, compared with thirty-five in Munster, thirty-four in Leinster and only eighteen in Connacht. The efficient administration of the Poor Law in Ulster was generally regarded as being facilitated by the small size of the unions. The Boundary Commissioners believed that many of the administrative problems prevalent in some of the western unions could be avoided if the size of the Poor Law unions was reduced.[45]

Following the introduction of outdoor relief in 1847, the problem of insufficient workhouse accommodation engaged the attention of many people involved in the administration of the Poor Law. As early as November 1847, Trevelyan recommended that a new union should be established in Erris, a very poor electoral division in the Ballina union. The Poor Law Commissioners, while agreeing that a separate union was necessary in Erris, felt that an equally strong case existed for establishing additional unions in each of the twenty-two distressed unions. The problem, however, was lack of funds: the local unions had no finances and the government was unwilling to advance even more money to the distressed unions. The Treasury compromised by allowing money to be loaned for the building of new workhouses at Belmullet, Berehaven and Dingle, which, apart from belonging to three of the poorest unions in Ireland, also had the distinction of being the three most disproportionately large unions, the paupers having to travel up to thirty miles to reach the workhouse. The Poor Law Commissioners were grateful for this concession, although they realised that it would not put an end to the problem of insufficient workhouse accommodation.[46] When giving evidence before a parliamentary committee in 1849 Twistleton, the Chief Poor Law

Commissioner, stated that in his opinion the building of additional work-houses and other changes in the Poor Law would have been unnecessary if the government had made more money available. If this had occurred, he believed, not only would the administrative machinery of the Poor Law have been more effective, distress and death would have been prevented.[47]

The British government also became directly involved in the debate about providing additional accommodation. The Whigs, increasingly sensitive to public criticism of their policies in Ireland, were questioned in parliament about what they were doing to solve this problem. The Home Secretary, in turn, questioned Trevelyan, who was increasingly regarded as the authority on Irish distress, as to the intentions of the Poor Law Commissioners regarding the size of the unions.[48] The Poor Law Commissioners believed that if the government wanted the Poor Law to provide relief efficiently and effectively, more permanent work-houses were necessary. Although 130 unions had been more than sufficient prior to the Famine, twice that number were now necessary. Twistleton, however, was pessimistic and thought that, due to financial constraints, the government would not be willing to allow such a large undertaking. He did not believe that in the prevailing economic and political climate, any additional financial assistance would be provided to the Poor Law unions. Without additional financial support, therefore, the Poor Law Commissioners felt unable to solve the problem of the large unions.[49]

At the beginning of 1848, the building of a new workhouse commenced in Dingle, Co. Kerry. The plans to build the two other new workhouses was suspended as, in March 1848, a Boundary Commission was appointed by the government. The new Commission consisted of Thomas Larcom, William Delves Broughton and the radical Ulster landlord William Sharman Crawford. The purpose of the Commission was to recommend alterations which could be made in the number and boundaries of both unions and electoral divisions within Ireland, bearing in mind the availability of finding local people capable of conducting the administration of the Poor Law. At the same time, they were also to look at the question of how poor rates could be made more equitable.[50]

Following twelve months of detailed and painstaking enquiry, the Boundary Commissioners made their initial report. Their findings confirmed the government's belief that some unions were inconveniently large and this impaired the efficiency of the Poor Law. The fact that relatively little outdoor relief had been provided in the localities in which the smallest unions were located appeared to confirm this. However, the

Boundary Commissioners recognised the vital role of the boards of guardians in ensuring that the relief provided was effective. In the large unions where the Poor Law had been working efficiently, the Boundary Commission attributed its successful administration to the interest and exertions of the local landlords.[51]

One problem to which the Boundary Commissioners were unable to reach any final conclusion was that of poor rates. The 1838 Poor Law Act had introduced the principle that each electoral division within a union was to pay for the support of the poor within its boundaries. The exceptional distress in some unions since the first appearance of the potato blight had demonstrated, however, that under such circumstances there was a limit to how far property could be made to support its own poverty. The Commissioners felt that in trying to enforce this policy, certain difficulties had arisen in the provision of relief in the poorest unions. At the same time, they recognised that an improvement could be effected if, as far as possible, electoral divisions were smaller and consisted as few properties as possible. Again, this was already the case within Ulster in which the highest number of electoral divisions were coterminous with properties. The Boundary Commissioners believed a reduction in the size of the electoral divisions in other parts of the country would act as a financial incentive to proprietors to take more interest in the level of pauperism on their properties. By making them more directly responsible, it was hoped also that ratepayers would provide the poor people on their estates with either employment or the means to emigrate.[52] This suggestion fitted in with the underlying philosophy of the Poor Law. It did not provide a solution to the problem of what was to be done if the resources of an area should ever again prove to be insufficient to meet the demands being made on them.

At the beginning of 1849, the Boundary Commissioners made a recommendation that fifty new unions should be created. Their list was based in order of urgency, the most immediate need being in the west of the country, that is for unions to be established in Belmullet, Castletown, Berehaven and Killala. The Boundary Commissioners had attempted to ensure that as a result of these changes, no part of the country would be situated more than eight miles from a workhouse. The size of electoral divisions was also to be reduced in the hope of encouraging the local ratepayers to take a more active role in their economic well-being. As might be expected, the recommendations had least impact in Ulster, where few changes were felt to be necessary. The Boundary Commissioners recommended that nineteen new unions should be established in Munster, fourteen in Connacht, thirteen in Leinster, and only

four in Ulster.[53] Ultimately, a total of thirty-three new unions were created, only one of which was situated in Ulster. This increased the number
of Poor Law unions from 131 to 163 and the number of electoral divisions from 2,050 to 3,429.[54]

The response of the Poor Law Commissioners to the recommendations of the Boundary Commissioners was guarded. As the worst of the
Famine was over, they no longer believed that it was necessary to create
the number of unions suggested. One of the main problems which the
Commissioners anticipated concerned the collection of rates, particularly
in the interim period before the administrative machinery of a new union
was in place. To facilitate effective rate collection, they recommended
that all of the new unions should be created simultaneously and not, as
had been suggested by the Boundary Commissioners, in order of
urgency.[55] The Commissioners also felt that if the changeover was to be
effective, the Treasury would need to provide financial aid to the unions
involved. This latter recommendation resulted in an argument between
the Commissioners and the Treasury regarding the provision of external
aid to help bring about this changeover. The Treasury was angered by
the Commissioners' assumption that it would provide financial aid. The
Commissioners, however, were adamant that such assistance was necessary. They did not believe that new unions could be created unless such
aid was forthcoming, and they threatened that they would not implement
these changes if the money was not provided.[56] The Treasury, although
furious with the Commissioners, felt that it had no option but to accede.
As a result, the money allocated by the Treasury for the use of the Poor
Law unions was larger than at any time during the Famine.[57]

The main concern of the local boards of guardians in relation to the
formation of new unions was a financial one. In the poorest unions,
where distress was still abnormally high, this was a particular problem. A
new union could not take with it any part of the funds of their parent
union, therefore, they were dependent on external funds until a new rate
could be collected. The new rates not only had to pay for the current
expenses of the union, but were also expected to commence immediate
repayment of the government annuities. Also, the loan made to the new
unions for the building of workhouses could only be equal to the amount
which had been repaid by the parent union for the original workhouse
loan. In general, many guardians regarded the creation of a new union
with alarm, particularly the additional expense of erecting, furnishing and
staffing a separate workhouse. In the unions in which the worst of the
Famine was over, many guardians considered the formation of a new
union to be an unnecessary extravagance at a time when pauperism was

decreasing and many workhouses had vacancies; in the unions where distress was still high, the guardians regarded it as a further burden on the already hard-pressed ratepayers.[58]

Apart from the financial difficulties, there were also administrative problems. Following the declaration of a new union, a suitable site for a workhouse had to be found and a new board of guardians elected as quickly as possible. Until this was done, the ex-officio guardians of the parent union were to manage the affairs of the new union.[59] Before the new workhouse was opened, a portion of space in the parent union was reserved for the use of the new union, although the new union was liable for its maintenance during this period. The Commissioners stipulated that this arrangement was not to exceed a period of more than three years. This arrangement was usually complicated. For example, in November 1850, the Ennis workhouse was maintaining the paupers of three other unions which were in the process of being established.[60] The formation of new unions had been intended to facilitate a more efficient administration of Poor Law relief and a corresponding reduction in union expenditure. Ironically, by the time the changes were implemented, there had been a drastic reduction in the level of pauperism and many workhouses were again less than half full.[61]

Poor Relief Act After 1850

The harvest of 1850, like that of the previous year, was healthy, with only isolated instances of blight appearing in some parts of the country. The general decline in crop yields compared to their pre-Famine level continued, however. This was due to a combination of factors, including a move away from the cultivation of labour-intensive potatoes; farmers, concerned about the possible reappearance of blight, growing fewer potatoes; and a general decline in the fertility of the soil after a number of years of intense blight. The trends which had been present in the provision of poor relief in the previous year continued, and there was an overall decrease in pauperism in the country and a further transition from outdoor to indoor relief. The guardians were informed that the number of auxiliary workhouses could safely be reduced, although it was recommended that they should keep an option on the lease of these buildings. The guardians were also advised that as pauperism was decreasing in most unions, they should begin to turn their attention to the efficient administration of the workhouses. Furthermore they should now regard the inspection and management of the workhouses under their control as the most important of their duties.[62]

One indication of the stabilisation that was taking place in the administration of the Poor Law was the fact that so many guardians were again turning their attention to the finding of gainful employment for all workhouse inmates. The original 1838 Poor Law Act had described pauper employment as an essential component of the workhouse test. Even during periods of extreme distress, the Commissioners continued to regard pauper employment as essential, both to deter people from applying for relief and to discipline those already in receipt of it. Stone-breaking was regarded as the most desirable form of employment for able-bodied men. Able-bodied females were responsible for all housework in the workhouse and sometimes for making the workhouse clothes. The Commissioners were particularly anxious that young females in the workhouse—of which there was a disproportionately large number—should be trained in all domestic duties in order to make them suitable candidates for emigration.[63] Even during the height of the Famine distress, therefore, the Commissioners ordained that paupers in receipt of either indoor or outdoor relief should be kept fully employed. In the 1850s, as many of the workhouses began to empty out, employment was again seen as an essential component of deterring paupers from seeking refuge in the workhouses.

The general improvement evident in many unions after 1850 did not apply to all parts of the country. Although many of the unions which had been designated 'distressed' were beginning to emerge from the years of devastation, this improvement did not encompass all unions in the west of Ireland. Following the harvest of 1850, both the government and the Poor Law Commissioners stressed the fact that the administration of the Poor Law was returning to its pre-Famine situation. They were, however, reluctant to admit that the condition of the poor in some unions was still continuing to deteriorate. The deterioration was most apparent in Co. Clare, an area which had suffered severely since the first appearance of potato blight, and which continued to show no signs of recovery. In the country as a whole in 1851, approximately 30,000 people were in receipt of outdoor relief. This was almost double the number receiving relief in the province of Connacht alone. In the three Clare unions of Ennistymon, Kilrush and Scariff, the Commissioners admitted that there existed, 'a degree of destitution which has no parallel in other parts of Ireland at the present time'.[64] These unions were still facing many of the problems which had been encountered by the distressed unions during the height of the Famine. The Ennistymon guardians were dissolved for the second time for not providing outdoor relief. The guardians explained that they had failed to do so as their funds were exhausted.[65]

Each of the unions in Co. Clare continued to experience unusually high levels of hardship in the early years of the 1850s, yet it was the Kilrush union in which it proved to be most severe and prolonged. The Kilrush union, in common with many others in Co. Clare, had experienced high levels of distress each year since 1845, due to the repeated failure of the potato crop upon which many of the local population depended for subsistence. In 1848, the union had achieved notoriety similar to that of Skibbereen due to the high number of evictions taking place each day. Following these evictions, the houses of the poor were generally demolished. By depriving such a large number of people of their homes and their livelihood, the evictions placed a further burden on the finite resources of the local Poor Law. This practice was a not unique to the Kilrush union but was particularly widespread there. The Poor Law Commissioners directed the local Inspector, Captain Kennedy, to report on the situation. At the same time, they informed him that:

> The Commissioners do not consider it to be within their province to interfere with the legal exercise of the rights of property; but when, owing to the demolition of houses, the poor rates of a union become liable for the support of destitute poor persons who have no house to go to, it becomes competent for the Commissioners to satisfy themselves, that such additions to the liabilities of the union are not occasioned by a violation of the law.[66]

In May 1848, Captain Kennedy informed the Commissioners that thirty to forty cabins were being demolished daily and 300 people being evicted as a consequence. Approximately a quarter of the population was already receiving poor relief, and this number was increasing. The evictions were legal, however, as many of the small occupiers were tenants at will. Kennedy believed that the main reason for these evictions taking place on such a large scale was the considerable number of very smallholdings in the unions. This threw a heavy burden on landlords whose property included a large number of holdings which were valued at under £4.[67]

As the situation in many parts of the country began to ameliorate following the 1849 harvest, in unions in Co. Clare distress was still increasing. Again, the Kilrush union was the most extreme example. The local Inspector informed the Commissioners that distress was so widespread that even if the full rate were collected, it would still prove insufficient to meet the financial needs of the union. Evictions continued to be numerous and showed no signs of abating. Captain Kennedy estimated that within two weeks in May 1849 alone, 1,200 people had been evicted.

Kennedy's reports were increasingly pessimistic about the condition of the poor people, and he warned:

> The condition of the poor daily becomes worse and the mortality more distressing. As soon as one crowd of houseless and naked paupers are dead or provided for in the workhouse, another wholesale eviction doubles the number who, in their turn, pass through the same ordeal of wandering from house to house or burrowing in the bogs or behind ditches until, broken down by privation and exposure to the elements, they seek the workhouse or die by the roadside.[68]

The condition of the Kilrush union did not improve following the harvest of 1849. In November 1849, there was a temporary suspension of relief in the union because the income from the rates was exhausted and the local contractors were refusing to allow any further credit. The guardians had asked the Poor Law Commissioners for financial assistance, but this was refused on the grounds that, in their view, local resources had not been used to their fullest possible extent. As a result, outdoor relief was discontinued for a period of several weeks. During this period, the workhouse inmates were fed on turnips grown in the workhouse grounds. A number of deaths from starvation were reported amongst persons dependent on relief for subsistence. The guardians repeatedly appealed to the Commissioners for financial assistance. When it failed to materialise, they stated that they considered that they were absolved from personal responsibility because they did not have the means at their disposal with which to combat this distress. Following the intervention of the local Inspector on behalf of the guardians, the Commissioners forwarded £100 to the union. The guardians regarded this with derision, as they estimated that it would not even provide relief for a week.[69]

In 1850, at the insistence of the MP, George Poulett Scrope, a select committee was appointed to enquire into the local administration of the Poor Law in the Kilrush union. Poulett Scrope was an English geologist and economist. He came to prominence in the 1820s as a result of his prolific writings on the conditions of the labouring poor. As a result, he became interested in the works of the political economists, but quickly became one of their harshest and most effective critics. One of Scrope's main concerns was that the leading political economists had elevated this philosophy to a 'science', complete with its own principles which they claimed were based on immutable economic laws. In his view much of political economy was, in fact, speculation. Yet, its proponents were:

> perpetually claiming for their science a paramount importance to the interests of mankind, and urging its conclusions on governments and legislatures, as the only infallible guide for securing the welfare of the state.

The consequence of this, Scrope believed, had been disastrous for the poor people of England and the famine-starved people of Ireland.[70]

The select committee was directed to establish whether the Poor Law had been administered effectively within the Kilrush union, and if not, what factors had prevented this. Its final report was critical. It stated that distress and consequent suffering of the poor people in the union had been 'intense to a degree almost beyond conception'. The population had decreased throughout the union from between 25 to 50 per cent even though there had been little emigration from the area. The committee concluded that, despite the fact that provisions had been both cheap and plentiful since 1848, insufficient relief had been provided through the mechanism of the Poor Law. As a consequence, they believed that many lives had been lost. The committee was also critical of the actions of local landlords, believing that many of them allowed themselves to be subsided by the government while failing to provide employment and, at the same time, carrying out large-scale evictions.

The select committee also criticised the role played by the British government in the provision of relief in Kilrush. They recognised that due to the high and continuing level of distress, the guardians and vice-guardians had been dependent on funds from external sources. The guardians, therefore, were dependent on the Poor Law Commissioners who in turn, were dependent on the Treasury. The Treasury, which had effectively been in charge of the distribution of the government's funds throughout the Famine, was careful in its application, aware of the increasing reluctance of parliament to provide money for this purpose. The attitude of parliament was partly based on their conviction that the resources within the local unions were not as exhausted as the ratepayers frequently claimed. The committee believed that, despite this, the government would not have allowed the situation to continue in the Kilrush and other distressed unions had they been aware of the deep and genuine suffering of many of the local population.

The select committee concluded that what had occurred in the Kilrush union and to a lesser degree in some of the other western unions, was an extreme example of the government, through the machinery of the Poor Law, attempting to force local resources to support local distress. The rigid adherence to this policy had resulted in a neglect of public duty. What the government had failed to take into account was the fact that, in some parts of Ireland, the local resources had collapsed almost completely and normal economic and social principles had ceased to function. The members of the committee did not believe that such a dogmatic approach would have been adopted had a similar situation prevailed in England:

> Whether as regards the plain principles of humanity, or the literal text and admitted principle of the Poor Law of 1847, a neglect of public duty has occurred and has occasioned a state of things disgraceful to a civilised age and country, for which some authority ought to be held responsible, and would have been long since held responsible had these things occurred in any union in England.[71]

At the same time, the committee also alleged that part of the blame lay with the people within the union itself, notably the local Poor Law administrators and the local landlords.

Within the Kilrush union, the findings of the select committee were unpopular. Many of the local ratepayers felt that the committee had judged them harshly, particularly in the light of the difficulties with which they had been faced. Sir Lucius O'Brien, a member of the select committee, who was both a local landlord and a Poor Law guardian in Co. Clare, vigorously rejected many of the committee's conclusions. He considered it unfair to condemn the local landlords as, during the years of distress and famine, they had been doubly penalised; many of them had not received rents for several years, yet had been paying very high poor rates. This was a particularly heavy burden in areas where the land was very sub-divided and the landlords were also liable to pay the rates on small-holdings. O'Brien did not agree that the local landlords and ratepayers were to blame for the inadequacies of the relief provided, but, in his opinion, the Poor Law system had failed to meet the needs of the distressed people and was 'wholly unsuitable to the Famine'.[72]

The report of the select committee had no immediate impact on the conditions within the Kilrush union. The on-going poverty of the union continued to attract public attention in Britain in the early months of 1851. This was primarily due to the publication of a new book, *Gleanings from the West of Ireland*, and the inclusion of a letter by its author in *The Times* in March 1851. Both of these publications criticised the way in which the Poor Law had been administered in the west of Ireland, particularly the way in which the affairs of the Kilrush union had been managed.[73]

In May 1851, 3,318 people were receiving outdoor relief and 4,903 people were in receipt of indoor relief in Kilrush. The guardians described these applicants for relief as being 'in low physical condition'.[74] The number of people receiving Poor Law relief in the union continued to increase during the summer of 1851, when 13,047 people were in receipt of outdoor relief and 7,645 persons were receiving indoor relief, out of a population of 51,247 persons. The burden of providing this on the local poor rates was heavy: poor relief in the twelve months following September 1850 cost £17,942 5s 5d out of a Poor Law valuation of £33,247.[75] This meant that the average poor rate in the Kilrush union for current expenditure only, not including any repayments, was 10s in the pound, far higher than the average national rate of 2s in the pound during the same period.

Although distress was most acute in the Kilrush union, other unions in the same locality were still experiencing severe distress. The continuation of the distress was of concern to the local boards of guardians. In September 1850, the chairmen of the Ballyvaghan, Corofin, Ennis, Ennistymon, Kilrush, Scariff and Tulla unions convened a meeting to discuss the administration of the Poor Law. Regardless of the formation of a number of new unions, the chairmen believed that more workhouses were still required in the vicinity. They appealed to the government for additional money to enable them to provide more extensive relief as their own funds were exhausted. This request was turned down.[76]

The Ennistymon union in particular was undergoing extreme financial difficulties. In the year ending September 1851, its current expenditure was £18,014 out of a valuation of £21,602, and this did not include the Rate-in-Aid or various other government repayments.[77] Mortality in the union was also increasing and the Commissioners suggested that the guardians should extend outdoor relief. The guardians, however, were unable to do so as their financial resources did not allow for any increase in the provision of relief. The local Poor Law Inspector sympathised with the guardians. He regarded them as a very efficient board and described the workhouses under their control as a credit to any union. Sir Lucius O'Brien, the chairman of the neighbouring Ennis union, also lent his support to the difficulties faced by the Ennistymon guardians. He informed the Commissioners that if the guardians were given external financial support, they would be able to provide sufficient relief. Despite this, the Poor Law Commissioners dissolved the board of guardians and re-appointed paid guardians.[78]

The continuing high level of distress in Co. Clare was accompanied by large-scale disease and mortality. The months from January to May 1851 were marked by a further increase in mortality in the area. The local doctor in the Kilrush union, Dr Madden, stated that he had never before seen such wretchedness. Mortality within the workhouse was particularly high, which Madden attributed to the debilitated condition in which many people entered the building, and the unnutritious food which they then received. Madden believed that many of the people who constantly congregated around the workhouse did so in the hope of being admitted so they could be buried in a coffin, regardless of the appalling conditions inside. Madden added that, notwithstanding the desperate situation confronting them, the board of guardians had always acted humanely. His report was corroborated by the local Poor Law Inspector who pointed out that these conditions were not confined to the Kilrush union, but existed in each of the unions in his district. He believed that a major factor in the illness of the people was the protracted insufficiency of nutritious food which had broken down the health of the poor people.[79]

The continuation of the problems of the Co. Clare unions resulted in a further government enquiry being established. The Lord Lieutenant appointed two men, Dr John Hill and Dr James Hughes to investigate the high mortality in some of the Clare unions. The enquiry took place between June and August 1851. In the course of their investigations, Hill and Hughes realised that the conditions within the workhouses and the scantiness of relief provided had actually contributed to the bad health and mortality of the population. Many of the workhouses in Clare were overcrowded and badly ventilated. The workhouse clothing was not warm enough for the cold, damp winters and, due to lack of water, was frequently not clean. The auxiliary workhouses, which had been hired to cope with the increased demands for relief, were often cold and ill-adapted to housing the sick and destitute. As a result of these conditions, healthy paupers had been reluctant to become inmates of the local workhouses and of those who did become inmates, very few could any longer be described as 'able-bodied'.[80]

Following the submission of this report, the local guardians were asked to act on some of the suggestions made by Hill and Hughes, particularly in regard to diet and overcrowding. At the same time, the Commissioners acknowledged that, due to the financial position of the unions and the difficulty in finding suitable additional accommodation, the guardians would find this difficult to do. Privately, the Poor Law Commissioners were worried that this report might be used by their enemies to prove maladministration by the Poor Law officials. Power, the

Chief Commissioner, pleaded with Trevelyan for the Treasury to allow more money to be used to retain the present number of Poor Law Inspectors in the Clare unions to help with the administration of relief.[81]

The Clare unions were not the only ones in which little improvement was evident following the harvest of 1849. In parts of counties Galway, Limerick, Mayo and Tipperary, isolated instances of blight appeared in the harvest of 1849, although it was not as widespread as in Clare. Pressure on the resources of the local Poor Law continued to be high and scenes reminiscent of the worst of the Famine months continued to be reported. In April 1850, the Castlebar workhouse and its auxiliaries were so overcrowded, and the guardians so short of funds, that there was no change of clothing for the inmates and only straw for bedding. The medical officer reported that the workhouses were so unhealthy that they were actually endangering the lives of the people within them.[82]

The financial condition of these unions showed little improvement following the harvest of 1850 in which isolated instances of potato blight again appeared in parts of the west. In the Ballina union, the guardians were in so much debt that the local sheriff took possession of the workhouse and put the workhouse clothes up for auction. The Kenmare guardians were unable to obtain any further credit from their contractors and their chairman was using his own money to obtain food for the paupers. When the board asked the Commissioners for financial assistance, they were told that they must strike higher rates in their union. The Kenmare guardians, who had often been in conflict with the Commissioners over the question of rates, again found themselves in dispute with the central authorities. The guardians attributed this to the fact that both the government and the Commissioners had an erroneous idea of the amount of money which the ratepayers could afford to pay in taxes. Twenty-five per cent of the population were in receipt of relief in their union, and some of the ratepayers were not much better off than the paupers. The Commissioners, however, who were under pressure to end the financial dependence of the unions on external funds, had no funds to give to the Kenmare guardians. Instead, they urged them to collect higher rates and warned them if they did not do so, they would be dissolved for a second time.[83]

One problem which was not confined to the poorest unions was that of sore eyes or, in its severest form, xerophthalmia, which was commonly referred to as ophthalmia. Ophthalmia was caused by a vitamin deficiency resulting from a prolonged absence of fat in the diet. Prior to the Famine, the Irish diet traditionally included Vitamin A in the form of milk, but this tended to disappear as the traditional potato diet was replaced by a far less nutritious grain-based diet.[84] In 1849, of the 932,282 persons admitted to the Irish workhouses, 13,812 were treated for an inflammatory disease of the eye. Of the people treated, 114 people lost the use of one eye and thirty-seven people lost the use of both eyes. In 1850, of the 805,702 paupers admitted to the workhouses, 27,200 were treated for this disease, 202 persons losing the sight in one eye and eighty persons losing the sight in both eyes. By 1851, although the government had sought the advice of various Irish oculists, including Professor Arthur Jacob and Sir William Wilde, the disease was still increasing. In 1851, 45,947 inmates of workhouses were treated for the disease. Of these, 656 lost the use of one eye and 263 lost the use of both. By 1852, as conditions within the workhouses, including diet, improved, incidences of this disease rapidly decreased. It had been most prevalent in the unions of Athlone, Cashel, Clonmel, Cork, Kanturk, Kilmallock, Kilrush, Limerick, Loughrea, Millstreet, Scariff and Tipperary and was particularly common amongst young children. In some instances, the Commissioners believed that the disease was feigned by the paupers in order to obtain better food or avoid doing work.[85]

The Famine and its immediate aftermath had clearly shown the limitations of the medical relief available within Ireland. This was particularly true of the medical facilities provided by the Poor Law, as the Famine had clearly demonstrated the close relationship between distress and disease. In 1851, the Medical Charities Act was introduced to improve and regulate the medical services provided by the Poor Law.[86] This Act provided for the establishment of dispensaries, to be financed from the local poor rates. Each Poor Law union was to be divided into dispensary districts for this purpose. The Medical Charities Act replaced the previous system which had largely been dependent on private subscriptions and voluntary county presentments by one based on a national system of taxation.[87]

It was not until the spring of 1852 that some signs of recovery were apparent in these unions, and the levels of distress and mortality began to decrease. In the twelve months ending September 1852, the number of people receiving relief in the whole country fell from 145,743 to 115,805. The 1852 harvest was healthy and virtually free from potato blight. The Commissioners hoped that as a result of this, an even greater decrease in the number of people in receipt of relief would take place in 1853.[88] By 1852, therefore, the worst of the Famine appeared to be over in all parts of Ireland, although the levels of disease, mortality and emigration throughout the country remained high.

Financing the Famine

As the Famine progressed, a growing disillusionment was apparent with the continuing dependence of a large portion of the Irish population on external agencies, particularly the Treasury. In contrast, the amount of money raised by the Irish people was frequently described in derisory terms. The Irish landlords were publicly denounced frequently for failing to come to the assistance of their fellow countrymen. The distressed people, on the other hand, were regarded as being only too willing to allow other people to provide for them. As a consequence of the perceived apathy of Irish people of all classes, therefore, the British government was forced, again and again, to intervene on behalf of the starving people. The cost of this intervention to the Treasury was high: from 1845 to 1852, the provision of relief cost the imperial Treasury £8,332,000. Initially, however, a large portion of this money (over half) was provided as a loan. The money advanced by the Treasury during the whole of the Famine was less than one-half per cent of the annual Gross National Product of the United Kingdom or, has been aptly pointed out, merely 10 per cent of what had been spent in one year alone during the Napoleonic Wars. Also, only a few years after the Famine, the government spent over £69 million on a disastrous foray in the Crimea.[89] In Ireland during the Famine, apart from voluntary subscriptions, the Irish ratepayers paid £8,332,351 in poor rates out of an annual Poor Law valuation of £11,372,413 in 1851.[90]

Increasingly, the successive relief policies introduced by the British government were intended not merely to provide assistance to urgent cases of distress, but also to help to bring about a long-term transformation of the Irish economy. The social and economic dislocation evident during the years of distress was regarded as an opportunity to bring about changes in the Irish economy and facilitate its transformation into a more streamlined capitalist society. The Quarter-Acre Clause, the workhouse test, and the burden of poor rates were some of the means by which the desired changes were to be effected. Eviction, emigration and high mortality, however, were part of the price to be paid. For the British government and some of its agents, determined to use the Famine as an opportunity to bring about these changes in Ireland, this price did not appear to be too high.

At the end of the Famine, it was evident that substantial changes had taken place in the country. In the 1850s, the Census Commissioners recorded that in the ten years from 1841 to 1851 the population of Ireland had fallen from 8,175,124 persons to 6,552,385 persons. They also estimated that if the Famine had not occurred, the population of

Ireland in 1851 would have been 9,018,799.[91] Notwithstanding this, the Census Commissioners believed that Ireland had derived various advantages from the years of distress. Regardless of the high social and economic cost, the Census Commissioners suggested Ireland had benefited from the Famine. In their report, they stated:

> In conclusion, we feel it will be gratifying to your Excellency to find that although the population has been diminished in so remarkable a manner by famine, disease and emigration between 1841 and 1851, and has been since decreasing, the results of the Irish census of 1851 are, on the whole, satisfactory, demonstrating as they do the general advancement of the country.[92]

This revealing comment by the Census Commissioners brought them into the realms of socio-economic commentary. It is unlikely that such remarks would have been made in such a highly influential document unless the Census Commissioners were certain that their sentiments would be received favourably by their administrative and political superiors. This example of *post hoc* rationalisation comes close to suggesting that mass starvation, death, eviction, and large scale emigration were legitimate tools of social engineering.

Their Sorrowful Pilgrimage: Emigration

1847–55

Years of famine and distress had an impact on the rate of emigration from Ireland. Emigration was not a new phenomenon. In the eighteenth century, over a quarter of a million persons sailed to colonial America. These emigrants were predominantly from Ulster and, because they were mostly of Scots descent, were referred to as Ulster-Scots. The rate of emigration slowed down during the French Revolutionary and Napoleonic Wars, but between 1815 and 1845 an estimated one million people left the country and the number appeared to be increasing. During the Famine, the scale and pace of emigration rose sharply. One to one-and-a-half million people left Ireland between 1845 and 1851 and as many as a further two million in the subsequent twenty years. Famine emigration did not truly commence until the end of 1846, following the more widespread second appearance of blight, and it peaked in 1852, long after the potato blight had disappeared from most of Ireland. Even when the Famine was over, the high level of emigration continued and, in the following sixty years, an additional six million persons left. As a consequence, by the end of the nineteenth century, an international network of Irish communities had been established.

The prime destination of the emigrants was overwhelmingly the United States, with approximately 80 per cent choosing to go there. The next most significant destinations were Britain, British North America (Canada) and Australasia. The precise number of people who left Ireland during and immediately following the Famine is not known. Passenger lists are relatively rare although where they do exist they provide useful insights into the origins and destinations of the emigrants. The Emigration Commissioners estimated the Famine and immediate post-Famine emigration as follows.

Table 24: Emigration Rates, 1847–55[1]

1847	-	219,885 persons
1848	-	181,316
1849	-	218,842
1850	-	213,649
1851	-	254,537
1852	-	368,764
1853	-	192,609
1854	-	150,209
1855	-	78,854

The reasons for choosing to leave Ireland varied throughout the nineteenth century. Before the Famine, some contemporary commentators regarded emigration as a safety valve, necessary because the stagnating agrarian economy was unable to support the large, impoverished and fast-growing rural population. The large population, and the consequent sub-division of land in several parts of the country, was often blamed for the poverty of the country. It was generally agreed, however, that an even higher level of emigration was required as a pre-requisite to the modernisation of Irish agriculture. During the intermittent periods of distress and scarcity in the early part of the century also, emigration was regarded as a means of providing immediate amelioration to the most impoverished portions of the population. Not all social theorists, however, viewed emigration in this way. Malthus, for example, did not regard it as a long-term solution to problems of over-population.[2] Notwithstanding the fact that emigration was frequently correlated with poverty, emigration prior to the Famine was not confined to the poorest parts of Ireland. Most emigrants came from the relatively wealthy province of Ulster rather than the west of Ireland and had a different motivation for choosing to leave their country of birth. For many of these people, emigration provided a way of realising rising materialist goals in the industrialising nations of America and Britain. To a large extent, therefore, emigration was a rational and reasoned response to prevailing economic and social circumstances, other countries being seen as providing more opportunities for advancement than existed in Ireland. The process of emigration was also facilitated by the introduction of steam packets which were used increasingly on the main emigrant routes, thus making the decision to move both cheaper and more accessible than previously had been the case.[3]

After 1845, successive years of potato blight acted as a catalyst to the decision to emigrate. Emigrants were drawn from all parts of Ireland and all social groups, although as successive years of blight took their toll, the number of impoverished and pauper emigrants, for the first time ever, became a significant portion of the total number. At the same time, however, a large number of emigrants continued to be drawn from areas which did not include the poorest sections of the population, including south Ulster, east Connacht and the midlands of Ireland. This indicated that the general desire to leave Ireland during these years was not only confined to the portion of the population directly affected by the loss of the potato crop. The counties which demonstrated the largest increase in emigration over their pre-Famine levels were Clare, Kerry, Kilkenny, Limerick and Tipperary, in which approximately 16 to 18 per cent of the local population emigrated. Emigration was lowest from counties Antrim (7 per cent), Down (6 per cent), Dublin (3 per cent), and Mayo (8 per cent).[4] Overall, emigration was highest from areas which were poor, but not absolutely destitute, which usually meant that the population possessed the means to emigrate. The fact that emigration was not highest from the areas most devastated by the distress was due to the complex factors involved in the decision to emigrate; apart from financial considerations, emigrants needed to possess the necessary will, motivation, information and health to move.

The Famine exodus did not commence until the end of 1846 although its extent did not become apparent until 1847. During the latter year, emigration was 100 per cent higher than in 1846. In some ways, 1847 marked a watershed in Famine emigration. As the year progressed, it was obvious that emigration was no longer the preserve of able-bodied labourers and professionals who, in an orderly and rational manner, had sought an increase in their fortune elsewhere. Instead, emigration had increasingly become the last refuge of a desperate population who believed that their only hope of survival lay outside Ireland. Although many of the emigrants were drawn from the poorest and least skilled sections of society, a large portion were also drawn from the substantial farming class. This caused one northern newspaper to despair that the majority of emigrants were 'the flower of the people'. Much of this emigration was carried out in a mood of despair, anxiety and hysteria, the emigrants even being willing to risk hazards of an autumn or winter crossing rather than the traditional, safer, spring and summer ones, in their determination to be anywhere but Ireland. After 1847, the sense of urgency and desperation evinced by a large number of emigrants became less obvious. The rate of emigration did not decrease, however, until after 1852, even through the worst of the Famine was long over in many districts. Following this, it began to settle down again into the regional and social patterns, with emigration from the west, notably Connacht, gaining a new prominence.[5]

The reduction in the rate of emigration which became obvious after 1853 was greeted with relief by some members of the British government. The government had chosen to keep its intervention in the process of emigration to a minimum, but regarded it as beneficial to the Irish economy. By 1853, however, official reports estimated the number of emigrants in excess of one and a half million persons, a large number of whom were aged under thirty. The Emigration Commissioners warned the government that if this outflow continued, it would erode the labouring population of Ireland to an unacceptable level. Even more worrying, perhaps, was the general scarcity of Irish seasonal labourers in England, who were heavily relied upon during the harvest season.[6] To the relief of the government, however—who were as unwilling to intervene to prevent emigration as they had been to intervene to promote it—after 1854, Irish emigration declined rapidly and by 1858, was lower than its pre-Famine level. This decline was not due to financial reasons as the remittance system was sufficient to allow even larger scale emigration. The Emigration Commissioners attributed the decrease to improvements within Ireland which, in turn, were due to the removal of a large portion of the population.[7] These improvements, however, did not prove sufficient to sustain the economy without the support of an on-going programme of emigration, which proved to be particularly useful during intermittent periods of recession within Ireland throughout the late nineteenth century.

Making the decision to emigrate was the easiest part of the whole process. The subsequent parts of the journey were frequently perilous. This was most obvious in 1847 and 1848 when the eagerness of the emigrants to leave Ireland and the desire of the shipping companies to maximise their profits superseded all other considerations. The coincidence of frequent gales at sea, winter sailings, overcrowded and insanitary conditions in both the interim boarding houses and on board ship, and inadequate quarantine facilities when they arrived at their destination, proved to be a fatal combination for many emigrants.[8] Even the soubriquet 'coffin-ships' and the greeting 'Irish need not apply' did not deflect would-be emigrants from leaving Ireland.

Emigrating could be unpleasant. Many cases were reported to the government, and many more remained unreported, of fraud and deception by unscrupulous shipping companies and their agents. Often those concerned were attempting to obtain additional money from the unsuspecting emigrants for various services which were unnecessary or overpriced.[9] Even arrival at the port of destination did not bring to an end the problems, as a sophisticated business emerged in the exploitation of the new arrivals. The widespread existence of this business was generally acknowledged:

> As soon as a party of emigrants arrive in Liverpool they are beset by a tribe of people, both male and female, who are known by the name of 'mancatcher' and 'runner'. The business of these people is, in common parlance, to 'fleece' the emigrant, and to draw from his pocket, by fair means or foul, as much of his cash as he can be persuaded, inveigled or bullied into parting with . . . But these are not the only class of the man-catching fraternity, nor do they confine their operations to an exorbitant profit upon passage money. The mancatchers keep lodging houses for emigrants—wretched cellars and rooms, destitute of comfort and convenience, in which they cram them as thickly as the places can hold.[10]

The problem became so prevalent that the government appointed a select committee to advise whether any further protection was required for the emigrants beyond the existing, and inadequate, Passenger Act.

The Committee reported that the majority of abuses occurred in Liverpool, particularly on the American passage. They attributed this to the fact that the numbers travelling through Liverpool were so vast that 'considerable abuses have become systemless in the trade, and the emigrant is exposed to frauds and malpractices from which in other ports he is comparatively secure'.[11] The committee found that the most common abuses were practiced by runners or 'crimps'. The most successful of these were those who were Irish themselves and therefore had a reassuring familiarity for the new arrivals. The runners met the emigrants as they disembarked; carried their luggage for a fee; offered to negotiate any additional passages on their behalf, for which they received a commission; directed the emigrants to a lodging house on whose behalf the runner was acting; advised the emigrants as to the provisions which would be necessary for the longer voyage—much of which was in fact unnecessary—and arranged for the purchase of these items at exorbitant prices. Finally, the runners offered to exchange the emigrants' money for dollars, not only deducting commission in the process, but sometimes even giving the unsuspecting emigrant some other foreign coin. Because many migrants spent only forty-eight hours in Liverpool before embarking for the next stage of the journey, the majority remained unaware of the extent of the deception and did not have the time to seek redress anyway.[12]

The select committee lamented the extent of abuses practised on Irish and, indeed, other emigrants in Liverpool, which the Passenger Act patently did not protect them against. Despite this, they were not willing to recommend any major intervention by the government that would involve additional expenditure or restrict the number of persons leaving Ireland. Instead, the select committee gave support to a continuation of the minimalist approach adopted by the government even during the height of the Famine. The committee justified its stance on the grounds that:

> . . . more systematic efforts may be made and ought to be made by the local authorities, and fuller powers granted to them, if deemed necessary for the purpose, before so great a departure from principle should be sanctioned as the undertaking by the State of functions which are legitimately within the province of private enterprise.[13]

It was not only the British government that was indifferent to the problems faced by the Irish emigrants. An unforeseen impediment to the Irish Famine haemorrhage came from some of the host countries themselves. As the number of Irish people seeking refuge elsewhere greatly increased during 1847, so to did their reputation for being both pauperised and disease-ridden. The reputation acquired by the Irish migrants was not unfounded. Many of them, even before they left the shores of Ireland, were unwittingly incubators for and carriers of various diseases. Others were merely debilitated as a result of two or more years of shortages, and a diet based primarily on stirabout or soup, which was as un-nutritious as it was unfamiliar to the Irish palate. The same countries that had contributed so generously to Irish distress in 1845 and 1846 now closed ranks and tried to control the Irish influx by hurriedly introducing a number of restrictions and taxes on immigration, as the scenes of distress moved too close for comfort.[14] The Irish immigrants were disliked for a number of reasons: they were feared as carriers of disease, as potential burdens on the local taxes and, of particular worry to the native labouring population, as competition for jobs. Some attempts were made to discourage the Irish influx. The Governor of Nova Scotia, Sir John Harvey, even took the precaution of writing to the Colonial Secretary, Earl Grey, to inform him that employment prospects in Canada had been greatly exaggerated and, in fact, that very little labour was available. This letter was widely publicised in Ireland, as Harvey had wished, in an attempt to discourage any further emigration to the area.[15]

Regardless of the difficulties associated with emigration, the numbers leaving Ireland showed no signs of abating until the 1850s, and continued to be an integral part of the Irish lifecycle in the second half of the nineteenth century. Not surprisingly, emigration acquired the properties of a paradox. Leaving Ireland simultaneously represented both escape and exile. As the century progressed, a culture of exile emerged, reinforced by a whole system of leave-taking, which included American 'wakes', a bottle night and supper, a farewell procession of friends and neighbours and a final blessing from a local priest.[16] All of this created, quite deliberately, a powerful and indelible impression on the mind of the departing emigrants. The idea of exile was further reinforced through the popularity of the emigration songs and ballads, most of which lamented having to leave Ireland and expressed the hope that one day they would return. Few emigrants, however, ever returned to Ireland. Regardless of all the difficulties, emigration represented an improvement in their material conditions which did not appear to be possible in the country of their birth.

By the end of the nineteenth century, the idea of involuntary exile and enforced banishment were used by the nationalist movement as evidence of British misrule. The image of Famine emigrants as victims—of enforced poverty, landlord tyranny, British misrule, official callousness and even religious oppression—proved to be a particularly enduring one to which subsequent generations of emigrants and nationalists paid lip-service. In 1909 a Celtic Cross was erected on Grosse Isle near Quebec City, a quarantine and inspection station where 4,572 Irish immigrants had died within a two-month period in 1847. The inscription, adhering to the stereotype of emigrants as being poor, oppressed and Catholic (which was far from true in Canada) stated:

> Sacred to the Memory of thousands of Irish emigrants, who to preserve the faith, suffered hunger and exile in 1847–48, and stricken with fever, ended here their sorrowful pilgrimage.[17]

The vast majority of emigration was privately financed, the government, with few exceptions, choosing not to interfere with the process, whilst landlord-assisted emigration accounted for only about 5 per cent of the total movement. As a consequence, cost was extremely important and the poorest emigrants often only went as far as England, Scotland and Wales, the passage fare to America being beyond their means. This also influenced the decision of many Irish people to travel through Liverpool, where the cheapest passages were to be obtained, and from there, to choose to emigrate to Canada, the cheapest destination. Increasingly, as the Famine continued, the remittance system, often in the form of pre-paid tickets, became an essential part of this process. The official estimate of remittances, which probably underestimated the amount sent to Ireland, was as follows.

Table 25: Remittances to Ireland, 1848–51 [18]

1848	£460,000
1849	£540,000
1850	£957,000
1851	£990,000

Remittances contributed to a system of chain migration, which reinforced the existing patterns of settlement overseas. The remittances also provided an often irresistible reason for emigrating, whilst holding out a promise of untold wealth to be earned beyond Ireland. It also removed from the government the necessity to intervene and provide large-scale state subsidies. Government officials also observed, with satisfaction, that a further consequence of the chain migration was:

> The numbers who have already emigrated and prospered remove the apprehension of going to a strange and untried country, while the want of means is remedied by the liberal contribution of the relations and friends who have preceded them.[19]

As early as 1848, therefore, a system of chain migration had been established which was greatly facilitated by the growth of a remittance system based on the notorious 'American letter' with its welcome enclosure of money. Once this system had commenced, it proved to have its own irresistible momentum, and newly arrived emigrants to North America no doubt realised that one of their first duties was to send both news and money back home. To those who remained in Ireland, no more convincing argument of the benefits of emigration could be offered. Also, if the early Famine emigrants had departed in a mixture of haste and hysteria, those who followed could not have been better briefed, better prepared, and more readily financed. Subsequent emigrants were able, if they so chose to do so, to slip easily into a comfortable network established by the earlier Famine emigrants.

Estimates of the number of emigrants who left during the Famine vary, and precise numbers will probably never be known. In the 1850s, the Census Commissioners calculated that between 1841 and 1851, the loss of population was 1,649,330 persons. They stated that 1,289,133 of these persons had been lost through emigration. The level of excess mortality implied by these figures is extremely low, and is not even borne out by their own independent estimates of mortality. They regarded the emigration as having contributed to a general improvement in the state of the country, but they were worried that it was heavily concentrated among one section of the population, that is, people aged between twenty and thirty years old, who accounted for 40 per cent of all emigrants. Thus, they warned, the emigrants included 'a large proportion of the youngest, the healthiest and most energetic of the population'. Those who had not emigrated, on the other hand, included 'the old, the most feeble, and the most destitute' or as one Census Commissioner subsequently described those who remained in Ireland as, 'the poor, the weak, the old, the lame, the sick, the blind, the dumb, and the imbecile and insane'.[20]

Government Intervention

Regardless of the theoretical approval of the government for emigration, in practical terms little support was forthcoming. In the years following the ending of the Napoleonic Wars, politicians, economists, government officials, and many Irish landlords agreed that the economy of the country did not have the resources to sustain such a large and fast growing population. Prominent economists, including John Stuart Mill and Nassau Senior, lent their support to the view that emigration could help to bring about social improvement in Ireland although, in general, they disapproved of state-assisted emigration. The benefits of emigration were two-fold. The rural economy could not modernise until subdivision was ended and property was consolidated. At the same time, emigration would relieve Ireland of her excess population and provide British colonies with much needed settlers.[21]

The question of Irish settlement in Britain was less straightforward. Britain had long been a popular destination for Irish migrants and this increased in the early part of the nineteenth century. The proximity of Britain, the availability of employment in the rapidly expanding industrial sector, the higher wages paid, and the fact that, in 1801, an Act of Union had united the kingdoms, made Britain a favourite choice for many migrants, either on a permanent or seasonal basis. This presented a dilemma for the British government, anxious that nothing should hinder the expansion of her economy. Select committees appointed in 1826, 1827 and 1830 warned that a substantial increase in migration to Britain would ultimately have a depressing effect on the British economy, by reducing the condition of the British labouring classes to the same impoverished state as those in Ireland. The 1826 committee warned the government that it was necessary to decide whether emigration:

> . . . shall be turned to the improvement of the British North American Colonies, or whether it shall be suffered and encouraged to take that which will be and is its inevitable Course, to deluge Great Britain with Poverty and Wretchedness, and gradually, but certainly, to equalise the State of the English and Irish peasantry.[22]

To a large extent, the emigration debate centred on the question of the desirability of state-sponsored compared with voluntary emigration. The desire for large-scale, government-assisted emigration was particularly intense in the wake of the sporadic periods of distress in the first half of the nineteenth century. Direct intervention by the government was, however, rare. An exception to this occurred following the crop failure in 1821–2, when the government financed a small emigration scheme, of 2,300 persons, to Canada. The government paid not only the cost of the journey, but also for a settlement for the emigrants and their support for eighteen months following their arrival.[23] The cost of this—approximately £20 per head—was judged to be very high. In 1847, when in a mood of urgency and desperation the question of state-assisted colonisation from Ireland was again considered, the cost of pursuing a similar scheme was regarded as prohibitive.[24]

In the 1830s the question of a Poor Law for Ireland was increasingly discussed by the legislature, and emigration was generally regarded as an integral part of any system of poor relief. Opinion about the exact form that this should take was divided. The Poor Inquiry Commission of 1833–6 was chaired by Archbishop Whately, an advocate of state-funded emigration. The committee, following three years of painstaking investigation, concluded that, in the short term, emigration was essential to bring about an improvement in the condition of Ireland. They were clear, however, that emigration should not be regarded as 'an Object to be permanently pursued upon any extensive Scale'. The Commission further recommended that the government's involvement in the process of emigration be increased in order that:

> Those who desire to emigrate should be furnished with the Means of doing so in safety, and with intermediate Support, when they require it, at Emigration Depots. It is thus, and thus only, that the Market of Labour can be relieved from the Weight that is now upon it, or the Labourer be raised from his present prostrate state.[25]

The proposals of the Poor Inquiry commission were unpopular with many leading members of the Whig government, including Lord John Russell. George Cornewall Lewis and Nassau Senior were requested to produce an official review of its contents. Although they also advocated the large-scale emigration of the poorest sections of the Irish population, they disagreed with the Commission as to how this was to be funded, disapproving of a system which encouraged dependence on the government. Lewis and Senior did not believe that emigration should be a charge on the imperial government, but suggested that, as a temporary expedient, a loan fund could be established, obtained from the sale of waste land in the colonies. In the longer term, it was to be made clear to the Irish that emigration was not to be regarded as a public charge but, as was the case throughout the rest of Europe, was to be financed by the emigrants themselves.[26] The Report of the Poor Inquiry Commissioners and the response to their recommendations provided an early indication of the adherence of the government to a policy of non-interference in the 'free' market. The government persisted in this policy during the Famine, paying lip-service to the notion of 'free' choice rather than taking any positive remedial action to lessen the impact of the crisis.

Other suggestions of the Poor Inquiry Commissioners regarding poor relief in general was also criticised. George Nicholls, an English Poor Law Commissioner, was sent to Ireland to re-examine the issue of poor relief. In keeping with many earlier commentators, Nicholls attributed the poverty of the country partly to its large population. In parts of the west and south, where the population was particularly excessive, he stated, 'emigration seems to be the only immediate Remedy, or rather, Palliation'.[27] Nicholls also completely overturned the recommendations of the Poor Enquiry Commissioners with his proposal that a Poor Law, similar to the 'new' English Poor Law of 1834 and based on the workhouse test, should be introduced into Ireland. He subsequently suggested that the local administrators of the new system of relief should have the power to apply a portion of the local poor rates for the purpose of assisting emigration. Many of Nicholl's suggestions, including the extension of the workhouse system to Ireland and the introduction of the emigration provision, found favour with leading members of the government. The recommendations of the Poor Enquiry Commissioners were ignored and in their place, a Poor Law, based on the reports of George Nicholls, was introduced into Ireland in 1838.[28]

Notwithstanding the frequent appeals for more official involvement in the process of emigration, the various governments in the early nineteenth century demonstrated little inclination to do so. With the exception of the short-lived emigration schemes in the 1820s, and an experimental scheme of sending orphaned females to Australia in 1831 and 1834, the 1838 Poor Law was the first legislative measure which included a provision for emigration. The Devon Commission, which was appointed in 1842, although recognising that a variety of measures were essential to improve the condition of Ireland, stated 'a well organised system of emigration may be of very great Service, as one among the measures which the Situation of the Occupiers of Land in Ireland at present calls for'.[29] In 1843, an amendment was introduced to increase the powers of the Poor Law guardians to assist emigration. None the less, the number of emigrants aided by the poor rate remained small: in 1844, the guardians assisted thirty-one paupers to emigrate, seventy-six in 1845, and 197 in 1846.[30]

A select committee appointed in 1846 to examine the operation of the Poor Law came out very clearly in favour of increased government intervention in emigration. The committee pointed out that emigration was most essential in districts where there was the greatest imbalance between the need for emigration and the resources of the population to pay for it. They therefore recommended that, 'increased Facilities for the emigration of poor Persons should be afforded, with the Co-operation of the Government'.[31] These recommendations were made before the full extent of the potato blight was known. Following the almost total failure of the potato crop in 1846, a further select committee was appointed to examine how colonisation might be used as a supplementary measure to improve the condition of Ireland. After only nineteen days enquiry, the committee submitted a report, although they made it clear that this report was not conclusive. They did, however, state their approval of additional emigration and suggested that it should be brought 'to the earliest attention of the Legislature'.[32] The committee approved of colonisation, explaining that:

To transplant our Domestic Habits, our Commercial Enterprise, our Laws, our Institutions, our Language, our Literature, and our sense of Religious Obligation, to the more distant regions of the Globe, is an enterprise worthy of the character of a great maritime Nation. It is not only in its Progress the Pursuit and the Attainment of Glory, but in its success is the Performance of a high Duty, and the Accomplishment of a noble destiny.[33]

Despite the mounting crisis in Ireland and the numerous suggestions that government assistance was necessary to help the poorest people to emigrate, the government continued to refuse to deviate from its chosen policy of minimum intervention.

Emigration and the Poor Law

Regardless of the general consensus that emigration from the poor, highly subdivided and densely populated regions of the west of Ireland would be beneficial, the 1838 Poor Law was the first sustained measure which made legislative provision for the emigration of poor people. The original Poor Law Act and the amending Act of 1843 provided that either the guardians or the ratepayers of a Poor Law union could authorise the expenditure of local rates to assist poor persons to emigrate. These Acts stipulated that pauper emigrants had to have first been inmates of the workhouse for three months.[34] These provisions were, however, little used. The 1847 Poor Law Amendment Act increased the powers of the guardians to assist poor persons, notably smallholders, to emigrate. It provided that if a person who occupied land valued at under £5 gave up their property to their landlord, and if the landlord was willing to pay two-thirds of the cost of emigration, the guardians could pay the remaining third of the cost. Expenses for this purpose were to be raised as an additional charge to the poor rates of the electoral division in which the provision was situated. Unlike earlier provisions, the persons assisted to emigrate did not have to have been inmates of the workhouse for any specified period.[35] This amendment appears to have been a deliberate attempt by the government to encourage small occupiers of land to relinquish their property without simultaneously becoming a permanent burden on the poor rates.

In spite of the increased powers of the Poor Law guardians to provide assistance to emigrants, in 1848, only £3,429 raised from the poor rates was spent on emigration. Assisted migration, therefore, remained relatively insignificant. The power of the Poor Law to finance emigration was further extended in 1849, based on the recommendations of the 1849 select committees. The provisions of the 1849 Act, which were popularly known as the Mansell Act, marked a liberal departure from earlier legislation. It provided for guardians or vice-guardians to borrow the cost of emigration from the Exchequer Bill Loan Commissioners if both the Treasury and a majority of ratepayers agreed. This money could be used to help not merely people in receipt of poor relief, but also poor persons resident in the union to emigrate to any foreign state.[36] This legislation meant that the state, through the mechanism of the Poor Law, was willing to provide a limited form of assistance to the poorest classes. Following its introduction, Poor Law emigration did rise significantly, reaching a peak in 1852 when 4,386 persons were assisted to emigrate by the Poor Law, at a cost of £21,010 5s 4d. Compared to the overall number of emigrants in that year—an estimated 190,322 persons—Poor Law emigration can be viewed as relatively insignificant. Also, although the number of persons assisted to emigrate did increase, they did not come from the poorest unions where emigration could have been most beneficial. The Commissioners attributed this to the financial difficulties of these unions which made them reluctant even to borrow money.[37]

Table 26: Persons Assisted to Emigrate under 1849 Poor Law Amendment Act[38]

Period	No. assisted to emigrate
Aug. 1849 – March 1851	2,592
Year ending March 1852	4,386
1853	3,825
1854	2,691
1855	3,794
1856	830
1857	802

The Rate-in-Aid Act, introduced in 1849, allowed the Treasury to use a portion of the monies raised to assist emigration.[39] Initially, the Treasury was reluctant to allow this provision to be used extensively. The continuing distress in some of the western unions, and the on-going dependence on outdoor relief, however, resulted in the Treasury agreeing that a portion of the Rate-in-Aid could be used for this purpose. In 1851 and 1852, £15,000 of Rate-in-Aid money was used to assist pauper migration. Many of the recipients of this money were from the poorest unions in counties Clare and Kerry, and their destinations were America, Australia and Canada.[40] Within a year, the Commissioners requested that an additional sum of money should be allocated for emigration, primarily of women and children. This was because, while a renewed demand for labourers within the country had removed large numbers of men and boys from the workhouses, a disproportionately large number of able-bodied women and girls still remained within these institutions. The Treasury agreed that a further and final sum of £10,000 could be used to assist young females from the poorest western unions to emigrate. These females were sent to Canada on the grounds that an 'unabated demand' for this class of person existed there. Fifteen thousand female emigrants were sent to Canada in this way. The Emigration Agent in Quebec informed the Poor Law Commissioners that the emigrants had immediately found employment and that he could have found employment for twice that number.[41]

To a large extent, the reluctance of many relief officials and government ministers to finance Poor Law emigration was due to a prevailing ambivalent attitude regarding the value of assisted emigration. Although emigration itself was regarded as necessary, the benefit of providing financial assistance was less clear. Some members of the government feared that if the assistance provided by the Poor Law was too generous, persons who were not absolutely in need of relief might be encouraged to enter a workhouse in order to obtain a free passage to the colonies. If this became widespread, the resources of the local poor rates would be further stretched and would serve to increase the demands on the Treasury.[42]

To a large extent, the administrators of the Poor Law were anxious to promote pauper emigration as far as possible. The Commissioners directed the local Inspectors to point out the benefits of emigration. Able-bodied females who had been in the workhouse for over twelve months were regarded as being suitable candidates for sending to Canada. The financial benefits to the union of this form of emigration were emphasised. One Inspector suggested to the boards of guardians in his district that if this class of paupers were sent to Canada:

> some of the permanent dead weight in the workhouse may be got rid of at a cost to the electoral division of about five pounds, or one year's cost of maintenance.[43]

In some instances, the cost of pauper emigration was even less than £5. An increasing number of remittances sent to the local workhouses meant that a number of paupers required only a suit of clothing or a small additional sum to enable them to emigrate.[44]

The whole process of pauper emigration was closely monitored by the

Poor Law Commissioners and ultimately by the Treasury. If a board of guardians proposed to assist a group of paupers to emigrate, the local Inspector was personally to inspect each of the proposed candidates. Paupers who were emigrating to a British colony were not to be chosen unless it appeared that they had a reasonable prospect of being able to support themselves and their families. The Commissioners also recommended that the emigrants should arrive at their destinations in the summer when most employment was available.[45]

As large numbers of females continued to be in the workhouses, able-bodied females (particularly orphans) were regarded as the most suitable candidates for emigration. The Commissioners recommended that all females should be protected and their virtue guarded both during the journey and upon arrival. Young widows with large families and women with illegitimate children were not regarded as suitable, as it was deemed unlikely that they would be able to support themselves in the colonies.[46]

The boards of guardians most actively involved in promoting emigration were not necessarily those where distress was most severe. The Strabane guardians, for example, devoted much of their time in 1850 and 1851 to devising schemes for pauper emigration, even though the worst of the Famine was over in the union by 1849. In most cases, the guardians provided a supplementary amount of money or an outfit of clothing to paupers who already possessed their passage fare. At the beginning of 1851, the Strabane guardians decided that all paupers who had been in the workhouse for two years should be considered eligible for emigration to Canada. Fifty-eight of these persons received the approval of the local Inspector. The group sailed from Derry to Quebec in April 1851. Before they left, the friends of the emigrants were allowed to visit them in the workhouse. As prescribed by the Commissioners, each emigrant was provided with a new outfit of clothes, cooking utensils, food and bed clothes for the journey. Upon arrival in Canada, each emigrant was given 10s. The total cost of the emigration was £3.10s 0d for each adult, and £2 per head for each person under sixteen.[47]

In a number of the poorest unions the guardians were anxious to empty their workhouses of potential long-term inmates through a policy of emigration. The Kenmare guardians were one of the most active boards in this regard. At the beginning of 1850, when relief was still extensive within the union, the guardians appointed an Emigration Committee. All people who were aged between fifteen and forty and had been in receipt of relief for over a year, were potential candidates. The committee decided to choose paupers who, due to their character and industrious habits, were likely to be able to earn their livelihood in a new country. Two groups of sixty and a hundred paupers respectively were sent to Quebec. The cost varied from £6 and £10 for each emigrant. The guardians also appealed to large proprietors in the union to subsidise further emigration, recommending that to do so would reduce the burden on the local rates.[48]

A number of landlords, like the guardians, viewed emigration as a long-term economic investment. This was especially true of landlords who wanted to clear their estates of smallholdings in a humane manner, but did not want to place a permanent burden on the local poor rates. One of the most well-publicised examples of this practice occurred on the Marquis of Lansdowne's estate in Co. Kerry. The estate, which was about 60,000 acres in extent, was partially situated in the Kenmare union, one of the poorest in the country. The agent of the estate, William Stuart Trench, described it as being 'swamped with paupers' and estimated that 3,000 residents of the estate were in receipt of poor relief. There was little prospect of employment within the district. It was likely, therefore, that the paupers would have to remain within the workhouse indefinitely, at an estimated cost of £5 per annum for each pauper. Trench calculated that the cost to Lansdowne of maintaining the paupers on his estate was £15,000 per annum. The total rental of the estate was £10,000, a large portion of which had not been paid for a number of years. If, however, every person on the estate was offered the option to emigrate, at no cost to themselves, the cost to the estate would only be £13,000—less than the cost of one year's poor relief.

The paupers who participated in this scheme were allowed to choose whether to travel to Boston, New York or Quebec, departing initially from Cork. The scheme was popular, and in little more than a year, 3,500 paupers took part in it. Within a four-year period, 4,600 persons had been helped to emigrate in this way. This left approximately fifty persons in the Kenmare workhouse who were chargeable to Lansdowne's estate. The speed and thoroughness with which Lansdowne cleared his estate resulted in some accusations of eviction and enforced emigration. Both Trench and Lansdowne denied this, although they admitted that some emigrants had attempted to jump ship in Cork and Liverpool. Overall, they judged the scheme to have been a success: the ships carrying the emigrants had all arrived safely, each of the emigrants had found employment and many were sending remittances back to Ireland. The large-scale removal of smallholders also benefitted the estate, and in the years following the emigration, Trench reported that the estate was prospering financially.[49]

Landlords such as Lansdowne, who prompted emigration on a large scale, were unusual, although it was possibly more common than had traditionally been recognised. Prior to the Famine, Irish landlords had been one of the strongest advocates of assisted emigration, but although many believed it to be desirable, they were unwilling to supply the money to make it possible. During the Famine years, however, landlords as diverse as Lord Monteagle of Limerick, Sir Montague Chapman of Westmeath, Colonel Wyndham in Co. Clare, the Fitzwilliams in Co. Wicklow and Shirley in Co. Monaghan, provided financial support for the emigration of their tenants. This form of assistance was most common after 1847, following the transfer to Poor Law relief, when the combination of unpaid rents and spiralling poor rates provided a powerful incentive to clear an estate of paupers. Landlord-assisted emigration was at its highest in 1849 and 1850, but declined rapidly after this. In total, it accounted for no more than 5 per cent of all emigration from Ireland which, although small, was higher than either state-assisted or Poor Law emigration during the same period.[50]

The small amount of legislative assistance provided to emigrants disguised the fact that many high-ranking relief officials believed that large-scale emigration was necessary if the Irish economy was to improve. Not only was it necessary for paupers to emigrate, but the emigration of small ratepayers was regarded as highly desirable by members of the government. The removal of a large portion of the population and the resultant consolidation of smallholdings which would facilitate the long desired transformation from a subsistence to a wage-earning economy was an aspiration of many key members of the Whig administration during the Famine. This was an essential part of their long-term vision for Ireland. Many members of the government regarded the various relief measures as providing an opportunity to bring about an improvement within the economy. Emigration financed from the local poor rates, however, was regarded as being less desirable than privately financed emigration. In consequence, the 1847 Poor Law Amendment Act attempted to encourage an increased amount of landlord-sponsored emigration. Again, in areas where distress was most intense, there was an inverse relationship between the desirability of large-scale emigration and the ability of the local guardians and landlords to finance it. The fact that landlords were liable for rates on property valued at lower than £4 was an additional incentive to evict these smallholders or encourage them to leave their property. For tenants valued at under £4 who were exempt from poor rates, the constrictions of the Quarter-Acre Clause on the one hand and the spectre of the workhouse or possibly starvation on the other would also have provided incentive to emigrate, if this was financially feasible.

After 1847, the Poor Law was increasingly used by the government as a way of encouraging additional migration. This was facilitated by the stringency of the various provisions of the Law, notably the workhouse test, the high poor rates and the Quarter-Acre Clause. The burden of poor rates, especially in the unions in the south and west of the country, provided a powerful incentive for many small ratepayers to emigrate. The Treasury approved of this and, despite appeals by the Poor Law Commissioners, refused to provide financial assistance to this class of persons unless they were threatened with starvation. Following a request for financial assistance to the distressed unions, Trevelyan explained to Twistleton in an unofficial letter that this was not possible on the grounds that:

> I do not know how farms are to be consolidated if small farmers do not emigrate, and by acting for the purpose of keeping them at home, we should be defaulting at our own object. We must not complain of what we really want to obtain. If small farmers go, and their landlords are reduced to sell portions of their estates to persons who will invest capital, we shall at last arrive at something like a satisfactory settlement of the country.[51]

This view of emigration was not confined to Trevelyan, but was shared by other leading officials involved in the relief operations especially those who were advocates of political economy. Wood, the Chancellor of the Exchequer, agreed that a vigorous collection of the rates was necessary to encourage even more emigration. He believed that if the rate collection was enforced 'the pressure will lead to some emigrating . . . what we really want to obtain is a clearance of small farmers'.[52] The Prime Minister, Russell, was less dogmatic. He realised that the poor rates were a heavy burden on many people, but felt that this was necessary if the aims of the government were to be achieved. He summed up the situation thus: 'it is better that some should sink, than that they should drag others down to sink with them'.[53] The Poor Law, and its various amendments, provided both the means and the incentive for many people to emigrate, at little additional cost to the government.

Orphan Emigration

In contrast to most European emigration, Irish emigration was unique in that as many women as men emigrated throughout the nineteenth century. The majority of these women were young, unskilled and unattached. Emigration provided their only possible route to either employment or marriage. Little is known, however, about the experiences of these women and girls or their impact on the various host countries. Their contribution to the emigration process has been largely underestimated or ignored.[54] A well-documented scheme that commenced in 1847, to take young, orphan females from the workhouses of Ireland to Australia provides many unique insights in the attitudes of the authorities to female emigration.

The orphan emigration scheme was carried out at no cost to the government, the major part of the expenditure being met by the colonial authorities themselves. It was one of the few exceptions to the government's policy of non-intervention in the process of emigration. Traditionally, emigration to Australia had been far smaller than emigration to America. Since 1788, Australia, or Botany Bay as it was known, had been used as a penal colony by the British government. By the 1820s, however, both the government and the settlers were anxious to dissociate themselves from the image of Australia as a land of convicts and kangaroos. In Australia, also there was a gender imbalance, men exceeding women by up to eight to one. The colonial authorities wanted more females to settle in the colony for their house-keeping skills, their child-bearing capabilities and most importantly, their civilising influence.

At the beginning of 1847, the Governor of South Australia suggested that a portion of the South Australian Land Fund should be used to assist emigration to the colony. This idea was enthusiastically received by the British government, who were already considering sending orphans from workhouses in Britain to Australia. Sir George Grey, the Home Secretary, recommended that, in the first instance, 10,000 British orphans of both sexes should be sent.[55] The British government initially favoured sending orphans of both sexes but both the Emigration Commissioners and the Australian authorities believed that it should be restricted to females. The candidates who participated in the scheme were all to be volunteers who wanted to emigrate to Australia. It was decided that initially the females should be inmates of workhouses in Britain. The money provided by the colonial authorities was channelled through the Colonial Land and Emigration Commissioners. The number of vessels sailing to Australia was increased from fifty-four to seventy-two to carry the additional passengers.[56]

When the quota of emigrants from Britain was not reached, it was decided to extend the scheme to Ireland. Female Irish orphans who were inmates of a workhouse were allowed to volunteer to emigrate to Australia, at no cost to themselves. The Emigration Commissioners were anxious that, as the scheme was being financed by the Australian government, only suitable candidates should be chosen. They were concerned that if all of the candidates were taken from workhouses, this might prove difficult. They warned the government:

> The Colonists are desirous of adding to their body not the idle and worthless, but those whose education and moral and religious training affords a reasonable guarantee that they will become active and useful members of a society which is in a state of healthy progress.[57]

To ensure that only suitable candidates were chosen, the Emigration Commissioners appointed Lieutenant Henry to visit the participating Irish workhouses and examine the females. Eligible females were to be aged between fourteen and eighteen, those nearest to eighteen being given preference. The Emigration Commissioners also recommended that each ship carrying the emigrants should be provided with a teacher, even though this would have to be paid for by the British government.[58]

The government was reluctant to bear any additional expense for the emigration of Irish orphans and ruled that the cost of their superintendence and education during the voyage was to be paid for by the Irish administration. The Lord Lieutenant also decided that as a large portion of the females would probably be Roman Catholic, they should be accompanied by chaplains and religious instructors. The low wages offered for these positions, however, meant that few people applied for them. The government also decided that the cost of transferring the orphans from the Irish workhouses to Plymouth, the embarkation port for Australia, was to be paid by the unions to which the females belonged.[59]

Although the Treasury was not initially involved in this scheme, with his usual thoroughness, Trevelyan attempted to impose his own views on it. Characteristically, he insisted that the Emigration Commissioners should submit to him personally regular reports of their activities. In a confidential and controversial letter to the Irish Executive, Trevelyan also suggested that as Australia was a British, and hence, Protestant colony, it would be preferable to send Protestant rather than Catholic orphans from the Irish workhouses. Trevelyan believed that Protestant females would also have had a better 'moral education' than their Catholic counterparts. He also predicted that there would be resistance within the colony to a disproportionate number of Catholics being sent there.[60] The Lord Lieutenant responded to this suggestion angrily, accusing Trevelyan of Ultra-Protestantism. Trevelyan, however, was unrepentant. He retaliated to the criticism of the Irish Exeuctive by enlisting the support of the Colonial Office. The Colonial Office agreed that, in the first instance, the unions participating in the scheme should be those in which the greater attention had been paid to training the females, particularly in needlework and washing. Trevelyan was confident that these unions would be situated in the north of the country where the population was predominantly Protestant anyway.[61]

The scheme to assist orphaned workhouse inmates to emigrate was welcomed by the Poor Law Commissioners. They believed that it would be of long-term benefit to the Poor Law as almost 50 per cent of the inmates of the workhouses were children aged under fifteen, and many of them were orphans. It was also a way of relieving the impoverished western workhouses of some of their excess population at relatively little cost. This did not, however, prove to be the case. Trevelyan's insistence, supported by the Emigration Commissioners, that only females who had been well trained would be allowed to emigrate, meant that the poorest unions only had a limited involvement in the scheme. This was because, as the Poor Law Commissioners acknowledged, the poorest unions generally contained the worst educated paupers. At the same time, many of the guardians of these unions were unable to afford the cost of the outfit necessary for each female.[62]

In recognition of the overcrowded state of many workhouses, the emigration scheme was put into effect quickly. Each board of guardians was requested to compile a list of eligible females who were willing to emigrate to Australia. Although the cost of the voyage was to be paid for by the colonies, the guardians were to provide each selected female with an appropriate outfit. The women were to be fully briefed about the scheme and about what they could expect to find in Australia. The lists compiled by the guardians were thoroughly scrutinised by the local Poor Law Inspectors, but the final selection of the females was made by Lieutenant Henry, the government's agent. The medical officers of the selected unions were then to examine each of the candidates. Those whom they considered to be healthy were vaccinated. The whole selection process was completed in approximately four weeks.[63]

Although the Poor Law Commissioners wanted the emigration scheme to be implemented as quickly as possible they realised that its continuation would depend largely on the successful selection of young persons from the outset. To ensure this was the case, the local Inspectors were informed that they should only recommend females who proved to be 'the most orderly and best educated'.[64] The Commissioners were aware that the continuation of the scheme depended to a large extent on a good impression being created by the first batch of emigrants. The government, however, was dissatisfied with the way in which the Poor

Law Commissioners were implementing the scheme, thus causing a delay in sending out the orphans. The government complained that they did not receive a list of emigrants until 8 May 1848, which meant that the first vessel could not sail until the beginning of June, and the second one until the end of July. Although the government stated that they were reluctant to send out further ships until they had received news of the progress of the first ones, additional sailings were scheduled for September and November 1848 and February 1849. Despite this, many members of both the government and the Irish Executive expressed their dissatisfaction with the low numbers that had emigrated compared with the original estimations.[65]

In their Annual Report for 1849, the Poor Law Commissioners stated that they were satisfied with the progress made in the orphan emigration scheme. Within twelve months, 2,219 orphans from eighty-eight separate unions had sailed to Adelaide, Port Philip and Sydney. The cost of the migration to the unions was approximately £5 per head. The scheme had proved to be popular with both the guardians and the females in the workhouses and an even larger number had shown interest in participating. This had not been possible due to an initial ceiling of 2,500 emigrants which had been decided on by the Emigration Commissioners. Shortly after this, the Emigration Commissioners agreed to allow more orphans to emigrate. By May 1850, a total of 4,175 female orphans had emigrated to Australia, representing 118 separate unions.[66]

The majority of boards of guardians regarded the orphan emigration scheme favourably as it provided a way of emptying their workhouses of a class of paupers who were, potentially, a long-term burden on the poor rates. For the poorest unions, however, even the relatively small amount of capital outlay required was beyond their means and this limited the number of orphans whom they could afford to send. Notwithstanding this, the desire of the guardians to participate in the scheme was so great that, in September 1848, the Poor Law Commissioners decided that no additional names were to be added to the existing lists of candidates. In the middle of 1849, guardians were again invited to submit the names of suitable candidates for emigration. Again this was short lived. In November 1849, the Poor Law Commissioners informed the guardians that the funds which had been put at the disposal of the Emigration Commissioners were almost exhausted and that they could hold out no hope of further emigration under this scheme.[67]

All of the emigrants were volunteers, eligible candidates in the selected unions being invited to put their names forward. Among female paupers, the possibility of free emigration was popular. Even before a union was officially involved in the scheme, a number of guardians were independently approached by inmates, who requested to be included.[68] Candidates who were selected by the emigration agent and pronounced fit by the medical officer were provided with a new outfit and various other items including a hat, boots and a comb, which were considered to be essential by the Commissioners. Each was to remain in the local workhouse until directed to commence the journey. The waiting time could range from a few weeks to a few months. When departure time arrived, the orphans, usually in groups of twenty, travelled to Cork or Dublin and then to Birkenhead or directly to Plymouth. From Plymouth, they sailed to Australia.[69] This part of the journey was generally successful and achieved with little trouble. Edward Senior, the Poor Law Inspector in east Ulster, recommended that the females from Ulster should be kept separate from orphans from the rest of the country on the basis that they differed in race, religion and outlook from the others. The government refused, not wanting to be accused of religious bias. They did insist, however, that the Irish orphans were to be kept separate from the English orphans, and were sent from Plymouth in different vessels.[70]

A number of complaints concerning both the immorality and lack of house-keeping abilities of the first batch of orphans, most of whom were from Ulster, resulted in further stipulations being made regarding the selection of orphan emigrants. Following this, they insisted that more emphasis should be put on the 'moral character' and domestic training of subsequent candidates. Accordingly, the local Inspectors and other officers involved in the selection process were directed to ensure that potential emigrants were of 'unblemished moral character'. If any doubt existed regarding any individual orphan, she was to be eliminated from the list. To ensure that this was acceded to, a certificate of character and health for each prospective emigrant was to be sent to the emigration officer.[71]

The first vessel carrying Irish orphans to arrive in Australia was the *Earl Grey*, with 219 females. The voyage was reported to have been healthy with only two emigrants dying en route. Even before the females arrived in Australia, however, a number of unfavourable reports had preceded them. The Emigration Commissioners, afraid that this might make it harder for the females to find employment, attempted to play them down. This proved difficult: immediately upon arrival, a scandal erupted which was publicised widely. The immediate cause was a complaint made by Dr Douglass, the surgeon superintendent on the *Earl Grey*. He claimed that over two-thirds of the women, many of whom were from the Belfast union, had behaved badly during the voyage. Douglass reserved his most severe criticisms for fifty-six of the women whom he described as being of 'abandoned' and 'disreputable' character, and whose immoral behaviour had been a by-word during the journey. There was even a suggestion that two of the women had become pregnant at sea and that an abortion had been performed.[72]

The Australian authorities, anxious to limit any damage caused by this report, sent the recalcitrant females to a separate location from the others. The remainder were kept in Sydney where they were to receive religious instruction pending a report by a Committee of Investigation appointed by the Australian authorities. The report, when submitted to the Australian authorities, was overwhelmingly favourable to the orphans. They were described as being orderly, obedient and industrious. Following this, the girls were allowed to seek employment, and each of them quickly found it either in or close to Sydney. All but one of the remaining fifty-six girls who had been sent to the country also found immediate employment.[73]

Despite the favourable report on the orphans and the fact that the vast majority of them had quickly found employment, the Australian government continued to be unhappy with the way in which the emigration had been carried out, particularly in regard to the choice of females. The British government was reluctant to attract any further adverse publicity to the scheme, but reluctantly promised that a 'searching enquiry would be made'.[74] The Home Office initiated an enquiry, and in Ireland the Lord Lieutenant was directed to institute an investigation into the choice of orphans with a view to ensuring that a similar incident would not again occur. Privately, the Home Secretary confided in the Irish government that he believed that a number of officers of the Poor Law had been guilty of 'a very culpable failure'.[75]

The enquiry initiated by the Lord Lieutenant took almost six months to complete. As a result, it became apparent that a number of irregularities had occurred. In some instances, the females were found not to have been orphans, to be aged over eighteen or even, as was the case in one union, to have been a widow in her thirties with three dependent children. In spite of these and other small irregularities, the enquiry reported that none of the officers involved were aware of the deceptions, but had attempted to ensure that the best selection possible had been made. Naturally, this was welcomed by the Home Office which was determined to keep the whole incident as quiet as possible. The government had also received information regarding the arrival of subsequent parties of orphans, all of which were favourable. The Home Office, therefore, decided to play down the complaints. They stated that the problems which had occurred were attributable to the fact that many of the females were from large manufacturing towns, particularly Belfast. Young females from such towns, they added, were not typical of those from other districts in Ireland.

The unions involved in the incident were reprimanded, but the Home Office chose to view it as an isolated event in an otherwise successful project. To prevent similar incidences occurring again, however, the Poor Law Commissioners were told that in future orphans were to be selected from rural unions rather than the manufacturing towns of the north-east. The severest Home Office criticisms were reserved for Douglass, the Surgeon Superintendent who made the initial complaints. The Home Office stated:

> There appears sufficient proof that Dr Douglass made charges of too sweeping a nature . . . casting a general and indiscriminate stigma upon a large body of young women, several of whom must be presumed from the present evidence to have been undeserving of such blame.[76]

The Emigration Commissioners were also anxious that the incident should be kept as quiet as possible. They wanted the scheme to continue as it conferred upon the females an opportunity of obtaining an independent livelihood. The Emigration Commissioners admitted that a number of the females had behaved badly, but believed that the majority of them had acquitted themselves creditably. The news received about the females from the colony had also been favourable and the colonists had stated that they were willing to take even more orphans.[77]

The professed optimism of the Emigration Commissioners and the British government disguised the fact that the scheme was, in fact, facing a number of problems. In Australia, as further groups of Irish orphans arrived, they increasingly encountered hostility from the colonists. Even before the Home Office enquiry was concluded, the government had received a number of unfavourable reports from Australia. In accordance with the wishes of the British government, an Irish Orphan Emigration Committee was established. It included prelates from both the Anglican and Roman Catholic Churches, a Presbyterian Minister, a Wesleyan Minister, two members of the Legislative Council, the Advocate General, the Proctor of Aborigines, and two notable colonists who did not hold office in local government. At the second meeting of the Committee in September 1848, they reported that the majority of colonists were of the opinion that the orphan emigrants should not be predominantly from Ireland, but should include a larger proportion of English and Scottish females.[78] A few months later, the Australian government informed the Emigration Commissioners that they desired that only a further 300 to 400 orphans should be sent to them, but this should not include any females from Ireland. The reason provided for this decision was that even though the Irish orphans had quickly found employment, the number of reports concerning their character and immorality was increasing. If this continued, the Australian government believed that it would be difficult for any further emigrants from Ireland to find employment.[79]

The apprehensions of the Australian government quickly proved to be correct. In 1849, the Orphan Committee informed the British government that the girls who had arrived that year were finding it difficult to find employment. They attributed this to the fact that supply was beginning to exceed demand for female servants. Consequently, they requested that no further females be sent to the colony. As a result, in July 1849, the orphan emigration scheme was brought to a close. During its brief existence, over 2,000 females from Ireland had participated in the project. In the parts of Ireland which were continuing to undergo both distress and famine, the closing of the scheme was greeted with dismay. The Poor Law Commissioners, the guardians and the paupers themselves all requested that it be resumed.[80]

Following pressure from the British government, the scheme did recommence towards the end of 1849 primarily with orphans from unions situated in the south-west of Ireland. The problems, however, did not disappear. One batch of orphans, upon arrival in Plymouth, had been found to have 'the itch'. Despite this, they were allowed to continue their journey. A group of fifteen females from the Clonmel workhouse also behaved badly and their language was described as being 'vile in the extreme'. A report on their conduct described them as being:

> ... refractory, insubordinate and extremely troublesome during the passage, setting at defiance all authority, mixing with the sailors and threatening that if extreme measures were resorted to for the purpose of restraining them, they would get the sailors to help them.[81]

In both cases, the Poor Law Commissioners contacted the local Poor Law authorities involved and urged them to take more care in selecting candidates. Again, the Poor Law Commissioners and the British government chose to view these incidents as isolated, on the grounds that the reports concerning the majority of the females continued to be favourable.[82]

Within a few months, however, the emigration scheme was again experiencing problems. The immediate cause was the alleged inability of the Irish orphans to perform housework. At the end of 1849, the Orphan Emigration Committee stated that females from the Irish workhouses were ignorant of the duties of household servants, and therefore were less acceptable to Australian employers than other female emigrants. At the time this report was made, 200 of the Irish orphans were unemployed. The Committee recommended to the British government that in 1850, the total number of females sent to Australia should not exceed 800.[83] These allegations were taken seriously by the British government who regarded the lack of housekeeping skills far more seriously than any earlier charges of immorality, fearing that such allegations would damage the employment prospects of all subsequent female emigrants from Ireland. The government commanded the Irish Executive to direct its attention to the important area of providing girls in the workhouses with further instruction in the duties of domestic servants. If this was done, the government were sanguine that the colonists would be willing to take an even larger consignment of female orphans.[84]

At the beginning of 1850, yet another scandal arose centred on the Irish orphans. This began with the publication in the *South Australian Register* of a letter which stated that the Irish orphans were 'filthy brutes' and the depot in which they stayed until they found employment was, in fact, a brothel which was being maintained at public expense.[85] The Children's Apprenticeship Board, which was in charge of caring for the girls when they first arrived in the colony, investigated these allegations. In their report, they stated that some of the claims, notably the one concerning the brothel, were unfounded. They were, however, very critical of the Irish orphans in general and stated that the physical description of the girls had been provoked by 'the extreme filthiness and unimaginable indelicacy of some of those workhouse girls'. The Apprenticeship Board stated that, in general, the emigration of these girls to work as servants had been both costly and ineffective. They considered, therefore, that it was a misapplication of the funds of the Australian government. As a consequence, they suggested that it would be inappropriate to receive any further Irish orphans.[86]

The inauspicious ending of the orphan emigration scheme gave rise to a number of acrimonious accusations and counter-accusations between the relevant authorities in Britain and in Ireland. Both the British government and the Emigration Commissioners blamed it on shortcomings in the Irish Poor Law, notably the lack of training and inadequate education which young people received in the Irish workhouses. If this had not been the case, they believed that the colony would have been willing to accept a far larger number of orphans and this, in turn, would have been of immense benefit to the Irish unions.[87] The Poor Law Commissioners, understandably, resented the interpretation which the government placed on the closing of the scheme. They were also indignant at the numerous allegations and counter-allegations concerning the orphans, particularly the imputation that the scheme could have continued if the females had been better educated. The large majority of females had found employment easily and the reports concerning them continued to be favourable. Only a few appeared to have become morally degraded as a result of the emigration. The Poor Law Commissioners added that they had given the matter their 'mature consideration' and yet were still unable to ascribe the outcome of the scheme to any previous defect in the training of the females whilst inmates of the workhouse.[88]

Overall, the Poor Law Commissioners felt that a large share of the blame for the various problems arose from the way in which the project had been conceived and executed by the government. The colonies could not expect to receive high quality emigrants by limiting the scheme to workhouse orphans who, because of their youth, were unlikely to possess the appropriate training in housework. The British government were also culpable in having had such high expectations from the females because:

> It must have been manifest when this branch of emigration was first proposed, that the materials from which the selection was to be made were not altogether of a hopeful character, consisting as they did exclusively of the most indigent peasantry in the world, brought up from their earliest years in habits inseparable from extreme indigence, and afterwards maintained in large numbers in the workhouses in a state of absolute dependence on the public.[89]

The Commissioners were also critical of the operation of the orphan depot in Adelaide. A similar facility had not been established for English and Scottish orphans and the Commissioners felt that, overall, it had harmed rather than benefited the Irish females. The management of the institution was very lax as the girls were free to come and go as they pleased. As a result of this, some of the girls treated the depot as an asylum and, the Commissioners believed, this had resulted in a number of girls leaving their jobs, without any provocation, knowing that they could return to the depot. This was particularly true of those who had found employment in the countryside, but preferred to stay in a town. The

Commissioners, although recognising that the management of the establishment had been benevolent, felt that more discipline and control should have been imposed. Also, as the depot had proved expensive to maintain, this had placed a heavy burden on the funds provided by the Australian government. The Poor Law Commissioners were optimistic that if a revised scheme was allowed to continue, the girls would be better trained for finding employment. They believed that a provision introduced into the Poor Law in 1848 which allowed unions to acquire farms specifically for the training of young boys in farming and agricultural work and young girls in the domestic duties of servants, would facilitate this.[90]

In spite of the apparent optimism of the Commissioners, the orphan emigration scheme was not revived. The Emigration Commissioners officially recorded that the scheme had been ended at the request of the colonial authorities because, while the emigration as a whole had been well conducted, a number of the girls proved to be totally ignorant of the domestic duties for which they were wanted. During its short life, 4,114 females from Irish workhouses had been taken to Australia; 2,253 to Sydney, 1,255 to Port Philip, and 606 to Adelaide.[91] There were suggestions that from the outset the Australian authorities had been reluctant to take such a large number of Irish orphans, but had been coerced into doing so by the Colonial Secretary, Earl Grey. The British government had also thrown their weight behind the scheme as it had provided a way of emptying the workhouses of a group of inmates who would have found it difficult to emigrate otherwise, and all at no cost to the emigrants or the government. In short, the needs of the colonists were secondary to the interests of the government.[92]

The ending of this scheme did not fully bring to an end assisted emigration from Irish workhouses to Australia. Many boards of guardians were anxious that, if possible, the workhouses should be cleared of female orphans, and many applied to the Emigration Commissioners for financial aid for this purpose.[93] By this stage, the Australian authorities had made it very clear that they were reluctant to receive a disproportionately high number of emigrants from Ireland, particularly females. The Emigration Commissioners explained to the local unions that it was their duty to look to colonial interests rather than employ the funds at their disposal for the purpose of relieving distress in Ireland. They could hold out no hope of assisting any further emigration from Ireland. In a more controversial statement, they also further stated that emigrants from Ireland had found it difficult to obtain employment because of their religion.[94]

Although assisted emigration for any category of Irish person appeared to be no longer possible, the Emigration Commissioners were able to offer assistance to persons who were willing to emigrate to Van Diemen's Land (Tasmania). Women of good character aged between eighteen and twenty-five were considered to be the most suitable candidates. On average, twenty to thirty women from each union were to be allowed to participate. The unions involved had to contribute £1 for each accepted candidate and to provide them with a suitable outfit. The cost of the journey from the point of embarkation in England was to be paid from colonial funds. The Poor Law Commissioners agreed to participate in this scheme with some reluctance as they were still annoyed by the opprobrium which had been directed at the Irish orphans who had gone to Australia, most of which they considered to be unwarranted. They also stated that they believed such schemes to be of unequal benefit to the unions as they primarily benefited those which still had financial resources at their disposal, rather than the most needy ones. The Commissioners suggested to the Treasury that a portion of the Rate-in-Aid could be used to help the poorest unions, but the Treasury refused to allow it to be spent in this way.[95]

The experiment of assisting emigration from the Irish workhouses was short lived and although it was initially welcomed by both paupers and Poor Law Commissioners alike, ultimately it disappointed the pauper emigrants and the Poor Law Commissioners were discredited. The authorities in Australia, who financed the emigration were also disappointed with the return which they received for their expenditure. To a large extent, the failure of the scheme was due to the insistence that it should be limited to workhouse orphans aged between fourteen to eighteen. By imposing such limitations, the needs of the colonists in Australia were made subservient to the desire of the British government to promote emigration, particularly of the 'deadweight' in the Irish workhouses. The government, and its agent the Treasury, favoured the scheme primarily because it could be carried out at no cost to themselves. Its ultimate benefit to either Ireland or Australia was of secondary importance.

Emigration to Britain

Even before the appearance of the potato blight, Britain had been a favoured destination of many Irish emigrants. In the decades following the ending of the Napoleonic Wars in 1815, the stagnation of the predominantly rural, Irish economy contrasted sharply with the expansion of the industrialising British economy. As a result, the pace and scale of emigration from Ireland to Britain, both seasonal and permanent, increased significantly. For Irish emigrants, Britain had the advantage of being familiar, easily and quickly accessible and, of particular importance during periods of recession, relatively cheap to reach. Since 1800 also, Britain and Ireland had been joined together politically by the Act of Union. During the Famine, the number of persons emigrating to Britain increased substantially. The majority of emigrants to Britain, in common with those who went further afield, were escaping from the impact of successive years of potato blight. They crossed the Irish Sea in the expectation of finding what was no longer available to them in their own country—work, poor relief, or assistance from friends. Other emigrants travelled to Britain merely to use the country as the first step in a longer chain of emigration.[96] In 1841, the Census enumerators calculated the number of Irish-born people living in Britain at 419,000 (52 per cent of whom were male). As a result of the influx of Irish people during the Famine years, this increased to an estimated 717,000 persons in 1851, and it continued to rise until it peaked in 1861 when it reached 805,000, or approximately 3 per cent of the population, although there were marked regional diversities. It is probable, furthermore, that the calculations of the Census Commissioners consistently underestimated the number of Irish-born in Britain; nor did they include persons born of Irish parents.[97]

The profile of Irish emigrants to Britain was similar to those who chose other destinations. The majority were young and single. Almost 50 per cent were female. This social composition made Irish emigrants unique within Europe: most other European emigration consisted of family groups and single men, women travelling as wives or appendages rather than as migrants in their own right. The majority of the Famine emigrants to Britain settled in the ports or the areas surrounding them, most particularly, the ports of Liverpool, Glasgow and London and their hinterlands, and to a lesser degree, Bristol, Swansea, Neath, Cardiff and Newport. To a large extent, these patterns conformed to earlier settlement trends, confirming the importance of networking or chain migration. The towns that contained the largest number of emigrants following the Famine influx were London, with a recorded 5 per cent, Manchester with 13 per cent, Glasgow with 18 per cent, and Liverpool with 22 per cent.[98]

Many contemporary and subsequent accounts suggested that all Irish immigrants to Britain were poor. Although this was generally the case during the Famine, throughout the nineteenth century a sizeable minority of Irish immigrants were skilled workers, or possessed capital. These groups emigrated to Britain—the undoubted 'workshop of the world'—

with the time-honoured aspiration of all emigrants of achieving social and economic improvement. For the majority of Famine emigrants, however, choosing to migrate to Britain was an economic decision, born out of desperation, and frequently arising from the emigrants' inability to afford to venture further afield. Despite their overwhelmingly rural background, they settled in towns in Britain, the problems associated with urbanisation adding to the unfamiliarity of their new life. Skills and education were rarely part of the luggage of this class of immigrants and many of them found employment in low-skilled and low-paid occupations. Many settled in Irish 'ghettoes'. All of this inevitably reinforced the low status and separateness of the newcomers to Britain. To a large extent, therefore, the Irish emigrants were merely exchanging their rural poverty for urban poverty.

Poverty was not the exclusive preserve of the Irish in the fast industrialising and urbanising Britain. The low economic and social status of many of the Irish was strengthened by other factors which separated them from their neighbours and work-mates: their religion (whether a Mayo Catholic or an Antrim Presbyterian), their race, dress, and accent, all added to their distinctiveness. They also had a reputation for being dirty, lawless and drunken. The poverty of many Irish immigrants, therefore, combined with their congregation in the lowest paid jobs and the most run down slums and tenements of the poorest neighbourhoods, made them an easily identifiable target for social commentators and for the opprobrium of their hosts.

The stereotyped image of the Irish in Britain, reinforced by the Famine experience, proved both powerful and enduring. It viewed Irish emigrants as poor and outcast, fleeing from poverty and starvation in their own country. This perception continued long after the Famine was over. It was reinforced by cartoons, such as those which appeared in *Punch*, which gave Irish men ape-like features. It refused—possibly deliberately—to take into account the fact that, during the course of the nineteenth century, the Irish in Britain were, in reality, a diverse group and a sizeable proportion of them (perhaps as large as 30 per cent) were distributed in the higher echelons of the social and economic hierarchy. Furthermore, by regarding the Irish immigrants as an outcast group, it ignored the fact that for almost half a century, Ireland and Britain had been joined to form a 'united kingdom'. Regardless of this, the Irish were generally regarded as inferior to their British counterparts.[99] 'Paddy', and his female equivalent 'Biddy' were traditionally depicted as poor, dirty, stupid, lacking in both skills and social graces, having a high propensity to both alcohol and crime, Papist and extremely fertile—the latter two were believed to go together anyway. Yet the image of Irish immigrants was also ambivalent as, in spite of these apparently unattractive characteristics, Paddy could be (when he was not misbehaving) lovable, in a childlike and roguish way.

The image of Irish immigrants preceded the Famine influx. The idea of communities of Irish emigrants existing in many British cities, known as 'Little Irelands', where poverty, disease, alcoholism, crime and children were endemic, was made popular as early as 1831 when Dr James Kay wrote a pamphlet describing the poverty and squalor of such districts. Although this pamphlet was hurriedly written in response to a cholera epidemic which, it was feared, could have disastrous effects on the urban population, the assertions made by Kay both informed and shaped the view of the Irish in Britain for many decades.[100] Even Friedrich Engels, writing on the eve of the Famine, admitted his anthropological debt to Kay and at the same time helped to reinforce the association of Irish immigrants with urban slums and sordidness. He described one of the Little Irelands in Manchester thus:

> But the most horrible spot lies on the Manchester side, immediately south-west of Oxford Road and is known as Little Ireland . . . A hoard of ragged women and children swarm about here, as filthy as the swine that thrive upon the garbage heaps and in the puddles. In short, the whole rookery furnishes such a hateful and repulsive spectacle as can hardly be equalled in the worst court on the Irk. The race that lives in these ruinous cottages, behind broken windows, mended with oilskin, sprung doors, and rotten door-posts, or in dark, wet cellars, in measureless filth and stench, in this atmosphere penned in as if with a purpose, this race must really have reached the lowest stage of humanity.[101]

As Irish immigration to Britain increased at the end of the 1840s, a climate of prejudice intensified. The initial sympathy which had been felt for the victims of the potato blight quickly dissipated as the victims crossed the Irish Sea in unprecedented numbers. The emigrants were regarded as carriers of disease, competitors for jobs, and a burden on the poor rates. This one-dimensional view of Irish emigrants focused almost exclusively on the poor and pauper immigrants, the small yet not insignificant number of middle-class Irish emigrants becoming an invisible minority. This antagonism had been evident even before the increased Famine influx and it endured well beyond the Famine years.

The antipathy to the Irish immigrants was increasingly given support by a number of writers and social commentators who attempted to provide a racial dimension to this prejudice. As early as 1841, J.A Froude described Irish emigrants as being 'more like tribes of squalid apes than human beings'. This theme was further developed by the middle-class journal, *Punch*, when, in 1862, it devoted an article to explaining the link between apes, negroes and Irish immigrants. In mock Darwinian fashion it declared:

> A creature manifestly between the gorilla and the negro is to be met with in some of the lowest districts of London and Liverpool . . . It belongs in fact to a tribe of Irish savages . . . When conversing with its kind it talks a sort of gibberish. It is, moreover, a climbing animal, and may sometimes be seen ascending a ladder laden with a hod of bricks.[102]

Many of the emigrants to Britain chose the Liverpool route on the grounds of economy. To meet the increased demand, there were frequent sailings to Liverpool from the ports of Dublin, Drogheda, Dundalk and Newry. Liverpool was also the primary port of embarkation for emigrants from all parts of Europe for onward passage to North America. Potential emigrants were well aware of the options available to them and the cost of each option, due to the aggressive and highly competitive advertising campaign of the shipping industry. Emigration to Britain did increase in 1846, but it was not until the early months of 1847 that the mass exodus really commenced. Extensive emigration occurred in the first months of the year, the emigrants deciding not to delay until the traditionally more popular summer months. The Famine emigrants were not drawn exclusively from the poorest sections of society, that is, those affected most immediately by successive years of potato blight. The majority of the early emigrants came from counties Cavan, Kilkenny, King's County, Leitrim, Queen's County and Tipperary, rather than the western counties where both the potatoes and, increasingly, the relief mechanisms, had failed. A large portion of emigrants who left Ireland at the beginning of 1847 were described as being financially 'snug'. The first groups also included a large number of 'fine able young fellows of the labouring classes'. As the year progressed, however, the emigrants were increasingly described as being drawn from the poorest sections of society, many of whom regarded the purchase of a sailing ticket as their final chance of survival.[103]

Many of the healthy and seemingly solvent emigrants of early 1847 were going further afield than Britain, using Liverpool as the first step in their trans-Atlantic journey. The emigrants who remained in Liverpool or its industrial hinterland were often drawn from the poorer sections of society. In April 1847, the parish authorities in Liverpool estimated that since the beginning of the year, 90,000 Irish persons had arrived in their city. Of this number, they estimated that 30,000 had continued their journey overseas, leaving 60,000 who had either remained in Liverpool or sought work in one of the neighbouring industrial towns. The local authorities described these emigrants as being overwhelming poor or paupers. Due to the large volume of emigrants, they were highly visible and the authorities in Lancashire complained of being crowded with new arrivals. As the Irish emigrants continued to flood into Liverpool, the association of Irish emigrants with poverty, and increasingly with dirt and disease, created an uncomfortable and unpalatable impression on the mind of the host country.[104]

As the influx of the Irish intensified during 1847, public opinion in Britain became more overtly concerned with the impact of such large-scale emigration. Increasingly, it was accepted that the Irish immigrants who remained in Britain were the poorest and most debilitated, whilst the healthy, able-bodied emigrants went further afield. This contributed to a growing resentment against the Irish immigrants. The Liverpool Poor Law authorities were one of the first to worry about the impact that such unchecked immigration would have on their city. As early as December 1846, they had contacted the Home Office requesting that the government should regulate the emigration. They suggested that the emigrants should be screened in Ireland before they embarked, and that paupers who were sick or had no money should be prevented from leaving. They also suggested that a portion of the Consolidated Fund should be allocated to Liverpool and other ports that were being flooded with Irish immigrants. The government, however, replied to this and other similar requests by stating that it was not within their jurisdiction to intervene.[105]

The outbreak of fever in Liverpool and a number of other British ports in the spring of 1847 confirmed the worst fears of the local port authorities. Appeals were made repeatedly to the government to intervene and regulate the influx of Irish emigrants to Britain although, again, the government refused to take any action. The Liverpool authorities, in desperation, started to clean public areas with a chlorine of lime in order to prevent the spread of fever and other diseases. One Liverpool newspaper warned that the problem was only beginning:

The first flush of good weather will spread disease and death into hundreds of streets. The filthy state in which the poor people arrive and the shocking dark, damp, dirty places in which they herd—as many as thirty in a cellar—are the most certain constituents of malignant fever, and deeply shall we suffer in a few weeks by the loss of many of our valued townsmen and townswomen if the evil now growing around us be not stayed.[106]

This pessimistic view of the situation was confirmed by a number of doctors in Liverpool, including the Medical Officer for Health. They contacted the Home Secretary directly and warned him that if the situation was allowed to continue, an epidemic was inevitable.[107]

No record was kept of the number of Irish immigrants to Liverpool and other British ports during the Famine years. Many of the people who travelled did so with the intention of emigrating further afield but abandoned that intention if they found employment. Others, however, sought work in Liverpool as a temporary expedient until they had obtained sufficient funds to continue the journey. After 1849, the police in the main ports compiled information on immigrants, although they admitted that the figures were not totally accurate. It was not until 1854 that any reduction in the number of emigrants was evident, although immigration still continued to be higher than its pre-Famine level. One of the main concerns of the authorities was to differentiate the number of paupers, who were potentially seeking poor relief, from the merely poor, who were seeking employment in Britain. The police authorities in Liverpool estimated the numbers of immigrants to the port in the five years from 1849 to 1853. Their estimates are summarised in Table 27.

Table 27: Estimate of Immigrants to Liverpool, 1849–53[108]

	Deck Passengers Labourers	Deck Passengers Paupers	Total
1849	160,457	80,468	240,925
1850	173,236	77,765	251,001
1851	215,369	68,134	283,503
1852	153,909	78,422	232,331
1853	162,229	71,353	233,652

In other parts of Britain, the arrival of the Irish paupers proved to be a heavy burden on the local Poor Law authorities. In 1848, 30 per cent of all expenditure in England and Wales for the relief of Irish paupers was provided by the Manchester union, burdened by an influx of Irish migrants. In Lincoln, the workhouse was extended specifically for the purpose of accommodating the additional Irish paupers, but within a few months, even this proved to be insufficient. Many other boards of guardians appealed to the English Poor Law Board for assistance in treating the diseases, notably typhus fever, which they attributed to the arrival of Irish immigrants.[109]

The inhabitants of Glasgow also were apprehensive about the influx of Irish paupers into their city and the Lord Provost petitioned the government asking for stricter controls to be introduced. Although the subject of Irish immigration to Britain was debated heatedly in parliament, the blame for many of the problems was again placed on the Irish landlords not only for dereliction of duty, but also for allegedly having paid the passages of many emigrants in an effort to clear their estates of their poorest tenants.[110] The government, however, continued to be reluctant to intervene or do anything which might impede the flow of migrants from Ireland, something which they believed would ultimately be beneficial to Ireland and which, furthermore, was taking place at no cost to the state.

The unwillingness of the Whig administration to amend the existing legislation governing immigration resulted in some of the local port authorities imposing their own restrictions on entry. The parish authorities in Liverpool placed a steam boat in the river Mersey for the purpose of allowing medical officers to board all ships arriving from Ireland before they docked. Passengers who were found to be suffering from infectious diseases were sent to a lazaretto. Any ship which was carrying passengers infected with fever was put in quarantine for fifteen days.[111] Apart from the medical threat associated with the Irish immigrants, it increasingly became obvious that due to the sheer volume of immigrants to cities such as Liverpool, and the debilitated condition of many of the new arrivals, it was highly unlikely that they would be able to support themselves financially. In April 1847, even before the main influx of emigrants had commenced, 11,000 Irish people were in receipt of Poor Law relief from the parish authorities in Liverpool.[112]

The growth in the volume of Irish persons travelling to Britain resulted in a more extensive use of the powers of removal by the British authorities. The removal of a pauper to his or her parish of origin or place of settlement had been an integral part of the English Poor Laws since the seventeenth century. The so-called Laws of Settlement which permitted this were a complex body of legislation which determined the liability of a parish for the provision of poor relief. They ruled that any person inhabiting a tenement of less than £10 valuation per annum and seeking relief other than in their parish of birth was deemed to have no settlement rights and could be removed. Despite the fact that by the nineteenth century, the Laws of Settlement were increasingly regarded as an impediment to the free movement of labour, the amended English Poor Law of 1834 did not abolish or even reform these laws.[113] In 1846, the concept of 'irremoveability' was introduced, whereby five years' continuous residence in a parish conferred the right on a person to receive poor relief in that parish.[114]

There was no comparable provision regarding settlement in the Irish Poor Law and this imbalance had been a source of unresolved conflicts since the introduction of the Irish Poor Law in 1838.[115] Also, the provisions regarding people born outside England and Wales were even more stringent. Parish authorities had the right to remove to their place of origin any person born in Ireland, Scotland, the Isle of Man or the Isles of Scilly. The fact that the removed paupers, who were predominantly Irish, were frequently left at a port of entry, was a source of much dissatisfaction. Initially it was unclear whether the more liberal provisions of the 1846 Act applied to persons born in Ireland but, after some deliberation, it was decided that they did. The introduction of this legislation coincided with the beginning of the massive Famine influx and a period of economic recession in Britain. As a result of this, many parish officials in Britain, particularly those located in ports, were determined to remove any Irish paupers before they could acquire the status of irremoveability. A government select committee appointed in 1847 to examine the whole question of removal and settlement recommended the abolition of the principle of settlement. At the same time, the committee recommended that ports such as Liverpool should be granted special powers to protect them from a sudden influx of Irish paupers. The government, however, was unwilling to abolish settlement at such a sensitive period and thus incur the wrath of many Poor Law authorities. A further select committee on removal was convened in 1854, but again the government chose not to interfere with the principle of removal. Instead settlement, and the consequent removal, was allowed to remain in place.[116]

The unwillingness of the government to amend its settlement legislation confirmed the continuation of settlement and removal as an integral part of the English Poor Law. In the late 1840s and early 1850s, the power of removal was invoked to an extent previously unknown against Irish immigrants. The Poor Law authorities in Britain regarded the Laws of Settlement as a necessary protection against undue demands on their finite resources. The Irish Poor Law authorities regarded them as cruel and punitive and, since Ireland had no reciprocal legislation, as reflecting the unequal status of British and Irish paupers. Inevitably, these provisions continued to be an on-going source of controversy between the British and Irish Poor Law authorities. Regardless of numerous protests from the latter, the Laws remained in place with only few amendments for the remainder of the century.[117]

It was not only the poverty of many of the Irish immigrants which made them such unwelcome guests in Britain, but also the fact that this was often combined with disease, particularly fever. An outbreak of fever in 1847 was blamed on the recent arrival of infected Irish paupers.[118] In the Cardiff union in Wales, many of the newly-arrived Irish immigrants were so ill or debilitated that they were unfit to seek employment. In addition to the burden which this placed on the local poor rates, the guardians were also concerned that if this was unchecked, disease would spread to all parts of their city, putting all the inhabitants at risk. In 1848, the Cardiff guardians appointed a special committee, under the provisions of the Nuisance Removal Act, to deal with the distressed paupers arriving at the union. This did not prove sufficient, however, to prevent an outbreak of cholera in the union in the following year. The expenditure on cholera treatment in the Cardiff union in 1849 was £1,670 3s 0d, the majority of the patients being Irish. The Cardiff guardians feared that the arrival of further Irish paupers would exacerbate the spread of cholera and other diseases. To limit the impact of this, they started a programme of large-scale removal of Irish paupers reaching the port. When this became known, a number of captains took the precaution of landing their Irish passengers a short distance from the port. The Cardiff guardians responded by offering a £10 reward for information which could lead to the conviction of any ship's captain involved in this practice.[119]

The combination of a potato failure in Ireland with an economic recession in Britain was an unfortunate coincidence for many Irish paupers. The English, Welsh and Scottish Poor Law authorities responded to the unprecedented influx of Irish poor with large-scale removal, some of which was not only indiscriminate but also illegal. Furthermore, many of the removed paupers were abandoned at the nearest port in Ireland rather than being taken to their place of origin. The number of removal orders from Liverpool—the primary destination of many of the Irish poor—peaked in 1847 when 15,008 paupers were removed to Ireland at a cost of £4,175 11s 3d to the union. By 1849, removals from Liverpool had dropped to 9,509 persons, at a cost of £2,568 3s 10d, and in 1851, it had fallen to 7,808 which cost the Liverpool Poor Law authorities

£1,968 19s 10d. By the middle of the 1850s, the numbers from Liverpool had stabilised at approximately 4,500 each year—a figure which was far in excess of its pre-Famine level.[120]

The number of persons removed from Scotland, which had a separate Poor Law and Law of Settlement legislation, also rose dramatically during the Famine. Again, it was used overwhelmingly against Irish immigrants. In 1848, 1,072 Irish persons were removed from Scotland, compared with only eleven persons removed to England during the same period. Removal from Scotland to Ireland continued to increase until 1851 when it reached 2,272 persons. Removal from the Welsh Poor Law unions also peaked at the beginning of the 1850s; by 1853, only a total of 112 paupers were returned to Ireland from Wales. By the early 1860s, the number of removals to Ireland had fallen drastically and the total number of Irish persons removed from England and Wales had dropped to approximately 200 each year.[121]

Although the number of removals from Britain to Ireland during the Famine was high, the figures have to be measured against a backdrop of a slump in the British economy, the enormous increase in immigrants, and an increase in crime which was attributed to a number of paupers preferring the shelter of a British gaol to the possibility of being sent back to Ireland. Nor is the sudden and substantial growth in the number of removals during the Famine years the whole story. The number of Irish poor relieved outnumbered all others by approximately three to one.[122] The attitude of the British Poor Law authorities towards the Irish immigrants was not totally lacking in compassion. This was particularly evident in Liverpool despite the high number of removals from the city. A number of local doctors, including Dr Duncan, the respected Medical Office of Health for Liverpool, did what they could to ameliorate the condition of sick Irish immigrants and attempted to improve the sanitary condition in which they lived. The sheer volume of immigrants, however, meant that their efforts made little impact. Mr Rushton, the stipendiary magistrate in Liverpool, who was renowned for his humanitarianism, was appalled by the condition in which many of the Irish poor arrived in Liverpool. He informed the government that they were, 'half naked and starving' and he suggested, that as an act of humanity, the number of deck passengers travelling on each packet from Ireland should be limited for the protection of the passengers.[123] The government, however, was not willing to intervene in this area, choosing to let market forces be the primary determinant of the comfort and safety of ships' passengers.

A number of boards of guardians showed little sympathy to the Irish immigrants and used the Famine as an excuse to get rid of all Irish paupers indiscriminately, no matter how long their residence in the area. The Bradford guardians informed the Poor Law Commissioners in 1848 that they were removing all Irish paupers, irrespective of their length of residence in the area. Four years later, they admitted that they had sucessfully removed nearly all Irish paupers from their union.[124] This may have deterred some Irish paupers from applying for relief, preferring to rely on the limited resources of their families or friends instead, or even move to another union. Despite actions such as these, the power of removal was generally employed with restraint throughout the course of the nineteenth century. During the 1840s and 1850s, powers of removal were invoked against the Irish paupers to an extent previously or subsequently unknown but, apart from a short period during the Famine, wholesale removal was unusual. The Poor Law authorities in Britain mostly used removal as protection against a sudden influx of paupers, especially if it coincided with a period of recession. One English Poor Law authority described the Laws of Settlement as a 'flexible deterrent' which could be used judiciously when demand for poor relief was unusually high. Due to the cyclical and short-term nature of depression in the newly industrialising British economy removal, a long-term solution, was not always necessary. The nature of the Famine influx was such, however, that for a while, more extreme measures appeared unavoidable.[125]

In Ireland, the impact of the increase in removals was especially severe on unions which were also ports, such as Dublin, Belfast, Cork, Dundalk, Drogheda and Waterford. The most common practice was to leave the returned paupers at the port of entry rather than return them to their union of origin. As there was no similar Law of Settlement in Ireland, the Irish paupers were legally entitled to receive relief in these unions. The burden which this put on the local poor rates was an on-going source of dissatisfaction to the guardians and ratepayers. Providing relief, even in the short term, proved to be a strain on the resources of the unions involved. The Lord Mayor of Dublin established a special fund to pay for removed paupers, but so many demands were made on it that, by the end of 1847, it was exhausted.[126]

The Dublin boards of guardians frequently discussed the problem of returned paupers. They regarded the principle of settlement and removal as unfair and, at the same time, objected to the way in which it was implemented against the Irish paupers. The British unions which sent paupers back to Ireland were generally anxious to do so as quickly and as cheaply as possible. Many were given no food for the return journey, even though it could take over twelve hours, and women and children were sent back as deck passengers even in winter. Following the death on board ship of two returned paupers in 1847, the anger of the Irish guardians became evident. The guardians of the North Dublin union demanded that the Irish Poor Law Commissioners prosecute the English Poor Law Board for negligence. Regardless of the iniquities and abuses of the Laws of Settlement, however, they were not charged.[127]

Other seaports in the east of the country faced similar problems to the Dublin unions. The Belfast union was the primary recipient of removed paupers from Scotland. The Scottish Poor Law, which had been introduced in 1846, included a provision which enabled natives of England, Ireland and the Isle of Man to be removed to their own country if they applied for relief. Some Scottish boards of guardians, notably that in Edinburgh, quickly acquired a reputation for removing all Irish applicants for relief. In the eighteen-month period following July 1847, the Belfast union received 351 paupers from England and 5,657 paupers from Scotland alone. On some days, as many as forty were removed to Belfast. They were automatically entitled to relief from the Belfast union even though it may not have been their parish of origin. The Belfast guardians regarded this as an unfair burden on the local taxpayers. To ease the burden of paying for them, the guardians appointed a special committee to raise voluntary subscriptions to return them to their places of origin within Ireland. The Belfast guardians also disapproved of the way in which the removed paupers were treated, particularly the fact that they were not supplied with food for the journey. Although the Belfast guardians, like their southern counterparts, frequently petitioned both the Poor Law Commissioners and the British government for a change in the Law, no change was made.[128]

If some British Poor Law authorities acquired a reputation for removing all Irish paupers as soon as they applied for relief, a number of Irish unions were equally prompt in denying their responsibility for the returned paupers. One such case involved an Irish weaver who had been resident in Scotland for eight years. Following an application for relief in 1851, he was returned to Ireland accompanied by a Poor Law official. The official took the pauper to his native Strabane, but the local guardians refused to accept custody of him on the grounds that he was legally relievable in Scotland. They returned him to the care of the officer with instructions to take the pauper back to Scotland. The officer, however, deserted the pauper at Derry, on the pretence of buying some tea. The pauper returned to Strabane and again applied to the guardians for relief. Defeated yet undaunted, the Strabane guardians appealed to the Poor Law Commissioners to end the injustice of removal.

The Strabane guardians also were involved in the case of a female pauper who, originally a native of Dublin, had spent fourteen years in Scotland. The woman had become ill and, upon applying for admittance to hospital, had been removed back to Ireland, in this case, Derry. The Derry guardians responded by removing her to the Strabane union. The Strabane guardians again complained to the Commissioners about the injustice of the system of removal, and appealed to their local Member of Parliament to protect them from such unfair charges.[129]

One case of unfair removal did result in a parliamentary enquiry. It involved John McCoy, who was removed from the Newcastle-upon-Tyne union to Armagh. McCoy had lived in the same parish in England for fifteen years. In 1848, when he applied for poor relief for the first time, he was instantly removed to Ireland. The guardians of the Armagh union, to which he was returned, complained to the Poor Law Commissioners that under the provisions of the English Poor Law this man was irremoveable, and the removal was therefore illegal. The Irish Poor Law Commissioners supported the Armagh guardians in their appeal. This case highlighted some fundamental differences between the English and the Irish Poor Laws. In England, the local boards of guardians could make a legal appeal chargeable upon the poor rates, but this was not possible in Ireland. The Armagh guardians were required to make themselves personally responsible for the costs of the case. Furthermore, the Irish Poor Law Commissioners, who did not have the same powers as the English Board, could not initiate an appeal without the prior consent of the latter.[130] In this instance, the English Poor Law Commissioners refused to initiate an appeal. They admitted that they did not want to antagonise the local English administrators by becoming involved in this or similar cases. They pointed out that as John McCoy could not prove conclusively that he had been resident within one parish for the stated number of years, no appeal should be made. More significantly, they added that the central issue in all cases of removal involving Irish paupers was whether any Irish immigrant at any stage officially acquired the status of irremoveability, which they doubted.[131] The inability of an Irish pauper to acquire the same entitlements as a British pauper reinforced the unequal status of Irish paupers in Britain and highlighted the difficulties which faced all Irish immigrants, no matter how long their residence in Britain.

This incident was not untypical and the Irish Poor Law Commissioners received many similar complaints. They sympathised with the Irish guardians but, due to their unequal powers *vis à vis* the English Board, their hands were tied by legal and financial constraints which rendered them almost powerless. The Irish Executive, who were repeatedly appealed to by the Irish guardians for support, were also sympathetic, but believed it was unlikely that any change would be made in the law. They pointed out to the guardians that the large numbers of persons emigrating to Britain was proving a great burden on the ports in the west of the country, and they concluded that while the distress continued, it was a disadvantage to be a seaport in either country.[132] A legal opinion on the matter in 1849 decreed that Irish people could indeed become irremoveable but this ruling made little difference in practice. In 1848, the Irish guardians made 102 requests concerning removal, compared with only fourteen in 1846. By 1851, the number of official complaints had risen to 147 and, even as late as 1853, seventy-one complaints were made. Furthermore, it is probable that an even higher number of complaints would have been received but the costly and complicated process of instituting an appeal acted as a disincentive to the Irish guardians to pursue additional cases.[133]

Regardless of the frequency of complaints against the Laws of Settlement and the way in which they were implemented, the British government proved to be reluctant to abolish or even amend them. In 1861, long after the Famine influx had ended, an Amendment Act was passed, but it only made minor modifications. Removals from Britain to Ireland continued, much to the dissatisfaction of the Irish guardians. The numbers peaked at the beginning of the 1850s and declined rapidly in the 1860s, tending only to rise during cyclical slumps in Britain. The Laws of Settlement were not finally abolished until 1948. Although in the years after the Famine their use was limited to periods of economic depression, the continuation of these Laws was a constant reminder that Irish immigrants to Britain were there as guests and not by right.

9

Conclusion

1845–5
2

The Famine that affected Ireland from 1845 to 1852 has become an integral part of folk legend. In the popular imagination, the Famine is associated with nationwide suffering, initially triggered by the potato blight, compounded by years of misrule and consolidated by the inadequate response of the British government and Irish landlords alike. The resultant large-scale emigration took the tragedy of the Famine beyond the shores of Ireland to an international stage. Recent scholarly studies of the Famine have attempted to move away from this traditional view. In doing so, a sanitised alternative has emerged that has endeavoured to remove the patina of blame from the authorities involved in providing relief, while minimising the suffering of those who were most directly affected by the loss of the potato crop.[1]

Several specific issues need to be addressed in order to evaluate the varying responses of those in power. At a broad level there are three questions. First, what relief measures were implemented? Second, what were the determinants of the measures that were introduced? Third, and most significantly, how effective were they?

These questions are fundamental to an understanding of the Famine. There is still a widespread view that the Famine relief measures were inadequate. Much of the blame is laid at the door of the British government, and to a lesser degree, Irish landlords. Is this an unfair assessment, especially when seen in the context of the perceived role of government in the middle of the nineteenth century?

Early in the nineteenth century, Ireland was widely regarded as a poor country, dominated by a stagnant subsistence agriculture based substantially upon the ubiquitous potato. On the eve of the Famine, the Irish economy supported a population in excess of eight million people which was large by European standards and represented a sizeable portion of the United Kingdom population as a whole—the population of England and Wales at the same period was approximately sixteen million, and of Scotland, under three million. On the eve of the Famine, the economy of Ireland supported its own population and supplied food for a further two million mouths in Britain. Ireland, therefore, should have been a significant consideration in any social or economic policies that affected the United Kingdom as a whole.

The onset of the Famine was unexpected although partial crop failures and food shortages were not unusual. In 1845, therefore, the potato blight, regardless of the lack of understanding of either its origins or an antidote, was not regarded with undue alarm. Although approximately 50 per cent of the main subsistence crop failed in 1845–6, the consequence of the resultant shortages was not famine, nor did emigration or mortality increase substantially. The role played by the government, local landlords, clerics, and various relief officials was significant in achieving this outcome. The second, more widespread, blight of 1846 marked the real beginning of the Famine. Ominously, the impact of the shortages was apparent in the period immediately following the harvest. Inevitably also, the people undergoing a second year of shortages were far less resilient than they had been twelve months earlier. The government responded to this potentially more serious situation by reducing its involvement in the import of food into the country and by making relief more difficult to obtain.

The distress that followed the 1847 harvest was caused by a small crop and economic dislocation rather than the widespread appearance of blight. The government again changed its relief policy in an attempt to force local resources to support the starving poor within their district. The government professed a belief that this policy was necessary to ensure that a burden which it chose to regard as essentially local should not be forced upon the national finances. This policy underpinned the actions of the government for the remainder of the Famine. The relief of famine was regarded essentially as a local responsibility rather than a national one, let alone an imperial obligation. The special relationship between the constituent parts of the United Kingdom forged by the Act of Union appeared not to extend to periods of shortage and famine.

To what extent was a famine or other disaster inevitable when viewed within the context of the general, and some would say increasing, poverty of Ireland? This assumption of Irish poverty, which underpinned political prescription during the Famine, perhaps owed more to distantly derived dogmas than to the reality. For example, a number of recent studies have suggested that height is a reliable indicator of 'nutritional status' (that is, 'the balance of nutritional intake with growth, work, and the defeat of disease'). Surveys of nineteenth-century British military records indicate that Irish recruits were taller than recruits from the rest of the United Kingdom. This implies a sustained nutritional advantage within Ireland. Also, it is now widely accepted that Ireland's pre-Famine economy was more diverse, vibrant, dynamic and responsive to change than has traditionally been depicted. In contrast to this situation, recent quantitative studies of the British economy have reassessed the impact of industrialisation in the first half of the nineteenth century and concluded that, throughout this period, Britain's economic growth remained 'painfully slow'.[2]

In the middle of the nineteenth century, economic hardship was not the monopoly of Ireland. The horrors of life within the industrialising towns of mid nineteenth-century Britain, so vividly depicted by Friedrich Engels, Elizabeth Gaskell, John Smith, and other contemporaries, and the endemic poverty of some agricultural areas, most notably the Scottish Highlands, show that British poverty, in some cases, largely mirrored Irish rural poverty.[3] Nor was vulnerability the sole preserve of the Irish poor. In Britain and other parts of Europe, cyclical depressions and slumps occurred frequently within the industrial sector and poor harvests did have an impact on the poor within urban areas. What was common to the poor of both Britain and Ireland was their dependence on an external agency—increasingly represented by the state—to provide a safety net during periods of shortage; whether caused by an accident of nature, such as the potato blight, or the imperfect calculations of man.

The unusual, and previously unknown, potato blight which triggered the Irish Famine had its origins in America. It spread across the Atlantic in the early 1840s and by 1845 there were reports of it in mainland Europe and the south of England, which heralded its appearance in Ireland. This unexpected and, as it proved, uncontrollable potato disease, exploded upon an agrarian economy in Ireland in which approximately one-third of the population relied upon the potato as the main ingredient of their subsistence diet. To a large extent, the faith in the potato was justified: although potato harvests were intermittently poor, for the most part bad harvests tended to be localised and rarely lasted beyond one season. Also, crop failure was not unique to the potato and food shortages caused by poor harvests were a feature of eighteenth-century and early nineteenth-century Europe.

The potato blight, which appeared in varying degrees throughout Ireland from 1845 to 1852, was remarkable for its longevity and its geographic spread. Unfortunately, the arrival of the blight coincided with a period of rapid population growth and relative economic stagnation. The livelihoods of a large number of poor people were increasingly precarious. For this group of people, the blight could not have occurred at a worse time. A few decades earlier, and dependence on the potato would not have been so acute; a few decades later, and the economy could probably have made its own internal adjustments.[4]

If the blight is judged to be an unforeseen ecological disaster, beyond the control of man, which struck Ireland at a particularly vulnerable time, it was especially important that the intervention of man (as represented by Irish merchants, landlords, and the policy makers within the British government amongst others) should compensate for the failings of nature. It was the failure of these key groups to meet the challenge and implement effective action which transformed the blight into a famine.

The 1830s and 1840s were decades of widespread and virtually unprecedented economic dislocation and social unrest in Britain. For the government, a disquieting feature of this unrest was that it was apparent amongst both the middle and the lower classes. The Anti-Corn Law League, for example, was an influential lobby group whose main aim was to bring about a repeal of the Corn Laws. The repeal of these Laws in 1846 owed more to the unrelenting campaign mounted by this group than to food shortages in Ireland. In repealing the Corn Laws, Peel committed political suicide and paved the way for a Whig government, led by Lord John Russell, just as Ireland was about to enter its second year of shortages. The Whigs, and Russell in particular, had been responsible for the introduction of the 1832 Reform Act and the 1834 'new' Poor Law in England. They had a reputation for being a party of reform and of high expenditure. Having obtained power almost by default, however, Russell's government was particularly sensitive to public opinion and aware of the force of popular protest—especially when harnessed to a powerful lobby group. The Whigs, therefore, were unlikely to risk rocking their own precarious power base for policies which they believed would be unpopular. It was an unfortunate coincidence that one of a series of cyclical economic depressions afflicted Great Britain and the industrialised north-east of Ireland during the height of the Famine, in the autumn of 1847. Although the recession was short lived, its impact was devastating, especially in the industrial and (since 1832) politically powerful, north-west of England. At the same time, other parts of the United Kingdom, particularly the highlands of Scotland, suffered crop failures and resultant hunger. Continental Europe was also faced with economic problems. The conjunction of an economic crisis (both in the industrial and agricultural sectors) and political discontent was held responsible for the revolutionary movement which swept Europe in 1848. The rising which took place within Ireland in this year can be seen as part of this revolutionary continuum rather than an isolated or peculiarly Irish incident. The international situation, and a fear of revolution, undoubtedly coloured the relief policies pursued by the British government.

The slump of 1847 was a sharp reminder to the government of the problems on its own doorstep. During the autumn of 1847, news of Irish distress vied increasingly for column space in the English newspapers with stories of hardship, unemployment and bankruptcies in England, notably in Lancashire, the flagship of industrial Britain. Poverty and distress, therefore, were not confined to Ireland but were also evident in one of the wealthiest parts of the British Empire.[5] The demands of the Irish poor were now in direct competition with the demands of the urban poor within Britain. An obvious comparison was drawn between the distress of the feckless Irish peasants and their irresponsible and greedy landlords, with the distress of the hard-working factory operatives and the enterprising entrepreneurs upon whom, it was believed, much of the success of the British Empire rested. Since the reign of Elizabeth I, Poor Law philosophy had drawn a distinction between the 'deserving' and the 'undeserving' poor. The English factory operatives, unemployed through no fault of their own, were regarded as deserving poor; it was apparent that the Irish peasants could be regarded with equal justification as falling into the latter category.

A hardening attitude to Irish distress was illustrated by the response to appeals for additional assistance as a third year of shortages became inevitable. An early indication of a resistant official response occurred in October 1847, when a group of Catholic bishops and archbishops appealed to the government for an increase in official aid. They were informed, in a widely published response, that such a request was unreasonable, particularly as it implied that:

> the means for this relief should be exacted by the government from classes all struggling with difficulties, and at a moment when in England trade and credit are disastrously low, with the immediate prospect of hundreds of thousands being thrown out of employment or being as destitute of the means of existence as the poorest peasant in Ireland.

An appeal for funds in the form of a second 'Queen's Letter' was also published in October 1847 and read out in all churches throughout England. It elicited more criticism than cash.[6]

The government remained committed to the policy of forcing Ireland to depend on its own resources as far as possible, chiefly through the mechanism of the Poor Law. Within the domestic economy, however, the government did depart from its declared *laissez faire* policy and intervened to allow the terms of the 1844 Bank Charter Act to be relaxed in order to aid the industrial sector. By the end of 1847, the financial crisis in Britain was over and a period of prosperity was under way. The Great Exhibition of 1851 was a triumphant demonstration of Britain's international industrial and economic supremacy. In the same year, in a different part of the United Kingdom, the west of Ireland, a portion of the population was about to confront a seventh consecutive year of famine and shortages.

The contribution of outside charitable bodies was mostly confined to the early years of the Famine. By 1847, most of these sources had dried up or, as in the case of the Quakers, they had decided to use their remaining funds to concentrate on long-term improvements rather than immediate relief. Significantly, the Quakers' men on the ground who toured the west of Ireland in the winter of 1846–7 were critical both of absentee landlords and the policies pursued by the British government alike. The British Relief Association, which remained operative after 1847, allowed its funds to be allocated through the medium of the Treasury. This was not without problems. Count Strzelecki, the Association's local agent, fought a hard battle with the Treasury to ensure that a successful scheme to feed schoolchildren was continued, regardless of the disapproval of Trevelyan.

A fundamental policy position of government, enforced rigorously throughout the Famine, as noted earlier, was the determination to make local resources support local distress. The Irish landlords were singled out continually as a group that needed to be reminded of, and occasionally coerced into, undertaking their duties to the poor. Following the 1845 blight, however, the money contributed voluntarily by the landlords and other subscribers was the highest amount ever raised. Regardless of this achievement, the Irish contribution was represented as derisory and the landlords increasingly targeted as the object of public opprobrium. Irish landlords undoubtedly provided an easy and obvious scapegoat both as a cause of, and as contributors to, the Famine. This was a view taken both by their contemporaries and by some later historians.[7]

Initially, a portion of the contributions to the relief funds were voluntary, but increasingly this money was raised through compulsory local taxation. The transfer to Poor Law relief in 1847 marked the completion of this process. The government justified this shift of responsibility on the grounds that unless firm action was taken, a duty which rightfully belonged to the Irish ratepayers would be thrown onto the taxpayers of Britain. There is no doubt that the burden of taxation within Ireland was uneven, a disproportionate amount falling on landlords, especially those whose estates were greatly subdivided. Other key economic groups within the country, notably industrialists and, significantly, the corn merchants, would have felt relatively little increase in the amount of poor rates which they paid.

Although the way in which relief was provided was determined by the government and allocated almost exclusively by the Treasury, from the outset the governments of both Peel and Russell described their respective roles as supplementary to that played by the Irish people themselves. It was perhaps ironic that as the demand for relief increased markedly in 1846, Russell's government was determined that its involvement should decrease. Within the framework of local responsibility, the diverse roles played by merchants, landlords, tenants, Poor Law officials and paupers within Ireland was crucial. The role of the landlords, despite being an easy scapegoat for the ills of Ireland, was diverse, ranging from those who mortgaged their estates to help their poor tenants to those who, insulated by their absenteeism, chose not to set foot in the country during this period.

The involvement of the local gentry in poor relief was a traditional one, both as members of relief committees and providers of subscriptions. In the years 1845–6, they performed this role successfully although in the following year, like all other relief officials, they were overwhelmed by the fact that the demand for relief far exceeded what was in their power to deliver. In the latter years of the Famine, as more demands were placed upon the taxpayers of Ireland, there was a discernible hardening in the attitude of landlords and farmers towards their tenants and a corresponding increase in evictions. The moral obligation between landlords and tenants and even between the poor and their neighbours proved vulnerable to years of distress and spiralling taxation. Yet, generalisations about the role of landlords should be made with caution, particularly as the responses to the crisis and the manner in which responsibilities were discharged varied over time and place. It would appear, however, that the role of the local notables could be decisive in preventing the shortages from developing into famine.

The union of Dunfanaghy in Co. Donegal, which was the second poorest union in the country, is such an example. In 1847, although the local population suffered immense privations, there was little excess mortality or emigration. To a large extent, this was due to the involvement of local landlords and merchants—notably the energetic Lord George Hill —who actively participated in relief schemes in their various guises, including grand juries, relief committees, and the Poor Law board. It is significant that in the crucial winter of 1846–7, the committees in this area flouted the strict guidelines of the government and sold corn to the population at below the market price and before the designated time. In areas where the local relief committees had neither the capital, the foresight, nor the motivation to initiate an effective remedy, the local population bore the fatal consequences of the government's short-sighted policy.

To what extent, however, can any individual group, organisation or state body be blamed for the degree of suffering that resulted from successive years of potato blight? Would the outcome of the years of shortages and suffering have been different if the response of the authorities, various charitable organisations, and other key individuals to successive years of blight had been different?

There is no doubt that the part played by the government was pivotal within the whole relief endeavour. Was it, however, within the remit of the government—either ideologically or financially—to provide sufficient relief to keep suffering, emigration, and mortality to a minimum level? The policies of the government, and the way in which it perceived its role, are crucial to an understanding of the Famine years. The changing perceptions and strategies of the British government determined the type of relief provided and the methods and timing of its allocation. The role played by the Treasury, both in implementing the various relief policies and in advising the government, was critical. Charles Wood, the Chancellor of the Exchequer, together with his colleague, Charles Trevelyan, represented a school of economic orthodoxy which advocated both non-intervention and fiscal rectitude. A populist version of their views found a wider audience in the columns of *The Times* and the cartoons of *Punch*. It was also supported in the learned contributions to the *Edinburgh Review* and the fledgling *Economist*. In the wake of the financial and monetary crisis of 1847, the demand for retrenchment was also welcomed by a politically influential industrial middle class. The Treasury, in effect, became not only the guardian of the relief purse, but—mainly due to the energetic and prolonged involvement of Charles Trevelyan—was increasingly deferred to by members of the government as the oracle of all wisdom regarding Ireland. Although no one person can be blamed for the deficiencies of the relief policies, Trevelyan perhaps more than any other individual represented a system of response which increasingly was a mixture of minimal relief, punitive qualifying criteria, and social reform.

The Treasury's agenda for Irish relief went far beyond the mere allocation of government funds. Its imprint was evident throughout both the public and private sectors. Not only did it arbitrate on the crucial issue of who deserved to be given financial support and how much they should receive, but increasingly it attempted to control the day-to-day administration of relief. No other organisation played such a sustained role or showed such an obvious interest in the affairs of Ireland. The government, which was in the midst of a foreign crisis, an economic depression, and a year of revolutions and uprisings in Europe which extended both to Britain and Ireland, was no doubt glad to be able to allow the Treasury to shoulder such a large portion of the Irish relief burden. Also, despite evidence to the contrary, many officials, including even the well-informed Trevelyan, publicly declared the Famine to be over in 1848.[8] The problems of Ireland, therefore, were necessarily a low priority to a government at the centre of a large and still expanding Empire. However, by allowing the Treasury to play such a pivotal role in the provision of relief, it was perhaps inevitable that the need to 'balance the books'—an excellent objective in Treasury terms—should at times overshadow the need to provide adequate relief. By using the Treasury in such a capacity, its role far exceeded that of guardian of the public purse and extended both to influencing public policy and, even more significantly, to final arbitrator in the provision of relief.

The role of the various relief officials within Ireland was also significant. As the local agents of the government, it was their duty to determine how policies should be implemented on the ground. They were relied upon to provide information on local conditions. Many of them also simultaneously carried out a confidential correspondence with Trevelyan, in which he urged them to be frank. Not surprisingly, many of the officials who shared confidences with Trevelyan also professed to share his view on how relief should be provided. In the west of Ireland, however, where shortages were most intense and most prolonged, the relief officials were less sanguine about the impact of the government's policies. Many of them were increasingly frustrated both by lack of resources and by the constraints which official legislation placed upon them.

This frustration was even more evident amongst the central relief officials in Dublin, most notably the Irish Executive and the Poor Law

Commissioners. Increasingly, as the Famine progressed, the advice of these officials was ignored or dismissed. A dichotomy between the official government response to the Famine in Britain and the official preferred response within Ireland became apparent. Lacking independent financial resources, the power of the latter group was severely restricted. At times, the frustration of the officials in Dublin was barely concealed. This divergence reached a public climax with the resignation of Edward Twistleton, the Chief Poor Law Commissioner, in 1849.

The British government contributed in the region of £10m for Irish distress, mainly in the form of a loan, part of which was interest bearing. This amount was equalled by the contribution made by the ratepayers of Ireland from a total annual valuation of approximately £13m pounds. Inevitably, the burden fell most heavily on the ratepayers in the west of the country. In view of the great imbalance of the incomes of the two countries, the amount provided by the British Treasury was derisory. It has been estimated as only 0.3 per cent of the annual gross national product of the United Kingdom. To put this in a different context, the British contribution to Famine relief represented only about 20 per cent of the amount expended on the Crimean War a few years later, in 1854–6.[9] Regardless of such comparisons, even when it was evident that local resources were either unable or unwilling to support local distress, and where mortality was an inevitable outcome, the government was reluctant to increase its level of involvement.

The Famine was a disaster of major proportions, even allowing for an inevitable statistical uncertainty on its estimated effect on mortality. Yet the Famine occurred in a country which, despite concurrent economic problems, was at the centre of a still-growing empire and was an integral part of the acknowledged workshop of the world. There can be no doubt that despite a short-term cyclical depression, the combined resources of the United Kingdom could either completely or much more substantially have removed the consequences of consecutive years of potato blight in Ireland. This remains true even if one accepts Trevelyan's proud assertion that no government had done more to support its poor than Britain had done during the Famine years.[10] The statement implies that not only was enough done to help the suffering people in Ireland, but that it was accompanied by a generosity that patently is not borne out by the evidence. To have fed in excess of three million people in the summer of 1847 was a worthy and notable achievement. It also dispels the frequent assertion that the British government did not possess the administrative capability to feed such a large number of starving people. But if the measure of success is judged by the crudest yet most telling of all

351

measures—that of mortality—the British government failed a large portion of the population in terms of humanitarian criteria.

In this context, Trevelyan's comment reveals the separateness of Ireland from the rest of the United Kingdom. His perception mocked the precepts of the Act of Union. It should not, however, be forgotten that the government and the Treasury had to provide a system of relief that would satisfy both parliamentary and public opinion. If measured by this criterion alone—accepting, however, the individual criticisms of the opposition party—the relief measures were undoubtedly regarded as successful, and to some, even over-generous.[11]

The policies of the government increasingly specified criteria that disallowed external assistance until distress was considerable and evident. The leitmotif of relief provided by the central government throughout the course of the Famine was that assistance would be provided only when it—or, in fact, its agent, the Treasury—was satisfied that local resources were exhausted, or that if aid was not provided, the distressed people would die. By implementing a policy which insisted that local resources must be exhausted before an external agency would intervene, and pursuing this policy vigorously despite local advice to the contrary, the government made suffering an unavoidable consequence of the various relief systems which it introduced. The suffering was exacerbated by the frequent delays in the provision of relief even after it had been granted and by the small quantity of relief provided, which was also of low nutritional value. By treating the Famine as, in essence, a local problem requiring a local response, the government was, in fact, penalising those areas which had the fewest resources to meet the distress.

The government response to the Famine was cautious, measured and frequently parsimonious, both with regard to immediate need and in relation to the long-term welfare of that portion of the population whose livelihood had been wiped out by successive years of potato blight. Nor could the government pretend ignorance of the nature and extent of human tragedy that unfolded in Ireland following the appearance of blight. The Irish Executive and the Poor Law Commissioners sent regular, detailed reports of conditions within the localities and increasingly requested that even more extensive relief be provided. In addition, Trevelyan employed his own independent sources of information on local conditions, by-passing the existing official sources of the Lord Lieutenant. This information revealed the extent of deprivation caused by the Famine. It also showed the regional variations arising from the loss of the potato crop; and it exposed the inability of some areas to compensate for such losses from their own internal resources. There was no shortage of detailed and up-to-date information. What was crucial was the way in which the government used this information.

While it was evident that the government had to do something to help alleviate the suffering, the particular nature of the actual response, especially following 1846, suggests a more covert agenda and motivation. As the Famine progressed, it became apparent that the government was using its information not merely to help it formulate its relief policies but also as an opportunity to facilitate various long-desired changes within Ireland. These included population control and the consolidation of property through a variety of means, including emigration, the elimination of small holdings, and the sale of large but bankrupt estates. This was a pervasive and powerful 'hidden agenda'. The government measured the success of its relief policies by the changes which were brought about in Ireland rather than by the quality of relief provided *per se*. The public declaration of the Census Commissioners in the Report of the 1851 Census, which stated that Ireland had benefited from the changes brought about by the Famine, is a clear example of this.[12]

For landlords also, who were able to ride the storm of diminished rentals and heavy taxation, the Famine ultimately brought both social and financial benefits. As Lord George Hill, a 'reforming' landlord who had attempted without success to consolidate his estates prior to 1845, admitted:

> The Irish people have profited much by the Famine, the lesson was severe; but so rooted were they in old prejudices and old ways, that no teacher could have induced them to make the changes which this Visitation of Divine Providence has brought about, both in their habits of life and in their mode of agriculture.[13]

The clues to understanding the policies chosen by the government can be discerned in a number of key elements within that policy. Despite the overwhelming evidence of prolonged distress caused by successive years of potato blight, the underlying philosophy of the relief efforts was that they should be kept to a minimalist level; in fact they actually decreased as the Famine progressed. The reduction in the relief provided both in real terms and in nutritional value inevitably had a detrimental, and frequently fatal, impact upon the health of the distressed population. A number of relief officials employed the theories of Adam Smith and other leading political economists to justify minimal interference, or even non-intervention, in the market on the grounds that it contained a self-adjusting mechanism.[14] The employment of this theory was most evident in the months following the second appearance of blight in 1846 when the government promised the Irish corn merchants that they, the government, would play a secondary role in the importation of food into the country. They also agreed that government food would not be sold below the local market price and that the food depots would not open until 1847.

The consequences of this policy were disastrous. Insufficient food was imported into the country and no restrictions were put on food leaving Ireland. Furthermore, the delay in opening the food depots left some of the population without access to any food for a number of weeks; and even after the depots had opened, the government insistence that corn should not be sold below the market price placed it beyond the reach even of those in receipt of cash wages from the public works. This change of policy, and a dogmatic adherence to it, marked the true beginning of the Famine. The government's commitment to this general and simplistic dogma was not, however, absolute. It was clearly absent in other areas of imperial policy at the time. Instead, the policy of non-interference was employed with determination by a government which used it to achieve aims beyond the mere provision of relief.

The policy of closing ports during periods of shortages in order to keep home-grown food for domestic consumption had on earlier occasions proved to be an effective way of staving off famine within Ireland. One of the most successful uses of this policy occurred, perhaps significantly, prior to the Act of Union. During the subsistence crisis of 1782–4, at the instigation of the Lord Lieutenant, an embargo was placed on the export of foodstuffs from the country. The immediate effect had been to reduce food prices within Ireland. When the crop failed again in 1783, in addition to the continuation of the embargo, a sum of money was also set aside by the Irish government to be used as bounty payments for food brought into the country. Although the Irish merchants lobbied against this measure and were vociferous in their antagonism towards it, their protests were over-ridden. The Lord Lieutenant recognised that the interests of the merchants and of the distressed people were irreconcilable.[15] The outcome of this humanitarian and imaginative policy was successful. The years 1782–4 are barely remembered as years of distress. By refusing to allow a similar policy to be adopted in 1846–7, despite the recommendations of the Lord Lieutenant, the British government ensured that 'Black '47' was indelibly associated with suffering, famine, mortality, emigration and to some, misrule.

In 1845, the administrative machinery for the provision of relief was better equipped to deal with distress than ever before. This was due largely to the introduction of the Poor Law in 1838 which, for the first time ever, established a national and compulsory system of relief in Ireland. As a consequence, a national framework existed for the provision of relief, complete with its own administrative structure including officials and local wardens. Twistleton, the Chief Poor Law Commissioner, repeatedly stressed that in his view the failure of relief was not an administrative one but a financial one.

The response of Russell's government to the Famine combined opportunism, arrogance and cynicism, deployed in such a way as to facilitate the long-standing ambition to secure a reform of Ireland's economy. In the midst of dealing with a famine in Ireland, increasing reference was made to the need to restructure agriculture in Ireland from the top to the bottom. This had been the ambition of a succession of governments prior to 1845, but the Famine provided a real opportunity to bring about such a purpose both quickly and, most importantly, cheaply.

In the early decades of the nineteenth century, for example, state-sponsored emigration had been recommended by select committees, social theorists and government advisors alike, all of whom agreed that it would be beneficial to Ireland; but the government had refused to involve itself in the additional expenditure that an active pursuit of this policy would involve. The Famine, however, gave the impetus to emigration to flourish, without imposing an additional financial burden on the government. It, therefore, provided opportunities for change. The Whig administration, through legislation such as the Quarter-Acre Clause and the Encumbered Estates Acts, ensured that such opportunities were not wasted.

If the potato blight had been confined to 1845, its impact would have been insignificant and it would have been remembered only as one of the many intermittent subsistence crises which affected Ireland and all agricultural societies. Even though over half of the crop was lost through blight in 1845, the increase in excess mortality and emigration was insignificant. In 1845–6, as had so clearly been demonstrated in the subsistence crisis of 1782–4, if the political and social will existed, a subsistence crisis did not necessarily have to become a famine.

In the 1840s, the policy of the British government was shaped by a prevailing economic dogma, inspired by a particular interpretation of free market economics. The champions of this philosophy were Adam Smith and his successors such as Nassau Senior and Harriet Martineau. In the context of providing poor relief in Ireland, this influential philosophy decreed that ultimately such relief was damaging and that genuine improvements could be achieved only through self-help. In its more extreme form, the principles embodied in this dogma denied any government responsibility for the alleviation of distress. Proponents of such theories even managed to suggest that during periods of extraordinary distress it could be better for those affected not to have access to extraneous relief lest the self-righting mechanisms of the economic system—the allegedly ubiquitous yet truly imperceptible 'invisible hand'—became ensnared by unwarranted interference. The outcome of a slavish adherence to these self-adjusting mechanisms would inevitably be human suffering. Yet this appeared to be of little consequence to those who worshipped at the altar of *laissez faire*. Short-term suffering appeared to be a small price to be paid for long-term improvement, especially if the theoreticians did not have to participate directly in the experiment.[16]

Despite the fashionable adherence to these theories at the time of the Famine, they were only one of the many influences upon political decision-making. It is clear that such theoretical dogma could be dismissed when prevailing pressures demanded: the intervention by the government in the autumn of 1847 to alleviate the impact of a slump in the manufacturing districts of England providing a concurrent example. The philosophy of non-interference was in practice employed selectively and pragmatically. Its content and application changed as the government considered necessary. Within the Whig government itself, there existed differences of opinion regarding the level of financial intervention in Ireland. Significantly, those who favoured a minimalist approach, spearheaded by the men at the Treasury, were in the ascendant. Nevertheless, during the crucial period in the provision of Famine relief, that is, after the complete devastation of the potato crop in 1846, there is no doubt that this economic theory had powerful public support and, more significantly, enjoyed a popular appeal among many of the ruling elite, particularly those most directly responsible for determining the extent and means of providing relief.

From the perspective of a political response to the Famine, the most substantial deviation from the purist theories of free market economics came about in Ireland itself. This deviation was motivated by the less than purist desire to seek a major reform of the Irish economy, especially in the 'potato economy' districts in the west. In these areas, the free market clearly had failed to deliver spontaneously the desired result, particularly in terms of larger, more efficient holdings, and the British government chose to use the Famine as a means of facilitating and imposing their own reforms. The Famine provided a unique opportunity to bring about long-term structural changes in Ireland's agrarian sector.

During the latter part of the Famine, notably following the transfer of relief to local responsibility through the mechanism of the Poor Law in the autumn of 1847, a 'hidden agenda' of reform is increasingly apparent. Much of this was covert. The government and its agents were not willing to admit openly that the suffering of many people in Ireland, and the consequent high levels of mortality and emigration, was being employed to achieve other purposes. The government was able to use the chaos caused by the Famine to facilitate a number of social and economic changes. In particular, it took the opportunity to bring about a more commercial system of farming within Ireland which no longer would offer refuge to a variety of non-productive elements—whether they were landless labourers or apathetic landlords. If, due to its ultimate aim, this policy could be judged as altruistic, its implementation, based on the prevailing view of the Irish, cannot be. Irish peasants, feckless and indolent as they were perceived to be, were judged less 'worthy' to receive relief than their counterparts in Britain. One consequence of this perception occurred in 1846 when Ireland was not allowed to receive imports of food until supplies had been delivered to Scotland first.

Irish landlords were an even more obvious target for the wrath of the British government. Some of the criticisms levelled against the Irish landlords did have a basis in truth. However, the invective with which such criticisms were delivered frequently was petty and politically motivated. More significantly, by its insistence on local responsibility, the government was able to minimise its own role in the provision of relief and, at the same time, offer an easy scapegoat to blame when the level of suffering appeared to be unacceptable. But where did the line of acceptable suffering lie? A government enquiry in 1851 stated that the level of suffering was unacceptable and queried whether a similar level would have been allowed in England. If the loss of population is taken as the ultimate measure of suffering, how could any government justify the outcome of its policies in a country that had lost between 20 and 25 per cent of its population? Ireland may have been a part of the United Kingdom, but its place within it was hardly that of an equal partner or even that of a young sibling: in the words of Trevelyan, Ireland was a 'prodigal son' who had to be forcibly brought under parental control. If, as some people stated, the Famine was a punishment from God, the punitive relief measures did nothing to diminish this belief.

To achieve the aims of the 'hidden agenda' required little action by the government other than to ensure that pressure was maintained within Ireland and not transferred elsewhere. Effective relief entailed extraneous aid, but this would have perpetuated the existing system of agricultural production. If distress was to be used as the mechanism to forge a new

economic order within Ireland, it was essential to manage relief programmes carefully and to find a shield that would deflect or neutralise
the inevitable political pressures to do more. It is perhaps ironic that this
pressure increasingly came from leading relief officials within Ireland.
Lacking political weight, however, such officials were easily ignored or
dismissed as the situation required.[17]

To achieve its ultimate aims, the government's strategy was based on
two underlying principles: that of issuing the minimal amount of relief
consistent with political acceptability; and that of imposing the maximum
possible burden on local resources in order to force a restructuring of
Irish agriculture. It is perhaps no coincidence that the areas perceived to
be in greatest need of agrarian reform were those that suffered most from
the impact of the potato blight. The minimalist approach to the provision of relief took several forms. Approximately 50 per cent of the relief
provided was given in the form of loans to the distressed areas which first
had to be matched by equal funding from some of the poorest localities
within the British Empire. The actual distribution of relief was delayed
to the last minute possible, even where this was contrary to the advice of
local relief officials.

The transfer to Poor Law relief after 1847 emphasised the burden of
local responsibility and, through the raising of local poor rates, placed an
especially heavy burden on landlords whose estates were subdivided into
very small holdings. The government introduced new legislation to reinforce its policies, the most obvious being the Gregory Clause which
denied access to relief to anyone in possession of more than a quarter of
an acre of land. The transfer of properties was also facilitated by the
Encumbered Estates Acts. Ostensibly, therefore, the government may
have invoked the theory of a free market policy, but in practice its actions
departed from such purist dogma. Instead, it was replaced by an even
more entrenched and righteous philosophy based on the premise that
changes were necessary for the future well-being of Ireland and, by
implication, the whole of the United Kingdom. The Famine provided an
ideal opportunity for both encouraging and fostering these changes.
Effectively, this approach, far from observing *laissez faire* principles, was
closer to a model of opportunistic interventionism.

The invocation of free market theory by the government also had a
further useful purpose. By supposedly basing a whole area of policy upon
this theory, especially in the face of an unfolding human tragedy, it was
possible to divert attention from many of the real problems confronting
the government—most especially the economic one. It is evident that
had the government sought to respond to the Famine, based on their

knowledge of local circumstances, a compelling case for massive financial intervention would have been difficult to resist. In its place, an exposure of the nature of the problem was replaced by abstract theory, and a behind-the-scenes attempt at social engineering substituted for the provision of resources commensurate with the real needs of the situation.

In conclusion, therefore, the response of the British government to the Famine was inadequate in terms of humanitarian criteria and, increasingly after 1847, systematically and deliberately so. The localised shortages that followed the blight of 1845 were adequately dealt with but, as the shortages became more widespread, the government retrenched. With the short-lived exception of the soup kitchens, access to relief—or even more importantly, access to food—became more restricted. That the response illustrated a view of Ireland and its people as distant and marginal is hard to deny. What, perhaps, is more surprising is that a group of officials and their non-elected advisors were able to dominate government policy to such a great extent. This relatively small group of people, taking advantage of a passive establishment, and public opinion which was opposed to further financial aid for Ireland, were able to manipulate a theory of free enterprise, thus allowing a massive social injustice to be perpetrated within a part of the United Kingdom. There was no shortage of resources to avoid the tragedy of a Famine. Within Ireland itself, there were substantial resources of food which, had the political will existed, could have been diverted, even as a short-term measure, to supply a starving people. Instead, the government pursued the objective of economic, social and agrarian reform as a long-term aim, although the price paid for this ultimately elusive goal was privation, disease, emigration, mortality and an enduring legacy of disenchantment.

Appendix 1

Analysis of Loss of the Potato Crop in 1845-6

This analysis is based on information collected by the local constabulary on behalf of the government following the first appearance of the potato blight in 1845. The information was collected by electoral divisions within counties. Electoral divisions were new administrative units which had been introduced by the Poor Law Act of 1838. Each comprised a group of townlands. Electoral divisions varied greatly in size, with the largest ones in the west. They did not conform to any previous administrative unit and, occasionally, even breached county boundaries.

The data provided by the constabulary is arranged as a series of classifications, giving for each county the number of electoral divisions which have lost a portion of the potato crop. The classification of the extent of crop failure is arranged into bands of ten per cent: for example, the number of electoral divisions in a county where the potato failure was over 30 per cent of the crop but less than 40 per cent.

The data thus suffers from a degree of imprecision. The actual extent of potato crop loss in each electoral division is not stated; there is no indication either of the relative size of each electoral division or the amount of potatoes which was actually grown within it. Such information would allow an estimate of the importance of the potato in relation to other forms of agricultural output in each area. Thus each electoral division in the analysis has to be given an equal value due to the imprecision of the data. Moreover, data were not available for every electoral division, leading to gaps in the analysis. Thus there is no data for Co.

Carlow and incomplete data for King's Co. and for counties Mayo, Cavan and Westmeath. Despite these difficulties, it remains possible to construct a broadly indicative picture of the relative magnitude of the potato crop failure in 1845. These data are shown according to county for the following two bands:

i. The percentage of electoral divisions (EDs) in each county that experienced a loss of at least 30 per cent of the potato crop.

ii. The percentage of EDs with a loss of at least 40 per cent of the potato crop.

For all EDs in Ireland the result is:

Results for Counties

	Overall % of EDs	Standard Deviation	Coefficient of Variation
At least 30% failure	72.3	16.1	22.2
At least 40% failure	42.6	20.9	49.1

This analysis indicates substantial differences in the volume of crop failure as the proportions move from 30 per cent to 40 per cent. At the higher level (in EDs losing at least 40 per cent of their crop), a considerable increase in the variability between one county and another takes place, i.e. the geographical difference in the extent of crop failure becomes more starkly apparent. The following tables provide a statistical analysis of this.

	% of EDs in County	
Basis of Classification (over 40%)	**high**	**low**
Mean +/- standard deviation	**63.5**	**21.7**
Counties	*over this*	*under this*
	Antrim	Armagh
	Monaghan	Wicklow
	Clare	Fermanagh
	Waterford	
	Kilkenny	
	Louth	

	(over 30%)	high **88.4**	low **56.2**
Counties		*over this*	*under this*
		Antrim	Donegal
		Clare	Fermanagh
		Waterford	Londonderry
		Kilkenny	Tyrone
		Roscommon	Mayo

Notes on the Analysis

Table a) For counties with EDs with 40 per cent or more failure—Mean = 42.6 per cent + 1 sd of 20.9 = 63.5 per cent. Any county in the top 36.5 per cent (100–63.5) has relatively high failure, i.e. with a relatively high proportion of EDs experiencing at least 40 per cent of the potato crop failed.

Mean = 42.6 per cent - 1 sd of 20.9 = 21.7 per cent. Thus the bottom 21.7 per cent of EDs with at least 40 per cent failure rate are defined here.

Table b) The same as above, except that the band of EDs is widened to include those divisions with at least 30 per cent of the crop failing. At the top end, it is to be expected that an overlap with the 40 per cent plus group will occur in the list of affected counties.

Analysis of the Variation of Employment on the Public Works in 1846

The sharp variations in the use of public works, if they are correlated broadly with the incidence of distress, suggest that a partial loss of the potato crop, a high level of dependency on the potato, and a more general vulnerability of the local economy were the primary combined influences that ignited a demand for public works when a 'threshold' of need was reached. For example, the concentration of the scheme into a small number of counties is evident:

County	% of all persons employed on public works	% of national population
Clare	21.4	3.5
Limerick	14.0	4.0
Galway	12.4	5.4
Roscommon	9.8	3.1
Mayo	8.4	4.8
Tipperary	7.2	5.3
Cork	5.5	10.4

It can be seen from the above statistics that the leading five counties which made use of the public works accounted for 64.8 per cent of all relief works, whilst only representing 21.4 per cent of the Irish population. The top seven counties accounted for 77.5 per cent of the people employed on the public works, and 37.1 per cent of the Irish population.

At the height of the Public Works scheme, in August 1846, the average number of persons employed per day was 98,000 or 2.8 per cent of the Irish workforce as enumerated in the Census of 1841. The following table provides an indicator of the significance of the scheme within each of those counties using a relatively high proportion of its resources.

County	Employed on Public Works week ending 8 August 1946*	Total Workforce in 1841*	Relief Workers as % of Workforce
Clare	20.0	120.5	16.6
Limerick	13.1	114.9	11.4
Galway	11.6	180.5	6.4
Roscommon	9.2	99.8	9.2
Mayo	7.9	169.7	4.7
Tipperary	6.8	171.7	4.0
Cork	5.1	303.5	1.7

* (numbers in thousands)

This table helps to place in perspective the impact of the public works in the counties in which they were most used. In the most heavily affected areas, the scale of relief was significant but does not justify the accusation of the government and other relief officials that the demand was 'excessive', although such a term is inherently ambiguous.

Nevertheless, a major feature of the pattern of relief is the wide disparity in the level of uptake. The most plausible general explanation for this pattern is that the use of the scheme mirrors need, as already suggested. For example, the affected counties have a relatively high dependence on agriculture, and within that context, a heavy dependence on the potato. This lack of economic diversity contributes to the vulnerability of some areas and hence their dependence on external aid, as represented by the public works. For example:

County	% of people employed in agriculture in 1841
Clare	61.9
Mayo	62.8
Roscommon	64.5
All Ireland	51.0

The public pronouncements of the government regarding the alleged 'over-subscription' of the public works do not, in fact, reflect the true situation. It may be noted, however, that the official description of the statistics are themselves misleading, as they continually refer to the 'Number of Persons Employed on the Relief Works' and then quote numbers which, in fact, refer to the number of man-days of work undertaken. Thus one person working a six-day week is counted as six 'persons'. It is not possible to say whether the use of such terminology and the type of data provided, either deliberately or inadvertently, helped to create a false impression of the scale of the scheme. It does, however, require careful interpretation of the official data to obtain a true perspective of the limited local impact of the public works, even in areas of high usage.

Appendix 3

Analysis of Variability in the take-up of Soup Rations in the Poor Law Unions of Ireland in 1847

1. For a limited period during 1847 daily food rations were issued in Ireland, for the most part gratuitously, to those qualifying as being in need of assistance. As an indicator of the geographical distribution of distress during an intense period of scarcity and famine, the take-up figures for food rations, expressed as a percentage of the population of each Poor Law union, provides some insights into the demand for relief, although there are some problems associated with this source of information. The advantages and disadvantages of the data are indicated below:

Advantages

    i. The rate of take-up is less constrained by a limit on supply than earlier forms of relief e.g. workhouse relief has a capacity constraint, both public works and government food depots are of limited value as indicators of demand for relief—determined by the success in bringing a public work to the area and by the amount of corn which had been imported by the government. It is also free from earlier restrictions imposed on the claimants for relief, e.g. the 'destitution' requirement necessary to gain access to workhouses or the £6 valuation clause to be enforced by the relief committees. Because it was free from such restrictions, the issue of food, usually in the form of soup, in the summer of 1847 is more clearly an indicator of unrestrained, but genuine demand for relief, and, as such, is likely to be a more accurate indicator of distress.

366

ii. Data is available for the whole country on a uniform basis, i.e. according to Poor Law union.

Disadvantages

i. The issue of rations could be subject to some (unspecified and unmeasurable) abuse that is likely to exaggerate the numbers using the system, despite the existence of controls. However, unless it is assumed that there are wide disparities in the propensity to commit fraud (in effect, an assumption that the population of one county is less honest than that of another), the effect on patterns of take-up is likely to be limited.

ii. The provision of gratuitous food rations was not the only form of relief in the summer of 1847. Workhouse relief was still available throughout the country. Relief extraneous to the government food ration scheme was also available, although on a much limited scale. For example, some additional soup kitchens were opened by individuals and private charities. The existing evidence for this is scarce but suggests that the incidence of private relief occurred mainly in the wealthier Poor Law unions of Ulster. The provision of local, private relief indicates less dependence on external aid such as a government loan to fund a soup kitchen and more reliance on local resources. Overall, however, private activity was limited. By far the greatest amount of relief was provided through the government's relief scheme, the agent for which was the newly reconstituted relief committees.

2. Using these data, an analysis was constructed on the following basis:

i. for each Poor Law union, the maximum number of rations issued in any one day was expressed as a percentage of the population as enumerated in the 1841 Census. This rate was computed for 127 of the 130 Poor Law Unions—the Belfast, Antrim and Newtownards unions did not avail of the government scheme.

ii. using the above data, the following statistics were calculated as shown:

	value
Mean (x)	36.11
Standard deviation (sd)	21.62
Coefficient of variation o/x	0.598
(N = 127)	

367

3. The purpose of these calculations was to assist in the construction of an indicator of the geographical distribution of distress in the summer of 1847 using the percentage of the population receiving rations as a measure. It is not suggested that this measure is any other than one of several indicators of distress, although it does possess a uniqueness in view of its ability to display a less restricted (as opposed to earlier systems of relief) demand for assistance in the form of food, as discussed earlier.

4. As a simple method of classifying the Poor Law unions into varying levels of distress, the following divisions were used, based on the relationship of the standard deviation (sd) from the mean (x):

General description	Basis of measure	Threshold values	No. of PLU
Very high distress	x + 2 sd	79.35	6
High distress	x + 1½ sd	68.54	11
Fairly high	x + 1 sd	57.81	22
Average	x +/- 1 sd		51
Fairly low	x - 1 sd	14.49	19
Little distress	x - 1½ sd	3.68	3

Explanation of terms:
sd = Standard deviation
(1)= refers to the use of these values. A value falls into a given category. Forty per cent of Poor Law unions have values that are within the range x +/- 1 sd.

5. The distribution of Poor Law unions values indicates a relatively dispersed pattern. For example, the 'normal distribution', although a statistical concept, would anticipate 68 per cent of values to lie within one standard deviation of the mean, compared with the 40 per cent indicated above. This is partly the evidence of 'skewness', or the extent to which the distribution of Poor Law union values departs from a symmetrical pattern. The measure of skewness in this distribution -0.53 (it is zero for a normal or symmetrical distribution). This figure suggests a significant departure from symmetry, with a consequently dispersed set of values. Moreover, as the above table indicates, the skewness has a bias in a particular direction, namely in favour of a relative concentration upon higher values, which in this analysis indicates higher levels of distress.

Map 3 shows the geographical distribution of those values that are greater than one sd difference from the mean. Clear concentrations emerge from a high/very high level of distress in the west of Ireland, with low levels being concentrated in the north, north-east and around Dublin.

Note:- The following alternative names are sometimes used:
Irvinestown for Lowtherstown; Newtown Limavady
for Limavady.

Map 3: Take-up of Soup Rations as an Indication of distress, by Poor Law Union, in the summer of 1847

Very High Distress: **79.35 or more per cent**: Ballinrobe, Clifden, Gort, Swinford, Tuam, Westport

High Distress: **68.5 to 79.3 per cent**: Ballina, Castlebar, Ennistymon, Galway, Newcastle

Fairly High Distress: **57.8 to 68.5 per cent**: Bantry, Cahirsiveen, Ennis, Kanturk, Kenmare, Kilrush, Lismore, Listowel, Rathkeale, Roscommon, Scariff

Therefore, the statistical analysis and the visual evidence of the mapping levels of distress demonstrate the existence in the summer of 1847 of significant contrasts in the geographical distribution of distress in Ireland.

Diversity Within Poor Law Unions

While it is possible to demonstrate considerable diversity in the intensity of distress between Poor Law unions, the next part of the analysis examines the extent of diversity within Poor Law unions. The analysis is based upon the following data and calculations:

a. within a selected group of Poor Law unions, the proportion of the population receiving food rations in 1847 in each electoral division was calculated;

b. these data were then used to estimate the mean and the standard deviation in each of the Poor Law unions. From these estimates, a calculation of the coefficient of variation was made.

The limited number of electoral divisions within each Poor Law union places obvious constraints upon the confidence limits associated with this statistical analysis. However, as a general indicator, which is as much qualitative as quantitative, the coefficient of variation has been used as a convenient method of comparing, from a sample of Poor Law unions, the extent of diversity between:

    i. all Poor Law unions within Ireland

    ii. selected poor Law unions within each of the statistical bands outlined above, whose internal diversity is measured. The analysed unions were chosen on the basis of selecting the median value within each statistical band.

Poor Law Unions: Analysis of internal diversity on the basis of the percentage of the population in each electoral division receiving gratuitous rations in the summer of 1847

Category	PLU	No. of EDs	xp	xe	ve
x + 2sd	Westport	10	85.7	87.1	0.16
x + 1½sd	Castlebar	10	75.9	81.4	0.16
x + 1sd	Kilrush	13	62.3	53.4	0.26
	Limerick	19	54.03	65.0	0.26
x + - 1sd	Mallow	13	39.96	44.6	0.33
	Manorhamilton	10	16.14	15.5	0.31
x - 1sd	Cookstown	16	10.74	10.1	0.32
x - 1½sd	Kilkeel*	3/10	2.12	-	-
All Ireland			36.1		0.598

* No scope for meaningful analysis in this union as only three out of the ten electoral divisions came within the government's scheme

Key:

   xp = population average of take-up

   xe = average take-up calculated as the mean value of the individual EDs

   ve = coefficient of variation

(See further notes below on the statistics.)

These results indicate that the level of variability in the incidence of distress is much greater between Poor Law unions than within Poor Law unions. This does not suggest that significant differences do not occur between the electoral divisions that comprises each Poor Law union as measured by the coefficient or variation (v) as shown above. The results of this analysis of sample Poor Law unions indicates:

a. The variability of distress at the national level of all Ireland is much greater than at the local level. However, there is significantly more variation within Poor Law unions than have 'middling' overall levels of distress, than in others facing severe distress, as revealed by the (ve) values above. The scope for variation is, of course, greater away from localities with very high overall figures of take-up of rations.

b. Within the Poor Law unions, the range of values recorded is wide, e.g.

Division	*Highest Figure*	*Lowest Figure*
Castlebar	103.2	63.7
Kilrush	87.2	32.7
Limerick	107.07	37.2
Mallow	69.0	15.2
Manorhamilton	25.7	11.4
Cookstown	14.1	3.2

Notes on the Analysis

i. The results for Kilkeel indicated a position where 70 per cent of the electoral divisions did not record any use of the government soup kitchens. This resulted in too few observations for a viable statistical analysis. A similar pattern to this is apparent in a few other unions, for example in the Dunfanaghy union, where only one of the ten electoral divisions established a government soup kitchen.

ii. The calculation of the mean and the standard deviation (sd) on the basis of electoral divisions resulted, of course, in an unweighted average (denominated as xe) compared with the true overall mean of (xp). The calculation of xe is a necessary step in the estimation of ve.

References

GLOSSARY OF ABBREVIATIONS

BG	Board of Guardians
BRA	British Relief Association
CSORP	Chief Secretary's Office, Registered Papers
NAD	National Archives, Dublin
NLI	National Library, Ireland
PLC	Poor Law Commissioner
PLI	Poor Law Inspector
PROL	Public Record Office, London
PRONI	Public Record Office, Northern Ireland
TRA	Temporary Relief Act

CHAPTER 1. BACKGROUND: THE RAGS AND WRETCHED CABINS OF IRELAND 1845 (pp. 1–30)

1. The view that a famine was inevitable has a long history and continues to be generally accepted by a number of British and American historians. Proponents of this view include Thomas Malthus, 'Newenham and Others on the State of Ireland', *Edinburgh Review*, July 1808; Nassau W. Senior, *Journals, Essays and Conversation Relating to Ireland* (2 vols, London 1868), vol. 1, p. 208; T.S. Ashton, *The Industrial Revolution* (London 1948), p. 161; K.H. Connell, *The Population of Ireland, 1750-1845* (Oxford 1951); Barbara L. Solow, *The Land Question and the Irish Economy* (Mass 1971); Samuel Clark, *Social Origins of the Irish Land War* (Princeton 1979), pp. 41-3; Peter Mathias, *The First Industrial Nation* 2nd ed. (Suffolk 1983), pp. 57-9, 177, 202; quote from

Thomas Malthus, *An Essay on the Principle of Population as it Affects the Future Improvement of Society* (first pub. London 1798, reprinted Cambridge 1992), book IV, chapter XI. For a reappraisal of this interpretation see Joel Mokyr, *Why Ireland Starved* (London 1983); J.S. Donnelly in W.E. Vaughan (ed.), *A New History of Ireland* vol.v (Oxford 1989); Kevin O'Rourke, 'Did the Great Irish Famine Matter?' *The Journal of Economic History*, vol. 51 (March 1991).

2. Mr and Mrs S.C. Hall, *Ireland, its Scenery, Character etc.*, 3 vols (London 1841-3); one-volume edition, ed. Michael Scott (London 1984), p. 406; Cormac Ó Gráda, *The Great Irish Famine* (Dublin 1989) p. 26.

3. Cormac Ó Gráda, *Ireland Before and After the Famine* (2nd ed., Manchester 1993), pp. 22-38; Liam Kennedy and Philip Ollerenshaw (eds), *An Economic History of Ulster* (Manchester 1985), preface, pp. 1-109; Jonathan Bardon, *A History of Ulster* (Belfast 1992), pp. 183-385; C. Feinstein and S. Pollard (eds), *Studies in Capital Formation in the United Kingdom* (London 1988).

4. E. Margaret Crawford, 'Subsistence Crises and Famines in Ireland: a nutritionist's view', in E. Margaret Crawford (ed.), *Famine, The Irish Experience, 900-1900* (Edinburgh 1989) pp. 207-9; P.M. Austin Bourke, *The Visitation of God? The Potato and the Great Irish Famine*, (Dublin 1993).

5. See, for example, quote on page xxx; Austin Bourke, *The Visitation of God?* pp. 67-71.

6. *General Report, Report of the Commissioners Appointed to take the Census of Ireland for the year 1841*, 1843 [504] xxiv, passim.

7. I am grateful to Angela Day of the Institute of Irish Studies, Belfast, for allowing me access to transcripts of the reports of the Ordnance Survey Officers who surveyed Ulster in the 1830s.

8. P.M. Austin Bourke, 'The Extent of the Potato Crop in Ireland at the Time of the Famine', *Journal of the Statistical and Social Enquiry Society of Ireland*, xx, part 3, 1959-60, p.11.

9. K. Theodore Hoppen, *Elections, Politics and Society in Ireland 1832-1885* (Oxford 1984); D.G. Wright, *Democracy and Reform 1815-85* (London n.d.), pp. 50-51.

10. A. Smith, *An Enquiry into the Nature and Causes of the Wealth of Nations* (first pub. London 1776; London 1976), p. 540.

11. J.S. Mill, *Principles of Political Economy* (London 1909), pp. 945-7; David Ricardo, *Works and Correspondence*; Thomas Malthus, *An Essay on the Principles of Population*; Thomas Malthus, *Principles of Political Economy* (London 1820); T.A. Boylan and T.P. Foley, *Political Economy and Colonial Ireland* (London 1992).

12. Edmund Burke, *Thoughts and Details on Scarcity* (London 1795).

13. Brian Inglis, *Poverty and the Industrial Revolution* (London 1971), p. 458.

14. *General Report of the Census Commissioners*, 1841, pp. v-liii; Mokyr, *Why Ireland Starved*, pp. 38-45; P.P. Boyle and Cormac Ó Gráda, 'Fertility Trends, Excess Mortality and the Great Irish Famine', in *Demography* xxiii (1986).

15. Ibid., pp. xvii-xxiii; Ó Gráda, *Ireland Before and After the Famine*, p. 36.

16. Malcolm Falkus, *Britain Transformed: an economic and social history 1700-1914* (Ormskirk 1987) pp. 60-75; Ó Gráda, *Ireland Before and After the Famine*, pp. 33-44; J. Brewer, *The Sinews of Power: money and the English state* (London 1989).

17. Lord George Hill, *Facts from Gweedore* (3rd ed. 1853), pp. 22-8.
18. Hall and Hall, *Ireland* (1984 ed.), p. xviii; see also *First Report of His Majesty's Commissioners for inquiring into the condition of the poorer classes in Ireland, with appendix and supplement*, 1835 [369], xxxii, part 1; *Third Report from His Majesty's Commissioners for inquiring into the condition of the poorer classes in Ireland*, 1836 [35] xxx, 1; *Report by George Nicholls to His Majesty's Secretary of State for the Home Department on Poor Laws, Ireland* 1837 [69] li, 353.
19. Malthus, *Essay on the Principle of Population*, book 1.
20. E.P. Thompson, *The Making of the English Working Class* (Hardmondsworth 1968), pp. 293-5; R.D. Collison Black, *Economic Thought and the Irish Question 1817-1870* (Cambridge 1960).
21. Eric J. Hobsbawn, *The Age of Revolution 1789-1848* (London 1962), passim; Eric J. Hobsbawn and George Rudé, *Captain Swing* (London 1969); Inglis, *Poverty*, pp. 301-2, 377-9: D. Thompson, *The Chartists* (London 1984).
22. Ibid. p. 445; J.D. Marshall, *The Old Poor Law 1795-1834* (London 1973), pp. 22-30; Michael E. Rose, *The English Poor Law 1780-1930* (Newton Abbot 1971).
23. Thompson, *The English Working Class*, p. 295; Eric Hopkins, *A Social History of the English Working Classes* (London 1986), pp. 89-91; Mark Blaug, The Myth of the Old Poor Law and the Making of the New, in *Journal of Economic History* xxiii, 1963.
24. 'Population and Growth in the United Kingdom', from Mitchell and Deane (1962) reprinted in Mathias, *The First Industrial Nation*, appendix, table 1; R. Schofield, D. Reher, and A. Bideau (eds), *The Decline of Mortality in Europe* (Cambridge 1991); E.A. Wrigley and R.S. Schofield, *The Population History of England, 1541-1871: a reconstruction* (Cambridge 1981).
25. Smith, *The Wealth of Nations*, book 1, quoted in Mathias, *The First Industrial Nation*, p. 174.
26. Ó Gráda, *Ireland Before and After the Famine*, pp. 1, 15-19.
27. Quoted in Joel Mokyr, *Why Ireland Starved*, p. 38.
28. Malthus, *An Essay on the Principle of Population*, book IV, chapter VIII, p. 270; in Inglis, *Poverty*, pp. 274-7.
29. Ibid., p. 284.
30. Black, *Economic Thought*, pp. 89-90; Inglis, *Poverty*, pp. 155-6; Friedrich Engels, *The Condition of the Working Class in England in 1844* (London 1892), pp. 196-8.
31. Quoted in Inglis, *Poverty*, p. 235.
32. James Kelly, 'Scarcity and Poor Relief in Eighteenth-Century Ireland: the subsistence crisis of 1782-84', in *Irish Historical Studies*, vol. xxviii, no. 109, May 1992, pp. 38-62.
33. Black, *Economic Thought*, pp. 91-104.
34. T.G. Conway, 'The Approach to an Irish Poor Law 1828-33', in *Eire-Ireland*, vol. vi, 1971, pp. 65-81.
35. *Dictionary of National Biography*, pp. 1334-40; *Third report of the Commissioners for inquiring into the condition of the poorer classes in Ireland.*
36. *Letter from N.W. Senior, on the Third Report of the Commissioners for inquiring into the condition of the poor in Ireland*, 1837 [90] li, 253, p. 4.
37. *Remarks on Third Report of the Commissioners*, by G.C. Lewis, 1837 [91] li, pp. 10-31.

38. Lord John Russell, quoted in *Royal Commission on the Poor Laws and the relief of distress. Report on Ireland*, 1909 [4630] xxxvii, p. 8.

39. John Prest, *Lord John Russell* (London 1972), pp. 113-14; Peter Mandler, *Aristocratic Government in the Age of Reform: Whigs and Liberals 1830-1852* (Oxford 1990).

40. Black, *Economic Thought*, p. 104.

41. Russell to Nicholls, *Report by George Nicholls to His Majesty's Secretary of State for the Home Department, on Poor Laws, Ireland*, 1837, [69] li, pp. 1-2; H.G. Willinck (grandson of G. Nicholls), in preface to George Nicholls, *History of the English Poor Law* (London 1898), p. xxxviii.

42. George Nicholls, *A History of the Irish Poor Law* (London 1856), p. 159.

43. Nicholls to Russell, *Report by George Nicholls . . .* , p. 9.

44. Ibid., p. 11.

45. *Second Report by George Nicholls to His Majesty's Secretary of State for the Home Department, on Poor Laws, Ireland*, 1837-8 [104], xxxviii, pp. 3-13.

46. R.B. O'Brien, *Fifty Years of Concessions to Ireland 1831-1881*, 2 vols (London 1883), p. 562; R.B. McGrath, 'Introduction of Poor Law to Ireland', unpublished M.A. dissertation, UCD 1965, pp. 171-90.

47. D. Large, 'The House of Lords and Ireland in the Age of Peel 1830-50', in *Irish Historical Studies*, vol. ix, 1955, p. 367; O'Brien, *Fifty Years*, p. 564.

48. *Hansard* 3, xlii, pp. 715-17 (30 April 1838); ibid., xliv, pp. 28-9 (9 July 1838).

49. Nicholls, *Irish Poor Law*, p. 150; Lord John Russell to Poor Law Commissioners, *Fifth Annual Report of Poor Law Commissioners 1839*, 11 August 1838; P.L. Commissioners to Joseph Burke, Assistant Poor Law Commissioner, Letter-Books of Joseph Burke (hereafter Letter-Books) (National Archives, Ireland), 23 June 1840.

50. 1 & 2 Vic. c. 56. An Act for the more effectual relief of the Destitute Poor in Ireland.

51. Black, *Economic Thought*, passim; Poor Law (P.L.) Commissioners to all Assistant P.L. Commissioners, Letter-Books, 11 September 1838; Nicholls, *Irish Poor Law*, pp. 238-45.

52. J.S. Mill, *Principles of Political Economy*, Book v, p. 946; Foley, *Political Economy*.

53. Rose, *The English Poor Law*; N.C. Edsall, *The Anti-Poor Law Movement 1834-44* (Manchester 1971), p.70; A. Brundage, *The Making of the New Poor Law* (London 1978) p. 131; Nicholls, *Irish Poor Law*, p. 245; *Appendix to Eighth Annual Report of P.L. Commissioners* (hereafter, *Annual Report*), 1842, p. 357; Eleventh Annual Report, 1845, p. 34.

54. P.L. Commissioners to all Assistant Commissioners, Letter-Books, 9 October 1838; Ibid., P.L. Commissioners to Burke, 27 June 1839; *Fifth Annual Report*, 1839, p. 62; Evidence of G. Gulson (Assistant P.L. Commissioner), *Reports of the Select Committee of the House of Lords, appointed to inquire into the operation of the Irish Poor Law, and the expediency of making any amendment in its enactments*, 1849 [192] xvi, pp. 88-90; ibid., evidence of E. Senior, pp. 146-8; ibid., evidence of A. Power, pp. 91-2.

55. Burke to P.L. Commissioners, *Letter-Books*, 21 December 1841; Minute Book of Belfast Union, 9 August 1842.

56. P.L. Commissioners to Chief Secretary, Dublin Castle, Chief Secretary's Office Registered Papers (CSORP) National Archives, Ireland, 0.6210, 27 February 1841, 25 May 1841.

57. Ó Gráda, *The Great Irish Famine*, pp. 19-20.

58. David Dickson, 'The Gap in Famines: a useful myth?', in Crawford (ed.), *Famine, The Irish Experience*, pp. 96-111; ibid. 'William Wilde's Table of Irish Famines, 900-1850', pp. 1-30; *Eighth Annual Report*, 1842, p. 50.

59. Ó Gráda, *Ireland Before and After the Famine*, p. 4.

60. T.P. O'Neill, 'The Famine of 1822', unpublished M.A. dissertation (NUI 1966).

61. *Ulster Times*, 29 August 1839; Minute Book of Killarney Union, 15 May 1841, 29 April 1843; Minute Book of Dunshaughlin Union, 24 January 1843.

62. Report to Chief Secretary, Dublin Castle, CSORP, 73/4145, 7 January 1839.

63. Minutes of P.L. Commissioners, quoted in *Report of Royal Commission on the Poor Laws*, 1909, (4630) xxxvii, p. 13.

64. *Morning Register*, 22 March 1839; *Sixth Annual Report*, 1840, p. 56; P.L. Commissioners to Burke, CSORP, 73/4488, 21 June 1839; Memorial from Castleblayney, CSORP, 73/4145, 7 January 1839; Nicholls, *Irish Poor Law*, p. 1258.

65. *Eighth Annual Report*, 1842, p. 50; Chief Secretary to Richard Hall (Assistant P.L. Commissioner in charge of the relief operations), CSORP, 00.7838, 18 June 1842.

66. Ibid., Hall to Chief Secretary, Carton 1097, 15 June 1842; ibid., Hall to Chief Secretary, 20 June 1842; ibid., Castlebar Guardians to Lord Lieutenant, Z.7430, 9 June 1842; ibid., P.L. Commissioners to Chief Secretary, 0.8664, 2 July 1842; Burke to Home Secretary, Letter-Books, 9 June 1842, 15 June 1842; ibid., Hall to Burke, 17 June 1842.

67. Hall to Chief Secretary, CSORP, Carton 1097, 20 June 1842; ibid., C. Otway (Assistant P.L. Commissioner) to P.L. Commissioners, Z. 9156, 6 July 1842.

68. *Eleventh Annual Report*, 1845, passim; Evidence of E. Senior (Assistant P.L. Commissioner), *Select Committee on the Irish Poor Law*, 1849, p. 133.

69. P.L. Commissioners to D. Phelan (Assistant P.L. Commissioner), Letter-Books, 18 October 1842; Sister P. Kelly, 'From Workhouse to Hospital: the role of the Irish workhouses in medical relief to 1921', unpublished M.A. dissertation UCG (1972).

CHAPTER 2. A BLIGHT OF UNUSUAL CHARACTER 1845-6 (pp. 31–70)

1. *Londonderry Journal*, 22 September 1845.

2. From *Gardener's Chronicle and Horticultural Gazette*, 16 August 1845, reprinted in *Londonderry Journal*, 26 August 1845.

3. Ibid., 2 September 1845, 9 September 1845.

4. *Gardener's Chronicle and Horticultural Gazette*, 16 September 1845.

5. *Londonderry Journal*, 9 September 1845.

6. E.M. Crawford, 'Subsistence Crises and Famines in Ireland: a nutritionist's view' in Crawford, *Famine, the Irish Experience*.

7. Cormac Ó Gráda, *The Great Irish Famine*, pp. 62-3.

8. E.C. Large, *The Advance of the Fungi* (London 1940) passim; P.M. Austin Bourke, *The Visitation of God?* (Dublin 1993), pp. 129-59.

9. *Londonderry Journal*, September and October 1845; *Dublin Evening Mail*, September and October 1845.

10. *Cork Examiner*, 10 October 1845, 20 October 1845; *Freeman's Journal*, 13 November 1845.

11. Sir Robert Peel to Sir James Graham, 13 October 1845, C.S. Parker, *Sir Robert Peel from His Private Letters* (2nd ed., London 1899), p. 233 (hereafter, Parker, *Peel*).

12. *Copy of the report of Dr Playfair and Mr Lindley on the present state of the Irish potato crop, and on the prospect of the approaching scarcity* 1846 [28], xxxviii; *Report of the Commissioners of Inquiry into matters connected with the failure of the potato crop, 6 February 1846*, 1846, [33], xxxvii.

13. Ibid., Sir Robert Peel to the Duke of Wellington, 21 October 1845, p. 226.

14. Ibid., Sir Robert Peel to the Duke of Wellington, 21 October 1845, p. 223.

15. Ibid., Dr Lyon Playfair to Sir Robert Peel, 26 October 1845, p. 225.

16. Ibid.

17. Peel to Sir Henry Hardinge, marked 'Secret', 16 December 1845, Parker, *Peel*, p. 280.

18. Ibid., Sir Thomas Fremantle to Peel, 5 November 1845, p. 229.

19. Report of Lindley and Playfair, passim.

20. *Freeman's Journal*, 19 December 1845.

21. Sir James Graham to Sir Robert Peel, 15 August 1845, in Parker, *Peel*, p. 533.

22. Torrens, *The Life and Times of Sir James Graham* vol. II (London 1863), pp. 413-14; Parker, *Peel*, p. 534.

23. Torrens, *Sir James Graham*, p. 418.

24. Norman Gash, *Sir Robert Peel: the life of Sir Robert Peel after 1830* (London 1972) passim.

25. Memorandum laid before Cabinet by Sir Robert Peel, 1 November 1845, Parker, *Peel*, p. 227.

26. Sir James Graham to Sir Robert Peel, 22 October 1845, Parker, *Peel*, p. 226.

27. Ibid., pp. 229-34; ibid., pp. 239-46.

28. Quoted in Mary Daly, *The Famine in Ireland* (Dundalk 1986), p. 69.

29. Torrens, *Sir James Graham*, p. 418.

30. Sir Robert Peel to Sir James Graham, 13 October 1845, Parker, *Peel*, p. 223.

31. Confidential letter from Sir James Graham, 2 December 1845, quoted in Torrens, *Sir James Graham*, p. 419.

32. Sir James Graham to Lord Lieutenant, 7 May 1846, *Correspondence explanatory of the measures adopted by Her Majesty's government for the relief of distress arising from the failure of the potato crop in Ireland*, 1846 [736] xxxvii, p. 184 (hereafter *Correspondence explanatory*).

33. Ibid., Routh to Trevelyan, 23 March 1846, p. 75.

34. Ibid., Trevelyan to Routh, 26 January 1846, p. 68.

35. Ibid., Routh to Trevelyan, 9 January 1846, p. 58.

36. Ibid., Trevelyan to Routh, 4 February 1846, p. 79.

37. Ibid., Trevelyan to Routh, 3 February 1846, p. 77.

38. Instructions to relief committees, February 1846, Relief Commission papers (NAI).

39. Routh to Trevelyan, 7 February 1846, *Correspondence explanatory*, p. 83.

40. Ibid., Routh to Trevelyan, 31 July 1846, p. 217.

41. Ibid., Routh to Trevelyan, 9 April 1846, p. 146.

42. Routh to Trevelyan, 14 February 1846, *Correspondence explanatory*, p. 86.
43. Ibid., Report of Edward Lucas, Chairman of Relief Commission, to Trevelyan, 20 January 1846, p. 1.
44. Ibid.
45. Routh to Trevelyan, 31 July 1846, *Correspondence explanatory*, p. 218.
46. Ibid., Graham to Lord Lieutenant, 7 May 1846, p. 181.
47. Ibid., Trevelyan to Routh, 20 February 1846, p. 95.
48. *Instructions to Committees of Relief Districts, extracted from Minutes of the proceedings of the Commissioners appointed in reference to the apprehended scarcity*, 1846 [171] xxxvii, p. 1.
49. Ibid.
50. Ibid., p. 2.
51. Ibid.
52. Amount of sums raised by local relief committees; *Dublin Evening Post*, 6 June 1846.
53. Ibid.
54. Ó Gráda, *Ireland Before and After the Famine*, pp. 118-22; 'The Arran Islands during the Great Famine', *Donegal Annual*, vol. x, 1971.
55. Routh to Trevelyan, 31 July 1846, *Correspondence explanatory*, p. 218.
56. Ibid.
57. Ibid.
58. E.M. Crawford, 'Subsistence Crises and Famines in Ireland: a nutritionist's view', in Crawford (ed.), *Famine, the Irish Experience*, passim.
59. Routh to Trevelyan, 31 July 1846, *Correspondence explanatory*, pp. 218-20.
60. Ibid., Routh to Trevelyan, 6 March 1846, p. 109.
61. Crawford, op. cit., pp. 213-15.
62. Edward Pine Coffin to Trevelyan, *Correspondence explanatory*, 30 March 1846, p. 136.
63. Ibid. Trevelyan to Routh, 20 February 1846, p. 136.
64. Ibid., Routh to Trevelyan, 31 July 1846, pp. 219-20.
65. Ibid.
66. Sums raised by relief committees.
67. Routh to Trevelyan, 31 July 1846, *Correspondence explanatory*, pp. 218-20.
68. Ibid.
69. Ibid., Trevelyan to Routh, 29 June 1846, p. 235; ibid., Trevelyan to Routh, 8 July 1846, p. 259.
70. Routh to Trevelyan, 31 July 1846, *Correspondence explanatory*, pp. 218-20.
71. *A statement of the total expenditure for purposes of relief in Ireland since November 1845, distinguishing final payments from sums which have been or are to be repaid*, 1846 [15], vol. xxvii, p.1.
72. Deputy Commissary-General Dobree to Trevelyan, 5 June 1846, *Correspondence explanatory*, p. 208; ibid., Trevelyan to Routh, 13 March 1846, p. 118.
73. Ibid., Routh to Trevelyan, 31 July 1846, pp. 218-22.
74. Ó Gráda, *Ireland Before and After the Famine*, pp. 108-9.
75. Routh to Trevelyan, 4 June 1846, *Correspondence explanatory*, p. 206.
76. Ibid., Trevelyan to Routh, 4 July 1846, p. 242.
77. Ibid., Trevelyan to Routh, 29 June 1846, p. 236.

78. Ibid. Trevelyan to Routh, 8 July 1846, p. 257.
79. Ibid., Commissary-General Hewetson to Trevelyan, 5 July 1846, p. 224; ibid., Captain Perceval to Trevelyan, 1 July 1846, p. 240.
80. Ibid., Trevelyan to Routh, 4 July 1846, p. 242.
81. Sums raised by relief committees.
82. Annual reports of Poor Law Commissioners, 1845-52.
83. Routh to Trevelyan, 1 April 1846, *Correspondence explanatory*, p. 139.
84. Ibid., Commissary-General Coffin to Trevelyan, 24 June 1846, p. 227.
85. Ibid., Routh to Trevelyan, 31 July 1846, p. 223.
86. Ibid., p. 222.
87. Ibid., Pole to Trevelyan, 10 April 1846, p. 148.
88. Ibid., Trevelyan to Routh, 29 April 1846, p. 177.
89. Ibid., Pole to Trevelyan, 18 May 1846, p. 148; ibid., Coffin to Trevelyan, 11 April 1846, p. 151; ibid., Dobree to Trevelyan, 24 April 1846, p. 175.
90. Ibid., Coffin to Trevelyan, 11 April 1846, p. 152.
91. Ibid., Trevelyan to Routh, 24 July 1846, p. 166; Routh to Trevelyan, 31 July 1846, p. 222; ibid., Routh to Trevelyan, 14 July 1846, p. 260.
92. *Final Report of the Board of Public Works in Ireland, September 1847* 1849 [1047], xxiii, p.3.
93. Memorandum on the relief of suffering arising from scarcity in Ireland, 24 February 1832, CSORP, National Archives Ireland (NAI).
94. A.R. Griffiths, 'The Irish Board of Works during the Famine years', in *Historical Journal*, vol. xiii, no. 4 (1970), passim.
95. Peel to Sir Thomas Fremantle, 3 November 1845, Parker, *Peel*, p. 229.
96. Acts, 9 Vic., cap.1; 9 Vic., cap.2; 9 Vic., cap.3; 9 Vic., cap.4.
97. *Final Report . . . Public Works*, p.3.
98. *Return of all sums of money either granted or advanced from the Exchequer of the United Kingdom, on account of the Distress and Famine*, 1849 [352] 48, p. 5.
99. Trevelyan to Fremantle, Chief Secretary, 26 February 1846, *Correspondence explanatory*, pp. 223-4; ibid., C. Trevelyan, Report on public works for the relief of scarcity in Ireland, 8 March 1846, p. 355.
100. Ibid., Lieutenant-Colonel Jones to Earl of Lincoln, 9 April 1846, p. 355.
101. Ibid., Commissioners of Public Works to Pennefeather, Under-Secretary, 9 February 1846, pp. 319-20; ibid., Fremantle to Trevelyan, 26 February 1846, p. 321.
102. Ibid., Report of C.E. Trevelyan on Grants for the Relief of Distress in Ireland, 15 April 1846.
103. Griffith, 'Board of Works', p. 636.
104. Jones to Trevelyan, 2 May 1846, *Correspondence explanatory*, p. 366.
105. Ibid., Commissioners of Public Works to Treasury, 7 July 1846, p. 385.
106. Ibid., 7 April 1846, p. 346.
107. Ibid., p. 347.
108. Ibid., 7 July 1846, p. 385.
109. Ibid., 8 August 1846, p. 404.

110. Ibid., Trevelyan to Jones, 16 March 1846, p. 331; ibid., Treasury Minute, 3 April 1846, p. 343.

111. Griffiths, 'Board of Works', p. 637.

112. Ibid., Treasury Minute, 26 June 1846, p. 382.

113. Ibid., Pennefeather to Trevelyan, 30 June 1846, p. 382.

114. Griffiths, 'Board of Works', p. 638.

115. Commissioners of Public Works to the Treasury, 8 August 1846, *Correspondence explanatory*, pp. 351-2; *Abstract return of the number of persons employed on the relief works for the week ending 8 August. Measures adopted for the relief of distress in Ireland, Board of Works series*, 1847 [764], l, pp. 80, 104. Return of men employed on Public Works for one week ending 18 July, *Correspondence explanatory. Board of Works series*, 1846 [735], xxxvii, p. 347.

116. Ibid.

117. Abstract of nos. employed . . . week ending 8 August, p. 80.

118. Census of Ireland for 1841 (Dublin 1843), p. 161.

119. Treasury Minute, 21 July 1846, *Correspondence explanatory*, pp. 393-4.

120. Office of Public Works to Board of Works, 25 August 1846, *Measures adopted . . . Board of Works*, p. 80.

121. Sir Randolph Routh to Trevelyan, 1 January 1846, *Correspondence explanatory*, p. 56.

122. C. Kinealy, 'The Irish Poor Law, 1838-62', unpublished Ph.D dissertation (TCD 1984), pp. 54-60.

123. Minute of Poor Law Commissioners, quoted in *Report of Royal Commission on the Poor Laws and relief of distress (Ireland)*, H.C. 1909 [4630] xxxvii, 1, p. 13 (hereafter, Royal Commission).

124. Sixth Annual Report of Poor Law Commissioners, 1840, p. 56 (hereafter, Annual Report); Commissioners to Joseph Burke, Assistant Poor Law Commissioner (APLC), CSORP, 1839 73/4488, 21 June 1839.

125. Burke to Home Secretary, Letter-Books of Joseph Burke, 9 June 1842.

126. Richard Hall, APLC in charge of relief operations, to Chief Secretary, CSORP, Carton 1097, 20 June 1842.

127. Joseph Burke to Home Secretary, Letter-Books, 9 June 1842; ibid., Richard Hall to Joseph Burke, 17 June 1842; Richard Hall to Chief Secretary, CSORP, Carton 1097, 15 June 1842.

128. Minute of Poor Law Commissioners, Royal Commission, p. 13.

129. Trevelyan to Routh, 4 February 1846, *Correspondence explanatory of the measures adopted by Her Majesty's government for the relief of distress arising from the failure of the potato crop in Ireland*, 1846 [735], xxxvii, p. 26 (hereafter, *Commissariat series*).

130. See Kinealy, 'Poor Law', chapter 1, passim; Sir James Graham to the Lord Lieutenant, PROL HO 45, 1080, Box 1, 7 May 1846.

131. Ibid.

132. Routh to Trevelyan, 14 February 1847, *Commissariat series*, pp. 33-7.

133. Routh to Trevelyan, 10 February 1847, *Correspondence explanatory*, p. 87.

134. Peter Froggatt, 'The Response of the Medical Profession to the Great Famine', in Crawford (ed.), *Famine: The Irish Experience*, p. 137.

135. Act. 6 & 7 Vic. c.92. (24 August 1843); Graham to Lord Lieutenant, 7 May 1846, PROL HO 45, Box 1, 7 May 1846.

136. Twelfth Annual Report of PL Commissioners, 1846.

137. Act 1 & 2 Vic. cap. 56 (31 July 1838).

138. Circular to all boards of guardians, 29 December 1845, *Twelfth Annual Report*, 1846, p. 102-3; Twistleton to Graham, PROL HO 45, 1080, 4 December 1845; P.L. Commissioners to Kenmare guardians, Letter-Books, 5 January 1846.

139. Act. 9 Vic. c.6.

140. *Twelfth Annual Report*, 1846, p. 50; Twistleton to Graham, PROL HO 45, 1080, 4 December 1845.

141. *Twelfth Annual Report*, p. 37; P.L. Commissioners to Burke, Letter-Books, 15 November 1845.

142. Summary of weekly returns of paupers in the workhouses in Ireland, Appendix to *Twelfth Annual Report*, p. 168.

143. Minute Book of Inishowen union, 16 November 1845; Minute Book of Belfast Union, 11 November 1845; *Twelfth Annual Report*, 1846, p. 51.

144. Circular to all boards of guardians, Minute Book of Kenmare Union, 15 November 1845; Circular to all boards of guardians, Minute Book of Belfast Union, 18 November 1845; *Twelfth Annual Report*, 1846, p. 41.

145. William Myles, Medical Officer, Arragh, Co. Cavan, *Abstracts of the most serious representations made by the several medical superintendents of the Public Institutions in the provinces of Ulster, Munster, Leinster and Connaught*, 1846 [120], xxxvii, p. 2.

146. Ibid., J.P. Evans, M.D., 18 February 1846, Newmarket-on-Fergus, Co. Clare, p. 3.

147. Ibid., passim.

148. Minute Books of Longford union, 3 August 1845, 4 October 1845, 25 October 1845, 6 December 1845, 20 December 1845, 30 January 1846.

149. Minute Books of Ballymoney union, 13 October 1845, 22 December 1845, 13 July 1846.

150. Minute Books of Enniskillen union, 22 December 1845, 14 July 1846, 18 August 1846.

151. Minute Books of Lowtherstown union, 29 October 1845, 12 November 1845, 7 January 1846.

152. Minute Books of Kenmare union, 3 May 1846, 13 June 1846; Weekly Reports of the Scarcity Commissioners, 14 March 1846, *Correspondence explanatory*, p. 329.

153. Minute Books of Belfast union, 29 April 1846.

154. Ibid., 24 March 1846.

155. Abstract of Constabulary Reports, March and April 1846, PROL HO 45, 1080.

156. Ibid.

157. Routh to Trevelyan, CSORP, 0.549, 9 July 1846.

CHAPTER 3: WE CANNOT FEED THE PEOPLE (pp. 71–135)

1. *Thirteenth Annual Report of Poor Law Commissioners*, 1847, passim.

2. Lord Bessborough to Lord John Russell, 6 October 1846, quoted in G.P. Gooch (ed.), *The Later Correspondence of Lord John Russell 1840-1878*, vol. 1 (London 1925), p. 150.

3. Ibid., Charles Wood to Russell, 22 September 1846, p. 147.

4. Ibid., H. Labouchere, Chief Secretary, to Russell, 24 September 1846, p. 174.

5. Ibid., Daniel O'Connell to Russell, 12 August 1846, p. 145.

6. Black, *Economic Thought*; Boylan and Foley, *Political Economy*; *The Times*, 6 January 1847; Russell to Charles Wood, Gooch, *Russell*, 15 October 1846, p.154; see also, Peter Gray, 'British Politics and the Irish Land Question', unpublished D.Phil thesis (Cambridge 1992).

7. Ibid., Russell to Bessborough, 11 October 1846, p. 151.

8. Ibid., Russell to Lord Lansdowne, 11 October 1846, p. 151.

9. Ibid., Russell to Wood, 15 October 1846, p. 154.

10. Routh to Trevelyan, 2 April 1846, *Correspondence explanatory*, p. 88; Colonel McGregor, Constabulary, to Trevelyan, August 1846, *Correspondence explanatory of the measures adopted for the relief of distress in Ireland from July 1846 to January 1847. Commissariat series*, 1847, i [761], p. 157 (hereafter, *Commissariat series*).

11. Ibid., Trevelyan to Routh, 14 October 1846, p. 157.

12. Russell to Duke of Leinster, 17 October 1846, Gooch, *Russell*, p. 157.

13. Routh to Trevelyan, 14 July 1846, *Correspondence explanatory*, p. 208; Trevelyan to Hewetson, 29 September 1846, *Commissariat series*, p. 99; ibid., Treasury Minute, 29 September 1846, p. 63.

14. Russell to Bessborough, 11 October 1846, Gooch, *Russell*, p. 151.

15. Routh to Trevelyan, 17 February 1846, *Correspondence explanatory*, pp. 39-41; Trevelyan to Routh, *Commissariat series*, 1 October 1846, p. 106; ibid., Trevelyan to Routh, 5 October 1846, p. 119; ibid., Treasury Minute, 29 September 1846, p. 63.

16. Routh to Trevelyan, 21 October 1846, *Commissariat series*, p. 183.

17. Ibid., Statement of corn and wheat purchased for Ireland by Mr. E. Erichsen & Co., 28 October 1846, pp. 208-11.

18. Bessborough to Russell, 6 October 1846, Gooch, *Russell*, p. 149.

19. Routh to Trevelyan, 29 October 1846, *Commissariat series*, p. 207.

20. Statement of corn and wheat purchased . . . 28 October 1846, *Commissariat series*, pp. 208-11; Ibid., Return of Indian Corn purchased and arrived in Great Britain. Purchases made through the agency of Mr Erichsen, p. 506.

21. Ibid., Summary of statement of purchase of Indian corn etc. purchased by Mr Erichsen, p. 211.

22. Ibid., Estimate of quantity of corn purchased . . . 3 October 1846.

23. Ibid., Return of Indian corn purchased . . . p. 508.

24. Capt. Mann to Trevelyan, 5 November 1846, *Commissariat series*, p. 239.

25. Ibid., Trevelyan to Routh, 30 October 1846, p. 211; ibid., Trevelyan to Routh, 31 October 1846, p. 211; ibid., Trevelyan to Routh, 6 November 1846, p. 240.

26. Circular issued by Sir Randolph I. Routh to all relief committees, 9 October 1846, Relief Commission Papers.

27. Capt. Mann, Kilrush, to Trevelyan, *Commissariat series*, p. 239.

28. Ibid., Routh to Trevelyan, 21 October 1846, p. 183.

29. Ibid., Trevelyan to Routh, 15 October 1846, p. 157.

30. Ibid., Routh to Trevelyan, 28 October 1846, p. 207.

31. Ibid., Routh to Trevelyan, 29 October 1846, p. 207.

32. Ibid., Mr N. Cummin, Cork, to Trevelyan, 28 October 1846, p. 206; *Roscommon and Leitrim Gazette*, 2 January 1847, 9 January 1847, 27 March 1847.

33. Russell to Bessborough, 11 October 1846, Gooch, *Russell*, p. 151.

34. Gooch, *Russell*, p. 143.

35. Trevelyan to Routh, 18 December 1846, *Commissariat series*, p. 382.

36. Trevelyan to Routh, CSORP, 0.1957, 12 January 1847.

37. Ibid., Mann to Trevelyan, 4 November 1846, p. 382.

38. Ibid., Deputy-Assistant Commissary-General Gem to Deputy Commissary-General Dobree, 16 December 1846, p. 382.

39. Lord Jocelyn, Tollymore Park, Co. Down, to Sir Robert Peel, 13 October 1846, Parker, *Peel*, p. 464.

40. Ibid., Graham to Peel, 26 September 1846, p. 464.

41. Trevelyan to Lieutenant-Colonel Douglas, 18 January 1847, *Commissariat series*, p. 501.

42. Russell to Sir Charles Wood, 3 January 1847, Gooch, *Russell*, p. 169 (Wood succeeded to a baronetcy on his father's death on 31 December 1846).

43. Ibid., Wood to Russell, 5 January 1847, p. 169.

44. Trevelyan to Routh, 15 October 1846, *Commissariat series*, p. 157.

45. Charles Trevelyan, *The Irish Crisis* (London 1848), pp. 52-9.

46. Wood to Russell, 5 January 1847, Gooch, *Russell*, p. 169.

47. Instructions for the formation and guidance of committees for the relief of distress in Ireland consequent on the failure of the potato crop in 1846, 8 October 1846 (hereafter Instructions).

48. Statement of the sums issued in donations authorised by the Lord Lieutenant in aid of subscriptions collected by relief committees in Ireland, 14 January 1847, *Commissariat series*, p.496; *Roscommon and Leitrim Gazette*, 9 January 1847.

49. List of Subscribers to Crossroads Relief Committee, Dunfanaghy, Relief Commission Papers for Co. Donegal, National Archives Dublin, 16 January 1847. For a comparison with the Skibbereen region see P. Hickey, 'A Study of Four Peninsula Parishes in West Cork, 1796-1855', unpublished M.A. thesis (UCC 1980) and Kieran Foley, 'The Killarney Poor Law Guardians and the Famine' unpublished M.A. thesis (NUU 1987).

50. Ibid., Memorial of parishioners of West Tullaghabegley to His Excellency the Earl of Bessborough, 14 October 1846.

51. Ibid. Wybrants Olphert, Ballyconnell House, Crossroads, Co. Donegal to Routh, 13 January 1847.

52. Instructions.

53. James Grant, 'The Great Famine in the Province of Ulster: the mechanisms of relief', unpublished Ph.D thesis (Queen's University, Belfast, 1986); Bardon, *A History of Ulster* (Belfast 1992), pp. 274-8.

54. Olphert to Routh, Relief Commission Papers, 13 January 1847.

55. Lord George Hill, *Facts from Gweedore*; Asenath Nicholson, *Light and Shades of Ireland: the Famine of 1847, 1848, 1849*, vol. III (Dublin 1850).

56. *Roscommon and Leitrim Gazette*, 27 March 1847, 8 May 1847; Patrick Hickey, 'Famine, Mortality and Emigration: a profile of six parishes in the Poor Law Union of Skibbereen 1846-7' in C. Buttimer, G. O'Brien and P. Flanagan (eds) *Cork: History and Society* (Dublin 1993), p. 882. Hill to Routh, Relief Commission Papers, 10 September 1846, 6 January 1847.

57. Ibid., Distress at Gweedore, 11 January 1847.

58. Ibid., Hill to Routh, 6 January 1847.

59. Trevelyan to Routh, 18 December 1846, *Commissariat series*, p. 381.

60. Ibid.

61. *Roscommon and Leitrim Gazette*, 2 January 1847, 9 January 1847, 24 April 1847, 22 May 1947; *The Times*, 4 January 1847, 7 January 1847.

62. Both Donnelly in *New History of Ireland* and Bourke, *God's Visitation*, p. 180 argue that closing the ports would have ameliorated the situation; Trevelyan to Routh, 18 December 1846, *Commissariat series*, p. 382..

63. *Final Report of the Board of Public Works in Ireland September 1847*, 1849 [1047], xxiii, p. 7 (hereafter, *Final Report*).

64. 9 Vic., cap. 1.

65. 9 & 10 Vic., cap. 107 (28 August 1846).

66. Routh to Trevelyan, PROL, T.64.366. C.1., 3 August 1846.

67. Monthly reports of Commissioners of Public Works to the Lords of the Treasury, 9 June 1847, p. 11.

68. See various monthly reports of Board of Public Works, 1846-7.

69. *Northern Whig*, 30 March 1847.

70. Return of all sums of money either granted or advanced . . . 1849 [352] 48, p. 5.

71. *Final Report*, p. 4.

72. Royal Commission on the Poor Law and relief of distress—report on Ireland, H.C. 1909 [4630], xxxvii, p. 16.

73. *Correspondence of Board of Works from July 1846 to January 1847 relating to the measures adopted for the relief of distress in Ireland (Board of Works series)*, part i, 1847 [764], p. 140 (hereafter, *Correspondence . . . July 1846 to January 1847*).

74. *Roscommon and Leitrim Gazette*, 2 January 1847; James H. Tuke, Report of the Society of Friends on distress in Ireland, NLI, Ir 9410859, December 1846.

75. S.W. Roberts, Castlebellingham to Board of Works, 5 February 1847, *Correspondence from January to March 1847 relating to the measures adopted for the relief of distress in Ireland (Board of Works series)*, part ii [797], ii, p. 69 (hereafter, *Correspondence . . . January to March*).

76. *Roscommon and Leitrim Gazette*, 27 March 1847; Jones to Trevelyan, 10 December 1846, *Correspondence . . . July 1846 to January 1847*, p. 334.

77. Jones to Trevelyan, 18 January 1847, *Correspondence . . . January to March*, p. 17.

78. A return of outrages, showing the names of the persons injured, nature of industry, date of occurrence when committed, the officer by whom reported, with the consequent local results etc., *Correspondence . . . January to March*, p. 60.

79. Ibid., pp. 60-69.

80. Captain Wynne, Miltown Malbay, Co. Clare (with enclosures to Mr Walker, Board of Works), 12 January 1847, *Correspondence . . . January to March*, p. 7.

81. Ibid., p. 66.

82. Ibid., pp. 60-69; *The Times*, 7 January 1847.

83. *Analysis of returns of poor employment under 9 Vic.c.1 and 9 & 10 Vic. c.107 from week ending 10 October 1846 to week ending 26 June 1847*, 1853 [169], xviii, p. 595.

84. Trevelyan to Jones, 5 December 1846, *Correspondence . . . July 1846 to January 1847*, p. 89.

85. Extract from the report of the Waterford Auxiliary Committee to the Central Relief Committee in Dublin, 7 February 1847, *Transactions of the Central Relief Committee of the Society of Friends during the Famine in Ireland in 1846 and 1847* (Dublin 1852).

86. Captain Froode, Swinford, to Walker, 8 January 1847, *Correspondence . . . January to March*, p. 6.

87. Ibid., Wynne, Milltown Malbay, to Walker, 12 January 1847, p. 7.

88. Ibid., Jones to Trevelyan, 13 January 1847, p. 7.

89. Ibid., Table showing the number of persons employed etc. up to 30 January, in Castlebellingham, Co. Louth, p. 69.

90. Treasury Minute, 10 March 1847, *First report of the Relief Commissioners, with Appendix*, 1847 [799], xvii; Jones to Trevelyan, 17 January 1847, *Correspondence . . . January to March*, p. 14.

91. *Final Report . . .* , p. 6.

92. Jones to Trevelyan, 13 Jones 1847, *Correspondence . . . January to March*, p.7; ibid., 17 January 1847, p. 14.

93. Ibid., 19 January 1847, p. 18.

94. Ibid., 13 January 1847, p. 8.

95. *Analysis of returns of poor employment under 9 Vic. c.1 and 9 & 10 Vic. c.107 from week ending 10 October 1846 to week ending 26 June 1847*, 1852 [169], xviii, p. 595.

96. Ibid.

97. *Final Report . . .* p. 4.

98. *Drainage works in operation throughout Ireland in March 1847, Reports of Board of Public Works in Ireland relating to the measures adopted for the relief of distress in March 1847*, 1847 [834], xvii, 6 April 1847, p. 7.

99. Ibid., Report of Board of Works for March 1847, p. 5.

100. Monthly Report of Board of Public Works for June 1847, *Reports of the Board of Public Works in Ireland relating to the measures adopted for the relief of distress in June 1847*, 1847, [860] xvii, p. 12.

101. Trevelyan, *Irish Crisis*, p. 43.

102. *Final Report . . .* , p. 7.

103. Ibid.

104. Monthly Reports of Board of Works for March, April, May, *Reports of Board of Public Works . . .* passim.

105. Ibid., Monthly Report of the Board of Public Works for May, p. 10.

106. Ibid., Monthly Report of the Board of Public Works for May, p. 10; *Roscommon and Leitrim Gazette*, 2 January 1847, 24 April 1847.

107. Monthly Report of the Board of Public Works for June, *Reports of the Board of Public Works . . . in June*, p. 11; *Roscommon and Leitrim Gazette*, 13 March 1847, 27 March, 1847, 3 April 1947; *The Times*, 6 March 1847, 27 March 1847.

108. *Final report . . .* , p. 7.

109. Ibid., p. 8.

110. Jones to Trevelyan, 13 January 1847, *Correspondence . . . July 1846 to January 1847*, p.334; *Roscommon and Leitrim Gazette*, 17 April 1847.

111. Jones to Trevelyan, 10 December 1846, *Correspondence . . . July 1846 to January 1847*, p. 334; *The Times*, 4 January 1847.

112. *Final Report . . .* , p. 7.
113. Minute Book of Lisnaskea union, 5 December 1846.
114. Circular to the Secretary of each relief committee, 8 December 1846.
115. 'The Jobbing on the Public Works', published in *The Sligo Champion*, reprinted in the *Northern Whig*, 6 March 1847.
116. *Northern Whig*, 11 March 1847.
117. Peter Gray, 'Punch and The Great Famine' in *History Ireland*, vol. 1 (Summer 1993); *The Times*, 23 March 1847.
118. Twistleton to Sir George Grey, 26 December 1846, *Copies or extracts of correspondence relating to union workhouses in Ireland (first series)*, 1847 [766], iv, pp 17-18.
119. Trevelyan, *Irish Crisis*, p.43; Trevelyan to Routh, 28 December 1846, *Commissariat series*, p. 425.
120. Circular to all Boards of Guardians in Ireland, Letter-Books, 10 September 1846.
121. P.L. Commissioners to Labouchere, CSORP, 0.18344, 17 October 1846; ibid., P.L. Commissioners to Redington, 0.19408, 31 October 1846; P.L. Commissioners to Labouchere, PROL HO 45, 1080, Box 1, 28 October 1846; Thirteenth Annual Report, 1847, passim.
122. *Roscommon and Leitrim Gazette*, 27 March 1847; Twistleton to Sir George Grey, 24 December 1846, *Copies or extracts of correspondence relating to union workhouses in Ireland (first series)*, 1847 [766], iv, p.13 (hereafter, *Correspondence relating to union workhouses*).
123. Thirteenth Annual Report, pp. 24, 38.
124. Burke to P.L. Commissioners, Letter-Books, 26 September 1846, 5 October 1846, 8 October 1846, 26 October 1846, 9 November 1846, 15 January 1847, 18 January 1847; ibid., P.L. Commissioners to Burke, 21 November 1846; correspondence of P.L. Guardians forwarded to Home Office, PROL HO 45, 1080, Box 1, 10 October 1846.
125. Burke to P.L. Commissioners, Letter-Books, 8 October 1846, 24 October 1846, 3 November 1846.
126. D. Phelan, Assistant P.L. Commissioner, 11 December 1846, *Commissariat series*, p.358.
127. P.L. Commissioners to Skibbereen Guardians, Letter-Books, 5 December 1846; *Roscommon and Leitrim Gazette*, 9 January 1847.
128. P.L. Commissioners to Grey, PROL HO 45, 1080, 28 September 1846; ibid., 7 October 1846; Burke to P.L. Commissioners, Letter-Books, 24 October 1846; ibid., P.L. Commissioners to Burke, 3 November 1846; ibid., P.L. Commissioners to Skibbereen Guardians, 23 October 1846, 5 December 1846; Minute Books of New Ross union, 21 October 1846, 4 November 1846; Minute Books of Dunshaughlin union, 3 November 1846, 10 November 1846, 12 January 1847; Minute Books of Trim union, 19 December 1846, 21 December 1846; Minute Books of Banbridge union, 23 November 1846; ibid., P.L. Commissioners to Redington, 0.23630, 20 December 1846; correspondence of P.L. Commissioners, forwarded to Home Office, PROL HO 45, 1080, Box 1, 10 October 1846, 23 October 1846.
129. Burke to P.L. Commissioners, Letter-Books, 18 January 1847; ibid., P.L. Commissioners to Burke, 3 November 1846; ibid., P.L. Commissioners to New Ross Guardians.

130. P.L. Commissioners to Redington, CSORP, 0.23630, 19 December 1846.

131. Ibid., Twistleton to Grey, PROL HO 45, 1682, 20 December 1846.

132. 'Table showing the name, population, number of electoral divisions and of guardians, the number of paupers for whom workhouse accommodation has been provided etc. during the year 1846', *Thom's Directory 1847*, pp. 1143-4.

133. P.L. Commissioners to Waterford Guardians, Letter-Books, 26 October 1846, 28 November 1846; Minute Books of Trim union, 21 December 1846; Thirteenth Annual Report, 1847.

134. Grey to Twistleton, 21 December 1846, *Correspondence relating to union workhouses*, p. 12.

135. Ibid., Routh to Trevelyan, 7 November 1846, *Correspondence explanatory*, p. 241.

136. Ibid., Trevelyan to Routh, 5 November 1846, p.226; ibid., 4 February 1846, p. 26.

137. Burke to Commissioners, Letter Books, 27 November 1846, 1 December 1846, 5 December 1846; Minute Books of Ballina union, 2 November 1846; Minute Books of New Ross union, 30 November 1846.

138. Routh to Trevelyan, 7 November 1846, *Commissariat series*, p. 241.

139. Minute Books of New Ross union, 9 December 1846, 30 December 1846.

140. Minute Book of Galway union, 2 September 1846, 16 September 1846.

141. Ibid., 30 September 1846.

142. Ibid., 30 December 1846.

143. Ibid., 24 February 1847, 3 March 1847, 17 March 1847, 31 March 1847.

144. Ibid., 26 May 1847, 9 June 1847, 16 June 1847, 23 June 1847, 30 June 1847.

145. P.L. Commissioners to Redington, CSORP, 0.23630, 18 December 1846, 19 December 1846; Twistleton to Grey, PROL HO 45, 1846, 20 December 1846; Minute Books of Dunshaughlin union, 29 December 1846.

146. Twistleton to Grey, *Correspondence relating to union workhouses*, 24 December 1846, p.14.

147. Ibid.

148. Ibid., Grey to Twistleton, 21 December 1846, pp. 12-13.

149. *Thom's Directory for Ireland 1850*, p. 112.

150. Minute Books of Ballina Union, 7 September 1846, 28 September 1846.

151. Minutes of Castlebar Union, forwarded to Chief Secretary, CSORP, 0.19716, 24 October 1846; *The Times*, 6 March 1847.

152. Minute Books of Westport union, 21 October 1846, 23 January 1846, 23 January 1847.

153. Minute Books of Ballina union, 8 January 1847; Minute Books of Westport union, 20 January 1847; Sub-Inspector Hunt to Inspector-General of Board of Works, 7 January 1847, *Correspondence relating to the measures adopted for the relief of distress in Ireland, Commissariat series, second part*, 1847 [796], II (hereafter, *Commissariat series II*) p.11; ibid., Fishbourne to Routh, 27 January 1847, p. 75.

154. Thirteenth Annual Report, 1847, p.45; Minute Books of Kenmare union, 12 September 1846, 25 December 1846; Minutes of Castlebar union, forwarded to Chief Secretary, CSORP, 1846, 0.19716, 24 October 1846; ibid., Minutes of Ennistymon union, 1846, 0.19600, 30 October 1846; ibid., Chairman of Westport union to Chief Secretary, 1846, 0.20106, 5 November 1846; ibid., Chairman of Ballinrobe Guardians to Chief Secretary, 1846, 0.20692, November 1846.

155. Minute Book of Stranorlar union, 12 September 1846.

156. Burke to P.L. Commissioners, Letter-Books, 18 December 1846.

157. Ibid., Burke to P.L. Commissioners, 28 January 1847.

158. Resolution of Westport Guardians, CSORP, 0.543, 13 January 1847; P.L. Commissioners to Ballyshannon Guardians, Minute Book of Ballyshannon union, 27 January 1847.

159. P.L. Commissioners to Redington, CSORP, 0.23630. 19 December 1846; Trevelyan to Philips, Secretary at Home Office, PROL HO 45, 1942, 12 April 1847.

160. Lord Lieutenant to Grey, 7 January 1847, CSORP, 1847, 0.341; ibid., Lord Lieutenant to Grey, 20 January 1847, 0.635.

161. H. Labouchere to Lord John Russell, 11 December 1846, Gooch, *Russell*, p. 163.

162. Grey to Bessborough [Lord Lieutenant], *Commissariat series II*, p. 230.

163. Wood to Russell, 2 December 1846, Gooch, *Russell*, pp. 161-2.

164. Mr Cardwell to Sir Robert Peel, Parker, *Peel*, 15 January 1847, p. 482.

165. Ibid., Mr John Young to Sir Robert Peel, 14 January 1847, p. 481; ibid., Memorandum from Peel to Trevelyan, marked 'Secret', 18 February 1847, p. 482.

166. Somerville to Redington, CSORP, 1847 0.580, 11 January 1847; ibid., 14 January 1847; ibid., Lord Lieutenant to Grey, 0.635, 20 January 1847.

167. Russell to Labouchere, 28 December 1846, Gooch, *Russell*, p. 166.

168. Commissioners to Grey, forwarding copies of correspondence with the Edenderry union on the subject of soup kitchens, PROL HO 45, 1706, December 1846.

169. Ibid., Copy of Treasury Minute, 8 January 1847, PROL HO 45, 1942; ibid., Routh to Bellew, 4 January 1847.

170. *Northern Whig*, 6 March 1847, 30 March 1847.

171. Ibid.

172. L.A. Clarkson, 'Famine and Irish History', in Crawford (ed.), *Famine, the Irish Experience*, p. 229.

173. Grey to Lord Lieutenant, CSORP, 0.1519, 23 January 1847.

174. Statement of sums issued under the authority of His Excellency the Lord Lieutenant of Ireland, to the Poor Law Commissioners for the maintenance of the poor in the undermentioned workhouses in Ireland up to 15 March 1847, CSORP, 0.4377, 16 March 1847.

175. Trevelyan to Philips, PROL HO 45, 1942, 12 April 1847; ibid., Treasury Minute, 5 March 1847; ibid., Treasury Minute, 12 April 1847.

176. Trevelyan to Routh, PROL HO 45 1942, 7 January 1847.

177. Minute Books of Galway union, 21 January 1847; Minute Book of Gort union, 19 February 1847.

178. Annual Reports of Poor Law Commissioners, 1846-50.

179. E.M. Crawford, 'Subsistence Crises and Famines in Ireland: a nutritionist's view', in Crawford (ed.), *Famine, the Irish Experience*, passim.

180. *Cork Examiner*, 22 December 1846; see also Hickey, 'Four Peninsula Parishes . . .'

181. Report of Inspector Coffin, 15 February 1847, *Commissariat series*, pp. 162-3.

182. *Northern Whig*, 11 March 1847.

183. Ibid.

184. *The Times*, 9 January 1847.

185. James H. Tuke, 'Report of the Society of Friends on distress in Ireland', NLI, Ms.Ir.9410859. (I am grateful to Mr MacArthur of Dunfanaghy for drawing my attention to this source.)

186. Ibid.

187. Ibid.

188. *The Times*, 4 January 1847, 7 January 1847, 23 March 1847 etc.; Transactions of the Central Relief Committee of the Society of Friends during the Famine in Ireland in 1846 and 1847, p. 212.

189. Report of the Society of Friends.

190. Report from Glenties, 16 December 1846, Appendix iii, Transactions of the Central Relief Committee of the Society of Friends.

191. Minutes of Belfast union, 15 December 1846, 22 December 1846, 29 December 1846, 26 January 1847, 2 February 1847, 2 March 1847, 16 March 1847, 4 May 1847.

192. *Northern Whig*, 23 March 1847.

193. Minutes of Belfast union, 22 March 1847.

194. *Northern Whig*, 22 April 1847.

195. Ibid., 20 April 1846.

196. *Northern Whig*, 23 March 1847.

197. Ibid., 1 April 1847.

198. Ibid.

199. Minute Book of Lurgan union, 15 October 1846, 7 January 1847, 28 January 1847.

200. Minute Book of Armagh union, 27 June 1846, 3 March 1847, 6 April 1847.

201. Minute Book of Enniskillen Guardians, 5 January 1847, 19 January 1847, 26 January 1847, 2 February 1847, 16 February 1847, 23 February 1847, 23 March 1847.

202. Ibid., 6 May 1847, 11 May 1847, 1 June 1847, 6 July 1847, 17 August 1847.

203. Provincial Bank to Wexford Guardians, CSORP, 0.9502, 7 April 1847; Commissioners to Redington, CSORP, 0.2061, 22 February 1847.

204. Minute Book of Killarney union, 2 January 1847; Minute Book of Ballyshannon union, 20 February 1847; Minute Book of Trim union, 29 May 1847; Minute Book of Kenmare union, 17 April 1847, 5 June 1847; 3 July 1847.

205. C. Kinealy, 'The Lisburn Workhouse during the Famine', *Journal of the Lisburn Historical Society* (Belfast 1991), passim.

206. Minute Book of Ballina unions, 1 February 1847, 8 February 1847, 2 July 1847; Minute Book of Westport union, 21 April 1847; Minute Book of Killarney union, 26 June 1847.

207. Memorial of Abbeyleix Guardians to Prime Minister, PROL, HO 45, 1080, 18 February 1847; Minute Book of Westport union, 1847, 27 March 1847, 31 March 1847, 10 April 1847.

208. Trevelyan, *Irish Crisis*, p. 111.

209. Ibid., p. 79.

CHAPTER 4: THE DEPLORABLE CONSEQUENCES OF THIS GREAT CALAMITY 1846–7 (pp. 136–174)

1. Return of all sums of money either granted or advanced . . . p. 5.

2. Treasury to Relief Commissioners, 10 February 1847, CSORP, Z.1591.

3. 10 & 11 Vic. c.7. 26 February 1847.

4. Treasury to Relief Commissioners, 10 February 1847, CSORP, Z.1591.

5. Trevelyan, *Irish Crisis*, p. 79.

6. *Rules and regulations for the Finance Committees, 10 March 1847, First Report of the Relief Commissioners constituted under the Act 10 Vic., cap.7. with appendices*, 1847 [799] xvii, p. 14.

7. Treasury to Relief Commissioners, 10 February 1847, CSORP, Z.1591.

8. See, for example, Daly, *The Famine in Ireland*, pp. 88-9; Ó Gráda, *The Great Irish Famine*, p. 45; James S. Donnelly, Jr, 'The soup kitchens', in W.E. Vaughan (ed.), *A New History of Ireland*, v: *Ireland under the Union 1: 1801-70* (Oxford 1989), pp. 307-15.

9. Treasury to Relief Commissioners, 10 February 1847, CSORP, A.1591.

10. Ibid.

11. *First report to the Relief Commissioners . . .* p. 12.

12. *First report of the Relief Commissioners . . .* pp. 39, 54.

13. Ibid., p. 9.

14. Ibid., Treasury Minute, 10 March 1847.

15. Ibid., p. 36.

16. *Northern Whig*, 13 May 1847.

17. *Third report of the Relief Commissioners constituted under the Act 10th. Vic., cap.7, with appendices, 17 June 1847*, 1847 [836] xvii, p. 3.

18. C. Kinealy, 'The administration of the Poor Law', chapter 1, passim.

19. *First report of the Relief Commissioners*, p. 14.

20. Ibid., pp. 7, 37.

21. Fifth report of the Relief Commissioners, 17 August 1847, *Fifth, sixth, seventh reports from the Relief Commissioners constituted under the Act 10 Vic., cap.7, with appendices*, 1847-8 [876] xxix, p. 5.

22. *First report of the Relief Commissioners*, pp. 14, 24.

23. General Order under Irish Relief Act, 4 March 1847, *Appendix to First Report of the Relief Commissioners . . .* p. 12

24. Ibid. p.9.

25. Ibid., *Regulations for Relief Committees under the Act 10 Vic. cap. 7., 8 March 1847*, p. 24.

26. *Third report of the Relief Commissioners* , p. 4; *Supplementary appendix to the seventh, and last, report of the Relief Commissioners*, 31 December 1847, 1847-8 [956], xxix, p. 4.

27. *First report of the Relief Commissioners*, p. 30.

28. *Supplementary appendix . . .*, p. 4; see also, Hickey, 'Four Peninsula Parishes', pp. 500-555; also unpublished autobiography of the Quaker, Alfred Webb, quoted in Foster, *Modern Ireland*, p. 329.

29. *Second report of the Relief Commissioners constituted under the Act 10 Vic., cap.7, with appendices, 15 May 1847*, 1847 [819] xvii, p. 3.

30. Inspecting Officer, Galway, to Relief Commissioners, PROL HO 45, 1942, 1 June 1847.

31. Ibid., Poor Law Commissioners to Lord Lieutenant, 12 June 1847.

32. Treasury Minute, 10 March 1847, *First report of the Relief Commissioners*, pp. 3-5.

33. Ibid.

34. Ibid; Circular No. 84, from the Office of Public Works, 10 April 1847, *Second report of the Relief Commissioners . . .* p. 7.

35. *Supplementary appendix . . .* , pp. 35, 79.

36. From *Cork Reporter*, reprinted in *Northern Whig*, 15 April 1847.

37. From *Ballinasloe Star*, reprinted in *Northern Whig*, 13 May 1847; from *Galway Vindicator*, reprinted in *Northern Whig*, 13 May 1847; *Roscommon and Leitrim Gazette*, 22 May 1847.

38. *Supplementary Appendix . . .* , pp. 22-86; *Roscommon and Leitrim Gazette*, 22 May 1847.

39. From *Western Star*, reprinted in *Northern Whig*, 22 April 1847; *Roscommon and Leitrim Gazette*, 29 May 1847.

40. From *Cork Constitution*, reprinted in *Northern Whig*, 15 May 1847.

41. From *Saunders' Newsletter*, reprinted in *Northern Whig*, 8 May 1847, 13 May 1847.

42. *Second report of the Relief Commissioners*, p. 5.

43. From *Saunders' Newsletter*, reprinted in *Northern Whig*, 15 May 1847.

44. *Third report of the Relief Commissioners*, p. 24; *Roscommon and Leitrim Gazette*, 22 May 1847, 29 May 1847 (from *Meath Herald*).

45. Ibid., p. 23.

46. Ibid. p. 25.

47. From *Saunders' Newsletter*, reprinted in *Northern Whig*, 15 May 1847.

48. *Northern Whig*, 15 May 1847; *The Times*, 7 January 1847.

49. *Second report of the Relief Commissioners*, p.4; *Roscommon and Leitrim Gazette*, 12 June 1847.

50. *First report of the Relief Commissioners*, p. 14.

51. *Second report of the Relief Commissioners*, p. 4; Malthus, *Essay on Population*.

52. *First report of the Relief Commissioners*, p. 9.

53. Ibid., p. 14.

54. *Third report of the Relief Commissioners*, p. 22.

55. Appendix C., *First report of the Relief Commissioners*, p. 22.

56. Ibid., p. 38.

57. *First report of the Relief Commissioners*, p. 23.

58. *Second report of the Relief Commissioners*, p. 4.

59. Central Board of Health to the Relief Commissioners, 21 June 1847, *Fourth report of the Relief Commissioners constituted under the Act 10 Vic., cap.7. with appendices*, 1847 [859] xvii, p. 18.

60. *Second report of the Relief Commissioners*, p. 6.

61. Ibid., pp. 6-7.

62. *Third report of the Relief Commissioners*, p. 5.

63. Central Board of Health to Relief Commissioners, 21 June 1847, *Fourth report of the Relief Commissioners*, p. 18; for further insights on this aspect of relief see, E. M. Crawford, 'Dearth, diet and disease in Ireland, 1850: a case study of nutritional deficiency' in *Medical History*, vol. 28, 1984.

64. *Fourth Report of Relief Commissioners*, p. 18; *Roscommon and Leitrim Gazette*, 29 May 1847.

65. *Second report of the Relief Commissioners*, p. 16.

66. Ibid., p. 18.

67. *First report of the Relief Commissioners*, pp. 16-55.

68. Ibid.

69. *Second report of the Relief Commissioners*, pp. 34-6; *Third report of the Relief Commissioners*, p. 29; *Fourth report of the Relief Commissioners*, p. 5; *Fifth report of the Relief Commissioners*, p. 6; *Sixth report of the Relief Commissioners*, p. 7; *Seventh report of the Relief Commissioners*, p. 7.

70. *Fourth report of the Relief Commissioners*, p .23; *Supplementary Appendix*, p. 6.

71. Maximum number of persons on rations in any one day as a percentage of the population by Poor Law union, *Supplementary Appendix*, pp. 18-21.

72. *Northern Whig*, 13 May 1847.

73. *Fourth report of the Relief Commissioners*, pp. 16-19.

74. *Fifth report of the Relief Commissioners*, p. 4.

75. Summary of the accountant's department, 19 July 1847, *Fourth report of the Relief Commissioners*, p. 4; Bourke, *The Visitation of God?*, p. 180.

76. *An account of the Receipt and expenditure of monies voted for the relief of distress in Ireland, during the Famine of 1847, administered by the Relief Commissioners, under Act 10 Vic., cap.7.*, *Supplementary Appendix*, pp. 16-17.

77. *Seventh report of the Relief Commissioners*, p. 3.

78. *Supplementary appendix*, p. 10.

79. *Sixth report of the Relief Commissioners*, p. 4; *Seventh report of the Relief Commissioners*, p. 3.

80. *Supplementary appendix*, pp 10-11.

81. *Seventh report of the Relief Commissioners*, p. 3.

82. *Seventh report of the Relief Commissioners*, pp. 24-7.

83. *Sixth report of the Relief Commissioners*, p. 3.

84. *Supplementary appendix*, pp. 13-14.

85. Ibid., *An account of the receipt and expenditure . . .* , pp. 16-17.

86. Relief Commissioners to the Lords of the Treasury, 31 May 1847, *Seventh report of the Relief Commissioners*, pp 30-31.

87. Ibid.

88. Ibid.

89. Ibid., pp. 26, 38.

90. Ibid., Treasury Minutes, 11 June 1847, 29 June 1847, 3 September 1847.

91. Board of Health to Redington, 4 September 1847, *Seventh report of the Relief Commissioners*, p. 41.

92. Act 9 Vic., cap. 6.

93. Act 10 & 11 Vic., cap. 22.

94. Sir William Somerville to the Board of Health, 9 September 1847, Seventh report of the Relief Commissioners, p. 40.

95. Ibid., Treasury Minute, 14 September 1847, p. 42.

96. Ibid.

97. Somerville to Trevelyan, PROL T.64.369.B, 18 September 1847.

98. Trevelyan to Somerville, PROL T.64.369.B, 21 September 1847.

99. *Seventh report of the Relief Commissioners*, p. 12.

100. *Supplementary appendix*, p. 13.

101. *Sixth report of the Relief Commissioners*, p. 3.

102. *Report of the Society of Friends . . .*

103. *Transactions of the Central Relief Committee*, pp. 55-6; Evidence of Joseph Bewley, *Report of the Select Committee of the House of Commons on the Poor Law (Ireland)*, together with minutes of evidence, H.C. (403) 1849, xv, second part, 169, pp. 952, 964 (hereafter, *Select Committee on Irish Poor Law*, 1849.)

104. Report of James Tuke from County Donegal, 10 December 1846, *Transactions of the Central Relief Committee* . . .

105. Ibid., Extracts from the letters of county correspondents, showing the general non-residence of landed proprietors, p. 212.

106. *Report of the Society of Friends* . . .

107. Statement of provisions and boilers shipped from Liverpool to the ports in the west of Ireland in January and February 1847, Appendix xi, *Transactions of the Central Relief committee* . . .

108. Ibid. 'Statements showing the number and value of grants for gratuitous distribution, distinguishing the several counties to which the grants were made', Appendix xxviii.

109. *Report of the Society of Friends* . . . ; Trevelyan to Lord Lieutenant, PROL T.64.369, B.1, 14 December 1847; Ibid., Trevelyan to J. Pim, Society of Friends, T.64.367.B.2, 24 August 1848.

110. Evidence of Bewley, *Select Committee on Irish Poor Law*, 1849, pp. 947-60.

111. Strzelecki to Trevelyan, PROL, T.64.369.B.3, 10 February 1847.

112. Treasurer of Hobart Relief Fund, Van Diemen's Land, to Secretary of State, PROL HO 45, 1794, 4 May 1847; Ibid., Chairman of the British Relief Association to Secretary of State, 17 June 1847, 1 October 1847; Woodham-Smith, *Great Hunger*, pp. 170, 382; Peter Gray, 'Punch and the Great Famine' in *History Ireland*, vol. 1, (Summer 1993), pp. 29-30.

113. Trevelyan to Chairman of British Relief Association, 20 August 1847, *Papers relating to proceedings for the relief of distress and state of the unions and workhouses in Ireland* (fourth series), 1847-8, liv, 29, p. 1.

114. Ibid., Minutes of Meeting of British Relief Association, pp. 2-3.

115. *First report of the Relief Commissioners*, reprinted in *Northern Whig*, 24 April 1847.

116. Woodham-Smith, *The Great Hunger*, pp. 56-8; *Roscommon and Leitrim Gazette*, 17 April 1847, 24 April 1847; for more information concerning the role played by Archbishop Murray, see Dublin Diocesan Archives (I am grateful to Cormac Ó Gráda for drawing my attention to this source).

117. Woodham-Smith, *The Great Hunger*, pp. 156-8; *Roscommon and Leitrim Gazette*, 10 July 1847.

118. *Northern Whig*, 1 April 1847, 15 April 1847, 8 May 1847; *Roscommon and Leitrim Gazette*, 17 April 1847.

119. Treasurer of Hobart Relief Fund to Secretary of State, PROL HO 45, 1794, 17 June 1847, 1 October 1847.

120. Further information on this donation and the recent commemorations of this connection can be obtained from the AFRI-project in Dublin.

121. Letter from Philadelphia, dated 25 February 1847, *Northern Whig*, 23 March 1847; *Roscommon and Leitrim Gazette*, 27 March 1847; the arrival of the sloop of war 'Jamestown', loaded with provisions from America, also attracted much publicity, *Dublin Evening Mail* 7 April 1847 etc.

122. Ibid.

123. Ibid., 17 April 1847.

124. Ibid., 8 May 1847.

125. Ibid., 1 May 1847.

126. Ibid., 15 April 1846.

127. Ibid., 1 April 1847; for some examples of the role played by landlords, see *Roscommon and Leitrim Gazette*, 2 January 1847, 9 January 1847, 20 March 1847, 3 April 1847, 24 April 1847, 1 May 1847, 8 May 1847; *The Times*, 6 and 8 March 1847, 1 October 1847; *Dublin Evening Mail*, 5 April 1847 etc.

128. Return of all sums of money . . . ; *The Times*, 5 October 1847, 6 October 1847, 7 October 1847, 9 October 1847, 12 October 1847.

129. I am indebted to Eileen Black of the Art Dept., Ulster Museum, for directing my attention to this.

130. *Northern Whig*, 24 April 1847; *Roscommon and Leitrim Gazette*, 9 January 1847, 10 July 1847.

131. *Northern Whig*, 24 April 1847.

132. Ibid.

133. Trevelyan to Ladies Relief Associations in Ireland, PROL HO 45. 1942, 10 October 1847.

134. *Northern Whig*, 6 March 1847.

135. Ibid., 13 May 1847.

136. Ibid., 1 April 1847.

137. Trevelyan, *Irish Crisis*, pp. 79, 139.

138. *Northern Whig*, 29 April 1847.

139. Table showing by provinces, counties and towns, the number of deaths in each year from 1841 to 1851. General Report of the Census Commissioners, *The Census of Ireland for 1851*, 1856 [2087], table xxxiii.

140. Ó Gráda, *Ireland Before and After the Famine*, pp. 104-11, 138-44; Grant, 'The Great Famine in the Province of Ulster'; Foley, 'The Killarney Poor Law Guardians'; Kinealy, 'The Irish Poor Law'; Mokyr, *Why Ireland Starved*, pp. 262-72.

141. Crawford, 'Subsistence Crises and Famines in Ireland: a nutritionist's view', in Crawford (ed.), *Famine, The Irish Experience*, p.201.

142. *Northern Whig*, 1 April 1847; Letter to Mr Monsell of Limerick Assizes, reprinted in *Roscommon and Leitrim Gazette*, 3 April 1847.

143. S.H. Cousens, 'The regional variation in mortality during the great Irish Famine, *Proceedings of the Royal Irish Academy*, lxiii, section C, No.3. (1963), pp. 132-3; Grant, 'The Great Famine in the Province of Ulster'; Foley, 'The Killarney Poor Law Guardians'; Kinealy, 'The Irish Poor Law'; S. Kierse, *The Famine Years in the Parish of Killaloe*, 1845-51 (Killaloe 1984); Proinnsias O Duigneain, 'North Leitrim in Famine Times' (Sligo 1986).

144. *Transactions of the Society of Friends* . . .

145. *Census for Ireland*, 1841-1901.

146. *Report of the Select Committee on Destitution (Gweedore and Cloughaneely); together with the proceedings of the committee, minutes of evidence etc.*, 1857-8 [412]. This report repeatedly refers to the fact that the condition of the local population in these areas

was far worse in the 1850s, than during the Famine. By the 1850s also, relations between the local landlords and tenants in the area had deteriorated considerably; C. Kinealy, S. Cannon and C. Cox, *The Famine in Dunfanaghy* (Dublin 1992).

147. *Northern Whig*, 15 April 1847; *Roscommon and Leitrim Gazette*, 27 March 1847, 29 May 1847.

148. See for example, Peter Frogatt, 'The response of the Medical Profession to the Great Famine', in Crawford (ed.), *Famine, The Irish Experience*, pp. 134-56; W.P. MacArthur, 'Medical History of the Famine' in Edwards and Williams, *The Great Famine*, pp. 263-315.

149. *Northern Whig*, 22 April 1847; *Roscommon and Leitrim Gazette*, 27 March 1847, 12 June 1847.

150. *Northern Whig*, 22 April 1847.

151. Ibid., 29 April 1847.

152. Ibid., 11 May 1847.

153. Ibid., from the *Cork Examiner*, 24 April 1847.

154. Ibid., 'Notes on the state of the country and progress of agricultural spring labour', No. iv., by C.A. 11 May 1847; *Roscommon and Leitrim Gazette*, 22 May 1847.

155. Crawford, 'Subsistence Crises and Famines in Ireland: a nutritionist's view', in Crawford (ed.), *Famine, The Irish Experience*, pp. 204-15; Crawford, 'Dearth, Diet and Disease in Ireland'; in *Medical History*, xxviii (1984); Crawford, 'Scurvy in Ireland during the Great Famine' in *Social History of Medicine*, No. 3. (1988).

156. Crawford, 'Subsistence Crises: a nutritionist's view', pp. 204-5.

157. *Northern Whig*, 22 April 1847.

158. Crawford, 'Subsistence Crises', p. 215.

CHAPTER 5: EXPEDIENTS WELL NIGH EXHAUSTED 1847–8 (pp. 175–231)

1. For example, Charles Trevelyan's book, *The Irish Crisis* (London 1848) ends in 1847; George O'Brien in *The Economic History of Ireland* (Longmans 1921) refers to 'the great famine of 1845–47'; Gooch, the biographer of the Prime Minister, Russell (op. cit.), refers to the period in Russell's administration following 1847, as 'Ireland after the Famine'; many of references in Edwards and Williams' (eds) book, *The Great Famine*, end after 1848.

2. *The Times*, 6 March 1847, 23 March 1847, 12 October 1847: Gray, 'Punch and the Great Famine'; Lord Palmerston to Russell, 19 August 1847, Gooch, *Russell*, pp. 172-3.

3. Letters written by the Prime Minister, *Russell*, and the Chancellor of the Exchequer, Wood, published in *The Kerry Evening Post*, 27 October 1847; Bardon, *A History of Ulster*, pp. 240-306; Lewis quoted in Mandler, *Aristocratic Government in the Age of Reform*, p. 253; Clarendon quoted in *The Times*, 7 October 1847.

4. Trevelyan, *Irish Crisis*, pp. 116-19; Jennifer Hart, 'Sir Charles Trevelyan at the Treasury', in *English Historical Review*, vol. 75 (1960), pp. 99, 110.

5. Nicholls, *First Report on Poor Law, Second Report on Poor Law, Third Report on Poor Law*.

6. 1 & 2 Vic. c.56. 31 July 1838.

7. 10 Vic. c.31. 8 June 1847; 10 & 11 Vic. c.84. 22 July 1847; 10 & 11 Vic. c.90. 22 July 1847.

8. 10 & 11 Vic. c.31, sections 1,2,3; General Order of the Poor Law Commissioners for regulating outdoor relief, 1 July 1847.

9. 10 & 11 Vic. c.31. sections 4-18.

10. 10 & 11 Vic. c.84.

11. Minute Books of English Poor Law Commissioners, PROL M.H.1.

12. Evidence of Twistleton, *Select committee on Irish Poor Law*, 1849, pp. 682-4.

13. Ibid., p. 682; *First Annual Report*, 1848, p. 6; Hart, 'Trevelyan at Treasury', passim.

14. Clarendon to Trevelyan, 3 January 1848, marked private, PROL T.64.367. c/1.

15. Routh to Trevelyan, 10 January 1847, PROL T.64.368.A; *The Times*, 12 October 1847.

16. Evidence of Edward Twistleton, *Select committee on Poor Law*, 1849, pp. 627-8.

17. *The Times*, 8 March 1847, 9 March 1847, October 1847; Russell to Wood, 26 March 1847, Gooch, *Russell*, p. 172.

18. Ibid., Russell to Wood, 28 June 1847, p. 172.

19. Evidence of Twistleton, *Select committee on Irish Poor Law* 1849, pp. 627-8.

20. Captain Pole, Sligo, to Trevelyan, 25 January 1847, PROL T.64.367. c/1.

21. Report of J. Lang, P.L. Inspector, Granard union, 23 April 1848, *First Annual Report*, 1848.

22. Lord Clarendon to Russell, 5 February 1848, Gooch, *Russell*, p. 220.

23. *First Annual Report*, 1848, p.9.

24. *First Annual Report*, 1848, p. 13; evidence of Alfred Power, *Select committee on Irish Poor Law*, 1849, pp. 16-17.

25. *Kerry Evening Post*, 25 September 1847; Memorial of Downpatrick Guardians, CSORP, 0.323, 12 December 1847; ibid., Commissioners to Downpatrick Guardians o.5152, 17 December 1847; Minute book of Lurgan Guardians, 19 August 1847, 16 December 1847; *First Annual Report*, 1848, p. 13.

26. Letter from R. Hamilton, Relief Commission Office, Dublin, reprinted in *Kerry Evening Post*, 11 August 1847.

27. Ibid.

28. Redington to P.L. Commissioners, CSORP, 0.6575, 29 May 1847; ibid., P.L. Commissioners to Redington, 0.6835, 4 June 1847; Circulars from P.L. Commissioners to local unions, 1 July 1847, 26 October 1847, *Papers relating to the proceedings for the relief of distress, and state of the unions and workhouses in Ireland* (fourth series), 1847-8 [896] liv, i, pp. 6-8, 25 (hereafter, *Relief of distress*, fourth series).

29. Redington to P.L. Commissioners, CSORP, 0.6575, 29 May 1847; ibid., Lord Lieutenant to various unions, 0.9273, 7 July 1847; Clarendon to Trevelyan, PROL T.64.367.A 15 October 1847; ibid., Somerville to Trevelyan, 20 October 1847.

30. Ibid., Twistleton to Trevelyan, 23 October 1847, T.64.367.A; ibid., Twistleton to Trevelyan, T.64.369. B.1, 14 December 1847; *The Times*, 12 October 1847; article from *Frankfurter Allegemeine Zeitung*, reprinted in *The Times*, 16 October 1847.

31. Sheriff of Co. Mayo to P.L. Commissioners, CSORP, 0.10579, 9 September 1847; ibid., P.L. Commissioners to Somerville, 12 October 1847.

32. P.L. Commissioners to Vice-Guardians of Ballinrobe, Castlebar and Westport unions, CSORP, 0.9345, 16 August 1847.

33. Twistleton to Trevelyan, PROL T.64.367.A, 23 October 1847.

34. John Ball, P.L. Inspector, to P.L. Commissioners, CSORP, 0.8211, 12 July 1847.

35. Twistleton to Trevelyan, PROL T.64.367.A, 23 October 1847.

36. P.L. Commissioners to Somerville, CSORP, 0.10409, 4 October 1847; ibid., P.L. Commissioners to Somerville, 0.10408, 4 October 1847.

37. Minute Books of Kenmare union, 11 December 1847.

38. Minute Books of New Ross union, 16 June 1847; Minute Books of Kenmare union, 10 July 1847; Minute Book of Wexford union, 7 August 1847; Minute Book of Dunshaughlin union, 21 August 1847; Minute Books of Ballina union, 4 October 1847, 11 October 1847; Minute Book of Trim union, 30 October 1847; *Reports from Mr Barron to the Poor Law Commissioners and correspondence relative to the dismissal of the late board of guardians of the Lowtherstown union*, 1847-8 (207), liii, passim.

39. *Kerry Evening Post*, 8 September 1847; *Dublin Weekly Register*, 17 July 1847; Minute Book of Enniskillen union, 17 August 1847, 26 October 1847.

40. Minute Book of Ballina Guardians, 12 July 1847, 2 August 1847; Minute Book of Killarney union, 13 September 1847, 23 September 1847; Minute Book of New Ross union, 22 September 1847.

41. P. Barron, P.L. Inspector, to P.L. Commissioners, CSORP, 0.9259, 9 September 1847; ibid., P.L. Commissioners to Donegal Guardians, 0.645, 28 December 1847.

42. Redington to Trevelyan, PROL T.64.369. B/1, 18 December 1847.

43. *Supplementary appendix*, pp. 18-21.

44. W.D. Broughton, P.L. Inspector, Swinford to P.L. Commissioners, CSORP, 0.13324, 18 December 1847; ibid., P.L. Commissioners to Redington, 0.7843, 7 July 1847.

45. Minute Book of Ballina union, 24 November 1847.

46. P.L. Commissioners to P.L. Inspector, Tralee union, CSORP, 0.13162, 18 December 1847; Evidence of Power, *Select committee on Irish Poor Law*, 1849, pp. 44-50.

47. Minute Book of Lurgan union, 8 July 1847.

48. Minute Book of Westport union, 25 August 1847, 8 September 1847.

49. Minute Book of Killarney union, 8 November 1847, 27 December 1847.

50. Minute Book of Kenmare union, 10 January 1848; extract from Minute Book of Listowel union, CSORP, 0.10480, 23 September 1847; ibid., report of Newcastle Guardians to P.L. Commissioners, 23 September 1847.

51. Captain Wynne, P.L. Inspector, Carrick-on-Shannon, 9 January 1848, *Papers relating to proceedings for the relief of the distress and state of the unions and workhouses in Ireland, Fifth series, 1848*, 919, p. 157; ibid., Vice-guardians Mohill union to P.L. Commissioners, 10 January 1848, p. 186.

52. Joseph Burke, P.L. Inspector, Letter-Book, 7 August 1847.

53. P.L. Inspector, Ballina to P.L. Commissioners, CSORP, 0.8271, 15 July 1847.

54. P.L. Inspector, Cork and Kerry to P.L. Inspectors, CSORP, 0.10190, 24 September 1847; ibid., P.L. Commissioners to Somerville, 28 September 1847.

55. Summary of financial returns showing the amount of poor rate collected in 1846 and 1847, *Relief of distress, fifth series*, p. 674.

56. Ibid.

57. P.L. Commissioners to Redington, CSORP, 0.13253, 27 December 1847; P.L. Commissioners to Home Office, 0.2842, 11 March 1848; Twistleton to Trevelyan, PROL T.64.370. C/4, 13 February 1848.

58. Ibid., Twistleton to Trevelyan, 12 February 1848; Gray, 'Punch and The Great Famine'.
59. Poor Rates. A statement for each union in Ireland, *First Annual Report*, 1848, pp. 162-4.
60. Wood to Russell, 6 February 1848, Gooch, *Russell*, p. 221.
61. Trevelyan to P.L. Commissioners, Treasury Outletters, T.14,31., 13 May 1848.
62. *First Annual Report*, 1848; *Second Annual Report*, 1849.
63. Burke to P.L. Commissioners, Letter-Books, 14 September 1847.
64. Crawford to P.L. Commissioners, CSORP, 0.10190, 24 September 1847, 0.11276, 1 November 1847; ibid., P.L. Commissioners to Somerville, 0.10190, 28 September 1847; ibid., Senior to P.L. Commissioners, 0.11473, 6 November 1847; ibid., Vice-guardians, Castlebar to P.L. Commissioners, 0.11034, 26 October 1847; ibid., 0.11223, 28 October 1847.
65. Circular of Poor Law Commissioners, 26 August 1846, *Relief of distress, fifth series*, pp. 123-4.
66. Circular to P.L. Commissioners, CSORP, 0.1171, 21 August 1847; *Second Annual Report*, 1849, p. 13.
67. Chairman of Rathkeale Guardians to Trevelyan, PROL T.64. 367. A/3, 12 November 1847; P.L. Inspector, Galway, to P.L. Commissioners, 0.13385, 19 December 1847.
68. Twistleton to Trevelyan, PROL T.64.369. B/1 13 December 1847; P.L. Inspector, Kenmare to P.L. Commissioners, CSORP, 0.410, 27 December 1847.
69. Report of P.L. Commissioners, CSORP, 5 January 1848.
70. Pauper returns in workhouses, *Relief of distress, fifth series*, pp. 680-81; ibid., Captain Kennedy, P.L. Inspector, Kilrush to P.L. Commissioners, 29 January 1848, p. 401.
71. Ibid., Captain Wynne, P.L. Inspector to P.L. Commissioners, 4 January 1848, *Relief of distress, fifth series*, p. 163.
72. Minute Book of Ballina union, 1 November 1847; P.L. Inspector, Ballina to P.L. Commissioners, CSORP, 0.13423, 18 December 1847; ibid., P.L. Inspector, Cahirciveen to P.L. Commissioners, 0.11632, 5 November 1847, ibid., 0.13423, 18 December 1847; ibid., P.L. Inspector, Listowel to P.L. Commissioners, 0.13399, 9 December 1847.
73. Burke to P.L. Commissioners, Letter-Books, 29 December 1847, 12 January 1848, 4 February 1848, 21 March 1848; ibid., P.L. Commissioners to Burke, 4 January 1848.
74. Burke to P.L. Commissioners, Letter-Books, 14 September 1847.
75. Minute of Ballymoney union, 27 September 1847.
76. Minute book of Lurgan union, 13 November 1847, 9 December 1847; Senior to P.L. Commissioners, CSORP, 0.10314, 25 September 1847.
77. Capt. Wynne to P.L. Commissioners, 25 January 1848, *Relief of distress, fifth series*, p. 165.
78. Ibid., Captain Hellard, P.L. Inspector to P.L. Commissioners, 19 December 1847, p. 455.
79. *First Annual Report* of P.L. Commissioners, 1848.
80. *Second Annual Report* of P.L. Commissioners, 1849.
81. Circular on the Provision of Outdoor *Relief, Relief of distress, fourth series*, 1 July 1847, p. 6; evidence of Twistleton, *Select committee on the Irish Poor Law*, 1848, p. 629.

82. Twistleton to Trevelyan, PROL T.64.370. C/4, 27 February 1848.

83. Ibid; *First Annual Report*, 1848, p. 14.

84. Twistleton to Trevelyan, PROL T.64.369. B/3. 7 March 1848; P.L. Commissioners to P.L. Inspector, Listowel union, CSORP, 0.1168. 15 January 1848; P.L. Commissioners to Ballina Guardians, Minute Books of Ballina union, 24 December 1847.

85. Twistleton to Trevelyan, PROL T.64.370. C/4, 27 February 1848.

86. P.L. Commissioners to Burke, Letter-Books, 5 February 1848; P.L. Commissioners to Redington, CSORP, 0.2376, 24 February 1848.

87. Vice-Guardians, Tuam union, CSORP, 0.3564, 21 March 1848; ibid., Memorial of ratepayers of Ennistymon union, 0.6504, 29 June 1848; confidential letter from able-bodied workers in Callan union to P.L. Commissioners, Letter-Books, January 1848.

88. Minute Book of Ballina union, 18 March 1848; evidence of Power, *Select committee on Irish Poor Law*, 1849, p. 12; resolution of Rathkeale and Lismore unions, CSORP, 0.4669, 8 May 1848.

89. Resolution of Kilmallock guardians, CSORP, 0.4835, 4 May 1848; P.L. Commissioners to Kenmare Guardians, Minute Books of Kenmare union, 29 July 1848.

90. Pauper returns in workhouses, *Relief of distress, fifth series*, pp. 680-81; *First Annual Report*, 1848, p. 24.

91. *First Annual Report*, 1848, p. 24.

92. Wynne to P.L. Commissioners, 31 December 1847, *Relief of distress, fifth series*, p. 153.

93. P.L. Inspector, Cahirciveen, to P.L. Commissioners, CSORP, 0.34. 17 December 1847; ibid., P.L. Inspector, Scariff, to P.L. Commissioners, 0.303, 1 January 1848; ibid., P.L. Inspector, Sligo, to P.L. Commissioners, 0.12730, 8 December 1847.

94. Burke to P.L. Commissioners, Letter-Books, 12 October 1847; Minutes of Kenmare union, 4 September 1847; Minute Book of New Ross union, 3 November 1847; P.L. Inspector, Kilrush, to P.L. Commissioners, 2 December 1847; extract of minutes of Newcastle Guardians, CSORP, 0.9877, 7 September 1847; report on Nenagh union in *Dublin Weekly Register*, 13 November 1847; extract of Nenagh minutes, NAI, Relief Commission Papers, 25 November 1847; P.L. Inspector, Galway, to P.L. Commissioners, CSORP, 0.948, 13 January 1848.

95. Quoted in Gooch, *Russell*, p. 218; ibid., Lord Clarendon to Lord John Russell, 30 March 1848, p. 221.

96. Ibid., Clarendon to Russell, 30 March 1848, pp. 221-2.

97. P.L. Inspector, Bantry to P.L. Commissioners, CSORP, 0.4739, 7 May 1847.

98. Twistleton to Trevelyan, PROL T.64.369. B/1, 9 December 1847; ibid., Twistleton to Trevelyan, 13 December 1847.

99. Rev. Dawson, Carrick-on-Shannon, 11 December 1847, *Relief of distress, fifth series*, p. 139.

100. Minute Book of Killarney union, 18 October 1847; Memorial of Skibbereen Guardians, CSORP, 0.12959, 25 November 1847.

101. Extract of Tralee minutes, RAP, 23 November 1847; *Kerry Evening Post*, 9 October 1847; Kilrush Guardians to P.L. Commissioners, CSORP, 0.707, 23 December 1847; *The Times*, 10 October 1847.

102. *First Annual Report*, 1848, p. 24; *Second Annual Report*, 1849, p.2; P.L. Commissioners to Home Office, PROL HO 45. 2472, May 1848.

103. P.L. Commissioners to Burke, Letter-Books, 24 July 1848; ibid. Circular to all Vice-Guardians and Guardians, 0.2187, 29 August 1848; Minute Book of Killarney union, August 1848; P.L. Commissioners to Westport Vice-Guardians, Minute Books of Westport union, 13 September 1848.

104. Twistleton to Trevelyan, PROL T.64.369. B/1, 14 December 1847; ibid., Wood to Treasury, 16 December 1847.

105. *Relief of distress, fifth series*, passim.

106. Ibid., P.L. Commissioners to Trevelyan, 19 January 1848, p. 11.

107. Minutes of Meeting of British Relief Association, *Relief of distress, fourth series*, pp. 2-3; Treasury Minute, PROL T.64. 369. B/1, 31 December 1847.

108. Strzelecki to each P.L. Commissioner of Distressed unions, 6 November 1847, *Relief of distress, fourth series*, p. 4; ibid., Resolutions of committee of British Relief Association, 26 August 1847, pp. 2-3.

109. P.L. Inspector, Skibbereen to P.L. Commissioners, CSORP 0.13177, 16 December 1847; ibid., P.L. Inspector, Clifden to P.L. Commissioners, 0.13380, 6 December 1847; ibid., P.L. Inspector, Swinford to P.L. Commissioners, 0.13244, 18 December 1847; ibid., P.L. Inspector, Kenmare to P.L. Commissioners, 0.13154, 19 December 1847; Strzelecki to British Relief Association, PROL HO 45. 1794, 3 January 1848.

110. J.J. Marshall to P.L. Commissioners, 29 January 1848, *Relief of distress, fifth series*, 613.

111. Twistleton to Trevelyan, PROL T.64.368/A, 3 January 1848.

112. P.L. Inspector, Mohill to P.L. Commissioners, CSORP, 0.13304, 24 December 1847; remittance of British Relief Association to Kenmare union, Minute Book of Kenmare union, 5 February 1848; P.L. Commissioners, forwarding remittance of British Relief Association to Wesport Vice-Guardians, Minute Book of Westport union, NLI Ms. 12,609, 5 April 1848, 26 April 1848; Twistleton to Trevelyan (marked confidential), PROL T. 64.369. B/3, 4 March 1848.

113. Strzelecki to British Relief Association, PROL T. 64.367. B/1, 19 March 1848; ibid., Strzelecki to Twistleton; 25 April 1848; ibid., Twistleton to Trevelyan, 13 May 1848; ibid., Twistleton to Trevelyan, 13 May 1848.

114. *Second Annual Report*, 1849, p. 8; evidence of Strzelecki, *Select committee on Irish Poor Law*, 1849, pp. 847-64; Strzelecki to Redington, PROL HO 45. 1794, 1 July 1848; British Relief Association to Twistleton, CSORP, 0.10468, 23 October 1848; ibid., P.L. Commissioners to British Relief Association, 25 October 1848; ibid., British Relief Association to P.L. Commissioners, 2 November 1848.

115. Trevelyan to Twistleton, PROL T.64.367. B/1, 6 June 1848; ibid., Twistleton to Trevelyan, T.64.367. B/2, 15 July 1848; ibid., P.L. Commissioners to Trevelyan, T.64.367. B/1, 10 June 1848; ibid., Twistleton to Trevelyan, T.64.367. B/2, 10 August 1848.

116. Trevelyan to Twistleton, PROL T. 64. 367. B/1, 13 June 1848.

117. Otway, P.L. Inspector, to P.L. Commissioners, CSORP, 0.9122, 4 August 1847; ibid., extract of minutes of Gort union, 08734, 24 July 1847.

118. Minute Book of Ballyshannon union, 10 January 1848; Minute Book of New Ross union, 8 December 1847; Burke to P.L. Commissioners, Letter-Books, 15 April 1849.

119. Extract from Ballymoney union, CSORP, 0.13329, 27 December 1847; ibid., P.L. Inspector, Ballina to P.L. Commissioners, 0.13172, 19 December 1847; ibid., P.L. Inspector, Kilrush to P.L. Commissioners, 0.298, 1 January 1848; ibid., P.L. Inspector, Newcastle to P.L. Commissioners, 0.1062, 5 January 1848; Twistleton to Trevelyan, PROL T.64.367. A/3, 19 November 1847.

120. Twistleton to Trevelyan, PROL T.64.367. A/3, 10 November 1847; P.L. Inspector, Ballina to P.L. Commissioners, CSORP, 0.13169, 14 December 1847; ibid., Memorial of Skibbereen Guardians, 0.12959, 25 December 1847; ibid., P.L. Inspector, Carrick-on-Shannon to P.L. Commissioners, 0.1019, 1 January 1848; *Roscommon and Leitrim Gazette*, 24 April 1847, 8 May 1847.

121. *First, Second, Third, Annual Reports*, 1848, 1849, 1850.

122. Twistleton to Trevelyan, PROL T. 64.370. C/4, 3 February 1848, 6 February 1848, 8 February 1848, 10 February 1848; ibid., Twistleton to Trevelyan, T.64.367. A.3. 19 November 1847; ibid., Twistleton to Trevelyan, T.64.366. A.4. 14 September 1848.

123. *Second Annual Report*, 1849, p. 11.

124. Twistleton to Trevelyan, PROL T.64.368. A/3, 4 January 1848; ibid., Twistleton to Trevelyan, T. 64.370. C/4, 3 February 1848.

125. *First Annual Report*, 1848, pp. 9-10; *Second Annual Report*, 1849, p.15.

126. P.L. Commissioners to Redington, CSORP, 0.10119, 20 July 1847; ibid., P.L. Commissioners to Somerville, 24 September 1847.

127. Twistleton to Trevelyan, PROL T.64.368. A/3, 4 January 1848.

128. Twistleton to Trevelyan, T.64.370. C/4. 6 February 1848.

129. Ibid.

130. Total amount advanced by the Relief Commissioners etc., *Supplementary appendix*, pp. 18-21.

131. *Armagh Guardian*, 28 September 1847; Memorial from Lowtherstown Guardians, CSORP, 0.10606, 7 October 1847; *First Annual Report*, 1848.

132. Burke to P.L. Commissioners, Letter-Books, 15 April 1849, 27 June 1849.

133. Ibid., P.L. Commissioners to Burke, 15 June 1849.

134. Ibid., P.L. Commissioners to Burke, 19 August 1848; Report of P.L. Commissioners showing Vice-Guardians, their names, late residence, and previous employment, PROL, T.64.370. C/4, 19 February 1848.

135. P.L. Commissioners to Vice-Guardians of Ballinrobe, Castlebar and Westport unions, CSORP, 0.9345, 16 August 1847; Twistleton to Trevelyan, PROL T.64.367.C1, 3 January 1848; extract of Tipperary Guardians Minutes, T.64.366.A., 9 January 1849.

136. Twistleton to Trevelyan, PROL T.64.370. B/1, 13 September 1847; ibid., Twistleton to Trevelyan, T.64.368.B. October 1848; evidence of Power, *Select committee on Irish Poor Law*, 1849, pp. 62-3.

137. Circular to all Vice-Guardians, Letter-Books, 9 May 1849; Minute Book of Listowel union, 28 March 1849, 9 May 1849, 18 June 1849.

138. Halliday to Trevelyan, PROL T.64.370. C/4, 20 February 1848; ibid., Dobree to Trevelyan, T.64.369. B/3, 1 March 1848.

139. Burke to P.L. Commissioners, Letter-Books, 17 May 1848, 19 July 1848; Twistleton to Trevelyan, PROL T.64.366.A, 14 September 1848.

140. 12 & 13 Vic. c.4.

141. *Copy of a letter from the Poor Law Commissioners in Ireland to the Secretary of State for the Home Department, dated 31 January 1849, with reference to the restoration of elected boards of guardians in certain unions in Ireland*, 1849 (61), xlviii, pp 1-3; *copy of an Order, dated 22 January, altering the dates of the proceedings of the annual elections of guardians, and of an Order dated 5 February, prescribing amended rules for the government of workhouses*, 1849 [82], xlvii, p. 2.

142. Hill, *Facts from Gweedore*, passim.

143. Quoted in Daly, *Famine*, p. 109.

144. Wood to Russell, 20 May 1848, Gooch, *Russell*, p. 228.

145. Daly, *Famine*, pp. 109-10; *Census for Ireland*, 1851, pp. xixiv.

146. Ibid.

147. 11 & 12 Vic. cap. 47, 14 August 1848.

148. Memorial by Lord Palmerston to Russell, 31 March 1848, Gooch, *Russell*, p. 225.

149. 10 & 11 Vic. c.31, section 10.

150. Twistleton to Trevelyan, PROL T.64.367. C/1, 3 January 1848; *Dublin Evening Post*, 15 January 1848.

151. *Dublin Evening Post*, 10 February 1848, 17 February 1848; *Armagh Guardian*, 4 May 1848; *Kerry Evening Post*, 14 April 1848.

152. Minute Book of Killarney union, 7 February 1848; Minute Book of Kells union, 12 January 1848, 28 March 1848, 15 April 1848.

153. Twistleton to Trevelyan, PROL T.64.367. C/1, 3 January 1848, 12 January 1848.

154. P.L. Commissioners to Mr Lynch, Westport, 19 January 1848, *Relief of distress, fifth series*, pp. 280-81.

155. Ibid., reply to above, 27 January 1848, p. 281.

156. P.L. Commissioners to Vice-Guardians, Ballina, CSORP, 0.2116. 7 February 1848; ibid., Vice-Guardians, Ballinrobe to P.L. Commissioners, 0.5139, 31 January 1848; ibid., Vice-Guardians, Castlebar to P.L. Commissioners, 0.2328, 3 February 1848; ibid., P.L. Inspector, Glenties to Commissioners, 0.2161, 15 January 1848.

157. P.L. Commissioners to Vice-Guardians, Ballina, CSORP, 10.2116, 7 February 1848; ibid., P. L. Commissioners to Vice-Guardians of Castlebar, Ballinrobe, Westport unions, 0.1048, 13 January 1848; *Dublin Evening Post*, 24 February 1848.

158. Lieutenant Hamilton, P.L. Inspector to P.L. Commissioners, 6 February 1848, *Relief of distress, fifth series*, pp. 90-91.

159. Ibid.

160. P.L.I. to P.L. Commissioners, CSORP, 0.13372, 16 December 1847; ibid., P.L. Commissioners to Redington, 0.10671, 13 November 1848.

161. P.L. Inspector, Carrick-on-Shannon to P.L. Commissioners, CSORP, 0.13372, 16 December 1847.

162. P.L. Commissioners to Redington, CSORP, 0.28, 21 December 1847; ibid., Home Office to Chief Secretary, 0.6588, 30 June 1848; ibid., P.L. Commissioners to Redington, 8 July 1848.

163. Circular from P.L. Commissioners, *Copies of correspondence upon which the Commissioners of the Poor Law in Ireland took legal advice as to the construction of the 10th section of the Act 10 Vic., c.31; and of the case submitted to them by counsel; and of the circular*

letter of the Commissioners issued thereon. 1847-8, liii, 519, p.4; ibid., opinion of Attorney-General, J. Henn, 15 May 1848, p.2; ibid., opinion of J. Monahan, 20 May 1848, p.4.

164. Ibid., Circular of the P.L. Commissioners, 8 June 1848, p.5.

165. Ibid.

166. Trevelyan to Twistleton, PROL T.64. 367. B/1, 12 June 1848.

167. Home Secretary to P.L. Commissioners, CSORP, 0.8186, 30 June 1848.

168. Twistleton to Trevelyan, PROL T.64.367. B/1, 15 June 1848.

169. Ibid., Twistleton to Trevelyan, T.64.367.A. 24 October 1847.

170. Ibid., Twistleton to Trevelyan, T.64.369. B/1, 14 December 1847.

171. Twistleton to Trevelyan, PROL T.64.367. B/1, 13 May 1848; Twistleton to Trevelyan, T.64.367. B/2, 15 July 1848; P.L. Commissioners to Trevelyan, CSORP, 0.6624, 8 July 1848.

172. Twistleton to Trevelyan, PROL, T.64.367. B/1, 13 May 1848; ibid., Twistleton to Trevelyan, T.64.367. B/2, 15 July 1848; P.L. Commissioners to Trevelyan, CSORP, 0.6624, 8 July 1848.

173. Trevelyan to Twistleton, PROL T.64.367. B/1, 6 June 1848.

174. Ibid., Twistleton to Trevelyan, T.64.367. B/2, 10 August 1848; ibid., P.L. Commissioners to Trevelyan, T.64.367. B/1, 10 June 1848.

175. Ibid., Trevelyan to Twistleton, 13 June 1848.

176. Ibid.

177. Ibid.

178. P.L. Commissioners to Trevelyan, CSORP, 0.6624, 8 July 1848.

179. Twistleton to Trevelyan, PROL, T.64.367. B/2, 9 July 1848.

180. Ibid., Trevelyan to P.L. Inspector, Kenmare, T.64.370. C/4, February 1848; ibid., Twistleton to Trevelyan, PROL HO 45. 2472, 9 February 1848.

181. Ibid., Twistleton to Trevelyan, marked confidential, T.64.370. C/3, 1 March 1848; ibid., Twistleton to Trevelyan, T.64.370. B/1, 13 September 1848.

182. Ibid., Twistleton to Trevelyan, T.64.366A, 26 February 1848; ibid., report of Trevelyan, March 1849.

183. *Report by G. Nicholls to Her Majesty's Secretary of State for the Home Department,* 1837 [69], li, p.22; Nicholls, *Irish Poor Law,* pp. 309, 357.

CHAPTER 6: MAKING PROPERTY SUPPORT POVERTY 1848–9 (pp. 232–264)

1. Circular to P.L. Inspectors requesting information on the state of agricultural crops, especially potatoes in the local unions, with replies, April 1848, *First Annual Report,* 1848; Bourke, *The Visitation of God?,* pp. 74-89; Joel Mokyr, 'Irish history with the Potato' in *Irish Economic and Social History* (1981); Ó Gráda, *Ireland Before and After the Famine,* pp. 80, 136.

2. Vice-Guardians, Bantry to P.L. Commissioners, CSORP, 0.6930, 18 July 1848; Twistleton to Trevelyan, PROL T.64.367. B/2, 15 July 1848, 15 August 1848; ibid., reports to Trevelyan concerning the state of the potato crop, T.64.367. B/1, 28 June 1848; Minute Book of Kenmare union, 5 August 1848.

3. Evidence of E. Senior, *Select committee on Irish Poor Law*, 1849, pp. 141-2; Senior to Trevelyan, PROL, T. 64.367. B/1, 2 May 1848; Grant, 'The Great Famine in the Province of Ulster'.

4. Senior to P.L. Commissioners, CSORP, 0.9353, 21 September 1848; evidence of A. Power, *Select committee on Irish Poor Law*, 1849, p.11; ibid., evidence of Senior, p. 138.

5. Senior to P.L. Commissioners, CSORP, 0.9353, 21 September 1848.

6. Kenmare Vice-Guardians to P.L. Commissioners, Letter-Book of Kenmare union, 4 November 1848; P.L. Inspector to P.L. Commissioners, PROL, HO 45. 2472, 17 November 1848; Vice-Guardians, Westport to P.L. Commissioners, CSORP, 0.11984, 5 December 1848.

7. Ibid., P.L. Inspector, Skibbereen to P.L. Commissioners, 0.11984, 23 November 1848.

8. P.L. Inspector, Kilrush union to P.L. Commissioners, PROL, HO 45. 2472, 12 June 1848, 12 November 1848, 19 December 1848.

9. Ibid., P.L. Inspector, Ballina to Commissioners, 0.11984, 5 December 1848.

10. Twistleton to Trevelyan, PROL T.64.366A, 9 November 1848.

11. Wood to Trevelyan, PROL T.64.367. B/2, 25 July 1848; ibid., Trevelyan to J. Pim (Society of Friends), 24 August 1848.

12. J. M. Holt, 'The Quakers in the Great Irish Famine', unpublished M. Litt thesis (TCD 1967), passim.

13. British Relief Association to Twistleton, CSORP, 0.10468, 23 October 1848; ibid., P.L. Commissioners to British Relief Association, 25 October 1848; ibid., British Relief Association to P.L. Commissioners, 2 November 1848; Trevelyan to British Relief Association, PROL T.64.366.A, 28 October 1848; ibid., Vice-Guardians, Bantry to P.L. Commissioners, 28 November 1848, *Papers relating to the aid afforded to the Distressed Unions in the west of Ireland*, 1849, xlviii, 7 (hereafter, *Distressed Unions*), p. 21.

14. Trevelyan to Twistleton, 24 September 1848, PROL T.64.366.A; ibid., 4 October 1848.

15. Twistleton to Trevelyan, PROL T.64.366.A, 15 November 1848.

16. Grey to P.L. Commissioners, 16 January 1849, *Distressed Unions*, p. 30; Twistleton to Trevelyan, PROL T.64.366.A, 13 September 1848, 15 November 1848, 21 January 1849, 6 February 1849.

17. Commissioners to Grey, 2 January 1849, *Distressed Unions*, p.26.

18. Ibid., P.L. Commissioners to Vice-Guardians, Bantry, 30 November 1848, p. 22; ibid., P.L. Commissioners to Grey, 16 December 1848, p.23.

19. Twistleton to Trevelyan, PROL T.64.366.A, 21 January 1849.

20. Ibid., Twistleton to Trevelyan, 15 January 1849, 31 January 1849, 6 February 1849.

21. *The Times*, 4 January 1847, 6 January 1847, 7 January 1847 etc.; *The Times*, quoted in *Northern Whig*, 15 February 1849.

22. *Dublin Evening Post*, 21 December 1848; *Dublin Evening Mail*, 21 December 1848.

23. *Northern Whig*, 17 February 1849.

24. Resolutions of Ballymena, Donegal, Downpatrick, Ennis, Kells, Listowel unions, December 1848 to March 1849, various Minute Books; *Dublin Evening Post*, 19 December 1848, 21 December 1848, 30 January 1849, 3 March 1849; Chairman of Tralee board of guardians to Trevelyan, PROL, T.64.366.A, 17 February 1849.

25. *Dublin Evening Post*, 1 January 1849, 23 January 1849, 30 January 1849, 7 February 1849.

26. Ibid; *Northern Whig*, 20 February 1849.

27. Twistleton to Trevelyan, PROL T.64.366.A, 15 January 1849, 31 January 1849, 6 February 1849; *Dublin Evening Post*, 8 February 1849, 2 March 1849.

28. Gooch, *Russell*, pp. 218-20.

29. Trevelyan to Walker, PROL T.64.357. B/2, 23 August 1848; Wood to Trevelyan, T.64.366.A, 14 November 1848.

30. Treasury Minute on Distressed Unions, 16 January 1849, *Distressed Unions*, pp. 3-4; *Dublin Evening Post*, 8 February 1849; Russell to Lord Clarendon, 24 February 1849, quoted in Mandler, *Aristocratic Government*, p. 252.

31. 12 Vic. c.5.

32. Return of all sums of money either granted or advanced, *Distressed Unions*, p. 5.

33. *Dublin Evening Post*, 8 February 1849, 10 February 1849, 15 February 1849; *Northern Whig*, 17 February 1849.

34. Treasury Minute, 16 January 1849, *Distressed Unions*, pp. 3-4.

35. Ibid.

36. Twistleton to Trevelyan, PROL T.64.366.A. 19 January 1849.

37. P.L. Commissioners to Trevelyan, CSORP, 0.8182, 5 August 1848.

38. Wood to P.L. Commissioners, PROL T.64.366.A, 9 September 1848; ibid., Russell to Trevelyan, 11 September 1848.

39. Twistleton to Trevelyan, PROL T.64.367. B/2, 15 August 1848; Treasury to P.L. Commissioners, NLI, m/f. T.14.31.17258, 8 August 1848, 11 August 1848; P.L. Commissioners to Burke, Letter-Books, 3 August 1848, 11 August 1848; ibid., Circular to Temporary Poor Law Inspectors, 29 August 1848; ibid., P.L. Commissioners to Burke, 30 September 1848.

40. Twistleton to Trevelyan, PROL T.64.366A. 13 September 1848, 17 September 1848.

41. Memorial of ratepayers and guardians of the Donegal union, CSORP, 0.8891, 11 September 1848.

42. Memorial of ratepayers of Roscommon union, CSORP, 0.6241, 26 June 1848; ibid., Memorial of Guardians of Swinford union, 0.12240, 26 December 1848; ibid., Memorial of Guardians of Tipperary union, 0.123, 4 January 1849; ibid., Carlow Guardians to Chief Secretary, 0.8756, 7 September 1848; Minute Book of Newry union, 27 January 1849; Minute Book of Wexford union, 22 July 1848.

43. P.L. Inspector, Scariff to P.L. Commissioners, CSORP, 0.12417, 22 December 1848; ibid., P.L. Inspector, Galway to P.L. Commissioners, 0.10525, 4 November 1848; ibid., Vice-Guardians, Westport to P.L. Commissioners, 0.10999, 23 November 1848; ibid., P.L. Inspector, Newcastle to P.L. Commissioners, 0.7802, 10 August 1848.

44. Wood to P.L. Commissioners, PROL T.644.366.A, 9 September 1848; Treasury to P.L. Commissioners, NLI, m/f, T.14.6305, 2 April 1849; ibid., Treasury to P.L. Commissioners, T.14.12539, 8 June 1849; Treasury Minute, 6 March 1849, *Distressed Unions*, p. 12.

45. Ibid., Twistleton to Trevelyan, 26 January 1849, 26 February 1849, 29 March 1849; ibid., P.L. Commissioners to Home Office, HO 45. 2521.A, 12 February 1849, 19 February 1849.

46. See, Jennifer Hart, 'Sir Charles Trevelyan at the Treasury', in *English Historical Review*, vol. 75 (1960); Smith, *Wealth of Nations*; Burke, *Thoughts on Scarcity*.

47. Treasury to P.L. Commissioners, NLI, m/f, T.64.2414, 31 January 1849, 10 March 1849.

48. Private Report by Trevelyan, PROL T.64.366.A. March 1849.

49. P.L. Commissioners to Grey, 31 March 1849, *Further papers relating to aid afforded to the Distressed Unions in the west of Ireland*, 1849, xiviii, 121, II, p.25 (hereafter *Distressed Unions*, II); ibid., P.L. Commissioners to Trevelyan, 26 April 1949, p.44.

50. Treasury to P.L. Commissioners, PROL T.14.12539, 8 June 1849.

51. Treasury to P.L. Commissioners, NLI, m/f, T.14.2414, 20 February 1849; P.L. Commissioners to Trevelyan, 7 March 1849, *Distressed Unions*, II, p. 14.

52. Table showing by provinces, counties and towns, the number of deaths in each year from 1841 to 1851, *Census of Ireland, 1851*, p.li.

53. Ibid.

54. Ibid., *General Report of Census Commissioners*, p. xlix.

55. Ó Gráda, *Ireland Before and After the Famine*, pp. 138–44.

56. *Second Annual Report*, 1849; *Third Annual Report*, 1850.

57. Froggatt, 'The Response of the Medical Profession to the Great Famine', in Crawford (ed.), *Famine, The Irish experience*, p. 147; Crawford, 'Dearth, Diet and Disease in Ireland, 1850: a case study in nutritional deficiency' in *Medical History*, xxviii (1984).

58. Minute Book of Armagh union, 14 April 1849; Minute Book of Omagh union, 18 January 1849; P.L. Commissioners to Burke. Letter-Books, 23 May 1849.

59. Minute Book of Belfast union, 13 December 1848, 20 December 1848, 7 February 1849; P.L. Commissioners to Chief Secretary, 21 December 1848, PROL HO 45. 1584.

60. Minute Book of Armagh union, 10 February 1849; ibid., Board of Health to Armagh Guardians, 10 April 1849; P.L. Commissioners to Burke, Letter-Books, 15 March 1849; Minute Book of Westport union, 28 March 1849; Second Annual Report, 1849, p.11.

61. P.L. Commissioners to Trevelyan, CSORP, 0.838, 2 April 1849, 11 April 1849.

62. Ibid., Treasury to P.L. Commissioners, 14 April 1849, 19 June 1849, 21 July 1849; ibid., P.L. Commissioners to Treasury, 17 August 1849.

63. Minute Book of Westport union, 8 May 1849; Minute Book of Belfast union, 8 May 1849, 11 June 1849, 28 July 1849; *Second Annual Report*, 1849, p.11; S.M. Cousens, 'The Regional Variation in Mortality during the Great Irish Famine', in *Proceedings of the Royal Irish Academy*, lxii, section c, no. 3, 1963, p. 143.

64. Treasury Minute, 4 May 1849, *Distressed Unions*, II, p. 48; ibid., P.L. Commissioners to Trevelyan, *Further papers relating to the aid afforded to the Distressed Unions in the west of Ireland* (hereafter *Distressed Unions*, III), 1849, xlviii, p.12; ibid., P.L. Commissioners to Lewis (Home Office), 30 April 1849, p.4.

65. Treasury Minute, *Distressed Unions*, II, 4 May 1849, p.48; Treasury Minute, 14 May 1849, Distressed Unions, III, p.13; ibid., Treasury Minute, 15 May 1849, p.13; ibid., P.L. Commissioners to Trevelyan, 8 May 1849, p.5; ibid., 10 May 1849, p.9; ibid., 11 May 1849, p.10; ibid., 12 May 1849, p.12.

66. Treasury Minute, 17 May 1849, *Distressed Unions, III*, p. 19; ibid., Waddington (Home Office) to P.L. Commissioners, 10 May 1849, p. 8.

67. Ibid.

68. Prest, *Lord John Russell*, p. 294.

69. *Select committee on Irish Poor Law*, 1849 (H.C.), p. 3.

70. 12 & 13 Vic. c.24.

71. Report of Trevelyan, PROL T.64.366.A, undated, probably March 1849.

72. Ibid.

73. *Northern Whig*, 22 February 1849, 1 March 1849, 3 March 1849.

74. *Third Annual Report*, 1850; Grant, 'The Great Famine in the Province of Ulster'.

75. *Hansard's Parliamentary Debates*, third series, col. 200, 5 March 1849.

76. Ibid., col. 62, 1 March 1849.

77. Ibid., cols 48-50, 1 March 1849.

78. *Northern Whig*, 8 March 1849, 10 March 1849.

79. *Hansard's Parliamentary Debates*, third series, col. 322, 6 March 1849.

80. Gooch, *Russell*, pp. 230-35.

81. *The Northern Whig*, 15 February 1849 – 6 March 1849.

82. See, for example, Minute Book of Belfast union, 21 February 1849; Minute Book of Newry union, 24 February 1849; Minute Book of Ballymena union, 27 February 1849; Minute Book of Armagh union, 27 February 1849; Minute Book of Omagh union, 1 March 1849; Minute Book of Londonderry union, 3 March 1849.

83. *Dublin Evening Post*, 27 December 1849; *Northern Whig*, 22 February 1849, 3 March 1849, 12 May 1849, 24 May 1849.

84. Senior to P.L. Commissioners, CSORP, 0.6883, 20 July 1849.

85. Return of accounts, *Rate-in-Aid (Ireland)*, 1852 [87] xlvi, pp. 128-31.

86. *Dublin Evening Post*, 10 March 1849 – 27 March 1849.

87. *Morning Chronicle*, quoted in the *Northern Whig*, 22 February 1849.

88. *Dublin Evening Post*, 17 March 1846.

89. Evidence of Alfred Power, *Select committee on Irish Poor Law* (H.L.), 1849 [192] xvi; Burke to P.L. Commissioners, Letter-Book, 12 March 1849.

90. Evidence of E. Gulson, *Select committee of Irish Poor Law* (H.C.) 1849 [209] xv, pp. 103-4; ibid., Evidence of E. Senior, pp. 149-51 (hereafter, *Select committee*, 1849).

91. George Nicholls, *A History of the Irish Poor Law*, (London 1856), pp. 356-9.

92. Evidence of Twistleton, *Select committee*, 1849, (H.L.), pp. 699-714; Twistleton to Trevelyan, PROL T.64.366.A., 24 March 1849.

93. Evidence of Twistleton, *Select committee*, 1849 (H.L.), p.947.

94. Ibid., p.717; a similar analogy with the cost of the Crimean War (over £69m) to the imperial purse had been drawn by Mokyr, *Why Ireland Starved*, p. 292.

95. *Third Annual Report*, 1850, p.4.

96. Lord Palmerston to Russell, 5 August 1849, Gooch, *Russell*, p. 235.

97. Ibid., Lord Lansdowne to Russell, 9 August 1849, p. 235.

98. Minute Book of Listowel union, 28 March 1849 – 9 May 1849; P.L. Commissioners to Burke, Letter-Books, 9 May 1849.

99. P.L. Commissioners to Trevelyan, 26 May 1849, *Distressed Unions*, III, p.30; ibid., 1 June 1849, p.38; P.L. Commissioners to Home Office, CSORP, 0.5256, 2 July 1849.

CHAPTER 7: THE GENERAL ADVANCEMENT OF THE COUNTRY 1849–52 (pp. 265–296)

1. *Third Annual Report*, 1850, p.6; *Fourth Annual Report*, 1851, pp. 9-10; Alfred Power to Trevelyan, PROL T.64.367. C/2, 1 April 1850, 2 October 1850; P.L. Commissioners to all Vice-Guardians, Letter-Books, 21 August 1849.

2. 12 & 13 Vic. c.104.

3. *Third Annual Report*, 1850, p.5.

4. *Third Annual Report*, 1850, pp. 5-7; *Fourth Annual Report*, 1851, pp. 9-10; Bourke to P.L. Commissioners, CSORP, 0.3576, 28 April 1849; ibid., Barron (P.L.I) to P.L. Commissioners, 0.7026, 2 August 1849; ibid., Lynch (P.L.I.), 0.7488, 19 August 1849; County Surveyor, Co. Mayo to Trevelyan, PROL T.64.370.A, 3 December 1849.

5. *Third Annual Report*, 1850, p. 8.

6. *Copy of a letter from the Poor Law Commissioners in Ireland to the Secretary of State for the Home Department, dated 31 January 1849, with reference to the restoration of elected boards of guardians in certain unions in Ireland*, H.C. 1849 [61] xlvii, pp. 1-3 (restoration of Boards).

7. 12 & 13 Vic. c.104; Twistleton to Trevelyan, PROL T.64.366.A, 14 September 1848.

8. Minute Book of Kenmare union, 14 December 1849, 21 December 1849, 28 December 1849; Minute Book of Glenties union, 16 November 1849, 7 December 1849; Burke to P.L. Commissioners, Letter-Books, 15 November 1849; Trevelyan to Wood, PROL T.64.370. C/1., 6 November 1849.

9. Minute Book of Lowtherstown union, 18 March 1848.

10. Minute Book of Westport union, 2 January 1850.

11. *Copies and reports and resolutions made by boards of guardians, either entered on their minutes or transmitted to the Poor Law Commissioners, in those unions where paid guardians have acted, relating to the management of those unions while under the superintendence of paid guardians*, 1850, [251], l, passim (hereafter, *Paid Guardians*).

12. Ibid., resolutions of various boards of guardians, p. 10-55; *Report from select committee of the House of Lords appointed to investigate and report upon the allegations and charges contained in the petition of the board of guardians of the union of Carrick-on-Shannon, complaining of the management and misconduct of the late Vice-guardians of the said union* 1850 [725], xi, passim.

13. Resolutions of Athlone, Enniskillen, Galway, Gort, Kenmare, Mullingar, New Ross, Scariff, Tullamore and Waterford guardians, *Paid Guardians*, pp. 10-55.

14. *Third Annual Report*, 1850, pp. 5-7.

15. *Fourth Annual Report*, 1851, passim.

16. Trevelyan to Wood, PROL T.64.370.A, 19 October 1849, 26 October 1849; ibid., Power to Trevelyan T.64.366.A, 13 July 1849.

17. Ibid., note written upon by Trevelyan; P.L. Commissioners to Waterford Guardians, CSORP, 0.228, 5 December 1849.

18. Abstract of return of liabilities of each union in Ireland on 31 December 1849, *Fourth Annual Report*, 1851.

19. Minute Book of Londonderry union, 6 December 1849, 20 December 1849; ibid., P.L. Commissioners to Omagh union, 13 December 1849; P.L. Commissioners to Waterford Guardians, CSORP, 0.228, 5 December 1849, 7 January 1849; ibid.,

Waterford Guardians to P.L. Commissioners, 13 December 1849, 20 December 1849; ibid., Mayor of Waterford to P.L. Commissioners, 24 December 1849; ibid., P.L. Commissioners to Chief Secretary, 0.1385, 28 February 1850.

20. P.L. Commissioners to Chief Secretary, CSORP, 0.1386, 28 February 1850; ibid., P.L. Commissioners to Chief Secretary, 0.1385, 28 February 1850.

21. Scariff guardians to Lord Lieutenant, and reply, CSORP, 0.1282, 12 February 1850.

22. Ibid.

23. P.L. Commissioners to Trevelyan, CSORP, 0.2710, 9 April 1850, 11 April 1850; Trevelyan to P.L. Commissioners, PROL HO 45, 2521.A, 7 November 1849; ibid., Treasury to P.L. Commissioners, 7 November 1849.

24. Alfred Power to Trevelyan, PROL T.64.367. C/2, 1 April 1850; ibid., Power to Trevelyan, T.64.370 C/1, 15 December 1849, 19 January 1850, 29 March 1850; ibid., P.L. Commissioners to Treasury, HO 45, 2521. A, 10 May 1850.

25. *Fifth Annual Report*, 1852; 13 & 14 Vic. c.14; *Thom's Directory*, 1850, p. 203.

26. Ibid., *Thom's Directory*, 1852.

27. *Third Annual Report*, 1850, p.7; Power to Trevelyan, PROL, T.64.367. C/2, 18 January 1851.

28. 12 & 13 Vic. c.77; Solow, *The Land Question*, chs. 3 & 4; Bardon, *A History of Ulster*, p. 317.

29. Trevelyan to Twistleton, marked confidential, PROL, T.64.370. B/1, 14 September 1848; ibid., Power to Trevelyan, T.64.370. C/1, 15 December 1849; Minute Book of Kenmare union, 9 December 1848, 22 November 1850.

30. Power to Trevelyan, PROL T.64.3657. C/2, 8 February 1851; ibid., Trevelyan to Wood, 26 June 1851.

31. Ibid.; Mandler, *Aristocratic Government in the Age of Reform*, pp. 272-82.

32. Resolution of Oughterard Guardians, CSORP, 0.5283, 1 September 1851.

33. Ibid., resolution of Belmullet Guardians, 0.5775, 3 August 1851.

34. Ibid., resolution of Roscommon Guardians, 0.5925, 29 September 1851.

35. Ibid.

36. Resolution of Rathdrum Guardians, CSORP, 0.5706, 16 September 1851; ibid., resolution of Killarney Guardians, 0.61586, 6 October 1851; ibid., resolution of Parsonstown guardians, 0.6285, 18 October 1851; ibid., extract from *Southern Reporter*, forwarded to Trevelyan, PROL T.64.367. C/2, 11 November 1856; ibid., Treasury Minute, T.64.368.A, 21 October 1851; ibid., Power to Trevelyan, T.64.367. C/2, 8 November 1851.

37. *Sixth Annual Report of Poor Law Commissioners*, 1853; *Seventh Annual Report of Poor Law Commissioners*, 1854; Mandler, *Aristocratic Government*, p. 272.

38. Minute Book of Strabane union, 31 December 1850, 7 January 1851.

39. P.L. Commissioners to Burke, Letter-Books, 8 January 1851, 20 February 1851.

40. *Fifth Annual Report*, 1852, p.11; Isaac Butt, *A Voice for Ireland: famine in the land* (Dublin 1847).

41. *First report of the Commissioners for inquiring into the number and boundaries of Poor Law unions and electoral divisions in Ireland*, 1849 [1015], xxiii.

42. *First Annual Report*, 1848, p.17; *Second Annual Report*, 1849, p.13.

43. Ibid., p.14.

44. *First Annual Report*, 1848, pp. 15-17.

45. *First report . . . Boundary Commissioners*, pp. 370-75; Bardon, *History of Ulster*, pp. 316–18.

46. Twistleton to Trevelyan, PROL T.364.367. A/3, 18 November 1847; ibid., Twistleton to Trevelyan, T64.369. B/1, 4 December 1847; ibid., Twistleton to Trevelyan, T.64.367. B/1, 3 April 1848.

47. *Second Annual Report*, 1849, pp. 13, 19; Twistleton to Trevelyan, PROL T.64.369. B/3, 7 March 1848; ibid., Twistleton to Trevelyan, T.64.367. C/1, 10 January 1848.

48. Ibid., Twistleton to Trevelyan, T.64.367. C/1, 10 January 1848.

49. Ibid., Twistleton to Trevelyan, T.64.368.A., 2 January 1848; ibid., Twistleton to Trevelyan, T.64.369. B/3, 7 March 1848.

50. *Second report of the Commissioners for inquiring into the number and boundaries of Poor Law unions and electoral divisions in Ireland*, 1850 [1146], xxvi, p. 5.

51. *First Report . . . Boundary Commissioners*, pp. 8-9, 12.

52. Ibid., p. 10; *Second report . . . Boundary Commissioners*, p.5; *Return of Electoral Divisions in Ireland which comprise the property of a single person, or of two properties only, showing the extent and population thereof*, 1847-8 [404], lvii; *Fourteenth report of the Boundary Commissioners*, 1850 [1278], xxvi, pp. 3-6.

53. *First report . . . Boundary Commissioners*, pp. 10-11, 380-91; *Eighth Report of Boundary Commissioners*, 1850 [1199], xxvi, pp. 3-5; *Fourteenth report . . . Boundary Commissioners*, pp. 3-6.

54. *Fourth Annual Report*, 1851, pp. 12-13; *Fifth Annual Report*, 1852, p. 15.

55. P.L. Commissioners to Boundary Commissioners, CSORP, 0.7487, 13 August 1849; P.L. Commissioners to Home Office, 2521.A, 8 March 1849; ibid., P.L. Commissioners to Home Office, November 1849.

56. P.L. Commissioners to Burke, Letter-Books, 29 May 1850, 19 June 1850; P.L. Commissioners to Home Office, HO 45. 2521.A, 8 March 1849.

57. Ibid., Treasury to P.L. Commissioners, 7 November 1849; ibid., P.L. Commissioners to Home Office, 24 December 1849.

58. P.L. Commissioners to Home Office, *Report of Irish Poor Law Commissioners on the measures taken for carrying into effect the recommendations of the Boundary Commissioners*, 1850 [1162], xxvii, pp. 1-3; P.L. Commissioners to Burke, Letter-Books, 10 June 1850, 19 June 1850; Memorial of guardians, landowners, ratepayers in the Nenagh union, CSORP, 0.229, 10 January 1850; Public Work Loan Commissioners to Omagh Guardians, Minute Books of Omagh union, 27 September 1849.

59. *Report . . . on recommendations of the Boundary Commissioners*, p.2; P.L. Commissioners to Burke, Letter-Books, 10 June 1850, 19 June 1850.

60. Reservation order, Minute Book of Westport union, 31 October 1849, 7 May 1850, 28 May 1850; Sir Lucius O'Brien, Ennis union, to Trevelyan, PROL T.64.367. C/2, 14 November 1850.

61. *Annual Reports*, 1848-54, passim.

62. Ó Gráda, *Ireland Before and After the Famine*, pp. 75-80; P.L. Commissioners to each P.L. Inspector, Letter-Books, 12 October 1850; ibid., P.L. Commissioners to Burke, 10 November 1850.

63. *Second Annual Report*, 1849, p. 8; *Third Annual Report*, 1850, pp. 9-10; *Fifth Annual Report*, 1852, p. 12; Burke to P.L. Commissioners, Letter-Books, 12 December 1848.

64. *Third Annual Report*, 1850, p. 7.

65. *Fourth Annual Report*, 1851, pp. 4-8.

66. *Report of the select committee appointed to inquire into the administration of the Poor Law in the Kilrush union since 19 September 1848*, 1850 [613] xi, p. viii (hereafter, *Committee on Kilrush union*); *Copy of report addressed to the Poor Law Commissioners by Inspector Bourke with reference to the condition of the Kilrush union*, 1850 [259], l.; ibid., Report of committee, *Committee on Kilrush union*, p. xii.

67. Captain Kennedy to P.L. Commissioners, 13 April 1848, *Copies of the correspondence between the P.L. Commissioners of Ireland and their Inspector, relative to the statements contained in an extract from a book, entitled, Gleanings in the west of Ireland*, 1851 [218] xlix, p. 6 (hereafter, *Evictions in Kilrush*).

68. Kennedy to P.L. Commissioners, 17 May 1849, *Distressed unions*, III, p. 16.

69. Report of committee, *Committee on Kilrush union*, p. xii.

70. Ibid., p. xiii; Inglis, *Poverty and the Industrial Revolution*, pp. 427-9.

71. Ibid., p. xiii.

72. Ibid., evidence of Sir Lucius O'Brien, pp. xvii-xviii.

73. Copy of a report made to the P.L. Commissioners by Mr Lucas, Temporary Inspector in charge of the Kilrush union, in regard to certain statements regarding the management of the Kilrush union, contained in a letter signed S. Godolphin Osborne, which appeared in *The Times* newspaper of 31 March 1851, 1851 [234], xlix.

74. *Third Annual Report*, 1850, p.7; *Fourth Annual Report*, 1851, pp. 4-8.

75. *Sixth Annual Report*, 1853.

76. Communication from Sir Lucius O'Brien, with copy of resolution of chairmen of unions in Co. Clare, regarding the administration of the Poor Law in Ireland, CSORP, 0.6066, 25 September 1850.

77. *Fifth Annual Report*, 1852.

78. Minutes of Ennistymon Guardians, 6 December 1851. *Copies of any correspondence which may have taken place in relation to the dismissal of the board of elected guardians of the Ennistymon union, and the appointment of paid guardians therein*, 1851 [203], xlix, p. 5.

79. Ibid., report of P.L. Inspector to P.L. Commissioners, 8 December 1850, 29 December 1850, pp. 6,18; ibid., Sir Lucius O'Brien to P.L. Commissioners, 6 January 1851, p. 21; ibid. P.L. Commissioners to Ennistymon Guardians, 28 December 1851, p. 17; Report of Dr Madden, CSORP, 0.3508, 2 June 1851.

80. Report of John Hill and James Hughes, MDs, PROL HO 45, 3696, 4 October 1851.

81. Ibid., Power to Trevelyan, PROL T.64.367. C/2, 1 November 1851.

82. P.L. Inspector, counties Tipperary and Limerick, CSORP, 0.7488, 19 August 1849; *Copy of report made to the board of guardians of the Castlebar union, on 20 April 1850, by Dr Ronayne, medical superintendent of the union, relative to the state of the workhouse*, 1850, [282], l.

83. Minute Book of Kenmare union, 1 November 1850, 15 November 1850, 29 November 1850, 28 December 1850.

84. Crawford, 'Subsistence Crises in Ireland: a nutritionist's view', in Crawford (ed.), *Famine, The Irish Experience*, p. 210.

85. *Fourth Annual Report*, 1851, p. 9; *Fifth Annual Report*, 1852, p. 14.

86. 114 & 115 Vic. c.68.

87. *Fifth Annual Report*, 1852, p. 15.

88. Ibid.

89. Ó Gráda, *Ireland Before and After the Famine*, p. 17, Mokyr, *Why Ireland Starved*, p. 292.

90. *Annual Reports of P.L. Commissioners*, 1845–53.

91. Table showing the number of persons in 1841 and 1851 in each Province, County, City and large town in Ireland . . . , *Census for Ireland*, 1851, p. xv; ibid., A table showing the probable number of inhabitants which would have been in Ireland in March 1851 . . . , p. xvi.

92. Ibid., *General report*, p. lviii.

CHAPTER 8: THEIR SORROWFUL PILGRIMAGE: EMIGRATION 1847–55 (pp. 297–341)

1. R. Dickson, *Ulster Emigration to Colonial America* (Belfast 1989); D. Fitzpatrick, *Irish Emigration, 1801-1921* (Dublin 1984), p. 4; Roy Foster, *Modern Ireland, 1600-1972* (London 1988), pp. 345–72; Cormac Ó Gráda, 'A note on Nineteenth-Century Emigration Statistics' in *Population Studies*, vol. 29 (March 1975). *Thirteenth general report of Colonial Land and Emigration Commissioners*, 1852-3 [164], xl, p. 10; *Sixteenth general report of Colonial Land and Emigration Commissioners*, 1856 [2089], xxiv, p. 10; *The Famine Immigrants; lists of Irish immigrants arriving at the port of New York, 1846-1851* (Baltimore 1983); Malthus, *An Essay on Population*, pp. 81-8.

2. *Report of the Select Committee of the House of Lords on Colonisation from Ireland*, 1847 [737] vi, p. vi (hereafter, *Colonisation from Ireland*).

3. Cormac Ó Gráda, 'Some aspects of nineteenth-century emigration', in L.M. Cullen and T.C. Smout (eds), *Comparative Aspects of Scottish and Irish Economic and Social History, 1600-1900* (Edinburgh 1977) passim; Kerby A. Miller, *Emigrants and Exiles: Ireland and the Irish Exodus to North America* (Oxford 1985), pp. 270-80; O. MacDonagh, *A Pattern of Government Growth: The Passenger Acts and their Enforcement* (London 1961).

4. *Census for Ireland*, 1851, p. liv.

5. *Thirteenth report of Emigration Commissioners*, p.10; *Sixteenth report of Emigration Commissioners*, p.10; *Armagh Guardian* quoted in *Roscommon and Leitrim Gazette*, 24 April 1847; Hickey, *Famine, Mortality and Emigration*, p. 907; Fitzpatrick, *Irish Emigration*, p. 9.

6. *Sixth Annual Report of P.L. Commissioners*, p. 9; *Thirteenth report of Emigration Commissioners*, p.10; *Fourteenth general report of Colonial Land and Emigration Commissioners*, 1854 [1833] xxvii, pp. 10-12.

7. *Twentieth general report of Colonial Land and Emigration Commissioners*, 1860 [2696] xxxix, p.14; *Sixteenth report of Emigration Commissioners*, p. 10.

8. *Northern Whig*, 11 May 1847.

9. *Report from the Select Committee on the Passenger Act with the proceedings of the Select Committee, minutes of evidence, appendices and index*, 1851, xiii, 632.

10. *Northern Whig*, 24 April 1847.
11. From *Morning Chronicle*, reprinted in *Northern Whig*, 15 July 1850.
12. *Report . . . on the Passenger Act*, pp. v-viii.
13. Ibid., p. xii.
14. Ibid., p. lvii.
15. *Northern Whig*, 24 April 1847.
16. *Illustrated London News*, 13 July 1850, 10 May 1851.
17. C.J. Houston & W.J. Smyth, 'The geography of Irish emigration to Canada', in *Familia: Ulster Genealogical Review* (Belfast 1988), p. 18.
18. *Census for Ireland*, 1851, p. lvi.
19. Ibid.
20. Ibid., Sir William Wilde, quoted in Fiztpatrick, *Irish Emigration*, p. 1.
21. Black, *Economic Thought and the Irish Question*, pp. 209–17; Cormac Ó Gráda, 'Across the Briny Ocean: some thoughts on Irish emigration to America 1800-1850' in T.M. Devine and D. Dickson (eds), *Ireland and Scotland 1800-50* (Edinburgh 1983), p. 121; MacDonagh, *A pattern of government growth*.
22. *Colonisation from Ireland*, p. vii.
23. Ibid., p. vi.
24. Ibid., pp. iii-vi.
25. *Third report of His Majesty's Commissioners for inquiring into the condition of the poorer classes in Ireland, with appendix and supplement*, 1836 [35], xx, p. 27; *Colonisation from Ireland*, p. viii.
26. Ibid., p. ix.
27. Ibid.
28. Lord John Russell to George Nicholls, 22 August 1836, *First report of Nicholls*, pp. 1-2; *Second report of Nicholls*, passim; 1 & 2 Vic. c.56, section 51.
29. *Colonisation from Ireland*, p. x.
30. 6 & 7 Vic. c.92, section 18; *Colonisation from Ireland*, p. xi.
31. Ibid., p. x.
32. Ibid., p. xvi.
33. Ibid.
34. 1 & 2 Vic. c.56. section 51; 6 & 7 Vic. c.92, section 18.
35. 10 Vic. c.24, sections 13-15.
36. *Twelfth report of the select committee on poor Laws (Ireland) together with minutes of evidence*, 1849 [403], xv, p. iii; 12 & 13 Vic. c.104, sections 26-8.
37. *Tenth report of the Colonial Land and Emigration Commissioners*, 1850 [1204], xxiii, p. 5; *Thirteenth general report of the Colonial Land and Emigration Commissioners*, 1852-3 [164], xl, p. 10; *Third Annual Report*, 1850, p. 11.
38. *Annual Report of the Local Government Board for Ireland for the year ending 1901*, Appendix G, No. 8.
39. 12 & 13 Vic. c.24, section 3.
40. *Fifth Annual Report*, 1852, pp. 11-12; *Sixth Annual Report*, 1852, p. 9.
41. *Seventh Annual Report*, 1854, p. 8.
42. P.L. Commissioners to Emigration Commissioners, CSORP, 0.7445, 22 June 1852.
43. Minute Book of Ballymoney union, 23 April 1849.

44. Minute Book of Lisnaskea union, 16 March 1850; Minute Book of Londonderry union, 21 April 1849; memorial of ratepayers of Skibbereen union, CSORP, 0.3609, June 1852; ibid., extract from Minutes of Balrothery union, 0.442. 24 December 1848; ibid., minutes of Balrothery union, 0.3608, 26 May 1852.

45. P.L. Commissioners to Burke, Letter-Books, 10 July 1849, 26 February 1851, 5 April 1851.

46. Ibid., 14 March 1851; P.L. Commissioners to Chief Secretary, CSORP, 0.2471, 27 March 1850.

47. Minute Book of Strabane union, 11 October 1850–23 March 1852.

48. Minute Book of Kenmare union, 3 May 1850, 14 June 1850, 30 August 1850, 28 December 1850, 3 January 1851, 7 March 1851, 21 March 1851, 11 April 1851, 8 August 1851.

49. W.S. Trench, *Realities of Irish Life* (London 1868), pp. 56-72.

50. S.H. Cousens, 'The Regional Pattern of Emigration during the Great Famine, 1846-51', in *Transactions and Papers of the Institute of British Geographers*, No. 28 (1960), passim; Edwards and Williams (eds), *The Great Famine*, p. 334; David Fitzpatrick 'Was Ireland Special?' in *Historical Journal*, 33 (1990); Fitzpatrick, *Irish Emigration*, pp. 15-16; Foster, *Modern Ireland*, p. 349; *Roscommon and Leitrim Gazette*, 20 March 1847.

51. Trevelyan to Twistleton, PROL T.64.370. B/1, 14 September 1848.

52. Ibid., Wood to P.L. Commissioners, T.64.366.A, 9 September 1848.

53. Ibid., Russell to Treasury, 11 September 1848.

54. Peig Sayers, *Peig* (Dublin 1936); Fitzpatrick, *Irish Emigration*, pp. 7-8; for the continuing absence of women in the history of emigration see, for example, Roger Swift and Sheridan Gilley (eds), *The Irish in Britain, 1815-1939* (London 1989).

55. Patrick O'Farrell, *The Irish in Australia* (New South Wales 1987), passim; Portia Robinson, *The Women of Botany Bay* (New South Wales 1988), passim; Trevor McClaughlin, *From Shamrock to Wattle* (Melbourne, 1985) passim; McDonagh, *Government Growth*, passim; Home Office to Governor of South Australia, PROL HO 45, 2252, 17 February 1847.

56. Colonial Office to Chief Secretary, CSORP, 0.6808, 23 August 1848; ibid., memorandum of Lord Lieutenant, 20 January 1849.

57. Emigration Commissioners to Colonial Department, 17 February 1848, *First Annual Report*, 1848, pp. 151-2; Emigration Commissioners to Colonial Office, PROL, HO 45, 1712, 17 February 1848.

58. Ibid.

59. Memorandum of Lord Lieutenant, CSORP, 0.6808, 20 January 1848.

60. Trevelyan to Clarendon, PROL T.64.367. C/1, 29 January 1848.

61. Ibid., 31 January 1848.

62. Ibid., Twistleton to Trevelyan, T.64.370. C/4, 17 February 1848.

63. P.L. Commissioners to each P.L. Inspector, April 1848; *First Annual Report*, 1848, p. 156; ibid., P.L. Commissioners to Medical Officer of each union, April 1848, p. 155; Burke to P.L. Commissioners, Letter-Books, 4 March 1848.

64. P.L. Commissioners to Redington, PROL HO 45, 2252, 4 March 1848.

65. Emigration Commissioners to Home Office, CSORP, 0.6808, 9 December 1848.

66. *Second Annual Report*, 1849, pp. 8-9; *Third Annual Report*, 1850, p. 11.

67. P.L. Commissioners to Burke, Letter-Book, 22 September 1848, 16 November 1849; ibid., P.L. Commissioners to Medical Officers of each union, 28 July 1849; Minute Book of Omagh union, 3 April 1849; 12 April 1849.

68. Minute Book of Omagh union, 5 April 1849; James S. Donnelly Jnr, *The Land and People of Nineteenth-Century Cork: the rural economy and the land question* (London 1975), p. 130.

69. Minute Book of Ballymoney union, 11 August 1849, 15 September 1849; Minute Book of Killarney union, 26 June 1848; Minute Book of Wexford union, 27 May 1848, 6 January 1849; Minute Book of Armagh union, 11 March 1848; Minute Book of Ballina union, 17 August 1848; P.L. Commissioners to Medical Officer of each union, *First Annual Report*, 1848, p. 155.

70. Senior to P. L. Commissioners, PROL T.64.369. B/3, 13 March 1848.

71. P.L. Commissioners to each P.L. union, Letter-Book, 11 August 1849; Minute Book of Omagh union, 30 August 1849; P.L. Commissioners to Armagh union, 28 August 1849; Minute Book of Strabane union, 5 November 1850.

72. *Ninth general report of Colonial Land and Emigration Commissioners*, 1849 [1082] xxii, p. 8.

73. C. Fitzroy, Government House, Sydney, to Colonial Office, CSORP, 0.9048, 19 December 1848; ibid., minute of Colonial Secretary on the above.

74. Ibid., Fitzroy to Colonial Secretary, 18 December 1848.

75. Ibid., Home Office to Chief Secretary, 19 May 1849.

76. P.L. Inspector to Guardians of Belfast union, Minute Book of Belfast union, 31 May 1849; ibid., P.L. Commissioners to Guardians, 6 June 1849; Home Office to Fitzroy, CSORP, 0.9673, 5 October 1849.

77. *Ninth Report of Emigration Commissioners*, p. 13.

78. H.E. Young, Adelaide, to Colonial Secretary, CSORP, 0.246, 10 September 1848.

79. Ibid., Colonial Office to Chief Secretary, 0.3081, 13 April 1849; Young to Earl Grey, 29 November 1848, *Ninth Report of Emigration Commissioners*, p. 52.

80. Superintendent, Port Philip to Colonial Officer, Sydney, CSORP, 0.8132, 8 January 1849; *Tenth Report of Emigration Commissioners*, p. 19.

81. Report from Melbourne, Letter-Book, 18 August 1849.

82. Ibid., P.L. Commissioners to Burke, 4 December 1849; P.L. Commissioners to Chief Secretary, CSORP, 0.2125, 29 April 1850; Report by Government Emigration Agent, Sydney, Letter-Book, 13 December 1849; ibid., P.L. Commissioners to Waterford Guardians, 24 August 1850; ibid., P.L. Commissioners to Waterford Guardians, 24 August 1850; Colonial Office to Chief Secretary, CSORP, 0.4779, 23 July 1850.

83. Ibid., Minute of Orphan Emigration Committee, 0.6423, 8 December 1849.

84. Ibid., Fitzroy to Colonial Secretary, 0.3337, 19 December 1849.

85. Ibid., Copy of letter to *South Australian Register*, 0.6479, 21 January 1850.

86. Ibid., Young, Adelaide to Colonial Office, 8 March 1850; ibid., Children's Apprenticeship Board to Colonial Secretary, 28 February 1850; ibid., Young to Colonial Office, 8 March 1850.

87. Ibid., Colonial Office to Chief Secretary, 10 October 1850.

88. Ibid., P.L. Commissioners to Chief Secretary, 27 November 1850.

89. Ibid.

90. Ibid.

91. Ibid., P.L. Commissioners to each union, 0.7068, 22 November 1850; *Eleventh general report of the Emigration Commissioners*, 1851 [1383], xxii, p. 14.

92. O. MacDonagh, 'The Poor Law, Emigration and the Irish Question' in *Christus Rex*, vol. 12 (1958), p. 34.

93. P.L. Commissioners to each union, 27 April 1850, *Second Annual Report*, 1849, p. 67.

94. *Tenth Report of Emigration Commissioners*, p.19; Emigration Commissioners to Kildysart union, CSORP, 0.7445, 22 June 1852.

95. Ibid., P.L. Commissioners to Emigration Commissioners, 6 July 1852; *Fifth Annual Report*, 1852, pp. 11-12.

96. D. Fitzpatrick, *Irish Emigration 1801-1921* (Dublin 1984), pp. 22-3.

97. Roger Swift 'The Outcast Irish in the British Victorian City: problems and perspectives' in *Irish Historical Studies*, xxv, no. 99, p. 264.

98. Colin G. Pooley, 'Segregation or integration? The residential experience of the Irish in mid-Victorian Britain', in Swift and Gilley (eds), *The Irish in Britain, 1815-1939*, p. 66.

99. L.P. Curtis, *Apes and Angels: the Irishman in Victorian caricature* (Newton Abbot 1971), passim.

100. Graham Davis, 'Little Irelands', in Swift and Gilley (eds.), op. cit., p. 109.

101. Friedrich Engels, *The Condition of the Working Class in England* (Leipzig 1845, London 1892), p. 934.

102. Quoted in Swift, 'The Outcast Irish', pp. 271-2.

103. From *Dublin Evening Post*, reprinted in *Northern Whig*, 11 March 1847; *The Times*, 17 February 1847; from *Sligo Journal*, reprinted in *Roscommon and Leitrim Gazette*, 20 March 1847.

104. From *Liverpool Times*, reprinted in *Northern Whig*, 15 April 1847.

105. Adam Hodgson to Sir George Grey, 23 March 1847, PROL HO 45, 1816; ibid., Sir George Grey, responding to various applications for government intervention, 27 March 1847; Frank Neal, *Sectarian Violence: the Liverpool experience, 1819-1914*, (Manchester 1987).

106. From *Liverpool Mercury*, reprinted in *Northern Whig*, 11 March 1847; from *Liverpool Times*, reprinted in *Roscommon and Leitrim Gazette*, 3 April 1847.

107. Dr Swift to Sir George Grey (Home Secretary), PROL HO 45, 1816, 3 April 1847.

108. Return of the number of Irish poor brought over monthly to the port of Liverpool from the coast of Ireland in each of the last five years; distinguishing, as far as possible, those who remain in this country and those who emigrate across the sea, *Report from The Select Committee of the House of Commons on poor removal*, 1854 [396] xvii, p. 751.

109. M.E. Rose, 'Settlement, Removal and the New Poor Law', in D. Fraser (ed.), *The New Poor Law in the Nineteenth Century* (London 1976) pp. 38-9; M.E. Rose, *The English Poor Law* (Newton Abbot 1971), p. 194.

110. *Northern Whig*, 1 April 1847; *Roscommon and Leitrim Gazette*, 24 April 1847.

111. *Northern Whig*, 13 May 1847.

112. Ibid., 17 April 1847.

113. 13 & 14 Ch. II, c.12; 8 & 9 Wm. III. c.30; 33 Geo. III. c.54; 35 Geo. III. c.101; Rose, 'Settlement removal . . .', passim.

114. 9 & 10 Vic. c.66; 10 & 11 Vic. c.110.

115. 1 & 2 Vic. c.56, section 41; 6 & 7 Vic. c.92, section 12.

116. *Report of the Select Committee on poor removal*, 1854 [396] xvii, passim; Rose, 'Settlement, removal . . . ', pp. 38-9.

117. Ibid., passim; *Annual Reports of Irish P.L. Commissioners* (reorganised as Local Government Board) 1848-96; 24 & 25 Vic. c.66.

118. Liverpool Board of Guardians to Home Office, PROL HO 45, 1816, November 1847.

119. Ibid., Cardiff Board of Guardians to Home Office, HO 100, 257, 7 June 1849; ibid., Notice of Cardiff Guardians, 2 June 1849.

120. Rose, 'Settlement, removal . . . ', pp. 27-38; *Committee . . . on poor removal*, pp. 570-607.

121. Ibid., *Returns of the number of Irish poor relieved out of the poor rates in the year 1848, in the city of London, Marylebone, Westminster, Lambeth, Southwark, Tower Hamlets and Finsbury respectively; and of the money value of the relief so afforded; similar returns as to Liverpool, Glasgow, Bristol, Cardiff, Newport, Merthyr Tydvil, Manchester, Salford, Preston, Bury, Leeds, Paisley and Edinburgh respectively*, 1849 [342], xlvii.

122. Evidence of R. Pashley, *Committee . . . on poor removal*, p. 473.

123. *Copy of a letter addressed to Her Majesty's Secretary of State for the Home Department by Edward Rushton, Esq., Stipendiary Magistrate of Liverpool, bearing the date 21 April 1849*, 1849 [266], xlvii, pp. 1-2; W.M. Frazer, *Duncan of Liverpool* (London 1947), pp. 30–70.

124. D. Ashford, 'The Urban Poor Law', in Fraser (ed.), *The New Poor Law*, p. 146.

125. Rose, 'Settlement, Removal . . . ', pp. 27–38.

126. *Dublin Evening Post*, 1 January 1848.

127. Ibid., resolution of North Dublin union, CSORP, 1847 0.9698, 8 September 1847.

128. Minute Book of Belfast union, 9 January 1848, 6 December 1848, 13 December 1848.

129. A. Patterson, 'The Poor Law in the Nineteenth Century', in Fraser (ed.), *The New Poor Law*, p. 186; Minute Book of Strabane union, 27 May 1851, 9 September 1851.

130. Clerk of Armagh union to P.L. Commissioners, 7 November 1848, *A copy of all correspondence between the Commissioners for administering the laws for the relief of the poor in Ireland and in England, relative to the removal of John McCoy from Newcastle-upon-Tyne to Armagh, including the opinion of counsel thereon*, 1849 [159], xlvii, p.3; ibid., P.L. Commissioners to the clerk of the Armagh union, 4 December 1848, p. 4; opinion of J. Henn QC, 22 January 1849, pp. 7-9.

131. Ibid., Viscount Ebrington to P.L. Commissioners, 6 May 1849, p. 9; ibid., P.L. Commissioners to Ebrington, 19 May 1848, pp. 10-12.

132. Lord Lieutenant to Belfast Guardians, CSORP, 0.11750, 16 December 1848; ibid., English P.L. Commissioners to Chief Secretary, 0.3136, 3 April 1851.

133. Ibid., opinion of J. Henn QC, 22 January 1849, pp. 7–9; *Seventeenth Annual Report of P.L. Commissioners*, 1864, pp. 30-70.

CHAPTER 9: CONCLUSION 1845–52 (pp. 342–359)

1. Edwards and Williams (eds), *The Great Famine*; Daly, *The Famine in Ireland*; Foster, *Modern Ireland*.

2. Roderick Floud, 'Standards of Living and Industrialisation' in *Recent Findings of Research in Economic and Social History*, No. 6 (1988), p. 2; Ó Gráda, *Ireland Before and After the Famine*, pp. 17-18, 67-76; J.G. Williamson, 'Why was British Growth so Slow During the Industrial Revolution?' in *Journal of Economic History*, xliv (1984); N.F.R. Crafts, 'The Industrial Revolution: economic growth in Britain, 1700-1860' in *Recent Findings of Research in Economic and Social History*, No. 4 (1987), p. 3.

3. Friedrich Engels, *The Condition of the Working Class in England in 1844* (London 1892); Elizabeth Gaskell, *Mary Barton* (Manchester 1848); John Smith, *The Condition of Scotland* (Scotland 1846); Brian Inglis, *Poverty and the Industrial Revolution* (London 1971); R. Woods and J. Woodward (eds), *Urban Disease and Mortality in Nineteenth-Century England* (London 1984). Bruce James, *Destitution in the Highlands, letters reprinted from The Scotsman* (Scotland 1847); John Prebble, *The Highland Clearances* (London 1963); Tom Devine, 'The Highland Clearances' in *Recent Findings of Research in Economic and Social History*, No. 4, 1987.

4. Cormac Ó Gráda, *Ireland Before and After the Famine*, pp. 40-41.

5. During 1846–7, governments throughout Europe responded to the widespread crop failures by opening soup kitchens, providing cheap food, prohibiting the export of foodstuffs, removing tariffs on food exports, and subsidising grain imports. These measures were generally very sucessful. See for example Jonathan Sperber, *The European Revolutions, 1848–51* (Cambridge 1994), pp. 106–8; Peter Mandler, *Aristocratic Government in the Age of Reform*; John Belcham, *Industrialisation and the Working Class: the English experience 1750-1900* (Aldershot 1990); D. Thompson, *The Chartists*, London 1984; *The Times* 1847, passim.

6. *St James's Chronicle*, 20 October 1847 passim; *The Times*, October 1847.

7. N. Senior, 'The Relief of Irish Distress in 1846 and 1847' in *Ireland. Journals* vol. 1, pp. 195–265; George O'Brien, *The Economic History of Ireland from the Union to the Famine* (London 1921); Gerald Keegan, *Famine Diary: journey to a new world* (Dublin 1991).

8. Trevelyan, *Irish Crisis*, passim; J. Mitchel, *Jail Journals*; N. Senior, *Journals*.

9. Ó Gráda, *Ireland Before and After the Famine*, p. 117, who also draws on the work of Joel Mokyr, *Why Ireland Starved*.

10. Trevelyan, *Irish Crisis*, p. 65.

11. See, for example, *Illustrated London News, St James's Chronicle*, especially August-October 1847; *The Times*, passim.

12. Report of 1851 Census Commissioners; see also Senior, *Journals*, vol. 2, pp. 3–5.

13. Introductory chapter to the third edition of Hill, *Facts from Gweedore* (1853), p. 9.

14. Trevelyan sent copies of the works of Adam Smith, Edmund Burke and of his own articles and book to relief officials in Ireland.

15. James Kelly, 'Scarcity and Poor Relief in Eighteenth-Century Ireland: the subsistence crisis of 1782-84', *Irish Historical Studies*, vol. xxviii, no. 109, May 1992, pp. 38-62.

16. This idea has been convincingly made by Black, *Economic Thought and the Irish Question*; Ó Gráda, *Ireland Before and After the Famine*; Boylan and Foley, *Political Economy and Colonial Ireland*.

17 See also R.J. Montague, 'Relief and Reconstruction in Ireland, 1845-49' (unpublished D.Phil. thesis, Oxford University 1976).

Bibliography

MANUSCRIPT SOURCES
REPUBLIC OF IRELAND

NATIONAL ARCHIVES, DUBLIN
Chief Secretary's Office, 1838-65
Distress Papers, 1840-55
Letter-Books of Joseph Burke (Assistant P.L. Commissioner), 1839-55
Official Papers, 1840-55
Relief Commission Papers, 1845-7.

NATIONAL LIBRARY OF IRELAND
Larcom Papers, Ms. 7,600
Mayo Papers, Ms. 11,186
Minute Books of Ballina Union, Ms. 12,000-04
Ennistymon Union, Ms. 12,766
Westport Union, Ms. 12,607-12
Moneagle Papers, Ms. 13,383; 13,352-4; 13,361
Reports of Society of Friends on distress in Ireland. Ir. 9410859
Treasury Outletters (microfilm) p. 284.

CUSTOM HOUSE, DUBLIN
Order Books of P.L. Commissioners, 1838-55

ST MARY'S HOSPITAL, DUBLIN
Minute Books of South Dublin Union

SOCIETY OF FRIENDS' LIBRARY, DUBLIN
Pim Manuscript

COUNTY LIBRARY, LIFFORD, CO. DONEGAL
Minute Books of Ballyshannon Union, BG.38.A
Glenties Union, BG.92.A

Inishowen Union, BG.97.A
Letterkenny Union, BG.109.A
Stranorlar Union, BG.147.A

DUNFANAGHY WORKHOUSE, DUNFANAGHY, CO. DONEGAL
Minute Books/Letter-Books of Dunfanaghy Union

COUNTY LIBRARY, GALWAY, CO. GALWAY
Minute Books of Ballinasloe Union
Clifden Union
Galway Union
Glenamaddy Union
Gort Union
Loughrea Union
Oughterard Union
Portumna Union
Tuam Union

COUNTY LIBRARY, TRALEE, CO. KERRY
Minute Books/Letter-Books of Dingle Union
Kenmare Union
Killarney Union
Listowel Union

COUNTY LIBRARY, NAVAN, CO. MEATH
Minute Books of Kells Union, BG.99.A.
Navan Union, BG.128.A
Trim Union, BG.155.A

COUNTY LIBRARY, LISMORE, CO. WATERFORD (COURTESY OF TRAMORE LIBRARY)
Minute Books of Dungarvan Union
Kilmacthomas Union
Lismore Union
Waterford Union

COUNTY LIBRARY, WEXFORD, CO. WEXFORD
Minute Books of Gorey Union
New Ross Union
Wexford Union

NORTHERN IRELAND

PUBLIC RECORD OFFICE, BELFAST
Minute Book/Letter Books of
Antrim Union, BG.1.A
Armagh Union BG.1.A
Ballymena Union, BG.4.A
Ballymoney Union, BG.5.A

Banbridge Union, BG.6.A
Belfast Union, BG.7.A
Clogher Union, GB.9.A
Coleraine Union, BG.20.A
Cookstown Union, BG.12.A. BG.12.B
Enniskillen Union, BG.14.A
Kilkeel Union, BG.16.A
Lisburn Union, BG.19.A
Lisnaskea Union, BG.20.A
Londonderry Union, BG.21.A
Lowtherstown Union, BG.15.A
Lurgan Union, BG.22A BG.22B
Magherafelt Union, BG.23.A
Omagh Union, BG.26.A
Strabane Union, BG.27.A

LONDON

PUBLIC RECORD OFFICE, KEW
Home Office Papers, 1838-55
Ministry of Health Papers, 1838-55
Treasury Papers, 1845-52
War Office Records, 1845-52

HOUSE OF LORDS RECORD OFFICE
Poor Law Papers, 1838-45

PRINTED CONTEMPORARY RECORDS

Annual Reports of Poor Law Commissioners, 1838-65
Annual Register: a review of public events at home and abroad, 1844-55
Hansard's Parliamentary Debates, 1835-55
Thoms' Irish Almanac and Official Directory of the United Kingdom of Great Britain and Ireland, 1844-64

NEWSPAPERS

Armagh Guardian
Cork Examiner
Dublin Evening Post
Dublin Evening Mail
Dublin Weekly Register
Edinburgh Review
Freeman's Journal
Gardener's Chronicle and Horticultural Gazette
Kerry Evening Post

Londonderry Journal
Morning Register
Northern Standard
Northern Whig
Roscommon and Leitrim Gazette
Sligo Champion
Sligo Journal
St James's Chronicle, Whitehall and General Evening Post
Tralee Chronicle
The Times
Ulster Times

BRITISH PARLIAMENTARY PAPERS

First Report of His Majesty's Commissioners for inquiring into the condition of the poorer classes in Ireland, with appendix and supplement. 1835 [369] xxxii

Third Report of His Majesty's Commissioners for inquiring into the condition of the poorer classes in Ireland, with appendix and supplement. 1836 [43] xxx

Second Report of His Majesty's Commissioners for inquiring into the condition of the poorer classes in Ireland, with appendix and supplement. 1837 [68] xxxi

Report by George Nicholls to His Majesty's Secretary of State for the Home Department on the Poor Laws, Ireland. 1837 [69] li

Letter from N. Senior on the Third Report of the Commissioners for inquiry into the condition of the poor in Ireland. 1837 [90] li

Remarks on the Third Report of the Commissioners for inquiry into the condition of the poor in Ireland by G.C. Lewis. 1837 [91] li

Second Report from George Nicholls to the Secretary of State on Poor Laws, Ireland. 1837-8 [91]li

Second Report from George Nicholls to the Secretary of State on Poor Laws, Ireland. 1837-8 [104] xxxviii

Third Report of George Nicholls. The result of an inquiry into the condition of the labouring classes and provision for relief of the poor in Holland and Belgium. 1837-8 [126] xxxviii

Report of the Poor Law Commissioners on the continuance of the Poor Law Commission and on some further amendments to the laws relating to the relief of the poor. 1840 [226] xvii

Reports of the Commissioners appointed to take the Census of Ireland for the year 1841. 1843 [504] xxiv

Copy of the Report of Dr Playfair and Mr Lindley on the present state of the Irish potato crop, and on the prospect of the approaching scarcity. 1846 [28] xxxvii

Report of the Commissioners of Inquiry into matters connected with the failure of the potato crop, 6 February 1846. 1846 [33] xxxvii

Abstracts of the most serious representations made by the several medical superintendents of the public institutions in the provinces of Ulster, Munster, Leinster and Connaught. 1846 [120] xxxvii

Instructions to Committees of Relief Districts, extracted from Minutes of Proceedings of the Commissioners appointed in reference to the apprehended scarcity. 1846 [171] xxxvii

A statement of the total expenditure for the purposes of relief in Ireland since November 1845, distinguishing final payments from sums which have been or are to be repaid. 1846 [615] xxxvii

Correspondence explanatory of the measures adopted of Her Majesty's government for the relief of distress arising from the failure of the potato crop in Ireland. 1846 [735] xxxvii

Correspondence of the measures adopted by Her Majesty's government for the relief of distress arising from the failure of the potato crop in Ireland. 1846 [736] xxxvii

Report from the select committee of the House of Lords on colonisation from Ireland. 1847 [737] vi

Correspondence from July 1846 to January 1847 relating to the measures adopted for the relief of distress in Ireland and Scotland. Commissariat series. 1847 [761] li

Correspondence from July 1846 to January 1847 relating to measures adopted for the relief of distress in Ireland. Board of Works series. 1847 [764] l

Copies of extracts of correspondence relating to union workhouses in Ireland (first series). 1847 [766] lv

Correspondence from January to March 1847 relating to the measures adopted for the relief of distress in Ireland. Commissariat series (second part). 1847 [796] lii.

Correspondence from January to March 1847 relating to the measures adopted for the relief of distress in Ireland. Board of Works series (second part). 1847 [797] lii.

First Report of the Relief Commissioners, with Appendix. 1847 [799] xvii.

Second Report of the Relief Commissioners, constituted under the Act 10 Vic., cap.7., with appendices. 15 May 1847, 1847 [819] xvii

Reports of Boards of Public Works in Ireland relating to measures adopted for the relief of distress in March 1847. 1847 [834] xvii

Reports of Boards of Public Works in Ireland relating to measures adopted for the relief of distress in March 1847. 1847 [834] xvii

Third Report of the Relief Commissioners constituted under the Act 10 cap.7., with appendices, 17 June 1847. 1847 [836] xvii

Fourth Report of the Relief Commissioners constituted under the Act 10 Vic., cap.7., with appendices. 1847 [859] xvii

Reports of the Boards of Public Works in Ireland relating to the measures adopted for the relief of distress in June 1847. 1847 [860] xvii

Reports of Mr Barron to the Poor Law Commissioners. Correspondence relative to the dismissal of the late board of guardians of the Lowtherstown Union. 1847-8 [207] liii

Copy of correspondence of Commissioners for inquiring into what alterations may be beneficially made in the number and boundaries of the Poor Law Unions and electoral divisions in Ireland, and a copy of instructions to the Commissioners. 1847-8 [214] lii.

Copies of correspondence upon which the Commissioners of the Poor Law in Ireland took legal advice as to the construction of the Act 10 Vic. c.31., and the case submitted to them by counsel, and of the circular letter of the Commissioners issued thereon. 1847-8 [442] liii.

Copies of correspondence upon which the Commissioners of the Poor Laws took legal advice as to the construction of the 10th section of the Act 10 Vic., c.31; and of the case submitted to them by counsel; and of the circular letter of the Commissioners issued thereon. 1847-8 [519] liii

Report from the select committee of the House of Lords appointed to inquire into the operation of the Poor Laws relative to the rating of immediate lessors. 1847-8 [594] xvii

Fifth, sixth, seventh Reports from the Relief Commissioners constituted under the Act 10 Vic. cap.7., with appendixes. 1847-8 [876] xxix

Papers relating to the proceedings for the relief of distress, and state of the unions and workhouses in Ireland. Fourth series. 1847-8 [896] liv.

Supplementary appendix to the seventh, and last, report of the Relief Commissioners, 31 December 1847. 1847-8 [956] xxix.

Papers relating to proceedings for the relief of the distress and state of the unions and workhouses in Ireland. Fifth series. 1848 [919] lli

Copy of letter from the Secretary of State for the Home Department, dated 31 January 1849, with reference to the restoration of elected boards of guardians in certain unions in Ireland. 1849 [61] xlvii

Copy of an Order, dated 22 January, altering the dates of the proceedings of the annual elections of guardians, and of an Order dated 5 February, prescribing amended rules for the government of workhouses. 1849 [82] xlvii

Copy of all correspondence between the Commissioners in Ireland and England relative to the removal of John McCoy from Newcastle-upon-Tyne to Armagh, including the opinion of counsel thereon. 1849 [159] xlvii

First report of the select committee of the House of Lords, appointed to inquire into the operation of the Irish Poor Law, and the expediency of making any amendments to its enactments. 1849 [192] xvi

Report from the select committee on the Irish Poor Law. 1849 [209] xv

Copy of a letter to Her Majesty's Secretary of State for the Home Department sent by Edward Rushton, Stipendiary Magistrate of Liverpool, dated 21 April 1949. 1849 [266] xlvii.

Return of number of Irish poor relieved out of the poor rates in the year 1848 in the city of London, Marylebone, Westminster, Lambeth, Southwark, Tower Hamlets and Finsbury respectively; and of the money value for the relief so afforded; similar returns to Liverpool, Glasgow, Bristol, Cardiff, Newport, Merthyr Tydvil, Manchester, Salford, Preston, Bury, Leeds, Paisley and Edinburgh, respectively. 1849 [342] xlvii.

Return of all sums of money either granted or advanced from the Exchequer of the United Kingdom, on account of the distress and famine. 1849 [352] iil.

Report of the select committee on Poor Laws, Ireland, together with minutes of evidence. 1849 [403] xv.

Notices served upon Relieving Officers of the Poor Law districts in Ireland by landowners and others under the Evicted Destitute Poor Act (11 & 12 Vic. c.47). 1849 [517] xlix

Papers relating to the aid afforded to the Distressed Unions in the west of Ireland. 1849 [1010] xlviii

Papers relating to the proceedings for the relief of distress, and state of the unions and workhouses in Ireland (eighth series). 1849 [1042] xlviii

Final Report of the Board of Public Works in Ireland, September 1847. 1849 [1047], xxiii

Further papers relating to the aid afforded to the Distressed Unions in the west of Ireland. 1849 [1060] xlviii

Further papers relating to the aid afforded to the Distressed Unions in the west of Ireland. 1849 [1077] xlviii

Reports relating to the evicted poor in the Kilrush union. 1849 [1089] xlix

Reports of Colonial Land and Emigration Commissioners:
  Ninth Report 1849 [1082] xxii
  Tenth Report 1850 [1204] xxiii
  Eleventh Report 1851 [1382] xxii
  Thirteenth Report 1853 [1647] xl
  Fourteenth Report 1854 [1833] xxviii
  Sixteenth Report 1856 [2089] xxiv
  Twentieth Report 1860 [2696] xxix

Reports of the Commissioners for inquiring into the number and boundaries of Poor Law unions and electoral divisions in Ireland:
  First Report 1849 [1015] xxiii
  Second Report 1850 [1145] xxvi
  Third Report 1850 [1147] xxvi
  Fourth Report 1850 [1147] xxvi
  Fifth Report 1850 [1148] xxvi
  Sixth Report 1850 [1148] xxvi
  Seventh Report 1850 [1155] xxvi
  Eighth Report 1850 [1199] xxvi
  Ninth Report 1850 [1191] xxvi
  Tenth Report 1850 [1223] xxvi
  Eleventh Report 1850 [1257] xxvi
  Twelfth Report 1850 [1277] xxvi
  Thirteenth Report 1850 [1277] xxvi
  Fourteenth Report 1850 [1278] xxvi

Copies of all reports and resolutions made by all boards of guardians, either entered on minutes or transmitted to the Poor Law Commissioners in those unions where paid guardians have acted, relating to the management of those unions while under the superintendence of paid guardians. 1850 [251] l

Copy of report addressed to the Poor Law Commissioners by Inspector Bourke, with reference to the condition of the Kilrush union. 1850 [259] l

Copy of Report made to the board of guardians of the Castlebar union on 20 April by Dr Roynane, medical superintendent of the union, relative to the state of the workhouse. 1850 [382] l

Report of the select committee appointed to inquire into the administration of the Poor Law in the Kilrush union since 29 September 1848. 1850 [613] xi

Report from the select committee of the House of Lords appointed to investigate and report upon the allegations and charges contained in the petition to the boards of guardians of the union of Carrick-on-Shannon, complaining of the management and misconduct of the late vice-guardians of the said union. 1850 [725] xi

Report of the Irish Poor Law Commissioners on the measures taken for carrying into effect the recommendations of the Boundary Commissioners. 1850 [1162] xxvi

Copies of any correspondence which may have taken place in relation to the dismissal of the board of elected guardians of the Ennistymon union, and the appointment of paid guardians therein. 1851 [203] xlix

Copies of correspondence between the Poor Law Commissioners and their inspectors relative to the statements contained in an extract from a book entitled 'Gleanings from the west of Ireland'. 1851 [218] xlix

Copy of a report made to the Poor Law Commissioners by Mr Lucas, Temporary Inspector in charge of the Kilrush union, in regard to certain statements regarding the management of the Kilrush union, contained in a letter signed S. Godolphin Osborne, which appeared in The Times *newspaper of 31 March 1851*. 1851 [234] xlix

Report from the select committee on the Passenger Act, with the proceedings of the select committee, minutes of evidence, appendices and index. 1851 [632] xiii

Rate-in-Aid (Ireland). 1852 [87] xlvi

Analysis of returns of poor employment under 9 Vic. c.1. 9 and 10 Vic. c.107 from week ending 10 October 1846 to week ending 26 June 1847. 1852 [169] xviii

Report of Sir C.E. Trevelyan on the Consolidated Annuities (13 Vic. c.14) and the modification of them for the year ending 30 September 1851, authorised by the Treasury Minute of 21st of the following month. 1852 [1463] xlvii

Analysis of returns of poor employment under 9 Vic. c.1 and 9 & 10 Vic. c.107 from week ending 10 October 1846 to week ending 26 June 1847. 1853 [169] xviii

Report from the select committee on Poor Removal. 1854 [396] xvii

Report of Messrs Bromley and Stephenson, 1854, relative to the Poor Law Commission etc. Ireland; and Treasury minute; and other papers. 1854-5 [28] xlvi

Reports of the Commissioners appointed to take the Census for Ireland for the year 1851. 1856 [2087] xxxi 1856 [2134] xxxi

Report of the select committee on destitution (Gweedore and Cloghaneely); together with the proceedings of the committee, minutes of evidence etc. 1857-8 [412] lxxxxi

Royal Commission on the Poor Laws and relief of distress—report on Ireland. 1909 [4630] xxxvii

SELECTED SECONDARY SOURCES

CONTEMPORARY WORKS

Banks, B., *Compendium of the Irish Poor Law*, Dublin 1872

Burke, Edmund, *Thoughts and Details on Scarcity, originally presented to the Right Hon. William Pitt in November 1795*, London 1795

Butt, Isaac, *A Voice for Ireland: famine in the land*, Dublin 1847

Dictionary of National Biography

Engels, Friedrich, *The Condition of the Working Class in England in 1844*, London 1892

Forbes, John, *Memorandums made in Ireland in the autumn of 1852*, 2 vols, London 1853

Gaskell, Elizabeth, *Mary Barton*, Manchester 1848

Godley, J.R., *Observations on the Irish Poor Law*, Dublin 1847

Hall, S.C. and A.M., *Ireland, its scenery, character etc.*, 3 vols, London 1841-3; one-volume edition, ed. Michael Scott, London 1984

Hill, Lord George, *Facts from Gweedore* 3rd ed., Dublin 1853

James, Bruce, *Destitution in the Highlands: letters reprinted from the 'Scotsman'*, Edinburgh 1847

Malthus, Thomas, *An Essay on the Principle of Population as it Affects the Future Improvement of Society*, 1st ed., London 1798

——*Principles of Political Economy*, London 1820

Martineau, Harriet, *Poor Laws and Paupers*, London 1833-4

McCulloch, J.R., *The Literature of Political Economy*, London 1845

Mill, J.S., *Principles of Political Economy*, London 1909.

Mooney, T.A., *Conpendium of the Irish Poor Law*, Dublin 1887

Nicholls, George, *A History of the Irish Poor Law*, London 1856

———*A History of the English Poor Law*, London 1898

O'Brien, George, *The Economic History of Ireland from the Union*, London 1921

O'Brien, R.B., *Fifty Years of Concessions to Ireland 1831-81*, 2 vols, London 1883

Parker, C.S., *Sir Robert Peel from His Private Letters* 2nd ed., London 1899

Perraud, Adolphe, *Ireland under English Rule*, Dublin 1863

Ricardo, David, *Works and Correspondence* (10 vols, ed. P. Sraffa and M.H. Dobb), Cambridge 1951–5

Sayers, Peig, *Peig*, Dublin 1936

Senior, Nassau W., *Journals, Essays and Conversations Relating to Ireland*, 2 vols, London 1868

Smith, Adam, *An Inquiry into the Nature and Causes of the Wealth of Nations*, London 1776

Smith, John, *The Condition of Scotland*, Edinburgh 1846

———*Transactions of the Central Relief Committee of the Society of Friends during the Famine in Ireland in 1846 and 1847*, Dublin 1852

Trench, W.S., *Realities of Irish Life*, London 1868

Trevelyan, Charles, *The Irish Crisis*, London 1848

LATER WORKS

Adam, W.F., *Ireland and Irish Emigration to the New World, 1815 to the Famine*, New Haven 1932

Aston, T.S., *The Industrial Revolution*, London 1948

Barber, Sarah, 'Irish Migrant Agricultural Labourers in Nineteenth-Century Lincolnshire', in *Saothar*, no. 8, 1982

Bardon, Jonathan, *A History of Ulster*, Belfast 1992.

Belcham, John, *Industrialisation and the Working Class: the English Experience 1750–1950*, Aldershot 1990

Black, R.D.C., *Economic Thought and the Irish Question 1817-70*, Cambridge 1960

Blaug, Mark, 'The Myth of the Old Poor Law and the Making of the New', in *Journal of Economic History*, xxiii, June 1963

Bourke, P.M. Austin, 'The Extent of the Potato Crop in Ireland at the Time of the Famine', in *Journal of the Statistical and Social Enquiry Society of Ireland*, xx, part 3, 1959–60

———*The Visitation of God? The Potato and the Great Irish Famine*, Dublin 1993

Boylan, T.A., and Foley, T.P., *Political Economy and Colonial Ireland*, London 1992

Boyle, P.P. and Ó Gráda, Cormac, 'Fertility Trends, Excess Mortality, and the Great Irish Famine', in *Demography*, xxiii, 1986

Bradshaw, Brendan, 'Nationalism and Historical Scholarship in Modern Ireland', in *Irish Historical Studies*, xxvi, no. 104, November 1989

Brewer, J., *The Sinews of Power: money and the English state*, London 1989

Brundage, A., *The Making of the New Poor law: the politics of enquiry, enactment and implementation 1832-9*, London 1978

Chambers, J.D., *The Workshop of the World: British economic history from 1820 to 1880*, London 1961

427

Checkland, S.G. and E.O., *The Poor Law Report of 1834*, London 1974

Clark, Samuel, *Social Origins of the Irish Land War*, Princeton 1979

Connell, K.H., *The Population of Ireland 1750–1845*, Oxford 1951

Conway, Thomas, 'The Approach to an Irish Poor Law 1828-33' in *Eire-Ireland*, vi, 1971

Cousens, S.M., 'The Regional Pattern of Emigration during the Great Famine, 1846-51', in *Transactions and Papers of the Institute of British Geographers*, no. 28, 1960

——'Regional Death Rates in Ireland during the Great Famine, 1846–51', in *Population Studies*, xiv, no.1, 1960

——'Emigration and Demographic Change in Ireland, 1851–61', in *Economic History Review*, ser. 2, xiv, no. 2, 1961

——'The Regional Variation in Mortality during the Great Irish Famine', in *Proceedings of the Royal Irish Academy*, lxii, section. c, no. 3, 1963

Crawford,E. Margaret (ed.), *Famine, The Irish Experience 900-1900: subsistence crises and famines in Ireland*, Edinburgh 1989

——'Dearth, Diet and Disease in Ireland, 1850: a case study of nutritional deficiency', in *Medical History*, xxviii, 1984

——'Scurvy in Ireland During the Great Famine', in *Social History of Medicine*, no. 3, 1988

Crafts, N.F.R., 'The Industrial Revolution: economic growth in Britain, 1700–1860', in *Recent Findings of Research in Economic and Social History*, no. 4, 1987

Crosby, T.L., *Sir Robert Peel's Administration 1841-46*, London 1976

Crotty, Raymond, *Irish Agricultural Production: its volume and structure*, Cork 1966

Cullen, L.M., 'Irish History without the Potato', in *Past and Present*, vol. 40, July 1968

Cullen, L.M. and Smout, T.C. (eds), *Comparative Aspects of Scottish and Irish Economic and Social History 1600–1800*, Edinburgh 1978

Daly, Mary, *The Famine in Ireland*, Dundalk 1986

Devine, Tom, 'The Highland Clearances', in *Recent Findings of Research in Economic and Social History*, no. 4, 1987

Dickson, R.J., *Ulster Emigration to Colonial America 1718–75*, London 1966

Donnelly, J.S. Jnr, *The Land and People of Nineteenth-Century Cork: the rural economy and the land question*, London 1975

——'The Irish agricultural depression of 1859–64', in *Irish Economic and Social History*, ii 1976

Droz, Jacques, *Europe Between Revolutions*, Glasgow 1967

Edsall, N.C., *The Anti-Poor Law Movement 1834–44*, Manchester 1971

Edwards, R.D. and Williams, T.D. (eds.), *The Great Famine: studies in Irish history*, New York 1957

Falkus, Malcolm, *Britain Transformed: an economic and social history 1700–1914*, Ormskirk 1987

Feinstein, C., and Pollard S. (eds), *Studies in Capital Formation in the United Kingdom*, London 1988

Finer, S.E., *The Life and Times of Sir Edwin Chadwick*, London 1952

Finnegan, F., *Poverty and Prejudice: Irish immigrants in York 1840–1875*, Cork 1982

Fitzpatrick, David, 'Was Ireland Special?', in *Historical Journal*, xxxiii, 1990

——*Irish Emigration 1801-1921*, Dundalk 1984

Flanagan, Patrick, O'Brien, E., and Buttimer, Cornelius (eds.), *Cork: History and Society*, Dublin 1993

Floud, Roderick, 'Standards of Living and Industrialisation', in *Recent Findings of Research in Economic and Social History*, vi, 1988

Foster, Roy, *Modern Ireland 1600–1972*, London 1988

Fraser, Derek (ed.), *The New Poor Law in the Nineteenth-Century*, London 1976

Gash, Norman, *Sir Robert Peel: the life of Sir Robert Peel after 1830*, London 1972

Glazier, Ira. A., and Tepper, Michael, *The Famine Immigrants: list of Irish immigrants arriving at the port of New York 1846-1851*, Baltimore 1983-1986

Gray, Peter, 'Punch and the Great Famine' in *History Ireland*, vol. 1, summer 1993

Gooch, G.P. (ed.), *The Later Correspondence of Lord John Russell 1840–1878*, London 1925

Griffiths, A.R., 'The Irish Board of Works during the Famine Years', in *Historical Journal*, xiii, no.4, 1970

Hart, Jennifer, 'Sir Charles Trevelyan at the Treasury', in *English Historical Review*, lxxv, 1960

Hobsbawm, Eric J., *The Age of Revolution 1789–1848*, London 1962

———*Industry and Empire*, Harmondsworth 1968

———and George Rudé, *Captain Swing*, Hardmondsworth 1969

Hopkins, Eric, *A Social History of the English Working Classes*, London 1986

Hoppen, K. Theodore, *Elections, Politics and Society in Ireland 1832–1885*, Oxford 1984

Houston, C.J. and Smyth, W.J., 'The Geography of Irish Emigration to Canada', in *Familia, Ulster Genealogical Review*, Belfast 1988

———*Irish Emigration and the Canadian Settlement: patterns, links and letters*, Canada 1990

Inglis, Brian, *Poverty and the Industrial Revolution*, London 1971

Keegan, Gerald, *Famine Diary: journey to a new world*, Dublin 1991

Kelly, James, 'Scarcity and Poor Relief in Eighteenth-Century Ireland: the subsistence crisis of 1782-84', in *Irish Historical Studies*, xxviii, no. 109, May 1992

Kennedy, Liam and Ollerenshaw, Philip (eds), *An Economic History of Ulster 1820–1939*, Manchester 1985

Kirse, S., *The Famine Years in the Parish of Killaloe*, 1845–51, Killaloe 1984

Kinealy, Christine, 'The Administration of the Poor Law in County Mayo, 1838–98', in *Cathair Na Mart: Journal of the Westport Historical Society*, vi no. 1, 1986

———'The Lisburn Workhouse during the Famine', *Journal of the Lisburn Historical Society*, Belfast 1991

———with S. Cannon and C. Cox, *The Famine in Dunfanaghy*, Dublin 1992

———'The Workhouse System in County Waterford 1838-1923', in William Nolan and Thomas P. Power (eds), *Waterford: History and Society*, Dublin 1992

Large, David, 'The House of Lords and Ireland in the Age of Peel 1832–50', in *Irish Historical Studies*, ix, 1955

Large, E.C., *The Advance of the Fungi*, London 1940

Mandler, Peter, *Aristocratic Government in the Age of Reform: Whigs and Liberals 1830–1852*, Oxford 1990

Mathias, Peter, *The First Industrial Nation: an economic history of Britain 1700–1914*, 2nd ed., Suffolk 1983

MacDonagh, Oliver, *A Pattern of Government Growth: the Passenger Acts and their enforcement*, London 1961

————'Irish Famine Emigration to the United States', in *Perspectives in American History*, x, 10, 1976

————'The Poor Law, Emigration, and the Irish Question', in *Christus Rex*, xii, 1958

Marshall, J.D., *The Old Poor Law 1795–1834*, London 1973

McClaughlin, Trevor, *From Shamrock to Wattle*, Melbourne 1985

McDowell, R.B., *The Irish Administration 1801-1914*, London 1964

Miller, Kerby A., *Emigrants and Exiles: Ireland and the Irish exodus to North America*, Oxford 1985

Mokyr, Joel, *Why Ireland Starved: a quantitative and analytical history of the Irish economy 1800-50*, London 1983 (revised 1985)

————'Irish History with the Potato' in *Irish Economic and Social History*, viii, 1981

————and Ó Gráda, Cormac, 'Emigration and Poverty in Pre-Famine Ireland', in *Explorations in Economic History*, xix, no.4, 1983

Murphy, Ignatius, 'Captain A.E. Kennedy, Poor Law Inspector, and the Great Famine in the Kilrush union, 1847–50', in *The Other Clare*, iii, April 1979

Neal, F., *Sectarian Violence: the Liverpool experience 1819–1914*, Manchester 1987

Nolan, William and Power, Thomas P. (eds), *Waterford: History and Society*, Dublin 1992

O'Brien, George, *The Economic History of Ireland from the Union to the Famine*, London 1921

O'Farrell, Patrick, *The Irish in Australia*, New South Wales 1987

Ó Gráda, Cormac, *Ireland Before and After the Famine: explorations in economic history 1800 –1925*, 2nd ed., Manchester 1993

————*The Great Irish Famine*, Dublin 1989

————'Across the Briny Ocean: some thoughts on Irish emigration to America 1800-50' in T.M. Devine and D. Dickson (eds), *Ireland and Scotland 1800-50*, Edinburgh 1983

————'Making History in Ireland in the 1940s and 1950s: the saga of the Great Famine', in *The Irish Review*, no. 12 (1992)

————'A note on Nineteenth-Century Emigration Statistics', in *Population Studies*, vol. 29, March 1975

O'Neill, T.P., 'The Irish Workhouses during the Great Famine', in *Christus Rex*, xii, 1958

O'Rourke, Kevin, 'Did the Great Irish Famine Matter?', in *The Journal of Economic History*, li, March 1991

Prebble, John, *The Highland Clearances*, London 1963

Prest, John, *Lord John Russell*, London 1972

Roberts, David, *Victorian Origins of the British Welfare State*, Newhaven 1960

Robinson, Portia, *The Women of Botany Bay*, New South Wales 1988

Rose, Michael E., *The English Poor Law 1780-1930*, Newton Abbot 1971

Schofield, R., Reher D., Bideau A., eds, *The Decline of Mortality in Europe*, Cambridge 1991

Schrier, Arnold, *Ireland and the American Emigration, 1850-1900*, London 1958

Sen, A.K., *Poverty and Famines*, Oxford 1981

Solow, Barbara L., *The Land Question and the Irish Economy*, Massachusetts 1971

Sraffa, P. and Dobb, M.H. (eds), *David Ricardo: works and correspondence*, Cambridge, 1951–5

Swift, Roger, 'The Outcast Irish in the British Victorian city: problems and perspectives' in *Irish Historical Studies*, xxv, no. 99, 1987

Swift, Roger, and Gilley, Sheridan (eds), *The Irish in Britain 1815–1939*, London 1989

Thompson, D., *The Chartists*, London 1984

Thompson, E.P., *The Making of the English Working Class*, Harmondsworth 1968

Vaughan, W.E. (ed.), *A New History of Ireland, vol. v: Ireland under the Union, 1801-70* Oxford 1989

Ward, T.J., *Sir James Graham*, New York 1967

Werly, J.M., 'The Irish in Manchester', in *Irish Historical Studies*, no. 18, 1972–3

Williamson, J.G., 'Why Was British Growth so Slow during the Industrial Revolution?' in *Journal of Economic History*, xliv, 1984

Woodham-Smith, Cecil, *The Great Hunger: Ireland 1845-9*, London 1962

Woods, R., and Woodward, J., (eds) *Urban Disease and Mortality in Nineteenth-Century England*, London 1984

Wright, D.G., *Democracy and Reform, 1815–85*, London, nd

Wrigley, E.A., and Schofield, R.S., *The Population History of England 1541–1871: a reconstruction*, Cambridge 1981

THESES

Burke, P.M.A., 'The Potato, Blight, Weather and the Irish Famine', Ph.D. thesis, University College, Cork 1965

Feingold, W.L., 'The Irish Boards of Poor Law Guardians, 1872–86, a revolution in local government', Ph.D thesis, University of Chicago 1974

Foley, Kieran, 'The Killarney Poor Law Guardians and the Famine, 1845-52', M.A. thesis, New University of Ulster, Coleraine 1987

Gray, Peter, 'British Politics and the Irish Land Question, 1843–50', D.Phil. thesis, Cambridge 1992

Grant, James, 'The Great Famine in the Province of Ulster: the mechanisms of relief', Ph.D. thesis, Queen's University, Belfast 1986

Hickey, P., 'A Study of Four Peninsula Parishes in West Cork, 1796-1855', M.A. thesis, University College, Cork 1980

Holt, J.M., 'The Quakers in the Great Irish Famine', M.Litt. thesis, Trinity College, Dublin 1967

Keep, G.R., 'The Irish Emigration to North America in the Second Half of the Nineteenth-Century', Ph.D. thesis, Trinity College, Dublin 1951

Kelly, Sister Patricia, 'From Workhouse to Hospital: the role of the Irish workhouses in medical relief to 1921', M.A. thesis, University College, Galway 1972

Kinealy, Christine, 'The Irish Poor Law', 1838–62, Ph.D. thesis, Trinity College, Dublin 1984

McGrath, Brigid, 'Introduction of Poor Law to Ireland', M.A. thesis, University College, Dublin 1965

Montague, R.J., 'Relief and Reconstruction in Ireland 1845–49', D.Phil. thesis, Oxford University 1976

O'Neill, T.P., 'The Famine of 1822', M.A. thesis, National University of Ireland 1966
———The State, Poverty and Distress in Ireland, 1700-1900, Ph.D. thesis, Trinity College, Dublin 1968

Solar, P.M., 'Growth and Distribution in Irish Agriculture before the Famine', Ph.D. thesis, Stanford University 1987.

Index